Don Heller

EQUITY AND EXCELLENCE
IN AMERICAN HIGHER EDUCATION

EQUITY AND EXCELLENCE IN AMERICAN HIGHER EDUCATION

William G. Bowen, Martin A. Kurzweil,
and Eugene M. Tobin

In Collaboration with
Susanne C. Pichler

UNIVERSITY OF VIRGINIA PRESS
Charlottesville and London

University of Virginia Press
© 2005 by the Rector and Visitors of the University of Virginia
All rights reserved
Printed in the United States of America on acid-free paper
First published 2005

1 3 5 7 9 8 6 4 2

Library of Congress Cataloging-in-Publication Data

Bowen, William G.
Equity and excellence in American higher education / William G. Bowen, Martin A.
Kurzweil, and Eugene M. Tobin ; in collaboration with Susanne C. Pichler.
   p.   cm. — (Thomas Jefferson Foundation distinguished lecture series)
Includes bibliographical references and index.
ISBN 0-8139-2350-6 (cloth : alk. paper)
1. Educational equalization—United States.   2. Discrimination in higher education—
United States.   3. Universities and colleges—United States—Admission.   I. Kurzweil,
Martin A., 1980–   II. Tobin, Eugene M.   III. Pichler, Susanne C., 1966–
IV. Title. V. Series.
LC213.2.B69   2005
379.2′6   2004023111

Contents

List of Figures

List of Tables

Acknowledgments

We wish, first, to thank our collaborator, Susanne C. Pichler, the exceedingly able librarian of The Andrew W. Mellon Foundation, for her tireless and highly effective work on this project. From the start of our planning for the 2004 Jefferson Lectures through the drafting of the manuscript and then the copyediting, Ms. Pichler has been invaluable in identifying good sources, drafting notes and other materials, reviewing the text and making substantive suggestions, checking and rechecking the accuracy of citations, and, in general, preventing as many mistakes as possible. Put simply, we could not have carried out the project without her.

The very useful appendix A, which describes the experiences of the University of Cape Town (UCT) in South Africa (and of higher education in South Africa more generally) in confronting equity and excellence issues in a very different setting, is the work of Ian Scott, Nan Yeld, Janice McMillan, and Martin Hall. The extraordinary difficulties faced by those in South Africa in the aftermath of apartheid puts in context the problems faced by those of us who have been spared those searing experiences. Through rigorous study and first-hand experience, the UCT team that worked on this essay is unusually well qualified to describe and analyze these issues.

Near the end of our drafting of the manuscript, we were fortunate to have Nirupama Rao join the staff of the Mellon Foundation as a research associate. Ms. Rao—a recent graduate of MIT, where she majored in economics—immediately contributed to the project in many ways: by reading and improving the text (particularly chapter 9 on K–12 education), by overseeing further work with the data in the expanded College and Beyond (C&B) database, which is described in chapter 1, and by serving as our principal contact with the University of Virginia Press throughout the editorial process.

Other colleagues at the Foundation who have been of great help include Neil Rudenstine, who made many suggestions for improving our discussion of worldwide developments in graduate education and research (in chapter 3) as well as other parts of the manuscript; James Shulman, the lead author of *The Game of Life*, a work that draws heavily on the C&B database, of which he is the principal creator, who has continued to offer good advice and sound counsel; Harriet Zuckerman and Pat McPherson, senior officers of the Foundation, who have made many substantive and stylistic suggestions for improving the content of the book and have, in addition, been constant sources of encouragement as well as good ideas; Joseph Meisel, program officer for research universities and humanistic scholarship, who was especially helpful in critiquing our treatment of "top-up" fees and educational reform in Britain (in chapter 8); Susan Anderson, in the Foundation's Princeton office, who prepared valuable background memoranda and made many useful editing suggestions; Pat Irvin, vice-president for operations and planning, who handled contract negotiations with various parties and assisted mightily in the "roll-out" of the book; Jacqueline Ewenstein, assistant general counsel, who navigated the legal route to obtaining the new C&B data; Lisa Bonifacic, the Foundation's assistant librarian, who provided invaluable research and helpful editing (particularly of notes and references) and also assisted in the preparation of the expanded C&B database; Cara Nakamura, a former research associate at the Foundation, who helped to collect the new C&B data from institutions and from the College Board; Kamille Davis and Lillian Ying, research assistants at the Foundation, who creatively, intelligently, and persistently tracked down facts, information, and statistics of all sorts; and, finally, Pat Woodford, Ulrica Konvalin, and Matthew Rowe, key staff members in the president's office, who took responsibility for logistical matters of all kinds.

Outside the Foundation, we are very fortunate to have had the help of a number of leading scholars. Sarah E. Turner, an economist at the University of Virginia who was a visiting scholar at the Russell Sage Foundation in New York when this research was being carried out, took an especially active role in advising us on econometric issues, directing us to important research contributions, and then reading and commenting extensively on the entire manuscript. We also thank the four other readers of the complete manuscript, whose detailed suggestions have improved it in many ways: David Breneman, dean of the Curry School at the University of Virginia; Michael McPherson, president of the Spencer Foundation; Stuart Saunders, former vice-chancellor of the University of Cape Town (who contributed an invaluable South African perspective); and Gordon Winston, professor of economics at Williams College. All of these readers were extremely helpful, and this brief mention fails to capture adequately our indebtedness to them.

For specific contributions we thank Alan Krueger and Jesse Rothstein, economists at Princeton, who worked with Sarah Turner to produce new simulations of the likely effects over the next 25 years of race-sensitive admissions policies (which are incorporated in chapter 6). Thomas Kane at UCLA helped us think through the effects of governmental grant programs and the impact of economic constraints on college access and choice. Caroline Hoxby at Harvard, another noteworthy contributor to the literature in this field (whose work, like the work of Kane, Turner, and other scholars listed above, is cited repeatedly throughout the study), took the time to comment on parts of the manuscript and to suggest an important line of inquiry—one pertaining to alumni giving—that we would have overlooked otherwise. (Professor Hoxby also deserves special thanks for having been such a fine teacher of one of us [Martin Kurzweil] and then for recommending him for appointment at the Foundation.) Lawrence Katz of Harvard read carefully chapter 9 (on pre-college preparedness) and made a number of helpful suggestions. Barnard College historian Robert McCaughey provided an exceedingly thoughtful and incisive critique of our "time line" (in chapter 2), and we are most grateful for his advice and direction. Mark Shulman, director of graduate studies at Pace Law School, provided us with a number of valuable editorial comments in chapter 2, and Jennings Wagoner Jr., of the University of Virginia's Curry School of Education, generously shared his insights, as well as documentation of Jefferson's views on education. Colin Lucas, former vice-chancellor of the University of Oxford and a trustee of the Foundation, was a great help in suggesting sources of commentary on the "top-up" fees debate in the United Kingdom and then reviewing carefully our discussion of that topic. Finally, we are grateful to Derek Bok, the former president of Harvard University and former dean of the Harvard Law School, for sharing his cogent assessment of research on contemporary undergraduate education (in chapter 10).

The expanded C&B database is at the heart of the new empirical research reported in this study. We thank the institutions that provided the necessary institutional records, as well as the College Board, which provided access to the Student Descriptive Questionnaire data that allowed us to link information about family backgrounds to institutional records. We also thank, specifically, the institutional researchers and administrators who put in often substantial efforts to deliver the data to us: Russell Adair, Yale University; Lawrence Baldwin, Wellesley College; Chrissie Bell, Smith College; David Brodigan, Williams College; Rebecca Brodigan, Middlebury College; Christine Cote, Bowdoin College; Randy Deike, Pennsylvania State University; Carrie Dirks, the College Board; Richard Fass, Pomona College; William Fitzsimmons, Harvard University; Richard Herman, University of Illinois; Bernard Lentz, University of Pennsylvania; Carol Livingstone, University of Illinois; Claudia Mitchell-Kernan, UCLA; Margaret Neall, Princeton University; Marian Pagano, Columbia University; Ross Peacock, Oberlin College; Jack Quinlan, Pomona College; Judith Richlin-Klonsky, UCLA; Lorne Robinson, Macalester College; John Romano, Pennsylvania State University; Ellen Sawtell, the College Board; Robin Shores, Swarthmore College; Marcia Snowden, Princeton University; Clayton Spencer, Harvard University;

George Stovall, University of Virginia; Michael Susi, Columbia University; Elizabeth Weiss, University of Illinois; Lew Wyman, Barnard College; and Elizabeth Yong, Harvard University.

There is also a broader group of individuals, too numerous to mention and many not even known to us by name, who contributed to this study by questioning and discussing the content of the 2004 Jefferson Lectures at the University of Virginia. Those in attendance at the lectures did not hesitate to challenge assumptions, to ask that key points be explained better, and to raise profound questions, such as what it really means (and will mean) to be a state university in an age when state appropriations are a smaller and smaller fraction of the budget.

On a personal note, we know that the weeks and months spent researching and writing this book have been made possible by the sacrifices of those whose support and interest in this project have sustained us. William Bowen thanks those who are by now, after many seemingly interminable projects, "the usual suspects," and especially Mary Ellen; Martin Kurzweil thanks his mother, father, and grandparents, as well as Rebecca, Molly, and especially Fiona, for their love, support—and patience; and Gene Tobin thanks Beverly, David, and Leslie for sharing many of their weekends and a vacation on the Jersey shore with the Mellon team.

Finally, we wish to thank Penelope Kaiserlian, Richard Holway, and their colleagues at the University of Virginia Press and Peter Strupp and his colleagues at Princeton Editorial Associates for their close attention to every aspect of the publication of this book. It has been a pleasure to work with them.

It is customary to end by excusing others from responsibility for errors that we have made or for interpretations of ours that people dislike— perhaps intensely. We are glad to conform to this tradition by accepting full responsibility for what we have written.

William G. Bowen
Martin A. Kurzweil
Eugene M. Tobin

August 2004

EQUITY AND EXCELLENCE
IN AMERICAN HIGHER EDUCATION

CHAPTER 1

Framework and Road Map

Americans feel very positively about the quality of their colleges and universities. A 2004 survey, for example, found that 93 percent of respondents consider our colleges and universities "one of the [country's] most valuable resources"; about 60 percent find the four-year institutions in their state (both public and private) of "high quality."[1] Praise for the education offered is glowing, and its value is appreciated; the "product," say Americans, is excellent (though they express some qualifications and worries about trends, which we will note in due course).

Survey respondents are, however, much more ambivalent about how and to whom access to this "valuable resource" should be provided. A robust majority worry that colleges are too expensive, and many parents express concern about being able to afford their children's education. Moreover, admissions policies that have veered from consideration of "objective" measures like SAT scores and grades are viewed with skepticism —three quarters disapprove of "legacy" preferences, and the nation is about evenly divided on the question of affirmative action for racial and ethnic minorities.[2]

In short, Americans want both excellence and equity in their higher education system. But while they feel good about the former (perhaps better than they should feel), there is much debate about the latter.

When we began this study of equity and excellence in American higher education—following an invitation to one of us (William Bowen) to speak on the subject as the 2004 Thomas Jefferson Foundation Distinguished Lecturer at the University of Virginia—the imbalance in attitudes toward these two topics became clear immediately. In many quarters, the impressive scale and high quality of American higher education are taken for granted, while the question of fairness in its provision engenders passionate and divisive debate. But it was also clear to us that the various arguments about what equity means and how to achieve it are inextricably linked to notions of excellence. In its most shallow construction, this linkage takes the form of a direct, zero-sum trade-off between the two ideals.

We are unsure when, in the context of American higher education, the claims of "equity" and "excellence" were first juxtaposed. But we do know that there has long been a simmering debate over whether it is better to educate a small number of people to a very high standard or to extend educational opportunities much more broadly—even if this means accepting a somewhat lower standard of performance and, in general, spreading resources more thinly. There has also been a more pointed debate, going back more than a century, over whether efforts to admit and educate students from a wide variety of backgrounds, including the children of new waves of immigrants and those from under-represented racial and ethnic minorities, threaten established educational verities and social mores.

As is evident from our description of this construction as shallow, we believe that the presumed tension between equity and excellence takes on a different (much more nuanced) character when we consider carefully what is meant by "excellence." Our country's success in pursuing excellence can be evaluated, after all, only in the context of an understanding of what our system of higher education seeks to accomplish (excellence in doing what?). Similarly, the "equity" objective takes on meaning only when we consider the distributional aspects of these goals and the criteria upon which access to resources is granted. Needed is a clear understanding of what it is that people want to achieve, for themselves and for their children (and for society in general), through the educational system. In short, we are driven back to a consideration of the root purposes of higher education.

PURPOSES OF HIGHER EDUCATION

A central purpose of higher education, in every setting, is to prepare talented young people to assume productive roles in their societies—to foster the creation of "human capital." In the colonial colleges, a main focus was on preparing young men for the clergy (though other needs were also recognized). Today, institutions of higher education are expected to prepare their graduates for careers in law, medicine, business, education, science, technology, and many other fields. This objective has both quality and scale dimensions.

Important as the formation of human capital is to the "productivity and prosperity" of society, American colleges have never seen themselves as serving merely "practical" (or narrowly vocational) objectives. W. E. B. Du Bois was eloquent—and succinct—in arguing: "There could be no education that was not at once for use in earning a living *and for use in living a life*" (our emphasis).[3] This emphasis on learning to "live a life" is one of the hallmarks of American higher education, and one of the reasons why residential experiences have been so highly valued here and elsewhere.

Since at least the latter half of the 19th century, colleges and (especially) universities have seen their purposes as encompassing the advancement and dissemination of knowledge, as well as the education of students. Ideas are vital components of a country's resource base. New ways of thinking—new discoveries—matter, as do the trained individuals in whom they are embodied and the educational environments that nurture them. Over time, the research function has become a more and more important responsibility of institutions of higher education worldwide.

Still another component of educational purpose might be termed "civic service," or even pursuit of "civic virtue," and colleges and universities have long regarded themselves as "civilizing forces." Thomas Jefferson believed passionately that education was essential to the survival of a republican form of government; citizens had to learn how to protect their rights, or they would surely lose them: "If a nation expects to be ignorant and free, in a state of civilization, it expects what never was and never will be."[4] Jefferson understood that higher education plays a key role in helping citizens develop the critical analytical skills necessary for formulating opinions and making decisions based on facts and rational processes, and that these skills and insights are immensely important for the responsible exercise of democracy.

THE COMPLEMENTARITY OF EQUITY AND EXCELLENCE

Even these brief descriptions of the purposes of higher education suggest self-evident ways in which the pursuit of excellence and of equity can be powerfully reinforcing.

- As part of their quest for excellence, colleges and universities want to attract the most promising students, and there has never been reason to believe that all outstanding candidates will be able to pay whatever fees are charged without help. At many colleges and universities, the best students have often been the recipients of need-based financial aid.[5] In Jefferson's oft-quoted phraseology, American education should seek to nurture the "natural aristocracy" of talent and virtue.[6]
- Moreover, the society at large can build the educational scale that it requires only if its institutions of higher education tap every pool of talent. America has achieved one of the highest levels of educational attainment of any country, but it runs the risk of losing its preeminent position unless it can help much larger numbers of students from poor families and from minority populations to participate and succeed at the tertiary level—and to do so requires improving markedly the college "preparedness" of such students.

- There are widely understood educational benefits associated with enrolling a student body that is both highly talented and diverse. The quality ("excellence") of the campus learning environment—both in the classroom and outside it—is improved for everyone when students from a wide variety of backgrounds are present. Students need to learn how to put themselves in other people's shoes.
- Participatory democracy requires intelligent and well-informed decision making by large numbers of citizens. Moreover, our republican system of government depends upon talented leaders who can represent and empathize with all members of an ever more diverse society. Higher education makes a direct contribution to the underpinnings of a well-functioning democracy by educating to a high level students from every background who will vote, govern, or legislate thoughtfully. Jefferson put it best when, in 1820, he wrote: "I know no safe depository of the ultimate powers of the society but the people themselves; and if we think them not enlightened enough to exercise their control with a wholesome discretion, the remedy is not to take it from them, but to inform their discretion by education. This is the true corrective of abuses of constitutional power."[7]

Beyond these important ways that the pursuit of equity can further the goals of higher education, many wise individuals throughout the history of the republic have considered improvements in access to opportunity, or the promotion of social mobility, a key purpose of education in and of itself. This goal has been important to some leaders of higher education and to some colleges from the early days of our country.[8] But it would be hard to argue that "equity," or the broad extension of "educational opportunity," was a clearly articulated goal of most institutions of higher education prior to the end of World War II. Determined, "activist" efforts to make higher education more inclusive, certainly in terms of the racial composition of student bodies, go back only three or four decades.

In any case, there is a broadly shared consensus today that individuals should be able to move up the ladder of accomplishment as far as their talents, character, and determination will take them. This simple proposition is especially important at a time when education is more critical than ever before in determining access not only to the best jobs (and the accompanying economic rewards), but also to a broad set of less tangible opportunities to "live a life." We are not, however, where we ought to be, and a principal thesis of this book is that much more needs to be done if the goal of enhanced opportunity is to be served adequately by American higher education.[9]

Enhancing equity or translating equity into high-quality educational opportunities for a wider range of people is far from an easy undertaking, or one without costs. Indeed, the real and imagined trade-offs associated with the simultaneous pursuit of equity and excellence are often confusing and difficult for many people to navigate. For example, in the context of the deeply divisive debate over affirmative action in higher education, there have been claims and counterclaims concerning the educational benefits of diversity: Does enrolling a racially diverse student body have strong positive consequences for the quality ("excellence") of the educational experience of students in general? Alternatively, does encouraging such diversity undermine the principle of meritocracy and distract us from the single-minded pursuit of excellence? Additional layers of complexity are added when we consider how our system of higher education distributes opportunity across groups defined by gender and socioeconomic status.

Apart from these conceptual questions, there are operational issues. Poorly conceived and poorly executed programs driven principally by ideology or by partisan political agendas can do no little harm. Resources are scarce, trade-offs have to be made, and emphasis must be placed on finding cost-effective ways to provide an excellent education to a broad spectrum of citizens. Finding the right policies is difficult, and there is generally no way of being sure what is the best approach. Careful analysis and a willingness to change directions in the face of evidence are essential. It is not enough to want to do the right thing. As one sage commentator observed: "Good intentions randomize behavior."

Still, there is a growing body of evidence that can provide guidance. In this study we will rely on historical research, detailed analysis of new data, and an increasingly rich literature to propose answers to some of these questions about equity, excellence, and their interaction.

ORGANIZATION OF THIS BOOK

The book is divided into two broad sections. In part I we discuss "where we have been and where we are now" in our pursuit of the equity and excellence objectives. Then, in part II, we look ahead and consider "where we are (and should be) going" by examining the major policy issues that present themselves to both educational institutions and policy makers at the state and federal levels.

Part I begins (in chapter 2) by providing some historical context—a "time line" that traces the equity-excellence relationships in higher education from the American Revolution through the work of the Truman Commission on Higher Education at the end of World War II. Not surprisingly, this time line does not represent a consistently virtuous or triumphant progression, because the exclusionary barriers posed by religion, race, ethnicity, gender, and class have been embedded in the nation's folkways and social fabric. The fact that well-meaning people of differing social and political persuasions persist in debating many of these questions testifies to the ways in which our colleges and universities continue to reflect the major policy divides in American society.

Chapter 3 examines the success of the U.S. higher education system in pursuing its excellence objectives from World War II to the present. This chapter includes data on educational attainment in the United States and in other countries, evidence of research accomplishments, and a discussion of the main reasons for our country's success in educating a large number of students to a high standard and in promoting graduate education and research. We document evidence of worrisome trends—in this country and abroad, some pertaining to the flow of foreign-born graduate students in the aftermath of the attacks of 9/11 and the responses to them by the U.S. government—which suggest that it may be difficult indeed to retain a pre-eminent position in graduate education and research and to continue to raise levels of educational attainment. At the end of the chapter we emphasize the clear dependence of further progress in building the scale of American higher education, and its quality, on our ability to reduce equity barriers inside the United States.

Chapter 4 explores the impact of characteristics such as socioeconomic status and race on college access, choice, and educational attainment (degree completion) at the undergraduate level, seen from a national perspective. This chapter analyzes the relationship between parental income and students' academic preparation, taking into account other family circumstances, race, neighborhoods, secondary school quality, funding inequities, and learning outcomes. We also explore the roles of financial constraints and information deficits in limiting access to college and choice among different types of institutions. Finally, chapter 4 discusses a troubling trend in rates of "stop out" (sporadic enrollment in school spread out over a longer period than is traditional) and suggests that it is unwise to focus solely on access to college and enrollment statistics; completion of educational programs in a reasonable period of time is in many ways more important. We do not address equity issues in graduate and professional education, important as they are; there is a limit to the ground that we thought we could cover effectively in this book.

Chapter 5 tackles one of higher education's most intriguing and, until now, unanswered questions: what is the status of socioeconomically disadvantaged undergraduates at the nation's most selective and expensive institutions? Using the expanded College and Beyond (C&B) database, a rich new dataset containing more than 180,000 student records obtained from 19 academically selective colleges and universities,[10] we explore how socioeconomic status affects the entire path through the educational process, from application patterns and admission decisions to choices made by students as to where to enroll, to academic performance in college, and, finally, to post-college outcomes. We are able to refine our understanding of the complex relationship between social class and the experiences of students at selective public and private institutions by placing these findings in the broader context of opportunities extended to other "special groups," such as recruited athletes, minorities, and legacies (alumni children). We were surprised by some of the results of this analysis, and we think readers will be too.

In part II we turn to a consideration of the most pressing equity-excellence issues going forward and suggest ways of framing the choices that need to be made.

Few debates have engendered more controversy than the use of race-based affirmative action in college admissions. In chapter 6 we discuss in some detail the history of this debate, focusing particularly on the recent Supreme Court decisions involving the University of Michigan's Law School and undergraduate admissions programs. We explore the current state of race-sensitive admissions in light of these decisions and identify what we regard as the important unresolved questions. These include the potential for future litigation and the implications of the Court's decisions for recruitment and enrichment programs, financial aid, and faculty recruitment. In many ways the most intriguing question is whether in 25 years affirmative action will still be permissible. It remains to be seen how a future Supreme Court will view Justice Sandra Day O'Connor's "expectation" that in 25 years race-conscious admissions programs will not be necessary. What is clear from the new simulations presented at the end of the chapter is that there is a real risk that our colleges and universities will be unable to maintain minority enrollments, particularly at the most selective institutions, if race-conscious preferences are terminated in a quarter century.

Chapter 7 picks up the thread of the broader debate over admissions policy introduced in chapter 5. We discuss the admissions advantages currently provided at the undergraduate level to underrepresented minorities, recruited athletes, early applicants, and legacies, particularly with regard to their implications for educational quality and for the country's equity goals. But this chapter focuses primarily on policies related to the admission and enrollment of students from modest backgrounds. Using new data for the 19 selective colleges and universities in our study, we simulate the effects of providing an admissions advantage to socioeconomically disadvantaged applicants. One important question is whether income- or class-based affirmative action is a suitable substitute for race-based affirmative action; we find that it is not. In addition to admissions policy, we discuss financial aid policies, including the increasing (and widely debated) use of "merit awards" by individual colleges and universities.

In chapter 8 we focus on other issues relating to the role of the state in higher education, at home and abroad. We cover issues associated with government-funded financial aid programs, which affect all college students, as well as the missions, tuition and financial aid policies, and funding and governance of public colleges and universities, which affect the vast majority of American students. In connection with this discussion of tuition charges and access, we examine the debate in Great Britain over so-called "top-up" fees—variable tuition charges that can be imposed by individual universities above a government-mandated base level that give universities greater freedom in determining their offerings and their charges. This controversy is a clear counterpart to the debate in this country over how flagship public universities should ration access to the educational opportunities that they offer.

Although the challenges facing primary and secondary education, and the social and environmental factors that exacerbate them, deserve more intensive study than we can give them, we cannot downplay the degree to which these challenges directly affect the nation's colleges and universities. In chapter 9 we draw extensively upon the findings of other scholars on the nature of these problems and suggest the basic outlines of a policy agenda that could improve, over the long term, the size, quality, and diversity of future pools of college applicants.

We end the main body of the book by providing "concluding thoughts" in chapter 10. After emphasizing that many of the most important educational developments (and successes) have occurred more recently than many people realize, we present our own "scorecard" of the nation's progress in meeting excellence and equity goals. Looking ahead, we then identify what seem to us to be the major problems and suggest ways in which we can do better in some areas (especially in extending opportunity) than we have done to date. We are persuaded that the goals of equity and excellence are interdependent. As Mamphela Ramphele, former vice-chancellor of the University of Cape Town (UCT) in South Africa, has said, "One cannot have one without the other."[11]

It is comforting to know that our country is not alone in confronting what are often vexing issues. We include, as appendix A, an essay by Ian Scott, Nan Yeld, Janice McMillan, and Martin Hall that explores the implications of pursuing both equity and excellence in the setting of a country in which many people were barred altogether from any kind of educational opportunity simply because of their race and gender. Our South African colleagues report on this history of enforced inequality, and present a fascinating account of the innovative policies developed at their institution and in their country to support national "development" at the same time that they help the disadvantaged majority realize the benefits of higher education.

A NOTE ABOUT THE NATURE AND ORIGINS
OF THIS BOOK

This study had its origins in The Thomas Jefferson Foundation Distinguished Lecture Series presented by William Bowen at the University of Virginia in April 2004.[12] The lectures also coincided with a series of events commemorating the centennial of the founding of the University's Curry School of Education, and we were delighted to participate in that anniversary celebration. We had been interested in producing a book-length study from the beginning of our work on the lectures and thus had assembled far more material than could be presented in three hour-long talks. In writing the book, we have retained some of the informal character—and rhetorical emphasis—of the lectures. We see no purpose in attempting to conceal our views on issues that are inescapably value laden. We have, however, accepted the obligation to give reasons—and evidence wherever possible—to support the propositions we advance.

Much of this evidence is quantitative and is presented in tables or graphs. We also make use of standard statistical methods in some of our analyses. However, everything in the text is presented in terms that we hope will be accessible to readers who have not had experience with quantitative methods. The discussions in the notes and in appendix B incorporate more technical explanations.

The book differs from the lectures in two respects. First, it presents much additional material, including a more fully developed historical context, a more thorough examination of the relevant literature, a fuller discussion of doctoral education, and many new empirical results at the undergraduate level that have grown out of our analysis of the expanded C&B database. In extending our research, we have modified some of the "messages" of the lectures. In particular, our discussion of the excellence objective is now considerably more nuanced than it was in the Jefferson lecture devoted to this topic. Second, the book is organized differently than the lectures, which had a topical rather than a thematic structure.

PART I

Where We Have Been and Where We Are Now

CHAPTER 2

An Equity and Excellence Time Line

On the eve of the American Revolution, the 13 colonies could boast of 9 colleges, all with denominational ties, extending from New Hampshire to Virginia, and enrolling approximately 750 students. By the turn of the new century, there were 18 colleges in the United States (with about 1,150 students enrolled), and each institution, in varying degrees, educated the sons of privilege as well as youth from more modest social and economic circumstances.

Historian David Allmendinger estimates that in the early 19th century between one-fourth and one-half of the students at Amherst, Bowdoin, Dartmouth, Middlebury, Williams, and other New England colleges relied on charity funds or had to teach school in order to cover tuition and other expenses. From their earliest colonial and Revolutionary War beginnings, most of America's colleges consciously embraced young men with intellectual curiosity who aspired to careers in the ministry and teaching, including many who came from humble beginnings.[1]

Individual institutions dealt with these "poor but hopefull [*sic*] scholars" in a variety of ways. At Harvard and Yale, as Stephan Thernstrom observes, when the amount of financial aid (in the form of gifts from wealthy patrons) did not keep pace with growing enrollments, aspiring students from modest backgrounds were forced to delay their matriculation. It was not uncommon for young men to work for a few years as school-teachers in order to save enough money to pay their own way, as Eli Whitney did prior to entering Yale in 1789 at the age of 24.[2] But even in the early national period there were significant differences, usually shaped by geography, institutional wealth, and trustee policy, which determined how individual colleges met their enrollment challenges. Urban and "commuter" schools such as Harvard, the University of Pennsylvania, and Columbia attracted many of their students from the more affluent families of greater Boston, Philadelphia, and New York; by contrast, most of the small New England colleges were forced to discount their tuition substantially in order to attract young men from rural, small-town backgrounds, those whom historian Samuel Eliot Morison famously called the "horny-handed lads from country districts."[3]

Still, there is little evidence to suggest that today's concerns about broadly extending educational opportunity and equity were ever part of most 19th-century contemporaries' thinking, nor does there appear to

be any reason why they should have been. Schooling beyond the rudi-
mentary levels of literacy and numeracy provided by the "common" primary or ward schools was not deemed essential (or even relevant) to one's
economic or social standing. Thomas Jefferson's thinking was frequently
an exception to conventional wisdom, and his "Bill for the More General
Diffusion of Knowledge" (1778) would, if adopted, have provided some
of the most talented male students in Virginia with free public and secondary education and access for the most outstanding of these to the
College of William and Mary. "By this means," Jefferson observed, "twenty
of the best geniuses will be raked from the rubbish annually," and, as the
"Bill" indicated, they would be chosen "without regard to wealth, birth,
or accidental condition." In addition, Jefferson's bill also called for the
creation of a statewide system of free elementary education for all (free)
male and female children.[4] Absent Jefferson's singular passion, as late as
1775, no colony outside New England had made public provision for *elementary* education, and it is estimated that barely one out of every thou-
sand colonists had been to college.[5]

Any chronological analysis of this kind risks making the assumption
that history is an unbroken progression of expanding opportunities: that
the present is always better, more open, and more tolerant than the past
and that the future, in one scholar's phrase, will bring even more "betterment."[6] This is rarely the case. Examining the relationship between
equity and excellence in higher education in the late 19th and early 20th
centuries is more like observing someone taking one step forward and
two steps backward than it is like watching a steady sequence of forward-
moving giant steps. Incremental periods of progress are often counter-
balanced by setbacks for specific groups; yet each success and failure
reveals much about the value and relevance that society ascribed to
higher education at a given time.

We begin our time line with one final caution about presentism:
although colleges and universities have become an increasingly common
destination for recent generations of high school graduates, we should
not forget that this is a relatively recent trend. Enrollments in higher
education among the traditional college-age (18- to 24-year-old) population remained below 5 percent until the early 1920s before rising to
approximately 15 percent in 1949 at the height of veteran activity under
the G.I. Bill. The fact that approximately 60 percent of current college-
age youth are enrolled in some form of tertiary education testifies to the
social and economic advantages of a college degree today.[7] For much of
our history (at least until the early 20th century), the perceived lack of
utility in attending college—even among the financially able—suggests
that the principal constraints on "college-going" were not always a lack of
academic preparation or the absence of funds but rather doubts about
higher education's relevance to social and economic mobility.

EDUCATING THE "LEARNED" AND "LABORING" CLASSES

America's Founding Fathers believed that a republican form of government depended on an educated citizenry. College and university proponents like Benjamin Rush (the founder of Dickinson College) and Jefferson (University of Virginia) sought to raise the existing level of higher education, but each understood this in terms of the differing needs of the "learned" and "laboring" classes.[8] As noted earlier, Jefferson's "diffusion bill" reflected his singularly passionate belief that "every citizen should receive an education proportioned to the *condition and pursuits* of his life" (our emphasis).[9] Implicit in that distinction was the assumption that one's position in the "learned" or the "laboring" class remained fairly immutable, with little expectation of social mobility.[10]

That assumption, however, does not explain the appearance in early 19th-century New England colleges of significant numbers of men, many in their mid- to late 20s, often the younger, ambitious sons of farm families, who left the limited opportunities of an overcrowded agricultural sector behind and invested their hopes in a college education. Though many had been inspired by the evangelical stirrings of the Second Great Awakening, other promising scholars from modest socioeconomic backgrounds viewed a college education as an important stepping-stone toward a professional career in medicine, education, or the law.[11] Overall, however, these graduates, as well as those of the antebellum Midwestern colleges, never represented more than a tiny percentage (about 1 percent) of college-age youth before the Civil War.

Such modest enrollments may strike a modern reader as being unusually low, but Colin Burke, a leading scholar in this field, contends that these percentages are high when two factors are considered: first, ministers, doctors, lawyers, teachers, and editors represented just over 1.5 percent of the mid-19th century's total workforce; and second, scholars estimate that only 2 percent of American families at this time had sufficient savings to support their children's college education.[12] Likewise, women and minorities, constituting well over half the population, were ineligible for admission. What seems just as important to note, however, is that students from modest social and economic circumstances were part of American higher education from its earliest, most formative beginnings.

Gentle Men from Humble Backgrounds

Although differences in social ambition and financial realities partially account for the limited presence of students from modest backgrounds in early 19th-century colleges, one is struck by the extent to which the

New England (and later the Midwestern) colleges adapted their social environments and financial policies to accommodate such students. In the years between 1815 and 1850, many institutions faced the prospect of going under because uncertain finances could not guarantee a vision or plan beyond a semester-to-semester operation. Under such circumstances, many colleges took those steps deemed necessary to ensure their survival in a tumultuous and relatively unforgiving economic climate. They cut their tuition and fees drastically, tailored academic calendars to the rhythms of older students (who needed time away from college to teach school or work as farm laborers), subsidized room and board, introduced cooperative boarding arrangements, and provided need-based "charity funds" to assist the neediest students.[13] In essence, they discounted their charges in the hopes of filling seats that would otherwise have gone empty.

The political realities of living in the "Age of the Common Man" led colleges to set aside some funds for "scholarship" students—disdaining the earlier references to "charity" students—but few institutions, families, or local churches had the means to meet students' full financial needs. Moreover, the Jacksonians' contempt for privilege, the persistent popular sentiment that a college education was an unnecessary—even dilettantish —pursuit, and some colleges' ambivalence toward and awkwardness in dealing with students from more modest socioeconomic backgrounds continued to raise questions about fairness and opportunity. As colleges struggled to accommodate the special circumstances of less affluent students while simultaneously satisfying the requirements of full-paying "gentlemen scholars," segregation by social class became increasingly common in the form of off-campus room and board arrangements, one variant of which gave birth to the fraternity system.[14]

In response to an ever-growing demand from needy students for financial assistance and an awareness of the potential benefits of developing a standardized method of raising and distributing funds, the American Education Society (AES) was born. During its heyday in the 1820s and 1830s, the AES, inspired by the Congregational Church, developed into the largest and most centralized source of student aid, assisting up to 1,000 students annually in the 1830s. It was a bureaucratic organization with a professional staff of fundraisers and evaluators that was far removed in tone, geography, and scale from the colleges, village churches, and local charity societies and benefactors on whom indigent students had once depended. Although the AES fell victim to the Panic of 1837 and the ensuing depression, which adversely affected investments, repayments, and fundraising, the scale of its activities testifies to the important role that financial aid had come to play in the lives of students from modest socioeconomic circumstances, and for the institutions in which they enrolled.[15] Of course not every institution fit the AES criteria or embraced the notion that meeting the needs of disadvantaged students was an important institutional goal. In 1827, for example, a committee of Harvard's Board of Overseers "scoffed at the idea that the University should 'exhaust its resources for the support of a large number of indigent persons.'"[16]

Educating the Elite

Opportunities to attend some of the more established, socially prestigious institutions in the East may have been constrained by selective entrance requirements, high tuition, and a rigid class system, but the entrance requirements of most institutions were minimal. In his analysis of the composition of the 19th-century Harvard College student body, Ronald Story notes that rising tuition costs and more demanding admission standards appear to have converged in the 1820s when scholarship support was still limited primarily to students seeking careers in the ministry. Story estimates that as late as the 1860s, "perhaps 15 percent of Harvard College students received aid."[17] Of course, as Stephan Thernstrom reminds us, "even though Harvard had the most extensive scholarship program in the nation, its student body remained predominantly middle, even upper middle class, in origin," reflecting parental wealth and the percentage of students who had been educated in private schools.[18]

At Princeton, the high cost of education, combined with relatively small offsets from an endowment or other non-tuition sources, forced the college to rely on full fee–paying students for its sustenance. The college's resulting recruitment from the Southern planter class led to a noticeable series of changes in the composition of the student body, changes exaggerated by the increasingly secular nature of society in the early republic. The numbers of students coming from farm families declined precipitously, falling from one-third of the student body on the eve of the American Revolution to less than one-tenth by 1794. By contrast, the proportion of students who were the sons of "gentlemen"—a category encompassing the planter elite, the Northern gentry, and the leisured class—represented between one-fourth and one-third of the student body. Though most Princeton graduates entered the professions, lawyers outnumbered ministers by a ratio of three or four to one throughout this period. "Paradoxically," as two scholars note, "the College had to learn to serve the affluent—not because it was rich, but because it was poor."[19]

In the 1820s and 1830s, Columbia, according to its most recent historian, "remained a bastion of class privilege catering to the city's tiny reservoir of property holders, and professionals, capitalists, and creditors. Its ninety dollar tuition, by the 1820s again the highest in the country, both reflected and reinforced its economic exclusivity."[20] Most institutions, of course, did not enjoy the luxury of admitting only full fee–paying students, and by the 1830s regional differences had begun to appear. In the Midwest, recently created denominational colleges successfully tapped into the region's strong evangelical ethos and community pride, and made use of vigorous fundraising efforts spearheaded by itinerant ministers who served as "college agents" to recruit students and raise the funds sufficient, in most cases, to keep these institutions solvent.[21]

Denominational Tolerance

Though nearly all colleges created in the first quarter of the 19th century had been founded by religious denominations, with most located within the Congregational and Presbyterian traditions, the major political debates and ecclesiastical in-fighting fueled by the passions of the First Great Awakening had largely subsided by the time of the American Revolution. In addition, the new states' increasing religious and ethnic heterogeneity, the absence of internecine conflict among denominations, the financial realities incumbent in running educational institutions dependent on both public and private funds, and the competition for students led college officials to make two important accommodations: the first was the rejection of religious tests for students and later faculty; the second was a more gradual adoption of nondenominational religious toleration—by which colleges meant the opportunity for students to worship in the *Protestant* church of their choosing.[22]

Religion does not appear to have been an impediment to the attainment of equity or excellence in higher education during the late 18th and early 19th centuries. The pluralism, homogeneity, and relative harmony that existed among America's mainstream Protestant churches, along with the increasing distinctions being drawn between church and state and, of course, the economic realities under which colleges operated contributed to an accommodationist embrace of religious diversity. Even after 1850, when sharper lines were drawn between secular and denominational concerns, prompting the creation of many of the nation's church-affiliated Baptist and Methodist colleges, the absence of perceived student or faculty "outliers" in numbers sufficient to threaten the prevailing social order delayed the introduction of the kind of exclusionary policies that would characterize college and university admission practices and faculty hiring after World War I, to which we shall turn later in this chapter.[23]

THE FERMENT OF ANTEBELLUM REFORM

Using rhetoric familiar to their 21st-century successors, early 19th-century college presidents identified their schools' educational missions with responsible citizenship and preparation for lives of usefulness. "If it be true no man should live for himself alone," Bowdoin College President Joseph McKeen observed in 1802, "we may safely assert that every man who has been aided by a public institution to acquire an education and to qualify himself for usefulness, is under peculiar obligations to exert his talents for the public good."[24] In practice, of course, college presidents and their institutions remained as conscious of their students' individual needs as they were of the expectations of "society."

Colleges sought to burnish their identities as advocates of social responsibility, public purpose, and civic virtue, but many Americans regarded these ideals with a combination of hostility, indifference, and suspicion, still not quite sure of their importance or necessity.[25] In fact, many young men from comfortable circumstances saw no need, irrespective of cost, to invest their time or energy in a college education whose utility was still unproven. For those students who did enroll, colleges served multiple purposes, as they do today, but their most transparent, if unintended, role in 19th-century America—as a differentiating force separating the "learned" from the "laboring" classes—was the most difficult to reconcile with rhetorically powerful commitments to the pursuit of equality.

Nowhere was the dilemma between elitist values and republican virtues better articulated than in the often-misunderstood Yale Report of 1828. The report rejected calls for a more practical, specialized, vocationally oriented curriculum, and argued that a college's primary goal was the development of "mental discipline" rather than the acquisition of knowledge, which the authors referred to as "the furniture of the mind." Still, the report endorsed the gradual introduction of new courses, so long as those electives strengthened mental discipline by expanding the powers of the mind. Frequently characterized, even by its defenders, as a stubborn, last-gasp defense of an obsolete classical curriculum, the report is more constructively viewed as an attempt by one of the nation's most prestigious, elite, and successful colleges to align itself with republican values at a time when traditional constraints on the maintenance of public order had broken down.[26] "Our republican form of government renders it highly important," observed the report's authors, "that great numbers should enjoy the advantage of a thorough [classical] education. . . . In this country, where offices are accessible to all who are qualified for them, superior intellectual attainments ought not to be confined to any description of persons. *Merchants, manufacturers,* and *farmers,* as well as professional gentlemen, take their places in our public councils. A thorough education ought therefore to be extended to all these classes."[27]

By the end of the antebellum period, most colleges were still being criticized as bastions of privilege, as Americans continued to question their relevance to social and economic mobility and their potential contributions to the public good.[28] In 1847, a debate over the creation of the Free Academy of the City of New York (now City College of the City University of New York) accurately captured the social divide over expanding educational access and the role and value of higher education. In response to critics' protestations that the municipally funded, tuition-free institution would create unrealistic expectations among children of the poor and exacerbate class tensions, academy advocates openly acknowledged the benefits of upward mobility, occupational satisfaction, and enhanced respectability that would accrue to the children of artisans and craftsmen once they had access to such "useful knowledge" as chemistry and the mechanical sciences.[29] The contrast with the Yale Report's emphatic preference for a classical over a practical curriculum is unintentionally revealing, as, of course, is the implied persistence of fairly rigid class barriers.

One is reminded of the skepticism with which Henry Adams described his upwardly mobile middle-class students' faith in education—"so full of pathos that one dared not ask them what they thought they could do with the education when they got it." And when Adams summoned the courage to ask, he was surprised by one student's answer: "The degree of Harvard College is worth money to me in Chicago." A good answer, Adams concluded; it "settled one's doubts."[30]

Gender and Race in 19th-Century Higher Education

On the eve of the Civil War, the egalitarian ideals of the abolitionist and women's rights movements were a growing but still far from established part of the public consciousness. North of the Mason-Dixon line, women, in particular, made the struggle for access to the nation's liberal arts and "multipurpose" colleges part of their struggle for civil and political rights.[31] Oberlin College, which provided a unique and heroic example as the first college to admit students without respect to color (1835) and the first to admit women (1837)—though not without its own travail—raised the equity bar far higher than most colleges were willing to reach.[32] Advocates for women's rights sought autonomy and educational equity, first through the single-sex instruction of female academies and seminaries, and later through the creation of women's colleges and coeducation.

Some women's academies and seminaries operated under conservative, anti-intellectual influences that prized domesticity, refinement, and social distinction over academic rigor. Even academies like those founded by Mary Lyon at Mount Holyoke and Emma Willard at Troy, which espoused a more serious academic approach, lacked instruction in classical languages, forcing the new women's colleges, such as Vassar and Wellesley, to establish "preparatory" departments or, in the case of Smith, to moderate entrance requirements.[33] Meeting the academic standards established by the most distinguished of the men's and soon-to-be coeducational colleges was always an underlying goal of women's college educators and trustees, but their motivation was never mere emulation. The driving force was the knowledge that their institutions' reputations and futures depended upon both access (equity) and excellence, and the latter, as they knew, required the kind of applicant pools that provided the schools both scale (numbers) and choice. In evaluating the impact of women's education and the expansion of coeducation, one is tempted to describe a glass half-full and half-empty. By 1870, as a result of the military-related demands of the Civil War, women represented 21 percent of the total undergraduate enrollment, but as one scholar notes, even "if the absolute numbers of women enrolled in colleges were increasing, as percentages of the total female population between the ages of eighteen and twenty-one, figures stayed low," as they did for men.[34]

Though the impulses behind the emergence of women's colleges shared a common idealistic foundation with the impulses behind higher education for blacks, they differed substantially in class origin and value systems, and for these reasons the former institutions were not so embattled as the latter. The educational prospects and opportunities open to free blacks on the eve of the Civil War were much more constrained than those open to women, and blacks, therefore, were much less successful than women working and studying in single-sex or coeducational environments. As Henry Drewry and Humphrey Doermann soberly observe, from 1826, when Amherst and Bowdoin granted degrees to the first two black graduates, to the end of the Civil War, when the nation's black population exceeded four million, only 26 other African Americans received baccalaureate degrees. Following patterns and motivations similar to those that led to the establishment of academies and seminaries for women, a number of black schools emerged in the antebellum period. Though most were transitory and none appear to have awarded baccalaureate degrees, the existence of institutions such as the Institute for Colored Youth in Philadelphia (1837), Avery College in Allegheny, Pennsylvania (1849), the Ashmun Institute, later renamed Lincoln University, in Chester County, Pennsylvania (1854), and Wilberforce University in Wilberforce, Ohio (1855) testifies to the practical and symbolic importance that advocates of black rights attached to education.[35]

MODERNIZATION, THE MODERN UNIVERSITY,
AND THE TWO MORRILL ACTS

Many of the technological, cultural, and scientific changes that we identify with the Civil War and associate with the modern university originated
before the war: the rise of science (and the emergence of "practical" curricula promoting "useful knowledge" in chemistry, engineering, agriculture, and mining); the transformative impact of the abolitionist and
women's rights movements; and efforts to make higher education "more
comprehensive, more advanced, and more available to more people" were
already under way before the first shots were fired on Fort Sumter.[36]

Henry Steele Commager once observed that Americans expected of
education what they expected of religion, that it be "practical and pay
dividends."[37] In many respects, the Morrill Land Grant Act of 1862,
which authorized the states to use proceeds from the sale of public lands
to establish state colleges of agriculture and the mechanical arts, embodied these objectives. Today, close to 10 percent of the nation's undergraduates are enrolled in land-grant institutions; these schools represent
six of the ten largest undergraduate campuses in the nation; and approximately one-third of all doctoral degrees are granted by these universities.[38]
In that regard, "they are prime actors at both extremes: in mass education with its emphasis on 'equal access,' and in graduate training with its
emphasis on research specialization."[39]

When Congress enacted Vermont Congressman (later U.S. Senator)
Justin Morrill's proposal, its supporters had several vague, overlapping,
and ennobling goals in mind, including elevating the status of the "laboring classes," promoting the long-term benefits of scientifically based agriculture, and harnessing the practical application of academic knowledge in the public interest.[40] What scholars refer to as the act's "assumed
intentions"—its myth-making uniqueness as creator of "people's colleges"
born of popular demand, and its putative role as the "prime mover in the
American agricultural and industrial revolutions" of the late 19th century—
represent a flourishing and thoroughly anachronistic "received wisdom"
that owed more to aspiration and conviction than to the ultimate realization of these ideals.[41]

The misconceptions surrounding the Morrill Act's intentions and the
"step-by-step incrementalism" that characterize the fulfillment of its
vision provide a convenient platform for reviewing the issues of educational access and quality after the Civil War. It is helpful to remember
that even before the law's enactment, 26 of the 33 states outside the
Northeast had had at least one state-controlled institution of higher education, and "a primary reason for state support [of such an institution]
. . . was to provide 'public goods,'" such as services relating to agriculture
and engineering.[42] But one of the most difficult challenges facing most

Morrill Act institutions was the absence of a suitable student pipeline. Though educational reformers had advocated tax-supported public high schools as early as the 1820s, it would be another 50 years before even a modest educational bridge would be constructed between the common schools and the land-grant colleges and state universities.[43]

In the meantime, faced with minimal student demand for access to the new institutions, most land-grant colleges scrambled to create their own preparatory or "feeder" programs, suffering quietly as critics derided the University of Wisconsin as "a High School for the village of Madison" and Pennsylvania State University, despite its collegiate aspirations, as "Farmers' High School."[44] Other colleges swallowed hard and lowered (or abandoned) already modest admission requirements, accepting students with only one year of work beyond the eighth grade. Though their standards, facilities, and quality of instruction would improve dramatically through the years, "ingrained in the land-grant idea," as one scholar observes, "was the concept of collegiate education for everyone at public expense. Against this popular democratic ideal, standards of excellence quite obviously would be at a disadvantage."[45] Nowhere was this more evident than in the post-Reconstruction South, where Jim Crow was ascendant and where equity and excellence were, therefore, greatly constrained.

When Congress enacted the first Morrill Act, the nation was engulfed in the Civil War, and almost 30 years would pass before the concept of public-supported, "separate but equal" agricultural higher education would be introduced to the states of the former Confederacy. By accepting the South's prevailing "folkways," the second Morrill Act (1890) codified the extension of segregationist practices (which included the provision of all forms of public accommodation) to include the historically black normal schools already in existence, as well as the new all-black land-grant colleges about to be created. Although intentionally funded at lower levels than white institutions, the black colleges and universities offered modest programs in teacher training, animal husbandry, and industrial education, reflecting the prevailing philosophy, espoused by Booker T. Washington, that vocational and mechanical training—rather than liberal education or political and civil rights—were the keys to black advancement. Black educational leaders, however, battled just as fiercely as their white counterparts had three decades earlier to ensure that the black land-grant colleges were not precluded from offering programs in more traditional academic fields.[46] Nevertheless, in assessing the status of the land-grant experiment during its first 35 years, one is reminded of Lord Bryce's characterization of many of America's late 19th-century state universities: they were, he wrote, "true universities rather in aspiration than in fact."[47]

The remarkable degree to which that assessment would change, in less than a generation, testifies to the active and increasingly influential "public" role that higher education would come to play in the affairs of the nation. Though one finds variations of "service" and "citizenship" themes throughout the history of higher education, the rise of the modern university is defined by three primary characteristics: an interest in curricula that address practical, utilitarian as well as traditional needs; an acknowledgment that the pursuit of research and advancing new knowledge is a legitimate function of higher education; and the recognition that universities have a public responsibility and obligation to extend the democratic benefits of such knowledge to the widest spectrum of society.[48]

Although the public expression of such ideas took many forms, one can hear the call for a partnership of the scholar and the state in Princeton Professor of Jurisprudence and Political Economy Woodrow Wilson's observation that if a college "is to do its right service . . . the air of [public] affairs should be admitted to all its classrooms," because "the school must be of the nation."[49] When Charles Van Hise, the distinguished early 20th-century president of the University of Wisconsin, observed that "the borders of the campus are the boundaries of the state,"[50] he was doing more than espousing a mission statement; he was articulating the "Wisconsin Idea," one of the modern American university's signal contributions and innovations. The premise behind the "Wisconsin Idea," Van Hise and Governor Robert M. La Follette's fusion of two old ideas in the concept of applying practical knowledge in the public interest, reflected the Progressive Era's optimistic belief in disinterested experts—university graduates who would use their human capital "to secure the social and political betterment of the people as a whole."[51]

It is not surprising that the "take-off" stage of the modern university and the Progressive Era's commitment to a variety of social, structural, and scientific reforms coincided with steady increases in the number of women enrolled in America's colleges and universities. Though women had long since entered the mainstream of educational consciousness, it was not until the early 20th century that the disparity between their educational achievement and its use emerged as a contemporary concern.[52] The late 19th- and early 20th-century settlement house movement represents one of the best examples of women graduates' applying their training in the emerging social sciences to address the contemporary challenges of urban America. Of course "settlement work"—like its sister professions, teaching and nursing—superficially emphasized women's nurturing qualities. In reality, settlement house leaders like Hull House's Jane Addams, the Henry Street Settlement's Lillian Wald, Greenwich House's Mary Simkhovitch, and many others worked closely with academic experts and political bosses, moving seamlessly between reference libraries and university laboratories and the back rooms of aldermanic deal-making to address such basic constituent needs as housing, child care, nutrition, public hygiene, municipal sanitation, and child labor reform.[53]

Women would not begin to approach relative numerical proportionality in higher education enrollment until the First World War (percentages would go up and down until the 1970s), and they would continue to face curricular and residential hurdles, first at the undergraduate level of coeducational institutions, followed soon thereafter by significant postgraduate barriers in specific disciplines. Yet in spite of these obstacles, their early 20th-century contributions to the national issues of their time reaffirmed the still contested premise that true educational excellence means educating a large number of people to a high standard. In the next chapter we will return to the contemporary role of women in their pursuit of educational attainment from the undergraduate level through professional and doctoral levels.

CREDENTIALS, CHARACTER, AND EXCLUSION

The determination of exactly *who* should have access to higher education, and how criteria establishing such access have changed over time, is part of a debate that is less than a century old. In *The Qualified Student,* a historical study of selective college admission, Harold Wechsler poses two related questions: "How legitimate . . . is higher education's regulation of social mobility?" and "What social strata [is] higher education supposed to sort out?" And he reminds us that these issues became a public concern in the early 20th century only after colleges and universities assumed roles as "social regulators" between—and, ultimately, among—socioeconomic classes and ethnic groups.[54]

The evolution of a process by which educational leaders became gatekeepers rationing access to undergraduate degrees, and then to the professions, is directly related to the fundamental economic, social, and cultural changes that transformed late 19th- and early 20th-century America. These changes stimulated an organizational revolution that touched nearly every facet of national life, ranging from corporate amalgamation and the federation of labor unions to the association of college and university professors and the consolidation of reformers. This "search for order" encompassed a variety of structural efforts designed to bring systematization, rationalization, and efficiency to everything from the standardization of rail gauges to the uniform certification of college entrance requirements. The organizational revolution was a direct response to the massive industrialization, urbanization, and immigration that transformed the nation between the end of Reconstruction and 1920. Its "foot soldiers" came from the members of an increasingly well-educated, bureaucratically oriented middle class whose leaders embraced the notion that a college degree was integral to upward mobility and social fulfillment.[55]

It is important to note that popular acceptance of the *degree* as representing the apex of educational achievement and the passkey to success was not widespread until the 1920s, when a national system of compulsory public secondary school education provided the critical bridge linking the public schools to a vertical network.[56] Though our equity and excellence time line focuses exclusively on colleges and universities, we should not forget that for much of the late 19th century, a loosely defined higher educational universe also included academies, normal schools, workingmen's and mechanic's institutes, and Chautauqua-like programs where students of various ages pursued course work, certificate programs, and lecture series. Well into the early 20th century, the absence of any modern sense of progressing up an academic ladder from kindergarten through college and on to professional school meant that many students entered the loosely defined educational "system" at various points of "unruly horizontality," often without strong external incentives. Equally important in shaping many universities' decisions, of course, was the annual financial pressure of filling seats. This helps explain, as Richard Angelo's work suggests, why the University of Pennsylvania Law School *Bulletin* asserted throughout the 1880s that students could matriculate at "any stage of their professional development" with the assurance that they would not be examined, nor would they need a college degree "or any previous line of study."[57]

For much of the late 19th and early 20th centuries, college and university admission officers used two distinct methods for selecting students. The first was a certificate system by which graduates of secondary schools whose curricula (and grades) met university standards were automatically certified for admission. The second approach, often called "conditioned admittance," which prevailed at many of the most elite schools, permitted students who failed qualifying exams to "make up [that] condition" by passing an introductory college course or taking the examination a second time, and, most important, preserved institutional discretion in determining admissions criteria beyond quantifiable test results or secondary school academic performance.[58]

Once universities strengthened their ties to existing graduate programs and professional schools, a college degree became much more of a necessity for aspiring professionals.[59] The rise of a credential-driven society—and the residue of class, racial, and ethnic tensions that rest just below the surface of American life—guaranteed that issues of "character" and "fitness" would emerge as significant factors in limiting access to higher education. In retrospect, what is most surprising is the longevity of such practices and the relative ease with which decision makers separated issues of equity and excellence from those of character and pedigree.

The simultaneous appearance of discriminatory admission policies and the passage of legislation restricting immigration in 1917, 1921, and

1924 accurately captures the xenophobia and nativism of American society at the end of World War I and the Red Scare that followed.[60] Both involved the introduction of quotas, but leaders of higher education were far more deceptive in their purpose and approach than were members of Congress, whose aims were clear and whose debates were filled with racial invective aimed at Southern and Eastern Europeans and Asians. Though they lacked transparency, the nation's elite higher educational institutions "deliberately, self-consciously, and articulately manipulated" admission policies to preserve a social order they correctly believed was under siege from the sons and daughters of the "new" immigrants.[61]

Today we value the diversity of American higher education, but 80 years ago, although there was some acceptance of women's colleges and co-education, most institutions placed limited value on the importance of admitting students from different racial, religious, ethnic, and socio-economic backgrounds. In 1927, Teachers College at Columbia University published the work of a young scholar whose research provides a revealing demographic profile of college students on the eve of the Great Depression. In *The Social and Economic Status of College Students* Edgar Reynolds analyzed data on ethnicity, family income, and parents' occupational and educational attainment from students at 55 colleges and universities nationwide, including women's and men's colleges, coeducational institutions, and state universities. The data offer a revealing snapshot of institutions that appear to have been frozen in time, though they were less than a generation away from potentially transformational change.

Occupationally, the highest percentage of students in the Reynolds study came from families headed by "proprietors" (businessmen), farm owners, and professionals; the lowest number came from families headed by parents in the "commercial, clerical, miscellaneous trades and manual labor groups." Not surprisingly, state universities had the largest number of students with families in the agricultural and manual sectors, while men's and women's colleges had the highest percentage of students from families in proprietary and professional service. Parental income, as Reynolds correctly observed, "is an index of the richness of the environment in which the student has lived, and hence indicates a common denominator of experience which usually determines cultural levels"—and, we would add, greater opportunities for child-rearing experiences that develop self-esteem, supportive relationships, and a respect for education. Reynolds found that family income was highest for parents of students attending women's colleges, followed closely by those of students at men's colleges, with families of students in the state universities and coeducational colleges trailing significantly behind.[62]

Writing near the end of the 1920s, after the last great surge of immigration, at a time when immigration quotas were in effect, Reynolds found that the overwhelming majority of students attending these 55 colleges were native-born, and that parents from the 15 nationalities represented in his survey were sending their children to college in numbers proportional to their percentage in the national population. After noting some truly unremarkable differences—"men's colleges draw more students from English and Irish descent, while women's colleges appear to attract the Scotch and Scotch-Irish"—Reynolds closed with a classic understatement: "It is the similarity in numbers of the several groups found in the various types of institutions," he observed, "that impresses one rather than the difference."[63] For Reynolds had confirmed the obvious: of the 15 nationality categories he had identified from the 1920 Census, 13 represented groups associated with the "old" immigration from Northern and Western Europe. "In the main," he concluded, "it is the fathers and mothers who were born in the Anglo-Saxon countries who are sending their sons and daughters to our colleges and universities."[64] This was the America, as David Halberstam has observed, "that existed before the coming of the G.I. Bill . . . when the people who went off to college were generally the people whose parents had gone off to college before them."[65]

The primary source of anxiety among educators at elite institutions was the growing number of Jewish students sitting in their classrooms; these were the children of Eastern European parents whose families had emigrated between 1890 and 1920 in the first sustained wave of the "new" immigration. Unlike the "old" English, Scotch-Irish, and German immigrants from Northern and Western Europe, most of whom were Protestant and whose descendants had long since assimilated into American life, the "new" Polish, Russian, Slovakian, and Italian immigrants from Southern and Eastern Europe seemed strange and exotic by comparison; they were notably different in appearance, language, religion, and customs. They were much more like the Irish Catholic immigrants of the 1840s. These "new" immigrants settled in the major cities of the Northeast, and the Jews, in particular, quickly identified education as one of the most accessible and expeditious ways of achieving upward mobility.[66]

The anxiety and distress caused by the sudden appearance of Jewish students on the doorsteps of the nation's institutions of higher education was far out of proportion to their actual numbers, but their presence was new, disorienting, and—for the institutions—potentially threatening. At a time when most elite colleges valued lineage, "legacies" (children of alumni/ae), and homogeneity, the appearance of Jewish students in their classrooms created paroxysms of anxiety and fear among administrators and trustees. This was particularly true at Harvard, Princeton, Yale, and Columbia, where the visibility ("clannishness") of "aggressive," socially awkward, and grade-conscious Jewish students threatened to repel these institutions' natural constituencies (and, therefore, their financial foundations)—particularly the socially refined, cultivated students from elite private schools who accepted the "gentleman's C" as a sign of "well-roundedness," and the alumni/ae, parents, and friends of these universities who served as pillars of their communities, guardians of the status quo, and the philanthropic underpinning of their alma mater.[67]

In spite of the paucity of scholarships and the clear preference of some admission offices for the graduates of elite secondary schools, Jewish students represented 25 percent of the Columbia student body on the eve of America's entry into the First World War; the comparable (freshman) numbers were 13 percent for Harvard, 9 percent for Yale, and 1.2 percent for Princeton.[68] The shared fear of university presidents such as Columbia's Nicholas Murray Butler, Harvard's Abbott Lawrence Lowell, and others was that the presence of large numbers of Jewish students would alienate the traditional Protestant elites who supported their universities. The so-called Jewish problem was not, however, a concern on all elite campuses, as evidenced by the growing number of Jewish students who were admitted to and matriculated at the University of Chicago and the University of Pennsylvania. Columbia represents something of a special case; even though it had a well-deserved reputation for active discrimination, it admitted far more Jewish students than did Harvard, Yale, and Princeton.[69] But for Columbia, like most of the nation's most prestigious institutions, including the leading liberal arts colleges, finding a way of controlling the growth of "Hebrews" was a present and continuing concern from the 1920s well into the postwar period.

At first glance, many of the institutional responses and solutions to this "problem" may strike us, in and of themselves, as non-invidious and even benign. After all, how can one object to familiar admission-related requests for interviews and photographs, or information about parental birthplaces and religious affiliations, character references, and results of standardized aptitude and personality tests? In today's highly competitive admission marketplace, institutional calls for "geographic diversity," for scholarships to be awarded on the basis of "character and promise," and for the preferential admission of children of alumni/ae and athletes appear increasingly familiar, if not altogether commendable in their longevity.[70]

That some of these non-academic considerations and procedures continue to play a role in contemporary admission practices—albeit, in some cases, for more virtuous and inclusive reasons—cannot disguise the fact that their implementation in the 1920s was rooted in attempts to limit the number of Jewish—and to a lesser degree, Catholic—applicants.[71] Even during the Great Depression, a decade in which the nation's most elite schools were forced to accept well over half of their applicants, there was an acceleration in the adoption of policies limiting the number of Jewish students. The fact that such policies remained a part of the higher education landscape well beyond the midpoint of the 20th century has a great deal to teach us about the complicated relationship that exists between an institution's perceived self-interest and what David Riesman termed "democratic meritocracy." Knocking down barriers to equity that exclude people on any basis other than merit, accomplishment, and potential remains the perennial challenge facing American society.[72] The struggle over access also marks the most fiercely contested terrain in higher education since the end of World War II, a period to which we now turn.

THE G.I. BILL: A DIFFERENTIAL BENEFIT

During the summer of 1943, President Franklin Roosevelt found an opportunity to reprise two of his most familiar fireside chat roles, "Dr. New Deal" and "Dr. Win-the-War." FDR asked Congress to pass legislation providing a variety of insurance and educational benefits for the nation's servicemen and servicewomen. According to historian Keith Olson, the president "defended his request on the grounds that veterans 'must not be demobilized into an environment of inflation and unemployment, to a place on a bread line or on a corner selling apples.'"[73] One year later, after accepting his party's nomination to run for an unprecedented fourth term, candidate Roosevelt remained consistent in portraying the Servicemen's Readjustment Act, now known as the G.I. Bill, as an anti-depression initiative designed to prevent unemployment during a post-war period of massive demobilization and transition from a wartime to a peacetime economy. Of course, as lawmakers (and authors) often discover to their shock and dismay, the public's perception of their work can be very different from what they intended, and such has been the case with the G.I. Bill.

From the beginning, the American public embraced the G.I. Bill of Rights as a veterans' bonus, a reward for past service. For many Americans, it also represented the advance guard of the "economic bill of rights" that FDR proposed in his January 1944 State of the Union address. In that talk the president called for a "second Bill of Rights" that would "guarantee every citizen a job, a living wage, decent housing, adequate medical care, education and 'protection from the economic fears of old age, sickness, accident and unemployment.'" Even though FDR's proposal never had a realistic chance of seeing the light of day, it captured the public's imagination.[74]

In December 1945, Congress responded to complaints voiced by the Veterans Administration and veterans' organizations by extending educational benefits for returning G.I.s from one year to four years, depending on length of service and age, and specifying that the inclusive period of service should extend from September 1940 (which had marked the introduction of the peacetime draft) through July 1947. Though the heart of the G.I. Bill dealt with employment, unemployment, mortgages, and various types of on-the-job training, it was the educational piece that attracted the attention of most contemporaries and historians.

"The story of the G.I. Bill," wrote its leading historian, "is a recording of success," and contemporaries agreed that it was "the most ambitious educational experiment in the nation's history. . . . At the college level alone a total of 2,232,000 veterans utilized their G.I. Bill, with over a million veterans crowding on American campuses during the banner year of 1947–1948."[75] College and university presidents lined up to endorse the statute's principled commitment to equity; faculty members sang the praises of returning veterans' motivation, focus, intensity, and seriousness; and most scholars continue to portray the enactment of the G.I. Bill as a significant, if not transformative, moment in the nation's commitment to higher education. Even early skeptics like the University of Chicago's Robert Maynard Hutchins and Harvard's James B. Conant, who feared that the absence of standards and the emphasis on vocationalism would inundate colleges and universities with unqualified students and create conditions where institutions would keep veterans on merely to cash in on government largesse, were ultimately won over.

Olson pointed to a Carnegie Foundation for the Advancement of Teaching survey of 10,000 students conducted in the spring of 1947 that offered some revealing insights into the G.I. Bill's underlying strengths and limitations. Most relevant to our consideration of equity and excellence was the acknowledgment by 10 percent of the veterans surveyed that they would not have gone to college without government support, while an additional 10 percent "probably" would not have attended. The G.I. Bill, as Olson observed, demonstrated that a significant percentage of the college-age population had the ability and the interest but lacked the resources to attend college.[76] By removing financial barriers for a minority of veterans and lowering them for the rest, Olson argued that the G.I. Bill introduced a new paradigm based on equality that deserved to be called "experimental" and "democratic." It was, as another scholar observes, "an entitlement . . . [with] no limit on the number of participants," and its tuition and benefits payments were portable to any college or university approved by the federal government.[77] The G.I. Bill also provided a generation of working-class Americans with "an unprecedented opportunity" to secure their economic well-being through a college degree, a ticket of admission to the middle class that quickly rivaled the union card as a significant economic lever of upward mobility.[78]

The Carnegie Foundation survey also confirmed the veterans' successful entry into some of the country's most selective institutions, including flagship state universities, Ivy League schools, and elite liberal arts colleges. Furthermore, judged by the frequency with which returning veterans dominated honor rolls, dean's lists, and commencement awards between 1946 and 1952, one can easily endorse Olson's claim that the G.I. Bill "demonstrated that [government] support of education, especially to a minority group (which the veterans were), paid rich dividends to a society and to the concept of democracy."[79]

The G.I. Bill reflected an eclectic practical partnership of civilian and military planners, pump primers and free marketers, but in the end, like so many of the New Deal's earlier legislative efforts, the G.I. Bill's actual implementation was influenced and controlled by state bureaucracies whose policies reaffirmed the axiom that all politics is local.[80] The G.I. Bill may have temporarily broken down class lines in higher education, but race and geography presented much more formidable obstacles. However race neutral and egalitarian the G.I. Bill may have been in statutory terms, it could not overcome generations of segregationist policies in the South that severely limited the funding for elementary through post-secondary education. One scholar has observed that in Mississippi, as late as 1950 black (public) schools received $32.55 in education funding per pupil, whereas white schools received $122.93.[81] Such limits effectively reduced the number of black veterans who possessed sufficient educational preparation to take advantage of the G.I. Bill's opportunities. Nor could advocates for African American G.I.s ignore the reality that Southern white Democratic congressional influence meant that a "separate" and "unequal" distribution of resources would prevail throughout the South.

The work of economists Sarah Turner and John Bound, who analyzed the effects of the G.I. Bill on educational attainment, demonstrates that black veterans, especially those born in the South, were severely constrained in their choices. "Across all private and public institutions in the South," they note, "white institutions accounted for 92 percent of total expenditures in 1943/44; among public institutions alone, colleges and universities for whites accounted for more than 94 percent of expenditures."[82] The historically black colleges and universities, both public and private, were understaffed, had fewer resources per student than their white counterparts, and frequently could not meet the physical demands for space required by black veterans. Turner and Bound argue that decentralized federal initiatives like the G.I. Bill, which lack regulatory mechanisms to ensure equal access and cede responsibility for administering benefits to the states, inevitably produce widely divergent outcomes. They regretfully conclude that "the G.I. Bill exacerbated rather than narrowed the economic and educational differences between blacks and whites."[83]

THE PRESIDENT'S COMMISSION ON HIGHER EDUCATION

The G.I. Bill's proponents initially were motivated primarily by their desire to avoid the reappearance of Depression era bread lines and the massing of disgruntled G.I.s bivouacking near the Capitol, as World War I veterans had done to the great political embarrassment of the Hoover administration. Government planners had been thinking since 1943 about the postwar economy and had focused their attention on developing training programs to facilitate the transition of the G.I.s into the workforce. But they and their successors soon found themselves dealing with an entirely different set of manpower questions unleashed by the veterans' friendly takeover of America's campuses. How long would or should this kind of access to higher education continue? How would differences of race, class, culture, ethnicity, and religion be reconciled to create meaningful cooperation and understanding? What *social* role should higher education play in American life?

In July 1946, President Harry Truman created the President's Commission on Higher Education and charged its members with evaluating the status and future role of the nation's colleges and universities, particularly in the context of America's changed international responsibilities, the increasingly technological society in which Americans would come to maturity, and the relatively new and vitally important role of the research university as a creator of new knowledge. Over the next two years, under the general title *Higher Education for American Democracy,* the Truman Commission produced a six-volume report covering such topics as the organization, financing, and faculty staffing of higher education and the barriers these arrangements presented to equalizing and expanding educational opportunity.[84] Writing in the shadow of an escalating Cold War, with totalitarianism lurking menacingly in the foreground, the commissioners offered a remarkably candid assessment of the nation's unfulfilled application of education to "the fuller realization of democracy," the solution of social problems, and international understanding.[85] In many respects this report, to which we now turn as the final piece in our time line, provides a clear, perceptive, and unusually detailed road map of the major issues facing higher education in the postwar period.

"One of the gravest charges to which American society is subject," the Truman Commission observed, "is that of failing to provide a reasonable equality of educational opportunity for its youth."[86] The commissioners were struck not only by the untapped resources their research uncovered, but also by the opportunity costs of not capitalizing on those resources. In particular, they pointed to an oft-cited 1943 National Resources Development Report, which suggested that 90 percent of high school–aged youth should be attending secondary school, and that 80 percent had the ability to graduate. This was both exhilarating and sobering news when viewed in the context of the 1940 Census, which revealed that 60 percent of the American population over 25 years of age had an eighth-grade education or less; fewer than 25 percent of the 25-year-old population had completed four years of high school or more, and only 10 percent had gone to college.[87]

In addition, the commission staff's analysis of data collected from the Army General Classification Test, the test of mental ability administered to almost 10 million servicemen during the war, led the commissioners to conclude that "at least 49 percent of our population has the mental ability to complete 14 years of schooling with a curriculum of general and vocational studies . . . and at least 32 percent of our population has the mental ability to complete an advanced liberal or specialized professional education." These numbers were so much higher than the national average of 16 percent of 18- to 21-year-olds who had attended college in 1940 that, when the commission incorporated evidence of extremely high postwar birth rates into its calculations, the members concluded that "the educational attainments of the American people are still substantially below what is necessary either for effective individual living or for the welfare of our society."[88]

The commissioners did not hesitate to identify the nature of the economic, social, racial, and religious barriers that stood in the way of the nation's commitment to equal opportunity: "For the great majority of our boys and girls, the kind and amount of education they may hope to attain depends, not on their own abilities, but on the family or community into which they happened to be born or, worse still, on the color of their skin or the religion of their parents." The commission made it clear that it considered inadequacies of family income and "the inequality of educational facilities provided by different states" two of the principal stumbling blocks to expanding educational opportunity.[89]

In acknowledging the "sobering inequalities" and maldistribution of family income that their research had unearthed, the commission cautiously steered clear of any public policy debates, choosing instead to express the hope that income patterns would change with an expansion of higher education opportunities. The commission was much more direct, however, when it came to discussing regional economic variations and urban-rural differentials: "The fact is that the future citizens of the Nation are being born in disproportionately large numbers in communities in which economic resources are the weakest, the plane of living the lowest, cultural conditions the poorest, and the home the least well equipped to contribute either to the physical well-being of youth or to their intellectual development."[90] Noting the significant, long-term educational deficits suffered by students living in the poorest states, in terms of both educational attainment and the relative rate of school and college enrollment, the commissioners proposed a *national* solution to "assure a common denominator of extended educational benefits" and equal educational opportunities.[91]

In specific terms, the commission recommended significant expansion of statewide community colleges to provide two years of tuition-free schooling for students seeking terminal degrees in both general education and vocational and technical training areas.[92] Students moving on to four-year colleges and universities would benefit from a federal program of national grants-in-aid and scholarships sufficient to support 20 percent of the non-veteran undergraduate enrollment, and graduate students would be supported by a new federal fellowship program that would provide up to 30,000 grants of $1,500 per year. The commission strongly urged public institutions to eliminate fees in students' 13th and 14th years and to reduce fees for instruction in professional school to 1939 levels. The commission answered its own rhetorical question—"Can America afford this program?"—with an unequivocal "Yes," and with an appropriately moral and ethical reminder that "higher education is an investment, not a cost. . . . It is an investment," the commission observed, "in social welfare, better living standards, better health, and less crime. . . . It is an investment in a bulwark against garbled information, half truths, and untruths; against ignorance and intolerance. It is an investment in human talent, better human relationships, democracy and peace." In short, as the commissioners observed, the nation could ill afford *not* to pay the cost of a strong program of higher education.[93]

The members of the Truman Commission understood, of course, that deeply entrenched in American society lay forces over which they had no control, including individuals who dismissed such altruistic rhetoric as misguided and whose defiance and self-righteousness mocked the very notion of equal opportunity. In an uncharacteristic moment of soul-searching, perhaps reflecting some of their own internal disagreements, the commissioners admitted that the "spiritual damage" done by such discriminatory social attitudes and behavior is not measurable; "indeed, it has never been recognized with complete honesty." Sounding as if they were drafting a future amicus curiae brief in a 21st-century affirmative action case, the commissioners observed that colleges and universities have "a unique opportunity to offer an experience in tolerance and understanding which grows out of democratic relations with students from various national and religious backgrounds. . . . To the extent that intolerant attitudes against members of minority groups are given support by our educational institutions," the commission noted, "the fabric of our democratic life is endangered."[94]

Seven years before the Supreme Court's 1954 decision in *Brown v. Board of Education,* the Truman Commission majority weighed in with its assessment of the "separate but equal" principle. "To maintain two school systems side by side—duplicating even inadequately the buildings, equipment, and teaching personnel—means that neither can be of the quality that would be possible if all the available resources were devoted to one system, especially not when the States least able financially to support an adequate educational program for their youth are the very ones that are trying to carry a double load." To their credit, the commissioners recognized the equally pernicious effects of de facto segregation outside the South, where social and economic discrimination contributed to the same kind of impoverishment and hopelessness that existed under Jim Crow. Wary of the possibility that their recommendation for equalizing educational resources among the states might be captured by local interests, the commissioners insisted that there be "no discrimination in the channeling of such funds" and that black institutions "by law receive their full proportionate share of all Federal and State funds destined for the support of college instruction."[95]

Writing at a time when a full understanding of the Holocaust was still unfolding, the commissioners noted that in the United States blacks and Jews were being victimized by "un-American" admission quota systems that were "European" in origin. "It is well to repeat the warning," they observed, that in making admission decisions "the only defensible basis is that total ability and interest—rather than quotas or ratios, however determined—be the criterion." A quota system "cannot be justified on any grounds compatible with democratic principles."[96] The commissioners recommended the removal from undergraduate and professional school application forms of all questions relating to religion, color, and national or racial origin; in addition, they urged institutions that might benefit from information about students' ancestry and religious affiliation to make such requests *after* students had been admitted. Though they made a passing effort at documenting discrimination against Jewish applicants in a variety of professional fields, such as medicine, dentistry, and college teaching, the commission attributed most of the blame to the professional associations that "tremendously influence" admissions policies.[97]

On balance, we conclude that the Truman Commission identified most of the "big issues" of its generation and succeeding ones with uncommon prescience and extraordinary insight. These reports still possess a timeliness and relevance; they surprise and sometimes embarrass us with their clarity and wisdom. Their data, research, and commentary on such monumental, unresolved, and contentious issues as race, class, and the proper role of the federal government in promoting and implementing national educational policy provide a rich legacy.

Of course the 28 commissioners and their chairman, George Zook, could not avoid missing some "big picture" issues, perhaps most notably the rapidly evolving role of women and how their levels of attainment at undergraduate, graduate, and professional levels would shape equity and excellence considerations into the future. The commission provided an unusually brief and inadequate discussion of what it termed "anti-feminism" in higher education, observing that "the denial of opportunity has largely disappeared in the present century except at the professional school level." In 1940, women had represented approximately 40 percent of enrolled undergraduates, and that number had jumped during the war years to 65 percent before falling to 32 percent at the time of the commission's report in 1947. The differential was even more significant at the graduate and professional school levels.[98] Still, as one historian notes, even as the proportion of women's enrollments relative to men's declined in the immediate postwar years, "the increase in the number of women degree recipients kept pace with the increase among men."[99]

In fairness to the Truman Commission, the postwar debates surrounding the education of women—and the soon-to-be familiar questions about marriage, family, career, life-cycle choices, and the "appropriateness" of liberal education for fulfilling women's multiple roles—were just beginning to enter the public domain. At one end of the spectrum, Mills College President Lynn White's sentimental, anti-feminist vision, *Educating Our Daughters: A Challenge to the Colleges* (1950), and its call for the integration of women's traditional nurturing and homemaking roles with liberal education, represented, in Paula Fass's judgment, "an appropriate opening to a decade in which conservative visions often became radical and progressive ideals took an unexpected turn."[100]

At the other end of the spectrum, Barnard College sociologist Mirra Komarovsky's *Women in the Modern World: Their Education and Their Dilemmas* (1953) satirized White's anti-feminist position without embracing what Komarovsky termed old-fashioned feminism's "militant hostility towards men, and its disparagement of the homemaker." Acknowledging value in White's calls for a well-rounded liberal education that accorded more recognition "to family values, to human relations, to creative arts and aesthetic appreciation," Komarovsky argued that the price of concentrating on the practical aspects of homemaking involved substantial intellectual, economic, and occupational sacrifices for women. Moreover, many of the applied fields related to the home, such as nutrition, food preparation, textiles, clothing, and budgeting, "would shrivel up in a generation were they not nourished by the theoretical disciplines."[101] A decade before Betty Friedan's *The Feminine Mystique* (1963) reignited the feminist movement, Komarovsky's research confirmed the unhappiness of students and alumnae "bored by housework and frustrated by child-rearing," who felt trapped by the constraints of domesticity and contemporary social expectations. But as Fass notes, Komarovsky believed that the solutions to "fragmented womanhood" lay not in changes in the curriculum; "the solution, if it existed, lay in the society and not in the schools."[102] In essence, women suffered not from too many choices but from unequal opportunities.

For all of its prescience, courage, conviction, and relevance to the critical national educational issues of the half-century to follow, the Truman Commission report has proven to be much more of a favorite among historians than it ever was among contemporaries. In some respects, it was the right report at the wrong time. At the completion of the commission's work in 1947, the nation had been buffeted domestically by postwar inflation, food shortages, and nationwide strikes. Internationally, Americans were becoming familiar with the theory of "containment" and were preparing to finance the rebuilding of the European economy as part of the Marshall Plan. Under these circumstances, a fiscally conservative and politically vulnerable Harry Truman lacked the means and the motivation to push expensive, polarizing higher education initiatives. Nonetheless, by staking out public, at times visionary positions on what the attainment of equity and excellence in education would require of the next generation, the Truman Commission created a new and, ultimately, permanent role for the federal government.

The chapters that follow will evaluate higher education's efforts since World War II to expand educational opportunity while concomitantly maintaining a standard of excellence in teaching and research. In meeting these objectives, we think it fair to observe that American higher education remains a work in progress.

CHAPTER 3

In Pursuit of Excellence

Presidential and national commissions occupy an interesting position in American political culture. They often emerge in reaction to a sense of vulnerability and crisis—as the Truman Commission did in addressing concerns about the nation's manpower needs and economic competitiveness in the early Cold War years, as Dwight Eisenhower's Commission on National Goals did in proposing a sweeping program of social reconstruction to counteract the perceived lack of national purpose as well as educational and scientific inferiority following the Soviet Union's launching of Sputnik, and as the Reagan administration's National Commission on Excellence in Education did in urging a renewed commitment to higher standards and academic rigor in order to counteract the alleged "rising tide of mediocrity" in the nation's schools and colleges.

If there is a common thread running through the recommendations that emanated from these reports, other than an often exaggerated sense of internal malaise and external threats, it is the recognition that our national security and international standing depend on having a highly educated populace. "The twin goals of equity and high-quality schooling," observed the authors of one of these reports, *A Nation at Risk* (1983), "have profound and practical meaning for our economy and society, and we cannot permit one to yield to the other either in principle or in practice."[1] We agree, and in this chapter we examine the results the United States has achieved in pursuing and sustaining educational excellence in the postwar era.[2]

"Excellence" in higher education can be thought of as high achievement in meeting core objectives. Broadly speaking, these core objectives, as they were outlined in chapter 1 and discussed historically in chapter 2, are to educate large numbers of people to a high standard and simultaneously to advance and disseminate knowledge. (We set aside, for separate discussion later, the "equity" objective, which can be thought of either as subsumed within the broad "excellence" objective or as complementary to it.) The pursuit of excellence pertains to both undergraduate and graduate teaching and to research, and it has both scale and quality dimensions—with "quantity" (numbers of students educated) and "quality" (of educational outcomes) constantly interacting. Ours is a large country, and to be regarded as "excellent" our higher education system must do more than produce a few good ideas and provide a small elite with an exceptionally fine, high-quality education.

The huge scale of the U.S. system of higher education is one of its distinctive characteristics, but so too is the wide range of institutions that it encompasses, extending from some of the most prestigious research universities in the world to small liberal arts colleges (some of which are highly selective and some of which have fewer resources and are far less selective), to comprehensive universities, to community colleges (that have important—but different—educational missions of their own). We will argue later in the chapter that this "institutional diversity" has been, and is, essential to achieving and sustaining the scale of the overall educational enterprise that we see today in the United States.[3]

EDUCATIONAL ATTAINMENT

The most commonly cited measure of success in creating human capital is educational attainment, and we begin by examining how well the United States has done in educating its populace (and citizens of other countries) in the post–World War II period. Impressive gains have been made. Today, more than a quarter of the U.S. population has a college degree, and one out of every three college graduates has an advanced degree.[4] In 2002, 40,000 research doctorates were conferred by American universities (with over 27,000 going to U.S. citizens or permanent residents). The scale of the American system of higher education can also be described in terms of the numbers of accredited degree-granting institutions: there are approximately 4,200 today, including just over 1,800 two-year colleges.[5] It is a commonplace to say that the American system of higher education is seen around the world as one of this country's greatest resources and as setting an international standard. While this is a true statement, it is also correct to say that America no longer enjoys quite as big an "edge" in higher education as it once did (in the immediate aftermath of World War II), and that other countries have made great strides in developing both undergraduate and graduate programs. It no longer seems right to speak so broadly of American "dominance" in higher education, though a sizable number of American universities remain preeminent—across a wide range of fields of study.

In documenting the impressive gains that have been made in building the scale of this country's system of higher education, we will emphasize three recurring themes.

- One is the key role that has been played by the increased enrollment of women at all levels of higher education. There have been dramatic increases in degrees earned by women, and while there may well have been some "crowding out" of men at the more prestigious institutions and in some professional programs in which capacity is limited, the increasing participation of women has surely been an important driver of overall increases in degree attainment.

- A second theme is the increased enrollment of foreign students at the doctoral level. The United States has become increasingly dependent on foreign graduate students at the same time that programs in other countries have become increasingly attractive and more successful in competing for these same students than ever before. Sustaining the inflow of talented students from abroad is a key challenge if the United States is to maintain its success in assembling the stock of human capital that drives our economic growth and is the envy of many other countries. At the same time, we need to recognize that the number of United States–born PhDs has declined, especially in branches of science and engineering.

- An even more daunting challenge, which we will describe briefly at the end of this chapter and then explore in greater detail in later chapters, is the capacity of the U.S. system of higher education to educate increasing numbers of our own citizens who are from racial minorities or poor families. In this important respect, our "excellence" and "equity" objectives are powerfully reinforcing. The existence of an equity barrier to continuing excellence is a major theme of the book as a whole, and if this barrier is not lowered, it will be difficult for the United States to continue to excel in educational attainment. Recognizing this reality tempers what might otherwise be an overly "sunny" picture of prospects for U.S. higher education.

Degrees Conferred: The Key Role Played by Increased Enrollment of Women

In 2002, over a quarter (26.7 percent) of the U.S. population aged 25 and over had completed college. Much of the increase in college completion rates has occurred over the past half-century or so. At the start of World War II (in 1939–40), 186,500 BAs were awarded in the United States, as compared with 1,244,171 in 2000–01; there has been roughly a seven-fold increase.[6] As recently as the 1950 Census, taken shortly after the Truman Commission Report was written, only 6 percent of those 25 and over had completed four or more years of college. During the period since the end of World War II, the overall growth in educational attainment, as measured by the percentage of the population with a college degree, appears at first blush to have been reasonably steady (figure 3.1a). However, closer inspection of the data reveals that there was a decided slow-down in the growth in educational attainment on the part of those

25–29 years of age from about the mid-1970s through the early 1990s (figure 3.1b).[7]

Educational attainment has increased markedly for both men and women, but in the past 10 to 15 years, in particular, the overall growth in the number of degrees conferred has been accompanied (and been driven, at least in part) by especially rapid increases in the educational attainment of women. If we focus on the 25- to 29-year-old age group (figure 3.1b), the pattern is easy to discern. The percentage of women in this age group with college degrees first exceeded the percentage of men in 1991; by 2002, the gap had widened to nearly 5 percentage points (31.8 percent for women and 26.9 percent for men). This is a clear instance in which progress in broadening educational opportunity for one group, women—enhancing "equity," as it were—has contributed to the broader goal of increasing overall educational attainment.[8]

Examination of trends in degrees conferred by level and type of degree reinforces our appreciation of the role that women have played in increasing overall levels of educational attainment. In total, the number of BAs awarded between 1970–71 and 2000–01 increased 48 percent; the number of MAs, 103 percent; and the number of doctorates, 39 percent—all healthy increases.[9] But if we count only degrees awarded to men, these percentage increases drop to 12 percent for BAs and 41 percent for MAs. PhDs awarded to men actually declined by 10 percent from 1970–71 to 2000–01. Looking at first professional degrees conferred in medicine, law, and business, we find that in 2000–01, women accounted for 43 percent of all MDs, 47 percent of all law degrees, and 41 percent of all master's degrees in business. In terms of gender equity, we have come a long way in 30 years. The corresponding shares of degrees earned by women in 1970–71 were 9 percent (medicine), 7 percent (law), and 4 percent (business).[10] In both medicine and law, there has been a substantial *decline* in the number of degrees conferred on men between the peak years of the late 1970s and early 1980s and today (a drop of roughly 25 percent in medicine and 20 percent in law).

There can be no mistaking the significance for the country of the interactive changes in hiring patterns, admission policies of professional schools, societal norms, and women's career aspirations that have combined to produce such a pronounced opening up of these fields to participation by women. At the same time, it would be a mistake to assume that increases in women's enrollment have driven up total enrollment by an equivalent amount. Especially in professional fields where the overall supply of places in entering classes is relatively fixed, at least in the short run (medicine is an obvious example), the increasing number of women candidates has surely displaced some number of men—either directly, via turn-downs in the admissions competitions, or indirectly by discouraging some men from applying at all, given the tougher competi-

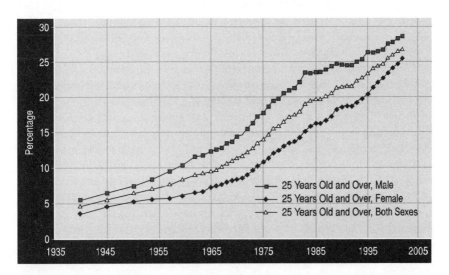

Figure 3.1a. Percentage of U.S. Population 25 Years Old and Over Who Have Completed College, Selected Years 1940–2002
Source: Adapted from U.S. Census Bureau, Population Division, Education and Social Stratification Branch, *Education Attainment*, historical table A-2.

Figure 3.1b. Percentage of U.S. Population 25 to 29 Years Old Who Have Completed College, Selected Years 1940–2002
Source: Adapted from U.S. Census Bureau, Population Division, Education and Social Stratification Branch, *Education Attainment*, historical table A-2.

tion for places.[11] As one reader put it, graduate programs are seeking "the best athletes," and whether they are men or women, U.S. citizens, or foreign-born candidates is not normally the main question.[12]

This is certainly the mindset at the doctoral level, which is highly competitive and of enormous importance to the entire system of higher education. Doctoral programs are of course the pipeline for the production of future teachers, scholars, and leaders of research enterprises of every kind. In addition, they are often a critical input in the process of creating new knowledge, especially in the sciences. There have been substantial changes in the composition of doctoral programs, and the same issues concerning possible "crowding-out" effects are present here: both the increased numbers of women candidates and the presence of large numbers of highly talented foreign applicants have changed the nature of the competition for places and then for jobs. The group that has experienced the greatest relative decline in numbers is without question white men. A recent government report noted that "among recent [science and engineering] doctorate holders employed in academia, the percentage of white males has fallen dramatically, from 73 percent in 1975 to 41 percent in 2001."[13]

These changes in the "mix" of degree recipients have to be seen in the context of trends in overall numbers of doctorate recipients. There has been a dramatic expansion in doctoral education in the United States since the end of World War II, but it has been episodic, with two periods of rapid growth (1961–71 and 1986–98) surrounding a plateau during the 1970s and most of the 1980s; then, most recently, there has been a moderate decline from the 1998 high point (figure 3.2). There have also been some changes in the pattern of degrees awarded by field. Over the past 30 years, the share of doctorates awarded in the life sciences has increased from 15 percent to 21 percent (with the absolute number rising from 5,084 to 8,350), the share in engineering has risen from 11 to 13 percent, and the social sciences have maintained a 17 percent share; the other fields have experienced declines in shares ranging from modest (in the humanities, whose share fell from 15 to 13 percent[14]) to rather sharp (in education, whose share fell from 21 to 16 percent). The absolute number of doctorates awarded fell only in education.[15]

Underlying these trends is the steady growth in the number of foreign-born recipients of U.S. doctorates, especially in certain fields. Each year the *Survey of Earned Doctorates* (*SED*) gathers a massive amount of information concerning new doctorate recipients—including citizenship status, field of study, race and gender, institution granting the doctorate, previous educational background, and plans following receipt of doctorate.[16] In the words of the most recent *SED* report: "The trend for *non*-US citizens earning doctorates from US institutions is generally one of increasing numbers. . . . *The growing numbers of doctorates awarded to foreign*

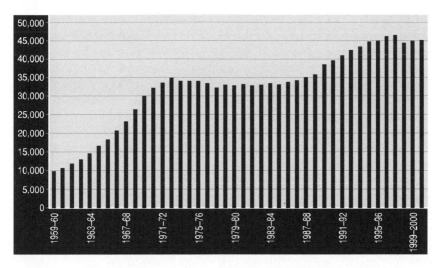

Figure 3.2. Doctoral Degrees Conferred by U.S. Institutions, 1959–60 through 2000–01

Source: U.S. Department of Education, National Center for Education Statistics, *Digest of Education Statistics, 2002,* table 246.

students on temporary visas has accounted for virtually all of the overall growth in the numbers of doctorate recipients since 1972" (our emphasis). Of the 2002 doctorate recipients in all fields with known citizenship status, only 70 percent were U.S. citizens; we suspect that a disproportionate number of those with unknown citizenship were also citizens of other countries, which means that the real percentage who are U.S. citizens could be closer to 65 percent.[17]

Between 1972 and 2002, the absolute number of doctorates awarded to U.S. citizens in all fields *declined* by more than 5 percent, with especially steep declines in the physical sciences and engineering. The explanation for this drop-off is, we believe, a combination of (1) increases in the number of well-prepared foreign applicants (which clearly causes some "crowding out" of U.S. candidates in the most selective programs that operate with relatively fixed numbers of places in each entering cohort);[18] (2) labor market conditions in the United States (which may provide stronger incentives for U.S. students to pursue career paths that do not mandate PhD study);[19] and (3) shifts in the intellectual "excitement" generated by different fields of study (one colleague has suggested that very bright U.S. students have come to think of parts of engineering and even physics and chemistry as somewhat passé, whereas in Asia and elsewhere, engineering and the hard sciences are very much in vogue).

The declines in doctorates awarded to U.S. citizens in at least some fields might conceivably have been even larger (though no one knows how

much larger) had it not been—again—for the increasing numbers of
women earning doctorates. In the words of the *SED* report: "The trend
towards the equal male and female representation in the doctoral
cohorts is particularly striking. . . . In 2002, 51 percent of all doctorates
awarded to US citizens went to women. . . . This marks the first time in
the *SED* that the majority of US citizens receiving a doctorate were
women."[20] Aggregate statistics can be misleading, however, because
women continue to be more likely to earn advanced degrees in fields
such as education and psychology than in economics or the physical sciences. To answer a question posed by one reader, if we exclude doctorates in education from these figures, women lose their majority position
—their share of doctorates outside the field of education is 46.5 percent.[21] Still, the share of doctorates earned by women has risen steadily,
decade by decade, in every broad grouping of fields of study, including
mathematics and the sciences (figure 3.3). It is relevant to note that a
recent international study shows that achievement gaps in both mathematics and science literacy have "largely disappeared" for 15-year-old
male and female students in the United States.[22]

Before examining trends in science and technology in more detail, we
want to pause for a moment to call attention to the worldwide context
within which broad measures of educational attainment in the United
States must be seen. International comparisons are difficult because of
differences in educational systems, but the Organization for Economic
Co-operation and Development (OECD) has worked hard to assemble

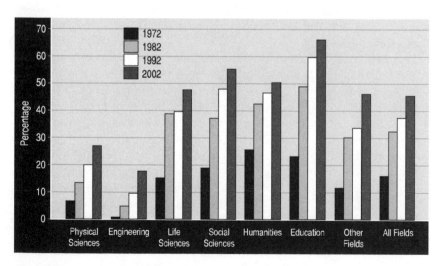

Figure 3.3. Percentage of Women Doctorate Recipients, by Broad Field of
Study, Selected Years 1972–2002

Source: Hoffer et al., *Doctorate Recipients from United States Universities.*

data showing trends in tertiary educational attainment (which include associate's degrees in the United States and the equivalent in other countries) between 1991 and 2002 for 30 OECD countries (table 3.1). Some readers may be surprised to see that while the United States ranks high, it is not at the top of the list—where we find Canada and Japan. The

TABLE 3.1
Percentage of the Population 25 to 34 Years Old Who Had Attained
Tertiary Education, OECD Countries, 1991 and 2002

| Country | Year | |
	1991	2002
Canada	32	51
Japan	n/a	50
South Korea	21	41
New Zealand	23	40
Norway	27	40
Finland	33	39
Sweden	27	39
United States	30	39
Belgium	27	38
Spain	16	37
Australia	23	36
France	20	36
Ireland	20	36
Denmark	19	31
United Kingdom	19	31
Iceland	n/a	29
Netherlands	22	28
Switzerland	21	26
Greece	n/a	24
Luxembourg	n/a	23
Germany	21	22
Poland	n/a	16
Austria	8	15
Hungary	n/a	15
Portugal	9	15
Czech Republic	n/a	12
Italy	7	12
Slovak Republic	n/a	12
Mexico	n/a	11
Turkey	6	11

Source: OECD, *Education at a Glance 2004.*
Note: n/a – not available.

United States is rather closely grouped with countries such as South Korea, New Zealand, Norway, Finland, Sweden, and Belgium. Next come Spain, Australia, France, Ireland, Denmark, the United Kingdom, and many European countries. It is beyond the scope of this study to attempt to explain this configuration of data, but we can note that the general pattern in 1991 was not very different from what it is today. The implication is that the increases in educational attainment in the United States reflect a worldwide conviction that it is worthwhile to invest more resources in education, including tertiary education—and especially in science, as we will see shortly.

It is evident that the United States cannot look with smug complacency on the successes of its own educational system when viewed alongside the rapid advances in educational attainment in other countries. The National Science Board makes this same basic point in an understated way: "Although the United States has historically been a world leader in offering broad access to higher education, many other countries now provide comparable access. The ratio of bachelor's degrees earned in the United States to the population of the college-age cohort remained relatively high at 33.8 per 100 in 2000. However, nine other countries also provided a college education to at least one-third of their college-age population."[23]

Degrees in Science and Technology: The Key Role Played by Foreign Students

The release by the National Science Board of *Science and Engineering Indicators 2004* (*S&E Indicators*) and its companion publication, *An Emerging and Critical Problem of the Science and Engineering Labor Force,* has called attention to trends in the fields of science and engineering that many find worrisome.[24] These reports raise issues of many kinds and contain a wealth of data that those particularly interested in science and engineering should consult directly. We will only highlight findings that seem especially germane to our broader interest in the excellence and equity objectives of American higher education. Of course many of the same issues are relevant in the humanities and other fields of knowledge, and we continue to hope that the voluminous studies overseen by the National Science Foundation in its own sphere of interest will encourage better data collection and more analysis in fields outside the sciences.

At the bachelor's degree level, *S&E Indicators* notes that "since 1990, bachelor's degrees in engineering [in the United States] have declined by 8 percent and degrees in mathematics have dropped by about 20 percent" —in the face of a general increase in the overall number of BAs conferred. In the physical and geosciences, the numbers of bachelor's degrees are

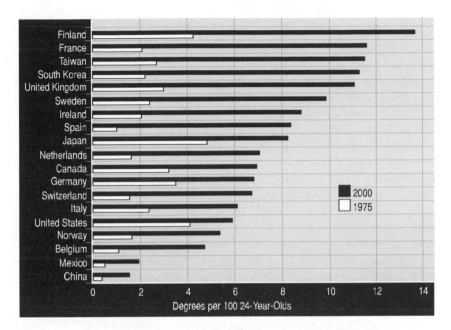

Figure 3.4. Ratio of First University NS&E Degrees to 24-Year-Old Population, by Country/Economy, 1975 and 2000 or Most Recent Year

   Sources: Adapted from National Science Board, *Science & Engineering Indicators 2004*, figure 2-34; data from OECD, *Education at a Glance 2002* and national sources.

   Note: NS&E (natural sciences and engineering) includes natural (physical, biological, earth, atmospheric, and ocean) sciences, agricultural and computer sciences, mathematics, and engineering.

well below the levels reached in the early 1980s.[25] The report adds: "There is evidence that many countries are trying to increase production of degrees in NS&E [natural sciences and engineering]. They appear to be succeeding in that goal well beyond what the United States has been able to achieve over the past 25 years."[26] We reproduce here a figure from *S&E Indicators* showing the ratio of first university NS&E degrees to the 24-year-old population in various countries (figure 3.4).[27] This figure demonstrates dramatically that in 2000, the ratio of NS&E first university degrees to the 24-year-old population in the United States was *below* the corresponding ratios for the great majority of the other countries shown in the figure. In 1975, in contrast, the United States was essentially tied with Finland for second place, just below Japan. The shift in relative position is unmistakable. *S&E Indicators* provides an even broader observation:

> The proportion of the college-age population that earned degrees in NS&E fields was substantially larger in more than 16 countries in Asia and Europe than in the United States in 2000. The United States achieved a

ratio of 5.7 per 100 after several decades of hovering between 4 and 5. Other countries/economies have recorded bigger increases: South Korea and Taiwan increased their ratios from just over 2 per 100 in 1975 to 11 per 100 in 2000–01. At the same time, several European countries have doubled and tripled their ratios, reaching figures between 8 and 11 per 100.[28]

One part of the explanation for these sharp differences in country ratios is that most other countries give their undergraduates less freedom to study an array of subjects and less freedom to change majors. This relatively early "channeling" by field of study is often accompanied by greater reliance outside the United States on the use of "manpower planning" approaches to direct young people into the fields that are thought to be most important to national well-being. In the United Kingdom (and other places as well), "manpower" needs have at times been assigned great importance in allocating funds across fields of study and institutions. By emphasizing broad preparation at the undergraduate level, including liberal education, the United States is something of an "outlier."[29] In general, other countries have chosen to concentrate their resources much more heavily in science and engineering.

High school preparation. It is often suggested that it is severe problems at the K–12 levels of education that are preventing larger flows of U.S. students into science and technology fields. There is no doubt that precollegiate education in America needs improvement, and later in this study we will talk about those issues (especially in the context of the need to do a better job of preparing students from minority groups and low-income families for higher education). However, *S&E Indicators* argues that available evidence fails to support the claim that a deterioration in preparation at this level is responsible for the fall-off in science and engineering degree attainment. The report states unequivocally: "Based on coursetaking, survey responses [to the Higher Education Research Institute (HERI) surveys] indicate that freshmen are at least as ready for college-level coursework as in the past. Respondents reported taking more of the recommended college-preparatory high school courses than in prior years." *S&E Indicators* also speaks positively about innovations in undergraduate S&E education.[30]

We are less convinced that K–12 education is not a substantial part of the problem. Many college faculty certainly have the impression that the quality of math and science instruction has fallen off, and the percentage of high school teachers of mathematics who have majored in mathematics is lower than it should be. According to *S&E Indicators,* "In 1999, 41 percent of eighth grade students in the United States received instruction from a mathematics teacher who specialized in mathematics . . . considerably lower than the international average of 71 percent."[31] Nor are international comparisons of student achievement encouraging: "In 1995, U.S. students performed slightly better than the international average in mathematics and science in grade 4, but by grade 8, their relative international standing had declined, and it continued to erode through grade 12." It is unsettling, to say the least, to learn that "U.S. student performance becomes increasingly weaker at higher grade levels."[32] One recent study found that 15-year-olds in the United States had scores in both mathematics and science literacy that were significantly below the scores of their counterparts in seven countries: Australia, Canada, Finland, Japan, New Zealand, South Korea, and the United Kingdom.[33]

It is entirely possible that the top 20 percent or so of high school students in the United States are as well prepared now as they were in earlier days (and these would be students included in the HERI surveys), even if they are not as well prepared as they should be. But what about the next 20 to 50 percent? One of the most disturbing sets of findings reported by *S&E Indicators* is this: "Achievement gaps between various racial/ethnic subgroups persist and have shown no signs of narrowing since 1990. For example, in NAEP's 2000 mathematics assessment of grade 12 students, 74 percent of white students and 80 percent of Asian/Pacific Islander students scored at or above a level deemed basic by a national panel of experts. In contrast, 31 percent of blacks, 44 percent of Hispanics, and 57 percent of American Indians/Alaskan Natives attained this level."[34]

Even if the absolute level of high school preparation has held up reasonably well, at least at the best secondary schools and for the strongest students, we suspect that the gap between high school preparation and college point-of-departure requirements is greater than it used to be. Students start at a more advanced point in the freshman year and are expected to move ahead at a very fast pace, with the consequence that a number of students who thought they would study math or science fall by the wayside. A study that focused on 1993 freshmen with a declared S&E major at 175 universities and colleges found that fewer than half had completed an S&E degree after six years. The same study documented that women and underrepresented minorities left S&E programs at higher rates than other students.[35]

A study of academic achievement in 2004 by the ACT, which is one of the two national organizations that offers college entrance tests, provides a still more sobering assessment. The ACT estimates that only 22 percent of the students who took its tests this year were ready for college-level work in English, mathematics, and science. In the words of the report: "Most of America's high school students are not ready for either college

or work. We've made virtually no progress in the last ten years helping
them to become ready. And from everything we've seen, it's not going to
get better any time soon."[36]

Doctoral programs. At the doctoral level, we have already noted that the
overall number of doctorates awarded to U.S. citizens in all fields has
declined by about 5 percent over the past 30 years, and that it has been
growth in foreign recipients that has offset the fall-off in the U.S. numbers. Of course graduate education in this country has been very attractive
to foreign students for a long time, especially in science and engineering.
S&E Indicators notes: "Over the years, their representation among all
S&E graduate students has approached 30 percent. Foreign students
with temporary visas represent half of all graduate enrollment in engineering, mathematics, and computer sciences, and one-third of enrollment in the physical, earth, ocean and atmospheric sciences combined."[37]
Doctoral degrees conferred show a similar pattern. In 2000, foreign students claimed more than one-third of all S&E doctoral degrees awarded
in the United States, and in certain sub-fields the share was much higher
than this (e.g., 65 percent in electrical engineering).[38] The share of foreign students earning doctorates was much lower in the social and behavioral sciences (just over 20 percent) and in the humanities (less than
15 percent).[39] More generally, the United States puts more emphasis on
the humanities and the social sciences in structuring its graduate programs than do most other countries.

The active participation of foreign students in U.S. graduate programs
has been exceedingly important for two reasons. First, the presence of
large numbers of talented foreign students unquestionably enriches both
the graduate education process and research programs. (The effects on
undergraduate teaching are more debatable. Indeed, there is a real concern that the "echo" effects of the recent upsurge of foreign-born doctorate recipients on staffing of American universities, and especially
teaching of undergraduates, will be adverse. At the same time, diversity
in faculty backgrounds can have positive educational effects.) Second,
the "stay rates" for foreign recipients of doctorates are very high. The
United States has been exceedingly fortunate to have remained an attractive employment destination for large numbers of the non-U.S. recipients of doctorates. The *SED* tracks carefully the plans of new recipients of
doctorates, and it reports: "In 1982, less than half (45 percent) of those
with temporary visas had firm commitments to positions in the United
States [following receipt of the doctorate]. A decade later, 59 percent had
firm commitments to stay in the United States; in 2002, the number had
increased to 71 percent."[40] This country's reliance on foreign-born holders
of doctorates for work in S&E fields can be seen clearly in census data on
employment, which show that in 2000 they constituted approximately

half of all doctorate holders among employed engineers; physical, life and computer scientists; and mathematicians.[41] The decisions of so many foreign holders of doctorates to stay in the United States, and to work here, means that these one-time graduate students subsequently make direct contributions to the nation's productivity and economic strength. In effect, the United States is benefiting from the heavy investments other countries have made in preparing their students at the pre-doctoral level to pursue doctoral programs at our universities and then enter our labor force.

It would be a mistake, however, to assume that the United States gains from educating foreign students only when they stay in this country. As Elias Zerhouni, director of the National Institutes of Health, commented in a *Science* editorial: "Some [foreign recipients of doctorates] will stay and improve US laboratories and facilities. Others will return to their own countries, increasing understanding in those countries of our science, cultural values, and good will."[42] It would be interesting to know how many of the leaders of other countries—finance ministers, diplomats, and administrators of educational institutions, as well as scientists—were educated in this country, and what the trend line has been. We know from anecdotal evidence that the "ambassadorial" effects of our having educated large numbers of such individuals can be very considerable, as important in the long run as shorter-term gains from employing foreign-born graduates in this country.[43]

There is no way of knowing if the current pattern of recruitment of foreign graduate students will continue. It is impossible to say with confidence how long the United States will be able to rely so heavily on regular infusions of foreign talent at the top of the educational pyramid to meet its needs in science and engineering. But several factors lead to concern about the ability of the United States to maintain its current level of "excellence" in educating and retaining highly trained scientists and engineers from all over the world. The raw data are troubling. Since 1997, there have been absolute declines in the overall number of doctorates awarded by U.S. universities (to U.S. citizens and to non-citizens) in every one of the major science and engineering fields.[44]

What is transpiring? First, it is clear that the United States no longer enjoys anything approaching a "near-monopoly" in the provision of doctoral training. There is no mistaking the strong desire of other countries to mimic the success the United States has had in building an exceptional educational base in science and engineering. One striking statistic tells the main story: in 2000, out of a worldwide total of 114,000 S&E doctoral degrees conferred, 89,000 (78 percent) were earned outside the United States.[45] There has been dramatic growth in doctoral education in China (which went from 234 doctoral degrees conferred in 1985 to 12,465 in 2001), Japan, South Korea, and the United Kingdom, among others.[46] However, as we will see later when we discuss measures of quality, the United States still holds a strong advantage "at the top," in that a large share of the highest-rated programs (and universities) are American.[47]

This welcome growth in doctoral programs worldwide means that more of a country's own students can stay at home for advanced study.[48] Of course costs are one important factor in shaping decisions about graduate education, and it may be that purely financial considerations will tilt the balance for some foreign students away from studying in the United States. The increasing number of graduate programs worldwide also means that foreign students from other countries have more choices in deciding where to study. There has been a pronounced increase in international student mobility, and many countries besides the United States have increased the fraction of foreign students in their educational programs at both undergraduate and graduate levels. *S&E Indicators* provides many examples of countries outside the United States that are recruiting foreign students. Japan set a target of 100,000 foreign students (most coming from Asian countries), which it is close to achieving. Universities in the United Kingdom, Canada, and France attract increasing numbers of graduate students from all over the world, not just from former colonies. Germany, having established some new programs taught in English, is said to be recruiting foreign students from India and China to fill its research universities, especially in engineering and computer sciences.[49]

The widening array of educational opportunities around the world is especially consequential in light of the attacks of 9/11 and the U.S. responses to them. There is already evidence of a sharp decline in the number of student, exchange visitor, and other high-skill-related temporary visas issued in 2002 and 2003. There was both a drop in applications for all visa classes, except exchange visitors, and higher visa refusal rates.[50] Important to our future ability to attract top students from abroad will be both how the United States is perceived around the world and how our government manages the delicate balance between a necessary concern for security and a desire to be welcoming to the "best and the brightest" from every country.

Data on foreign applications for graduate study beginning in 2004 are far from reassuring. Universities with well-regarded graduate programs that have become accustomed to attracting very large numbers of promising applicants from abroad report declines in applications (for 2004 versus 2003) that range from 16 to 17 percent to over 30 percent. In almost every situation, the largest fall-off has been in applications from China—with, in some instances, declines as large as 50 percent.[51] Not surprisingly, there have also been large drops in applications from Muslim countries.[52] To be sure, it is too soon to know whether this fall-off is the start of a long-term trend, a correction to abnormally high numbers of applications in the peak years of the late 20th century, a "blip" related in part to specific events such as the change in 2003 of the method used by the Educational Testing Service to administer the Graduate Record Exam in China (as a result of a strong suspicion of "sharing" of answers to questions), or a response to changing economic conditions (studying in the United States has grown less attractive in light of greater perceived uncertainty in U.S. employment prospects and expanding opportunities for highly skilled workers in Asian source countries).[53] Nor are we yet in a position to answer such key questions as how directly a fall-off in applications will affect enrollment or—even more important—whether it is the weaker applicants who are no longer applying. (Comments by faculty at leading universities such as Stanford and Yale suggest that the quality of the best foreign applicants is holding up quite well.)[54] These questions deserve careful study before seemingly authoritative pronouncements are made.[55]

Still, there are, as we have said, grounds for concern, and we dare not minimize the potential effects of our own policies. There is much anecdotal evidence to suggest that negative perceptions of the United States —combined with, and often aggravated by, new visa policies and procedures (related to worries about transfer of sensitive technologies as much as to the possibility of admitting terrorists)—are probably even more important. It is the unpredictability of the situation, and the lengthy delays, that are, in general, more troubling than actual refusals of visa applications. Also, difficulties encountered by foreign students and postdocs in returning to the United States after attending international conferences, visiting their families, or working with colleagues in their home countries can discourage attendance at U.S. universities and are certainly impediments to the fruitful exchange of ideas across borders. Tone, attitude, and just plain fear matter. Horror stories abound, and it is by no means only students from the Middle East who have been affected.[56]

In assessing the achievement of our country's system of higher education in educating large numbers of students, and especially graduate students, the United States has every reason to "count" foreign students and to take credit for having awarded PhDs to large numbers of them. We can be proud of the leadership foreign students educated in the United States have provided in the burgeoning development of graduate programs in their own countries. From the standpoint of serving educational values in an ever more interdependent world, we should not be so parochial as to focus only on our own citizens or even only on foreign students who make their careers here, important as their contributions are. For reasons that are both directly self-serving and idealistic, we want to continue to be a (if not *the*) preferred destination for outstanding students from every country and every culture. Fortunately, the pulling power, especially for the best students, of the exceptionally high quality

of this country's strongest doctoral programs is a powerful counterweight
—as is the broad appeal of research opportunities in the United States to
students who want to go where they believe they can do their best work.
And it is to the research dimension of the pursuit of excellence that we
now turn, before attempting to answer some of the still more fundamental questions about the quality of this country's educational system
and the factors that have, to date, allowed it to achieve so much.

SCHOLARSHIP AND RESEARCH

"Human capital" consists of ideas as well as the individuals who create
them and the educational and other environments that nurture them.
Thus, seeking to promote the "advancement and dissemination of knowledge" is certainly seen today as an over-riding obligation of higher education as well as of entities such as the Smithsonian Institution, historical
societies, museums, and independent research libraries. In his "Rockfish
Gap Report" of 1818, Thomas Jefferson anticipated what was to come
when he listed, as one of the purposes of the University of Virginia, "to
harmonize and promote the interests of agriculture, manufactures and
commerce, and by well informed views of political economy to give a free
scope to the public industry."[57] As Claudia Goldin and Lawrence Katz
argue convincingly, the growing specialization of knowledge and the
emergence of new disciplines did much, starting in the late 19th century,
to shape the modern research university with its emphasis on a fusion of
graduate training with scholarship and research.[58]

World War II demonstrated the importance to national security of a
strong research base in science and technology. The atomic bombs that
effectively ended that war were based on work at research centers like
those at the University of Chicago and the University of California. In
1945, Vannevar Bush, director of the Office of Scientific Research and
Development, submitted a report to President Harry Truman in which
he urged the creation of a new government agency to support research
at the nation's colleges and universities, "as long as they are vigorous and
healthy and their scientists are free to pursue the truth wherever it may
lead."[59] Public support for the research function of higher education
continues to be reflected in the budgets of the National Science Foundation, the National Institutes of Health, the National Endowment for
the Humanities, the research arms of other government agencies (including, of course, the Department of Defense), and appropriations by states
and even some municipalities.

In seeking to chart the contributions of scholarship and research to
the overall goal of educational excellence, we will of necessity concentrate on measurable indicators. But we do not for a moment suggest that

contributions that are less subject to quantification (and to "rankings" and rigorous international assessment), such as scholarship that enlarges our understanding of the historical roots of our values, gives us sharper insights into other cultures, and provides an improved intellectual framework for appreciating different modes of analyzing, communicating, and "seeing," are anything less than profoundly important. It is just that such outcomes are so devilishly hard to assess that we are driven back to citing specific research accomplishments, article citations, and prizes won.

Research Achievements ("Output") in Science and Engineering

Perhaps the most widely used measure of research accomplishments is winners of Nobel Prizes. The Sutton Trust in the United Kingdom has assembled a report containing the relevant data for the 532 winners of prizes that have been awarded between 1901 and 2002 in the fields of chemistry, economics, physiology or medicine, and physics who were affiliated with a university at the time of the award. The pattern is unmistakable (figure 3.5). U.S. universities have been the "primary" university association for just under half of all winners over this long period, and currently account for over 70 percent. Britain's share, which was consistently about 20 percent until the 1970s, has fallen to under 10 percent.

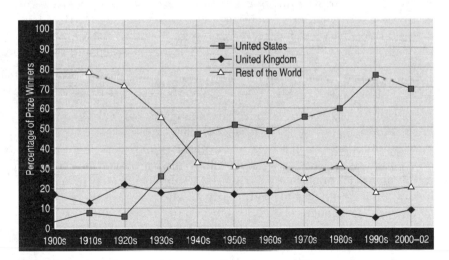

Figure 3.5. Percentage of Science and Economics Nobel Prize Winners from the United States, the United Kingdom, and the Rest of the World, by Nationality of Institutional Association, 1900–2002

Source: Figure constructed by the authors from values in Sutton Trust, "Nobel Prizes," table 3.

An examination of instances in which a laureate has won a Nobel Prize through work done at an institution outside his or her home country shows a definite "brain gain" by American universities. After reviewing other data, including citations in scientific papers (discussed later), the Sutton report concludes: "It is clear from all these indicators that the United States holds an increasingly dominant position in scientific research while other major countries' relative positions, including Britain's, have declined."[60]

There are, of course, many ways in which Nobel laureates can be classified, and focusing on citizenship rather than university affiliation alters the results considerably. In a front-page story in the *New York Times,* William J. Broad reported that the American share of winners in the 2000s was now "only" 51 percent.[61] The discrepancy between Broad's figures and those compiled by the Sutton Trust is not surprising—indeed, it is just what one would expect to find—given the marked increase in the percentages of foreign-born scientists educated and employed in the United States over the past 30 years. Although both ways of classifying have value, it is the university association at the time the award was made that provides the best information concerning the research contributions of universities in various countries. Still, in light of the pronounced expansions of doctoral programs outside the United States in recent years (noted in the previous section), we are skeptical that the Sutton Trust's characterization of the United States as "*increasingly* dominant" in scientific research (our emphasis) is correct—or, if it is correct today, whether it will be for long. Our colleague Harriet Zuckerman notes that there has been an increasingly long interval between the time of the work for which a Nobel Prize was awarded and the conferring of the award itself. Thus, the distribution of prizes by "institutional affiliations" is a less and less timely indicator of scientific strength.[62]

Articles published—and articles cited—are much more comprehensive measures of research output than prestigious prizes, and in the sciences and engineering elaborate sets of data exist and can be perused. Publication of articles in scholarly journals has long been the norm for disseminating and validating research results in scientific fields, and trends in articles published are watched closely as indicators of personal, institutional, and national productivity. In 2001, the United States had by far the largest share of S&E article output (articles published by individuals affiliated with U.S. institutions at the time of publication)—31 percent; the next highest-ranking country was Japan, with 9 percent.[63] However, *S&E Indicators* reports that article output by United States–based authors "has remained flat since 1992, even though real R&D [research and development] expenditures and the number of researchers continued to rise."[64] Article output has continued to grow strongly in Western Europe and Asian countries (figure 3.6), and the United States–

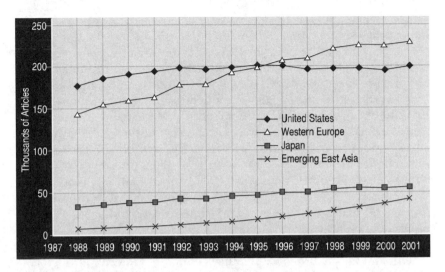

Figure 3.6. Output of S&E Articles by Selected Countries/Regions, 1988–2001

Sources: Adapted from National Science Board, *Science & Engineering Indicators 2004,*
figure 5-30; data from Institute for Scientific Information, Science Citation Index and
Social Sciences Citation Index; CHI Research, Inc.; and National Science Foundation,
Division of Science Resources Statistics.

Note: Emerging East Asia consists of China, Singapore, South Korea, and Taiwan.

based share of world scientific output has declined. The reasons for
the "flattening out" of U.S. output are said to be "unknown and under
investigation."[65]

The diminishing importance of national boundaries and the growing
internationalization of scientific research are illustrated by the increasing
number of collaborations that involve individuals from more than one
country. Technological advances (including tools as simple as e-mail) and
study abroad are clearly two factors, among others, that have fostered this
development. Over the 13 years from 1988 to 2001, the total number of
internationally co-authored papers more than doubled, increasing from
8 to 18 percent of all S&E articles. U.S. authors were particularly heavily
involved in these collaborations (participating in 44 percent of them in
2001), and America-based authors collaborated with scholars at institutions in 166 other countries. Even so, we see the same pattern noted in
other contexts: an extremely high overall level of U.S. activity accompanied by a downward trend in U.S. dominance. With few exceptions,
notably United States–China collaborations, the U.S. share of articles
involving a co-author from another country declined between 1988 and
2001—clearly a reflection of the growing number of centers of research
activity outside the United States that offer scholars improved opportunities to collaborate with colleagues in many other countries.[66]

The frequency with which an article is cited is one indication of its importance—but an imperfect one. (There is a not surprising tendency for authors to cite their own work, and the work of colleagues and friends.) As we would expect, the countries that produce the most articles also produce those that are cited most often. In 2001, the U.S. share of cited articles was 44 percent—a frequency more than five times greater than the next highest figure (8 percent for the United Kingdom). In some respects, a better measure of articles' importance is the "relative citation index," which adjusts for the share of published literature coming from the country in question. Even after this adjustment is made, the United States enjoys an extremely high ranking. One's confidence in the underlying data is strengthened by the finding that by this measure the United States ranks second, not first. Switzerland carried off top honors.[67]

There is no need to introduce more detail or other measures (such as patents and the citation data that they generate). However justified concerns about the future may be, there is no denying the pre-eminent position in scientific research enjoyed by the United States today. It is true that this country's relative position is being eroded, but the erosion process is gradual. And it may be that, over time, a somewhat more balanced international distribution of talent and of scientific contribution will prove to be healthy—not just for the world, but for the United States as well. Unequal partnerships often turn out to be less productive, in terms of the sharing of ideas and the promotion of mutual respect, than situations in which there is less "dominance" and all sides feel comfortable sitting at one table.

The Humanities

The unquestioned importance of scientific research sometimes seems to make people forget that there are other major branches on the tree of knowledge.[68] This is wrong on the merits—given the intrinsic importance of fields such as history, literature, and philosophy—and ignoring these other fields also leads to a discounting of the scholarly contributions of United States–based scholars. This country's system of higher education may well be at least as productive as any in the world when consideration is given to scholarly contributions in the social sciences (which are captured, though not emphasized, in the statistics reported in *S&E Indicators*) and in the humanities (which are excluded altogether).

The big problem is the lack of data, and of even a framework for assessment. Robert Solow, a Nobel laureate in economics, observed that while 1,200 pages of *S&E Indicators* are published biannually, "data-collection in the humanities [is] still at a primitive stage."[69] The comparative lack of data on the arts and humanities has not gone unnoticed; the American Academy of Arts & Sciences (AAAS), in the component of its Initiative for the Humanities and Culture that will "focus on building an infrastructure to improve the collection of data about the humanities and provide an empirical base for decision making by educators and policy makers,"[70] plans to create a set of humanities indicators. An introductory volume to the *Humanities Indicators* project, called *Making the Humanities Count: The Importance of Data* (authored by Solow and colleagues), has been published by the AAAS. This report includes several essays on the need and the potential for quantitative measures in the arts and humanities, along with "A Report to the American Academy: Evaluation of Existing Datasets for Policy Research on Humanities Fields" by Calvin C. Jones. Francis Oakley's essay ("Data Deprivation and *Humanities Indicators*") is particularly useful in illustrating how the lack of empirical measures leaves the humanities open to attack, as during the culture wars of the 1980s and 1990s, when an off-hand remark that Alice Walker's *The Color Purple* was likely taught in more English classes than the sum total of Shakespeare's plays was widely disseminated. Later research found Alice Walker's work to be represented in less than 1 percent of English classes.

Oakley also discusses the fact that if we rely solely on degrees earned we are left with the wrong impression, because students meeting general education requirements are responsible for a large part of the enrollment in arts and humanities classes. The OECD reports that in 2002, the United States ranked eighth out of 26 countries in the percentage (14.4 percent) of undergraduate degrees conferred in the arts and the humanities.[71] If account were taken of course enrollments outside students' major field, as Oakley suggests, the U.S. rank would surely be higher.

Data limitations notwithstanding, there are some things that can be said. In the humanities, where scholarly output takes many forms (including museum exhibits and musical scores), books and monographs are generally regarded as more important than articles in the presentation of scholarship. The American Association of University Presses counts 124 member presses in its 2003–04 *Directory*. Together, these publishers produce something on the order of 11,000 titles per year.[72]

With regard to journals, an analysis of 3,829 scholarly journals in the arts and humanities currently published in 12 countries, including the United States, the United Kingdom, Russia, Germany, China, and India, shows that over 40 percent are published in the United States. The United Kingdom, the country that comes closest to the United States in producing this type of journal, is responsible for 17 percent of the output.[73] The Institute for Scientific Information (ISI) publishes the *Arts and Humanities Citation Index,* a multidisciplinary index of articles published in 1,300 international arts and humanities journals, that allows us to learn about the institutional affiliations of the authors of articles published in arts and humanities journals. A search of the index for the years 1988, 1996, and 2002 shows that just under 30 percent of the articles in each of those years were published by authors affiliated with a U.S. institution. United Kingdom–affiliated authors published between 5 and 8 percent of the articles in those same years. Authors affiliated with institutions in India and Japan each published less than 1 percent of the articles in 1988, 1996, and 2002.[74]

The JSTOR electronic database, which contains the complete back files of more than 400 leading journals (overwhelmingly Western journals in the English language) offers an additional, relatively new, source of information.[75] More than 2,000 institutions in over 80 countries have subscribed to one or more of the JSTOR collections, which is itself testimony to the importance scholars attach to its content. Of the fields represented in JSTOR, history is the most popular in terms of the numbers of "meaningful accesses" to the database; language and literature is in fifth place, following economics, sociology, and political science. In the first six months of 2004, the history journals alone were accessed on more than 10.7 million occasions, and more than 1.3 million articles were printed. The extent of use outside the United States is also noteworthy, in that it serves as one measure of the value attached to this collection of journal literature by scholars in other countries. During the first six months of 2004, there were more than 3.6 meaningful accesses to history titles from outside the United States, 1.1 million to philosophy titles, and 1.7 million to literature titles.

Academic libraries and their attendant resources in the United States have expanded greatly since the middle of the 20th century. Although these libraries devote significant resources to the sciences and engineering, their role in supporting the arts and humanities is paramount. The number of print volumes alone in U.S. academic libraries grew by more than 4.5 million between 1974 and 2000.[76] Even more remarkable, perhaps, than the expansion of academic library collections is the development of tools and resources, such as union catalogs, abstracting and indexing services, and, more recently, full-text resources, including JSTOR, that help to maximize access to and dissemination of scholarly resources. The United States is home to two of the world's major bibliographic utilities, the Online Computer Library Catalog (OCLC) and the Research Libraries Information Network, each of which contains records of over 45 million books, journals, musical scores, archival collections, and visual resources. The larger of these two networks in terms of participants, OCLC, counted 45,402 member libraries from 84 countries in its most recent annual report; close to 20 percent of the member libraries are outside of the United States. Of 183 current abstracting and indexing services in the arts and humanities, such as the *MLA Inter-*

national Bibliography, the *Philosopher's Index,* and *Historical Abstracts,* one-half are published in the United States.[77]

The leaders of America's major research universities, such as the members of the Association of American Universities, recognize clearly the importance of the humanities and continue to encourage efforts to improve teaching and scholarship in these critically important fields.[78] But it is no easy task either to marshal the resources that are required or (first) to reach agreement on priorities.

JUDGING QUALITY

As scores of students of higher education have recognized, defining and measuring "quality" at any level of study is excruciatingly difficult. The subjective nature of the concept, the different purposes served by higher education (and by different kinds of colleges and universities), and the lack of readily comparable data all contribute to the problem. But there is an even more fundamental source of difficulty that is less frequently discussed: the "best" educational environment for one student may well not be the best environment for another student, even when the two students are similar in many respects. Two of us (Bowen and Tobin) spent much of our lives as university and college presidents attempting to convince prospective students that the key in making choices about colleges is to find the right "fit" between, on the one hand, the characteristics, motivations, and interests of the student in question and, on the other hand, what a particular institution is like—how its course of study is structured, what teaching practices are followed, what opportunities it offers outside the classroom, what it does well, and what it does badly. But of course prospective students and their parents want simpler, unequivocal answers to the question of what is "best"—even when such answers are inevitably flawed.

Rankings of Colleges and Graduate Programs in the United States

As one of our colleagues who did a study of college rankings observed: "There is a seemingly endless preoccupation in America with rankings, whether it's restaurants, doctors, hospitals, or colleges and universities."[79] There is a long history of efforts to compile relevant data, and an equally long history of disputes as to what it is that should be examined: is it perceptions of reputation; measures of resources; degrees of selectivity; test scores; outcomes of various kinds, including accomplishments of alumni/ae; or "best practices" in teaching?[80] It would be inappropriate for us to do more here than restate one basic point: undergraduate programs vary substantially in mission, in resources, and in perceived quality (however quality is defined). We see no reliable way of answering definitively either of two questions of interest: Is American undergraduate education better today than it was in the past? And is it better than undergraduate programs outside the United States? Certainly there are reasons for thinking it is probably better today (for example, laboratory and library resources, including electronic resources, are much improved), and the continuing flow of foreign students to U.S. college programs is one "revealed preference" measure of what students themselves think. Beyond that we will not go.[81]

At the doctoral level, ranking methodologies are better developed (the task is at least somewhat more focused), though they are certainly not free of controversy. The National Research Council is hard at work right now on a revised approach to the preparation of an ambitious analysis of 57 fields of study that is scheduled to be released in September 2007.[82] Again, these studies are helpful mainly in permitting cross-sectional comparisons of particular doctoral programs, and in allowing colleges and universities to gain some sense of whether their programs are improving relative to the programs offered by other American universities. But the appearance of these rankings every 10 years or so is relevant to this study in one larger way: these rankings allow us to assign graduate programs in defined fields to "quality tiers," and then to see how the production of PhDs is distributed by quality tier.

In an earlier study, Bowen and Neil Rudenstine charted the extraordinary growth in the number of PhD programs in the United States between 1958 and 1972 in six case-study fields: English, history, political science, economics, mathematics, and physics. They found that the number of doctorate-granting programs doubled over this 14-year period.[83] There was then a substantial contraction in the academic job market and the scale of the graduate education enterprise (with the number of doctorates conferred in these six fields declining by one-third between 1972 and 1988), and yet the overall number of programs increased modestly. Much of the contraction in program size (measured by numbers of degrees conferred) occurred at the most highly ranked, Tier I, programs. The overall result was that the share of all doctorates conferred by the Tier I programs in these six fields declined from 63 percent in 1958 to 44 percent in 1988; the share conferred by the lowest-ranked, Tier IV, programs rose from 6 percent to 16 percent. We also found that over this 30-year period there was a proliferation of very small programs (measured in terms of doctoral degrees conferred) that must surely have had difficulty operating efficiently—or effectively.[84] More recent research by Richard Freeman and his colleagues suggests that this problem of a growing presence of small, lower-ranked doctorate programs continues to the present day.[85]

It is hard to avoid the conclusion that, however much improvement there may have been in the quality of individual programs, the quality of the entire doctorate-granting enterprise is likely to have slipped at least somewhat. Still, as we saw earlier in the chapter, large numbers of foreign graduate students seek out U.S. programs. Moreover, there is every reason to believe—according to testimony from graduate deans and others —that the leading American universities attract absolutely outstanding students from abroad, and this is the graduate school version of the revealed preference test.

Worldwide Institutional Rankings of Universities

All of the problems present in creating rankings of programs and institutions within one country are multiplied many times when international comparisons are attempted. Recently the Institute of Higher Education at Shanghai Jiao Tong University published the results of its effort to rank the "top 500 world universities," and then the top 100 universities in (separately) America, Europe, and Asia. The creators of these rankings are to be congratulated for spelling out their criteria and the weights they assign to each. They focus on the institutional affiliations of Nobel laureates, the affiliations of highly cited researchers, numbers of articles published in *Nature* and *Science*, articles in the *Science Citation Index* and the *Social Sciences Citation Index*, and, finally, a "per faculty member" index that is intended to correct somewhat for the effects of size per se on the other measures. The authors recognize that these measures bias the results in favor of institutions that are strong in science, engineering, and some of the quantitative social sciences, rather than in the arts and humanities, and they regret their inability to obtain useful information in the latter fields. They write, rather plaintively, "We tried really hard but were not successful in finding special criteria and internationally comparable data for social sciences and humanities."[86]

Of the top 50 universities according to this ranking, 35 are in the United States (including 12 of the top 15); 5 in the United Kingdom; 2 each in Canada, France, and Japan; and 1 each in Germany, the Netherlands, Sweden, and Switzerland. The presence of so many American universities on this list, and at the very top of it, is not surprising, even in the absence of data on the humanities (in which the United States is relatively strong). One reason why international rankings in the humanities will always be difficult, if not impossible, to create is that the humanities—unlike math or the sciences, and some social sciences—has no common "symbolic languages" in which research and discovery are reported. Everyone, everywhere, who is a physicist can understand the latest findings. But the humanities are much more local or regional in terms of language, culture, methodology, modes of interpretation, and even which subjects are considered to be in the humanities (a term not even used in many countries). The humanities are multi-cultural by definition, just as the sciences are by nature trans-cultural.

In any case, the absence of wide-ranging assessments of programs in the humanities and related fields almost surely leads to an understatement of the relative position of U.S. universities (and undergraduate colleges). As noted earlier, the United States continues to devote more resources to the humanities, relative to the sciences and engineering, than is common in most other countries. Of course outstanding work in the humanities is done outside the United States; the United Kingdom, for example, has excellent historians, classicists, and art historians who are clearly equal to (and sometimes superior to) the best U.S. scholars, and Germany and France, as well as Canada, have first-rate classicists and historians. But in much of the rest of the world, including especially Asia, "excellence" is equated largely with work in the sciences and engineering, and work that is done in the humanities is often said to be somewhat mechanical.

Finally, and more generally, we should note that ranking *top* universities, however it is done, tells us nothing about the distribution of quality throughout an entire system of higher education, especially one as institutionally diverse as ours. Robert Stevens, who has long associations with colleges and universities in the United States and the United Kingdom, recently quoted one commentator as follows: "The US, with 4,000 institutions of higher education, probably has 50 of the best universities in the world and undoubtedly has 500 of the worst."[87] On this question, we are agnostic. Finding criteria for identifying the "worst" must surely be an even more daunting task than finding criteria for identifying the "best"!

A Market Test in the United States

Difficult as it is to assess "quality" at any level of educational attainment, there is a broad empirical test that can help us, in the U.S. context, answer a more limited question: does college education—and receipt of advanced degrees—have market value? One indicator that high educational attainment in the United States, and the large financial outlays that our country makes on tertiary education, are having a marked economic impact is to be found in earnings differentials. The U.S. Census Bureau recently produced a study called, appropriately, "The Big Payoff," which provides "synthetic" estimates of working-lifetime earnings associated with different levels of educational attainment. A principal finding is that present-day earnings differentials translate into very large differences over a projected 40-year working life: the estimate for high school graduates of $1.2 million compares with estimates of $2.1 million for those with bachelor's degrees, $3.4 million for those with doctorates, and $4.4 million for those with professional degrees.[88] The market is rewarding generously what it perceives as the large value added by formal education.

In addition, the economic benefits of higher education extend well beyond the individual. DeLong, Goldin, and Katz conclude that American economic growth during the 20th century—and perhaps especially the resurgence of productivity growth during the past 10 years or so—has been fueled principally by this country's unequaled stock of human capital: by the powerful combination of a highly skilled work force, technological advances, and the contribution of an educated workforce to "adoption and rapid diffusion of new technologies."[89]

Dating back to Horace Mann, civic benefits have been hailed as a justification for government intervention in the provision of primary and secondary education. According to research by Thomas Dee, these civic benefits extend to higher education as well. Dee finds that educational attainment beyond high school has strong positive effects on subsequent civic engagement, especially voter registration.[90]

FACTORS ACCOUNTING FOR EXCELLENCE— AND THEIR IMPLICATIONS FOR THE FUTURE

In this concluding section, we want first to draw attention to the major factors that account for the good results achieved by higher education in the United States to date before focusing on the "supply-side block" that we see as very threatening to the long-term ability of American higher education to achieve its potential. In an enumeration of the factors that have been so important to the present-day achievements of American higher education, the contributions of three different kinds of "resources" stand out as particularly important.[91]

First and most obvious is money spent. The Sutton Trust report says simply: "The US spends 2.7 percent of its GDP [gross domestic product] on higher education compared with an OECD average of 1.3 percent, and a UK spend of just 1 percent."[92] Moreover, this large differential in total dollars spent is by no means a function simply of a relatively large enrollment in the United States. The OECD also calculates expenditures per student, and at the tertiary level (higher education), U.S. expenditures per student are twice the OECD country mean ($22,234 versus $10,052); expenditures per student in the United Kingdom and Germany are slightly above the mean, and those in France are slightly below it.[93]

The strong connection between levels of expenditures and outcomes (both the scale of the U.S. system of higher education and its quality) is a result in large part of the substantial public and private subsidies provided in the United States. These subsidies create incentives for talented students to pursue their education, and they also help "allocate" the most promising students to the leading programs at undergraduate, professional, and doctoral levels. Bound and Turner have documented the history of U.S. subsidies to higher education and have argued as well that the United States subsidizes its system of higher education both more generously and more effectively (through the use of prices) than do most European countries.[94]

It would be a mistake, however, to assume that the funding patterns that have been so important to the unparalleled success of American higher education are assured for all time. The wealth of the United States and the vitality of its economic system will undoubtedly remain big "plusses." *In our view, however, one of the two most serious threats to the continued excellence of American higher education is the funding problems faced today by the public sector of higher education.* This topic is so important that we discuss it at length in chapter 8.

A second kind of "resource," not unrelated to dollars spent, is the general shape and character of the American "system" of higher education —if the word *system* is even appropriate. American higher education owes its success in no small part to this country's unique mix of private and public institutions and to the highly decentralized character of the entire enterprise, including sources of funding. Much decision making is vested in the states, but substantial power also resides in the federal government, in private donors, and in students and families "voting with their feet" as they decide where to apply and how much they are willing to pay for college. This pluralistic mix of funding sources has allowed the system as a whole to generate far more resources than would have been possible if it had been more monolithic. In addition, the decentralized, diverse, and highly competitive nature of higher education in this country has allowed "the system" to avoid the pitfalls of forced homogeneity and associated inefficiencies. Different kinds of institutions, costing different amounts of money to operate and to attend, have been able to serve the widely varying needs (and preferences) of multiple clienteles.[95]

This variegated structure, combined with this country's historical commitment to freedom of expression, has allowed students and faculty members to think creatively and independently, free (for the most part) of political tests and pressures to "think right."[96] This key feature of American higher education illustrates the importance of what Douglass North has referred to as "the rules of the game" in his path-breaking analysis of how such understandings, formal and informal, have a major impact on economic performance through time.[97]

One of our colleagues, Neil Rudenstine, who studied at Oxford, then served as provost at Princeton and as president of Harvard, is knowledgeable about worldwide higher education, and he is persuaded that the United States has basically the right model for funding and supporting higher education. In his view, the state-supported models of European countries—which rely so heavily on governmental funding, lack the incentives for private charitable giving that are so important in the United States, resist imposing substantial charges on students and families who can afford to pay, are reluctant to use "prices" to allocate students and ration places, and are more subject than the U.S. system to political pressures for "openness" and homogeneity—are unlikely to generate, over time, the resources and competitive structures needed to allow large numbers of their universities to compete internationally with major U.S. institutions.[98] These and other countries, including Asian countries, will be able to do well in selected fields and in strengthening carefully selected institutions if they are willing to concentrate their resources sufficiently, but it seems less likely that they will be able to match the United States in the overall excellence or "robustness" of its system of higher education.[99]

A third "resource" has been perhaps the most important of all, historically, in fueling the entire system of American higher education: the availability of a large pool of college-eligible students that is attributable to the earlier spread of elementary and secondary education across the country. Building on the work of many historians and other scholars, Goldin and Katz trace the origins of public education in the 19th century, citing the early ideas of Thomas Jefferson and others,[100] the development of "common schools," and the relentless advocacy of Horace Mann and the "school men" in the antebellum years. They conclude: "The creation of publicly funded common schools and their spread throughout much of America was the first great transformation of education in America. Even before free schooling spread throughout the states, with the abolition of the 'rate bills,' education in America had surpassed that in any other country.[101] Free public schooling, which had diffused nearly everywhere in the nation by the 1870s, set the stage for the next great educational expansion—the growth of public high schools."[102] By 1910, the secondary school enrollment rate outside the South was about 24 percent, and the high school graduation rate was about 10 percent; by the mid-1930s, about half of the relevant age group graduated in most states outside the South.[103] There can be little doubt that the subsequent "roll-out" of American higher education was made possible by the existence of this massive base of college-eligible students—a base unmatched anywhere else in the world.

However, as we saw earlier in the chapter, the growth in educational attainment in the United States has flattened in recent years, while it is

still rising in other countries. DeLong, Goldin, and Katz describe the
pattern as follows:

> Toward the end of the twentieth century . . . the rate of increase in years
> of schooling declined substantially in the United States. Beginning with
> the cohorts born around 1950, the growth in educational attainment for
> native-born Americans slowed perceptibly [figure 3.7]. By the 1980s, this
> slowdown had translated into a reduced rate of increase in the educa-
> tional attainment of the American labor force. . . . Among the advanced
> member nations of the Organization for Economic Cooperation and
> Development, the level of educational attainment is now increasing more
> rapidly in nations other than the United States, and the educational
> attainment of young American adults now lags that of young adults in
> some other countries.[104]

Delong, Goldin, and Katz add this trenchant observation: "The decel-
eration of growth in educational attainment [in the United States] has
occurred *despite rising economic returns to education during the past twenty
years* [figure 3.8]" (our emphasis).[105]

The potential "supply" of college graduates in the United States is
simply not responding to this extraordinary economic incentive. This
disjunction between incentives and behavior is the evidence that points
so strongly to the existence of a serious supply-side block. In our opinion,
this block is *the* major threat to the continuing excellence of American

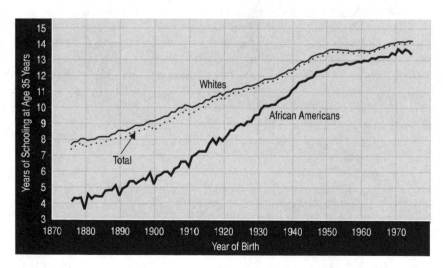

Figure 3.7. Years of Schooling of U.S. Natives by Birth Cohort and Race,
1876–1975
   Source: DeLong, Goldin, and Katz, "Sustaining U.S. Economic Growth," figure 1,
pp. 17–60.

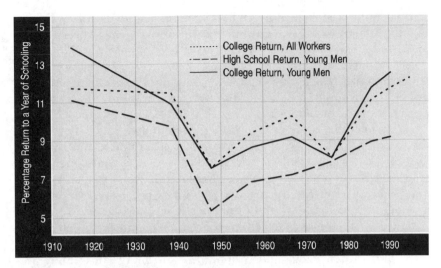

Figure 3.8. Educational Wage Differentials for All Workers and Young Male Workers, 1915–2000

Source: DeLong, Goldin, and Katz, "Sustaining U.S. Economic Growth," figure 2, pp. 17–60.

higher education—even more important than present and potential funding constraints. The root causes of this obstruction, we believe, are the barriers to educational advancement associated with socioeconomic status and race: there is a large group of disadvantaged Americans who are unable to achieve their full potential, mostly because of society's underinvestment in their college "preparedness."[106] The same can be said for a country like South Africa, where universities are trying hard to correct for the educational consequences of the apartheid system.[107]

"Preparedness," in the sense we use the term, depends on the effectiveness of elementary and secondary education as well as all the factors, at home and in neighborhoods, that condition how well young people take advantage of whatever pre-collegiate educational opportunities are presented to them. In subsequent chapters, we will examine the ways in which formal schooling and other factors such as family background and circumstances combine to influence educational outcomes. Colleges and universities are utterly dependent on the quality of their intake of students, which in turn depends on parental "investments" in children and on the quality of elementary and secondary education. Goldin and Katz attribute the extraordinary growth and diffusion of pre-collegiate education in America to features of our schools that were already in place in 1900—which they term "the 'virtues' of the past"—and which, they argue, "would determine U.S. educational development in the twentieth century and would enable the United States to lead the world in schooling for the masses."[108] The most important of these virtues were "*public provision by small fiscally independent districts, public funding, secular control, gender neutrality, open access, a forgiving system, and an academic curriculum*" (our emphasis). The authors recognize that "the virtues of the past need not be the virtues of today, and they also need not have been virtuous in all places and at all times in the past."[109]

We suspect that some of the "virtues" Goldin and Katz believe drove the expansion of elementary and secondary education in the 19th and 20th centuries have become vices today: decentralized control and responsibility for funding means massive differences (inequalities) in the availability of resources; the marvelously "forgiving" aspect of education in America in earlier days and in simpler settings, where everyone who wanted a second chance was given one, has degenerated too often into overly "permissive" approaches; and so on. None of this may have mattered much when family and community were more consistently pro-education and could be counted on to help. But today, in inner cities especially, inequalities and "relaxed" standards can be highly problematic when family and community issues (poverty, gangs, lifestyles) can work against an emphasis on educational values. We suspect that a new pre-collegiate model is needed. How to achieve such a thing is a daunting task—an understatement if ever there was one.

What is clear is that to continue to achieve excellence—defined, we repeat, as *educating large numbers of people to a high standard and advancing and disseminating knowledge*—we must enrich the pool of candidates for higher education by addressing *equity* objectives. There is no other way.

CHAPTER 4

Equity on a National Level
Socioeconomic Status and Race

At the end of the previous chapter, we saw that the United States is in danger of losing its human capital advantage because degree attainment has reached a plateau, and may even be decreasing. In this chapter we will explore how the limited college access and attainment of students from families in the bottom income quartile or from families with no experience of higher education contribute to the problem. Although we hope that our discussion of these issues will be informative, and we believe that we have cast a new light on some familiar issues, there is little in this chapter that will be wholly new to a student of "access and choice" in American higher education. The material presented here is, for the most part, intended as context for the chapter that follows, which contains a detailed analysis (based on a large new dataset) of the progression of students from the status of applicants to that of graduates at 19 selective colleges and universities.

It is rare today to find a college or university that restricts its pool of applicants by rule to one gender, one race, one religion, or a few prominent surnames. There are, of course, some notable exceptions; there are still examples of single-sex institutions, most significantly the women's colleges, whose enrollment patterns are analyzed in the next chapter. But in terms of both ethos and scale, today's barriers to entry are vastly different from those employed by the segregated public universities of the South, the all-male Ivy League, and the institutions that subscribed to the Jewish quotas of 50, 60, or 80 years ago.[1] Although explicit policies to keep certain people out have been eliminated, more "organic" barriers —such as poor academic and social preparedness, information deficits, and outright financial hardship—are limiting college opportunities for students from socioeconomically disadvantaged backgrounds (a group that contains more white students than minority students, even though racial minorities are disproportionately represented). These barriers are just as troublesome in their effects, and in many ways more difficult to overcome, than the explicit exclusion of individuals with unwanted characteristics. One is reminded of the long struggle, which continues to this day, against often subtle forms of racial bias, stereotyping, and stigma after de jure racial discrimination had been outlawed.

We begin this chapter by describing differences in access to a college education. The evidence shows that the United States has made progress in moving toward the goal of equity, but that socioeconomic status and race still play important roles in rationing access to opportunities. Weak academic preparation has the most significant and damaging impact. Poor and minority children frequently grow up in impoverished neighborhoods and attend primary and secondary schools that are far less well equipped to educate them than schools attended by their more privileged peers. Not surprisingly, then, controlling for academic preparation eliminates much of the enrollment deficit attributed to low socioeconomic status. However, some significant gaps remain. The literature indicates that financing problems explain only part of these remaining gaps; differential access to the information and assistance necessary to navigate the admissions and financial aid processes (also products of background and family circumstances) is in all likelihood more important.[2]

In addition to an enrollment gap, there is an attainment (college completion) gap that is also related to both socioeconomic status and race. We conclude the chapter with a brief discussion of the sources and implications of this additional impediment to meeting higher education's equity objectives.

COLLEGE ENROLLMENT

Overall, college enrollment rates have increased for all groups over the past 30 years (see figure 4.1).[3] Increases in real income, in student aid, and in the returns to college education have combined to produce this welcome result.

Socioeconomic Status and Enrollment

The fact that enrollment rates have gone up, as it were, "across the board," does not mean, however, that there is anything like equal access to college today. The groups of potential applicants from different SES categories started at different levels, and so, in the words of a recent College Board report, "an individual's chances of entering . . . college remain closely correlated with family background. Only 54 percent of high school graduates from the lowest income quartile enroll in college, compared to 82 percent of those with incomes above $88,675 [the top quartile]."[4]

Figure 4.1 shows that this gap in enrollment rates is now somewhat narrower than it was in 1970.[5] Yet economists David Ellwood and Thomas Kane, comparing data for 1980–82 graduates from the national High

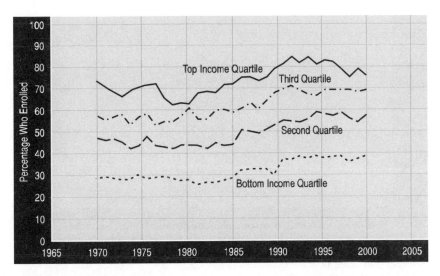

Figure 4.1. College Participation of Dependent 18- to 24-Year-Olds, by Family Income, 1970–2002

Source: "Chance for Bachelor's Degree by Age 24 and Family Income, 1970 to 2002," available at http://www.postsecondary.org, accessed June 25, 2004. Analysis based on U.S. Census Bureau school enrollment data.

School and Beyond database with data for 1992 graduates from the National Educational Longitudinal Study (NELS) database, find that "the role of family background in determining postsecondary training choices [and especially enrollment in 4-year colleges] seems to have *increased* over time" (our emphasis), causing a widening in the low income–high income enrollment gap.[6] This apparent discrepancy in findings can be explained by the use of different time periods in the two studies: the enrollment gap between high school graduates from poor families and others narrowed significantly in the 10 years before the period studied by Ellwood and Kane and narrowed slightly in the 10 years since.[7]

Race and College Enrollment

In addition to the socioeconomic gap in college enrollment, there is a clear race gap: students from certain minority groups (African Americans, Hispanics, and Native Americans) are much less likely to enroll in college than their non-minority peers (see figure 4.2). In 2001, around 65 percent of white 16- to 24-year-olds had enrolled in college compared to about 55 percent of African Americans and just under 50 percent of

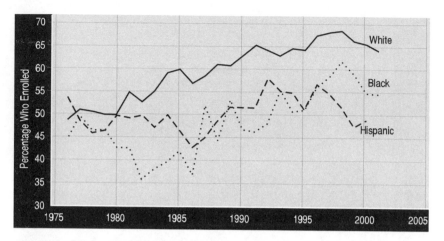

Figure 4.2. College Enrollment Rates for 16- to 24-Year-Old Recent High School Graduates, by Race/Ethnicity, 1976–2001

Source: U.S. Department of Education, National Center for Education Statistics. *Digest of Education Statistics, 2002,* table 183. This figure mirrors a figure found in the College Board report *Trends in College Pricing* (2003).

Note: Due to small sample sizes, a three-year moving average is used for Hispanics.

Hispanics of the same age.[8] Overall, there was a *widening* of the enrollment gap between 1976 and 2001, but this was due almost entirely to a substantial divergence between white and minority enrollment rates in the late 1970s and early 1980s. Since that time (over roughly the past 15 years) progress has been made in closing the gap.[9] Further good news is that, although the size of the gap has varied, enrollment levels have increased over this time period for each racial/ethnic group.[10]

The minority enrollment gap is primarily a result of the fact that underrepresented minority students are more likely than other students to come from low-income families. In 2003, the median income for white families with children under 18 years old was $61,970; for black families it was just $30,547, and for Hispanic families it was $32,073.[11] A glance at the bottom end of the income distribution helps to bring home the full extent of the income divide between the families of underrepresented minorities and other families. In 2003, 8.9 percent of white families with children under 18 years old and 10.9 percent of Asian American families with children under 18 were below the poverty threshold. Three times as many African American families with children, 28.6 percent, and nearly as many Hispanic families, 25.2 percent, lived in poverty.[12] When Kane explored the subsequent enrollment behavior of students who were eighth graders in 1988, he found that, after controlling for family income, the enrollment rates of African Americans and Hispanics were slightly *higher* than those of white students (but only the Hispanic advantage is statistically significant).[13] These enrollment rates, we should remember, reflect a range of affirmative action policies and are one measure of their success.

COLLEGE PREPAREDNESS

As a general rule, families that have high incomes and high levels of educational attainment when their children are of college age had high incomes and high levels of educational attainment when their children were young, and these persistent advantages enabled them to enhance the "college preparedness" of their children in reinforcing ways. As Pedro Carneiro and James Heckman note: "Children whose parents have higher incomes have access to better-quality primary and secondary schools. Children's tastes for education and their expectations about their life chances are shaped by those of their parents. Educated parents are better able to develop scholastic aptitude in their children by assisting and directing their studies."[14] It is the long-term, lasting effects of socioeconomic status on both cognitive and non-cognitive skills (including motivation, attitudes, social skills, and "proper" behavior) that Heckman and his various co-authors argue are the main determinants of differences in educational opportunity. Put another way, poor families have great difficulty investing sufficient resources to develop in their children, in the time before high school graduation, the abilities and outlooks necessary to enable their children to attend college and graduate.

Much has been written about the schools, family life, and neighborhoods of poor children and the cycle of negative reinforcement they engender, but the consequences of going to school and growing up in an impoverished community are so important that they deserve to be re-emphasized.

- The most stunning characteristic of schools attended by poor children is that a very large percentage of the children in these schools are poor, especially in urban areas: 1988 eighth graders with family incomes below $20,000 who lived in urban areas attended schools where 47 percent of students received free or reduced-price lunches.[15]
- Schools with large numbers of students from poor families are underfunded compared to schools in more affluent neighboring communities. In 2002, the average per-pupil spending was $6,383 at a school in a district with a poverty rate in the highest quartile nationally, compared to $7,731 at schools in districts with a poverty rate in the bottom quartile.[16] This contrast is especially powerful in the case of inner cities and their wealthy suburbs. New York City public schools spent

$11,112 per student in 2000–2001, while well-to-do suburbs like Rye and Scarsdale spent over $13,000. Detroit (with a child poverty rate of 27 percent) spent an average of $9,069 on each student in its public schools, compared to $12,653 in neighboring towns like Bloomfield Hills (where the poverty rate is less than 3 percent).[17]

- As might be expected, these funding inequities are reflected in characteristics that affect learning outcomes. In 2000, about 36 percent of schools where more than 75 percent of students receive free or reduced-price lunches had one or more teachers leave in the middle of the school year. In contrast, the corresponding figure at schools with fewer than 10 percent of students receiving free or reduced-price lunches was less than 6 percent.[18] The decision to stop teaching in a poor district is easier to understand when one considers the school environment: teachers at schools where more than 40 percent of students receive free or reduced-price lunches were more than twice as likely to report that absenteeism, tardiness, and behavior problems interfered with their work than were teachers at schools with less than 5 percent of students receiving free or reduced-price lunches.[19] In 1994, salaries were 28 percent lower for teachers in schools with high poverty levels than for teachers in schools with low poverty levels—a fact that must also have contributed to (or, since teacher pay is based on seniority, may have been a result of) low retention rates.[20] Jonathan Kozol has spent years visiting and writing about inner-city schools and describes other (harder-to-quantify) features that help to explain poor learning outcomes and teacher attrition. In a visit to Morris High School in the South Bronx, Kozol found "water cascad[ing] down the stairs [and] plaster . . . falling from the walls. Female students [told him] that they shower after school to wash the plaster from their hair." Despite advanced warning from the school's principal, Kozol was still "stunned to see a huge hole in the ceiling of the stairwell on the school's fourth floor."[21]

- A compounding factor is that minority students are disproportionately represented in the inner-city schools that Kozol describes. In 2003, approximately 80 percent of black and Hispanic fourth graders in schools located in central cities were attending schools in which more than half of the students were eligible for free or reduced-price lunches. Across the country, black and Hispanic fourth graders were approximately 10 times more likely to attend a school in which over 75 percent of students are eligible to receive free or reduced-price lunches than were white fourth graders.[22] Minority children are also increasingly likely to go to school only with other minority children. Indeed, at the 50th anniversary of *Brown v. Board of Education*, American schools are nearly as segregated as they were in 1954. In 2001–02, the average African American child attended a school that was 54 percent black and 12 percent Latino. The average white student attended a school that was nearly 80 percent white.[23] Outside the South and the West, between 40 and 50 percent of black students were in schools that enrolled between 90 and 100 percent minority students.[24] Even in the South, where aggressive desegregation efforts resulted in levels of integration that have never been seen in the North and the Midwest, secondary schools are more segregated today than they were 15 to 20 years ago—so, too, are the Topeka schools featured in *Brown*.[25]

- Of course the characteristics of the school he or she attends are not the only (or, perhaps, even the most important) factors in a child's academic and social development. In addition to self-evident differences in disposable income and education, there are other important systematic differences between the family situations of rich and poor children. Low-income children are almost twice as likely as wealthier students to come from single-parent families.[26] In 2000, children below the poverty line had a 12 percent chance of living in a home in which an individual was malnourished, whereas in families that were above the poverty line, there was just a 2 percent chance of being in that situation.[27]

- Outside of home and school, neighborhoods can have a further impact on how children view themselves and their life prospects. As we alluded to earlier, most poor children live in and go to school in communities that are overwhelmingly poor (and that are also overwhelmingly minority). In 2003, just under half (46 percent) of those living in central cities were from families with incomes that were 200 percent of the poverty threshold or less, while nationally, 33.6 percent of people had incomes in this category.[28] And the trends are dismaying: Paul Jargowsky found that economic segregation in large cities increased rapidly between 1970 and 1990.[29] Poor families in these predominantly poor neighborhoods experience a violent crime rate of 53.68 per 1,000 people, compared to 26.15 per 1,000 people for non-poor families.[30] There are also severe health effects related to living in a poor neighborhood (stemming from both environmental conditions and lack of health care resources), which are most prominently reflected in a much higher infant mortality rate (13.5 per 1,000 live births for poor families versus 8.3 per 1,000 for non-poor families).[31]

The Effects on Academic Preparedness of Growing Up Poor

What are the cumulative effects of growing up in these resource-poor environments? We know, first, that students from high-income families (and families with high levels of educational attainment) are encouraged from an early age to think about college, to take college preparatory courses, and to ready themselves to take the SAT and other tests used to assess college applicants. One simple reminder (and measure) of the consequences of this mindset is that students from well-to-do families are far more likely than students from lower socioeconomic categories to take the SAT in the first place (see table 4.1). Our analysis of NELS data charting the paths followed by students who were in the eighth grade in 1988 shows that less than a third of students from families in the bottom income quartile took the SAT, as compared with more than two-thirds of those from families in the top quartile. In addition, test-takers from families with high incomes and high levels of educational attainment do *much* better on the SAT than do students from other families. Among the test-takers, just over 7 percent of those from the bottom income quartile scored over 1200, as compared with more than 20 percent of those from the top income quartile.

Combining the probabilities of taking the tests in the first place and then scoring over 1200 on them demonstrates dramatically the advantages associated with coming from a high-SES family. *The odds of both taking the tests and doing very well on them were roughly six times higher for students from the top income quartile than for students from the bottom income quartile.* When we look at the test-taking behavior and results achieved by students from families with no experience of higher education, we find a very similar pattern (with even more pronounced differences): less than 1 percent of high school students from families with no college experience took the SAT and scored over 1200 on it—as compared with 6.6 percent of other students.

Furthermore, data we compiled from College Board reports on high school seniors show that differences in SAT scores associated with socioeconomic status have widened noticeably over the past 16 years, to the point that students whose parents have only a high school diploma earn scores (combined math and verbal) that are 200 points lower than the scores of students whose parents have one or more graduate degrees. Even more pronounced differences exist (roughly 300 points) between children of families in the highest income category (which is now $100,000 or more) and children in families with incomes of $30,000 or less (see figures 4.3a and 4.3b).[32]

Some may believe that this test-taking behavior is indicative of natural differences in cognitive ability or motivation. This is a difficult hypothesis to test, but one way to do so is to compare the test-taking patterns of students whose performance on earlier standardized tests indicated that they had similar ability levels. In order to focus on students who were potential college-goers, we limited our sample to students whose early standardized test scores placed them in the top decile. Of these presumably able students, only 68 percent with family incomes below $25,000 (in 1991) took

TABLE 4.1

Percentage of the 1988 Eighth-Grade Cohort Who Graduated from High School, Took the SAT, and Scored above 1200, by Family Income and Parental Education, from the National Educational Longitudinal Study

	Percentage of Cohort Who Graduated from High School (Diploma or GED)	Percentage of High School Graduates Who Took the SAT	Percentage of Cohort Who Took the SAT	Percentage of Those Who Took the SAT Who Scored above 1200	Percentage of Cohort Who Scored above 1200
Family Income					
Bottom quartile	79.9	34.2	32.2	7.4	2.4
2nd quartile	90.1	40.3	38.8	7.9	3.1
3rd quartile	94.8	50.9	49.3	12.0	5.9
Top quartile	97.1	70.1	68.4	21.4	14.6
Parental Education					
Neither parent attended college	76.9	30.8	28.0	3.3	0.9
At least one parent attended college	92.4	49.6	48.1	13.7	6.6

Source: National Center for Education Statistics, National Educational Longitudinal Study (1988–2000) database.

Note: Income quartiles are based on the 2000 Census, deflated to 1991 dollars. The third and fourth quartiles are slightly smaller than they should be, and the bottom two quartiles are slightly larger due to variable coding restrictions. The percentage of the cohort who took the SAT is not equal to the product of those who graduated from high school and the high school graduates who took the SAT, because there were non-graduates who took the SAT.

the SAT, compared to 88 percent of students with family incomes above $75,000 (the two categories represent, roughly, the bottom and top income quartiles). Likewise, 55 percent of those students whose parents had no more than a high school diploma took the SAT, compared to 77 percent of students whose parents had more than a high school diploma.[33]

The Minority Test Gap

Minority students also lagged behind their non-minority peers in observable measures of preparedness. For example, the average SAT I verbal test score for African Americans in 2003 was 431 (out of 800), while the average score for whites was 529 and the average score for Asians was

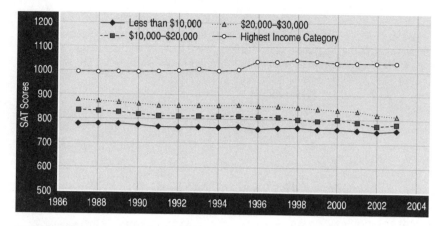

Figure 4.3a. Average Math and Verbal SAT Scores Combined, by Family Income and Year, All SAT-Takers, 1987–2003

Source: College Entrance Examination Board, College-Bound Seniors, 1992–2003.

Note: For 1996, the top income code changes from "$70,000 or more" to "$100,000 or more." All values are in current (unadjusted) dollars.

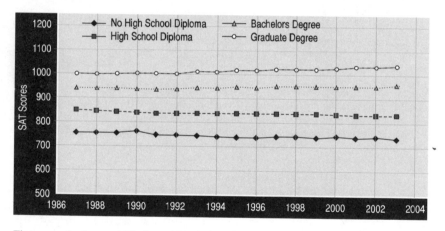

Figure 4.3b. Average Math and Verbal SAT Scores Combined, by Parents' Educational Attainment and Year, All SAT-Takers, 1987–2003

Source: College Entrance Examination Board, College-Bound Seniors, 1992–2003.

508. The average verbal score for Native Americans taking the test was 480, and the average score for Hispanics ranged from 448 to 457.[34] Another way of measuring the gap is to examine the distribution of minority scores compared to the scores of whites and Asian Americans. On the 2002 National Assessment of Educational Progress reading test, just 1 percent of African American 12th graders and 1 percent of His-

panic 12th graders in a nationally representative sample had scores at the "advanced" level, compared to 4 percent of Asians and 6 percent of whites. Even more disturbing, only 16 percent of African Americans and 22 percent of Hispanics reached the "proficient" level or higher, compared to 34 percent of Asian Americans and 42 percent of whites.[35]

Part of the racial gap in test scores can be explained by socioeconomic differences between minorities and non-minorities—but only part. Meredith Phillips and her colleagues estimated that differences in family income and parental education together account for about one-third of the gap in test scores.[36] When a more robust measure of family circumstances is used, including characteristics such as grandparents' education, the quality of the mother's schooling, and household size, two-thirds of the gap in test scores is explained.[37] A more recent study by Roland Fryer and Steven Levitt, using a rich new longitudinal dataset, found that the large (0.65 standard deviation) black-white test score gap observed when children enter kindergarten can be explained *completely* by controlling for a more elaborate set of background variables, including child's age, child's birth weight, socioeconomic status, participation in certain welfare programs, mother's age at first birth, and number of children's books in the home.[38]

A less encouraging finding from this same study is that, even with all these background controls in place, black students fall behind their white classmates during the first two years of school, at a pace of about 0.1 standard deviations per year. Fryer and Levitt tested a number of explanatory hypotheses, and the only one that appears to work pertains to school environments. The elementary schools that blacks attend are less satisfactory than those attended by whites on measures of safety, incidence of poverty among the families of students, discipline, and parental involvement—though the two sets of schools are remarkably similar on typical measures of quality such as class size and teacher education. This finding is strikingly consistent with the more qualitative findings of James Comer, who has spent a lifetime studying the effects of developmental factors on school outcomes.[39]

Another kind of explanation for the black-white test score gap, called "stereotype threat," has been advanced by psychologist Claude Steele, and studied in great detail by sociologist Douglas Massey and his colleagues. Steele and co-author Joshua Aronson describe stereotype threat as the condition in which minority students "must deal with the possibility of being judged or treated stereotypically, or of doing something that would confirm the stereotype."[40] Steele and Aronson hypothesize that stereotype threat can disrupt the performance of a minority student when the stereotype in play is in an area about which the individual cares deeply. Thus, they argue that it is academically interested minority students who are most likely to display the negative consequences of stereotype threat in their test scores.[41] Steele and Aronson have reported on a number of experiments they have conducted to test for the presence and effects of stereotype threat. They have found that "making African Americans more conscious of negative stereotypes about their intellectual ability as a group can depress their test performance relative to that of whites."[42] The mechanisms by which stereotype threat seems to affect performance are a loss of efficiency in answering questions and an increase in anxiety.[43]

Support for the stereotype hypothesis has also been found in empirical studies outside experimental settings. Douglas Massey and his colleagues, in their extremely thorough analysis of a survey of almost 4,000 college freshmen, found substantial evidence of stereotype threat as a cause of the racial disparity in academic performance. They found that African American and Latino students who had characteristics that made them particularly vulnerable to stereotype threat had lower grades and were more likely to fail a course in their first term than were other minority students. However, only 9 percent of African Americans and 7 percent of Hispanic students in their survey—which was already limited to relatively high-achieving students—had characteristics that predisposed them to suffering from stereotype threat.[44] While the effects of stereotype threat certainly seem to contribute to the preparation gap between underrepresented minorities and other students, the extent of the impact may be limited to the top end of the distribution, and then only to a fraction of this group.

There is a still more general, and to our way of thinking still more compelling, way of conceptualizing racial disparities in behavior and in performance. Glenn Loury has articulated the concepts of *racial stigma* and *biased social cognition* to explain how "the disadvantageous position of a racially defined population subgroup can be the product of a system of social interactions and not some quality intrinsic to the group."[45] America's past has conspired to create an underlying set of perceptions and social realities that to this day makes it very difficult for African Americans to be free of what Loury calls "spoiled collective identities." Activities as mundane as hailing a cab are, as Loury explains, affected profoundly. This history, and its after-effects, help us understand why it is especially difficult for blacks in America to claim their rightful shares of everything from taxi rides to high test scores.

The Effects of Family Income and College Preparedness on Enrollment

Having emphasized the strong correlation between family circumstances and academic preparation, we turn next to the question of how much of the enrollment gap this key relationship explains. In short, the answer is

"Much, but not all." In his Brookings Institution–sponsored study of the subsequent educational profiles of students who were eighth graders in 1988, Thomas Kane found that a person from a family in the top income quintile was 34 percentage points more likely to enroll in college than a person in the bottom quintile. Controlling for differences in math and reading scores reduces this gap substantially: to 21 percentage points. Including an additional control for parental educational attainment reduces the differential to 15 percentage points—but, as Kane emphasizes, this is still a highly significant difference. Kane also tested to see if his results held across ability levels, and he found that the gap in enrollment rates between the top and the bottom income quintiles was largest among the lowest scorers (18 points) but was also present among the highest scorers (11 points). In short, gaps in enrollment by family income are reduced, but not eliminated altogether, when the comparison is limited to those students who are the best test-takers.[46] Kane's main conclusion is that family income has an effect on enrollment "no matter what"—as does, obviously, preparedness.[47]

The effects of family income are more pronounced when we examine differences in enrollment related to race (using, again, Kane's analysis of the cohort of students who were eighth graders in 1988). We have already noted that the pattern of lower enrollment rates of African American and Hispanic students seen in the raw data disappears entirely when controls for socioeconomic status are added; it then *reverses* when controls for college preparedness are added (i.e., adjusted enrollment rates are now significantly higher for African American and Hispanic students than for white students).[48] This reversal in the racial enrollment gap after controls are added for both family income and preparedness is presumably best understood as a demonstration of the positive effects of the aggressive recruitment and admissions preferences associated with affirmative action policies.[49] As we will demonstrate in chapter 5, non-minority students from groups with lower socioeconomic status do not benefit from such admission preferences (at least at the 19 selective schools in our study). In chapter 7 we will return to the critically important policy question of whether highly qualified applicants from low-income families should be given more of a break in the admissions process—as we believe they should, if society is really committed to having higher education enhance social mobility.

Socioeconomic Status, College Preparedness, and College Choice

Of course using enrollment at any institution as a measure of access to higher education may hide substantial differences in the degree of college choice enjoyed by students from different backgrounds. In America's highly stratified system of higher education, there is a real premium attached, many have argued, to attending the wealthiest and most selective colleges and universities.[50] These colleges and universities tend to be more expensive and of course require more impressive academic credentials. One might therefore expect students from low-income families to be less likely than students from well-to-do families to attend the more academically selective institutions. The concern is, of course, that disadvantaged students may be systematically enrolling in institutions that are under-resourced and thus do not provide the caliber of education available at a wealthier school that allows an exceptionally capable student to achieve his or her full potential.

To test whether this has occurred, Michael McPherson and Morton Schapiro used a 1987 sample of students who scored well on the PSAT. They found that students from middle-income and below-middle-income families are proportionally less likely to apply to an institutional member of the Consortium on Financing Higher Education (COFHE), a group of 31 very selective private colleges and universities. Only 33 percent of these high achievers whose family incomes were in the lowest category (below $20,000) and 39 percent of those with families in the middle-income category ($40,000–$60,000) applied to a COFHE school, compared to 71 percent of those with incomes in the highest-income category (above $90,000). McPherson and Schapiro found that these talented students from low- and middle-income families were also less likely to be admitted to at least one of these institutions if they did apply, and were less likely to enroll in a COFHE college or university if accepted.[51] However, Richard Spies has tracked similar data for the past 30 years, and he has found that, when he controls for SAT scores directly, the application gap is greatly reduced, and that it has shrunk over time. The gap in 2000 was just 18 percentage points, after controlling for SAT scores.[52] (We will discuss Spies's studies in more detail in the next chapter.) Thus, there is reason to believe that the "application" gap (the reduced odds that a well-prepared student from a low-SES background will even apply to a selective school) has narrowed appreciably since the time of the McPherson-Schapiro study.

Instead of just looking at the high end of the preparedness and college quality spectrum, Caroline Hoxby has provided findings on the college enrollment of students from a broad range of ability levels at many different kinds of institutions—and, in addition, over a long time period. Working with national data for 1972 and 1992 high school graduates, Hoxby found:

> College is not less accessible now than it was 30 years ago; it is significantly more accessible. Moreover, there is no evidence that students are

being forced to enroll in inexpensive colleges that are inappropriate for their level of preparedness. In fact, the main group of students who appear to be getting displaced from very expensive colleges is the group of students from medium-high to high income families who have low college preparedness [i.e., low SAT scores and low high school grades]. They are being replaced by highly prepared students from low income families.[53]

But these data also reveal persistent—and in some cases widening—differences in college enrollment patterns by family income among students who are slightly less well prepared. For example, of all students from high-income families who demonstrated "medium-high preparedness" (SAT scores between 500 and 600 and rankings in the top third of their class), only 3 percent failed to go to college at all, and 52 percent went to one of the most expensive colleges; the corresponding figures for students from families in the bottom income quintile who demonstrated "medium-high preparedness" were 13 percent with "no college" and only 20 percent who attended one of the most expensive colleges.[54]

It seems clear that, from an equity perspective, the U.S. higher education system is moving in the right direction. But the gaps that remain are large at a number of SAT levels, and the apparently far more stringent limitations on college choice for students from poor families below Hoxby's top preparedness level (as contrasted with similarly prepared students from higher-income families) are especially troubling. We do not believe that every young person in America should attend college. Going to college could be the wrong decision for some students because of their interests and/or lack of adequate preparation. Indeed, not even all students with the same level of preparedness will benefit from attending college; as we will see at the end of the chapter, there may be quite a few students who enroll in college, realize that it was probably a mistake to do so, and stop out (enroll in school sporadically over a longer period than is traditional) or drop out. However, we surely do not want anything other than lack of ability and desire to prevent a student from enrolling or from enrolling in the institution best suited to his or her interests and talents. The most obvious potential barrier for students from low-income families who have high educational aspirations is the direct financial cost of college.

TUITION AND AFFORDABILITY

Headline writers and lawmakers alike focus on tuition when they discuss whether college is affordable and whether it has become more or less affordable as the years have passed. Looking only at tuition, the trend is certainly ominous. Between 1971–72 and 2002–03, enrollment-weighted tuition levels, in constant (2002) dollars, rose from $7,966 to $18,273 at private four-year colleges, from $1,646 to $4,081 at public four-year colleges, and from $840 to $1,735 at public two-year colleges.[55]

Whether the levels and rates of increase in tuition are "too high" is the subject of endless debate, but one proposition is abundantly clear: tuition levels have to be assessed in the context of family finances and available financial aid. Simply dividing listed tuition price by median family income does not provide a useful measure of whether price is (increasingly) the major barrier limiting collegiate educational attainment. In thinking about "affordability," and the relation between tuition and median family income, it is important to take into account shifts in the distribution of income itself, and not to focus solely on tuition. In recent years, the growing inequality of income in the United States has made it easier for the well-off to pay for college and harder for those at the bottom of the income distribution.[56] It can be argued that the increase in "tuition as a share of family income" cited by various commentators is due more to stagnating family income for low-income families than to tuition increases.

Catherine Hill, Gordon Winston, and Stephanie Boyd of Williams College have gone to great lengths to demonstrate that in 2001–02, the average net price actually paid by a student with a median family income at any of the selective schools in their study was just 34 percent of the average "sticker" price ("list" price). Net price was, on average, 22 percent of sticker price for families in the lowest income quintile.[57] It is true that aided students from families in the lowest income categories pay a higher share of their income in tuition (49 percent) than do aided students from higher-income families (21 to 28 percent) or un-aided students (21 percent).[58] However, in a 10-school sub-sample of the 28 schools studied, the net price as a percentage of quintile median income has fallen substantially (from 69 percent to 49 percent) for the lowest income quintile in just five years (1998 to 2003).[59]

As the Hill, Winston, and Boyd paper—with its emphasis on institutional aid policy—suggests, it is important to distinguish among types of schools when examining tuition increases. Hoxby divided colleges and universities into cost deciles and, for the years between 1970 and 1996, found: "Tuition has risen significantly [in real terms] . . . only for the 20 percent of college places that are most expensive."[60] When institutional aid is deducted from list tuition, the picture looks even better.[61] Hoxby also argues, persuasively in our view, that higher "net costs" (and the more rapid rise in real costs) at the most expensive places are justified by the quality of the education provided, and by the high returns to educational investments at the more expensive institutions.[62] These colleges and universities comprise the most competitive sector of higher education when it comes to selectivity in admissions, strength of faculty, and program quality.[63] Although it may be surprising to many readers, the high list tuition at these top-ranked institutions actually represents a substantial discount on the costs of the education that is provided—a discount that is made possible, for the most part, by endowments and other private gifts.

Some researchers, most notably Thomas Kane, disagree with Hoxby's analysis of tuition. Kane argues that combining public and private institutions in the same cross-tabulation and using constant dollar changes instead of percentage changes will always mask significant increases in tuition at public institutions, because the public institutions start from a much lower base than do private ones. Absolute dollar changes will always be much higher for private institutions. And it will appear that the large tuition increases were concentrated at these institutions, which represent only 20 to 25 percent of college enrollment.[64] It is also important to recognize that substantial increases in tuition at public institutions have occurred since the end date of Hoxby's analysis (1996)—the rate of increase has been especially rapid since 2001—and that it is the public institutions that provide educational opportunities for many economically disadvantaged students.[65] Despite these concerns, Hoxby's analysis indicates that explosive increases in tuition are not universal and that many institutions in the United States are still within the reach of most students. The public perception that college costs are spiraling out of control overstates the case.

Of course what matters is not the costs of college per se, but the effect that costs have on college-going behavior. To what extent are tuition and aid policies responsible for the persistent gap between enrollment rates of students from high-income and low-income families? Employing a number of tests of the effect of a change in tuition on enrollment rates, Kane has concluded that a $1,000 increase in public two-year college tuition would decrease total enrollment by 4.5 percent, and that a similar increase in public four-year college tuition would decrease enrollment by 0.8 percent.[66] Sorting students by family income, Kane finds that a $1,000 increase in public two-year college tuition would decrease the enrollment of students from families in the bottom 40 percent of the income distribution by 7.2 percent and would decrease the enrollment of those from families in the top 60 percent of the distribution by 4.4 percent.[67] These findings suggest that—notwithstanding generous financial aid programs—students from low-income families are financially constrained, at least to some extent.

One widely discussed aid program may be less certain in its effects, however, than many of us might surmise. Kane tested the impact of the introduction of the federally funded, means-tested Pell Grants in 1972 on enrollment rates and found that enrollment growth over the period immediately after the advent of Pell Grants was not significantly different from enrollment growth in the period immediately before, and in fact was slightly lower (though the difference was not statistically significant). This result is surprising because, as Kane points out, with a maximum Pell Grant equivalent to $4,200 in 1998 dollars, one would have expected an *increase* in enrollment of over 20 percent.[68] So, although college costs and the ability to pay clearly have some effect on enrollment patterns, the effects are not always as straightforward and predictable as one might assume. Several studies (which we will discuss in the next section) suggest that students and their parents, in making decisions about college, are not always performing a clear-cut cost-benefit analysis, or are not necessarily acting on the conclusions of such an analysis.[69]

INCOME, INFORMATION, AND SOPHISTICATION

Most economists, including Heckman and his colleagues, agree that so-called short-term credit constraints matter, and that they would matter much more in the absence of the well-developed financial aid programs found in America today. However, the number of students who are currently prevented from enrolling by a straightforward inability to pay is small; Heckman and Carneiro estimate that fewer than 8 percent of students fall into this category.[70] Still, higher-income families obviously have an easier time "paying the bills." Moreover, parents with high levels of educational attainment also foster college enrollment after their children's test score results are known by providing guidance, contacts, and knowledge about how the "admissions game" works. In their 1991 study, McPherson and Shapiro suggested that one reason why students sometimes failed to apply or enroll in COFHE schools was that they and their parents thought they would have to pay more than was in fact the case. They found that high-achieving students who either never applied to or were not accepted at a COFHE institution (and thus did not receive a financial aid offer) mostly overestimated the cost of a COFHE-type education—often substantially.[71] This "cognitive dissonance" (or simply "ignorance," because the availability of financial aid is often not well understood) is a likely explanation for the "economically irrational" reaction to the availability of Pell Grants described by Kane.

Indeed, one of Kane's main conclusions is that a simplified financial aid needs analysis and application, coupled with better advising, could go a long way toward improving the enrollment rates of students from low-income families (we discuss this proposal in more detail in chapter 8).[72] Kane has worked with Harvard economist Christopher Avery on a project in Boston called College Opportunity and Career Help, or COACH, which attempts to put this theory into practice. The program sends college students into disadvantaged high schools to advise their younger peers on the necessary steps for applying to and enrolling in college. Early results suggest that the "coaches" (who might be considered stand-ins for college-savvy parents or guidance counselors) improve the chances that students will make their way through the college enrollment process.[73]

Hoxby, also working with Avery, used data from a national sample of high-achieving high school students to test directly the economic rationality of students and their parents in the college enrollment and financial aid process. Hoxby and Avery found that, with the exception of those from high-income families, the students tended to value loans and work-study programs as much as grants, tended to pay more attention to financial aid as a share of list tuition than to total aid received, and to prefer grants that were named or were called scholarships. However, fewer than 7 percent of the parents of these students reported a lack of ability to pay as a reason why their children could not attend the institution of their choice (a fraction that is remarkably similar to Heckman's estimate of the number of credit-constrained students).[74] It seems that family finances have a fairly minor direct impact on a student's ability to attend a college (because of relatively low costs at less selective colleges and generous financial aid at more selective colleges), but are extremely important in developing the academic preparedness and the practical knowledge and skills that are ever more important in enabling students to attend. It is these myriad inter-connected, deep-seated, and long-lasting effects of socioeconomic status that make the educational opportunity gap so persistent—and so hard to close.

COLLEGE ATTAINMENT VERSUS COLLEGE ENROLLMENT

The differential college *graduation rates* of students from low- and high-income families, and of minority and non-minority students, exceed differences in enrollment rates and add another layer of complexity to the discussion of equity in educational opportunity. For 1992 high school graduates who started at a four-year institution, there was a 34-percentage-point difference in bachelor's degree attainment between those from families in the lowest income quartile and those from families in the top income quartile. The attainment rates were 44.2 percent for those from the bottom quartile and 78.2 percent for those from the top quartile.[75] There was also a large (roughly 15-percentage-point) gap in degree attainment between blacks and whites—and this gap has not closed at all over the past 50 years.[76]

Moreover, although college enrollment has risen over the past 30 years for all groups, Sarah Turner has found that the college completion rate has declined among those in their early 20s and stagnated for those in their early 30s, indicating that attainment rates have stalled while the time taken to complete a degree has unambiguously increased over the past three decades.[77] For example, in 1970, 51 percent of 23-year-old high school graduates had enrolled in college at some point, and 23 percent had completed a BA degree. In 1999, 67 percent of 23-year-old high school graduates had enrolled at some point, but just 24 percent had obtained a BA degree. The completion rate—degree earners divided by enrolled students—fell by about 25 percent. However, the college completion rate for 30-year-olds more than doubled during the same period, increasing from under 15 percent in 1970 to around 33 percent in 1999.[78]

Policies that encourage enrollment ("access") for all but then fail to provide the guidance and resources that allow students to translate participation into timely attainment—especially students who come from lower-income families—are in many ways a waste of both public and personal resources. As Turner points out, the private financial returns to college education accrue mainly to those who earn degrees, and the returns are highest for those who earn their degrees quickly.[79] Non-completers and slow completers invest their own money (and may go into debt) and are beneficiaries of contributions from both the government and their institutions in the form of financial aid; but for all that expense, the payoff is quite low. We understand and appreciate the argument (made by Gordon Winston, Thomas Kane, and others) that some students may need to experiment with college to determine if it is right for them. But experimentation should not last for 10-plus years.[80]

The most novel feature of Turner's analysis of what has gone wrong is her emphasis on the importance of "supply-side" considerations: the capacity of various kinds of educational institutions to expand when enrollment increases, the limited flow of additional resources to these institutions, and the concentration of some students who might not have gone to college in earlier years at schools with the most limited resources. "Persistence" could well be affected by the flow of marginal students into resource-poor institutions that are hard pressed to provide the academic, financial, and moral support that these students need.[81]

Here we have an important question for public policy: would it be wiser to invest more resources in the education of continuing student populations than in simply embracing access as an end in itself? We sit firmly in the camp of those who argue that the progress of current students toward their degrees should be emphasized. There is much to be said for allocating sufficient funds to institutions that bear the brunt of rising enrollments. We should help these schools meet the legitimate educational needs of larger populations of students who may not be able to complete their college degrees without considerable assistance.

The earlier stage of the educational process is also, of course, of critical importance. We agree with the proposition that students who are not prepared for college, or not motivated to go, are better off following other paths; generally speaking, we do not want improved "access" to turn out to be merely "fool's gold." Yet rather than using this line of argument as motivation to tighten admissions requirements at the least selective institutions or to diminish the generosity of financial aid programs, we would stress the need for more investment—creatively employed—in the *preparation* of the group of disadvantaged students whose ability and tastes place them on the enrollment margin. To be sure, the dictates of basic fairness argue strongly for improvement in the quality of the primary and secondary education provided to all disadvantaged students. But considerations of economic efficiency strengthen further the case for improving the college preparedness of the marginal students whose quest for a college degree may be frustrated not at the college gate, but after having passed through it.

Sorting out the reasons why students attend college (or attend different types of college) is not an easy task. As this survey of the literature and the available evidence suggests, there are many complicated factors at work. However, we can begin to sketch an overall picture—if a somewhat blurry one—from the points of agreement among scholars.

- First, there are real differences in the access to college of students from low-income and high-income families, and these differences are exacerbated by differences in the quality of the institutions that the two groups of students attend. However, the pattern has changed over the past 30 years. Higher education in general is now more accessible to students from low-income families, as are higher-quality institutions. The fact that gaps remain should not blind us to the real progress that has been made.
- The cumulative advantages associated with growing up in a well-to-do family (including receiving better-quality primary and secondary education and having more supportive peers and role models) are mostly responsible for the gap in enrollment. These take the form of both differences in academic preparedness and differences in sophistication about the college application and financial aid processes. Minority students (who are disproportionately represented among the socioeconomically disadvantaged) have academic preparation deficits that go beyond those we would anticipate on the basis of their family income alone.
- Financial constraints in the short term (at the time of college enrollment) are also a concern, but they do not seem to be a major source of the enrollment gap. Thanks in large part to current financial aid policies and subsidized tuition, only a relatively small group of

students are "constrained" in their ability to pay for college. Experience with the Pell Grants can be read to suggest that simply making financial aid policies more generous might not boost enrollment a great deal, but making them less generous (by allowing programs to stagnate) could well have dire consequences.

- Finally, it seems clear that enrollment maximization is not the best policy to pursue; college completion (in a timely fashion) is a more important goal. With the completion objective in mind, there is a great deal to be said for (1) bolstering the college preparation of students from low-income families who may be marginal college-goers (which we discuss in chapter 9), and (2) providing more resources to disadvantaged students, and to their institutions, as these students progress through college (which we discuss in chapter 8).

Perhaps the most complicated facts are those relating to college choice. There is no question that students from low-income families are underenrolling in the most selective, most expensive institutions, even after controlling for their college preparedness and other observable characteristics. Given the disproportionately high benefits that Hoxby and others have found that the selective schools offer, this is a troubling finding. What explains it? Are these institutions simply too expensive for college-goers from low-income families? Is the true capacity of these students to do first-rate academic work unappreciated or unobserved? Or are these students underenrolling as a result of false perceptions of their own or of misguided decision making? Moreover, at what point are they either failing to appear in the credible applicant pool or dropping out of it: do they underapply, are they underadmitted, or do they fail to matriculate if admitted? Are the selective colleges and universities making sufficient efforts to help these students attend their institutions and graduate from them? In the next chapter, we employ a rich new dataset to answer these and many other questions about the impact of socio-economic status and race on admission, matriculation, and graduation at 19 selective colleges and universities.

⊂♨◞

CHAPTER 5

The "Elite" Schools

Engines of Opportunity or Bastions of Privilege?

We turn now to a detailed examination of new data showing how socioeconomic status relates to admission, enrollment, and academic outcomes at 19 academically selective colleges and universities. The schools in this special study include 5 Ivy League universities (Columbia University, Harvard University, Princeton University, the University of Pennsylvania, and Yale University); 10 academically selective liberal arts colleges (Barnard College, Bowdoin College, Macalester College, Middlebury College, Oberlin College, Pomona College, Smith College, Swarthmore College, Wellesley College, and Williams College), 3 of which (Barnard, Smith, and Wellesley) are for women only; and 4 leading state universities (the Pennsylvania State University, the University of California–Los Angeles, the University of Illinois at Urbana/Champaign, and the University of Virginia). Thanks to the cooperation of these schools, and to the assistance of the College Board, we have at our disposal a rich new dataset that allows us to look "microscopically" at the more than 180,000 applications to these schools for places in the 1995 entering cohort, at the characteristics of those applicants offered admission, at the "yields" on those offers, and, finally, at the performance of the matriculants themselves as they moved through college to graduation.[1] At each stage along the way, we can see how outcomes differ according to the academic qualifications and socioeconomic status (SES) of the students.

We recognize that these schools are among the most selective colleges and universities in the country, and that results might well differ in many ways if we were considering a broader array of institutions (including some that were less selective and less wealthy). As always, it would have been desirable to look at more schools, but focusing on this group of highly ranked institutions is worthwhile because of the depth of the analysis that it permits and because many other colleges and universities want to know what these highly ranked institutions are doing. Some other schools would surely adopt similar admissions and financial aid policies if their circumstances permitted them to do so.[2] Furthermore, it is still often the case that the path to many positions of power and wealth in this country winds its way through these selective colleges and universities.[3] It is important, from a societal vantage point, to know who is attending them.

The fundamental question is whether these highly regarded institutions should today be considered "engines of opportunity" or "bastions of privilege." The president of one of them posed a central question to us early on in this project: "In applying to my university, is an applicant better off, other things equal, being rich or poor?" Put another way: is there an admissions advantage associated with being poor, or with being the first member of your family to go to college, that is comparable to the advantage associated with being a minority student, a legacy, or a recruited athlete? Alternatively, does coming from a wealthy family, in and of itself, increase an applicant's chance of admission? Although much is already known about the admissions results for other groups, this study represents, to the best of our knowledge, the first time anyone has been able to answer such questions about applicants of low (and high) socioeconomic status (SES) on a multi-institutional basis. Our data also allow us to break new ground in understanding how students from poor families fare throughout the college process—in the decision to matriculate or enroll, in academic performance, and in graduation—relative to other students. Combining these new data with earlier data from some of the same schools also allows us to describe trends and explore post-collegiate outcomes.

THE DECISION TO APPLY: GETTING INTO THE "POOL"

A "bridge" is needed between national data and these focused institutional data. We need to know about decisions to apply to these schools in relation to both academic preparedness and SES. In the previous chapter we discussed the extent to which family circumstances affect decisions to take the SAT in the first place and then the extent to which they affect test-taking performance (see table 4.1). We found that those in the top income quartile were about six times more likely to take the SAT *and* score above 1200 than were those in the bottom income quartile, and that young people with at least one parent who was educated beyond a high school diploma were nearly seven times more likely to achieve these high scores than those whose parents have no more than a high school diploma. Fewer than 2.5 percent of young people from low-income families, and fewer than 1 percent of the children of parents with low educational attainment, were in this category of high-scoring SAT-takers.

Of the candidates from low-SES backgrounds who do end up with high SAT scores, more apply to selective and expensive schools such as those in our study than one might have expected. Data in a recent report by Richard Spies (the fourth in a series that Spies began in the 1970s) indicate that, of all high-testing students from low-income families, about one-third apply to one or more of the 40 selective colleges that he chose as a reference group—a set of institutions that is generally similar to ours. However, more than half of the high-testing students from high-income families applied to these schools. Later in his study, Spies refers explicitly to "a difference of about 18 percentage points in the application rate between high and low-income students."[4] But we should not underplay Spies's "overarching conclusion," which is that "academic variables such as the SAT scores of the students are much more important factors in the college [application] process than financial variables such as family income."[5] Spies's data show, for example, that "a student with an SAT score of 1150 and an income of $57,000 is 38 percentage points less likely to apply than a student with a 1500 SAT and the same income. If, however, the SAT score is held constant at 1200, a student with an income of $57,000 is only 17 percentage points less likely to apply than a student with an income of $240,000." Spies also finds evidence that the impact of family income is considerably smaller now than it was in earlier years.[6]

Thus, progress has been made in encouraging high-ability students from modest circumstances to apply to expensive, academically selective schools—even though they remain less likely to do so than comparably prepared students from wealthier families. Apparently, the application process itself is not as much of a barrier for well-prepared students from low-income families as it used to be. One reason is that highly selective institutions have stepped up the recruitment of disadvantaged students. According to William Fitzsimmons, Harvard's dean of admissions and financial aid, direct mailings from Harvard reach over 75,000 high school students, representatives from Harvard and three other institutions (Duke, Georgetown, and Penn) travel together to over 130 U.S. cities per year, and Harvard's admissions officers travel by themselves to many more. A large part of this outreach effort is directed toward what Fitzsimmons calls "'non-traditional' families." Major efforts are made to demystify the application process and to emphasize the much greater availability of financial aid today.[7] The cumulative effects of years of this kind of aggressive recruitment, combined with improvements in the flow of information and increases in the mobility of the student population, have bolstered the number of high-ability students (including those from disadvantaged backgrounds) who apply to highly selective institutions.

Another product of this aggressive recruiting is high application rates for underrepresented minority students. We mentioned in the previous chapter that enrollment rates for minority students are higher than enrollment rates for white students, once differences in socioeconomic status are taken into account (despite the fact that minority candidates have test scores that are lower than their SES would suggest might be the case). This pattern is present at the selective schools in our study; minority students with a given SAT score are more likely to apply than are non-minority students with the same score.[8] These institutions seek out minority students and encourage them to apply even more aggressively than they recruit socioeconomically disadvantaged students. But beyond this, the selective institutions provide a substantial admissions preference to minority students (which we will describe in more detail later in the chapter), and their higher application rates represent a rational response to this incentive.

OVERVIEW: FROM APPLICATION TO GRADUATION

Applying to college is, of course, only the first step on the path from application to admission, to enrollment, and eventually to graduation. The unique aspect of our new data is that we are able to follow students through each of these steps. In figure 5.1 the path from application to graduation is charted (separately) for students from families with low incomes and low levels of parental education. "Families with low incomes" are those in the bottom quartile of the national income distribution of all families with 16-year-old children (the cut-off in 1995 was under $25,000) and "families with low levels of parental education" are those in which neither parent has education beyond a high school diploma (the college-going children are therefore sometimes referred to as "first-generation college students").[9]

There are two major conclusions to be drawn from these unadjusted, summary data. First, the percentage of students from low-income families and the percentage who are first-generation college students are both small. Students whose families are in the bottom quartile of the national income distribution represent roughly 10 to 11 percent of all students at these schools, and first-generation college students represent a little over 6 percent of these student populations.[10] Nationally, the bottom income quartile is, by definition, 25 percent of the population, while 38 percent of the national population of 16-year-olds have parents who never attended college.[11] Both groups are heavily underrepresented at the institutions in our study. When we combine the two measures of SES, and estimate the fraction of the enrollment at these schools that is made up of students who are *both* first-generation college-goers and from low-income families, we get a figure of about 3 percent (figure 5.2).[12] Nationally, the share of the same-age population who fell into this category was around 19 percent in 1992, making this doubly disadvantaged group even more underrepresented than students with just one of the two characteristics.[13]

The second main conclusion, which may surprise some, is that these percentages do not change very much as we move from the applicant pool to the group of students admitted, to those who enroll, and finally to

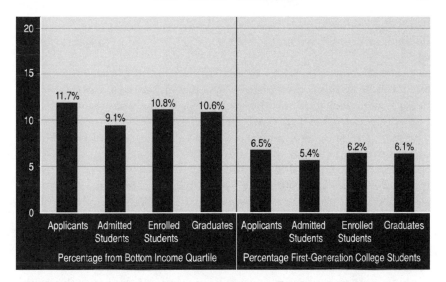

Figure 5.1. Percentage of Applicants, Admitted Students, Enrolled Students, and Graduates Who Were Socioeconomically Disadvantaged, All 19 Institutions, 1995 Entering Cohort

Source: Expanded College and Beyond database.

Note: Percentages based on non-foreign students who provided income and parental education data on the Student Descriptive Questionnaire.

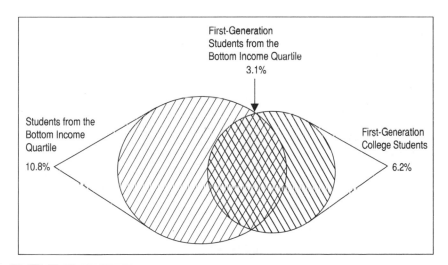

Figure 5.2. Percentage of Students Whose Families Were in the Bottom Income Quartile, Percentage Who Were First-Generation College Students, and Overlap Group, All 19 Institutions, 1995 Entering Cohort

Source: Expanded College and Beyond database.

Note: Calculations based on non-foreign students who provided income and parental education data on the Student Descriptive Questionnaire.

those who graduate. *This consistent pattern suggests that socioeconomic status does not affect progression through these stages.* Thus, even in this basic figure, which shows only "raw" data (and therefore does not take into account associated differences in SAT scores or other variables), we can begin to see the outline of what we regard as a striking finding: once disadvantaged students make it into the credible applicant pool of one of these highly selective schools (no easy accomplishment, to be sure), they have essentially the same experiences as their more advantaged peers. Much of the rest of this chapter will be devoted to verifying this pattern (which is, as it were, a kind of "dog that didn't bark" phenomenon), examining it in more detail, and attempting to parse out the meaning of this somewhat surprising "non-effect" of low SES at the different stages of a college education.

There is, naturally enough, some variation among our 19 institutions, but the differences are smaller than we had expected them to be—which is interesting, in and of itself. As one might expect, the share of enrolled students from the bottom income quartile is slightly higher at the public universities than at the private colleges and universities (11.8 percent versus 10.6 percent), as is the share who are first-generation college-goers (8.8 percent versus 5.5 percent). But these differences are hardly dramatic (figure 5.3). For reasons related primarily to the high degree of

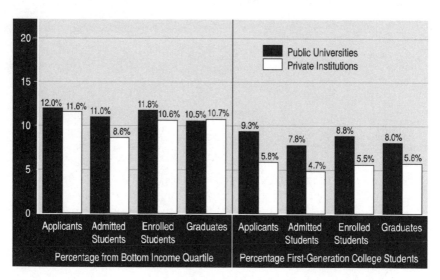

Figure 5.3. Percentage of Applicants, Admitted Students, Enrolled Students, and Graduates Who Were Socioeconomically Disadvantaged, Public versus Private Institutions, 1995 Entering Cohort

Source: Expanded College and Beyond database.

Note: Percentages based on non-foreign students who provided income and parental education data on the Student Descriptive Questionnaire.

selectivity of all these schools, to the high SAT scores that characterize them, and to the strong correlation between SATs and socioeconomic status, both sets of institutions enroll only very small numbers of students from families of modest circumstances. Only 4 percent of all students at the public universities are both first-generation college-goers and from low-income families, compared with just under 3 percent at the private institutions.[14] This "parallelism" of profiles raises important questions of mission and of institutional policy.

One group of institutions that does stand out is the set of three women's colleges: Barnard, Smith, and Wellesley. The average share of enrolled students from the bottom income quartile at these institutions is 15.7 percent, compared to 9.3 percent at the rest of the private institutions and 11.8 percent at the public universities.[15] The reasons for this greater representation of students from low-income families are not entirely clear. Differences in admissions policies and in yields are not the explanation. Nor is the explanation related to enrollment of minority students; women's colleges do not receive a higher percentage of their applications from (or enroll a higher percentage of) minority students than other institutions.

We believe that the explanation lies in the intersection between the financial aid needs of black women (as compared with black men) and the fact that women's colleges, by design, enroll only women. We know that black women are more likely to apply to, and enroll in, selective colleges than are black men, and black women applicants are more likely to come from the bottom income quartile than are black men who apply.[16] Thus, if women's colleges are as attractive to black students as other colleges, a higher share of their students will come from the bottom income quartile (because they are all women). In fact, at the women's colleges the overall share of African American students who are from low income families is 36 percent, while for the rest of our institutions the average share is just 23 percent. In any case, aside from the more substantial share of students from low-income families at the women's colleges, there is little difference between these colleges and the other private colleges in how applicants from low-income families fare. Henceforth, we will include the women's colleges with the rest of the private institutions in reporting findings.

ADMISSIONS

The question of *admissions preference* (which has, to this point, been referred to only implicitly) needs to be addressed directly—and can be, for the first time, with our data. Inspection of the raw percentages in figure 5.4 could easily lead one to think that admissions officers are

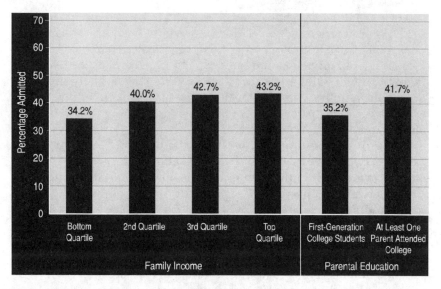

Figure 5.4. Percentage of Applicants Admitted, by Family Income and Parental
Education, All 19 Institutions, 1995 Entering Cohort

Source: Expanded College and Beyond database.

Note: Percentages based on non-foreign applicants who provided income and parental
education data on the Student Descriptive Questionnaire.

biased against applicants from modest socioeconomic backgrounds. The
"raw" probability of admission is clearly lower for students from lower
SES categories (whether defined by income quartile or parental education). But the raw data are misleading. The main missing variable is SAT
scores. Even within this highly select population of students, SAT scores
vary markedly according to family income and parental education. Average (combined) SAT scores of applicants are, for the most part, well over
100 points lower for applicants from families in the bottom income quartile or those with no parental history of college attendance.[17] The distribution of SAT scores by income and race demonstrates this pattern
clearly (figure 5.5). We should note that the distribution of the SAT
scores is more closely correlated with race than it is with income.

The clearest way to portray the importance of the different SAT distributions is by plotting the admission probabilities for various groups of
applicants in relation to SAT scores (in effect, holding SAT scores constant). This has been done in figure 5.6 for three groups of students:
non-minority students from bottom-quartile families, first-generation non-
minority students, and all other applicants (of higher SES) who are not
members of underrepresented minority groups. We see that *there was no*

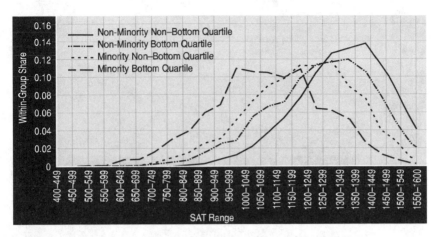

Figure 5.5. SAT Distribution of Applicants, by Race and Family Income, All 19 Institutions, 1995 Entering Cohort

Source: Expanded College and Beyond database.

Note: Distribution based on non-foreign applicants who provided income and parental education data on the Student Descriptive Questionnaire.

perceptible difference in the chances of being admitted, at any given SAT level, for students from the two low-SES categories and for all other (non-minority) students.

In a companion figure (figure 5.7), we show admission probabilities in relation to SAT scores for three other "special groups": underrepresented minority students, legacies, and recruited athletes.[18] It is evident that applicants in each of these special groups have a *decidedly* better chance of being admitted, at any specified SAT level, than do other students, including those from low-SES categories. (Note especially how much better a chance recruited athletes have of being admitted at relatively low SAT levels, albeit at levels that are above the cut-off for National Collegiate Athletic Association eligibility.) These substantial admissions preferences re-emphasize the lack of an admissions advantage (or, for that matter, a disadvantage) associated with being an applicant from a family in one of the low-SES categories.

More refined statistical analyses lend further support to this key finding. It is helpful to look at a summary measure that we call the "adjusted admissions advantage"—which is the average boost in the odds of admission provided to an applicant with certain characteristics relative to an otherwise identical applicant (table 5.1).[19] On an "other-things-equal" basis (adjusting for differences in race/ethnicity, legacy status, whether the applicant was a recruited athlete, whether the applicant applied through an early action or early decision program, and institutional

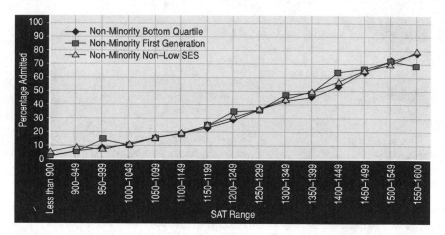

Figure 5.6. Percentage of Non-Minority Applicants Admitted, by Family Income, Parental Education, and SAT Score Range, All 19 Institutions, 1995 Entering Cohort

   Source: Expanded College and Beyond database.

   Note: Percentages based on non-foreign applicants who provided income and parental education data on the Student Descriptive Questionnaire.

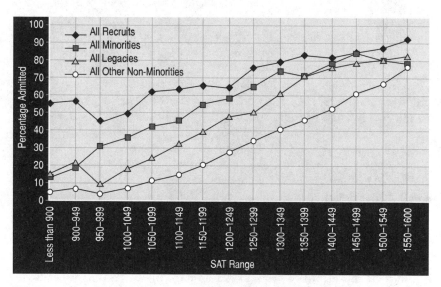

Figure 5.7. Percentage Admitted of All Minorities, All Recruits, All Legacies, and All Other Non-Minorities, by SAT Score Range, All 19 Institutions, 1995 Entering Cohort

   Source: Expanded College and Beyond database.

   Note: Percentage based on non-foreign applicants who provided income and parental education data on the Student Descriptive Questionnaire. Pomona, Swarthmore, and Wellesley do not have recruit data, and the University of Illinois does not have legacy data. They were excluded as appropriate.

TABLE 5.1

Adjusted Admissions Advantages Associated with Various Characteristics,
13 Institutions, 1995 Applicants

	Adjusted Admissions Advantage
Income (Relative to Middle Quartiles)	
Bottom quartile	−1.0
Top quartile	−3.1
Parental Education	
First-generation college student	**4.1**
Other Characteristics	
Recruited athlete	**30.2**
Underrepresented minority	**27.7**
Legacy	**19.7**
Early applicant	**19.6**

Source: Expanded College and Beyond database.

Notes: Numbers in **bold** are significant to 0.05. Predictions are based on a logistic regression with the dependent variable admission, and controls for SAT score, race, income, parental education, recruit status, legacy status, early application, and institutional dummy variables. Penn State, Pomona, Swarthmore, UCLA, the University of Illinois, and Wellesley were excluded due to missing values. Only data on non-foreign applicants who provided income and parental education information on the Student Descriptive Questionnaire were used. Observations with missing values were excluded.

idiosyncrasies, in addition to SAT scores[20]), we find that being a potential first-generation college student increases the odds of admission—but ever so slightly. First-generation college students get a statistically significant boost of 4.1 percentage points, which is quite modest against a "base" admissions probability of approximately 40 percent for otherwise similar students.

On the other hand, there is no statistically significant relationship (either way) between being from a family in the bottom income quartile and being admitted. Noteworthy is the clear finding that, while applicants from families in the bottom income quartile get no help in admissions, on an other-things-equal basis, neither do applicants from the families in the top quartile of the income distribution—who, surprisingly, pay a small "price" in admissions probabilities. (Although we have no quantitative evidence, informal conversations lead us to suspect that applicants from high-income families are more eagerly pursued by private colleges that are less well off financially.) Most of the 19 institutions in our study claim to be "need-blind" in admissions—to pay no attention whatsoever to the financial circumstances of their applicants.[21] These data suggest that in fact they are need-blind.

Admissions Advantages for "Special Groups"

The adjusted admissions advantages enjoyed by four groups of "special" applicants—recruited athletes, minority students, legacies, and (now added as an additional "special" group) early action/early decision candidates—are far greater, on an other-things-equal basis, than the advantage of 4.1 points enjoyed by first-generation college students (see the bottom panel of table 5.1). Recruited athletes receive the biggest boost at these institutions, about 30 percentage points, followed by under-represented minorities at 28 points, legacies at about 20 points, and early action/early decision candidates, also at about 20 points. The straight-forward interpretation of these estimates is that an applicant with an admissions probability of, say, 40 percent based on SAT scores and other variables would have an admissions probability of 70 percent if he or she were also a recruited athlete, 68 percent if a member of an under-represented minority group, and 60 percent if a legacy or an early action/early decision applicant.[22]

The reasons for giving admissions advantages to these four groups of applicants are radically different, and we will discuss and assess the ratio-nales used to justify the favorable treatment of each group in chapters 6 and 7 when we consider race-sensitive admissions and other institutional policies (such as preferences given to legacies). Here, when we are analyz-ing the "facts" of where we are today in admissions policies, these calcu-lations serve primarily as reference points.

SES Characteristics of the "Special Groups"

Of course minority applicants, recruited athletes, legacies, and early action/early decision candidates are not mutually exclusive groups. There are overlaps among them, and (more important, for our present purposes) there are correlations between SES and membership in these other groups. Given the admissions preferences that these groups receive, it is important to tease out these relationships.

Perhaps contrary to intuition, recruited athletes in our study were, overall, less likely than other applicants to be from families in the bottom income quartile or to be first-generation college students (5 percent of recruited athletes come from the bottom income quartile compared to 11.6 percent of other applicants, and 4.3 percent of recruited athletes were first-generation applicants compared to 6.4 percent of other ap-plicants).[23] Applicants from low-SES backgrounds were also under-represented among those who applied for early action or early decision, though this should come as less of a shock, because binding early accept-ance usually means that accepted students are unable to negotiate their financial aid package. Early applicants were less likely to be first-generation students (3.4 percent versus 5.7 percent) and were less likely to be from the bottom income quartile (7.9 percent versus 11.4 percent).[24] The group with the highest socioeconomic profile was (naturally) the legacy applicants. Even so, legacy applicants were more likely to come from the bottom income quartile than were recruited athletes (7.2 percent for legacies); no legacy applicants were first-generation students, by definition.

In contrast to the other special groups, underrepresented minorities are *far more likely* to come from disadvantaged backgrounds than other applicants and other students at these institutions. Over a quarter of the minority applicants in our study come from the bottom income quartile (25.7 percent), and 16.4 percent were first-generation applicants, while the corresponding shares for non-minority students were 9.5 percent and 4.8 percent. However, despite the greater likelihood that they will be from disadvantaged backgrounds, minority students do not comprise a majority of the disadvantaged students in the applicant pools or among the enrolled students from disadvantaged backgrounds at these institutions.[25] The reason for this result is simple demographics: on average, minority students make up only 12 to 13 percent of the student population at these schools. Nevertheless, the recruitment and admission of minority students certainly have the effect of increasing socioeconomic diversity at the academically selective institutions in our study.

How do all of these relationships and overlaps affect the admissions chances of students from low-SES backgrounds? The surprising answer is: not much at all. Due to the small differences in the proportion of students from low-SES and high-SES backgrounds who are recruits and early applicants, and because of the SAT distributions of legacies, controlling for these characteristics after already having controlled for SAT scores has very little impact on the admissions chances of students from low-SES backgrounds. The admissions relationship between race and SES is also the story of a "non-effect," even though there is substantial overlap between these groups. The reasons for this finding are more complicated, and we have relegated the explanation to an endnote.[26] The key point is that findings concerning the relationships between SES and admissions probabilities are not driven in any way by the disproportionate number of minority applicants who are in the low SES categories.

Public-Private Differences in Admissions

The general patterns in admissions are very similar for public and private institutions, but there are a few small differences.[27] The public institutions in our study give a modest adjusted admissions advantage to applicants from low-income families (about 5 percentage points), even though the private schools do not. On the other hand, the private schools give more of a boost to first-generation applicants than do public institutions (an adjusted admissions advantage of 4.3 points at private schools versus 2.0 points at the publics, both statistically significant).

The most substantial difference between the admissions practices of public and private institutions is in the awarding of a legacy preference. At the private institutions, the adjusted admissions advantage for legacies is about 21 percentage points, while the public institutions provide legacies with only a 5.5 percentage point advantage (which is nonetheless statistically significant). The adjusted admissions advantages for recruited athletes are roughly 31 points at both public and private institutions—though it must be remembered that with their higher "base" admissions percentage, this means that the public institutions are admitting recruited athletes at a much higher rate (about 82 percent versus 62 percent for the private institutions). Finally, minority preferences are about 6 points higher at the public universities than at the private institutions (30.6 points versus 25.1 points). Again, the difference in the base admit rate means that minority applicants to public universities are admitted at a very high rate (about 78 percent versus 54 percent at private institutions).[28] One important conclusion is that including various controls has little effect on the adjusted admissions advantage for students from low-SES backgrounds at both public and private institutions.

ENROLLMENT ("YIELD")

Once offers of admission go out, the locus of decision making shifts from the schools to the prospective students and their families. Their decisions as to whether to accept offers of admission determine how many students from various groups actually enroll (the school's "yield" is the fraction of offers of admission that are accepted). As we were able to infer from figure 5.1, students from lower socioeconomic groups enroll at disproportionately *high* rates. Figure 5.8a shows the enrollment rate differences explicitly. The yield for students from families in the bottom income quartile is 44.2 percent, and the yield for first-generation students is 42.6 percent, compared to 38.6 percent for students from the top income quartile.

Controlling for factors that are likely to affect enrollment decisions— such as athletic recruit status, early applicant status, race, and the number of other schools to which an applicant is assumed to have applied (using as a proxy the number of institutions to which a student sent his or her SAT scores)—actually *increases* the enrollment rate differential favoring students from low-income families and first-generation college students (see figure 5.8b).[29] Part of the explanation may be that we are not capturing fully the extent to which admitted students from high-income

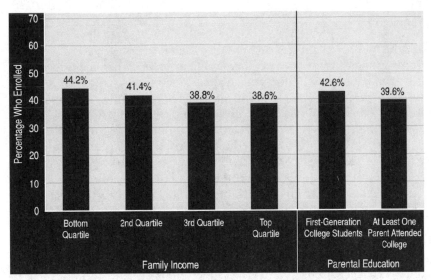

Figure 5.8a. Matriculation Rate of Admitted Students, by Family Income and Parental Education, All 19 Institutions, 1995 Entering Cohort

Source: Expanded College and Beyond database.

Note: Matriculation rates based on non-foreign admitted students who provided income and parental education data on the Student Descriptive Questionnaire.

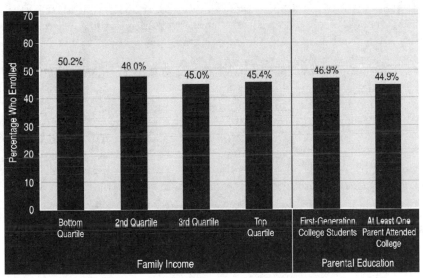

Figure 5.8b. Adjusted Matriculation Rate of Admitted Students, by Family Income and Parental Education, Controlling for Other Institutional and Individual Characteristics, 13 Institutions, 1995 Entering Cohort

Source: Expanded College and Beyond database.

Note: Analysis includes controls for SATs, race, recruit status, legacy status, early application, number of SAT reports, and institutional variables. Pomona, Penn State, Swarthmore, UCLA, the University of Illinois, and Wellesley were excluded due to missing values. Only non-foreign admitted students who provided income and parental education data on the Student Descriptive Questionnaire were included.

and high–parental education families have more options than other students. Students from poor families and first-generation college-goers who are admitted to these schools may also be much more dedicated to attending them; getting in and going may well be more significant accomplishments for them, and may be perceived as more important in their future lives, than for more privileged students. One reader of the manuscript (Michael McPherson) suggested another possible explanation for this pattern: students from wealthy families may be offered "merit-based" aid at less selective colleges and universities, and these offers could draw some of them away from our institutions, which offer mostly "need-based aid." It is much harder to attract highly able students from low-income families by offering merit-based aid because these students receive a great deal of need-based aid from almost all institutions they consider.[30]

Whatever is causing the higher enrollment rate for students from low-SES backgrounds, financial considerations certainly do not seem to be driving these students away, and this is surely a compliment to the generous financial aid programs of essentially all of the schools in our study. Indeed, this finding is a fairly strong repudiation of the existence of the much-debated "short-term credit constraints" discussed in the previous chapter, at least among the students from low-income families admitted to these institutions. It must be remembered, though, that these institutions are very wealthy compared to most institutions of higher education and offer the most generous financial aid; this is, then, a "best-case scenario." Also, this finding leaves open the possibility that enrollment rates for students from low-income families would be even higher if still more financial aid were provided.

Another interesting finding is that minority students who are admitted enroll at significantly lower rates than non-minority students (34 percent versus 41 percent). This result is not a statistical artifact: it holds up after the inclusion of our standard controls in the analysis. It is possible that high-achieving minority students, who are often especially heavily recruited and benefit from race-sensitive admission programs, have more options than other admitted students. This "other options" hypothesis is bolstered by the fact that minority students from low-income families and those who are first-generation college students enroll at higher rates than more advantaged minority students (and a similar pattern exists among non-minority students). Those students who, through a lack of financial aid concerns or through affirmative action—or both—are able to choose more freely and from among a wider array of institutions would seem to be the least likely to enroll at any given institution. Another possibility is that the combination of aggressive recruitment and the known presence of admissions preferences has encouraged some minority students to apply to these institutions even if they are not particularly inclined to attend. Unfortunately, we cannot, with our data, dig any more deeply into the reasons for this pattern.

ACADEMIC PERFORMANCE

Major Field of Study

How well students from low-income and low–parental education families did in their studies is obviously important, and grades earned will be the major focus of this section. But we are also interested in knowing which subjects these students elected to study. One might expect that they would be more drawn than other students to fields that hold the promise of high-paying employment right after graduation. Alternatively, there is the possibility that these students—who might not be as well prepared academically as their classmates or might have to hold a part-time or full-time job while in college—would congregate in fields that are thought to have easy grading policies or to be less work-intensive. *We find no evidence supporting either of these hypotheses; in fact, students from low-SES backgrounds disperse among the fields in essentially the same way as all other students do.*

Figures 5.9a and 5.9b show the distribution of students among four categories of majors (social science and business, humanities, natural science, and math and engineering) by family income and by parental education, respectively. The differences are slight. Looking first at figure 5.9a, the main difference is that students from the bottom income quartile are somewhat more likely to major in math or engineering; they major in the social sciences and in business in almost exactly the same proportions as other students, and they are ever so slightly less likely to major in the humanities or the natural sciences. In figure 5.9b we see that first-generation college students are overrepresented in the social science and business majors and in the humanities, and they are underrepresented in the natural sciences. But none of these disparities is large—especially when we compare them to the bunching of male recruited athletes in the social sciences and in business. In *Reclaiming the Game* Bowen and Sarah Levin found that between 50 and 60 percent of male recruits in the High Profile sports and 40 to 50 percent of male recruits in the Lower Profile sports could be found in a social science or business field, compared to around one-third of non-athletes.[31] In contrast to this pronounced overrepresentation, it seems clear that students from low-SES backgrounds are very much like their more advantaged classmates in their choice of majors.

Rank-in-Class

The next important question is how low-income and first-generation students perform academically after enrolling. Since these students enter with somewhat weaker academic credentials (on average) than their classmates, we would expect them to earn somewhat lower grades—and

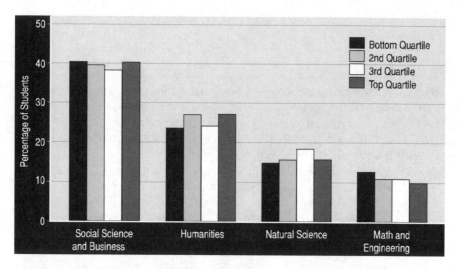

Figure 5.9a. Percentage of Students Majoring in Social Science and Business, Humanities, Natural Science, and Math and Engineering, by Family Income, All 19 Institutions, 1995 Entering Cohort
Source: Expanded College and Beyond database.
Note: Analysis based on non-foreign students who provided income and parental education data on the Student Descriptive Questionnaire.

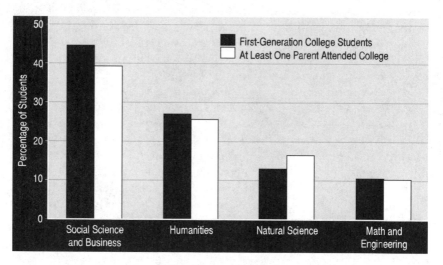

Figure 5.9b. Percentage of Students Majoring in Social Science and Business, Humanities, Natural Science, and Math and Engineering, by Parental Education, All 19 Institutions, 1995 Entering Cohort
Source: Expanded College and Beyond database.
Note: Analysis based on non-foreign students who provided income and parental education data on the Student Descriptive Questionnaire.

they do. The typical first-generation college student's cumulative grade point average (GPA) placed him or her at just under the 40th percentile in class rank; students from the bottom income quartile ranked in the 44th percentile (compared to the 53rd percentile for students from the top quartile of the income distribution). These roughly 10-point differentials are not trivial, but they are smaller than the corresponding differentials we found in past studies—when we compared athletes recruited for High Profile sports and other students, for example.[32] Updating these findings on the academic performance of recruited athletes and minority students (another group for whom we have found rank-in-class deficits in the past), we see that the GPA gap for all recruited athletes is 14 rank-in-class points; it is 30 points for male recruited football, basketball, and ice hockey players; and it is 19 points for underrepresented minorities at those institutions for which we have data.[33]

Both students from low-income families and first-generation college students are somewhat overrepresented in the bottom third of the class, but again, this overrepresentation is not nearly as pronounced as the overrepresentation of athletes recruited for High Profile sports at Ivy League universities and liberal arts colleges, two-thirds to three-fourths of whom are in the bottom third of the class.[34] We can also determine if students from low-SES backgrounds are over- or underrepresented at the highest levels of academic achievement—among those who earn honors or are elected to Phi Beta Kappa or Tau Beta Pi, for example. We have data on "head-of-the-class" performance for the five Ivy League universities as well as for UCLA and the University of Illinois. At these institutions, we find that about 34 percent of students from the top income quartile received honors of some kind, while only 20 percent of those from the bottom income quartile and 16 percent of first-generation college students did (figures 5.10a and 5.10b). Using an even higher hurdle, we find a similar pattern in the achievement of highest honors (summa cum laude) or election to an honor society like Phi Beta Kappa or Tau Beta Pi. Between 2 and 3 percent of students from the bottom income quartile and fewer than 1 percent of first-generation college students earn these highly prized distinctions, compared to between 5 and 6 percent of students from the top income quartile.

In short, students from low-SES backgrounds as a group are performing less well academically than their more advantaged peers, in terms of average grades as well as their presence at the very top of their classes. However, the raw data describing their performance are not nearly as disappointing as those for underrepresented minorities and (particularly) recruited athletes.[35] Of course all three of these groups begin college with less impressive formal credentials than students at large. We will now see how taking account of differences in SAT scores and other attributes affects our perceptions of these academic performance gaps.

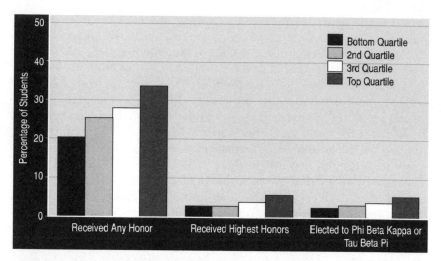

Figure 5.10a. Percentage of Students Receiving Any Honor, Highest Honors, and Elected to Phi Beta Kappa or Tau Beta Pi, by Family Income, 7 Institutions, 1995 Entering Cohort

   Source: Expanded College and Beyond database.

   Note: Analysis includes non-foreign students who provided income and parental education data on the Student Descriptive Questionnaire from Columbia, Harvard, Princeton, UCLA, the University of Illinois, the University of Pennsylvania, and Yale.

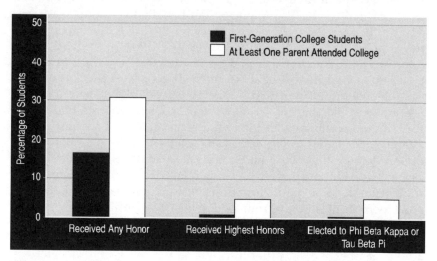

Figure 5.10b. Percentage of Students Receiving Any Honor, Highest Honors, and Elected to Phi Beta Kappa or Tau Beta Pi, by Parental Education, 7 Institutions, 1995 Entering Cohort

   Source: Expanded College and Beyond database.

   Note: Analysis includes non-foreign students who provided income and parental education data on the Student Descriptive Questionnaire from Columbia, Harvard, Princeton, UCLA, the University of Illinois, the University of Pennsylvania, and Yale.

Academic Underperformance

A key issue is not just how students from lower-SES backgrounds fare academically relative to their classmates, but how they perform relative to how they might have been *expected* to perform on the basis of their incoming academic credentials and other characteristics.[36] Determining how actual performance compares to expected performance provides us with a valuable measure of how students are achieving academically relative to their potential—and knowing this relationship permits us to explore the factors that affect the translation of academic potential into actual achievement.

Earlier research has shown that minority students earn lower grades than we would expect them to earn based on their SAT scores and other characteristics.[37] This phenomenon, which we refer to as "underperformance," is evident to an even greater extent among recruited athletes than among minority students.[38] Do students from disadvantaged socioeconomic backgrounds also underperform? The simple (perhaps surprising, but very encouraging) answer: *They do not. Students from low-income and low–parental education families do not exhibit any significant underperformance; they do almost exactly as well as we would expect them to do.* This important finding can be compared to the approximately 9-percentile-point underperformance of minority students and the 10-point underperformance of recruited athletes at the schools in our study (table 5.2). We can also report that the SES gaps in achieving honors and highest honors and in being elected to an honor society that are apparent in the raw (unadjusted) data disappear when we control for SAT scores, race, athletic recruit status, major field of study, and institutional idiosyncrasies. So these students from low-SES backgrounds are, from this perspective, taking full advantage of the educational opportunities that they are being given.

Recruited athletes and minority students underperform for different reasons.[39] In *Reclaiming the Game,* Bowen and Levin demonstrated empirically that the underperformance of recruited athletes was not primarily a result of the time they spent on the athletic field or the intensity of their athletic experience. The most startling evidence in support of this proposition is that recruited athletes underperform academically *whether they are playing or not,* while walk-on athletes, including those who compete actively, underperform very little or not at all.[40] There does seem to be a cultural aspect to the recruits' underperformance (for example, recruited athletes who major in fields that are heavily populated by other recruits underperform to a greater extent than do those in other majors).[41] But for the most part, the underperformance of recruited athletes appears to be directly related to factors associated with their recruitment and admission —to their interests and motivations.

TABLE 5.2
Academic Underperformance Associated with Various Characteristics,
All 19 Institutions, 1995 Entering Cohort

	Rank in Class Percentile Points
Income (Relative to Middle Quartiles)	
Bottom quartile	−0.5
Top quartile	**1.7**
Parental Education	
First-generation college student	0.4
Other Characteristics	
Recruited athlete	**−10.1**
Underrepresented minority	**−8.8**

Source: Expanded College and Beyond database.
Notes: Numbers in **bold** are significant to 0.05. Predictions are based on an ordinary least squares with the dependent variable rank in class and controls for SAT score, race, income, parental education, recruit status, graduation status, field of study, and institutional dummy variables. Only data on non-foreign students who provided family income and parental education on the Student Descriptive Questionnaire were used. Observations with missing values were excluded.

At all of the institutions in our study, coaches play a significant role in the admissions process; in some schools, they have a few "spots" that, assuming prospective athletes are over threshold, they can distribute more or less as they see fit (which is the case at the public universities, where teams have a specified number of athletic scholarships). At the Ivy League universities and some of the more athletically intensive liberal arts colleges, coaches generally provide lists of "preferred candidates," often in rank order, to the admissions office, which exercises some independent judgment but weighs coaches' rankings heavily—as demonstrated by the high admissions advantage enjoyed by recruited athletes on a coach's list. At some other schools, coaches make more general recommendations about candidates they believe would be strong contributors to their teams. Only the public institutions in our study provide athletic scholarships, which means that coaches at the private institutions have less leverage in encouraging a student to stay on the team once the student is enrolled. An important consequence is that coaches tend to be very careful in forming their lists of preferred candidates. They naturally favor those who are expected to be highly focused on their sport and to exhibit an unusual commitment to the team and the coach. In this process, other characteristics, such as intellectual curiosity or wide-ranging interests, which are normally highly prized by admissions officers, may be sacrificed or at least given less weight. The not-surprising result is that recruited athletes who, according to their grades and test scores, are capable of doing quite well academically, often fail to achieve their potential—and, for example, rarely earn honors or are elected to Phi Beta Kappa.[42]

It is conceivable that something similar happens to at least some minority students—that, for example, because admissions officers assign a preference based on a non-academic characteristic (race), other characteristics related to a high degree of academic success might receive less weight. But we do not think this is likely to be the case. Precisely because they are, in such cases, relying less on formal credentials, admissions officers can be expected to focus more, not less, on harder-to-measure attitudes and motivations in order to justify the admission of particular minority candidates. An alternative hypothesis explaining minority underperformance that has gained considerable empirical support is "stereotype threat," which we described in chapter 4. To recapitulate, stereotype threat is the anxiety that minority students feel when they are in a situation in which they could, through their actions or performance, confirm a negative stereotype about their group.[43] Claude Steele argues that the effects of stereotype threat are more likely to occur when students care deeply about their academic performance, and Douglas Massey's work confirms this hypothesis.[44] Thus, the academically oriented minority students at these highly selective colleges and universities may be among the students most vulnerable to stereotype threat.[45]

Students from low-income and low–parental education families are fortunate in *not* having the characteristics that can lead to underperformance by recruited athletes and minority students.[46] They are selected "in the regular way," on the basis of characteristics expected to lead to high academic achievement. Also, we would expect students who have had to overcome disadvantages of one kind or another in order to gain admission to be especially eager (determined) to benefit fully from the opportunities they have earned. Finally, though these students come from very different backgrounds than the more advantaged students, this difference in family circumstances is not readily apparent these days to professors or peers (thanks in part to present-day conventions concerning campus dress),[47] so any possible burden of stereotype threat is less likely to manifest itself. Moreover, the deeply rooted societal stereotypes and stigmas that are thought to play such a large role in the lives of many minority students are not present to anything like the same degree (and maybe not at all) in the case of white students from modest backgrounds.

The "Striver" Hypothesis and Overperformance

Some have argued that students from low-income families who make it into these institutions in spite of all the obstacles they have faced along the way might be expected to "overperform"—that these "strivers," as Anthony Carnevale calls them, will do better than expected based on their credentials.[48] Unfortunately, we do not find evidence that supports this appealing idea, at least in terms of average rank-in-class (later in the chapter we consider whether these students overperform in terms of post-collegiate outcomes). Of course we may be missing an important but unobservable measure of college preparation (such as study habits, comfort in academic settings, etc.), which, when added to the admissions equation, would predict lower academic achievement and thus (given actual academic outcomes) yield a finding of academic overperformance. However, this line of thinking does not fit well with the "striver" concept —which, in essence, suggests that formal credentials understate the true potential of students from low-income families. Our findings show that students from low-SES backgrounds at our schools perform, on average, neither better nor worse, but *exactly* as well as otherwise similar students from more advantaged backgrounds. Given the disadvantages many of these students have had to overcome, this is, we would submit, no small accomplishment.

Although it does not appear that the average student from a low-SES background overperforms academically, there are certainly individual students in this category who outperform their formal credentials. Isolating the characteristics that lead to this happy result could provide colleges with a useful tool to incorporate in the admissions process.[49] The most straightforward way to measure overperformance for students from low-SES backgrounds is to run a regression using only the pool of students from these backgrounds (in this case, we include students who meet either the criterion for low family income or that for low parental education, to maximize the number of observations), with rank-in-class as the outcome variable and with SAT scores and a variety of other characteristics that we would like to test as independent variables. The coefficients on the independent variables tell us if, and by how much, those characteristics boost grades. When we perform this exercise, we find that (perhaps as expected) SAT scores explain much of the variation in rank-in-class.[50]

After controlling for SAT scores (and minority status, which has a significant negative effect on grades), three variables stand out as having a substantial and statistically significant positive impact on rank-in-class. The first is, not surprisingly, high school rank-in-class. If a student from a low-income family is in the top 10 percent of his or her high school class, he or she can be expected to have a college rank-in-class around 9 points higher than a student from the bottom 90 percent of his or her high school class with the same SAT scores and race. The impact of the other two characteristics is not nearly as intuitively obvious. Students from low-SES backgrounds whose first language is something other than English have a smaller (3-point) but statistically significant advantage in their academic performance, after controlling for race, SAT scores, and even high school grades.[51] The last characteristic associated with overperformance is having musical interest and talent; seeking advanced placement credit in music has a large (6-point) coefficient that is just short of being statistically significant.[52] Understanding the relationship between these characteristics and academic performance, and identifying other overperformance variables, clearly has value.

GRADUATION

Extrapolating from national results, which show decidedly below-average graduation rates for college students from low-income families,[53] one might expect students from lower-SES backgrounds at these schools to be less likely to graduate than their classmates. In fact, first-generation college students graduate at almost exactly the same rate as their classmates, while students from the bottom income quartile are only slightly less likely to graduate than their wealthier classmates, with an 84 percent graduation rate compared to an 87 percent rate for other students (figure 5.11a).[54]

The graduation rate gap between students from the bottom income quartile and other students widens slightly when we control for SAT scores, race, and athletic recruit status; indeed, a small (non-significant) deficit in graduation rates between first-generation college students and others now appears as well (figure 5.11b). The income-quartile gap in graduation rates is small—just 4.7 percentage points between students from the bottom quartile and those from the top quartile—but it is statistically significant and at least mildly worrying because we cannot rule out financial concerns as the reason for it. On the other hand, if fewer than 5 percent of students from low-income families are not completing college because of an inability to pay, the schools they attended have reason to feel that they have done well in graduating so many of these disadvantaged students.

There is one other finding that is more troubling. The small overall difference in graduation rates by income category that exists across all 19 schools in our study masks the fact that there is a more substantial difference in graduation rates associated with socioeconomic status at the public universities. For students at the private colleges and universities, there is less than a 1-point difference in graduation rates between students from the bottom income quartile and those from the top quartile of the distribution; in contrast, there is a *12-point* difference for students at the public universities. Adding controls for other variables (including SAT scores, race, athletic recruit status, rank-in-class, and major field of

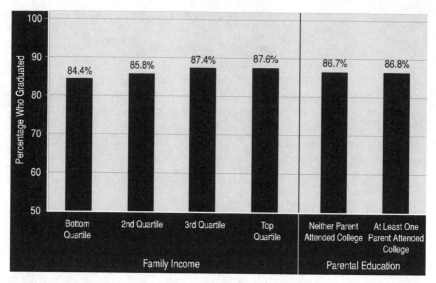

Figure 5.11a. Graduation Rate, by Family Income and Parental Education, All Institutions, 1995 Entering Cohort

Source: Expanded College and Beyond database.

Note: Graduation rates based on non-foreign students who provided income and parental education data on the Student Descriptive Questionnaire.

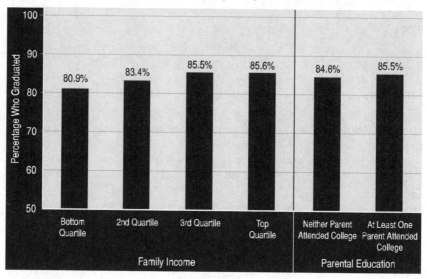

Figure 5.11b. Adjusted Graduation Rate, by Family Income and Parental Education, Controlling for Other Institutional and Individual Characteristics, 18 Institutions, 1995 Entering Cohort

Source: Expanded College and Beyond database.

Note: Analysis includes controls for SAT score, race, recruit status, and institutional variables. Swarthmore was excluded due to missing values. Only non-foreign students who provided income and parental education data on the Student Descriptive Questionnaire were included.

study) reduces the gap at the public universities to about 7 percentage points, but it is still statistically significant.

The explanation does not appear to be differences between the sectors in the distribution of SAT scores by income quartiles (which are so small as to be negligible). The availability of financial aid may play a role, though we would expect any systemic public-private differences in aid to manifest themselves in a gap in the relative enrollment rates of students from low-SES backgrounds—and there is no such gap. It is likely that disproportionate numbers of students from low-income families at public universities commute, another factor that could affect graduation rates. The percentage of undergraduates who live on campus is under 50 percent at the public universities in our study, whereas the on-campus percentages are often in the 90 percent range at the private institutions.[55] The percentage of students working cuts in the other direction. Although more students at highly selective public institutions worked full time in 1995 than did students in highly selective private institutions (2.3 percent versus 0.4 percent), nearly three times as many students at the private institutions had an on-campus part-time job, and nearly five times as many had a work-study job.[56]

One way to try to tease out the effect of these additional responsibilities is to look at graduation rates over more years. Presumably, some of the students who are working or commuting would simply take longer to graduate rather than drop out altogether. When we examine the graduation rates of these students as of 2003 (eight years after they matriculated), we find that there is still a substantial 10-point gap in the graduation rates of students from the bottom income quartile versus those from the top quartile (78 percent versus 88 percent). The differences narrow, which lends some credence to the proposition that some students from low-income families need more years in which to complete their studies, but these data show that a number of these students are not simply taking more time to graduate; they are not completing their degree programs at all, at least not at their original institution.[57]

We suspect that this result is driven mainly by differences in the scale of enrollment coupled with differences in the availability of institutional resources. Enrollment in the entering class in the public universities in our study averaged more than 4,000 in 1995; the average was under 1,000 at the private institutions.[58] Stanley Ikenberry, former president of the University of Illinois, suggested to us that students from poorer families, and from families that have never before sent a family member to college, are likely to need more help and more nurturing in college than are their classmates from families that are more experienced in dealing with the cultural, social, and academic challenges of college. At very large institutions, there is a somewhat greater risk that a student will simply "get lost."[59] Institutional scale and limits on the resources that can be devoted to undergraduate education per student could well take a toll on the completion rates of students from low-income families and first-generation college students (indeed, this is likely a part of the explanation for the completion/time-to-degree findings described in chapter 4).[60]

In contrast to students from low-SES backgrounds, who (with the exception of students from low-income families at the public universities) graduate at approximately the same rate as other students, minority students lag behind their non-minority classmates in graduation rates. Again we see a difference between public and private institutions, but this time it is only in the size of the deficits. At the public universities, there is a sizable, 13.5 percentage-point, gap between minority and non-minority graduation rates (71.5 percent versus 85 percent); at the private institutions, there is a smaller, but still substantial, 7.5 percentage-point gap (81.1 percent versus 88.6 percent). These gaps persist at the Ivy League universities, at the three most selective coed liberal arts colleges in our study (Williams, Pomona, and Swarthmore), and at the public universities after we include controls for socioeconomic status, SAT scores, athletic recruit status, and institutional fixed effects. However, at the women's colleges and the four other coed colleges, the graduation rate deficits disappear when these controls are added to the analysis.

We suspect that the reason for this mixed result is similar to the reason for the income-quartile gap in graduation rates at the public institutions: minority students, who often come to college from very different backgrounds than most of their classmates and may well have some problems adjusting to a new kind of environment, probably benefit from the additional attention that is available at a smaller institution. That is, they may experience the same difficulties in coping with the large scale of the public universities as do at least some students from low-income families.

LIFE AFTER COLLEGE

How students progress through their college careers is not, of course, the only outcome in which we are interested. A large part of the notion of colleges as "engines of opportunity" is that higher education confers benefits beyond the college experience itself; graduating from the colleges in our study should be expected to help students advance to stations in life that represent real social mobility. Although we do not have such data for members of the '95 entering cohort (who have been out of college for only a short time), we do have survey responses from members of the '76 entering cohort at 11 of our 19 institutions, obtained approximately 15 years after they graduated.[61] The life outcomes of this group of students, most of whom graduated in 1980, may not be an accurate portrayal of what will happen to the group who entered in 1995 and presumably graduated just five years ago; the labor market has evolved, interests and goals of students may be dissimilar, and the institutions themselves have changed in many ways. Still, this analysis provides at least some indication of how well these schools prepared an earlier cohort of disadvantaged students for life after college *relative* to other students who attended the same schools at the same time.

Earnings 15 Years Out of College

Perhaps the most straightforward measure of whether these colleges are succeeding as engines of opportunity is how well students from low-income families do financially once they graduate. Looking at the basic relationship between parents' income and the mid-working-life income of these students from the '76 entering cohort, we find that the earnings of those from families in the bottom quartile of the income distribution were noticeably lower than the earnings of those from families in the second or third quartile—and that the former students whose parental income was in the top quartile enjoyed a substantial earnings advantage over all the rest of their classmates (figure 5.12).[62] The average income in 1994 or 1995 of a former student from the bottom income quartile was over $67,000; former students from the middle two quartiles had average incomes of between $73,000 and $75,000; and those from the top quartile had average earnings of nearly $86,000.[63]

Looking beyond average earnings, we can ask whether there is a difference between students from wealthy or poor backgrounds in the likelihood that they will earn an extremely high income. We find that those from wealthy backgrounds were about three times as likely as those from low-income backgrounds to be in the top earnings category used in the survey (greater than $200,000). Just under 2 percent of former students from the bottom income quartile had a very high income 15 years out of college, while almost 6 percent of former students from families in the highest income quartile were themselves already in the top income category.

Of course it is entirely possible (even likely) that this difference in outcomes is the result of characteristics other than income per se that are correlated with socioeconomic background. In particular, high-income families are able to confer advantages of many kinds on their children after they graduate from college, in part because families with high incomes also tend to have high net worth as well as access to networks of contacts who can find promising positions for the recent graduate, make the right introductions, and so on.[64] After accounting for race, SAT scores, college rank-in-class, and sector of employment (for-profit, non-profit, government, or self-employed), as well as institution attended, we

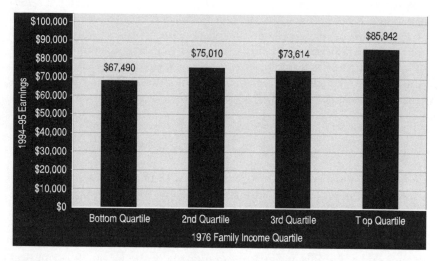

Figure 5.12. Average Individual Earnings of Alumni Who Worked Full Time in 1994–95, by Family Income Background, 11 Institutions, 1976 Entering Cohort

   Source: Expanded College and Beyond database.

   Note: Analysis based on non-foreign students who provided income data on the Student Descriptive Questionnaire.

find that the basic pattern evident in the raw data still holds. Although the adjusted average earnings of former students who were from families in the bottom income quartile are not significantly different from the earnings of those who come from families in the second and third income quartiles, the former students from the top quartile earned over $7,000 more than those from the middle group (and this difference is statistically significant). Likewise, when we estimate the probability of being in the top income category using regression analysis and the controls mentioned earlier, we find that those from families in the top quartile were significantly more likely to make it into the top income category themselves than were other survey respondents. *What is clear from this analysis of post-collegiate earnings is that the consistent, statistically significant, differences are between students from families in the highest quartile of the income distribution and all other students.* It is not that socioeconomically disadvantaged students are basically different from those just above them in the income strata (that is, those in the middle of the income distribution), but rather that the students from the most affluent families are very different, in their average earnings, from everyone else.

   In considering the economic progress made by graduates of these schools who came from modest backgrounds, we need to compare them to graduates of other colleges (and to those who were not fortunate enough to go to college at all), as well as to their classmates. By this criterion, students from low-SES backgrounds who attended these selective colleges and universities did very well indeed. The average 1995 income for *all* graduates of any college who are in the same age range as the '76 cohort included in the College and Beyond (C&B) survey was just under $49,000—nearly $20,000 below the average earnings of all students from low-SES backgrounds who attended the institutions in this study.[65] However, "all college graduates" is not an ideal comparison group, since presumably the average ability level (including earnings ability) is higher among the graduates of the more selective institutions than it is in the population of college graduates at large. To correct for this "ability bias" in an admittedly rough way, we make use of a small but nationally representative survey conducted specifically to facilitate comparisons with participants in the C&B survey.[66] Focusing on college graduates of the same "generation" as the '76 cohort who received "mostly A's" in college, we find that full-time workers earned an average of $55,654—almost $12,000 less than the alumni/ae of schools in the C&B study from low-income backgrounds. Thus, although they may not have earned as much as their classmates from more advantaged backgrounds, the students from families of modest means who attended these highly selective institutions earned far more than college graduates overall (never mind the large number of individuals from low-income families who did not graduate from any college). They also earned far more, on average, than high-ability college graduates, including those from high-income families, who attended other schools.

Advanced Degree Attainment and Occupation

How much one earns is only part of the story. We are also interested in the further education of graduates of the colleges and universities in our study and in what they do to earn a living. Accordingly, we look next at advanced degree attainment and then at career decisions, defined by sectors of employment. We might expect to find that students from low-income families are less likely to pursue advanced degrees—some, like law, medicine, and most masters programs, require substantial additional funds or loans, while all delay entry into the labor market. Students who are financially strapped may be disinclined to follow a path that consumes money and time.

Figure 5.13 shows advanced degree attainment by income background. Former students from the bottom income quartile were clearly less likely than former students from families with higher incomes to attain advanced degrees of any kind (as well as, more specifically, degrees in medicine or business, or a PhD)—though the gaps are not nearly as

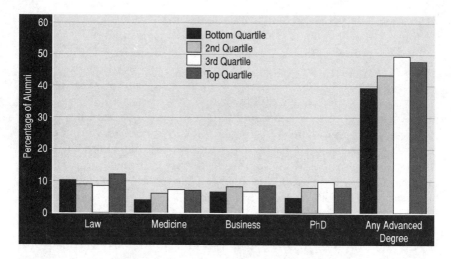

Figure 5.13. Precentage of Alumni Attaining an Advanced Degree in Law,
Medicine, or Business; a PhD; or Any Advanced Degree, by Family Income,
11 Institutions, 1976 Entering Cohort
  Source: Expanded College and Beyond database.
  Note: Analysis based on non-foreign students who provided income data on the Student
Descriptive Questionnaire.

large as one might have expected them to be. In the case of law, graduates from families in the bottom quartile of the income distribution are
actually more likely to earn a law degree than are those in the middle two
quartiles—but those from the top income quartile are even more likely
to earn a law degree. When we control for characteristics that may bias
the raw, unadjusted results (such as SAT scores, major field of study, race,
and rank-in-class), we find that the difference in advanced degree attainment between the bottom income quartile and the middle quartiles is
not statistically significant, but the top quartile still earns a significantly
larger number of professional degrees—thereby contributing to their
higher average earnings.

The advanced degrees most commonly earned by alumni/ae from the
bottom income quartile are law degrees and business degrees, which
could be interpreted as consistent with the proposition that these students need to earn money; both types of degrees require a short time
(two to three years) and are potentially very rewarding financially. However, the relative numbers of graduates from disadvantaged backgrounds
earning these degrees are not terribly different from the relative numbers of their more advantaged classmates—and the respective rates are
no different after controls are added for other variables. Furthermore,
while these degrees may offer high potential returns, they also require

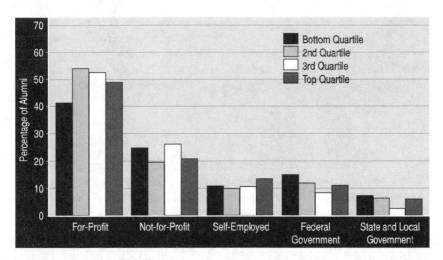

Figure 5.14. Percentage of Alumni Working in For-Profit, Not-for-Profit, Self-Employed, and Government Job Sectors, by Family Income, 11 Institutions, 1976 Entering Cohort

Source: Expanded College and Beyond database.

Note: Analysis based on non-foreign students who provided income data on the Student Descriptive Questionnaire.

high initial investments, as the grants and stipends that accompany most PhD programs are not normally available to students who wish to pursue law and business degrees. It seems, then, that former students from disadvantaged backgrounds are no more or less concerned about their labor market prospects than are their former classmates.

The pattern of advanced degree attainment gives some indication of the occupations into which graduates from low- and higher-income families move, but we can actually examine this question more directly. Although there are too few observations in our 1976 dataset to allow for an occupation-level analysis, we have grouped occupations into broad job sectors (for-profit, not-for-profit, self-employed, federal government, and state or local government). What we find (figure 5.14) is that graduates from low-income backgrounds, perhaps contrary to the intuition of some people, are less likely to work in the for-profit sector than are their more advantaged classmates. They are more likely than any other group to work for federal, state, or local governments, and they are more likely than all but those from the third income quartile to work in the not-for-profit sector. This could mean nothing more profound than that many of those who came from families of modest means were more familiar with jobs outside the for-profit sector than their classmates whose parents (generally their fathers) often had extensive experience with profit-making enterprises.

When we control for race, SAT scores, grades, and other characteristics, even these modest gaps mostly disappear. The overarching conclusion, as it has been throughout this analysis, is that the individuals from low-SES backgrounds who attend these selective schools behave in much the same way as their more advantaged, but otherwise similar, classmates.

Life Satisfaction and Civic Participation

As valuable as it is to be able to compare the earnings patterns and occupational choices of these former students from different SES strata, their work status alone does not come close to telling us everything we want to know about their post-college lives. As we stressed in chapter 1, two important goals of higher education are to help students in "living a life" and to instill in them a sense of civic responsibility. How well these selective institutions succeed in doing both for disadvantaged students is an important question.

The C&B survey of the '76 cohort included several questions on the respondents' satisfaction with various aspects of life as well as the impact of their undergraduate experience on their degree of satisfaction. The most relevant single question of this kind in the survey asked respondents to rate their overall satisfaction with life. We found (figure 5.15, left panel) that former students from the top three income quartiles were noticeably more satisfied with the general state of their lives than were those from the bottom quartile, with "only" 56 percent of former students from the bottom quartile reporting that they were somewhat or very satisfied with life compared to between 61 and 67 percent of those from the top three quartiles. When we asked a narrower question and focused on satisfaction with one's career (figure 5.15, center panel), we found that the share who were somewhat or very satisfied was essentially the same across quartiles, with former students from the bottom quartile actually having a slight edge. Moreover, the introduction of controls, including race, gender, SAT scores, college rank-in-class, income, and sector of employment, as well as institutional fixed effects, evens out any differences between the quartiles in both life and job satisfaction. In short, on an other-things-equal basis, degrees of satisfaction with life and with jobs were not affected by socioeconomic status.

We have two ways of estimating the impact of a person's alma mater on his or her personal sense of well-being. The first is by examining the answers to the direct question of how satisfied a former student was with his or her undergraduate experience (figure 5.15, right panel). Again we found that there was a difference between the bottom quartile and the top three quartiles in the percentage who said they were somewhat or very satisfied with their undergraduate experience (60 percent for those

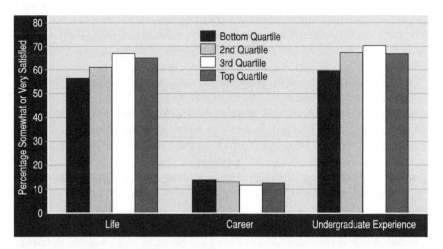

Figure 5.15. Percentage of Former Students Somewhat or Very Satisfied with Life, Career, and Undergraduate Experience, by Family Income, 11 Institutions, 1976 Entering Cohort

Source: Expanded College and Beyond database.

Note: Analysis based on non-foreign students who provided income data on the Student Descriptive Questionnaire.

from the bottom quartile versus 67 to 70 percent for those from the other quartiles). Once again, however, the gap does not stand up to the introduction of our standard controls.[67] The second measure is somewhat more subtle—we can examine the difference between the value that former students placed on certain skills and attitudes (such as ability to work independently, leadership skills, and ability to work cooperatively) and the degree to which they said that their undergraduate experience helped them develop in these areas. A smaller difference means that the former student was better served by his or her alma mater. Although these "value-development differences" are smaller (better) for respondents from the bottom income quartile than for those from the top two quartiles, the numbers are very similar. In sum, it seems that former students from the bottom income quartile are as satisfied with their lives and careers as otherwise similar students from higher quartiles. Those from socioeconomically disadvantaged backgrounds are generally also about as pleased with their undergraduate experiences as otherwise similar students, and they seem to feel that their alma maters met their most important expectations at least as often as, if not more frequently than, former students from wealthier families.

The next question to explore is what the students who attended these educational institutions have given back to their community, their polity, and society more generally. Being productive members of the economy (as these former students clearly have been) is, of course, one such benefit. But there are myriad other ways of making a constructive difference.

We begin with voting—one of the most basic, and also surely one of the most important, rights and duties of a citizen. Among the population at large, the percentage that votes in presidential elections typically hovers around 55 to 60 percent. In the 1992 presidential election, 61.3 percent of the population voted.[68] In contrast, close to 70 percent of the alumni/ae from the '76 entering cohort at our 11 institutions participated in that election. However, there were some differences in voting rates between former students from socioeconomically disadvantaged backgrounds and others. Alumni/ae whose parents' income was in the bottom income quartile had a 57 percent voting rate, whereas those from the top three quartiles voted at rates of between 67 and 72 percent. Adding our standard controls reduces the gap slightly, and the remaining difference is no longer statistically significant.[69]

Earlier research demonstrates that the members of the '76 cohort at the schools included in the C&B study were "noticeably more likely than [a] control group to participate in professional and trade associations, college-related functions such as fund-raising and student recruitment, cultural and arts activities, and environmental and conservation programs."[70] A second major conclusion was that black men, in particular, were more likely to participate in civic activities than were their white male classmates, and that they were even more likely to hold leadership positions: "In every type of civic activity [included in this analysis], the ratio of black male leaders to white male leaders is even higher than the ratio of black male participants to white male participants."[71] This truly striking finding reflects, we believe, both a strong desire on the part of these minority graduates to "give something back" and what can be termed a "supply-demand" relationship: the relatively small numbers of well-educated, well-qualified blacks in the pool of candidates for leadership positions, combined with the interest of many organizations in having a diverse leadership, must surely have contributed to the disproportionately high level of participation and leadership that was found.

The situation is clearly different for former students from low socioeconomic backgrounds (most of whom are white), and it is not surprising that we cannot replicate the findings for minority students for this group. In fact, when we control for associated differences (in race, income, and so on), we find no statistical differences in civic engagement seen in relation to socioeconomic status at the time of college enrollment. In one respect, this lack of association can be seen as a positive outcome. We might expect students who enter some of the nation's most highly rated institutions after having grown up in disadvantaged settings to be so focused on "getting ahead" financially that they would be less inclined than classmates to contribute time, effort, and money to volunteer causes. But there is no evidence that this has in fact been the case.

Later-Life Outcomes: Summing Up

It seems, then, that the general tendency for socioeconomically disadvantaged students to have the same outcomes in college as more privileged, but otherwise similar, students continues when we examine later-life outcomes. There are some important differences: former students from low-SES backgrounds earn somewhat less money and are less likely to pursue professional degrees than otherwise similar classmates from top-quartile families (though they are not less likely to do so than classmates from the middle two income quartiles). These differences bring into focus the limitations of higher education—even top-quality higher education—as a social equalizer. But the (adjusted) gaps are not particularly large, and the major take-away is that graduates from disadvantaged backgrounds are doing just as well as most of their classmates. These findings, however, do raise further doubts about the "striver" hypothesis. Just as the students from low-SES backgrounds—who, against the odds, were able to enroll in these selective institutions—achieve academically just as we predict that they should based on their other observable characteristics (no better and no worse), so, too, do they achieve in later life in much the same way as classmates with comparable characteristics.

The later-life outcomes of minority students serve as a useful counterpoint. In the raw data, minority alumni/ae from the '76 entering cohort at our 11 institutions earned slightly less than their non-minority classmates (about $5,000). However, when we add our standard controls (including parental income), minority alumni/ae earned more than their non-minority classmates, though the difference is not statistically significant. Minority graduates, like those from low-SES backgrounds, are relatively less satisfied with their lives generally and with their undergraduate experience than other classmates. However, minority graduates are more likely to say that they are satisfied or very satisfied with their jobs. These differences in satisfaction are all statistically significant, even after adding our controls. Minority alumni/ae are less likely to vote than their non-minority classmates, mirroring the deficit found for alumni/ae from low-SES backgrounds. But, as we have said, minority graduates are substantially more likely to participate in and lead organizations such as neighborhood associations. If there is a group that fits the "striver" definition in later-life outcomes—rising above one's disadvantaged background and succeeding beyond what one's formal credentials would suggest is likely—it seems that it is the minority graduates rather than those from low-SES backgrounds who best meet the criteria.

TRENDS

Having gone back in time to find students from disadvantaged backgrounds for whom we can measure later-life outcomes, the natural next step is to examine trends over the past 20 years. We begin by looking at changes in the numbers of students from low-SES backgrounds who enrolled and then compare academic performance in earlier cohorts with the academic performance of disadvantaged students in more recent years.

Enrollment

In studying trends in enrollment, we can take advantage of data for the '89 entering cohort in addition to the data for the '76 and '95 entering cohorts at the 11 institutions mentioned earlier. When we compare the presence of students from families in the lower income quartiles in these three cohorts, we find that there was a slight (but noticeable) increase: the number of students from the bottom income quartile (or, more accurately, the real income equivalent of the bottom quartile) increased from 10.0 percent to 10.8 percent of the class between 1976 and 1995. At the same time, students from the top income quartile increased their share of places tremendously, from 38.9 percent to 50 percent. These increases in the share of places occupied by students from low-income and high-income families were "paid for" by a decrease in the share of students from the middle income categories.[72] However, the change over this period was not continuous. There was a substantial erosion in the number of students from low-income families between 1976 and 1989; this fall-off was then more than compensated for by a sharp up-tick in the share of these students between 1989 and 1995 (from 8.7 percent to 10.8 percent).

We were originally somewhat unsure what to make of this finding, but our examination of other data sources, including the American Freshman Survey (AFS) and the roster of Pell Grant recipients, bolsters our confidence that this recent shift is real. AFS data on income distribution at highly selective institutions in 1981, 1989, 1995, and 2002 indicate that the students from families with the real incomes equivalent to our 1989 bottom quartile decreased in the 1980s and then increased markedly in the 1990s. The AFS also shows that the percentage of students receiving Pell Grants at the survey's highly selective institutions increased substantially from 1989 to 1995.[73] The same trend is apparent in the Pell Grant data for our 19 institutions and for the 145 most selective institutions according to *Barron's* guide.[74] Between 1989 and 1995, Pell Grant recipients at our 19 institutions increased from 13.9 percent of all undergraduates to 16.7 percent. At Barron's most selective 145 institutions, Pell Grant recipients increased from 14.3 percent in 1989 to 16.9 percent in 1995.[75]

On the other hand, there was a *drop* in the share of first-generation college students, from 6.4 percent in the '89 entering cohort to 5.7 percent in the '95 cohort (comparable data for the '76 cohort are not available). But this could be due simply to a decrease in the number of parents in the relevant age range who never attended college. Holding real income constant when looking at income quartiles avoids this problem of a changing base. When we attempt an analogous "correction" by looking at the change in parental education between the 1990 Census and that for 2000, we find that the percentage of all 16-year-olds who were potential first-generation college students fell from 45.3 percent to 38.1 percent, a 16 percent drop. The fall in first-generation college students at our institutions was, relatively, somewhat smaller (an 11 percent decline).[76]

Academic Performance and Graduation Rates

In addition to tracking shares of the student population by socioeconomic status, our data allow us to examine trends in college outcomes, such as academic performance and graduation rates. One major finding deserves to be highlighted. The basic similarity between students from low-SES backgrounds and other students in college grades (once SAT scores are accounted for) is a relatively new phenomenon. For the 11 schools for which we have comparable data, there were gaps between the average rank-in-class of the socioeconomically disadvantaged students and their more privileged peers in the raw numbers for all three cohorts. The gap in rank between students from the top and the bottom quartiles ranged from 10 points in the '95 cohort to 14 points in the '89 cohort. Similarly, there were gaps between the rank-in-class of the first-generation college students and other students of between 12 and 15 points in the two cohorts ('89 and '95) for which we have data. When we add controls for SAT scores, race, gender, athletic recruit status, and institutional fixed effects, we find that students from the bottom income quartile showed slight but statistically significant academic underperformance in both the '76 and the '89 cohorts, whereas, in sharp contrast, *the students from low-income families in the 1995 cohort did not underperform at all.* Also, there was no statistically significant underperformance among first-generation college students in either 1989 or 1995.

The basic equality of graduation rates for students from low- and high-SES backgrounds also seems to have been true only in recent years. About 77 percent of students from low-income families who entered these schools in 1976 eventually graduated, compared to 86 percent of those in the top income quartile; for the '89 entering cohort, the comparable statistics were 78 percent and 89 percent.[77] But the gaps disappeared by the graduation of the '95 cohort; in this cohort, students from the bottom income quartile graduated at an 87 percent rate, compared to an 88 percent rate for students from the top quartile. A similar pattern can be found when comparing students by parental education. In the '89 cohort, 81 percent of first-generation college students graduated compared to 88 percent of other students. By the graduation of the '95 cohort, the graduation rates of these groups were virtually even at 88 and 90 percent, respectively. It appears that, in addition to increasing (somewhat) the share of their students who come from low-SES backgrounds, these highly selective colleges and universities have in recent years been more successful in helping these students perform academically up to their potential (or have become better at choosing students from low-SES backgrounds who are likely to do so).

Sources of These Trends

The Spies studies show that income has played less of a role over time in the decision to apply to highly selective and expensive institutions. Similarly, research by Caroline Hoxby demonstrates that, in an increasingly national and integrated market, the best colleges and universities compete vigorously for the best students, regardless of these students' family circumstances.[78] Recall also Dean Fitzsimmons's description of the intense recruitment of all students and the focus on identifying and encouraging high-achieving students from modest backgrounds. We suspect that these efforts have had a strong cumulative effect, as high schools that enroll students from poor families have heard the same story over and over—and as they have been visited by earlier graduates of their secondary schools who have gone on to graduate from selective colleges and universities. It seems clear that these institutions are becoming better at finding talented students from every background, persuading them to apply and enroll, and then encouraging them to do well academically in college.

Another shift in institutional circumstances, and in institutional policies, may help explain these trends. The improved financial condition of at least the private institutions in the 1990s (when endowments increased dramatically), with attendant increases in financial aid, presumably mattered. In contrast, severe financial constraints in the late 1980s may have had a great deal to do with the decreases in socioeconomic diversity that we observe between the '76 and '89 cohorts.

CONCLUSION

Cutting through all of this analysis, there is one major take-away: *for those applicants who took the SAT, did well on it, and applied to one of these selective institutions, family income and parental education, in and of themselves, had surprisingly little effect on admissions probabilities, on matriculation decisions, on choices of majors, on subsequent academic performance and graduation rates, and even on later-life outcomes such as earnings and civic participation.* This is certainly not to suggest that socioeconomic status has little or no effect on college enrollment and degree attainment at these academically selective schools, or on lifetime earnings and other outcomes. It has had (and still has) a huge effect. But "the effect" occurs early on, in the years before college application, when "preparedness" is shaped through the persistent, cumulative development of cognitive skills; motivation, expectations, and other non-cognitive qualities; and practical knowledge about the college admissions process. When well-prepared applicants from poor families, or from families without prior college experience, appear in applicant pools (often as a result of the efforts of dedicated parents and teachers, as well as aggressive recruiting by the colleges and universities), these candidates are treated in admissions in very much the same way as everyone else. And, once enrolled, they then perform as they would be expected to perform. *But the odds of getting into this highly competitive pool in the first place depend enormously on who you are and how you grew up.*

The question is whether the glass is "half full" or "half empty." By providing an increasingly straight path to entry and graduation for academically talented students from all socioeconomic strata, these prestigious institutions are fulfilling their historical promise to serve as "engines of opportunity." On the other hand, the disproportionately large number of graduates of these schools who come from the top rungs of American society indicate that they also remain "bastions of privilege."[79] Vigorous recruiting notwithstanding, the applicant pools of these schools contain only a small number of well-prepared students from families of modest circumstances. This is the "controlling reality." Given this reality, the key question is this: can reliance on the traditional need-blind admissions approach enroll enough of these students to satisfy the commitment of these schools to be true engines of opportunity? Are the claims of "equity" really being met through a need-blind approach in a society in which students are so stratified by socioeconomic status in their pre-college years? These are the large questions to which we will return in part II of this study. We believe that American higher education can do still better than it has done to date.

PART II

Where We Want to Go: Policy Issues

CHAPTER 6

Race in American Higher Education
The Future of Affirmative Action

It is significant—and not surprising—that discussions about race in America are excruciatingly difficult for many people. This has certainly proved to be the case in higher education, where policies governing admissions and the propriety of taking race explicitly into account in selecting a class have been contentious, not always well understood, and often pursued without clear explications of the policies themselves or their consequences. Our goal in this chapter is to clarify as best we can the issues associated with affirmative action in admissions, with an emphasis on understanding their consequences for the pursuit of equity and excellence in higher education.

THE LONG SHADOW OF AN "UNLOVELY HISTORY"

The historical record of the role played by race in American life is far more than just a "backdrop" to consideration of policy issues in the present day. In chapter 2 we saw how painstakingly slow was the process whereby black Americans obtained access to even the most basic forms of educational opportunity. The heroic efforts of many courageous pioneers notwithstanding, by the end of the Civil War, as we noted earlier, only 28 African Americans had received baccalaureate degrees.[1] The stories recounted by Drewry, Doermann, and others of the struggles of determined individuals to achieve an education, against what must have seemed overwhelming odds, are a vivid reminder of the long shadow cast by slavery, "Jim Crow" laws, and the stereotypes of African Americans that have been so deeply ingrained in the thinking of otherwise far-sighted people, such as Thomas Jefferson.[2]

From World War II to Brown v. Board of Education *and Its Aftermath*

In 1940, at the outset of World War II, less than 2 percent of blacks aged 25 to 29 held a college degree, a statistic that sums up how little progress was made over the decades that followed the Civil War. World War II is widely seen as having accelerated the pace of change in race relations and, as we noted in chapter 2, the members of the Truman Commission (appointed in July 1946) were articulate—and far ahead of their time— in acknowledging that the "spiritual damage" done by discriminatory social attitudes and behaviors was not measurable and "indeed . . . has never been recognized with complete honesty."[3] Yet educational opportunities for black Americans did not change immediately or markedly after the war. Even in the case of the G.I. Bill, beneficial effects for blacks were dampened by generations of segregationist policies in the South, which had severely limited the funding available to blacks at all levels of education.[4] Outright segregation persisted in much of the South, and in other parts of the country economic and social disadvantages continued to impede educational opportunities for black students.

In the fall of 1951, black students averaged less than 1 percent (0.8 percent) of the entering class at the 19 College and Beyond (C&B) institutions for which we have data.[5] The Supreme Court's *Brown v. Board of Education* decision in 1954 was, of course, a watershed event. But it was far more important for what it promised than for what it delivered in the near term. John Payton, a lead attorney in the recent University of Michigan affirmative action cases (which we will discuss in detail later in this chapter), participated as a speaker at several celebratory events held in conjunction with the 50th anniversary of *Brown,* and he was eloquent in emphasizing that *Brown* was an absolutely monumental turning point in the struggle for racial justice. As Payton explains:

> *Brown* heralded a fundamental change in the country. Not immediately, to be sure, but the trend was unmistakable. Overt oppression would come to an end. Overt segregation would come to an end. . . . Equally important, the rationale that justified racial segregation and oppression began its slide into obscurity. Today the once respectable arguments in favor of white privilege have virtually disappeared from public discourse. . . .
> *Brown* resulted in the transformation of the assumptions of our society. It ended the accommodation that the Progressives had made with racial oppression.[6]

In preparing for one of his talks, Payton examined how law reviews treated the *Brown* decision 50 years ago. He found that there was *no* analysis of *Brown,* either immediately or for several years, in the law reviews of the University of Chicago, Columbia, Stanford, or Yale (though there was commentary in the law reviews of New York University and the University of Pittsburgh). Harvard did include *Brown* in its "Supreme Court Term" for 1954, but published no separate article or comment. Later, Payton tells us, there was an article in the *Harvard Law Review* by Alexander Bickel that focused on the intent of the framers of the 14th Amendment and was critical of *Brown.*

Later still, in 1959, Herbert Wechsler published "Toward Neutral Principles of Constitutional Law," an influential article "arguing that *Brown* could not be squared with any set of acceptable neutral principles." In the article Wechsler referred to an incident of segregation that had occurred over two decades earlier when he and the late Charles H. Houston —former dean of Howard Law School, first special counsel to the National Association for the Advancement of Colored People, mentor to *Brown* lawyer Thurgood Marshall, and the architect of the legal strategy that culminated in *Brown*—could not eat in the white-only cafeteria that served the U.S. Supreme Court. Wechsler asserted that Houston "did not suffer more than I in knowing that we had to go to Union Station to lunch together during recess." Payton's response: "Are you kidding me?" Then he continues: "Amazingly, Wechsler sought to deny this truth right in front of him. Instead of [focusing on] white supremacy and its attendant oppression and degradation, he trivialized his own experience of white supremacy into a nuisance that he imagined affecting him as much as Charles Houston or any Black person."[7]

As Payton then reminds us, the aftermath of *Brown* should have been sobering for Wechsler or anyone else: "Massive resistance, open defiance, public displays by the Ku Klux Klan. And in 1955, the entire country was riveted by the hideous spectacle of the murder of Emit Till, the refusal of an all-white Mississippi jury to convict the white men accused of the murder, and the 1956 publication in *Look* magazine of the murderers' lurid story of the murder that they could then, freely and with impunity, proudly admit to."[8] Just eight years later, in 1962, the enrollment of James Meredith at the University of Mississippi led to violence and bloodshed.[9] These realities of the "not that long ago" should help us understand the depth of feeling associated with race in America, the extent to which many white people who certainly did not think of themselves as racists lived "in denial," and the slow pace of change.[10]

This country's long history of exclusion and then of indifference, if not hostility, to the aspirations of black students has left a lasting imprint not just on the individuals caught up in this often tragic drama but on the educational system itself—with implications for Justice Sandra Day O'Connor's 25-year pronouncement in the majority opinion of the *Grutter* case, to which we will return. "Separate" and "[un]equal" have taken a tremendous toll, and, as our choice of tense connotes, they still do.[11] It is historically indefensible and morally wrong to think of race as "just another" dimension of disadvantage—or, in the language of much of the debate over affirmative action, as "just another" dimension of diversity. As Ronald Dworkin has put it, "The worst of the stereotypes, suspicions, fears, and hatreds that still poison America are color-coded."[12]

The after-effects of this long history, and their deep-seated stereotypes, limit opportunities and create divides that demean us all. This social reality, described with searing precision by Glenn Loury in *The Anatomy of*

Racial Inequality, explains why persistence is required to overcome, day by day, the vestiges of our country's "unlovely racial history."[13] Racial disparities—what W. E. B. Du Bois once trenchantly identified as "the problem of the color-line"—remain, in our view, by far the most daunting of the challenges to achieving equity in American higher education—and real opportunity in American society.

Active Recruitment of Minority Students

It was in 1961 that President John F. Kennedy first introduced the term "affirmative action" in the employment context, and the idea then spread to other arenas, including higher education.[14] By the mid-1960s, stimulated by the Civil Rights Movement, many colleges and universities began to recruit minority students, first haltingly, not knowing quite how to go about it, and then much more aggressively. It is easy, in retrospect, to assume that changes in admissions policies were easy to accomplish. But that was certainly not the case at Yale, where President Kingman Brewster's appointment of R. Inslee Clark as director of admissions in 1965 provoked a debate within the Yale Corporation that is almost unimaginable today. It is worth quoting Geoffrey Kabaservice's account at some length:

> In the spring of 1966, admissions director R. Inslee ("Inky") Clark was summoned before the Yale Corporation to report directly on the changes in policy he had implemented since his appointment by Brewster in the year before. . . . Clark briefly described the process leading up to the admission of his first class, the Class of 1970, and the new emphasis he had placed on talent spotting, merit, and diversity. One of the Corporation members who had "hemmed and hawed" through Clark's presentation finally said, "Let me get down to basics. You're admitting an entirely different class than we're used to. You're admitting them for a different purpose than training leaders." Unspoken but understood by all was that the dean of admissions' new emphasis had rejected unprecedented numbers of wealthy, WASP applicants from preparatory schools, many of them alumni sons, who had been Yale's longtime constituency. Clark responded that in a changing America, leaders might come from nontraditional sources, including public high school graduates, Jews, minorities, even women. His interlocutor shot back, "You're talking about Jews and public school graduates as leaders. Look around you at this table"— he waved a hand at Brewster, Lindsay, Moore, Bill Bundy, and other distinguished men assembled there. "These are America's leaders. There are no Jews here. There are no public school graduates here."[15]

There were, needless to say, no African American members of the Corporation either. Nonetheless, Brewster, Clark, and Yale persevered and provided visible leadership in overturning long-held presumptions about who did and did not "belong" at selective colleges and universities. By the time of the '76 entering cohort, the percentage of black students at the selective schools in our database had increased from less than 1 percent (in the '51 entering cohort) to about 5 percent.[16] But true *inclusion* of minority students turned out to be anything but simple.

One serious mistake made by many colleges and universities was to fail to appreciate that it was not good enough simply to enroll more minority students. Offers of admission and the provision of scholarship dollars were necessary, but they were not all that was needed. The much earlier success of many schools in enrolling "poor but pious youth" was misleading in this context. It was one thing to enroll the son of an impecunious minister who may have had an excellent pre-collegiate preparation, perhaps even at a private school, and who "fit right in"—and it was quite another to enroll a minority student who might well have attended an inner-city high school and was quite likely to feel isolated and uncomfortable at a predominantly white college or university. Often black students from more privileged backgrounds also felt ill at ease.[17]

Not surprisingly, colleges and universities struggled mightily with issues of all kinds—with admissions criteria (were blacks from ghetto areas to be favored over other black applicants?); with support programs (especially programs that were designated "remedial" and hence sparked a whole set of unanticipated consequences); with residential patterns (the issue of "self-segregation"); with curricular offerings (the desirability of having black studies programs); and with the implications of having very small numbers of black faculty members. Student protests in the mid- to late 1960s and early 1970s—often tied to the Vietnam War and other issues, such as investments in companies doing business in South Africa —were a visible manifestation of the recurring tensions that accompanied efforts to reconcile differences in perspectives and priorities. At bottom, the challenge was to find the most effective ways of not just enrolling, but *educating*, a diverse population of students.[18]

Over this period, there was, as one would expect, criticism of affirmative action as well as support for it. In 1978, the *Bakke* case—a formal challenge to racial preferences citing the Civil Rights Act of 1964— reached the Supreme Court. The Court was sharply divided, with four justices finding the two-track admissions policy of the medical school at the University of California–Davis to be discriminatory and four others concluding that it was necessary to overcome the effects of past discrimination. Justice Lewis Powell's deciding opinion condemned the use of quotas but concluded that it was permissible to take race into account, as one among several factors, in seeking to secure the educational benefits of diversity.[19] On the authority of Justice Powell's opinion, virtually all selective colleges and professional schools have continued to consider race in admitting students—albeit not without recurring challenges, which culminated in the University of Michigan cases heard by the Court in 2003.[20]

Controversies notwithstanding, black and Hispanic educational attainment have risen sharply over recent decades at both the undergraduate and the graduate/professional levels. Between 1959 and 2003, the percentage of blacks aged 25 to 29 who had graduated from college increased from 4.6 percent to 17.2 percent; the percentage of Hispanic college graduates increased from 5.7 percent in 1974 to 10 percent in 2003.[21] Eleven years after *Brown,* in 1965, barely 1 percent of all law students nationwide were black, and over one-third of them were enrolled in all-black schools; barely 2 percent of all medical students were black, and more than three-fourths of them attended two all-black schools.[22] The number of black students attending law school has more than doubled, and the number of Hispanic law students has increased more than sixfold, since 1971. Between 1978 and 2002, the number of black students attending medical schools increased by about a third, while the number of Hispanic students more than doubled.[23] Blacks and Hispanics have also made progress in earning PhDs, even though the absolute numbers of doctorates earned outside the field of education remain low.[24]

ASSESSING RACE-SENSITIVE ADMISSIONS

In the late 1990s, Derek Bok and one of the authors of this book (Bowen) embarked on a major empirical study of the actual effects of race-sensitive admissions policies, as they could be discerned through a detailed analysis of a database built at the Mellon Foundation between 1995 and 1997—the original College and Beyond (C&B) database—that contained the in-college records of basically all matriculants in the student cohorts that entered 28 academically selective colleges and universities in 1951, 1976, and 1989. We were also able to link these records to detailed College Board data describing pre-college family characteristics and to the results of a large-scale survey of post-college experiences.[25] In light of the increasingly contentious public debate over the role played by race in admissions, legislative actions in California and the state of Washington prohibiting any consideration of race, the sweeping *Hopwood* decision in Texas that threatened to overturn *Bakke,* and the strong likelihood that there would be a further Supreme Court review of affirmative action, the time seemed right for a comprehensive empirical review of how these policies had actually worked. We sought to "find the facts," as best we could.

The findings of this research were reported in *The Shape of the River: Long-Term Consequences of Considering Race in College and University Admissions,* and here we will summarize as succinctly as we can the principal lessons learned through this research, the debate engendered by it, and follow-on and companion studies. Five propositions stand out:[26]

1. *The presumed educational benefits of diversity have been strongly affirmed.*
    Patricia Gurin and her colleagues at the University of Michigan
    have made by far the most comprehensive effort to assemble and
    assess masses of evidence (including the findings in *Shape of the
    River*) of the effects of diversity on both "learning outcomes" and
    "democracy outcomes." Gurin concludes: "We have documented a
    consistent picture from both our research and the research of
    other scholars that shows a wide range of educational benefits
    when students interact and learn from each other across race and
    ethnicity."[27]

2. *Race-sensitive admissions policies have increased substantially the number
    of well-prepared minority students who have gone on to assume positions of
    leadership in the professions, business, academia, the military, government,
    and every other sector of American life—thereby reducing somewhat the con-
    tinuing disparity in access to power and opportunity that is related to race
    in America.* The evidence presented in *Shape of the River* shows that
    minority students admitted to academically selective colleges and
    universities as long ago as the mid-1970s not only have graduated
    at very high rates but have completed rigorous graduate programs,
    done well in the marketplace, and, most notably, contributed in the
    civic arena out of all proportion to their numbers.[28] Although Jef-
    ferson might not have seen it as such, this has been a near-perfect
    demonstration of his propositions concerning the importance of
    education for the responsible exercise of citizenship.[29]

3. *The costs of race-sensitive admission policies have been modest and are well
    justified by the benefits; most of the alleged negative effects of race-sensitive
    admissions are, on examination, seen to be minor or non-existent.*
    Specifically:

    a. *There is no evidence that, overall, race-sensitive admissions policies
        "harm the beneficiaries" by putting them in settings in which they are
        overmatched intellectually or "stigmatized" to the point that they
        would have been better off attending a less selective institution.* That
        assertion withers in light of the evidence. The most com-
        pelling and relentlessly consistent data in *Shape of the River*
        show that, far from being stigmatized and harmed, minority
        students admitted to selective colleges under race-sensitive
        admissions policies performed very well. Indeed, the more
        selective the college they entered (holding their own SAT
        scores constant), the more likely they were to graduate and
        earn advanced degrees, the happier they said they were with
        their college experience, and the more successful they have
        been in their careers.[30] This result is precisely the opposite of
        that which proponents of the "harm-the-beneficiary" line of
        thinking would have predicted.[31]

b. *Evidence also disposes of the argument that substituting race-neutral admissions policies for race-sensitive policies would have removed from campus a marginal group of mediocre students, leaving only a distinctly superior "top tier" of well-qualified minority students.* Examination of the later accomplishments of those students who would have been "retrospectively rejected" under race-neutral policies shows that they did just as well as a hypothetical reference group that might have been accepted if admissions officers had given black students and white students with the same grade point averages and test scores exactly the same consideration. There are *no* significant differences in graduation rates, advanced degree attainment, earnings, civic contributions, or satisfaction with college.[32] These striking results testify, we believe, to the excellent job done by admissions officers in "picking and choosing" among the large number of applicants from minority groups as well as other candidates who are well over the admissions threshold—many of whom are rejected.[33]

c. *Contrary to what is often supposed, eliminating race-sensitive admissions policies entirely would have increased the admission rate for white applicants at these academically selective institutions by less than two percentage points, from roughly 25 percent to 26.5 percent.* At all selective colleges and universities with a plethora of well-qualified candidates, the "opportunity cost" of admitting any particular student is that another strong applicant is not chosen. A rejected applicant—and the applicant's parents—sometimes assume that he or she would surely have gotten in had it not been for "reverse discrimination." In fact, race-sensitive admissions policies have not reduced appreciably the chances of well-qualified white applicants to gain admission to the most selective colleges and universities. In fact, in many situations, recruited athletes receive larger admissions "breaks" and displace more other applicants than do minority students.[34]

4. *Progress has been made in narrowing test score gaps between minority students and other students, but gaps remain—and so does the need for race-sensitive admissions policies.* At a group of liberal arts colleges and universities examined in 1976 and 1995, average combined SAT scores for minority students rose roughly 130 points at the liberal arts colleges and roughly 150 points at the research universities. The test scores of other students rose too, but by much smaller amounts. In short, test score gaps narrowed over this period, and the average rank-in-class of minority students on graduation improved even more than one would have predicted on the basis of test scores alone.[35] Still, test score gaps remain, and more

progress needs to be made. At the 10 C&B institutions for which we have limited data on the '99 entering class, there was a 137-point gap between the SAT scores of minority students and those of non-minority students.[36]

5. *One unanticipated consequence of the publication of "The Shape of the River" is that a number of African American students who attended the selective schools included in the study found the highly positive findings very reassuring; the findings served to counter hurtful "suggestions" that they did not really deserve to be there.* After we made a presentation to the American Council on Education, a young black woman came up and introduced herself as a Harvard graduate. She said that she had found *Shape of the River* "liberating" and added: "I guess I have been walking around with a kind of cloud over my head, which I didn't really understand was there, and it's gone now. . . . We did pretty well, didn't we?" We responded, "Yes, you did very well indeed." She nodded and said, with emphasis, "Thank you. I'm ready now to stand up and fight!"[37]

THE SUPREME COURT DECISIONS
IN THE MICHIGAN CASES

The legislative challenges to race-sensitive admissions policies in California and Washington, and the issues posed by the *Hopwood* case in Texas, all pale in comparison to the importance of the two University of Michigan cases heard by the U.S. Supreme Court in 2003.[38] One does not have to quarrel with Payton's assertion that the two Michigan cases were less important than *Brown*—as essentially all race-related cases have been—to underscore their significance. Before the decision, Charles Vest, president of the Massachusetts Institute of Technology (MIT), saw all that has been accomplished, and all that can be accomplished in the future, as "hanging by a thread." Vest's concern, shared by many others, was that the "thread" represented by Justice Powell's seemingly innocuous phrase in *Bakke* justifying the use of race "as one of many factors" in admissions decisions, could be severed by "one snip of the judicial scissors."[39] The clear goal of the plaintiffs and their backers in the Michigan cases was to eliminate altogether the freedom of colleges and universities to consider race in deciding whom to admit.

Avoiding a flat prohibition on consideration of race was, then, the bullet to be dodged—and it was dodged, to the immense relief of the leaders of the higher education community and legions of others who believe strongly in the importance of continuing to take race into account. The central message of the majority opinion in *Grutter v. Bollinger et al.* (the law school case) was summarized well by Linda Greenhouse: "The result of today's rulings was that Justice Powell's solitary view that there was a 'compelling state interest' in racial diversity, a position that had appeared undermined by the court's subsequent equal protection rulings in other contexts and that some lower federal courts had boldly repudiated, has now been endorsed by five justices and placed on a stronger footing than ever before."[40] The Court's opinion, as Justice O'Connor delivered it, is unequivocal:

> Today, we hold that the Law School has a compelling interest in attaining a diverse student body.[41]
> ... The Equal Protection Clause does not prohibit the Law School's narrowly tailored use of race in admissions decisions to further a compelling interest in obtaining the educational benefits that flow from a diverse student body.[42]

At the same time, in its decision in *Gratz v. Bollinger et al.*, the Court invalidated the admissions policy used by Michigan to admit students to its undergraduate College of Literature, Science, and the Arts.[43] The difference was in the approach taken to admissions: whereas the law school considered all candidates in an "individualized" manner, the undergraduate college used a point system based in part on race that was deemed to violate the Equal Protection Clause because it was too mechanical and not narrowly tailored (every underrepresented minority applicant was automatically awarded 20 points toward the 100 points needed to guarantee admission).[44] Moreover, while making it clear that quotas and mechanical systems were not permissible, the *Grutter* decision recognized the desirability of achieving a "critical mass" of minority students through other means. This is an important outcome, because having a critical mass encourages the presence of a range of viewpoints, which in turn counteracts tendencies to view minority students as "all alike."

There is every reason to believe that higher education not only can "live with" this decision (the University of Michigan moved immediately to change its undergraduate admissions policies to conform to the requirements of the Court[45]), but may be better off because of it. We find individualized, non-mechanical methods of evaluating applicants to be more desirable. The judgment of seasoned admissions staff is invaluable in choosing among candidates who have comparable formal qualifications—and an individualized approach also makes it harder for applicants and parents to "game" the system.

At the same time, it should be recognized that depriving a school of the option of simply assigning bonus points based on race can make it more difficult to recruit and enroll minority students. After the Court rendered its decision, the University of Michigan added new essay requirements to its application, in part to help its admissions staff take account of barriers overcome by applicants of all races, and it also spent an additional $1.8 million on admissions and recruiting. The more complex application and admissions procedure at Michigan appears, in its first year, to have been associated with a drop of about 25 percent in the number of black applications.[46] No one knows if this was a one-time blip or if this year's experience heralds a basic shift in the university's ability to attract black applicants. In any case, we continue to believe that a move away from the more mechanistic approach of previous years was not only needed to comply with the Court's ruling but was right on its own terms. If there is a "cost" (especially a near-term cost) in terms of the number of minority applicants, and even matriculants, that is, in our view, a price worth paying.

The *Grutter* case without question strengthened President Vest's "thread" (turning it into a "rope," as it were). It did this, first, by replacing a "fractured," "splintered" decision in *Bakke* with a solid five-justice opinion supporting diversity as a compelling state interest. In addition, the Court expanded dramatically the rationale for enrolling a diverse class to include not only the on-campus educational benefits of diversity but also the preparation of larger numbers of well-educated minority candidates for leadership positions in the professions, business, academia, the military, and government—a second principal objective of race-sensitive admissions that the evidence in *Shape of the River* demonstrates has been achieved. Many of us have long regarded Justice Powell's sole focus on what Patricia Gurin calls "learning outcomes"[47] as an unnecessarily narrow and limited justification for race-sensitive admissions policies. By now embracing *both* the improvement of learning outcomes and the preparation of more minority students for important roles in national life (what Joel Goldstein calls the "instrumental rationale") as components of a "compelling state interest" in racial diversity, the Court has aligned its reasoning with the thinking and stated missions of almost all of American higher education.[48]

This is why *Grutter* is much more than "bullet-dodging"; it is a strong, positive step forward—a real cause for celebration. This decision is also of fundamental importance for a broader reason: it rebuts the idea that the Court understands the 14th Amendment as endorsing only the "anti-classification" principle (that "government may not classify on the basis of race"). Fortunately, the "antisubordination" principle ("the conviction that it is wrong for the state to engage in practices that enforce the inferior social status of historically oppressed peoples") is alive and well, much as the Court may have disguised its endorsement of it.[49]

The Court's decision is gratifying in and of itself, and it is also encouraging to see the numerous references in the Court's opinion to the role played by social science research in bolstering the arguments for this conclusion.[50] Also, there is a sea change to be noted between 1954 and 2003 in the positions taken by the American establishment.[51] In *Grutter* the Court refers to briefs submitted on behalf of American businesses "making clear that the skills needed in today's increasingly global market-place can only be developed through exposure to widely diverse people, cultures, ideas, and viewpoints." The contrast with "business opinion" at the time of *Brown* is striking. As John Payton has reminded us: "No corporations supported the plaintiffs in *Brown*, [whereas] an array of corporations supported the University of Michigan. In fact, no corporations supported the other side." He adds: "[Similarly,] while the military had fiercely opposed integration during World War II, in the Michigan cases we were supported by a spectacular amicus brief by a Who's Who of retired Generals, Admirals, and other officials."[52] In the words of the Court's opinion: "High-ranking retired officers and civilian leaders of the United States military assert that, 'based on [their] decades of experience,' a 'highly qualified, racially diverse officer corps . . . is essential to the military's ability to fulfill its principal mission to provide national security.'"[53]

The Court then takes a still broader tack, which hearkens back to sentiments expressed by Jefferson: "This Court has long recognized that 'education . . . is the very foundation of good citizenship.' . . . For this reason, the diffusion of knowledge and opportunity through public institutions of higher education must be accessible to all individuals regardless of race or ethnicity. . . . Effective participation by members of all racial and ethnic groups in the civic life of our Nation is essential if the dream of one Nation, indivisible, is to be realized."[54] After next emphasizing the particular importance of law schools as training grounds for a large number of our nation's leaders, the Court observes: "In order to cultivate a set of leaders with legitimacy in the eyes of the citizenry, *it is necessary that the path to leadership be visibly open to talented and qualified individuals of every race and ethnicity*" (our emphasis).[55] These stirring words introduce the concept of "democratic legitimacy" as one of the principal societal needs that race-sensitive admissions addresses. The eloquence with which the majority states its conclusions—indeed, its *convictions*—is striking.

Another important part of the O'Connor opinion is its skepticism about the claim that "race-neutral means exist to obtain the educational benefits of student body diversity that the Law School seeks."[56] In response to the hypothetical question of whether an institution must attempt every conceivable race-blind approach to admissions before settling on affirmative action, the Court says flatly: "We disagree. Narrow tailoring does not require exhaustion of every conceivable race-neutral alternative." What it does require is "serious, good faith *consideration* of workable race-neutral alternatives that will achieve the diversity the university seeks" (our emphasis).[57] The Court is dismissive of ideas such as using a lottery system, lowering admissions standards for all students, and adopting "percent plans" such as the one in use in Texas, whereby all high school students above a certain class-rank threshold (10 percent in Texas) are automatically guaranteed admission to the University of Texas.[58] The combination of this opinion and the considerable research done by Professors Marta Tienda, John Kain, Glenn Loury, and others leads us to conclude that, for all intents and purposes, the "percent plans" have had their "day in the sun" and will no longer attract the backing that they once did.[59] Further support for this conclusion comes from reports emanating from Texas that describe a variety of objections to the 10 percent rule and "second thoughts" about it. Objections have been raised by parents, the president of the University of Texas at Austin, and Governor Rick Perry.[60] It is not even clear that the percent plans, if challenged in the courts, would stand up to legal scrutiny, given the fact that they are so mechanical and so lacking in individualized consideration of candidates.

Americans have an endless appetite for the "painless alternative," but all of the work that has gone into examining various approaches to achieving diversity persuades us all over again that the most straightforward way of proceeding—by explicitly taking race into account as one factor among others—is the most sensible and efficient.[61] There is much to be said for avoiding charades and for not dissembling.

We are also persuaded that colleges and universities must do a much more careful and systematic job than most have done heretofore in studying the outcomes achieved as a result of the admissions policies that they have adopted. The O'Connor opinion (correctly in our judgment) respects the Court's "tradition of giving a degree of deference to a university's academic decisions, within constitutionally prescribed limits."[62] But it surely follows that academic institutions, in turn, need to be accountable for the uses they make of the discretion they are given. When college and university presidents first dealt with the issues of race and admissions in the 1970s, many (including one of the authors of this study) were reluctant to focus on the measurement of outcomes. At that time, presidents were concerned that they might not like what they found. There was also concern about the possible effects of such studies on the perceptions of minority students (their self-perceptions and others' perceptions of them). It now seems clear that focusing on outcomes is necessary both to understand internally how policies are working and to satisfy the obligation of accountability.

OPEN QUESTIONS AND NEW CHALLENGES

Risks of More Litigation: Evidence of Continuing Opposition to Affirmative Action

One large question is whether the decisions reached in the University of Michigan cases will "stabilize" this area of the law, at least for a time, or whether they will provoke other suits. Justice Antonin Scalia, in his dissenting opinion, seemed almost to invite more challenges:

> [T]oday's *Grutter-Gratz* split double header seems perversely designed to prolong the controversy and the litigation. Some future lawsuits will presumably focus on whether the discriminatory scheme in question contains enough evaluation of the applicant "as an individual." . . . Still other suits may challenge the bona fides of the institution's expressed commitment to the educational benefits of diversity that immunize the discriminatory scheme in *Grutter.* (Tempting targets, one would suppose, will be those universities that talk the talk of multiculturalism and racial diversity in the courts but walk the walk of tribalism and racial segregation on their campuses.) . . . And still other suits may claim that the institution's racial preferences have gone below or above the mystical *Grutter*-approved "critical mass."[63]

In crafting their admissions policies, colleges and universities will need to follow closely the clear guidance provided in *Grutter,* and we presume that the overwhelming majority will do so; in fact, most conform today. Also, we agree with Justice Scalia that those in higher education who have been (properly) extolling the virtues of "cross-racial understanding" and "learning through diversity" should align their practices with their educational philosophies in all facets of college and university life. There is, as Justice Scalia argues, much to be said for "walking the walk" as well as "talking the talk."

Organizations like the Center for Individual Rights and the Center for Equal Opportunity will continue to challenge institutions they believe are close to, if not over, the edge of compliance with applicable law. An "information-gathering campaign" was launched by these organizations in the spring of 2004, when they began to force the disclosure of the details of race-conscious admissions policies by threatening legal action against institutions that refused to do so. Their intent is both to collect ammunition with which to challenge the legality of policies that appear to be outside the Supreme Court's guidelines and "to place colleges under public and political pressure to abandon race-conscious policies even if they are operating within the law."[64]

Strong opposition to affirmative action also continues to be seen at the state level. In California, in the spring of 2004, the then-chairman of the Board of Regents, John J. Moores, argued that the University of California–Berkeley was using race as an "unstated factor" in admissions, in violation of Proposition 209 (the state ban on race-sensitive admissions).[65] There is also a petition drive in the State of Michigan to ban racial preferences that may be on the ballot in 2006. In Colorado, a bill that would have banned affirmative action in the state was defeated by one vote in the state senate.[66]

These continuing assaults are all too real and are not to be taken lightly. But there are also new political (as well as judicial) realities for these oppositionist groups to contemplate. Without question, the extraordinarily strong support for race-sensitive admissions reflected in the outpouring of briefs on Michigan's behalf is a factor to be weighed. It is more than mildly ironic that in instigating and supporting the *Grutter* and *Gratz* challenges, the anti–affirmative action groups provoked the formation of a broad-based alliance of businesses, labor unions, religious groups, professional and scholarly associations, the military, and a wide range of academics that created something approaching a societal consensus (within the "establishment," at least) in favor of taking race into account in admissions decisions. The breadth and depth of support was truly amazing to behold.[67]

Recasting Recruitment and Enrichment Programs: MMUF

Outside the realm of admissions per se, the logic and language of the Michigan decisions reinforced concerns about racially exclusive programs and have already led to some recasting of policies. Race-exclusive "recruitment and enrichment" programs were, of course, under attack prior to the Court's decisions in *Grutter* and *Gratz*. The widely publicized challenge to MIT's summer enrichment/recruitment program for minority students, MITE²S, by the Center for Equal Opportunity and the Department of Education's Office for Civil Rights, made it clear in the winter of 2003 that any race-exclusive program might be shut down by injunction.[68]

In the same time frame, the Mellon Foundation embarked on a major review of its own MMUF program (then called the Mellon Minority Undergraduate Fellowship program), which has been highly successful in encouraging talented minority students to pursue PhD programs and consider academic careers (over 100 MMUF students have already earned PhDs).[69] Some institutions participating in MMUF received letters very similar to the one that precipitated the debate over the MIT program, and they naturally turned to the Foundation for advice. A brief "insider's" account of the Foundation's response to these assaults on enrichment/recruitment programs may be instructive to others facing similar challenges.[70] The Foundation's trustees voted in June 2003, shortly after the Michigan decisions were announced, to reaffirm in the strongest terms their unequivocal commitment to the fundamental goals of MMUF. At the same time, it seemed wise to be *proactive* in making changes that might both reduce the program's legal vulnerability and perhaps strengthen it in significant ways.[71]

The most vulnerable aspect of MMUF was, of course, its race exclusivity, which was reflected in its original mission statement, its selection criteria, and its name. For the program's first 15 years, only members of "underrepresented minority groups" were eligible to apply. In light of the Michigan decisions and the evolving needs of higher education, the MMUF mission statement was broadened: "The fundamental objectives of MMUF are to reduce, over time, the serious underrepresentation on faculties of individuals from certain minority groups, *as well as to address the attendant educational consequences of these disparities*" (our emphasis). Then, to ensure that the Foundation's intentions were understood, the criteria for program eligibility were made more inclusive, so that students of all races and ethnic backgrounds would know that they are eligible to apply for participation in MMUF. The new selection criteria include race as one factor among others (since "preference" related to race is permitted), and they also emphasize the importance of a "demonstrated commitment" to the fundamental purposes of the program. In addition, it was explicitly stated that there was to be no "goal" of enrolling a specific number of minority or non-minority participants; the Foundation's expectation, however, was (and is) that a very large fraction of MMUF participants will continue to be minority students. Finally, there was a change in the name of the program: to celebrate its success and to signal both the restatement of its objectives and its high hopes for future contributions, the Foundation renamed it the Mellon Mays Undergraduate Fellowship program in honor of Dr. Benjamin E. Mays, the noted African American educator and former president of Morehouse College, who exemplifies so many of the goals of the program.[72] Fortunately, the MMUF acronym, which has become so significant in its own right, remains unchanged.

Making these changes was no easy process—in large part because of considerable resentment of the aggressive tactics used by well-financed groups of anti–affirmative action advocates. There was, not surprisingly, an initial tendency to say: "No way; we have a great program, and we are staying right where we are!" Further reflection, and much discussion, led to a more thoughtful, more constructive response. The emphasis of the Supreme Court in the Michigan cases that race can be only one factor among others considered in admitting candidates makes race-exclusive programs of recruitment and enrichment increasingly vulnerable to legal challenge.[73] As this reality became clearer and clearer, the desirability of modifying MMUF *on our own terms,* and in advance of potentially debilitating attacks, became widely accepted by campus coordinators and others whose continued allegiance was essential. There is every reason to be optimistic that the modified program design will work well. Those of us who were involved in making the changes described here are persuaded that it would have been a major mistake just to sit by and defend a race-exclusive formulation that, however sensible it may have seemed 16 years ago, is no longer viable. Just getting mad is not an effective response. Nor is giving up entirely on worthy goals, as some programs have done.[74]

Other Open Questions: Financial Aid and Faculty Recruitment

Debate continues among lawyers and within the higher education community as to whether race-targeted financial aid awards are permissible in the aftermath of *Grutter* and *Gratz*. (One irony is that Pepperdine University, with its strong ties to the conservative movement, is nonetheless battling with anti–affirmative action groups to retain its minority-only scholarship program.)[75] Similarly, there is uncertainty as to what colleges and universities can and cannot do in efforts to recruit and promote a more diverse faculty. These are large questions, different in some important respects from the questions about the legality of race-sensitive admissions and race-exclusive "enrichment" programs; they are not as simple as they may at first seem to be. We can do no more here than single out these issues as deserving further study and reflection. We are skeptical, however, that there will be many, if any, settings in which race exclusivity is going to be permitted.[76]

IN 25 YEARS?

The "open question" that has received the most attention, and is the most challenging, has to do with the permissible duration of race-sensitive admissions policies. Was O'Connor's widely quoted 25-year comment ("We expect that 25 years from now, the use of racial preferences will no longer be necessary to further the interest approved today"[77]) merely a hope, expressed as a prediction (estimate), or did it impose a binding limit? This is an interesting legal question, but until there is further jurisprudence, there is no way of being sure.[78] Both Derek Bok and Glenn Loury have described this part of the Court's decision as, at the minimum, a "wake-up call."[79] Those of us interested in closing racial gaps of all kinds should certainly want to help create conditions in which racial preferences in admissions are unnecessary—as quickly as possible.

Practical Possibilities

However desirable it may be to meet the 25-year goal, is it possible from a practical perspective? The basic reason racial preferences are needed at present is that underrepresented minorities still do significantly less well on traditional measures of college preparation (especially test scores)

than whites and Asians. Can *preparation gaps* be eliminated over the next
25 years? The sizes of the current gaps tell us that this is a daunting task.
For example, as we noted in chapter 4 when we reported the results of
national reading tests, only 16 percent of blacks and 22 percent of Hispanics have reached the "proficient" level or higher, compared to 34 percent of Asian Americans and 42 percent of whites. The race gap is so
large and deeply rooted that any reasonable person has to be skeptical
that there are quick fixes. The extent of the black-white test score gap is
shown in figure 6.1a; figure 6.1b provides a particularly vivid illustration
of the extreme underrepresentation of black test-takers among those
with the highest scores.[80]

At the same time, there is evidence that the black-white gap in test
scores has been closing. But will it close fast enough? Alan Krueger, Jesse
Rothstein, and Sarah Turner have simulated the likely effects of "convergence" trends on black-white gaps in preparedness over the next quarter
century, and their initial results indicate that eliminating the need for
race-sensitive admissions over this period will be a very challenging
assignment. Let us reduce a mass of data and some complicated assumptions and calculations to a few "bottom-line" numbers for the 17 selective
schools for which we have the relevant data.[81]

The single factor most likely to lead to reductions in test score gaps
over the next 25 years is income convergence. There are reasons to
expect that the large gaps in income between black and white families
with children of college age that exist today will diminish over time, and
Krueger, Rothstein, and Turner assume that "half of the black-white
income gap will close in the next generation."[82] Family economic
resources clearly have a large impact on SAT scores, as we noted in chapter 4 and as many others have observed. Based on their analysis of the
relation between family income and SAT scores (which includes the effects
of income on the likelihood both of taking the tests and of doing well on
them), Krueger, Rothstein, and Turner suggest that, in 25 years' time,
income convergence alone might be expected to raise the percentage of
admitted students who are black from 5 percent of all black and white
students (which is what today's percentage would be on a race-neutral
basis, with white admit rates applied to all applicants) to about 7 percent.[83]

This result should be compared with the actual share of black matriculants in the '95 entering cohort at these selective schools, which was
about 11.5 percent (of all black and white matriculants) with race-
sensitive admissions policies in place. It is evident that income convergence cannot be expected to get us back to the current level of black
enrollment (used here as a proxy for enrollment of all underrepresented
minorities)—never mind failing to continue the progress that has been
made in recent years in closing racial gaps.

Krueger, Rothstein, and Turner also examine the possibility that test
scores could converge *within income categories*. Data on trends in student

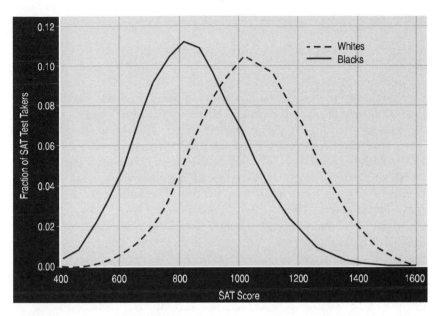

Figure 6.1a. Distribution of SAT Scores, Black and White Test-Takers

Source: Alan B. Krueger, Jesse Rothstein, and Sarah E. Turner, "Race, Income and College in 25 Years: The Legacy of Separate and Unequal Schooling," unpublished draft, October 1, 2004.

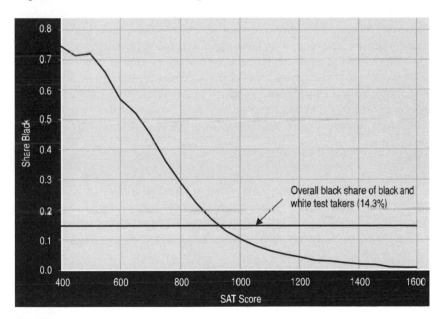

Figure 6.1b. Shares of Black, and Black and White, Test-Takers, 1995 Entering Cohort

Source: Alan B. Krueger, Jesse Rothstein, and Sarah E. Turner, "Race, Income and College in 25 Years: The Legacy of Separate and Unequal Schooling," unpublished draft, October 1, 2004.

achievement tests show that there was some convergence in both math and reading test scores between the early 1970s and 1998. In one set of simulations, the authors assumed that the average rate of convergence over this entire period will continue for the next 25 years. This projected rate of improvement translates into a further projected increase in black enrollment of about 2 to 2.5 points, leading to a black enrollment rate of just under 10 percent.[84] This is a much more encouraging result—though it, too, fails to get us back to the current level of black enrollment.

However, there are two reasons for being highly skeptical about the likelihood of doing this well. First, as Krueger, Rothstein, and Turner point out, some part of this test score convergence may be due to income convergence, which has already been built into their projections.[85] A second, and in our view much more serious, issue has to do with the time path of test score convergence. Scholars have noted that the overall reduction in the test score gap since the 1960s has not been continuous. The narrowing occurred until the late 1980s or 1990, after which the gap held steady or, in the case of science and mathematics, actually widened slightly.[86] If we focus on what has been happening over the past 15 years, rather than over the past 40, we see no basis for being optimistic about score convergence.[87] It is also sobering to note that the underrepresentation of blacks in the top tenth of the test score distribution has not changed in recent decades.[88] Of course it is candidates from "the top tenth" who would have the best chance of gaining places at the most selective colleges and universities in the absence of race-sensitive admissions programs.

What are we to conclude? There is no reason to believe that the need for race-sensitive admissions will end within the next 25 years simply as a result of trends and policies already in place. If 25 years is a firm limit, it is not a well-thought-out one. The goal is laudable, and we can certainly anticipate some progress. But elimination of the need for racial preferences will not "just happen."[89]

New Efforts That Are Needed

The persistent gaps in preparation and performance that bedevil us are not going to be corrected by the firing of a single "silver bullet." It would be splendid, for all sorts of reasons, if it were possible to eradicate the underlying racial disparities in socioeconomic status and family background that have so much to do with creating a "preparedness gap"—or even to accelerate the "convergence" noted by Krueger, Rothstein, and Turner. It would also help enormously if we could somehow bring the quality of primary and secondary schools attended by underrepresented minority students up to the level of those attended by whites and Asians—and by "quality" we mean the entire learning environment, not just teacher education and student-teacher ratios. How easy it is to state this goal, and how hard it is to identify the resources, gain the pedagogic know-how, engage families and communities in improving the education of their children, and marshal the political determination needed to address this fundamental problem.[90] There is also the sobering fact that secondary schools are more segregated today, in both the North and the South, than they were 15 to 20 years ago.[91] Residential segregation is obviously a huge part of the problem. As John Payton has observed, "Virtually none of the things that would have to change in the next 25 years to meet this challenge really have anything to do [directly] with higher education."[92] The truly "heavy lifting" has to be done by society at large (we discuss some approaches in chapter 9).

Still, there can be no denying the need for colleges and universities—including, of course, leading schools of education—to extend their own efforts to provide both academic and infrastructure support for pre-collegiate education.[93] Colleges and universities can also help by being more proactive in addressing the problem of academic underperformance among minority students on their campuses. Freeman Hrabowski's work at the University of Maryland, Baltimore County, is especially impressive. His experiences (and the experiences of others) suggest that remedial programs are often harmful rather than helpful, and that the wiser strategy is to challenge minority students to perform to higher standards. Encouraging students to work together in groups and in special "honors" programs seems to help.[94] Improving the academic performance of undergraduates contributes directly to the pools of good candidates for graduate and professional programs—and, in turn, helps reduce the impact of the stereotypes and problems of perception that may be an important source of underperformance itself.[95] Scholars at colleges and universities can also help by continuing to do careful research on which pre-collegiate programs and approaches seem the most promising.[96] Progress has been made, but there is still much that needs to be done.

The simulations of Krueger, Rothstein, and Turner assume a continuation of current admissions policies, and it is worth considering whether rather fundamental changes should be made in these policies. In the next chapter, we will urge the most wealthy and selective colleges and universities to consider moving beyond need-blind admissions and giving a positive boost to the admissions chances of well-qualified candidates from poor families and from families with no college-going history. Such a change in admissions policy would, in our view, be a good thing in its own right; it would advance this country's equity objective. It would also, indirectly, increase the numbers of minority students on these campuses beyond what they would be if race-sensitive admissions policies were no longer allowed. But, as we will show in detail in the next chapter, changes of this kind would not by themselves do all that needs to be done.

MORALITY, JUSTICE, AND PERSISTENCE

We would like to conclude this chapter by emphasizing what we see as the moral essence of the problem of race in American higher education—and in America. This country's "unlovely racial history" continues to afflict all of us, whatever the racial category to which we belong. Glenn Loury is right when he stresses the difficulty each of us has in overturning and discarding ways of thinking about ourselves, and about others, that contain a racial component. He is right in stressing "the stubborn social reality of race consciousness in America."[97] It is in this historical context that we see the need to address continuing racial disparities as a *moral* obligation—an obligation to do "what is right" for that reason alone—quite apart from the other educational, social, and practical considerations that argue in favor of taking fuller advantage of what minority groups can contribute.

Do we believe that this "stubborn social reality" will be gone in 25 years? No, we do not. It is a fantasy to imagine a "virtually painless exit from the nation's racist history."[98] Jonathan Reider recalls that early in the busing boycott, Martin Luther King Jr., spoke in prophetic terms: "It is not enough for us to talk about love. . . . There is another side called justice. . . . Justice is love correcting that which revolts against love." As Reider goes on to point out: "[We need] to recall a darker side of our history: that blacks [in fighting segregation] were mainly on their own; that, all too often, liberals were less than heroic; that even respectable whites who forswore racism were often clueless and grudging in response to black claims. The point is not to pick at old wounds; it is that too much love and not enough justice betrays those who suffered then and sullies those who forget now."[99]

So we do not favor being in too much of a hurry to pretend that we live in a color-blind world when we do not—or in too much of a hurry to say "let bygones be bygones" when what happened before still matters so much. Rather, we favor facing up to where we have been, as a country, acknowledging the long-lasting effects of our "unlovely history," and staying the course: trying to make things better by taking account of race, in sensible ways, at the same time that we work to reduce the need for racial preferences.

CHAPTER 7

Broadening the Quest for Equity
at the Institutional Level
Socioeconomic Status, Admissions Preferences, and Financial Aid

A theme of the first part of this book is that the continued *successful* pursuit of excellence in American higher education depends on opening the gates of opportunity wider. Historically, colleges and universities have been far more welcoming to white male students of European descent who were of the "right" religious persuasion, and usually from families able to pay, than they have been to others. Fortunately, as we saw in chapter 2, substantial progress has been made in eliminating the most blatant forms of discrimination based on religion, gender, and national origin. But there is clearly more work to be done.

Race in America, and especially the treatment of African Americans, has been, and continues to be, the hardest marker of "disadvantage" to counter—in large part because "color" is such a visible marker and is associated with deeply ingrained stigmas and stereotypes. This is why we began this part of the book by considering the racial dimension of limitations on educational opportunity. However, important as race is, it is by no means the only lens through which to look in seeking to open the gates of opportunity wider. The major purpose of this chapter is to discuss ways in which at least the more "privileged" colleges and universities (as defined by both financial resources and selectivity in admissions) might do more, at the institutional level, to address the disadvantages associated with low socioeconomic status (SES).

At the outset of this discussion, we should remind ourselves why, in today's world, there is such a strong case to be made for being broadly inclusive in "crafting a class."[1] There are three principal reasons, which were discussed in chapter 1, but are worth reiterating here:

1. As part of their quest for excellence, colleges and universities want to attract the most promising students, and there has never been reason to believe that all outstanding candidates will be able to pay whatever fees are charged without help. At many colleges and universities, the best students have often been the recipients of need-based financial aid.[2] Society at large needs all the trained talent it

can marshal. True as this statement is for the United States, it has much broader applicability. In South Africa, for instance, "inequality of access" is not a minority problem; there is simply no way South Africa can develop the talent it will need to compete internationally unless it is able to educate to a high level a much larger fraction of the native African population than it has done historically.[3]

2. The quality ("excellence") of the campus learning environment is improved for everyone when students from a wide variety of socio-economic backgrounds are present. Students need to learn how to put themselves in other people's shoes.[4]

3. Finally, a commitment to this form of inclusiveness is an essential part of a broader affirmation of opportunity and is at the center of our concern for equity.[5] An important societal goal is to enable individuals to move up the ladder of accomplishment as far as their talents, character, and determination will take them. This proposition, central to a well-functioning democratic society, is especially important at a time when education is more critical than ever before in determining access not only to the best jobs (and the accompanying economic rewards), but also to a broad set of less tangible opportunities that help us "live a life." Moreover, the sense of democratic legitimacy is undermined if people believe that the rich are admitted to selective colleges and universities regardless of merit while able and deserving candidates from more modest backgrounds are turned away.

In this chapter we first describe the evolution of need-blind admissions policies and emphasize how important they have been in changing the mix of students attending selective institutions. To provide a context for the detailed discussion of SES that is to follow, we next summarize the extent of preferences ("admissions advantages") given to four special groups—underrepresented minority students, legacies and "development cases," recruited athletes, and early decision applicants—and assess the arguments for and against conferring these preferences. (To our way of thinking, the case for some is much stronger than the case for others.) Against this background, we examine in detail the somewhat peculiar juxtaposition of (1) stated support by leading colleges and universities for giving preferences to students from modest backgrounds and (2) the new evidence demonstrating that no such preferences are in fact given by the 19 institutions in our study. We next make a case for putting a "thumb on the scale," as it were, when considering applications from outstanding candidates from modest backgrounds. We illustrate the effects (and costs) of a hypothetical policy of this kind by using simulations that demonstrate that such preferences could be a valuable part of an overall admissions policy but that they are far from a full substitute for race-sensitive admissions. Finally, we discuss (and assess) the reasons for the trend toward more emphasis on merit aid at the institutional level.

NEED-BLIND ADMISSIONS POLICIES
AT ACADEMICALLY SELECTIVE INSTITUTIONS

One of the key determinants of the composition of the student body at academically selective colleges and universities (including the 19 in our special study) is the decisions made by the admissions office in choosing among large numbers of well-qualified candidates. Two other key determinants are the characteristics of the applicant pools (who applies) and the yields on admission offers (who comes). We know from the evidence presented earlier for the schools in our study that these factors combine to produce entering classes in which 10 to 11 percent of the students typically come from families in the bottom income quartile, just over 6 percent are first-generation college-goers, and only about 3 percent meet both criteria—that is, are from low-income families with no previous experience of college (refer back to figure 5.2).

These percentages are clearly low in relation to the percentages in the underlying population. But it would be churlish in the extreme not to recognize how much these prestigious institutions, with their high degree of selectivity and their established constituencies, have accomplished. Success in enrolling the present number of students from low-income families can be attributed to a combination of active recruitment of candidates from diverse backgrounds, a "need-blind" admissions philosophy, and a financial aid policy that meets the full need of all admitted students who elect to matriculate. In 2003, all but 4 of the 19 colleges and universities in our study reported that they were fully "need-blind" in admitting students; that is, their admissions offices pay no attention to the financial circumstances of the student or the student's family in making admissions decisions (and the other 4 are very close to meeting the need-blind criterion, as we explained in chapter 5). These colleges and universities also devote substantial resources to financial aid and do very well in meeting the full need of their admitted applicants.[b]

Need-blind admissions policies at many of the private institutions in our study evolved in the late 1950s and 1960s (starting with the universities in the Ivy League) in conjunction with the establishment of a larger "Overlap Group," representing 23 East Coast colleges, that agreed on expected family contributions for students who were admitted to more than one of the schools in the group. The purpose was to concentrate limited financial aid on students with demonstrated need and to avoid "bidding wars" that might serve only to divert scarce resources from where they were really needed.

The development of this elaborate machinery for defining what need-based aid meant took place at a time when many of these schools had no well-thought-out financial aid policy and, in many cases, lacked the financial resources needed to meet the commitments they would have liked to make. The primary purpose of need-blind admissions was to reassure students from modest circumstances that their lack of money would not be held against them in the admissions competition. The understandable fear of many applicants was that schools would prefer to admit students from families that would have no difficulty meeting the costs of their college education from their own resources—a practice that surely existed historically when colleges were struggling to pay their bills and that exists today at many financially hard-pressed colleges and universities. The key point is that the motivation behind the adoption of need-blind admissions, in conjunction with need-based aid, was to help students from poor families, not to act against them. These policies remain in place today even though the Overlap Group (and the machinery used to agree on expected family contributions) was disestablished in the early 1990s as a result of a highly controversial anti-trust case brought by the Department of Justice.[7]

Establishing these policies was no easy task and was accomplished only some years after the philosophy of need-blind admissions was articulated. In chapter 2 we discussed other early 20th-century barriers to the enrollment of larger numbers of students from poor families, especially when family economic circumstances intersected with such factors as religion, social class, and the secondary schools that students attended. The situation at Yale in the mid-1960s is described vividly by Geoffrey Kabaservice in his account of the changes that Kingman Brewster and his colleagues (including the newly appointed director of admissions, "Inky" Clark) brought to Yale. We described in the previous chapter the interrogation that Clark experienced when trying to make the case for recruiting and admitting a class of students very different from the classes that had been common up to that time. Later in his book, Kabaservice describes "the wall of biases against an applicant from an excellent, competitive public high school, such as New York's Bronx High School of Science in the 1950s":

> The student came from a public high school, which Yale's admissions officers did not visit. He scored highly on aptitude tests, which Yale discounted. He had a specialized education, which many influential Yale faculty members thought unfitted him for the liberal arts. He focused on science or technology, which Yale had traditionally considered unsavory. He was almost certainly from a nonwealthy family, which handicapped him in the era before need-blind admissions. And he had no Yale alumni connection or feeder school tradition to boost his candidacy. Furthermore,

even if the candidate from Bronx Science was not Jewish himself, he came from a school that was predominantly Jewish . . . , at a time when anti-Semitism in Yale's admissions was covert but active. . . . It is not surprising to find that during [President A. Whitney] Griswold's first five years in office, Bronx Science sent only 7 graduates to Yale, while Andover (not nearly as selective) sent 275. Over the same five-year span, almost all alumni sons who applied were accepted.[8]

It is one thing to overturn atavistic policies and practices of the kind that Kabaservice describes and to agree that a very different admissions philosophy is called for; it is quite another to find the resources required to implement a full need-blind admissions policy and a meet-all-need financial aid policy.[9] In considering the feasibility of enrolling more students from poor families, resource constraints have to be taken into account. Throughout the 1970s, even as wealthy a university as Princeton, with an exceedingly generous student aid endowment, struggled to find ways to meet the full need of all admitted students.[10] Many liberal arts colleges outside the Northeast (Oberlin is a good example) have frequently been unable to meet full need, and we will say more later in the chapter about their circumstances when we discuss merit aid.[11] Brown University was not able to move to a full need-blind approach until 2002, when it established a policy that was to take effect with the admission of the Class of 2007.[12] Other excellent schools, such as Tufts, are continuing to try to find the additional resources required if they are to be fully need-blind in admissions and to meet the full need of those offered admission.[13] Also, it was not until 2001 that Princeton met the full need of foreign students—and it is likely that many schools that say they meet full need today are really referring to support for American students.

Resources plainly matter, and later in this chapter we provide dollar estimates of what it would actually cost to adopt one hypothetical approach to going beyond need-blind admissions in order to enroll more students from low-income families at academically selective colleges and universities. But first we need to hearken back to the factual picture of how applicants from low-SES backgrounds are faring in the current admissions competitions at the 19 schools in our case study—in relation to applicants from more advantaged families and also in relation to special groups who already receive preferential treatment (minority students, legacies, and recruited athletes).

PREFERENCES FOR SPECIAL GROUPS

The most striking single finding to emerge from the mass of empirical work reported in chapter 5 relates to SES: *the probabilities of admission at the*

19 schools in our special study are essentially identical, at any given SAT level, for three groups of non-minority students: those from the bottom income quartile, those who are potential first-generation college-goers, and all others. (We exclude minority students from these comparisons because we know that they benefit from race-sensitive admissions policies, and we do not want to confound the results of this analysis of how applicants from low-SES backgrounds fare by mixing together the treatment of race and the treatment of SES.)[14] The curves that plot admission probabilities against SAT scores for the three groups of non-minority applicants are so close together that it would be difficult to put a piece of paper between them (refer back to figure 5.6). More refined statistical analysis confirms that, on an other-things-equal basis, *applicants from low-SES backgrounds, whether defined by family income or parental education, get essentially no break in the admissions process; they fare neither better nor worse than other applicants.*[15]

The obverse side of this core finding is that, overall, students from affluent families also get no special break once they enter the admissions pool; at these schools at least, they have the same overall chances of admission as otherwise similar applicants.[16] These 19 schools say, overwhelmingly, that they pursue need-blind admissions policies. And our robust empirical findings suggest that in fact they are need-blind—and to a greater degree than most of us would ever have assumed to be the case. For these schools, the real question is whether being need-blind is good enough.

The results for three special groups of applicants—underrepresented minority students, legacies, and recruited athletes—stand in sharp contrast.[17] Members of each of these groups have a *decidedly* better chance of being admitted, at any specified SAT level, than do their fellow applicants, including those from low-SES categories (refer back to figure 5.7 and to table 5.1). The "adjusted admissions advantage"—the average boost in the odds of admission provided to an applicant with certain characteristics relative to an otherwise identical applicant—is about 30 percentage points for a recruited athlete, 28 points for a member of an underrepresented minority group, and 20 points for a legacy.[18] As we explained earlier, the straightforward interpretation of these estimates is that, for example, an applicant with an admissions probability of 40 percent based on SAT scores and other variables would have an admissions probability of 70 percent if he or she were a recruited athlete, 68 percent if an underrepresented minority, and 60 percent if a legacy. Applicants who participate in early decision programs also enjoy a definite admissions advantage—about 20 percentage points at the 13 institutions for which we have data.

The question for faculty, administrative officers, and trustees responsible for setting policy is simply stated: looking ahead, is this set of preferences the best way to allocate scarce places at highly selective institutions?

Needless to say, the reasons for giving admissions advantages to these various groups of applicants are radically different, and we believe that some justifications are much more persuasive than others.

Rationale for Giving Preference to Underrepresented Minorities

As we argued in detail in the previous chapter, we believe that minority preferences serve several basic educational and societal goals. To recapitulate briefly: First, as was acknowledged by the Supreme Court in *Grutter v. Bollinger,* a diverse student body provides educational benefits to all students. Second, as Justice Sandra Day O'Connor's majority opinion also emphasized, it is important that these highly regarded schools—which are in many ways gateways to wealth and power in this country—are seen to be accessible to students from all racial backgrounds. Finally, minority preferences correct at least in part for disadvantages that these students, as a group, have experienced—and will experience—in a country that is still affected profoundly by racial stigmas. Race matters in America, and that reality needs to be acknowledged.[19]

Rationale for Giving Preferences to Legacies and "Development Cases"

Legacy preferences serve to enhance the ties of alumni/ae to their alma mater. Schools have an understandable interest in keeping alumni/ae —who can and often do promote their institutions with an evangelical fervor—feeling positively about their institutions. As Harvard's dean of admissions, William Fitzsimmons, puts it: "[The school's alumni/ae] volunteer an immense amount of their free time in recruiting students, raising money for their financial aid, taking part in Harvard Club activities at the local level, and in general promoting the college. . . . They often bring a special kind of loyalty and enthusiasm for life at the college that makes a real difference in the college climate . . . and makes Harvard a happier place."[20] Children of alumni/ae are expected to carry historical ties and commitments into a new day—to "keep the past alive." In addition, all of these institutions rely heavily on alumni/ae donations, and rejecting a reasonably well-qualified legacy applicant can not only end support from the parent(s) but also damage relations with other alumni/ae.

To the extent that earlier cohorts were almost entirely wealthy and white and current cohorts are mostly wealthy and white, legacy preferences serve to reproduce the high-income/high-education/white profile that is characteristic of these schools. At the 18 schools for which we have legacy data, 50 percent of legacy applicants come from the top quartile of the income distribution, compared with 39 percent of non-legacy applicants.[21] Of course today's legacy pools include children of minority graduates, but this is a relatively recent phenomenon. Cameron Howell and Sarah Turner have estimated that, by 2020, the legacy applicant pool at the University of Virginia will have the same racial distribution as the current cohorts.[22] But today, just 6.7 percent of legacy applicants at these 18 institutions are underrepresented minorities, compared to 12.5 percent of all other students.

The issue of fairness (equity) involved in legacy preferences was thrust into prominence in the context of the Supreme Court's consideration of minority preferences at the University of Michigan. Even though a legacy preference does not raise the same kinds of constitutional questions as a racial preference, the two kinds of preference have become intertwined politically. Indeed, Justice Stephen Breyer asked explicitly about the relationship between the two types of preference, and the university systems in both Georgia and California prohibited legacy preferences after legal prohibitions ended racial preferences.[23] Former senator John Edwards has criticized legacy preferences as "giv[ing] more to kids who already have more," and Theodore M. Shaw, a lawyer for the National Association for the Advancement of Colored People's Legal Defense Fund, posed his question this way: "What does legacy preference do to advance fairness and merit?"[24] Those who find legacy preferences inappropriate in today's world would like to see them explicitly prohibited.[25]

In assessing the actual extent of legacy preference today, it is important to use the right numbers. The comparative admit rates for legacies and other applicants published regularly by schools themselves and then by the press serve only to confuse a subject that needs more careful, more dispassionate, judgment brought to bear on it. We are told, for example, that "Harvard accepts 40% of legacy applicants, compared with an 11% overall acceptance rate. Princeton took 35% of alumni children who applied last year, and 11% of applicants overall. The University of Pennsylvania accepts 41% of legacy applicants, compared with 21% overall."[26] These comparative percentages may be useful to college and university leaders who want alumni/ae to know that they are respected and loved, but they are deceptive because they fail to take into account the fact that legacy applicants have stronger academic credentials than other applicants and would be accepted at higher rates if there were no legacy preference at all. Comparing legacies in competitive admissions situations with other candidates who present similar credentials gives a better sense of the extent of the true "break" legacies actually are given.[27]

Dean Fitzsimmons notes that at Harvard "legacy status is basically used as a tie-breaker between comparable candidates,"[28] and our data confirm that legacy preferences are generally reserved for candidates with strong credentials. When we assign the applicants to the 13 colleges and universities for which we have sufficient data on legacies to three SAT categories, we find that the legacy advantage is much more pronounced in the highest SAT range than elsewhere, a pattern that is also evident in figure 5.7 (where we see that the vertical distance between the admissions probability for a legacy applicant and the probability for other applicants increases as we move up the SAT scale). The adjusted admissions advantage for legacies with combined SAT scores below 1100 is just over 6 percentile points (and not statistically significant), the advantage for those with SAT scores between 1100 and 1300 is 18 percentile points, and the advantage for those with SAT scores of 1300 and above is 25 percentile points (the latter two admissions advantages are statistically significant).[29]

It is important to recognize how much change there has been since the mid-1960s. At the time Brewster and Clark undertook to reform the Yale admissions process, more than two-thirds of alumni sons who applied to Yale were accepted, even though, we are told, "a disproportionate number flunked out or were placed on probation."[30] In those days, preferences for alumni children were deeply connected to privileges of many other kinds having to do with family background, social class, prep school education, and the like. In thinking about legacy preferences today, it is well to remember how much progress has been made in eliminating the worst kinds of exclusivity and "social favoritism."[31]

Defenders of legacy preferences as they are conferred at present argue that the admissions bar is still a high one, that relatively small numbers of applicants benefit from legacy preferences, and that the financial gains to colleges and universities from giving some weight to alumni/ae status are relevant.[32] In addition, many colleges and universities also pay special attention in the admissions process to other candidates whose parents or other relatives are likely to make large donations, sometimes known as "development cases" or candidates on "the president's list." As John McCardell, the former president of Middlebury College, puts it: "If a handful of slots go to deserving applicants whose families can at least have the potential to improve in dramatic ways the quality of the education at Middlebury College, we would not be fair to our successors or predecessors if we were to overlook that reality."[33]

Duke is the university that has attracted the most attention in discussions of development cases, presumably because of the degree to which it has institutionalized the practice of favoring children of wealthy parents. According to a long story in the *Wall Street Journal:*

> Through its own network and names supplied by trustees, alumni, donors and others, the development office identifies about 500 likely applicants with rich or powerful parents who are not alumni. . . . It cultivates them with campus tours and basic admissions advice; for instance, applying

early increases their chances. It also relays the names to the admissions office, which returns word if any of the students forget to apply—so development can remind them. The development office then winnows the initial 500 into at least 160 high-priority applicants. Although these names are flagged in the admissions-office computer, admissions readers evaluate them on merit, without regard to family means. About 30 to 40 are accepted, the others tentatively rejected or wait-listed. During an all-day meeting in March, [the admissions director] and the senior vice president for development debate these [remaining] 120 cases, weighing their family's likely contribution against their academic shortcomings. . . . Most of the 120 students are admitted. . . . Once these children of privilege enroll, the development office enlists their parents as donors and fund raisers. . . . The strategy appears to be paying off. For the last six years, Duke says it has led all universities nationwide in unrestricted gifts to its annual fund from nonalumni parents: about $3.1 million in 2001–2002. . . . While 35% of alumni donate to Duke, 52% of parents of last year's freshman class contributed to the university—besides paying $35,000 in tuition and room and board.[34]

Duke emphasizes that all of these candidates are over threshold and graduate at high rates. Also, "no bargains are struck." Nonetheless, serious questions have been raised about the extent to which admissions decisions are tied to the fundraising machinery. A former president of Duke, Keith Brodie, is said to have trimmed the number of such cases to 20 a year. Brodie is quoted as saying: "A Duke education is too valuable an asset to squander." The same story in the *Wall Street Journal* references a report to the trustees by a university committee on admissions that called for a one-third cut in applicants accepted for development reasons, and the admissions director is said to have planned to reduce the number of such admissions to about 65 per year. So the cross-pressures are evident. Duke has a smaller endowment than a number of its major competitors, the percentage of its alumni/ae making annual gifts is also below the norm for its peer group, and the University thus finds itself under keen pressure to raise more money. But some on campus worry about the effects on intellectual vitality and diversity.[35]

In our view, there is a clear trade-off between the goals of equity (which are not advanced by preferences of this kind) and excellence (which does depend on generating resources from alumni/ae and other donors).[36] But to make the excellence argument, it is necessary that legacy/development preferences be conferred with something approaching surgical precision, that great care be taken in deciding how much of a "break" to give which candidates, and that the numbers not be too large. One faculty member commented to us that he would not object at all to having some number of "tie-breaker" preferences go to individuals whose families could make a real difference to the school *if* he were persuaded that in fact such slots were not often wasted on "friends of friends" and other applicants with modest qualifications whose families are not in fact likely to help the school financially.

In sum, we favor placing tight limits on preferences related to legacy status—and even tighter limits on those related to family wealth—because of their adverse impact on equity objectives, including the need for more, not less, socioeconomic diversity. But we do not think that ideological arguments against all such preferences should be allowed to overwhelm the legitimate interests of colleges and universities in maintaining a real sense of historical continuity on their campuses and in attracting the resources that they need to pursue their excellence objectives. (Another highly relevant finding is that legacy matriculants exhibit very little underperformance—1.4 percentile points in class rank.) More generally, we believe that all forms of preference, and all policies concerning tuition and financial aid, need to be examined together to see if an appropriate balance is being struck in pursuing the complementary goals of equity and excellence.

Rationale for Giving Preferences to Recruited Athletes

Whereas minority admissions preferences serve educational and societal purposes, and legacy/development preferences serve institutional purposes tied to the pursuit of educational excellence, the preferences given to recruited athletes serve primarily the narrower purposes of the institution's athletic establishment and the interests of trustees and alumni/ae with strong feelings about athletics.[37] This set of preferences reflects the dictates of a college sports culture that continuously ratchets up levels of competition. Athletes are recruited so that college teams can compete with teams from other colleges that are also recruiting athletes. There is no evidence that athletic accomplishments have any significant effect on giving or on how alumni/ae in general view their institution (actually, a majority favor placing less emphasis on intercollegiate athletics).[38]

Thought of in the right way—as one component of an overall educational experience—athletics can be a valuable learning experience and a fine addition to other aspects of college life. Many of us know from personal experience that intercollegiate competition can be great fun, a healthy counterbalance to long hours in the library or laboratory, and, in all respects, a valued complement to academic pursuits. Regrettably, however, college sports in their current form represent a distinct threat to academic values and educational excellence. Anyone who reads the papers is aware of the blatant perversions of values (and not just academic values) represented by so much of big-time sports in present-day America. But that is far from the end of the story; indeed, from our perspective, it is not even the most important part. Recent research reveals all too clearly the ways in which intercollegiate athletics conflicts with core academic values at many of the country's most selective colleges and universities that *do not offer athletic scholarships.*[39]

The increasing intensity of athletics at every level of play, combined with the "dynamic" of a competitive system that transfers problems from one set of sports to another and from one set of institutions to another, has led to an ever-widening academic-athletic divide. Today recruited athletes, men and women alike, at the Ivy League universities and at leading liberal arts colleges, enjoy, as we have seen, a huge admissions advantage. Recruited athletes are less and less representative of their classes (clustering in certain fields of study and bunching heavily in the bottom third of the class), they underperform academically (earning much lower grades than they would be expected to earn on the basis of their high school credentials), and they are far more isolated socially from their classmates than were their predecessors. One of the most fascinating findings is that it appears to be the recruitment/admissions process itself that is primarily responsible for these troubling outcomes. This is a story that has much more to do with "selection" (i.e., with the interests and motivations of recruited athletes, as well as of the coaches who recruit them) than with "treatment" (i.e., with time spent practicing and competing)—a conclusion that is supported strongly by the very different academic outcomes achieved by "walk-on" athletes as compared with those of recruited athletes, even recruited athletes who do not end up playing.

It is also clear that, contrary to what is often assumed, recruited athletes as a group do not contribute to racial or socioeconomic diversity. As Bowen and Sarah Levin point out in *Reclaiming the Game,* "Recruited athletes in the schools in our study are in general appreciably less likely than students at large to be from underrepresented minority groups."[40] Furthermore, just 6 percent of recruited athletes enrolled at the institutions in our study are from the bottom income quartile, compared to 12 percent of other students. In short, giving admissions preferences to recruited athletes does little if anything to promote the equity goal of higher education (and may, in fact, detract from it) at the same time that it raises troubling issues for the pursuit of educational excellence.

Why does all of this matter?

- First, there is a serious risk that failing to reverse the direction now so evident will undermine the real value of intercollegiate sports on campuses that continue to see athletics as an integral part of an educational mission.
- Second, there can be large "opportunity costs." Students eager to take advantage of the special educational opportunities a particular

college has to offer may be turned away because places in the entering class (as many as 25 percent or more at some liberal arts colleges) have been claimed by recruited athletes who are less likely to participate fully in the educational life of the institution.

- Third, there are serious issues of institutional integrity and truth-telling. It is discouraging to see the "disconnect" that exists today between stated principles (for example, the assertion that athletes will be academically "representative" of their classes) and present-day realities. Truth-telling is important, especially for institutions that pride themselves, as colleges and universities should, on standing for the highest level of integrity.
- Fourth, we should not underestimate the "signaling effects" of current practices on secondary schools, prospective students, and their families.[41] The obvious "story line" is that the development of sports skills should be given high priority by those (parents and secondary schools) who want to send their students to the most selective institutions.
- Fifth, today's intercollegiate athletic programs, even at the Division III level, involve substantial financial outlays, especially when we consider the capital costs of facilities alongside rising personnel costs and operating expenses.

In sum, the drift into recruitment-driven, high-intensity athletic programs at many of the country's leading educational institutions, while not perhaps a "fatal flaw," does indeed compromise the pursuit of excellence. It does so directly, by distorting priorities and misallocating resources (including highly coveted places in the entering classes of the most selective institutions). And it does so indirectly, by raising questions about our core commitments—about what matters most in crafting a class and in defining a campus ethos.

Rationale for Giving Preferences to Early Decision Applicants

Although they are not defined by demographic characteristics or by their interest in a particular activity such as varsity sports, early decision applicants can also be considered a "special group" from the standpoint of admissions preferences. Our data confirm the findings of Christopher Avery, Andrew Fairbanks, and Richard Zeckhauser: students who apply through early decision programs enjoy a decided admissions advantage.[42] We find that applying early to one of the 13 institutions for which we have data, provided (in 1995) an adjusted admissions advantage of 19.6 percentage points.[43] This is a striking statistic, and we must remember that the early application "craze" did not really start until 1999 or 2000. Only about 8 percent of applicants to our institutions applied through early application or early decision programs for entry in 1995, as compared to the nearly 30 percent of applicants who applied early to similar institutions in 1999–2000.[44]

We recognize that early decision and early action programs are valued by prospective students who definitely know where they want to go to school and wish to be spared the agony of waiting until spring for the school in question to act on their application. From a larger perspective, however, what is most troubling about this form of preference is that it rewards applicants who are fortunate enough to know that applying early can benefit them substantially and who attend secondary schools, or are from families, with sufficient sophistication to know how to meet the early application deadlines. This group includes students at top-tier secondary schools, those with close connections to the college or university to which they are applying, and recruited athletes. (Coaches urge the athletes whom they are recruiting to apply early in order to enhance their chances of admission and to "lock them in"; athletic recruiting increasingly depends on early application programs.)[45] Also, the very nature of early decision programs—which require students offered admission to matriculate at the school in question—makes it impossible for students who have financial need to compare financial aid offers from various schools in which they are interested. Minority students are of course disproportionately represented in the "need-sensitive" category.[46]

These programs do not support the equity objectives that concern us in this study. Moreover, early decision programs can have harmful effects on secondary education by trivializing the final year of high school, as President Richard Levin of Yale has stressed.[47] These programs also encourage prospective students to "game" the system, in ways that Avery and his colleagues explain very clearly. For instance, an applicant may be tempted to apply for early decision at his or her second-choice school (assuming it is less selective than the first choice school) rather than taking a chance on not getting into either the first- or second-choice school in the regular round. Application decisions always involve striking a balance between where a student would most like to go and where a student can be admitted. But early application shifts the equilibrium (too far, in our view) toward the latter. Early decision can also prevent a prospective student from taking the time to compare educational opportunities before making a binding decision. For all of these reasons, early decision programs are troublesome not only in terms of their implications for the equity objective, but also because they cannot be said to promote the excellence objective of higher education. They are attractive to particular schools because they can help them recruit candidates who might otherwise have gone to a competitor. In addition, early decision programs increase an institution's attractiveness by raising its yield and reduce the workload in its admissions office by diminishing the number of applicants and spreading the workload out over the year. But these institutional benefits seem far from compelling, especially when one counts the equity costs and takes a system-wide perspective.

SOCIOECONOMIC STATUS AND ADMISSIONS: PREFERENCES BASED ON INCOME OR "CLASS"

Against this backdrop of evidence of admissions preferences bestowed on various groups of applicants, for reasons that seem to us compelling in some instances (underrepresented minority candidates) and unpersuasive in others (recruited athletes), we return to the central question of this chapter: how should students from poor families and from families with no previous history of college attendance be treated in the admissions process? If we were to poll presidents of leading colleges and universities, we are confident that a large majority would want their schools to be more than "neutral" in considering such candidates. The brief submitted to the Supreme Court in conjunction with the University of Michigan cases by Harvard, Brown, Chicago, Duke, Dartmouth, the University of Pennsylvania, Princeton, and Yale is unequivocal on this point. The relevant section reads as follows:

> Admission factors begin, of course, with the core academic criteria, including not just grades and test scores but teacher recommendations and state, regional, national, and international awards. In some cases, those criteria will be all but decisive, either positively (very rarely) or negatively (more often). In the vast majority of cases, however, they are not themselves decisive, and the process continues. *Admissions officials give special attention to, among others, applicants from economically and/or culturally disadvantaged backgrounds,* those with unusual athletic ability, those with special artistic talents, *those who would be the first in their families to attend any college,* those whose parents are alumni or alumnae, *and those who have overcome various identifiable hardships.*[48] (our emphasis)

What is striking is the juxtaposition of this clear statement of intent with the equally clear empirical finding that, at the schools in our study, there is absolutely no admissions advantage associated with coming from a poor family and only a very small advantage (about 4 percentile points) associated with being a first-generation college-goer; at least that was the case for the '95 entering cohort. We do not believe that this disjunction is due to any desire to be disingenuous or to "gild the lily." Rather, we believe it is due to a combination of a lack of data at the institutional level on the background characteristics of all applicants (data that are hard to assemble), financial aid constraints, a commitment to being need-blind (and therefore purposefully ignoring SES), and the lack of vocal champions for students from low-income families when tough choices are being made among a large group of very well-qualified candidates.[49]

This last point deserves emphasis. The president of one of the universities in our study told us that, on reflection, and on the basis of what he had seen in the admissions process at his own university, he was not at all surprised by the finding that admissions at these highly selective institutions is truly need-blind, but not more than that. He said that when the admissions staff was considering an outstanding soccer player, it was as if "lights went on" in the room; everyone paid close attention, and everyone knew that the coach and athletic director were, in effect, watching closely and would have to be dealt with. Similarly, when the staff considered a legacy candidate with strong ties to the university, it was clear that representatives of the alumni office, the development office, and perhaps even the president's office, were "present" in spirit if not in person. Minority candidates also were considered carefully and sympathetically, in part because of the active involvement of recruiters and admissions staff members with a special commitment to racial diversity. But, the president continued, when an otherwise "normal" applicant from a family of modest circumstances was considered, the process just moved right ahead without anyone making a special plea—perhaps, at least in part, because the immediate institutional interests to be served (as contrasted with the societal interests) are less evident, or more diffuse, in the case of socioeconomic status.

Reasons to Favor Preferences Based on SES

It is one thing to understand the disconnect between what is said about SES and what actually happens in the admissions process, and it is quite another to regard the status quo as acceptable. We do not think that it is. Consistent with the general theme of this chapter, there are four reasons that we favor giving some preference to well-qualified applicants from modest backgrounds.

- First, this group of students is poorly represented in the most selective institutions at the present time. Students from families in the bottom quartile of the national income distribution represent roughly 10 to 11 percent of all students at these schools, and first-generation college students represent a little over 6 percent of the student population. Only 3 percent of the students are *both* first-generation collegegoers and from low-income families, whereas the national share of the same-age population in this category is nearly 20 percent (see chapter 5). Enrolling more such students would clearly increase diversity, with its attendant educational benefits.

- Second, enrolling more students from economically as well as racially disadvantaged backgrounds would unquestionably promote social mobility and be seen as representing a school's serious commitment to enhancing opportunity in America.[50]
- Third, it is essential to remember the odds that students from modest backgrounds had to overcome in order to get into the credible applicant pool in the first place. Recall (from chapter 4) that students from families in the top income quartile were more than twice as likely as students from the bottom income quartile even to take the SAT. Among the test-takers, the odds of scoring over 1200 were three times higher for those in the top quartile as compared with those in the bottom quartile. Combining these probabilities, the key fact is that *the odds of both taking the tests and doing very well on them were roughly six times higher for students from the top income quartile than for students from the bottom income quartile.* When we look at the test-taking behavior and results achieved by students from families with no experience of higher education, we find even more pronounced differences. In short, family circumstances have an enormous impact on the chances of applicants' even being considered by the admissions staff at an academically selective college or university. Those who have "bucked the odds" to get into the credible pool would surely seem to deserve special recognition.
- Fourth, enrolled students who come from modest backgrounds do very well academically; in contrast to both recruited athletes and minority students, this group of students does not underperform. Also, there is evidence that they do well in later life (see chapter 5).

For all of these reasons, relying simply on a traditional need-blind approach to admissions does not seem to us to be sufficient. Are the claims of equity really being met through a need-blind approach in a society in which prospective students are so stratified by SES in their pre-college years? Later (in chapter 9) we discuss the multiple strategies that can be used to improve the pre-collegiate preparedness of these students, but we see no reason to wait (and perhaps to wait a very long time) for such strategies to make a real difference. Meanwhile, we believe that colleges and universities could take additional steps now to increase socioeconomic diversity on their campuses and to enhance social mobility in America.

To be sure, it is necessary to maintain perspective and not exaggerate the nationwide consequences of enrolling more students from low-income families at schools of the kinds included in our study. As one commentator put it, "Even if Harvard were tomorrow to get its share of low SES students up to the share of the overall population, the national SES gaps in enrollment and educational attainment would remain very much what they are today." Of course this is true. Not even the most determined efforts by the highly selective institutions can be expected to have a major quantitative impact nationwide. Other policies, at all levels of government and at all levels of the educational system, are needed if major progress is to be made. But we should not allow the enormity of the overall problem to justify inaction at the "local" level. The symbolic as well as the substantive benefits of actions by leading colleges and universities should be recognized.

One Approach: A Hypothetical "Thumb on the Scale"

Those of us who favor encouraging academically selective colleges and universities to do more than they are doing at present to enroll students from modest family backgrounds need to examine the implications of adopting specific, realistic alternatives to the traditional approach that combines need-blind admissions and need-based aid. The most direct alternative is simply to "put a thumb on the scale" when weighing the qualifications of applicants from lower-SES categories, much as colleges do now when they consider minorities, legacies, and recruited athletes—an approach sometimes called "class-based affirmative action."[51] But what kind of thumb—and how heavy a thumb? What would be the effects of such an approach on the composition of the entering class (including the number of minority students), the academic qualifications of enrolled students, and financial aid requirements?

To provide tentative answers to these questions, we have simulated the effects of one particular thumb type and size for the schools in our study. After considering several alternatives, we decided to explore the implications of putting a hypothetical "legacy thumb" on the scale. That is, we decided to see what would happen if students with family incomes in the bottom quartile were given the same admissions advantage, within each SAT range, now enjoyed by legacies. We want to emphasize again that this is a purely hypothetical exercise, intended to serve only illustrative purposes. Any number of other "hypotheticals" could be tried out, and any school interested in doing more for applicants from low-income or first-generation families would have to devise its own approach.[52]

The idea of a "legacy thumb" appeals to us in part because there is a nice kind of symbolic symmetry associated with it. Why not give the least privileged group of applicants, who presumably have had to overcome many obstacles to become qualified candidates for admission, the same advantage in the admissions process that is now conferred on those whose parentage has given them a special place in the competition for admission? We like the "legacy thumb" approach for another reason. As we pointed out earlier in the chapter, the general practice, at least at the most selective private colleges and universities, is to give legacies a significant boost *only after they have done very well on their own in building a strong academic record, and to give those with stronger records bigger boosts.* There is, in our view, much to be said for giving special consideration to applicants who have demonstrated considerable achievement on their own. In the case of candidates from low-SES backgrounds, this approach has special resonance. It says, in effect, "You have done great, in the face of many obstacles. Now we will give you a well-deserved helping hand." Using the actual admissions advantages currently enjoyed by legacies as a rough metric has the further advantage of emphasizing that, within each SAT interval, holistic assessments of all applicants would continue to be made—as opposed to more or less automatically taking all applicants from lower-SES backgrounds whose credentials placed them over some threshold.

What do we find, in our simulations, when applicants from low-income families receive the same admissions advantage as legacies (and, in our initial simulations, underrepresented minority groups also retain their current degree of admissions advantage)?[53] The admissions probability for such candidates at the schools in our study could be expected to increase substantially—from 32 percent at present to 47 percent—which is, coincidentally, essentially the same as the admissions probability for minority applicants (see table 7.1). The admissions probability for nonminority students from the bottom income quartile would increase even more dramatically—by almost 20 percentage points, from 30 percent to nearly 50 percent. Especially interesting is the effect on the admissions probability for all other applicants: it falls, as it would have to, but only by about 1 percentage point—from 39 percent to 38 percent. The explanation is, of course, the relative sizes of the applicant pools.

Turning to enrollment, our simulations show that the share of the class comprised of students from low-income families could be expected to increase from 11 percent to about 17 percent. The minority share would (by assumption) stay constant at just over 13 percent, and the share of all other students would decline from 79 to 74 percent. (These percentages add to more than 100 percent because there is an overlap between students from low-income families and minority students. The two groups together could be expected to constitute 26 percent of the student population, not 30 percent.) A side-effect of this kind of shift in admissions policies might be to reduce somewhat the number of students from wealthy families at the most selective institutions and, in effect, redistribute some of them to other liberal arts colleges and universities—which might be healthy all around. There is another potential

TABLE 7.1
Simulation of the Effects of Income-Sensitive Admissions Preferences
Based on Legacy Preferences, Retaining Race-Sensitive Preferences,
18 Institutions, 1995 Entering Cohort

	Current Policy	Income-Sensitive Preferences
Admissions Probabilities		
Non-minority, bottom income quartile	29.6%	49.2%
Minority, bottom income quartile	39.9%	40.7%
Minority, non–bottom quartile	51.4%	51.7%
All bottom income quartile	**32.1%**	**46.6%**
All minority	**48.3%**	**48.8%**
Non-minority, non–bottom quartile	**39.4%**	**38.2%**
Percentage of Admitted Students		
Non-minority, bottom income quartile	5.9%	10.5%
Minority, bottom income quartile	3.3%	3.3%
Minority, non-bottom quartile	12.2%	12.1%
All bottom income quartile	**9.2%**	**13.8%**
All minority	**15.5%**	**15.5%**
Non-minority, non–bottom quartile	**78.6%**	**74.0%**
Percentage of Enrolled Students		
Non-minority, bottom income quartile	7.2%	13.4%
Minority, bottom income quartile	3.4%	3.4%
Minority, non–bottom quartile	9.9%	9.9%
All bottom income quartile	**10.6%**	**16.7%**
All minority	**13.4%**	**13.2%**
Non-minority, non–bottom quartile	**79.4%**	**73.5%**

Source: Expanded College and Beyond database.
Note: The University of Illinois is excluded due to missing legacy data. Numbers may not
sum correctly or may differ slightly when they should be the same due to rounding.

effect: giving a "boost" to applicants from low-income families might
encourage more such applicants to apply to highly selective schools.[54]

There are three kinds of potential "costs" associated with this hypothetical "legacy thumb" policy (not counting the political/relationship
costs—or gains—associated with a change in philosophy that, as always,
would anger some and please others). First, there could be effects on the
academic profiles of the institutions and on academic outcomes. It would
not be unreasonable to worry about some reduction in average SAT scores
if high-scoring students from high-SES backgrounds were replaced by
less well-prepared students from low-SES categories. But in fact, in our
simulation the average SAT score of the members of the entering class
remains essentially unchanged. A large part of the explanation is that at
present large numbers of high-testing students from low-income families

are being turned down; they are suffering the same fate as many other disappointed candidates with high test scores who applied to these selective institutions. For example, figure 5.6 shows that rejection notices were sent to just over half of the applicants from low-income families with SAT scores between 1350 and 1400. Another reason for the modest impact on SAT scores is that the legacy admissions advantage is greatest at the higher reaches of the SAT distribution (and is virtually non-existent at the lower end). Thus, relatively speaking, it is the students with high SAT scores from low-income families who would benefit disproportionately from receiving legacy-type admissions preferences.[55] Nor is there any evidence to suggest that the relatively small number of additional students from low-income families to be admitted under this regime would fail to perform academically at the level of other students. More aggressive changes in admissions policies might have deleterious effects of this kind, but the relatively modest initiative under investigation here seems unproblematic from this standpoint.[56]

Second, there would be—no question about it—significant dollar costs involved in providing financial aid to a larger number of needy students (and perhaps some additional institutional expense for support services). We estimate that for our group of private liberal arts colleges, with an average of 500 students per class, grant aid funds would have to increase about $460,000 per class, per year, or just under $2 million for all four classes per year (an approximately 12 percent increase), if current financial aid policies were maintained. For the private universities in our study, with 1,500 students per class, the necessary increase could be expected to be about $1.4 million per class, per year, or between $5 and $6 million for all four classes (which is also approximately a 12 percent increase).[57]

The third potential cost is also related to institutional finances. These institutions rely heavily on alumni/ae donations, and it is reasonable to ask whether enrolling a substantially higher number of students from low-SES backgrounds would result in less wealthy or less generous alumni/ae.[58] We know from the findings presented in chapter 5 that alumni/ae from the '76 entering cohort with low-income family backgrounds earn the same amount as otherwise similar classmates from the two middle income categories, but that those from the top income group earn significantly more than the other three groups. We also have data on donations (through 1999) by alumni/ae from the '76 entering cohort for nine institutions.[59] Analyzing the raw data for this limited set of institutions, we found that alumni/ae who came from the bottom income quartile in 1976 were somewhat less likely than their classmates to have made a donation in the nearly 20 years that they had been out of school. Former students from the bottom income quartile gave at a 38 percent rate, compared to rates of 50 to 59 percent for those from the two middle quartiles and a 62 percent rate for those from the top quartile.

The decision to make a gift to one's former school is influenced by many factors, such as one's experience at school, one's general attitude toward charitable giving, one's responsibilities to family members—and of course one's income and wealth. Controlling for gender, race, SAT scores, college grades, employment status, sector of employment, and income, we find that the giving gap between alumni/ae from the bottom income quartile and other former students disappears.[60] There are no significant differences between the bottom quartile and any other quartile in giving rates or in being a top giver. Thus we find that enrolling more students from low-income families could be expected to diminish alumni/ae donations, but because of characteristics other than socioeconomic background per se, especially choices of sectors in which to work. In other words, there is no "future donations" trade-off between *similarly situated* alumni/ae from different socioeconomic categories. However, we know that alumni/ae from low-SES backgrounds will not be, in general, "similarly situated."

The costs of additional financial aid and forgone future donations would presumably vary substantially from one institution to another, as would the capacity of the institution to absorb these costs or to offset them by increases in tuition. We understand the need to live within what are often tight institutional budget constraints, and we certainly do not mean to suggest that putting a thumb on the scale, on behalf of students from low-SES backgrounds, would be a painless process for any institution. Trade-offs always have to be considered, and they are not limited to choices within the admissions and financial aid domains. Faculty have to be recruited and retained, libraries have to be supported, and so on. "Absolutist" policies ("We will do *X*, no matter what") are always suspect. When resources are limited, principles collide.

Still, substantial as these financial costs may be, it is easier (at least for us) to imagine moving some distance in the direction of admitting students from lower-SES backgrounds by means of admissions policies—as far as resource constraints would allow—than it is to believe that the powerful pre-college "conditioning" of the pool of applicants can be fixed any time soon. We are strongly in favor of doing whatever can be done to enhance college preparedness for students from disadvantaged backgrounds, but that will be a long and difficult process (see chapter 9). Meanwhile, there is, in our view, a strong argument in favor of doing more at the undergraduate level to help some substantial number of deserving students almost immediately.

Institutions interested in doing more for potential students from low-income families may also elect to provide even more generous financial aid to these students than they do already. Harvard and the University of

Virginia have both elected to replace loans with grants for students from lower-income families in an effort to increase enrollment of students from economically disadvantaged backgrounds.[61] We hope that these initiatives succeed. However, we suspect that giving a boost in admissions may be more effective in altering the socioeconomic composition of classes than improving financial aid offers to those who are admitted. The relatively high yields on current offers of admission to applicants from low-income families (higher than the average yields on all offers of admission) suggest that present-day financial aid policies are less of a problem than is reliance on need-blind admissions. It is fine to be more generous—and being more generous certainly could increase yields further and help with recruitment—but we think consideration should be given to the alternative of putting a thumb on the admissions scale (maybe even a thumb and a half). And if any institutions are going to take the lead in moving beyond need-blind admissions, it is almost certainly going to have to be the wealthy, academically selective institutions that we have studied.[62]

THE INTERACTIONS BETWEEN CLASS AND RACE: CAN "CLASS-BASED" AFFIRMATIVE ACTION SUBSTITUTE FOR RACE-SENSITIVE ADMISSIONS?

We turn now to the last major question that has been part of this discussion (and, for some, the thorniest one): what would happen if institutions were to provide a boost to applicants from low-income families *and* stop giving any explicit preference to those who are members of under-represented minorities? Since the families of minority students are disproportionately represented in the bottom income quartile, giving consideration to family income (or parental education) presumably would benefit them to some extent, relative to other applicants.[63] But by how much? What would happen to minority enrollments if, hypothetically, minority preferences were eliminated at the same time that a "legacy-like" preference was given to those from low-income families? The answer provided by our simulations is that minority enrollments could be expected to fall by nearly half—from 13.4 percent to 7.1 percent (see table 7.2).[64]

Do these patterns differ appreciably between public and private institutions? To answer this important question, we ran separate simulations for the public universities and the private colleges and universities in our set of schools. The results are similar.[65] At the public universities, using the "legacy thumb" for applicants from low-income families and simultaneously eliminating any explicit minority preference would reduce the share of minority students from 17.4 percent to 8.0 percent; the corresponding reduction at the private institutions would be from 12.5 percent

TABLE 7.2

Simulation of the Effects of Income-Sensitive Admissions Preferences
Based on Legacy Preferences, Eliminating Race-Sensitive Preferences,
18 Institutions, 1995 Entering Cohort

	Current Policy	Income-Sensitive Preferences
Admissions Probabilities		
Non-minority, bottom income quartile	29.6%	49.2%
Minority, bottom income quartile	39.9%	27.0%
Minority, non–bottom quartile	51.4%	26.3%
All bottom income quartile	**32.1%**	**43.3%**
All minority	**48.3%**	**26.6%**
Non-minority, non–bottom quartile	**39.4%**	**40.5%**
Percentage of Admitted Students		
Non-minority, bottom income quartile	5.9%	10.7%
Minority, bottom income quartile	3.3%	2.5%
Minority, non–bottom quartile	12.2%	5.6%
All bottom income quartile	**9.2%**	**13.1%**
All minority	**15.5%**	**8.0%**
Non-minority, non–bottom quartile	**78.6%**	**81.3%**
Percentage of Enrolled Students		
Non-minority, bottom income quartile	7.2%	13.0%
Minority, bottom income quartile	3.4%	2.7%
Minority, non–bottom quartile	9.9%	4.4%
All bottom income quartile	**10.6%**	**15.7%**
All minority	**13.4%**	**7.1%**
Non-minority, non–bottom quartile	**79.4%**	**79.9%**

Source: Expanded College and Beyond Database.
Note: The University of Illinois is excluded due to missing legacy data. Numbers may not sum correctly or may differ slightly when they should be the same due to rounding.

to 6.9 percent. The relative fall-off would be slightly greater in the public institutions, but only slightly.[66] In Thomas Kane's words: "It's important to be very clear that income and race are not substitutes."[67] Nor are parental education and race substitutes. Simulations for first-generation college students suggest that the fall-off in minority enrollment would be even greater under a policy favoring applicants from families with low levels of parental education than it would be under a policy favoring applicants from the bottom income quartile.[68]

The results of a similar simulation at graduate and professional schools would surely be even more dramatic, but we lack the data needed to present formal results. A recent account of decisions reached at Texas A&M is, however, right on point. Texas A&M decided not to take race into account at the undergraduate level and succeeded in enrolling a considerable number of minority students through aggressive recruiting. However, at the graduate/professional school level, the university leadership recognized that it is necessary to pay explicit attention to race and ethnicity. There was just one Hispanic student and not a single black student among the 59 medical school graduates at Texas A&M in 2003–04. Accordingly, the university is "relenting" on its opposition to affirmative action at the graduate level. The administration "announced that it would begin allowing admissions officers at its health-science school to explicitly take race into account when it comes to granting interviews or sending out acceptance letters."[69]

If some would like to believe that consideration of SES can be as effective as race-sensitive admissions in increasing minority enrollments—and are disappointed when the data demonstrate that this is not the case— others are concerned that focusing on the overall racial mix of an enrolled class can obscure the modest number of minority students from certain backgrounds who are enrolled. In highly publicized discussions at Harvard, this issue was raised pointedly in the context of claims that only about a third of all African American students at Harvard are from families in which all four grandparents were born in this country.[70] In their comprehensive study of the achievements of minority students at 28 academically selective colleges and universities in the original College and Beyond database, Douglas Massey and his colleagues found that 9 percent of the black students had been born abroad, and that more than 20 percent reported that either their mother or father had been born abroad.[71]

As the commentary on the Harvard discussion indicates, opinions vary widely as to the importance of the native-born distinction.[72] The larger question is the one we have been discussing: how should institutions view race, socioeconomic status, and the interaction between the two in the admissions process? Our answer is that, first, for all the reasons given in this chapter, more efforts should be made to recruit and enroll students of all races from modest backgrounds. Second, for reasons elaborated in chapter 6, we also believe that race needs to be considered on its own terms. We do not accept the proposition that it is only minority students from poor families who should receive special consideration in the admissions process. It is useful to recall Justice Thurgood Marshall's observation in his separate opinion in Bakke: "the racism of our society has been so pervasive that none, regardless of wealth or position, has managed to escape its impact."[73]

The ramifications of this fact of life are reflected in two important statistical findings concerning academic underperformance. First, we have seen that low SES is not, in and of itself, associated with underperformance, whereas race is. Second, when we look within the minority population, we find that underperformance runs across all SES categories and that minority students from the bottom income quartile are actually less likely to underperform than are minority students from the top three quartiles. At the 18 institutions in our study for which we can perform the analysis, minority students from the bottom income quartile exhibit rank-in-class underperformance of just under 6 percentile points, whereas those from the top three quartiles exhibit underperformance of just over 9 percentile points. These results are consistent with the thesis that stereotype vulnerability can afflict *all* minority students, and there are surely other factors (not fully understood) that also affect the academic performance of minority students in general.

If we are to disabuse ourselves and others (including minority students themselves) of the attitudinal constraints that can be so damaging, we need to include in campus communities minority students who come from a wide variety of backgrounds and who will go on to set standards and lead by example. In *The Shape of the River,* Bowen and Bok recount a discussion that occurred when a distinguished black educator visited the Mellon Foundation:

> [The black educator] noted, with understandable pride, that his son had done brilliantly in college and was being considered for a prestigious graduate award in neuroscience. "My son," the professor said, "needs no special consideration: he is so talented that he will make it on his own." His conclusion was that we should be indifferent to whether his son or [his son's] white competitors got the particular fellowship in question. We agreed that, in all likelihood, all of these candidates would benefit from going to the graduate school in question and, in time, become excellent scientists or doctors. Still one can argue with the conclusion reached by the parent. "Your son will do fine," another person at the meeting [James Shulman] said, "but that isn't the issue. *He may not need us, but we need him!* Why? Because there is only one of him."
>
> That mild exaggeration notwithstanding, the relative scarcity of talented black professionals is all too real. It seemed clear to a number of us that day, and it probably seems clear to many others, that American society needs the high-achieving black graduates who will provide leadership in every walk of life.[74]

It is not, in our view, a matter of either/or. We believe that institutions should consider both socioeconomic status and race in the admissions process.

THE "MERIT AID" DEBATE

In this final section of the chapter, we will summarize another aspect of the debate over how institutions treat SES—but this time from the perspective of student aid policies rather than admissions. We will broaden our frame of reference to include colleges and universities generally, not just the 19 highly selective schools for which we have detailed data. This discussion of institutional policies will be brief (in part because the available data are so limited). It will focus on defining issues, identifying broad trends, and emphasizing that certain principles may work better in some institutional settings than in others. This consideration of financial aid at the institutional level will then lead to a still broader discussion in the next chapter of Pell Grants, various governmental merit aid and loan programs, and related policy choices at the federal and state levels.

Concepts and Definitions

We put "merit aid" (sometimes called "non-need-based aid") in quotation marks because this is an instance in which nomenclature is confusing and clear definitions are hard to find. At one level, everyone understands that "merit aid" refers to grants and other forms of assistance offered by colleges and universities to students because of their "merit" (however defined[75]) rather than because of their "need" (as determined by a complex needs analysis that takes into account family circumstances and the costs of the college or university at which the student is enrolled). One complication to note is that "merit aid" will often go to students with demonstrated need (in combination with, or in place of, other need-based aid), and the total of what is *called* "need-based aid" will therefore understate the overall amount of financial aid that serves to meet demonstrated need (even though merit aid grants may not meet full need).

At the same time, the composition of "need-based aid" packages often reflects judgments based in considerable measure on perceived merit. Financial aid officers sometimes speak of an approach called "merit within need," a concept that Michael McPherson explains this way:

> The canonical case would be a school that says that it awards no "merit aid." All aid is need-based and the school meets the "full need" of all students. But the package of aid that meets need is very different for different students, depending on their attractiveness to the institution. So a highly attractive student may get all her aid in the form of grants, while the least attractive students may have a $7000 loan as part of the package. Student A and student B have the same total "need," say $20,000, but student A gets a set of grants (federal, state, and institutional) totaling $20,000 while student B gets $13,000 in total grants and $7,000 in loans. Both have their need "fully met," but clearly the student with more merit gets a better deal. So, to my mind "merit within need" refers to "packaging" decisions. . . . Nobody need be receiving anything called a "merit award," but the need-based aid packages are better for students who are judged to have higher merit.[76]

Finally, it should be recognized that schools themselves generally report how much of their aid is "need-based" and how much is "merit-based" using their own definitions of these somewhat arbitrary categories. The consequences are that "some colleges find it to be effective marketing to re-label need-based aid as a merit scholarship while others, in an attempt to minimize the percentage of their aid budget reportedly allocated in terms of merit, do just the opposite."[77]

Trends: The Re-emergence of Merit Aid

This semantical jungle provides a clear warning that no one should pretend to understand fully what institutions are doing or be overly confident about the reliability (never mind the precision) of published data. Taking one step back, however, it is possible to describe broad trends at a wide range of institutions that have implications for both equity and excellence objectives (as opposed to the trends in need-blind admissions or meet-full-need policies described at the beginning of this chapter, which apply mostly to very selective, wealthy institutions). As several good histories of the "need" versus "merit aid" debate make clear, a critical event was the creation of the College Scholarship Service (CSS) in 1954 for the express purpose of applying a uniform methodology in the determination of financial need (in an effort to discourage "bidding wars"; the correspondence to the motivation for forming the group of "overlap schools," described earlier, is clear). By the 1960s, the CSS system of needs analysis had become generally accepted and widely used. The growing national concern for equity, reflected in initiatives such as the War on Poverty and the development of need-based governmental aid programs, encouraged the adoption of a need-based approach at the institutional level. Through the 1970s, there was a growing emphasis on the desirability of meeting applicants' "full need" and of downplaying merit awards, though many schools continued to make them. Then, as competition for students increased in the late 1970s and the 1980s, policies changed and student aid came to be seen increasingly as an "institutional tool" to be employed in enrollment-management programs. As many people observed, the merit award programs that expanded in the 1980s and the 1990s were in many respects a "return to prior policies."[78] The era of strong, broad-based support for the "need-based ideal" was relatively brief.

According to a national survey of colleges and universities: "Approximately three-quarters of the four-year institutions offered no-need ['merit'] awards to accepted applicants in 2000. . . . Between 1979 and 2000, the offering of no-need awards increased in all sectors except for two-year private institutions."[79] In 2000, these no-need awards went to a variety of groups of students: among the four-year private institutions, 66 percent of the schools made awards to the academically talented, 44 percent to students with special nonacademic talents, 38 percent to athletes, 35 percent to racial/ethnic minorities, and 27 percent to disadvantaged students.[80] The same survey reports that half (52 percent) of four-year private institutions answered "Yes" to the following question: "Type of financial aid offered is related to academic ability of student?" Just about a quarter (26 percent) of four-year public institutions gave the same response.[81]

One recent government study (the National Postsecondary Student Aid Study, or NPSAS) presents a similar picture of broad trends but adds important information related to family income, types of awards received, and school selectivity. The main findings are summarized succinctly:

> This study found that the percentage of full-time students receiving institutional grant aid increased measurably between the early and late 1990s. Increases in aid were especially apparent for students in the highest income quartile, and much of the increase was awarded in the form of merit aid. The study also found that students who achieved high academic merit in high school were more likely to receive institutional grant aid if they attended less selective rather than very selective institutions. . . . In very selective institutions (in both the public and private not-for-profit sectors) the likelihood of high-merit students receiving institutional grant aid increased with their financial need.[82]

Michael McPherson and Morton Schapiro are actively engaged in analyzing microdata collected through the three waves of the NPSAS in order to determine—for the first time, with sound empirical methods—the interrelationships among family income, SAT scores, and the awarding of institutional aid. A principal early finding is that "both income background and SAT scores play a large role in determining how much aid a student receives." At private four-year institutions, by far the largest amount of aid goes—as one might have hoped would be the case—to students with high SAT scores from the lowest income bracket ($9,541 per student, on average), but students with high SAT scores from the top income bracket also receive substantial aid ($3,406, on average). The amount of aid falls off sharply within each income bracket as SAT scores fall—an apparently clear indication of the importance of merit. The average amount of aid also falls off as income increases, but much less sharply. Even within the category of "need-based grants," the amount of grant aid varies directly with SAT scores: for example, students with high SAT scores from the low-income category receive an average of $6,954 in need-based grants, whereas students with mid-range SATs scores from the same income category receive $3,113 and students with low SAT scores (in the context of this generally high-testing student population) receive $1,614.[83] This would seem to be rather clear evidence of "merit within need." However, McPherson and Schapiro warn that their results do not control for the effects of school selectivity. And it is important to recognize that students with high SAT scores are more likely to attend expensive schools—and thus to require more aid—than students with low SAT scores.

In terms of trends, a troubling (preliminary) finding is that "affluent students are receiving larger and larger tuition discounts [financial aid awards] while those from low income backgrounds for the most part are not."[84] Between 1996 and 2000, students with high SAT scores from high-income families saw their average amount of financial aid go up by over 40 percent in real terms (from an average of $2,378 to $3,406, in year 2000 dollars). Students from upper-middle-income families also received larger percentage increases in awards (at all SAT levels) than did students from low-income families. The absolute amounts of aid provided to students from low-income families remain appreciably higher than the amounts provided to students from high-income families, but the differences in awards between students from low-income families and those at the same SAT levels from middle-income families have narrowed markedly.[85]

Principles and Policies

At the most abstract level, equity considerations would seem to require that institutionally provided aid be distributed primarily, if not solely, on the basis of need. However, as McPherson and Schapiro argue in an earlier study:

> The simple morality of the "need-blind, full-need" approach is both too simple and too limited to provide a general guide to colleges and universities in shaping their aid policies. . . . The handful of schools that practice a "need-blind, full need" approach to financial aid are distinguished mainly by the exceptional resources, both of endowment and of affluent high-quality applicants, that allow them to sustain the practice. . . . When representatives of this relatively privileged set of institutions advocate "need-blind, full need" policies for all of higher education, their position is both impractical and, in some measure, even if unconsciously, self-serving.[86]

From the perspective of the most selective schools, the pure need-based approach (or relatively pure, remembering the "merit within need" qualification) has a great deal to be said for it. It would be wrong, many of us would argue, for these schools to "waste" resources by providing merit aid to students whose families can afford to pay the fees that are charged—though we must remember always that these fees do not come close to covering the full cost of the education that is provided and that, therefore, these schools are already providing substantial subsidies to every one of their students, whatever the family's financial circumstances.[87] Moreover, if these top-ranked schools lose some students to other institutions because the other schools provide merit aid, they have a large reservoir of outstanding applicants ready to enroll.

The situation is different, however, at schools that are harder pressed financially (and thus may not, as a practical matter, be able to meet the full need of all admitted students) and that lack the luxury of being able to choose among a very deep pool of exceptionally well-qualified applicants. Many of the Ohio colleges studied by Duffy and Goldberg fit this description, and their case studies, replete with quotations from presidents and others at these colleges, explain well why these schools elected to employ some combination of need and merit awards when competition for well-qualified students intensified in the 1980s and 1990s. Alfred MacKay, the acting president of Oberlin during the 1991–92 school year, criticized a need-based aid policy that "offers all admitted students the same financial aid package whether or not the students are specially wanted by us or by others" as foolishly utopian and costly. These colleges, and others like them, used merit aid "to attract high-ability students who otherwise might not have considered attending a small liberal arts college in the Midwest."[88] At the conclusion of their study, Duffy and Goldberg write:

> When we began our research on this book, we were opposed to merit aid. However, as we learned more about the evolution of financial aid in this country and the particular situations and practices at the colleges in our study, we adopted a more nuanced attitude toward merit scholarships. . . . Spending large amounts of financial aid on students who barely meet admissions cutoffs, as some of the colleges we studied were doing before they began merit and preferential packaging programs, makes little sense for either institutions or the students thus enrolled. If you believe, as we do, that the composition of a class affects the education students receive, then colleges that no longer have competitive admissions should be able to invest their money to attract diverse, well-qualified students from the full range of socioeconomic backgrounds. If, as supporters of merit aid imply, the existence of such programs will encourage high school scholars, like high school athletes, to excel, so much the better.[89]

In summing up this discussion, there are five points that we would like to underscore:

- First, there is evidence that the "peer effects" on learning outcomes mentioned by Duffy and Goldberg are real. To the extent this is the case, there is a clear "excellence" trade-off to be considered in situations such as those faced by the Ohio colleges. Being able to attract some number of outstanding students who otherwise would have gone elsewhere—perhaps to a different kind of institution altogether (such as a private college in the Northeast or a public university in the Midwest)—can have multiple positive and reinforcing effects: on the interest of other good students in applying to the school in question, on campus ethos and intellectual vitality, and on the pleasure that faculty derive from teaching good students.[90]

- Second, judicious use of merit awards need not have as damaging an effect on funds available for need-based awards as is sometimes assumed. In fact, careful use of targeted student aid funds can improve the overall financial situation of a college rather than weaken it. There is often at least a modest amount of excess capacity at a school that is struggling to meet its enrollment target, and admitting one more qualified student who can cover some part of his or her educational costs may make sense financially as well as educationally. The evidence examined by Duffy and Goldberg does not suggest that, at the schools they studied, increases in merit aid led to anything like proportionate reductions in need-based aid. Of the schools in their study, all but one increased their need-based aid at the same time that they were expanding merit aid, and most were funding at least 90 percent of demonstrated need. The picture in more recent years appears murkier, however.[91]

- Third, the word "judicious" in the previous paragraph is important. A college can become so obsessed with its standing vis-à-vis its competitors, and especially historic rivals, that it yields to the temptation to attempt to "buy" a student who simply prefers to go to some similar school. It is this use of merit awards that is most difficult to justify (along with athletic scholarships, which are also a type of "merit" award). It is hard to see what societal values would be served by having schools within the Ivy League, for example, bid against each other for high-achieving students from wealthy families, given the likelihood that most of these students would end up somewhere within the broad set of "Ivy-like" schools in any case. Nor is it evident that efforts to "buy" students will work, given the "game theory" aspect of such competitions for students. Attempting to bid a student away from another college may simply stimulate offsetting bids, and colleges may end up receiving less revenue from essentially the same students as before—a classic outcome of price wars.[92]

- Fourth, the trends toward more no-need aid, and toward concentrating such aid on relatively affluent students, cause one to question whether these policies are being pushed too hard. At some point, the "equity" costs of such policies cannot be justified in terms of claims that they are offset by gains in educational quality.

- The fifth and last conclusion that we take away from this discussion, and from our review of the relevant literature, is an obvious one: individual colleges and universities must be expected to act in what they perceive to be their own best interests. If the circumstances of a particular college threaten its ability to maintain its character or quality, and if it believes that merit scholarships will help "right the ship," no amount of exhortation from outside is likely to convince the school that its first obligation is to meet the full need of the entire range of students that it admits.

We are *not* proposing that the freedom of institutions to make such decisions (including decisions concerning tuition levels and educational costs as well as types and amounts of financial aid awarded) be limited. On the contrary, as we argued in chapter 3, it is precisely the decentralized and variegated structure of this country's higher education system that gives it so much vitality. The point we are making is simply that the full consequences of the sum total of the decisions reached by individual institutions need not reflect the larger values or objectives of the society. No institution should be expected to put someone else's sense of societal interests ahead of its own priorities, which is why government programs are needed—to function alongside the initiatives taken by individual institutions and to address squarely barriers to the achievement of core societal values such as equal opportunity. In the next chapter we examine how well such policies actually work, at both national and state levels, and whether they can be improved.

CHAPTER 8

Government Support of Higher Education

The higher education market, left to itself, cannot be expected to produce socially optimal results. Imperfect information, credit constraints, and externalities ("spill-over benefits") are all relevant. Potential students may underinvest in their own education, and the interest of society as a whole in outcomes such as preparation for citizenship, the promotion of social mobility, and the advancement of learning may not be served adequately if market mechanisms alone have to be relied upon to determine the resources available to higher education and their allocation. Government, at every level, has a significant role to play in correcting imperfections and seeing that the needs of the entire society are taken into account.

This chapter focuses on government policies at the tertiary level that are related to the provision of undergraduate education at four-year institutions. State-supported two-year colleges, which play an increasingly important role in educating students from disadvantaged backgrounds, warrant further study. Their specific concerns, however, are not dealt with here. Similarly, government support of graduate education and advanced research is a subject all its own, one we do not address. Finally, we reserve for chapter 9 discussion of the considerable role government (and especially local government) plays in college preparation from preprimary through secondary education.

With respect to equity, the goals of government in supporting undergraduate education are, in our view, quite clear: to increase the college-going rate of those who are prepared for college, to increase the likelihood that students will be able to attend a college that is a good match for them, to minimize the risk that students will leave college for financial reasons before attaining their degrees, and to do all of this in a cost-effective way.[1] This is, needless to say, much easier said than done! Developing a policy that will achieve just one of these goals is no easy task. There are innumerable assumptions that have to be made in establishing operational definitions for each goal, and there are certain to be conflicting views as to how much money should be spent, how a program should be administered, and so on. When the resolution of these complicated questions takes place in a legislature or other political forum—as it must, when it is governmental policies that are at issue—there is bound to be compromise.

In the federal system of the United States, there are of course several levels of government that may be involved in setting policy, sometimes cooperatively and sometimes independently. The bulk of public higher education funding and activity takes place at the state level, primarily through the mechanism of state government appropriations to public colleges and universities—which totaled nearly $68 billion in 2003.[2] State governments also provide student-level support through grants and loans, but the federal government provides most of the financial aid for students. In this chapter we will address what we see as the major policy questions in providing financial aid to students and institutional support through appropriations to public colleges and universities. We conclude the chapter with an examination of the controversy in the United Kingdom over "top-up" fees, which raises many of the same choices and political issues debated in the United States. Similar debates are going on in many other countries, but we focus on the situation in the United Kingdom, treating it as a case study.

GOVERNMENT-FUNDED FINANCIAL AID
AT THE UNDERGRADUATE LEVEL

In recent years, the debate over how best to structure financial aid for undergraduates has coalesced around two major issues.

- The first we will call "targeting." This part of the debate revolves around the question of who should receive government money to assist in paying for college and whether the current distribution of funding maximizes enrollment and retention. The advent in the mid-1990s of broad-scale, state-sponsored merit aid programs (such as the Georgia HOPE Scholarship program) has been a natural focal point for this debate, but the more recent introductions of federal tax credits for tuition payments and tax-favored college savings plans are also controversial and deserve careful consideration.
- The second broad issue that has inspired passionate debate is one we call "resources versus mechanisms." The nub of contention is whether existing programs can be strengthened most effectively by increasing the amount of money dedicated to them (using mechanisms essentially in their present forms) or by adjusting the mechanisms through which current funding is distributed.

Analyzing every major federal and state financial aid program is well beyond the scope of this study. What we will do here is sketch the boundaries of these two debates and offer our perspective on each, using the results of recent research to inform the discussion.

Targeting Government Financial Aid: Principles and Practices

Traditionally, federally funded financial aid has been need-based. Eligibility for the two largest federal student aid programs, the Pell Grants and the Stafford Loans, is determined by a complex formula that uses income, assets, and family size (as provided by the student on the Free Application for Federal Student Aid, or FAFSA) and is limited to those whose financial need is substantial. One study estimates that 90 percent of dependent students who receive federal grants are from families with incomes below $40,000.[3]

In recent years, however, and especially since the early 1990s, a number of states have adopted a different approach. Over a dozen have created merit-based aid programs that typically provide "tuition and fees to young residents who have maintained a modest grade point average in high school."[4] (Although this is a departure from the tradition of providing need-based financial aid at the federal level, in some ways it can be seen as a continuation of the tradition of providing non-need-based subsidies through state appropriations to public colleges and universities.) The best known of these programs is Georgia's HOPE Scholarship program, which provides scholarships that cover tuition at any Georgia public institution and subsidizes tuition at Georgia's private institutions for students with a high school GPA above 3.0, regardless of financial need.

Since the late 1990s, the federal government has also established programs that depart from adherence to purely need-based eligibility criteria. During the Clinton administration, two tax credits for parents with children in college (or for college students who are financially independent) were written into the tax code—the Hope Scholarship (named after Georgia's merit scholarship program) and the Lifetime Learning Credit.[5] These are "tax reduction" programs in that they are non-refundable (i.e., they can be used only to reduce one's taxes and hence are of no value to families that pay no taxes), and both reimburse families only for out-of-pocket tuition expenditures. Furthermore, tax reduction payments may be disbursed months after fall term tuition payments are due, creating short-term liquidity crunches for students who depend on these credits. As a result, these programs are regressive, providing very little benefit for low-income families who not only have low tax burdens but also receive need-based grants that defray much if not all of their out-of-pocket tuition expenditures.[6]

During roughly the same period, the federal government and state governments authorized savings plans that allow parents to make investments on behalf of their children, which, if used to pay for college tuition, will not be taxed (either principal or interest). Families at all income levels are eligible for these "529" savings plans, which have features similar to those of an Individual Retirement Account (IRA) (though there are slight differences among the 529 plans in different states and between them and the federal Coverdell Education Savings Account). Not surprisingly, given the structure of state and federal tax systems, the advantages of these plans are strongly correlated with economic circumstances: families with higher incomes benefit much more from participating in the plans than do those with lower incomes.[7]

The creation of these non-need or "merit-based" aid programs is seen by critics as a clear shift not just away from government-funded aid policies that are progressive, but toward regressive policies. As we just pointed out, tax incentives such as the Hope Scholarship and the Lifetime Learning Credit, and savings plans like the 529 and the Coverdell plans, provide very little benefit to poor students and their families. Merit aid plans like the Georgia HOPE Scholarship are awarded more frequently to students from higher-income families than to those from lower-income families because students from higher-income families tend to perform better academically. The regressive nature of the state-level HOPE Scholarship program is compounded by the fact that it is funded with lottery revenue (as are similar programs in other states), which comes mainly from the pockets of low-income people.[8] Furthermore, when state aid money is committed to merit-based programs, there is an inevitable worry that such funds may be diverted from need-based programs.

Beyond the basic issue of fairness, there are also serious questions as to whether these programs serve the country's equity and excellence goals: Are they inspiring capable students to enroll in college who would not enroll otherwise? Do they allow students to move from less expensive to more expensive institutions, to which they may be better suited? Do they encourage students who enroll to persist to graduation? For the savings plans, it may be too early to tell; they have not been in place long enough for suitable data to be collected. However, it is already clear that these accounts are held predominantly by individuals who are better educated and wealthier than the general population of parents, and it seems highly unlikely that these savings plans will be found to have much of an impact on enrollment. Children from families who elect to participate in the savings plans almost surely would go to college in any case. The savings plans may, however, enable middle-class students to choose to attend a more expensive college.

The impact of the federal tax credits, which have a similar distribution profile, may provide a clue as to the effects that the savings plans are likely to have. One study finds that the Hope and Lifetime credits did not benefit low-income students or boost their college enrollment rates, but were used mainly by middle-class families with income between $30,000 and $75,000. Unfortunately, the available data do not allow an analysis of the effect of the tax credits on college choice.[9]

In contrast to what has been learned about the effects of federal tax incentives, Susan Dynarski, among other researchers, found that the

Georgia HOPE merit scholarship program, designed in part to keep talented students in-state, did increase the share of young people attending college by between 6 and 8 percentage points, relative to young people in other Southern, non–merit aid states. And while the HOPE Scholarship does not seem to have improved the enrollment of black and Hispanic students in Georgia, in the three other states that Dynarski studied, the enrollment effects of state scholarship programs for black and Hispanic students are greater than the enrollment effect for whites.[10] Moreover, Dynarski found that the merit aid programs she studied increase the probability that students will enroll in four-year institutions, suggesting that the awards improve access to more expensive institutions.[11]

Despite these positive results, this type of merit aid is highly suspect from the standpoint of cost effectiveness. Although there certainly seems to be a net increase in the share of young people enrolled in college as a result of these programs, the bulk of students receiving merit aid awards are, according to Dynarski, from "infra-marginal . . . families whose schooling decisions are unaffected by their receipt of aid."[12] Most recipients do not seem to use the additional resources to purchase more or better education. Instead, many of the families who received this windfall simply increased their non-education consumption—by buying a new car, for example.[13] There also appears to be an unanticipated negative effect on academic quality due to the fact that the HOPE Scholarship and many of its offspring have college GPA requirements that students must meet in order to continue to receive the awards. There is some evidence that these requirements are causing students to take fewer credits or easier courses.[14] Grade inflation at the high school level may also weaken actual achievement and result in a larger pool of eligible students.

In sum, merit aid—unlike savings plans and tax credits—does seem to encourage students to enroll and does increase the financial aid provided to some low-income students (perhaps in part by encouraging them to obtain Pell Grants[15]). However, merit aid programs also achieve their effects at a high cost. Georgia lawmakers recently had to rein in the program to avoid a predicted $434 million deficit.[16] There are also serious questions concerning how merit aid dollars are distributed, with the bulk of the money providing a windfall for students from the middle and upper-middle income classes who would have gone to college anyway. In short, merit aid programs are poorly targeted in that— viewed in the context of the goals articulated at the beginning of this chapter—they spend considerable resources to achieve a relatively small improvement in college-going rates of students from low-income families.

However, there is another side to this argument that deserves consideration. Some scholars (most notably social scientists Theda Skocpol and

William Julius Wilson) have noted the political potency of what Skocpol calls "targeting within universality." The key proposition is that for a program to be viable politically, the public must feel that it is open to everyone, even if it disproportionately benefits the disadvantaged. This explains the great popularity of programs like Social Security.[17] However, there is one major difference between the set of financial aid programs being discussed here (tax credit programs, tax-favored savings programs, and merit aid programs) and programs like Social Security: the former disproportionately benefit advantaged families, whereas Social Security disproportionately benefits the disadvantaged.[18]

One further point about targeting. If the goal is to use aid dollars most effectively, then a need-based framework is best, but there may be room within that framework for differentiation based on merit or other characteristics. (As discussed at the end of the previous chapter, this is the approach many individual colleges and universities use in applying their "merit-within-need" philosophies.) Governmental programs use a variant of this approach in that students receive need-based aid only up to the amount of their college costs, which are higher at more selective, more expensive institutions. But the mechanism for providing aid—and the amount available through some programs, such as the Pell Grant program—is the same whether the student is 18 and a dependent or 48 and a parent, whether the student has a 1500 SAT score or a GED, and whether the student is attending a state flagship university and studying physics or is gaining vocational certification at a for-profit proprietary institution.[19]

It is extremely difficult to structure a set of incentives that will provide appropriate degrees of differentiation, and the current situation is, in many ways, the result of a political balancing act, with proprietary institutions playing a particularly powerful hand.[20] Nor are most of us entirely comfortable deciding (or, for that matter, having the government decide) which higher education pursuits are more valuable than others. Nevertheless, some effort should be made to ensure that, after targeting aid to those who need it most, the distribution of financial aid is weighted toward those who will put it to the best use. In principle, aid should be targeted so as to maximize the expected societal return on the investment of public funds.

More Resources or Better Mechanisms?

There is no question that, in principle, the most efficient financial aid programs are those that are very well targeted. However, even if the eligibility rules are appropriate, it is possible for an aid program to be ineffective. As we saw in chapter 4, Thomas Kane and others have found very little evidence that the Pell Grant program—the country's largest need-based aid program—had any substantial effect on enrollment when it was first introduced and provided generous assistance.[21] That brings us to the second "hot topic" in the financial aid debate: whether need-based programs, like the Pell Grant program, can be improved more by increasing their funding or by changing the way they are defined and administered.

The "more resources" partisans note that in 1986 the average Pell Grant covered 98 percent of average tuition at public four-year colleges; in 1999 it covered just 57 percent.[22] The conclusion they draw from this is that the Pell Grant program is ineffective today because the grants are no longer large enough to make college affordable for the poorest students. However, there is evidence that Pell Grants did not increase the enrollment of low-income students even in the 1970s, when the program began and grants covered close to full tuition (as they also did in 1986).[23]

Kane suggests an alternative hypothesis for the ineffectiveness of the program. He notes that, in contrast to the experience with the Pell Grant program, students from low-income families exhibit definite enrollment responses to changes in tuition, to merit-based aid programs, and to changes in other payouts that are not means tested. Each of these other approaches provides clear guidelines on how much money is involved and how the "benefits" affect the students (reduced tuition if they enroll in a particular school, X dollars toward tuition if they have a "B" average in high school, and so on). The Pell Grant program, on the other hand, relies on a complicated process of need analysis that a student is not allowed to complete until the spring before the student enrolls in college. It is then up to the college to inform the student how much aid he or she will receive under the program. So it is only those who are on the verge of enrolling in college who can learn whether they are eligible for a Pell Grant and other means-tested federal financial aid, and how much they will receive.[24]

Other prospective students (those who are uncertain about whether to attend college, and might be swayed to do so by an offer of sufficient aid) may be unaware of the support to which they are entitled and confused about how to get it. One literature review from the early 1990s found that students from low-income families and their parents often do not understand the application process or their own eligibility for aid.[25] Beyond simply being unaware of what resources may be available, the potential applicant from a poor family may find that the application itself poses a substantial challenge. As Kane writes: "For those who itemize their taxes, the financial aid form may be less complicated than a tax form; but for those who do not itemize, the application form is likely to be *more* vexing."[26] Kane's argument is that the culprits for the lack of impact of the Pell Grant may be the complexity of the application and the obscure connection between family characteristics and aid, rather than the amount of money provided through the program. His recommendation is to simplify the need analysis formula (perhaps just to a grid of family size and income) and minimize the application burden.[27]

The Advisory Committee on Student Financial Assistance (ACSFA), a congressionally created council on financial aid, disagrees with Kane's approach. ACSFA argues that federal aid application forms are straightforward and that early information about financial aid could be more discouraging than encouraging. Then, having concluded that existing "mechanisms" are fine, ACSFA's main policy proposal is to increase the maximum award amount of the Pell Grant.[28] In our view, there is sufficient evidence casting doubt on the effectiveness of the current mechanisms to justify pursuing Kane's approach. For example, early research on the College Opportunity and Career Help (COACH) project (described in chapter 4) found that assistance with the college and financial aid application processes in the last year of high school increased knowledge about these processes and likely improved college enrollment among disadvantaged students.[29] Also, evidence from Georgia suggests that there may be numerous students who are eligible for Pell Grants but do not fill out the FAFSA in the absence of some stronger external motivation (such as the desire to obtain a HOPE Scholarship by completing the form).[30] A further argument in favor of simplifying the eligibility criteria and the application process is that one could do so virtually costlessly. There is much to be said for adopting inexpensive approaches, such as simplifying the need analysis formula, as a first order of business.[31]

ACSFA's focus on increasing grant aid is illustrative of another aspect of the resources versus mechanics debate. Those advocating the investment of more resources typically lament the fact that the amount of federal support dedicated to grant aid has declined relative to the amount dedicated to loans. For example, the National Center for Public Policy and Higher Education reported that in 1981 loans accounted for 45 percent of federal aid, and grants accounted for 52 percent, whereas in 2000 some 58 percent of federal aid was in the form of loans and 41 percent was in grants.[32]

Loans clearly are not as valuable to the individual as grants, because the principal and interest must be paid back over time. However, from a system-wide perspective, an aid policy weighted toward loans may be a more cost-effective approach. Loans are less of a boon to the borrower than grants are to the recipient, but they are also less expensive to the lender or grantor. This means that, given a limited capacity to provide financial aid, more students can be helped through loan programs than through grants, and the average loan can be larger than the average grant.[33] The drawback of loans is, of course, that the amount of debt students must incur may dissuade them from taking loans in the first place —and this concern is especially real in the case of poor students and their families, who may not have experience with large loans, who may have had bad experience with other kinds of debt (like credit card debt), and who may simply be more apprehensive about the future than those with higher income. The concern about taking out loans to pay for education is compounded by the fact that education itself is a risky venture because outcomes are not guaranteed—and there is no way to diversify the risk faced by an individual. To the extent that students from low-income families are more likely to be on the fence about going to college (given their lower levels of college preparedness, described in chapter 4), their perception of risk is likely to be even higher.

One possible solution is a relatively straightforward income-contingent loan repayment plan of the kind proposed by Kane. Under this plan, the payment schedule (though not the obligation to pay) would depend on a student's income after college, thereby reducing the risk involved in accumulating student debt. Income-contingent methods of paying for college have been debated for decades, and any feasible plan has to guard against adverse selection. There are two ways to provide relief to low-income borrowers—to extend the term of the loan for those who struggle in the job market after college or to provide some loan forgiveness to low-income borrowers. The current federal income-contingent loan primarily extends the term of the loan, which can be done at relatively low cost. However, the cost of any additional loan forgiveness for low-income borrowers would have to be borne by taxpayers. It would be difficult to make such a scheme self-supporting by charging high-income borrowers high rates, because the high-income borrowers would simply opt out of the system.[34]

More generally, some variant of the income-contingent approach has the great appeal of reducing the risk that a debt-encumbered student who goes into a low-paying job (such as teaching) or encounters health problems will end up in dire straits. This is surely one reason—a politically important reason—why in the United Kingdom the recent introduction of higher tuition rates anticipates deferring collection of these fees until after a former student has reached a certain income threshold.[35] By its forward-looking nature, an income-contingent plan has the benefit of providing "insurance" for students from middle- and higher-income families—although, since their potential earnings are lower, it will disproportionately benefit disadvantaged students. This is a good example of the kind of politically practical "targeting within universality" approach mentioned earlier, but one that does not involve providing another entitlement unrelated to need.

We should emphasize that we are not advocating anything like a complete shift from grants to loans, because a substantial grant component in aid packages certainly makes the decision to go to college much easier for the poorest students. But we do believe that there is much to be said for using loans to supplement grants for students from low-income families and as the primary source of government aid for those in the middle (especially the upper-middle) part of the income distribution.

We would hope that simplifying the federal need analysis formula and decreasing the risk associated with borrowing through an income-contingent approach would improve the appeal of existing need-based financial aid programs. In terms of cost-effectiveness, and thinking in terms of likely effects on enrollment, these seem to us to be more logical next steps than simply raising the level of funding provided through the existing Pell Grant system (though that may also be needed to prevent erosion of current levels of support).

We recognize that one objection to the "simplify, simplify, simplify" approach we are advocating is that forcing applicants to jump over some number of hurdles before receiving assistance may have value in discouraging students from enrolling in college without having really thought through what is best for them.[36] But we do not believe the proposals we have endorsed reduce the "costs" of enrolling in college to such a low level that ill-prepared and basically disinterested students will flood the system. The prospective student must still value education more than whatever job is available without attending college, must apply to and be accepted by a college (if the point of entry is anything other than an open-admissions institution), and must still repay loans, even if they are subsidized and repayment schedules are income contingent.[37] Other "mechanism" adjustments (such as making access to the benefits of the income-contingent repayment plan dependent on attaining a degree and increasing institutional investment in supporting marginal students) can be employed to limit the downside risks.

In addition to lending directly to students and families, the federal government subsidizes and supports student loan provision through the Federal Family Education Loan (FFEL) program, which guarantees loans made by private lenders to postsecondary students and their families. The yield private lenders earn on FFEL loans is determined by a formula mandated by Congress—a formula that has led to substantial windfall subsidies to private lenders despite measures intended to correct these riskless transfers. The yield was reduced as interest rates fell, but grandfather clauses and loopholes actually caused the amount of loans guaranteed at the old 9.5 percent rate to mushroom from $12 billion at the end of 2002 to $17 billion by July 2004.[38] Setting the interest rate on these loans by congressional mandate rather than market mechanisms (perhaps through a contract auction) prevents the process from incorporating information about the lender's costs and interest rate expectations.[39] Reforms that correct only the rate level will not take these information asymmetries into account. A more comprehensive restructuring may be needed to streamline the federal student loan system and make it more efficient.[40]

To sum up: on both equity and efficiency grounds, we believe that aid should be targeted toward those who will benefit most and whose behavior can be most positively affected. So we do not support policies that redirect aid from the bottom of the income distribution to the upper-middle and top end, nor do we support those policies that provide benefits to all regardless of their financial status. But we can learn something important from experience with these policies—namely, that having clear eligibility criteria and "transparent" benefits can encourage prospective students to take advantage of available financial aid resources. Applying this line of thought to means-tested programs such as the Pell Grant program could improve their effectiveness. Some may question the political practicality of these policies; merit aid programs like the HOPE Scholarship program are extraordinarily popular among the general public, and the "more resources" advocates (including those associated with for-profit proprietary institutions) comprise a powerful constituency within higher education circles. But when governmental resources are severely limited (as we expect they will be for the foreseeable future), there is no alternative to fighting hard to make sure that each dollar of funding is put to its best use if the goals of equity and excellence are to be pursued successfully.

PUBLIC UNIVERSITIES: FINANCE, GOVERNANCE, AND RELATIONSHIP TO THE STATE

Although we suspect that when most people think of government support of higher education their attention is drawn to federal aid programs like those that offer the Pell Grant and the Stafford Loan, by far the largest transfer of government money to higher education occurs via the appropriations made by state governments to public colleges and universities. Public institutions receive more than one-third of their funds from state governments, approximately one-tenth from the federal government, and approximately one-fifth each from tuition and fees and from sales and services.[41] Yet, important as they continue to be, state appropriations have been declining for some years now, relative to other sources of support for public and private institutions of higher education. A 2003 Brookings Institution study by Thomas Kane and Peter Orszag begins with this succinct summary of funding trends:

> Over the past two decades, state financing of higher education has declined as a share of personal income. State appropriations have fallen from an average of roughly $8.50 per $1,000 in personal income in 1977 to an average of about $7.00 per $1,000 in personal income in 2002. Tuition increases have only partially offset the decline in state appropriations in allowing public institutions to keep up with private ones.

As a result, educational spending per full-time equivalent student has declined at public institutions relative to private institutions, from about 70 percent in 1977 to about 58 percent in 1996.[42]

In an earlier paper, Kane and Orszag attributed the decline in state higher education appropriations to expansions in Medicaid costs and interactions with the business cycle.[43] Medicaid costs are projected to continue to rise, and to rise dramatically. Unless there is a sudden shift in the willingness of the American people to pay for a larger share of the costs of health care at the national level, the prospects for reversing this funding trend are far from encouraging. It is also clear that the political context in which tuition levels are set imposes limits on the degree to which tuition revenues can be used to offset reductions in appropriations —a point to which we will return shortly.[44]

Kane and Orszag also cite a number of measures that suggest strongly that the decline in relative spending on higher education has affected the quality of the public universities:[45]

- Public universities have lost ground relative to private universities in the national rankings of universities. In 1987, 7 of the 26 top-rated universities in *U.S. News & World Report* were public institutions; by 2002, only 4 of the top 27 universities were public.
- Faculty salaries at public universities have declined relative to salaries at private universities. Kane and Orszag found that faculty salaries at public and private institutions were essentially equivalent prior to 1980, but by 1998 full professors at public universities earned just 82 percent as much as their colleagues at private institutions.
- The gap in student-teacher ratios between private and public institutions has widened. Between 1971 and 1997, the student-teacher ratio at private universities fell from 17.3 to 15.7, but the ratio rose from 21.1 to 21.5 at public universities.
- SAT scores of incoming undergraduate students dropped significantly at public universities relative to private universities between 1986 and 2000.
- Surveys indicate that faculty members at public universities are more likely than their counterparts at private universities to believe that the quality of education at their institutions has declined.

Because of the scale of the public sector (where roughly three-quarters of U.S. students are educated), this downward trend in measures of quality across the board is worrying. Furthermore, there is clearly cause to question the capacity of the best public universities to keep pace with the strongest of their private competitors. This situation is grounds for serious concern because of the reliance of the overall system of higher education on the "complementarities" provided by the existence of strong public and private institutions. Clark Kerr, as president of the University of California and then as head of the Carnegie Commission on Higher Education, never failed to emphasize that the health and vitality of this country's system of higher education depended on the continuing, mutually reinforcing contributions of both private and public institutions; the two sectors depend on each other for new ideas, for the stimulation that guards against complacency, and for mutual protection against inappropriate forms of political pressure.[46]

In considering the funding of public higher education, it is helpful to make use of two concepts: differentiation and devolution. State-sponsored higher education is not a monolith: there are vast differences in mission, resources, and clientele between the most selective public research universities and the less selective regional colleges, universities, and community colleges. For all intents and purposes, the leading state "flagship" schools are national, not state, institutions. Imposing one-size-fits-all regulations on them, and setting policy for them strictly on the basis of rather narrowly construed state interests, harms them more than it helps them or the state. The modest portions of the budgets of these flagships that state appropriations cover do not justify this level of control. At the same time, the regional institutions often suffer from having to compete with the more selective institutions for state funding and attention. These under-resourced institutions are where the most marginal college students enroll—a dangerous combination, as we explained in chapter 4.[47] "Differentiation" pertains in another sense. The support and guidance these institutions have received from the state since their inception have led the most selective public institutions to be more responsive to local economic needs (for instance, supporting departments in vocational fields), more conscious of ensuring access, and generally much larger (in terms of number of students) than their private university peers. Simply turning the public flagships into private institutions would not suit the purpose of any constituency and certainly would remove the benefit that results from the complementary contributions that the two types of institutions can make. But granting state flagship schools greater freedom and autonomy from legislative controls through a market-driven form of devolution—a development discussed later in this chapter—strikes us as a more efficacious way of balancing resources while reaffirming American higher education's complementarities.

The Public Flagships: Tuition and Governance Issues

Finding the resources needed to maintain top-quality institutions is one of the most fundamental challenges to the continuing excellence of the American system of higher education. There is no denying that the cost of science, in particular, has risen dramatically. Nor is there any denying the force of what Charles Clotfelter calls "unbounded aspirations" or the consequences of the fierce competitive drives that make the best people and the best places dissatisfied with their present circumstances.[48] In addition, the "handicraft" nature of personalized instruction—especially at the graduate level and in small-group settings at the undergraduate level—has played a role in causing university costs to rise faster than the Consumer Price Index for at least a century.[49]

State appropriations have not kept up with the increasing need for resources, and the consequences have been severe, particularly for the highly selective state flagship institutions.[50] In a recent editorial the *New York Times* was forceful in arguing: "The United States has been sabotaging its future for decades by starving the public colleges and universities that have moved millions of Americans into the middle class. . . . The gap between state aid and the real cost of an education is glaringly evident at the flagship public colleges, which often receive a pittance from the legislature while maintaining expensive, world-class programs that compete with those of top private colleges and universities."[51]

But although state governments provide a low and diminishing share of the necessary resources, they inhibit public universities from raising funds in other ways. An article in the *Chronicle of Higher Education* details pressures on (and by) state legislatures to put caps on tuition increases. David Breneman, the dean of the University of Virginia's Curry School of Education, is quoted as saying: "It's a silly game that is utterly predictable. . . . Governors and state legislators cut funds from state colleges knowing the cuts can be made up through tuition increases, and the public starts to squawk about affordability." Then, as Breneman observes, "A newly elected governor or legislature comes in on a white horse and says, 'You awful universities; you're squeezing people. I'm going to turn around and cap you.'"[52] We agree with Breneman and others that the worst possible situation is one in which states provide inadequate appropriations and then prevent the universities from setting tuition at what the institutional leaders believe is the appropriate level.[53]

The funding crunch caused by this dynamic affects the institutions themselves, their students, and the state. Insufficient resources cause public research universities to lose faculty members, students, and reputation relative to their more fiscally flexible (and nimble) private competitors. Tight budgets also often prevent these institutions from offering as many courses as students need or would like. One article on cutbacks at state universities describes a student "troll[ing] the university's Web site like a day trader, checking every few hours for the stray course opening that might suddenly appear."[54] States offer two motives for supporting top-flight universities: one is to develop the skilled workforce and the academic and research infrastructure that they need to maintain or strengthen their economy, and the other is to provide their citizens with access to high-quality higher education. Preventing these institutions from obtaining the resources they need hinders pursuit of both goals.[55]

Some of the most prominent public universities are fighting back. The *New York Times* editorial quoted earlier continues:

> The top public colleges have begun to balk at this arrangement. . . . In Virginia, the three most important public campuses [the University of Virginia, Virginia Tech, and William and Mary] . . . are seeking a so-called charter arrangement under which they would take a fixed amount of state money in exchange for more freedom from state regulations and the ability to raise tuition rates as they see fit. . . . This effort is clearly being driven by the University of Virginia, where the state's contribution now accounts for a piddling 8 percent of the budget. With state support shaky and declining, the University of Virginia and other elite schools are in danger of losing reputations and programs that took decades to build.[56]

Major public universities in other states have also started to react and have developed similarly novel solutions. David Breneman has drafted an informative paper that describes and analyzes a variety of initiatives in seven states (including Virginia) that in one way or another would alter the relationship between state governments and public higher education. A common feature of these proposals is that they involve more "market" features than have been common in public higher education. Some examples include an effort in Colorado to deliver state higher education funds in the form of vouchers to students instead of appropriations to institutions; a plan in Florida that calls for funding based on "performance contracts," whereby the state's major universities would receive lump sums of money and tuition control for agreeing to meet performance goals; and the passage in Texas of HB 3015, which allowed the state's universities to set tuition without legislative intervention.[57]

Perhaps the most notable of these plans is the one proposed in the spring of 2003 by James Garland, the president of Miami University in Oxford, Ohio. Garland recommended that the level of in-state tuition, then listed at $7,600, be raised to the level of out-of-state tuition ($16,300, at the time). The rationale was that the strong demand by out-of-state students for a Miami education had demonstrated its market value, that the university's chief competition came from the private sector, and (an unspoken assumption) that there was no reason that in-state families of means should be subsidized so heavily.[58] In the fall of 2004, with the approval of the Ohio legislature, all Miami students received tuition bills in the amount of approximately $19,640, but every in-state student also received an Ohio Resident Scholarship of $5,000, which was slightly more than the per-student subsidy provided by the state. This part of the proposal countered the obvious objection that Ohio residents had already paid for access to Miami through their taxes.

One large question concerns the equity aspects of such a plan. Thirty-five years ago, Lee Hansen and Burton Weisbrod argued persuasively that state subsidies that lowered tuition across the board would confer disproportionate benefits on higher-income families.[59] Miami University officials contend, however, that the increased revenue generated by the new tuition plan will assist Ohio's middle-income families who make too much money to qualify for federal aid programs but still have financial need. Under the Miami plan, additional student aid will be available in the form of an Ohio Leader Scholarship of between $5,000 and $6,200, with amounts varying according to merit, need, and a student's intention to major in subjects considered critical to the state's economic growth.[60] In general, we are more comfortable with a wholly (or largely) need-based approach to distributing these moneys than we are with providing merit aid to some students who may not really need it.[61] But we recognize that some modest differentiation according to merit, where there are substantial differences among students in achievements and potential, can benefit the learning environment at a school such as Miami University (refer back to the discussion of merit aid and peer group effects at the end of chapter 7). Also, we agree with the notion that a "high-tuition/ high-aid" policy would likely increase access to education for students from less well-off families.

Constraints on tuition policy are the most onerous limits that states put on their public universities, but they are hardly the only ones. Many states require that their public flagships enroll a certain portion of their class from among the pool of state residents. Others have very active, politically appointed trustees who involve themselves to varying degrees in university business from faculty hiring to football practice.[62] "Sunshine laws" have hampered the presidential search process in several states, because many potential candidates are understandably cautious about having their candidacy for a position made public (given ties to institutions where they are presently employed, or simply the potential embarrassment of being passed over for the job).[63] These kinds of intrusions make it more difficult for a public university searching for top leadership to compete with private institutions that have fewer constraints. Moreover, the degree of oversight is hard to justify when viewed in relation to the current level of financial support that most leading state universities receive from their legislatures.

Most public research universities, their students, and the states themselves would be better off if these institutions had more freedom to govern themselves, even if the consequences were further reductions in state appropriations. Evidence in support of this proposition is provided by the examples set by leading professional schools at many of these institutions. Law schools and business schools such as those at the University of Virginia and the University of Michigan charge tuition at more or less market levels, have active fundraising programs similar to those of their private competitors, are more open to residents of any state than are the undergraduate programs at the same schools, and receive very little state funding. It is no coincidence that they are, in many ways, the most successful and highly regarded units at these prominent state universities. However, it is necessary to add that causation surely flows in both directions: greater freedom to chart its own path can unquestionably strengthen an already strong program, but it is also far easier for an already strong program, than for a struggling program, to move ahead on its own.

As we said earlier, we are certainly not advocating eliminating the differences between public and private research universities in purposes and other characteristics—even if such a step were possible, which it plainly is not. Leading state universities offer work in fields that are crucial to the local economy (a good example is the Department of Dairy Science at the University of Wisconsin–Madison). In addition, their generally affluent student bodies notwithstanding, state flagship universities offer access to a high-quality university education to qualified state residents for whom out-of-state education may be unattractive or unaffordable. There are opportunities, we believe, for creative efforts to use some of the resources generated by higher tuitions and more aggressive fundraising (as well as continued state support) to pay for the recruitment and admission of students from modest backgrounds, especially those who live in resource-poor sections of the state, through application of the kind of "thumb on the scale" approach that we advocated in chapter 7. In this way, major public universities could continue to serve their historic missions within their states while also using some part of the same pool of resources to maintain the national standards necessary to serve the country's excellence objectives. This is another instance in which the goals of equity and excellence can be reinforcing.

The Regional Public Institutions: Investments with Potentially High Returns

In contrast to the state flagships, the other public institutions in a state typically do not recruit undergraduate students on a national level; they are more regionally oriented. Furthermore, these institutions are focused on access in quite a different way than the flagships. While the highly selective public universities offer residents of their states access to some of the best faculty in the world, well-equipped laboratories, and outstanding libraries and other resources, the more regional public institutions are typically attended by students who are closer to the margin of attending college, and the resources made available to them are of the more basic kinds (although there are, of course, some number of outstanding faculty, specialized resources, and high-achieving students in every setting). Recognizing that there are pronounced differences between these regional institutions, with some much stronger than others, we should point out that the resources available to them are often too basic; many are severely underfunded and can afford neither the personnel, the facilities, nor the tools necessary to assist students who require extra attention. The result, as we noted in chapter 4, is that a large fraction of these students drop out or "stop out."

If state resources and attention focused on the flagships continue to decline—either because of the forces already at work or as a consequence of new "bargains" whereby schools obtain greater institutional autonomy by giving up some claim on state resources—the state should be able to re-invest those freed-up funds in the regional institutions that are not in as strong a position to raise tuition or private funds. Tuition at these institutions could remain low as a result of this additional funding provided by the state, and the equity costs of across-the-board tuition subsidization documented by Hansen and Weisbrod are likely quite small in such situations, where many students are from poor or working-class families. Additional resources could also be used to improve the teaching and counseling capacities that would enable more marginal students to do college-level work and persist to graduation.[64]

As we noted in chapter 4, there are powerful economic as well as equity arguments for dedicating enough resources to ensure that students who enter college earn their degrees in a timely fashion, and especially for targeting these funding interventions toward those students whose attainment chances can be most affected by such investments. Although improving college preparedness beginning at younger ages is the best long-term strategy for improving college outcomes, focusing more resources on the institutions that provide many of these less well-prepared students with their higher education may be the most effective policy in the short run.[65]

———

Public colleges and universities, both selective and less selective, have a crucial role to play in American higher education. The sheer scale of the sector guarantees this. We suggest that careful consideration be given to assisting the major flagship universities in the public sector by giving them more authority over their own tuition and other policies and by encouraging them to raise money from the private sector—as of course they are already doing. It may then be possible over time to redistribute some amount of state funds to the less selective, less well-off public institutions.

At the same time, states should continue to subsidize as generously as they can the most clearly "public benefit" aspects of their most selective universities (as contrasted to subsidizing students from well-to-do families who attend either undergraduate or professional school programs at these prestigious institutions). This approach implies actively promoting access by well-qualified students from modest family backgrounds. None of this will be easy, especially in politically charged settings, but the need has never been greater for carefully honed programs designed to pursue both equity and excellence goals within state systems.

ATLANTIC CROSSINGS: THE PURSUIT OF EQUITY AND EXCELLENCE IN GREAT BRITAIN

Martin Wolf, the chief economics commentator for the *Financial Times,* has observed that a first-rate university system meets five criteria— excellence, diversity, freedom, resources, and access.[66] Though far from perfect and still very much a work in progress with respect to meeting these criteria, America's decentralized, institutionally diverse, public-private approach to higher education provides a case study of one democratic society's efforts to educate the largest number of its citizens to the highest possible standard.

Few nations have followed the educational successes and failures of the United States with more intense interest, occasional envy, or bemusement than our friends in the United Kingdom. Our institutions' reactions to issues of race, affirmative action, and political correctness are on public display across the Atlantic and are much debated. We believe that this chapter's discussion of public university finance and governance in the United States would benefit from the consideration of comparable developments in Britain, particularly the government's efforts to strengthen tertiary education by granting universities more autonomy in determining fees, improving "attainment" (college preparedness), and opening participation to underrepresented socioeconomic groups. In many respects, the almost decade-long argument in the United Kingdom over allowing universities to charge "top-up" fees—tuition charges above the current government-mandated and -funded maximum—is a surrogate for a more fundamental debate over the role of education in promoting opportunity and social mobility.[67]

By the early 1990s, the United Kingdom had leaped (seemingly overnight) from the ranks of industrialized nations with the least accessible system of higher education into the upper echelon of those with the highest proportion of young people earning degrees.[68] Unfortunately, like their Conservative predecessors Margaret Thatcher and John Major,

Prime Minister Tony Blair and the Labour majority did not initially allocate adequate resources to meet the growth in the student population
or provide universities with the means of funding the increase in enrollments. Indeed, until recently, no British government has been willing to
ask students and their families to help pay for expansion, either directly
through fees or indirectly through taxes.

When Prime Minister Blair pledged at the 1999 Labour Party conference to make higher education available to 50 percent of Britain's young
adults by 2010 (33 percent were enrolled in 2000) and that a large proportion of the new students would come from less privileged backgrounds, he placed the issues of equity and excellence on the national
political stage. It was a signal of the Labour government's intention to
complete Britain's transition from an elite system of higher education
to one open to the masses.[69] The growth of higher education enrollment
without a commensurate infusion of government funding or other
income stream has had predictable results in the United Kingdom: the
student-faculty ratio at most institutions increased from 9 to 1 in the
early 1990s to 18 to 1 in 2002. Faculty compensation has not kept pace
with either the private sector or with other public sector occupations,
deferred maintenance costs have risen substantially, research laboratories
and libraries at many universities are woefully deficient, faculty morale
has plummeted, and half the country's universities are running deficits.[70]

Social Class and the Origins of the Welfare State

The media have treated "top-up" fees as part of a constellation of par-
ticularistic concerns and national anxieties. Editorials range from calls
for university autonomy and financial independence to allegations of
"dumbed-down" admissions policies. They express fears of ever-widening
gaps between the social classes aggravated by variable fees that pressure
students to choose courses and universities on the basis of cost, and issue
sober warnings about the comparative failure of British universities to
attract the brightest students and the most esteemed and productive
scholars. Never far from the surface are the internal culture wars and par-
liamentary in-fighting that are pitting Old Labour's egalitarianism
against New Labour's commitment to modernization, along with the customary byplay among Labour, Conservatives, and Liberal Democrats
vying for constituent support from unions, civil servants, middle England,
the moneyed elite, and the lower-middle and working classes. Add a historic (at times irrational) suspicion, envy, and resentment of Oxford and
Cambridge into the mix, and you have an irresistible melodrama worthy
of Fleet Street.

In a society where the government classifies citizens in two ways—first by social class based on occupation ("skill"), and second by socio-economic group according to employment status—questions of equity are not easily separated from deeply ingrained social, cultural, and political identities.[71] Indeed, the controversy over top-up fees represents a much more deep-seated debate within Britain about access, privilege, and opportunity. In order to gain perspective, we will pick up the historic threads of the narrative during World War II.

In a democracy, the degree of wartime sacrifice and suffering that citizens experience on the home front is often related directly to the enactment of social reform legislation in the postwar period. In December 1942, Britain's wartime coalition government issued a report—*Social Insurance and Allied Services,* better known as the Beveridge Report—which proposed a cradle-to-grave, state-operated system of national insurance that was more comprehensive than any that had previously existed. When enacted after the war, the new social welfare benefits included a National Health Service, as well as unemployment and social security insurance.[72] Banishing "want," as the report stated, also required an attack on "ignorance." As late as 1943, families could send their children to secondary school only on a fee-paying basis, with the result that over 80 percent of children did not study beyond the primary grades. But when Parliament passed the Education Act of 1944, it introduced universal free secondary schooling (state-supported elementary education having been introduced in 1870). Under the Butler Act, as it became known, the "school-leaving" age was raised to 15 and the basis was laid for the financial support of students admitted to university. However, by 1950 less than 2 percent of the college-age cohort went to university, and a national system of "maintenance" grants was not introduced until the early 1960s.[73]

In chapter 2 we noted the differences between President Franklin D. Roosevelt's call for a universal bill of economic rights and the practical constraints that limited the implementation of that vision to returning veterans. In his memoir of English higher education, Robert Stevens reminds us that "as GI's raced back from the Second World War to take the benefits of the GI Bill at universities and colleges across America, the British Tommies returned to a society where tertiary education was virtually unknown" to all but 2 percent of the college-age cohort.[74] The economic challenges that a war-weakened Britain faced substantially affected the ability of postwar governments to improve school quality and extend the reach of higher education. British public policy was heavily influenced by the widely held belief that higher education, unlike old-age supports, unemployment insurance, and medical care, remained an elite prerogative. In part, this contributed to what one observer calls

Britain's private-public divide—"two systems of education: one for the top of society, and another for the rest."[75]

Even after enactment of the Butler Act, generations of British students emerged from primary school to face an uphill battle in a tripartite educational system in which their placement was determined—along with their futures—by the results of examination at the age of 11. Except for the students of upper-class families who could afford the elite "public" schools (what we call private or independent schools in the United States), 11-year-olds who failed to win a place in the highly selective, academically rigorous, state-supported grammar schools were "streamed" by means of social class distinctions into largely mediocre secondary "modern" schools and an underdeveloped system of secondary technical schools. Here their educations effectively ended at age 15 with a school-leaving certificate or, after a fifth year, with a General Certificate of Education (later re-named a Certificate of Secondary Education).

In many respects, developments in British secondary education over the past 40 years have revolved around efforts by successive Conservative and Labour governments, motivated by different ideological concerns, to temper the social class divisions created by the "11+" examination system. The last major effort at transformation, begun under a Labour government in the mid-1960s, involved shutting down the high-ability grammar schools and replacing them with open-admission "comprehensives" loosely modeled on the American high school. The resultant "over-promotion of mediocrity and . . . under-exploitation of talent" prompted one critic's caustic question: "How long can we base good universities on indifferent schools?"[76]

Higher education institutions have also labored under the fierce, uncompromising attachment of the British middle and upper classes to one of the most valuable perquisites of the postwar welfare state—a university education. Cambridge University historian Stefan Collini has observed that "in Britain, entrance to a university is almost the only widely desired social good that cannot be straightforwardly bought."[77] "Straightforwardly" is the operative word, because many middle- and upper-class families send their children to private schools with the hope and expectation that a very good secondary school education will improve their sons' and daughters' chances of earning a place at "Oxbridge" (a tongue-in-cheek British conflation of the two elite schools, Oxford and Cambridge) or at another of the United Kingdom's leading universities. This is what George Walden calls the "unspoken British educational settlement"—the belief that citizens whose taxes support the state-maintained schools have earned the right "to the best the state could offer."[78] As one critic has observed, "The middle classes, whose children are, and will certainly remain, the predominant users of universities,

firmly believe in the need for lower public spending, but only on everybody else."[79]

The notion that all but the poorest undergraduates should pay the
same fee, whether they attend an internationally renowned research university or a former polytechnic (a local or regional vocationally oriented
institution) will strike most Americans as being incompatible with a market economy, but for many Brits the premise is entirely plausible. In the
United Kingdom, as Martin Trow notes, both the government and universities use the rhetoric and vocabulary of the market—customers,
market share, efficiency, and brand—but "since government controls the
price universities can place on their services, and the amount of services
they can sell, universities currently operate not in a market but in something more like a command economy."[80] In fact, when the subject of
top-up fees first arose, the notion that universities might be granted the
latitude to charge variable rates produced a storm of controversy.

Top-Up Fees and the Higher Education Act (2004)

"The whole debate over top-up fees," observed the *Economist*, "has been
fueled by resentment that the value of a degree is a reflection on the
prestige of the university that has awarded it, and that the market will
therefore allow those universities to charge more."[81] Predictably, Universities UK, higher education's trade association, opposed any funding solution that would divide the sector or "give priority to addressing the financial problems of one group of institutions at the expense of others."[82] It
is hardly surprising, snickered the *Economist*, "that the body that represents all universities prefers mediocrity for all to world-class funding for
a few."[83] The lack of trust and goodwill evident in such sentiments is the
inevitable byproduct of a formerly elite university system whose recent
expansion and adoption of a public service mission has yet to translate
public trust into political capital.[84]

Successive British governments have pursued the goal of increasing
university participation with varying degrees of enthusiasm and financial
support. The Dearing Report (1997), commissioned at the end of John
Major's Tory government, offered a glancing look at the consequences of
continued government funding reductions as enrollments grew and state
support declined. Although its euphemistic language spoke of "savings"
and "efficiency gains," the report did introduce the long-overdue idea
of student payments, recommending that students should contribute
approximately 25 percent of the cost of their education through fees on
earnings following graduation.[85] A year later, the new Labour government introduced a compromise, stopgap measure, imposing modest up-
front tuition fees tied to the retail price index, and initially capped at

£1,000 (approximately $2,000 in 2004 dollars). At the same time, the government replaced maintenance grants with a new system of loans, thereby increasing the financial burden on U.K. students.

Six years passed before a working consensus emerged around the principles that "those who benefit from higher education should contribute to its cost," and that universities need the freedom and discretion to obtain additional resources from higher fees.[86] A variety of elements combined to delay the emergence of a consensus: entrenched forces representing the values of the postwar welfare state opposed any form of change, and the university community was divided, as was the Labour Party. Finally, the higher education debate became ensnared in the political compromises necessitated by such domestic and international issues as the debate over whether the United Kingdom should adopt the Euro, Scottish and Welsh devolution, the Good Friday agreement (involving plans for a devolved government in Northern Ireland), and the war in Iraq. But perhaps the most succinct explanation of the extended debate over the future of higher education comes from the *Economist*—"What caste is to India and race is to America," the editors observed, "class is to Britain."[87] In sum, the Brits are dealing with deeply held attitudes, folkways, and belief systems that shape personal and national identity. Given our own contentious, unresolved 400-year struggle with issues of race, we can understand the enormity of trying to reverse whole tides of national history, and the fear and enmity generated by such efforts.

In July 2004, the Blair government took a potentially transformational step for the future of British higher education when Parliament voted final approval of the Higher Education Act (2004) authorizing universities in England to charge variable fees of up to £3,000 (approximately $5,750 in 2004 dollars) beginning in 2006. (Wales was to decide later, and the legislation does not affect Scotland.) English universities will have greater freedom in determining the price and nature of the education they provide. In concert with the awkwardly named "access regulators" in the Office for Fair Access (OFFA) who oversee outreach efforts to increase the number of applications of students from low socioeconomic backgrounds, universities can now set their own fees and vary charges between courses at their own institution and at other universities. When the current up-front fee contribution ends in 2006, the government will provide universities with income equivalent to the value of the new fee, and the Blair government has reaffirmed its intention to treat all income from higher fees as additional. Under the proposal's "graduate contribution scheme," students will repay the interest-free fee loan after graduation through taxes, once their annual incomes exceed £15,000 (approximately $27,000 in 2004 dollars).[88]

Throughout the build-up to presentation of the government's white paper and final passage of the Higher Education Act, the National Union of Students (NUS) argued that the introduction of variable fees would force students to select their course of study according to cost. Citing the American experience, NUS alleged that one in three students entering higher education in the United States "base their choice of institution on fee levels and/or financial aid offers, not on their grades" or the appropriateness of the course.[89] In addition, NUS argued that students from low-income families are more likely to graduate with larger debt loads than their classmates, to earn less as graduates, and therefore, to take longer to repay loans. NUS called the Higher Education Act's passage "a tragic day for the future of education in the UK" and promised that the "student movement will never forget what has happened with this Bill."[90]

In order to encourage more students from lower socioeconomic groups to attend university, the government announced several additional initiatives in support of the Higher Education Act (2004): these include the provision of new up-front maintenance grants of up to £2,700 a year, higher maintenance loans to meet average basic living costs, and also a promise to write off any outstanding student loan debt after 25 years. Students who receive the full £2,700 maintenance grant and whose university fee is £3,000 per year will also receive at least £300 a year in extra financial support, such as a bursary (scholarship) from their university.[91] None of these steps appears to have assuaged the NUS, which pledged to defeat the members of Parliament who "gave their word that they would vote against top-up fees but reneged on that promise."[92]

In many respects, focusing on the "hated fees," as opponents derisively called the top-ups, narrows the context of the debate in a misleading fashion. Though money and resources stand at the heart of this national conversation, the passion unleashed during this debate reflects deep-seated perceptions and stereotypes that compromise access and equality of opportunity. When Secretary of State for Education and Skills Charles Clarke presented Parliament with the government's January 2003 white paper, *The Future of Higher Education,* he called the social class gap "a national disgrace." Clarke observed, "Thirty years ago, students received full grants and there were no tuition fees. Despite this, students from middle-class backgrounds were three times more likely to go to university than those from poorer backgrounds. Over the [past] thirty years the numbers going to university have more than trebled but the gulf in access has remained the same."[93] Peter Scott, vice-chancellor of Kingston University and former editor of the *Times Higher Education Supplement,* has noted that "the student mix in elite universities has changed remarkably little since the 'golden time' of the 1960s; to the extent the system has become more open it has been because of the addition of new institutions with wider student constituencies." Higher education participation may have become "universal" for the middle class, but as Scott observes, attending university remains an atypical experience for academically able and highly motivated working-class students, who tend to be concentrated in less prestigious institutions.[94] The British experience since World War II is a powerful answer to those in the United States who argue that access issues can be solved by holding down student charges.

Social Class and the Preparation Gap

Most close observers of U.K. education agree that the main barrier to university entry for disadvantaged students is low pre-collegiate "attainment" (preparation). According to a recent government report:

> At least three-quarters of the 30 percentage point social gap in higher education participation [between children in the higher and lower social classes] can be attributed to differences in the level of attainment by the age of 16. Thirty percent of children whose parents are in unskilled occupations achieve five or more GCSEs [General Certificate of Secondary Education, commonly known as the School Leaving Certificate], compared to 69 percent of children whose parents are in professional or managerial occupations.[95]

Recognizing that the most significant educational differences appear in a child's earliest years, the Blair government has proposed free part-time nursery education for three- and four-year-olds, more and better early education through the Sure Start program (similar to America's Head Start program), and the introduction of higher standards in primary and secondary school, much like America's recent testing and accountability plans.[96] The latter proposals have already become part of the run-up to the next general election.[97]

Recent government data collected by the Higher Education Funding Council for England (HEFCE) suggest that the next British government will face an "aspiration" as well as an attainment (or preparation) gap. In 2001 half of the U.K. population identified themselves as working in skilled (manual), partly skilled, or unskilled occupations, but only 19 percent of the student-age cohort from these family backgrounds enrolled in higher education. Even though this represented an 8 percentage point improvement over 1991 data, the corresponding increase in participation by young people from families with professional and non-manual occupations was 15 percentage points (from 35 percent to 50 percent), and indications are that this gap between the highest and the lowest social classes is growing.[98]

There is some good news to report: nine out of ten students who earn two or more passes on A-level examinations (standardized examinations taken by students who wish to attend university) enter higher education, and this result holds true for students from lower-income as well as higher-income families.[99] However, on a broader basis, social class remains the principal determinant of differential participation in higher education. For example, only 23 percent of those from manual work backgrounds pass two or more A-levels by the age of 18, compared to 47 percent from non–manual work backgrounds. The data also indicate that there is an 8 percentage point gap in applications to the highest-rated universities between the top and the bottom three social groups, even though there is only a 1 percentage point difference in the admissions rates of those who apply.[100]

Social class differences in enrollment are most apparent when a variety of universities are studied. In a report commissioned by the Department for Education and Skills (DfES), an examination of 13 universities identified by the Sutton Trust[101] revealed that well-qualified students from state secondary schools are less likely to apply when compared with students from independent schools (35 percent versus 55 percent), but that when acceptances are considered, state and independent school students with the same A-level points are admitted at an equal rate. (We note, parenthetically, that these results are again highly consistent with our findings for the United States.) Another HEFCE study revealed that 35 percent of students who earned three A grades in the A-level examinations did not apply to Russell Group universities, a self-selected group of large research universities often described as Britain's version of the Ivy League.[102] Clearly, as DfES understatedly concluded, "a significant number of young people who would seem to have the potential to benefit from going to university are missing this opportunity."[103]

Facing strong pressure from the university community, which insisted on retaining sole control over admissions, the Blair government ultimately retreated from its initial plans to tie university fee increases to access regulators' approval of recruitment and outreach efforts.[104] However, Prime Minister Blair and Education Secretary Clarke did not back away from their pledge to establish an OFFA to work with universities on outreach efforts aimed at increasing the quality and number of applications from students from lower socioeconomic groups.[105] With financial assistance from the government, many initiatives, including special admissions recruitment visits, summer camps for students to help break down stereotypes about elite institutions, and transparency in terms of access to information and availability of financial aid, have been introduced.[106]

Access, Access, Access

The government has strongly suggested that universities could do more to recruit academically able students from all socioeconomic backgrounds, in part by increasing their understanding of why talented students from lower socioeconomic groups may be "put off" from applying to the nation's elite institutions by what the English commonly refer to as Oxbridge's white-flannel, *Brideshead Revisited* reputation.[107] Wherever one comfortably places such comments on a scale ranging from truth-telling to posturing to harmless nonsense, such sentiments capture the enduring —and, many would say, harshly unequal—nature of contemporary British education.

In Britain, as in the United States, an accumulation of interconnected, deep-seated, and persistent factors—such as family income and stability, parental education, quality of primary and secondary schools, and influence of teachers and other adult role models—affects students' academic preparedness and aspirations. The challenge to Britain's top universities is to broaden access and expand opportunity for talented disadvantaged students. As Sir Colin Lucas, then vice-chancellor of Oxford, noted, such efforts must be conducted "in a way which maintains the highest academic standards."[108] And here is the source of concern. One-third of all students who earn three A grades in the A-level examinations are the products of private (independent) schools that educate only 7 percent of the total student population. The picture is actually bleaker if one eliminates consideration of grades in such secondary A-level subjects as general studies, media studies, and business studies, and focuses on the A-levels of most interest to top universities. In physics, 40 percent of all the A grades go to students attending private schools, and the corresponding percentages for chemistry (45 percent), French (51 percent), and classics (80 percent) confirm the glaring inequities in secondary education, and underscore the complex equity (and excellence) challenge facing the United Kingdom's most prestigious universities.[109] Unfortunately, we do not have data for Great Britain that are comparable to the data used in the earlier chapters of our book. Yet when one considers that approximately one-third of U.K. children live in the poorer areas of the country, and that these students make up only 6 percent of the population at the nation's top educational institutions, the immensity of the challenge facing government and the universities in closing a preparation gap heavily influenced by culture and economics becomes clearer.[110]

In our review of the media coverage addressing issues of equity and excellence in the United Kingdom, we were struck by the social disincentives, what one observer calls a "bias against aspiration, which runs through large sections of British society and disfigures our educational system." The writer, Anthony Smith, goes on to describe the lack of educational aspiration that occurs when a schoolteacher tells a parent that "she will never see her child again" if the student goes to Oxford or Cambridge, or the burden carried by talented students when they are advised by their teacher that "only class traitors" apply to Oxbridge.[111] Similar stereotyping and discouragement can be found in every country, and certainly in our own, but perhaps not to this degree.

The 64,000-Dollar Question

We began this review of Britain's efforts to maintain quality while expanding access to higher education with the observation that a first-rate university system should demonstrate a commitment to meet five criteria—excellence, diversity, freedom, resources, and access. As our colleagues across the Atlantic prepare for the full implementation in 2006 of the Higher Education Act, they are maintaining their commitment to academic excellence and have taken the first steps toward freeing their universities from a form of centralization that has not always encouraged fresh thinking. Whether the nation can provide the resources sufficient to maintain academic excellence, while meeting the needs of an expanding educational system that is both open and inclusive, is what the British would call the 64,000-dollar question. Resources, as much as resolve, will determine the success or failure of this latest initiative.

In celebrating the passage of the Higher Education Act, Secretary Clarke declared that it would "provide universities with the funding they need to improve laboratories and lecture theatres, student accommodation and lecturers' salaries."[112] But not even Whitehall can change the bottom lines of university income statements and balance sheets. Most observers agree that the top-up fee maximum (£3,000) is much too low, because the actual cost of educating an undergraduate at the best universities is at least £10,000 in the humanities and much more in science and technology courses. Even with the £10 billion that the government has pledged to invest in 2005–06, public spending on higher education is still projected to remain under 1 percent of gross domestic product, prompting a growing number of universities to accelerate their search for additional revenue sources. For the most renowned research institutions this entrepreneurial process has been under way for decades, and there have been modest successes in the areas of industrial spin-offs and technology transfer partnerships. But the reality, as the *Economist* observed, is that all universities must become better at earning and raising money, "whether through developing profitable new programmes such as selling courses abroad or mastering that mainstay of the American system, private fundraising."[113] Since the most successful development programs in the United States are geared toward ensuring lifelong, "cradle-to-grave" associations with alma mater—relationships that require significant and continual institutional investment and benefit from strong residential campus communities—it remains to be seen whether the less affluent U.K. universities, in particular, can afford the infusion of resources so necessary to nurture and construct the ties that build endowments and bind their graduates for life.[114] In the meantime, most experts anticipate that the current £3,000 maximum fee will need to be adjusted upward reasonably soon.

———

Whether the Higher Education Act proves to be a milestone in the history of the United Kingdom or a temporary fix to protect "an invaluable, but wasting asset,"[115] we feel compelled to close this discussion with an important reminder: whatever their financial limitations, privileged attitudes, and bureaucratic failings, U.K. universities cannot be regarded as primarily responsible for the class divide that permeates British society, or for the pre-collegiate underperformance that contributes to the underrepresentation of students from lower socioeconomic groups. Universities have a role to play in addressing these issues, but the class divide in education, and in society at large, will narrow only when families, communities, schools, and government use their social and financial capital to nurture, inspire, and prepare young people to compete equitably in the marketplace.[116]

The situation in the United States is, in many ways, much the same: a major increase in attendance at prestigious colleges and universities by students from modest backgrounds depends on societal change and on improved college "preparedness"—the subject of our next chapter.

CHAPTER 9

Improving College Preparedness

Throughout this study, we have argued that differential college prepared-ness of advantaged and disadvantaged young people is *the* major deter-minant of differences in educational attainment. Government support of tertiary education in the United States, in the form of both the provision of financial aid (primarily through federal programs) and state appropri-ations to public universities, has as one of its principal objectives improving college access for disadvantaged students by making higher education more affordable. The "thumb on the scale" admissions policies we propose in chapter 7 would represent a still more activist approach by individual colleges and universities committed to enrolling a larger number of under-graduates from modest backgrounds. The combination of admissions advantages and institutional, federal, and state aid could certainly improve access for the current generation of applicants from low-socioeconomic-status (SES) backgrounds and signal greater opportunity for subsequent cohorts—in part by strengthening incentives to be high achievers in sec-ondary school and by encouraging these students' application to and enrollment at the colleges and universities best suited to their needs.

Policy changes at the collegiate level alone, however, will not tap fully the potential of disadvantaged students. There is an even more funda-mental need for larger, better-prepared pools of applicants from low-SES and minority backgrounds: improving their college preparedness should be a major objective of national policy. We are persuaded that a compre-hensive approach is needed, with consideration given to the sources of the preparedness gap from birth through adolescence and to both schooling and the out-of-school environment. Required are early invest-ments that improve cognitive development at the pre-primary stages, in-school programs that build on early gains, and, finally, programs designed to narrow gaps in access to information so that talented stu-dents from low-SES backgrounds can compete successfully with their more advantaged peers. The best solutions will require more than gen-erous funding and a clear recognition that the problems of collegiate access are broader than those caused by income disparities (though these surely play a large role). In this chapter our objective is to identify and discuss key issues on the long path from birth to college and to point to the principles, at least, of promising policies going forward.[1]

We considered earlier (in chapter 4) some of the reasons why there is a gap in such measures of pre-collegiate academic preparation as test scores between children from privileged families and other children—including differences in family resources, neighborhoods, and schools—but we did not note, at the time, the lingering controversy over the significance of these factors. There is a school of thought—most prominently represented by the book *The Bell Curve*—that argues that educational and life outcomes are rooted in genetic differences in innate intelligence.[2] To be sure, individual ability, including genetic endowments, is an important determinant of life outcomes, but the extreme proposition that family circumstances do not matter, or that a child's broader external environment is not a factor, has been discredited.[3] There is little or no evidence that a significant portion of the variation in life outcomes across socioeconomic or racial groups can be explained by genetic differences.

Others argue that family life and other experiences before and outside of school, primarily in early life, are the defining elements of a child's educational preparation.[4] We agree that early influences—and some early interventions—may yield the most lasting benefits, but we also believe that later disadvantages can erase early gains or exacerbate early setbacks. Similarly, attitudes and capacities formed by events outside school can be either reinforced or countered by in-school experiences.

In short, we believe that schooling, all the way from pre-primary programs to the end of high school, can either mitigate or exacerbate non-school influences on children; that it is the accumulation of (often small) advantages and disadvantages over the course of the first 18 years of life that leads to massive preparation differences by the time of college application.[5] But while the disadvantages, like the advantages, are cumulative and reinforcing, it is also true that later disadvantage can cause harm without the presence of early disadvantage. Likewise, later forms of support can mitigate earlier disadvantage, at least to some extent.

Thus a sensible set of policies must, as we have said, be comprehensive: addressing the early educational problems of poor and minority children is of first importance, but programs targeted to the early years must be reinforced by subsequent investments at each successive step up the educational ladder. Moreover, it is not enough to focus only on the formal educational aspects of a disadvantaged child's life before college. Disadvantage outside of the classroom can play a significant role and must be addressed as well. Of course governments cannot raise children; parents, guardians, and other family members have the largest impact and the greatest responsibility. But governments can certainly touch the lives of disadvantaged youth through macro-level social programs, including structuring incentives for young people and their families as well as providing support for the institutions that are charged with helping them. At the very least, government has a responsibility not to compound problems.

In the remainder of this chapter we will expand our discussion of accumulating disadvantages by focusing on some of the major problems facing disadvantaged students in their homes, neighborhoods, and schools—and on some of the proposed solutions to them. Our commentary is based heavily on a growing body of empirical research by scholars who have specialized in this field.[6]

OUTSIDE THE SCHOOLHOUSE: NEIGHBORHOODS, HEALTH, AND PRE-PRIMARY EDUCATION

Families and communities, and the values, role models, and health and educational resources they provide, are key determinants of a child's development—and of his or her college readiness. The influence of these factors begins early in life (or, in the case of prenatal care, before birth), and well-conceived policies may be most potent at this stage. But children born to disadvantaged families in impoverished or economically isolated communities generally live in these environments through adolescence, if not longer, and the consequences continue, and accumulate, over time.

Communities disconnected from the economic mainstream, whether they are urban or rural, lack the positive peer and social networks that the neighborhoods of more advantaged children afford. In chapter 4 we documented some of the harsh characteristics of impoverished urban neighborhoods, noting in particular the concentration of poverty that is prevalent in these areas. Sociologist William Julius Wilson has studied the burden of living in urban neighborhoods with high unemployment and crime rates, few legal businesses, and the absence of a middle class. He posits that the lack of college-educated role models for children (particularly minority children) helps to reinforce the cycle of poverty.[7] A similar dearth of role models likely dampens the educational aspirations of capable students in the poor and isolated segments of rural America.

In many states, poverty rates in rural areas exceed urban poverty rates—with the compounding difficulty that geographic isolation makes government services even less accessible. While 11.6 percent of the metropolitan population was below the federal poverty line in 2002, 14.2 percent of the non-metro, or rural, population qualified as poor—a poverty gap that has persisted over the last half century and remains regardless of how rates are broken down by race, age, ethnicity, and family structure. The 2.6 million rural children who live in poverty constitute 35 percent of the rural poor, and racial disparities are as striking here as in urban areas: while on average one of every five rural children is poor, nearly half of all black children in rural areas live in poverty. Although the economic expansion of the 1990s reduced poverty rates across the board, since 1985 the rural child poverty rate has never dipped below 18 percent, and persistent poverty remains most prevalent in rural areas.[8]

The educational progress of students who grow up in rural areas illustrates well the cumulative effects of a difficult environment (and of poor school quality). Rural students perform about as well as suburban students (and much better than urban students) on National Assessment of Educational Progress (NAEP) exams in both the fourth and the eighth grades. But by the twelfth grade these test score advantages disappear even in raw terms; rural seniors have much lower scores than suburban seniors, below the national average and roughly equal to those of urban seniors. Despite graduating from high school at higher rates than both urban and suburban students, only 54 percent of rural students apply to college, while 57 percent and 62 percent of urban and suburban students apply, respectively.[9]

To assess scientifically the extent to which neighborhood characteristics affect the social well-being of low-income families, a federally funded urban relocation experiment was undertaken in 1994. The demonstration project, known as Moving to Opportunity (MTO), was carefully designed so that treatment effects could be definitively measured and analyzed. Empirical studies of this multi-state randomized housing experiment found surprisingly moderate impacts on children who were moved to a "better" neighborhood. While short-term educational and health outcomes were promising, the results are more mixed several years out—long-term test scores showed no improvement.[10] Interestingly, girls showed real gains in terms of high school attendance and college-going. Boys, on the other hand, appear to have been negatively affected by relocation in a variety of social dimensions.[11] Obviously relocating young people to improve their college preparedness is not a practical long-term national policy, but the MTO project is exactly the type of well-designed experiment that can reveal the extent to which various neighborhood characteristics contribute to outcomes important for college preparedness. The results of this research highlight the importance of role models and peers (both possible factors in the gender difference seen in the results), as well as the significance of the formal educational environment vis-à-vis the out-of-school experience (in this experiment, the children's school quality was not drastically affected by residential relocation).[12]

Empirical tests of peer effects within school environments and groups of friends have shown mixed results, but there is evidence that heterogeneous peer groups can improve the performance of low achievers without affecting high achievers.[13] Jonathan Guryan used the time variation in school desegregation plans during the 1970s to assess their effects on the high school dropout rates of black students. He found that within-district integration plans led to a significant decline in the black dropout rate, with no discernible effect on the high school completion rates of white students.[14] Boston's Metropolitan Council for Educational Opportunity (Metco) program, which sends mostly minority inner-city students to suburban receiving districts on a voluntary basis, gives rise to an experimental setting in which researchers found that increasing the number of typically low-scoring Metco students had only isolated and short-lived negative effects on students from the receiving district.[15]

An analysis of an open enrollment program in Chicago's public schools, which employed a lottery to distribute spots in oversubscribed schools, does not show academic gains for the students who move from schools with low-achieving peers to schools with high-achieving peers, but the researchers do find improvement in non-cognitive outcomes, such as disciplinary problems and arrests, that almost certainly affect educational attainment.[16] Once again, these policies are not practical for all communities; open enrollment and busing are impossible for isolated, sparsely populated rural districts, for example. However, this research provides important insights into how the sorting of young people into groups and the relationships resulting from this sorting affect the development of a child's college preparedness. Taking steps to bring disadvantaged young people and their more privileged peers into contact with one another in both educational and extracurricular settings appears to be a wise policy—and it should clearly be done in a way that allows researchers to analyze the results in detail.

Childhood health is another important factor in educational, psychological, and of course physical development. Children living with low-SES families are more likely than children living in more advantaged homes to suffer from certain ailments, to be exposed to unhealthy conditions, and to have less access to medical services. The link between SES and health has been widely documented, and researchers continue to explore the pathways of transmission between health and SES.[17] We know that a child's weight at birth is strongly correlated with SES, and that low birth weight has a significant negative impact on future test scores.[18] Researchers have found that disadvantaged children are more likely to experience "health shocks" such as chronic illness or accidental injury, and to experience them more frequently (throughout their lives) than more advantaged children. These shocks are associated with lower test scores and eventually with reduced college readiness.[19]

Efforts to mitigate the effects of low SES on children's health in order to improve, among other things, their chances of doing well in school, need to address both environmental factors associated with poor health and issues related to access to care. Government healthcare interventions that minimize the frequency of health shocks—through the provision of access to better preventive healthcare—can do a great deal of good at relatively low cost. For example, the State Children's Health Insurance Program (SCHIP), which provides low-premium or no-premium health insurance to children, has reduced the percentage of children from low-income families who lack health insurance by a third since 1997.[20] Access to preventive care for approximately 5.3 million children was improved at a cost of roughly $1,000 per child in fiscal year 2002.[21] Improving the availability of prenatal care may reduce some of the most troubling developmental setbacks children from low-income families face. Sound and enforceable policies on pollution and equitably distributed municipal services will also minimize health risks for disadvantaged children. Progress on these fronts can help more disadvantaged children arrive at school better able to meet the challenges that await them—in the first 12 years of school and beyond.

Perhaps the clearest difference in the pre-primary lives of children from low-SES and high-SES backgrounds is in the formal education they receive during this time: participation in preschool programs has consistently varied with income. In 1993 well over half of all children from high-income families attended preschool programs, whereas only a quarter of low-income children participated in these programs. Data from the Department of Education suggest that similar patterns exist today.[22]

In an effort to narrow this gap, Head Start was created in 1965 and today provides over 900,000 economically disadvantaged children with pre-primary nutrition and education programs.[23] Head Start seems to be at least as effective as most other preschool programs attended by low-income children. However, the effects do not seem to be particularly long-lasting. Researchers have found that both white and black children who have attended the program show significant short-term test score improvements of about 7 percentile points over children who have not attended preschool.[24] Unfortunately, these immediate improvements in academic achievement fade out almost entirely (and quickly) for black children and are greatly diminished for white children.[25] Head Start closes about one-third of the test score gap between low-income white children and their more advantaged peers and reduces the chance that a low-income white student will repeat a grade by 16 percent relative to low-income white children who did not attend preschool.[26] The only source of long-term gain for black children that has been identified is increased access to and use of preventive healthcare.[27]

The differential gains for minority and non-minority children are without doubt the most serious imperfection in the Head Start program, but they may not be attributable to the program itself. There is some evidence that subsequent differences in school quality are responsible for the speedier and more complete erosion of Head Start gains for black students: *while white Head Start students attend primary schools comparable to those attended by other white children, black Head Start participants are dis-proportionately more likely to attend schools of lower quality—in terms of average test scores—than those attended by other black children.*[28] The fact that the real and lasting gains of Head Start are so sensitive to primary school quality highlights the importance of continuing support. (One may draw a similar conclusion, as we have noted, from the educational paths of poor, white, rural students and from the research of Roland Fryer and Steven Levitt—described in chapter 4—on black-white test score gaps in the early years of school.)

Head Start certainly has *not* been a failure—at the very least, we can say that for many participants it is better than having no access to any pre-school program—but it has not been a rousing success. Continued research would be worthwhile, but so too would be exploration of new models. Since 1995, Georgia has mandated that every school district in the state provide preschool for all four-year-olds, regardless of income, and has provided the districts the funding to do so.[29] Although no rigorous study of this program has been conducted, it has the potential to be more effective than Head Start in certain respects. The fact that the program is universal may result in higher funding and more institutional support than Head Start has received, because the middle class and the wealthy are likely to be more willing to pay for and defend a program through which they receive a benefit. A school district may well have stronger incentives and greater expertise than the federal Department of Health and Human Services (which runs Head Start) to provide students with the preparation they need to succeed in the schools of that district. Decentralization is also likely to encourage more experimentation in the design of programs. On the other hand, a universal program is more costly than a targeted program, and providing the additional schooling to more advantaged students could lead to the Catch-22 of being cost-ineffective if it has no impact on their academic achievement or of widening the achievement gap if it does prove to have an impact. In any case, universal preschool represents the type of innovative public policy alternative that is worthy of careful evaluation.

Disparities in extramural enrichment during the years when a child is in school also seem to have an effect on college preparedness. Researchers tracking the long-term academic performance of 800 randomly selected Baltimore students who entered first grade in 1982 found that students from high-SES backgrounds substantially outperform students from low-SES backgrounds when they enter school and that the achievement gap between the two groups expands over time. During the school year, children from low- and high-SES families posted identical math and reading score gains in elementary school. But while students from high-SES families continued to improve during the summer months, disadvantaged students' achievement stalled or declined.[30] Equalizing educational opportunities in the summer months requires interventions in the same spirit as those provided by Head Start: where differential opportunity exists, additional resources and programs must be provided. Directly providing summer school or offering vouchers to offset the tuition costs of private summer programs may help to enrich the educational environments of disadvantaged children, but quality differences could be as important as availability differences. Research based on the results of a policy change in the Chicago Public Schools suggests that remedial summer school boosted student performance in reading and mathematics, with stronger impacts on younger children.[31] While individual studies of the effectiveness of summer school programs have found mixed results, meta-analyses have concluded that, overall, these programs positively affect student achievement.[32]

Taken together, these studies make clear the importance of continuing to invest in the education of students from low-SES backgrounds, and of minority students from low-SES backgrounds in particular, both in school and out of school, right up to the time they graduate from high school. Failing to do so endangers these students' long-term prospects and erodes the value of prior taxpayer investments. Structuring these continuing investments so as to reap real gains is no easy task. Moreover, there is a prior problem: raising and distributing funds among school districts in a more equitable way is a formidable challenge in and of itself.

FINANCING PRIMARY
AND SECONDARY EDUCATION

For most of their history, American schools have been funded by local property taxes. This is one of the "virtues" of the late 19th and early 20th centuries that Lawrence Katz and Claudia Goldin cite as a root cause of the rapid spread and early success of American primary and secondary schooling (see chapter 3). But, as we suggested earlier, this virtue has a downside. Local funding means that differences in property wealth and in voter tax rates will translate into disparities in educational resources. It is only one more step to the conclusion that districts with a high proportion of poor or uneducated residents, or with a stagnant economy, will have fewer educational resources.

Stylized economic models based on the public goods theory of Charles Tiebout have predicted that, if public school quality and the tax burdens it requires were capitalized into housing prices, families would sort among districts according to their housing and educational preferences and budgets.[33] However, these theoretical propositions rely on assumptions that in many cases are counterfactual. In addition to assuming the availability of a nearly infinite array of housing and schooling

combinations and perfect residential mobility, the Tiebout model of public education funding assumes that parental choices uniformly reflect
their children's best interests. Moreover, even if the conditions for perfect sorting efficiency were achieved, increased productivity in all public
schools would not necessarily narrow the equity divide.

Caroline Hoxby's empirical analysis of the effects of Tiebout choice suggests, though not without controversy, that increased inter-district choice
boosts the productivity of schools in a metropolitan area, improving
achievement on a number of measures while simultaneously decreasing
school spending.[34] But increases in inter-district choice do not seem to
close the gap between advantaged and disadvantaged students; the productivity gains are not significantly different for poor and non-poor children or for minority and non-minority children.[35] This finding is heart-
ening in one sense (greater inter-district choice does not seem to worsen
the situation), but nonetheless suggests that enhancing the freedom of
choice among public school districts cannot alone help disadvantaged
children catch up to their more advantaged peers. Traditional Tiebout
choice inherently helps only those with the means and the opportunity
to move.

Beginning in the 1970s, there was a reaction to the inequities of traditional patterns of local school finance: many states (often as the result of
court decisions) enacted what are known as school finance equalization
(SFE) plans. These plans come in several different forms, but in general
they redistribute local property taxes so that a per-pupil spending floor is
instituted. It is important to recognize that, by dedicating the same tax revenue stream to a district's own school spending and to the pool for redistribution, these policies change the tax-setting behavior of both potential revenue-receiving and potential revenue-generating districts. Research
has shown that, where SFE plans were effective in equalizing per-pupil
spending, the plans led to a leveling down of spending, as districts were
effectively taxed by the state government for taxing themselves. Worse yet,
the design of the most stringent plans in some states actually *decreased*
spending in the disadvantaged districts that SFE was supposed to benefit.[36]
The point is not that redistribution is inevitably self-defeating, but that
financing equalization is tricky territory that is best navigated with a careful eye on the perverse incentives such plans can create; if the full incentive
effects of reform are taken into account, SFE could be more successful.[37]

Although SFE policies have often been instituted to comply with state
court orders for greater equity in the distribution of school resources,
some state supreme courts have ruled that school financing inequities do
not violate state constitutional provisions and have thwarted schemes
that directly redistribute revenue raised to fund local schools.[38] Redistribution plans that avoid adverse taxing incentives and rely on a less sensi-

tive tax base can begin to correct the underinvestment in the education of disadvantaged students in a more constitutionally acceptable way. A system of so-called categorical aid may redistribute resources more productively to districts whose residents are poorer or who have children that are more costly to educate. Categorical aid systems provide additional funds to school districts specifically to increase their investment in "categories" of students who receive insufficient resources, such as students from low-income families or those with disabilities. But categorical aid systems must be carefully designed as well, as they can promote their own forms of unintended consequences. Basing aid on characteristics that are difficult to confirm—for example, attention deficit disorder (ADD) —can lead to misrepresentation and "gaming" of the system, and thus to a poor distribution of funds.[39] It is also crucial that the categorical aid funds come from revenue streams, such as income or consumption taxes, which are independent of the local funding process. If structured correctly, categorical aid can increase funding to targeted populations without distorting effects.[40]

REFORMS WITHIN THE SYSTEM

How funds are raised and how they are distributed are important questions, but simply putting money into the hands of school districts is not an education policy. The correction of current inadequacies requires more than generous funding; money must be spent effectively. Unfortunately, the record of American primary and secondary schools in this regard is not good. Average achievement test scores have improved, but only modestly, for 30 years.[41] Improvements in educational attainment have slowed considerably for birth cohorts after 1950, and progress toward meeting goals related to high school graduation rates (after excluding those receiving general equivalency diplomas) has stalled.[42] During the same period, education spending per pupil doubled.[43] Taken together, these trends suggest a decline in the productivity of spending on education over the past 30 years.

This macro-level loss of productivity has led some to argue that increasing spending on educational inputs—for example, reducing class size, increasing teacher salaries, and improving the maintenance of school buildings—has little effect on academic achievement.[44] Research shows, however, that additional funding for some inputs has the *potential* to improve achievement, and where increased spending has been found to help, it has disproportionately helped minority children and those from low-SES backgrounds.[45] Analyses of the long-term impacts of Tennessee's randomized experiments in class size reduction by Alan Krueger and

Diane Whitmore reveal that lower student-teacher ratios in the early grades improved students' standardized test performance and increased the likelihood of their taking the ACT or the SAT, with disadvantaged and minority students experiencing the largest improvements. While the average test scores of white students educated in smaller classes in grades K–3 increased by 3 to 4 percentile points, the scores of black students improved by 7 to 10 percentile points. Once students returned to regular-sized classes in the fourth grade, these gains shrank to 1.5 percentile points for white students, whereas black students retained a 5-point gain.[46] On average, reducing class size narrowed the black-white college entrance testing gap by 54 percent.[47] This differential benefit suggests that, in addition to enhancing equity objectives, concentrating resources on disadvantaged children is the most *productive* use of additional funding.

However, not all estimates of the effect of class size reduction have been as encouraging. Research analyzing the effect of class size changes as a result of natural population variation in Connecticut found that increasing class size from a base of 15 to 30 students had no appreciable impact on student achievement.[48] One possible explanation for these disparate results is that the Tennessee experiment may have shifted teacher incentives, because positive outcomes would make permanently smaller classes more likely. On the other hand, the "natural experiment" that occurred as a result of population variation in Connecticut is not tainted by altered incentives, because the subjects were unaware of the "experiment." Of course, if class size reduction efforts generate incentives that lead teachers to improve educational results, that is a desirable outcome—if only in the short term.

It is important to assess the full impact of any policy change, and state incentives to reduce class size led some California schools to combine students from different grades into the same class—a change that was so detrimental to the test scores of these students that in aggregate it may have outweighed the positive effects of smaller classes for the 85 percent of the students who were educated in single-grade classrooms.[49] Class size reduction initiatives may also entail hiring many new teachers, and the marginal hire is likely to be of lower-than-average quality. Nevertheless, Tennessee's experience with class size reduction suggests that additional resources do benefit students who receive inadequate educational support at home. Targeting the resources devoted to factors such as class size toward disadvantaged youth will not only help these students, but will also improve macro-level productivity.[50] This conclusion is consistent with an "accumulating disadvantages" view of the path toward college preparedness. Those who in early life experience disadvantages, both in and out of school, have the most to gain from subsequent programs of support, while those who have done well as a result of accumulated advantages can expect a much smaller return on additional investments. This same point is made with great force by those who have studied educational problems in South Africa. According to Luis Crouch and Thabo Mabogoane, "In poor communities, with illiterate or poorly educated adults, the quality of the school has a greater influence on the life chances of learner than it has in the more privileged communities."[51]

Several constraints hinder the careful distribution of funds and the development of innovative programs. Apart from the politicking that is standard in these kinds of local financing situations, school districts have to contend with the influence of often-powerful teachers' unions. Teachers in almost three-quarters of the school districts in the United States are represented by a union or some other organization in contract negotiations, and in some parts of the country virtually all school districts are covered by collective bargaining agreements.[52] The motives of teachers are almost always admirable. However, the incentives that strong unions bring to bear on school spending can have a negative effect on productivity.[53] While most of the teachers in a union (including its leaders) have a strong interest in, and are often vocal advocates for, maximizing the educational value their students receive, the entirely understandable organizational goal of the union is to improve the financial and nonfinancial aspects of teaching careers for its members.

Collective bargaining agreements generally incorporate policies pertaining to class size, criteria for hiring and firing, and teaching assignments, as well as pay scales, and can cause spending to be shifted accordingly.[54] One careful study of the effects of increased unionization (defined as the advent of meaningful collective bargaining power) finds that it raises per-pupil spending substantially, that three-quarters of the additional spending goes to reducing class size and increasing teacher salaries, and that, on an other things equal basis, dropout rates increase.[55] Teachers have the right to organize in the pursuit of their own best interests, and labor markets in which employers have disproportionate power have undesirable consequences of many kinds. The objective should be to find ways to achieve a closer alignment of union incentives with the educational goals of parents, school boards, and most of the teachers in the union.[56]

PUBLIC PROVISION OF EDUCATION, COMPETITION, AND SCHOOL CHOICE

Growing contingents of scholars and policy makers have argued that relying on the almost completely public provision of K–12 education (another of Goldin and Katz's "virtues" of late 19th-century pre-collegiate education) stifles the ability of parents to help their children achieve educational goals. Private schools, of course, provide an alternative, but over 85 percent of primary and secondary students attend public schools —and for many of the disadvantaged students upon whom we focus, private school is not a realistic option.[57] On one level, school choice initiatives in recent years, such as the creation of charter schools and voucher programs, are intended to give disadvantaged students the opportunity to attend better schools. But another, more significant, goal of these policies is to create a system of incentives—through competition for students and the public dollars they carry with them—for public schools to make their programs more attractive to all students and parents.[58] High-SES parents often have this kind of market power already: they are mobile enough to relocate if necessary to improve educational prospects for their children, politically astute enough to mobilize for changes in their public schools, and wealthy enough that they *can* make the choice to send their children to a private school (the threat alone is often sufficient to cause local schools to improve). In a sense, school choice programs targeted at disadvantaged families can conceivably provide a mechanism that will give them something like the degree of choice that more advantaged families already enjoy.

In a charter school system, the school district authorizes an organization (perhaps a group of teachers and administrators, public-minded citizens, a for-profit company—or in some cases a religious group) to run a school within a district on the basis of a proposal submitted by the organization. The school receives funding from the district on a per-pupil basis, with the funding amount typically about 45 percent of what the local public schools spend per pupil.[59] In a voucher system, school districts (or the state) furnish parents with a stipend that can be employed at a public school or used to subsidize tuition at a private school. In practice, the voucher amount is typically between 14 and 29 percent of the district per-pupil average.[60] Under a charter school system, providers first compete to win school contracts and then compete for students with traditional public schools and other charter schools; under a voucher system, existing public and private schools compete against each other to win students.

Experiments around the country have provided opportunities to better understand the effects of charter schools and vouchers, though many choice programs have not been optimally designed for careful empirical research. It is not surprising, therefore, that studies of some of these programs have yielded conflicting results and have been controversial. Nonetheless, several studies have found positive effects associated with the mostly small-scale voucher and charter experiments.[61] The results of one voucher program, in Milwaukee, stand out because they come the closest to representing system-wide general equilibrium effects. The program is unique because of its scale and generosity; vouchers are available to any student at or below 175 percent of the poverty line, and the voucher amount is over $5,000. Equally important, public schools lose a substantial fraction (23 percent) of per-pupil state funding for every student who opts out of the public system and uses his or her voucher at a private school. Oversubscription is handled by a lottery system.[62] Cecilia Rouse examined the treatment effects of this voucher plan and found that, relative to control groups of lottery losers or a random sample of Milwaukee public school students, students educated at private schools through the voucher program improved their math test scores significantly.[63] In a related study, Caroline Hoxby found that Milwaukee *public* schools exposed to the greatest degree of competition (as measured by the percentage of students eligible for vouchers) experienced substantial gains in achievement and productivity relative to similar schools elsewhere in Wisconsin.[64]

Charter schools have yet to be evaluated through carefully designed demonstration projects, though improved efforts to conduct such studies are under way.[65] Quasi-experiments and observational studies point to results that are both promising and conflicting. Although an earlier evaluation of Michigan charter schools found that charter school competition did not affect public schools, differences in pre-existing degrees of competition may have confounded the results. More recent examinations of North Carolina's large-scale charter program suggest that traditional schools post significant achievement gains when exposed to competition from charter schools.[66] The results from a study of Chicago's charter schools suggest that students who apply to attend a charter school, win oversubscription lotteries, and then enroll in the district's charter programs in early grades post higher test scores in reading and math than do other students. Students who enroll after the third grade do not experience statistically significant achievement gains, though this may be a result of a smaller pool of such students.[67]

These positive findings, however, are specific to the conditions underlying the programs studied and to their particular features; the success of these programs is very sensitive to the details of their design and implementation. For example, vouchers that cannot cover a substantial fraction of private school tuition could lead more expensive private schools to skim students from wealthy families and high-ability students from low-income families (by providing financial aid), leaving in public schools and inexpensive private schools the lower-ability students from low-income families or those students whose parents are less involved in their education.[68] Low-value vouchers (or a voucher system that leaves public budgets unchanged by design) would also provide weaker incentives for public schools to offer higher-quality education, because their finances would not be impaired when students left.

Charter schools are by definition less regulated than traditional public schools and therefore vary enormously in their curricula, philosophies, and quality. Issues abound, ranging from sometimes subtle effects on the staffing and financing of the standard public schools in the area to worries about possible religious or ideological domination. Questions about accountability are very real. Also, adverse selection problems could arise in either charter school or voucher systems if enrollment were restricted in some way—by an admission test or interview, for example (though neither is currently permitted). Both types of programs have very little potential in rural or other isolated areas, where there are too few schooling options (public or private) to provide any real choice. Finally, given the high degree of de facto choice already enjoyed by students from well-to-do families, subsidizing additional school choice for them is unlikely to be a good use of scarce public funds.

The importance of getting the school choice programs "just right" calls for more experiments designed to yield clear findings about what works and what does not work—or in which settings various approaches yield the most positive outcomes.[69] But whatever the source and character of the underlying research design and data collection, great care has to be taken to explain clearly what the data do and do not show. There was much controversy associated with press accounts in August 2004 of "findings" pertaining to the performance of charter schools in a report by the American Federation of Teachers (AFT) that was based on raw data released earlier by the Department of Education. The AFT analysis of these data showed charter schools lagging behind traditional schools; the simple cross-tabulations summarized in the AFT report clearly raised questions about the effectiveness of charter schools. The AFT performed a service by challenging the government to explain why these data were released without any kind of public announcement (perhaps suggesting a politically motivated interest in causing them to "go away").[70] Critics of the AFT report are also right, however, in calling attention to the lack of adequate controls for potentially important differences in the characteristics of students who attended charter schools and other public schools (the classic problem of selection bias); also, the AFT report ignored entirely the question of educational progress over time.[71]

Some commentators have suggested that the AFT story led less to a meaningful debate than to a "firestorm among ideologues."[72] In our opinion, the only broad judgments about charter schools that can be rendered at this juncture are that the jury is still out, and that it is wise to avoid coming too quickly to sweeping conclusions based on limited evidence. A larger concern is that this issue has become so politicized on both sides that there is reason to worry about the prospect for even solid evidence to be effective in changing people's positions. There is an obvious need for some standard method of presenting data on educational outcomes with as much objectivity as can be mustered. The system used to measure and report economic data could provide a model.[73]

CHANGING THE ATMOSPHERE: ACCOUNTABILITY VERSUS COMMUNITARIAN APPROACHES

After funds are allocated and various policy decisions have been made, the question of how a school should actually be run—and in what kind of atmosphere students are best educated—remains. This question is of particular importance in the case of disadvantaged students, for whom interactions with adults and peers and the general social structure provided by a school can offset, at least in part, insufficient (or absent) experiences of this kind outside of school. In recent years, two sides to this debate have emerged: there are those who endorse what has become known as "accountability" and those who support a system in which the concept of "community" is key. The idea behind the increasingly common systems of high-stakes testing and standards—codified at the national level by the 2001 No Child Left Behind Act—is that stagnant achievement is a result of low expectations (for children and schools) and a lack of accountability for poor academic performance.[74] The proposed solution is to increase the frequency with which achievement is measured, establish standards of performance using those measures, and create punishments for students and schools that fail to meet the standards (such as students being held back a grade, schools losing funding, or school administrations losing institutional control).

The concept behind accountability programs is similar to that behind school choice in that it is intended to force underperforming schools to improve through incentive structures. Indeed, many supporters of accountability programs also support school choice. But there is an important difference between the two systems: under school choice, the pooled judgments of education consumers determine which schools are performing well or poorly, to what extent they are doing so, and what the consequences are to be; under accountability programs, the government makes these decisions. If accountability programs were seen to improve the performance of schools, it would be according to the measures chosen by the government, which are not necessarily those valued by parents, students, or (later) colleges and employers. Moreover, pursuit of a government's inevitably rather rigid standards can lead to outcomes that are inefficient or potentially harmful.

There is a great deal of evidence that accountability programs have increased students' performance on standardized tests—surely a positive result.[75] However, it is much less clear whether these score improvements are the result of actual educational progress or if they derive from an increased pedagogical focus on the test (at the expense of other learning), or possibly even from reassignment of students and changes in test-taking procedures to "game" the test. Several studies have found that the introduction of an accountability program resulted in more students' being assigned special education status, which exempts them either from taking the test or from having their scores included in the official measure.[76] Research also shows that the introduction of high-stakes tests causes teachers to preemptively hold back low-achieving students to prevent them from taking the test, and that academic resources are diverted from subjects (such as science and social studies) in which students are not tested. Finally, there is some evidence that achievement gains measured were ephemeral and test-specific. In a study of Chicago public school children, scores on the high-stakes tests improved, but scores on "less important" standardized tests did not.[77] What is particularly important to note about all of these findings is that the worst subversions of the program were found at the most disadvantaged schools. Still, accountability programs have shown the power that a clear system of incentives can have (with both good and bad results); refinement is entirely possible and is certainly worth the effort.

In contrast to the top-down approach associated with the emphasis on accountability, communitarian approaches to schooling generate their standards and incentives through interactions among parents, teachers, administrators, and students. Indeed one might say that communitarian methods (exemplified by the School Development Program [SDP] of Yale psychiatrist James Comer) rely on the commitment and involvement of a school's constituents as the means of ensuring accountability. Comer and other communitarians note that low achievement and discipline problems are concentrated at "schools in communities that are dysfunctional for a variety of economic and resultant social and psychological reasons."[78] The key insight of the advocates of communitarian approaches is that schools can be used to foster the sense of belonging and the supportiveness necessary for development.[79] To achieve this, schools need to create an environment in which staff, parents, and students feel invested in the school, in the concerns and emotions of other members of the school community, and in the efficacy of the educational process.[80]

Many schools already incorporate some of these elements in their educational process, but most schools are stuck, to at least some extent, in what Comer calls the "intelligence and will" model. Developmental levels are taken for granted, and students are expected to respond to academic materials (and succeed or fail in doing so) solely on the basis of their native intelligence and their willpower.[81] Transitioning from this kind of environment to the more supportive, communal environment recommended by Comer and others is perhaps the greatest challenge to communitarian approaches. Developing a sense of community is not something, like test score standards, that can be imposed by law. Most communitarian programs involve sending a team of experts into a school to train school leaders or even to introduce and operate the program. Making the transition takes time, and it can be both expensive and very sensitive to the quality of the leaders and experts involved.[82]

Anecdotal evidence suggests that these programs have been largely successful in increasing commitment to schooling, improving discipline, and in some cases raising test scores. However, the few systematic empirical studies of the academic effects of communitarian approaches have produced mixed results.[83] Meredith Phillips provides one of the more sophisticated analyses and reports that the characteristics of communitarian environments that she studied did not significantly improve test scores or attendance for middle school students.[84] However, a more recent study of different *types* of communitarian programs found that three of them (including James Comer's SDP) had strongly positive achievement results, and that SDP, in particular, did so at a relatively low cost.[85] It seems that communitarian reforms can be effective, but that (as in the case of school choice plans) their effectiveness depends on their details—including the singular drive and charisma of their leaders, such as Comer—and that their benefits must be weighed against the financial costs of instituting and managing an approach that is in fact more complicated than it may seem to be.

THE LAST FEW YARDS: OUTSIDE-THE-CLASSROOM INFLUENCES ON STUDENTS IN THEIR ADOLESCENT YEARS

Early investments through health and preschool programs are essential first steps to college preparedness. High-quality primary and secondary schooling are needed to retain and build on gains from early childhood programs. But college preparedness also requires encouraging students to have high educational aspirations, building their confidence, and imparting to them knowledge of how to navigate the application process. Communities devoid of role models experienced in and connected to higher education may have trouble fostering the social skills and behaviors that help students transition to the application stage of this long process of getting ready for college. Recent studies of mentoring programs that match adults familiar with higher education (sometimes college students themselves) to disadvantaged students suggest that these out-of-school support systems can change the mindsets and broaden the educational goals of students from low-SES backgrounds.

One study based on random assignment of adult mentors within the Big Brothers/Big Sisters program found that only 18 months after being matched with mentors, student participants were less likely to engage in self-destructive behavior or skip classes, had higher average grades, and felt more confident of their academic abilities.[86] While Big Brothers/Big Sisters emphasizes broad, general mentoring support, Philadelphia's Sponsor-A-Scholar (SAS) program specifically emphasizes educational development and aims to help area high school students transition to college. The SAS program provides mentoring through high school and the first year of college, separate academic support, advice on the college application and financial aid processes, as well as financial support during college—a comprehensive approach if ever there was one. Researchers used samples of Philadelphia students matched by demographic characteristics and prior achievement to measure the effectiveness of the SAS program. Participating in the program was found to result in significantly higher grade point averages and a 22 percent increase in the rate of college-going.[87] In Chicago, the LINK Unlimited program provides college-preparatory educational opportunities for economically disadvantaged African American children. Sponsors provide mentoring, friendship, and financial support toward a student's tuition in one of the city's parochial schools, and assist in students' college search and application processes. In New York City, Prep for Prep, the oldest and arguably most successful model for many pre-collegiate enrichment and leadership programs, is currently in its third decade with over 3,000 graduates. Prep identifies talented students from disadvantaged backgrounds, puts them through an intensive, academically rigorous summer and year-long leadership development program that prepares them for placement in independent schools, and then follows up with post-placement services.[88]

The SAS, LINK Unlimited, and Prep for Prep programs require substantial funding, and all of these long-term programs demand a significant time contribution from volunteers and professionals. But shorter-term interventions directed specifically at the college application process can also have an impact. The COACH program in Boston, run by economists Christopher Avery and Thomas Kane, sends area college students into disadvantaged local high schools to assist juniors and seniors with their college applications and essays and has shown promising preliminary results.[89] We think that approaches of this kind have great potential, not least because they are targeted, relatively inexpensive, and can have a nearly immediate effect. Moreover, helping in this way can be a valuable form of social service for many college students.

———————

Overshadowing all of the debates over specific policies and programs are larger issues of political will, resources, and priorities. Today we lack the sense of urgency, the idealism, and the optimism that accompanied the enactment of such visionary 1960s War on Poverty programs as Head Start and Community Action, in part because those programs have not fulfilled their unrealistically high expectations. The approaches discussed in this chapter for improving the extramural lives of poor children and the schools they attend cannot be expected to solve all problems—and the problems they will solve will not be solved quickly. Persistence is going to be required.

Perhaps the biggest challenge is to convince contemporary policy makers and the American public to take on the intractable, unglamorous infrastructure problems of early childhood, primary, and secondary education—especially in poor communities. Above all, people in general have to regain and reassert a sense of the "joint and several" responsibility of all of us to provide greater educational opportunities for those so easily left behind. "What we're learning," as Kati Haycock, director of the Education Trust, has observed, "is that education is not like an inoculation, where if you do it once, you are set for life. It is more like nutrition, where you have to do it right and then keep doing it right."[90] Education at all levels—and especially at the pre-college levels—needs and deserves a higher place on the nation's list of priorities. The temptations to "look away," to assume that nothing really can be changed, are all too real. But it will not do to give up on improving college preparedness, especially for those who are most prone to experience the accumulated disadvantages that limit educational opportunities so severely.

The truth is that, with considerable effort, we may be able to maintain current levels of equity and excellence in higher education even if no significant changes are made in improving preparedness. But preserving the status quo without tackling the accumulated disadvantages that children carry with them throughout their lives would ultimately erode a half century of progress in enhancing the capacity of our colleges and universities to serve the country's core values. In our view, the nation can ill afford to pay such a price.

CHAPTER 10

Concluding Thoughts

Today the American "system" of higher education, though not without flaws and weaknesses, represents the highly successful fruition of an essentially uncoordinated series of efforts—by many actors, private and public, acting at many levels, over many years, often with quite different objectives in mind—to meet a broad array of societal needs. Judged by the standards of the world around us, this country can take justifiable pride in the degree to which its diverse, heterogeneous institutions of higher education, taken together, serve the goals of excellence and equity. No other nation has demonstrated as sustained a commitment to educating large numbers of students to a high standard, while simultaneously contributing in unprecedented ways to the advancement and dissemination of knowledge. Nor can any other nation claim as unbroken a record of expanding opportunity. Warts abound, as everyone recognizes, and in this final chapter we will focus on how we can make an impressive system better yet. Still, it would be wrong to begin this discussion, in which we will provide less a summary of findings than some concluding thoughts, without paying tribute to how much has been achieved.

A HISTORICAL PERSPECTIVE

In order to determine how the American system has evolved into its current decentralized public-private partnership, we reviewed more than 200 years of history to re-discover the system's distinctive strengths as well as its idiosyncrasies. This was an instructive exercise, and we are even more persuaded now than we were at the outset that history really matters—more than many of us appreciate.

One rather obvious conclusion, which nonetheless deserves to be highlighted, is that many of the elements that account for the present-day strength of American higher education are of unusually recent vintage. To be sure, from the earliest days of the republic our most prescient leaders—among them Washington, Adams, Hamilton, and Jefferson—acknowledged the critical importance of education in a democratic society. The need for an educated citizenry was clear to these men, but their sense of what that implied was quite different from what we envision today. What did "an educated citizenry" mean at the start of the 19th century? And who would pay for the education needed to produce it? Reformers like Horace Mann, who championed public or "common" primary schools, believed that young children should be trained to be numerate and literate. But the key to understanding 19th-century schoolmen's passion for primary education rests in their belief that the inculcation of commonly held public ideals was essential for "social harmony" and political stability, themes of increasing importance as the nation absorbed generations of new immigrants.[1] A modern-day emphasis on the *economic* contributions of education would not come until much later.

However, "getting there" was not accomplished quickly or without real struggle. We risk romanticizing Americans' commitment to public education at the elementary and secondary levels if we fail to acknowledge both the inertia and the obstreperousness that delayed nationwide acceptance of tax-supported compulsory public education. As every schoolchild once learned, in 1852 Massachusetts became the first state to enact a mandatory attendance policy requiring parents to send children between the ages of 7 and 14 to school for a minimum of 12 weeks a year. Far from creating a groundswell of support, the Massachusetts statute produced resounding silence across the nation. Decades would pass before other states required some form of mandatory schooling, and even then progress was painstakingly slow.

Well into the late 19th century, as historian Judith Sealander notes, state legislators and taxpayers fought vociferously against the premise that "the property of all could be taxed to educate the children of all." In many communities across the nation, "public" schools were financed by a combination of tuition fees and voluntary contributions, and in the South even this minimal schooling was denied to many school-age children, regardless of race. It was not until 1918 that Mississippi required children to go to a state-approved school at least part of the year.[2] By the turn of the 20th century, a high percentage of children, especially outside the South, attended elementary school, but "only about one-half who entered first grade went further than the sixth. Barely one in three completed the typical eight-year grammar school curriculum. Fewer than one in five went to high school, and of that number five out of six failed to graduate."[3]

The triumph of mandatory school attendance, the emergence of the high school, and the attainment of a high school diploma as a necessary and desired student objective—and therefore the beginnings of the nation's modern college and university "feeder system"—all owe a great deal to the fear and anxiety engendered among old-stock Protestants by the great waves of Southern and Eastern European immigrants who entered the United States between 1890 and 1920. The same nativist sentiments that fueled passage of the immigration restriction laws of the early 1920s and the introduction of admission quotas at the nation's most prestigious colleges and universities also stimulated state legislatures' passage of mandatory public schooling laws. By the early 1920s, every state required school attendance for children between the ages of 6 and 16, with enforcement mechanisms in place for prosecuting truancy violators.[4] The modern American high school had arrived, touted as the best institution to unify the nation's increasingly disparate population. Enrollments doubled between 1890 and 1940, and on the eve of World War II, close to half of the population had graduated from high school; at the end of the 20th century, the percentage of high school graduates (not counting those who earned general equivalency diplomas and other equivalencies) stood at 80 percent.[5]

For those of us inclined to take achievements for granted (thinking "surely it has always been this way"), it is useful to recognize that contemporary debates about equity and excellence in American higher education lack context or relevance until the early 20th century, when a national secondary education system was put into place. Claudia Goldin and Lawrence F. Katz are right in emphasizing that today's successes at the higher education level are built squarely on this massive base of college-eligible students—a base unmatched anywhere else in the world.[6] The rapid development of higher education in the United States after World War II would have been impossible without these pools of candidates for admission.

In considering the future of this country's higher education system, a supreme irony is that the very foundation of what has been built so successfully to date, the elementary and secondary education system, is today widely thought to have deep-seated problems of its own—problems that, as we have argued throughout this book, now threaten both the equity and excellence objectives of American higher education. (A related irony is that some of the "virtues" of the late 19th and early 20th centuries that Goldin and Katz credit as having contributed to the effective spread of mass education—especially "public provision by small fiscally independent districts"—are today seen as serious impediments to improving the quality of education at the pre-collegiate level. See chapter 9.)

Another historical legacy that can never be overlooked is this nation's "unlovely racial history." We continue to struggle today—and will struggle for many decades into the future—with the after-effects of centuries of racial subordination and discrimination. Fortunately, other indefensible exclusions—of Jews, Catholics, other unwanted immigrants, and, for a time, women—have been largely if not entirely corrected.[7] To mention one other irony, it is the rapid increase in the enrollment of women and foreign students in graduate and professional programs that has been the principal driver of recent progress in educational attainment at this top level of the educational pyramid. Learning to be more inclusive has had clear-cut benefits for higher education, the economy, and our society. It is also worth noting that, the most troubling aspects of our history notwithstanding, we have been largely spared the divisive issues of "class" that continue to be so daunting in the United Kingdom, the extreme versions of the ideology of "openness" and "free education" that have created such problems in continental Europe, and of course the dreadful history of apartheid that has had such corrosive effects on South Africa. History creates mindsets that are generally much harder to change than rules and policies.

AN "EXCELLENCE AND EQUITY" SCORECARD

It is a fact that many of the world's political and educational leaders "cast envious and wondering eyes at the American university system."[8] But it would be simplistic, and simply wrong, to believe that American higher education has achieved all that it needs to achieve, that it has done equally well in serving all of its objectives, or that it has any basis for complacency. On the basis of the findings reported in this study, we would like to fill in our own scorecard, as a prelude to discussing what we see as the major challenges ahead and the policies that seem to us to represent promising ways of addressing these challenges.

Starting with the "excellence" objective, we are comfortable assigning a grade of "A," and perhaps even an "A+," for this country's achievements in graduate education—and also in research and scholarship (in the humanities as well as in the sciences), which together constitute the major contribution of this nation's research universities to America's culture and to the world economy. The top rankings customarily assigned to America's premier universities are well deserved. However, the decline in the number of U.S. recipients of doctorates in major fields of science is a concern. (See chapter 3 for a discussion of the factors involved, including both preparation at the K–12 level and labor market incentives for top college graduates.)

At the undergraduate level, we would propose a grade of "A–" for the results the United States has achieved in educating a large number of students to a high standard, and in providing a valuable mix of curricula designed to meet different needs, from the liberal arts to more vocationally oriented programs of study. One important caveat is that there are potentially serious issues associated with the preparation at the undergraduate level of enough students interested in science and engineering and capable of pursuing these subjects at higher levels; the United States now ranks well below many other countries in the ratio of first degrees conferred in science and engineering to the 24-year-old population. Another caveat applicable to undergraduate education, offered by a thoughtful commentator, is that many students are not making the substantial intellectual gains one would like them to make in part because some methods of teaching ignore important empirical findings about what constitutes effective teaching and learning.[9]

The U.S. educational system has been less successful in pursuing society's equity objective, though definite progress has been made in opening up opportunities for an ever wider range of students. A "B" seems an appropriate overall average grade. Historically, through at least the mid-1950s, we would have had to give our system a "D" (maybe even an "F") for its treatment of racial minorities. A better grade for improving opportunities for racial minorities is appropriate today, but surely no higher than a "C+." We have been much more successful in eradicating barriers related to religion and gender, and we have also made progress in moving toward need-blind admissions (and it is achievements on these fronts that justify the overall average grade of "B"). But there is much more progress to be made in opening up opportunities for students from poor families.

It remains true that, as the College Board puts it, "An individual's chances of entering . . . college remain closely correlated with family background."[10] One of the stunning findings reported in chapter 4 is that the odds of getting into the pool of credible candidates for admission to a selective college or university are *six* times higher for a child from a high-income family than for a child from a poor family; they are more than *seven* times higher for a child from a college-educated family than they are for a child who would be a first-generation college-goer. A consistent theme of this study is that doing better on the equity front is both essential in and of itself and critical for continued progress in achieving scale and excellence.

Sustaining the Excellence of American Higher Education

We see no need for "systemic reform" of higher education in America; we hear no cries for a fundamental overhaul of the decentralized, variegated "system" that has served the country so well. The elements of the basic "model" include a healthy respect for freedom of expression and critical inquiry, a willingness to make use of market mechanisms, and a pluralistic set of decision makers and funding sources—which generate, in total, more resources than a monolithic system would produce. The resulting diverse and highly competitive structure has allowed the system to avoid the pitfalls of forced homogeneity and associated inefficiencies that one finds in many other countries. Different kinds of public and private institutions, costing different amounts of money to operate and to attend, serve the varied needs (and interests) of multiple clienteles.

The comparison that our colleague Neil Rudenstine makes between the U.S. model and the state-supported European model (and other national models) is telling. These other models rely heavily on government funding, lack incentives for private charitable giving, resist imposing substantial charges on students and families that can afford to pay, are reluctant to use "prices" to allocate students and ration places, and are more subject than the U.S. model to political pressures for "openness" and homogeneity. Mr. Rudenstine is doubtful—and we share his skepticism—that these alternative national models will be able, over time, to generate the resources and create the incentives needed to allow large numbers of their universities to compete effectively with the major U.S. universities.

If we have got the basic model more or less right (as we believe to be the case), what is required for continued success in educating large numbers of students to a high standard, at both undergraduate and professional levels? The most basic need is for steady infusions of two kinds of resources: dollars and talent.

Obtaining adequate financial resources is a particularly acute problem for public universities. Even the strongest and most prestigious of these institutions struggle to compete with their private counterparts for students, faculty, and research money, mostly because state appropriations have continued to decline and all too often the same state-supported institutions are prevented by their legislatures from increasing tuition or raising money in other ways to make up for shortfalls in appropriations. The decline (at least in terms of relative standing) of the public "flagship" universities (see chapter 8) threatens the quality of a sector that is both extremely important in and of itself and a crucial "balance wheel" in the overall system of higher education. The great public universities complement what private universities do and provide healthy competition for them. Under-funding has also impacted the regional public institutions, which are responsible for the education of large numbers of students—including many under-prepared students from disadvantaged backgrounds. These students, who are among the most likely to drop out or stop out, often need more help than they can be given with the resources currently available to their institutions.

National priorities, and especially the declining willingness to raise and spend public funds for public purposes, are, in our view, a major part of the problem. But even within current budget constraints, there are positive steps that can be taken. In particular, we favor giving the flagship universities much more freedom to set their own tuition fees, thereby reducing somewhat the unnecessarily large subsidies provided to students from wealthy families who could, and should, pay a larger share of the costs of their own education. Intelligently crafted student aid policies can be used to cushion the effects of higher tuition on students of modest means. In the case of the "regional" universities and many state and community colleges, a different mix of policies is in order, with lower tuition accompanied by more generous funding from state and federal sources.

The second critical resource that is needed—an unceasing flow of talented students—has both an international dimension at the highest level of educational attainment and a "local" dimension at the undergraduate level. Graduate and professional programs have come to depend on large numbers of exceptionally talented foreign students, and this resource cannot be taken for granted. Other countries are strengthening their own universities, and foreign students have an ever wider set of choices for graduate study. This is not a development to be decried, but it is a reality that must be taken into account in fashioning policies in this country. We can easily make our problems worse than they have to be, and many observers have noted that changes in visa policies growing out of security concerns, if not administered carefully and sensibly, can discourage attendance at U.S. universities by highly talented students from abroad who are important to the quality of this country's higher education system.

The problem at the undergraduate level is of an altogether different kind. The flow of talent needed at this level has to come predominantly from our own school systems. What we have termed (in chapter 3) a "supply-side block" at the "local," or pre-collegiate, level constitutes the most serious threat to the continuing ability of institutions of higher education to extend their reach and enhance the quality of the education that they offer. The evidence is compelling. There has been a plateauing of educational attainment at the BA level *in spite of rising economic returns to higher education over the past 20 years.* In short, the potential supply of college graduates is not responding to clear economic incentives. Why is this? The answer, surely, is the combination of factors (in homes, in neighborhoods, and in elementary and secondary schools) that dampen the aspirations, achievements, and prospects of many children from a very young age. The quality and size of the pool of students who can attend or truly benefit from college is limited due to the weak college preparedness of many young people, and especially those from poor families and minority groups. This is what we mean by a "supply-side block," and here is where equity and excellence concerns merge powerfully.

From the perspective of the excellence objective alone (setting aside, but just for the moment, the fundamental issue of fairness that is paramount), the nation's changing demography gives us no choice but to tap more effectively the talent that resides in these "less traditional" pools comprised of students from racial or ethnic minorities and from poor families. There simply will not be enough "more traditional" candidates to meet the needs of our country in an ever more "brain-intensive" age.

People of all political persuasions should be able to relate to this key proposition. Interestingly, this is precisely the situation that confronts South Africa, which is why it too has no choice—on "developmental" grounds alone—but to do a better job of educating new groups of students who will arrive at universities afflicted by the legacy of apartheid, and certainly without the benefit of all the advantages enjoyed by many of their white contemporaries (never mind their white predecessors).[11]

Promoting Equity

There is no need to repeat here the extensive documentation provided throughout this study of continuing disparities in access to educational opportunity and of continuing differences in educational attainment—all related to race and socioeconomic status. Let us focus instead on what might be done to improve things, and to justify giving America a higher grade on this metric than the composite "B" grudgingly proposed earlier.

The place to begin, surely, is with pre-collegiate preparation. In the long run, the ability of this country's higher education system to educate larger numbers of students from diverse backgrounds to a high standard will depend more than anything else on our success in addressing the panoply of problems that combine to limit the college preparedness of so many young people. Stated simply, poor families have great difficulty investing sufficient resources of all kinds (personal time and encouragement, as well as money) to develop in their children, in the time before high school graduation, the abilities and inclinations they need to attend college, do well, and graduate. "Preparedness" gaps are due to a variety of interacting causes, from poor health to "neighborhood effects" to poor schools plagued by limited funding and other problems. Children from privileged families have more resources at home and access to better-quality primary and secondary schools. The ever accumulating benefits that they enjoy do not just result in stronger cognitive skills; they also lead to higher aspirations, better coping and social skills, and access to information about how to prepare for college and then compete successfully for admission and financial aid.

The only way to fix this problem in the long run is to attack it at its roots—by improving the health, out-of-school environment, and pre-collegiate education of disadvantaged students. In chapter 9 we point out the close connections between socioeconomic status and these factors, and then describe some ways of weakening certain of these links. Changes need to be made in the way schools are financed (with less emphasis on local property taxes) and the way money is spent. We emphasize the importance of properly structuring incentives and high-light the potential for using competition to improve the efficiency of primary and secondary education—while recognizing the dangers of causing unintended consequences. We also believe that James Comer is right in saying that it is not enough to rely solely on the "intelligence and will" approach to learning. Improvements in the social and develop-mental contributions of a school or classroom, through methods of the kind incorporated in Comer's School Development Program, can make a difference. But all of these approaches take time to put in place and then require more time to produce an effect. The deeper goals are, in large measure, profound social changes, not just changes in education policy. They are worthy goals—and they must be pursued—but instant results cannot be expected.

One real danger is that, as we work at improving the prospects of young children, another generation (or two or three generations) will be lost. These children, born too early to reap the benefits of pre-collegiate reform, will have the same disappointing educational outcomes as their parents, and they will then see the same cycle repeat with their own chil-dren. Fortunately, there are steps that can be taken at the college level to improve the lot of those who are too old to benefit from (what we hope will be) ongoing improvements in primary and secondary education. Here American educators might benefit from studying South Africa's example (see appendix A), particularly the higher education community's post-apartheid emphasis on establishing curricular flexibility and differential entry levels to accommodate genuine learning differences.

At the federal and state levels, financial aid programs can be re-aligned and re-designed to have greater effect—and to be much more cost-effective. Many current forms of aid, such as non-refundable tax credits, tax-favored savings plans, and state merit aid, are politically pop-ular, but either do not have a large impact on the college outcomes of those who are on the margin of attending college or have an impact but at a very high cost. These programs are wasteful, in that they allocate scarce resources to students and families that do not really need them. However, they do provide a lesson in efficacy. Even though disadvan-taged students may not always be the primary beneficiaries, they seem to know about and be influenced by programs like the HOPE Scholarship in Georgia, with its "if X, then Y" funding formula. Simplifying the eligi-bility criteria and the application process for federal need-based aid to achieve a HOPE-like degree of straightforwardness could improve the effectiveness of federal programs such as the Pell Grant program.

It is also possible to improve the effectiveness with which we use avail-able financial aid channeled through governmental loan programs. We favor experimentation with a type of income-contingent repayment plan (preferably operated through the tax system) that would avoid the problems of adverse selection. The plan adopted in the United Kingdom, whereby the government in effect advances "top-up" fees to the colleges students attend and then collects the fees from students after they graduate and after they cross certain income hurdles, is worth studying carefully.

"Merit aid" (really "non-need-based aid") has also become increasingly prevalent at the institutional level, and the evidence suggests that higher and higher shares of this money go to students from well-to-do families. Here, too, we worry about the efficiency of giving financial aid dollars to students who could afford to attend college without them. However, as we discuss at the end of chapter 7, there is room for some merit-based awards within a need-based structure. We understand the thinking of those colleges that have chosen to assign limited grant aid funds to those students in need who are most promising and who seem likely to get the most out of the education provided by the college. Beyond this, there is a case, based on anticipated learning outcomes, for providing some amount of aid to students whose exceptional qualifications will improve the education of their peers—*if* they enroll. This is an important "if," because merit aid awards offered by institution A may simply provoke a similar, offsetting, response from institution B; the resulting price war may serve mainly to siphon revenue from the entire set of schools involved. Moreover, at some point the equity costs of such merit aid policies (however effective or ineffective they may be from the perspective of a single institution) may outweigh whatever gains are to be achieved in terms of educational quality.

Decisions concerning the principles used in allocating institutional aid are only one component of efforts at the institutional level to achieve a greater degree of equity within higher education. Particularly vigorous efforts have been made over the past 30 years to increase the racial diversity of campus communities. "Race-sensitive" admissions policies have become ubiquitous at selective institutions that are able to choose among a large group of well-qualified applicants. Overall, these policies have worked very well. They have also been highly contentious, and it is only in the aftermath of the Supreme Court's decision in *Grutter v. Bollinger et al.* that institutions can be reasonably confident that well-crafted policies emphasizing individualized choices among applicants (rather than mechanical approaches such as awarding some number of points to all minority candidates) will survive judicial scrutiny.

In reviewing the Court's opinion in *Grutter,* as expressed by Justice O'Connor (chapter 6), we are particularly impressed by the significant broadening of the Court-approved rationale for the use of such policies, which now includes not only the on-campus educational benefits of diversity stressed by Justice Powell in *Bakke* but also the importance of meeting national needs for larger numbers of well-educated minority students and the "democratic legitimacy" associated with making it plain that the most selective undergraduate and graduate/professional institutions are genuinely open to individuals of all races. As strong supporters of race-sensitive policies, we were also encouraged by the substantial political support for such policies—across many establishment groups whose members do not always agree with one another—that was stimulated, however inadvertently, by the opponents of affirmative action.

Colleges and universities can legitimately take pride in the contributions that they have made in helping to close the gaps between underrepresented minorities and other students in both educational and life outcomes. But this is not the time to relax these efforts. Race remains the most nefarious divider in American society, and it is impossible to know whether the objectives of race-sensitive admissions will have been achieved within Justice O'Connor's "expected" 25-year time limit. New simulations carried out by our colleagues suggest that this putative deadline will not be met if we simply count on a continuation of current policies and trends in income convergence. Additional proactive efforts at both collegiate and pre-collegiate levels are needed.

An approach discussed more and more frequently is to provide admissions preferences to applicants on the basis of socioeconomic status (an approach termed "class-based affirmative action"). An obvious first question is, are such preferences being given now? One of the most striking new empirical findings to emerge from our research is that at the 19 selective schools for which we have detailed data, *there is no perceptible difference in the odds of being admitted, at any given SAT level, between applicants from poor families and applicants from rich families* (see chapter 5). Almost all of these colleges and universities claim to follow "need-blind" admissions policies (meaning that family circumstances should not affect admissions outcomes)—and we now know that, in fact, this is exactly what they do. More generally, our research demonstrates that other outcomes are similarly unaffected by socioeconomic status. Specifically, we find that for those secondary school students who took the SAT, did well on it, and applied to one of these selective institutions, family income and parental education, in and of themselves, had surprisingly little effect. Overall, they have little if any discernible influence not only on admissions probabilities, but also on enrollment decisions (yields), choices of majors, subsequent academic performance and graduation rates, and even on later-life outcomes such as earnings and civic participation.

As we emphasize in chapter 5, this is certainly not to say that socioeconomic status has little or no impact on one's educational opportunities or life chances. It has a huge impact, but the effect occurs earlier on, when college preparedness is shaped by the persistent, cumulative development of cognitive abilities, motivation, expectations, and coping and social skills. Once a student from a modest or disadvantaged background gets into the "credible admissions pool," that individual is treated pretty much as everyone else is treated. *But the odds of getting into this privileged pool in the first place depend enormously on one's race and on how one grew up.*

Is this situation cause for celebration or regret? It is certainly preferable to the situation that prevailed at many colleges prior to the reasonably widespread adoption of need-blind admissions in the late 1960s, when children from privileged backgrounds often enjoyed a huge admissions advantage (far greater, we are sure, than the advantage enjoyed today by legacy applicants). But are the claims of equity really being met today by a policy that gives no positive weight to having come from a poor family—and having somehow overcome all of the attendant barriers in order to compete with a candidate from a very different background for a place in the class? We do not think so, and in these concluding remarks we want to express again our hope that the most privileged colleges and universities, in particular, will think carefully (and sympathetically) about the arguments for "putting a thumb on the scale" when considering candidates with outstanding credentials who come from poor families.

Our simulations suggest that even a modest-sized "thumb" could make a considerable difference in the fraction of enrolled students coming from the bottom income quartile, raising the percentage from about 11 percent today to about 17 percent. It is also worth emphasizing that this hypothetical thumb-on-the-scale approach need not entail any reduction in academic standards: at present, the schools in our study are rejecting roughly *half* of all applicants from the bottom income quartile who have SAT scores in the 1350–1400 range. In short, the composition of the present pools of candidates at these selective institutions offers a real opportunity to take a next step in promoting social mobility and opportunity. Well-qualified candidates are there, and the evidence suggests that, once enrolled, these students can be expected to do very well; unlike both recruited athletes and minority students, they show no tendency to underperform academically.

We say "next step" because we do not believe that "class-based affirmative action" can replace race-sensitive admissions. Having simulated the effects of policies of both kinds, alone and in combination, within our set of 19 selective public and private institutions, we found that shifting to income-sensitive preferences, and eliminating race-sensitive preferences, would cause the share of undergraduate students who are underrepresented minorities to fall by *half*. At graduate and professional levels, the fall-off would be even greater. For us the conclusion is clear: preferences based on income or parental education are not a substitute for race-sensitive admissions. However, preferences for socioeconomically disadvantaged applicants, if properly tailored, could serve as a useful *complement* to race-sensitive admissions.

More and more questions are being raised these days about admissions advantages conferred on a very different group of applicants, legacies, and the "politically correct" approach appears to be to eliminate legacy preferences. We favor a more nuanced approach that would limit the use made of legacy preferences but would recognize that such preferences are justified in some circumstances. Used judiciously, as they are at many institutions, these preferences can advance the excellence objective of colleges and universities even though they do entail some cost from an equity perspective. The case for athletic preferences is, in our view, much weaker, since these preferences advance neither equity nor excellence objectives (chapter 7).

Financial aid can also be used more aggressively than it has been used in the past, and recently several leading universities have proposed more generous financial aid programs for students from low-income families as a way of encouraging more of them to apply and enroll. The signaling effect of such plans could be strong, and lightening the financial burden of poor students is admirable. However, our research suggests that providing more aid to students from low-income families without changing admissions policies may not have as large an impact on enrollment as is hoped; once offered admission, these students already enroll at higher rates than other students, which suggests that present financial aid policies are generally adequate. The key, we believe, is to admit more of these students, choosing especially those who, in the face of obstacles of many kinds, have excelled academically in their pre-collegiate studies. This would be a way of saying to an applicant (in words used in chapter 7): "Hey, you have done great. Look at all that you have accomplished without the advantages enjoyed by most other applicants. Now it is our turn to give you a helping hand."

We also want to stress the value of active programs of recruitment, and especially of targeted efforts to assist students from low-income families, and those from families with no college experience, in navigating the "process" of applying for admission and financial aid. A pilot program in Boston (the COACH program) is one illustration of how this kind of assistance can be provided. This approach is relatively inexpensive and can, we hope, harness the idealism and desire to help of student volunteers who have already "made it" in that they are currently enrolled in college.

In concluding these thoughts on ways in which we might do better on the equity front, we wish to emphasize how high the stakes are. The purely economic value of higher education to individual students and to society at large is greater than ever before and increasing. Many economists credit America's stock of human capital with making possible much of the 20th century's economic growth, and especially with bringing about the "productivity miracle" of the 1990s and the early 2000s.[12] Given the growing economic importance of technology, the need for a highly skilled workforce can only become more acute. The consequences for individuals on both sides of the "education-training divide" are apparent. In chapter 3 we noted the million-dollar difference in lifetime income expectations between those who graduate from high school and those who earn a bachelor's degree.[13] If we fail to enable more students from low-income families to gain the knowledge and skills they will need to succeed in the marketplace, today's large income inequalities—which are already a problem—will become even more pronounced. Ironically, by providing an excellent education to large numbers of students from the most privileged backgrounds, America's colleges and universities will have contributed to the problem rather than to its solution. As Harvard President Lawrence Summers has argued eloquently: "Increasing disparity based on parental position has never been anyone's definition of the American dream."[14]

THE VALUE OF RESEARCH

In reflecting on the research by many scholars that we have found informative in thinking about these issues, we are struck by the importance of using the findings from such studies and the difficulty at times of persuading policy makers to reject argument by anecdote in favor of argument by evidence. In the past decade there has been a tremendous increase in the social science literature relevant to proposals to improve preparedness, and there is certainly room for more good work of this kind. Similarly, the research on student aid has been very helpful in calling into question convenient assumptions about programs such as those offering the HOPE Scholarships in Georgia and the federal Pell Grants. We expect that work being done now on merit aid, using the National Postsecondary Student Aid Studies, will be equally informative. And, as we suggested in the previous section, close scrutiny of the effects of permitting "top-up" fees to be charged in the United Kingdom, along with the proposed graduate repayment plan, could be helpful to educational leaders and policy makers in both countries. Similarly, we believe that the imaginative rethinking of testing and course development in South Africa offers lessons for America as well as for South Africa.[15]

One encouraging development is that colleges and universities seem to be much more interested in empirical studies of outcomes than they used to be. It was gratifying to see how the marshaling of social science evidence, on learning outcomes and on the other effects of race-sensitive admissions policies, helped to inform the Supreme Court's decisions in the Michigan cases. Going forward, it will be very important for colleges and universities to continue to monitor the effects of various admissions initiatives, including some—such as the admissions advantages conferred on recruited athletes—that raise serious questions of both fairness and the effective use of resources. Careful empirical study of early decision programs reveals that they have been much more important in favoring some groups of students than most admissions officers have realized, and this is another example of the potential usefulness of rigorous social science research. It is sadly still too often the case that administrators—and especially *experienced* administrators—assume that they "know" the facts, when actually they do not. As we complete work on this manuscript, we are considering a further expansion of the College and Beyond database to include a wider range of institutions and to collect additional data pertaining to gender. We hope that colleges and universities, as well as governmental policy makers, will continue to welcome efforts of this kind. We believe that they will.

THE ESSENTIAL COMPLEMENTARITY
OF EQUITY AND EXCELLENCE

The final theme we would like to underscore is the essential complementarity of equity and excellence goals all over the world. Because this volume ends with an appendix devoted to the experience of the University of Cape Town (UCT) in South Africa in promoting both equity and excellence, and because the leaders of that university community have a well-earned reputation for thinking freshly about these issues, we conclude by quoting from the inaugural address given in 1996 by Mamphela Ramphele, who was then vice-chancellor of UCT. Dr. Ramphele spoke eloquently of her "vision of a higher education system which strives for *excellence with equity*" (our emphasis). She went on to say:

> One cannot have one without the other. Excellence is undermined by discriminatory policies and practices, which rob society of opportunities to draw from the widest pool of talent available to pursue intellectual activities. Equally destructive are policies that purport to pursue equity at the expense of excellence. Contrary to popular myth on both the left and the right, poor people in this country did not struggle for liberation in order to have equal access to mediocrity—they are passionately seeking to gain access to the best this country can offer. . . . The challenges facing South Africa, as it enters the 21st century, are primarily centered on the need to produce high levels of skilled human resources to drive a modern competitive economy, which equitably offers opportunities to all citizens to realize their full potential and to exercise their citizenship rights.[16]

Dr. Ramphele is surely wise to insist that there is nothing to be said for "equal access to mediocrity." Nor should we ever be satisfied with achievement of a pristine "excellence" that confers access to privilege on a favored few. Pursuing policies with these principles—this *balance*—in mind is the key to maintaining and enhancing the role of American higher education as a driver of the nation's economy, as an engine of social mobility, and as a key contributor to this nation's commitment to democratic values.

Equity and Excellence in Higher Education

The Case of the University of Cape Town

Ian Scott, Nan Yeld, Janice McMillan, and Martin Hall

In the apartheid period, South Africa's higher education sector was highly fragmented. In addition to a distinction between universities and technikons (vocationally oriented higher education institutions), the institutions were divided by race. Among the universities intended only for white students, there was an unofficial but firm division between the English-medium and Afrikaans-medium institutions. The English-medium universities followed a broadly liberal tradition, and preferred to be known as the "open" universities because of their own commitment (constrained in practice by apartheid legislation) to admitting students on academic merit, regardless of race.

As one of the English-medium, open universities, the University of Cape Town (UCT) resisted the 1959 legislation that imposed racial segregation on the higher education sector. Subsequently, and particularly under the leadership of Dr. Stuart Saunders as vice-chancellor through the 1980s and the first half of the 1990s, UCT had a strong anti-apartheid record, including stretching the bounds of apartheid law in admitting black students in increasing numbers when opportunities to do this started to arise in the late 1970s, and opening residences to students of all races in 1981.[1] Financial aid was made available to support talented but indigent black students, and a range of initiatives were put in place to assist these students academically. While focusing on equity through means such as these, UCT retained a central commitment to academic excellence in its teaching and research. Consequently, the university's equity-related initiatives have often been controversial, resulting both in tensions within UCT's academic community and in the need to balance—and, where possible, reconcile—the tensions between equity and excellence.

This tension is widely characteristic of contemporary South Africa. The idea of "transformation"—involving breaking decisively with the inequalities and divisions of the apartheid past and fostering a social and economic dispensation in which all sections of the population can share

—is a dominant one. The essence of transformation is changing the distribution of benefits to include historically excluded groups. For higher education, this means widening participation but recognizing that increasing access is not in itself sufficient. Unless the quality and the relevance of higher education are maintained and improved, the benefits it provides will lose value. Moreover, the benefits obtainable from higher education extend well beyond the interests of those directly involved in it. Thus the nature, forms, and intent of knowledge production in the higher education sector, which have a material effect on the society at large, represent as much a transformation issue as does who participates, and raise important questions about different forms of excellence.

One of the key implications of this is the importance of examining traditional structures—in the case of higher education, particularly the structures of provision—inherited from the exclusionary past, and being willing to change them. In relation to access to higher education, this raises the key question of the extent to which the institution should adapt to meet the needs of the students as opposed to simply requiring the students to meet the traditional demands of the institution.

THE APARTHEID LEGACY

In the late 1950s and early 1960s, universities in South Africa became subject to many restrictions in terms of whom they could admit. In 1953 the notorious Bantu Education Act restructured schooling along racial and ethnic lines, and in 1959 the ironically named Extension of University Education Act extended this restructuring to higher education. This ensured that there was a mechanism for excluding students on racial grounds, in line with the increasingly pervasive system of apartheid.

By its nature, apartheid ideology produced compartmentalization of all structures in the sociopolitical order, not the least in education. The evolution of "grand apartheid" required that there be separate education authorities and institutions for each race or "population group," the main categories being white, colored, Indian, and black (African). When "homeland" territories were established for the black ethnic groups, each had its own education structure as well, though the central government's black education authority, which became known as the Department of Education and Training (DET), remained dominant.[2] Higher education did not escape these divisions, and institutions fell under one or the other of the race-based departments. The apartheid legislation and structures, and the inequalities they entrenched, profoundly affected all the higher education institutions, not the least with regard to access, as outlined in this appendix.

In the wake of the Extension of University Education Act, from 1959 to the late 1960s, there was a considerable decrease in the numbers of black (particularly African) students at residential universities. These numbers, however, had never been high. By 1969, there were only 4,886 African students in "white" universities, compared to 68,559 white students in these institutions.[3]

In the 1970s, however, black enrollments began to increase at the open universities, whose administrations went to great lengths to obtain permits for prospective students. Permits were usually granted only if students registered for certain courses (such as Italian or archaeology) that were not available at the few institutions set aside for black students. This permit system, while inimical to academic planning, was fairly easily manipulated by institutions and students because students, once they had been admitted, could transfer to other courses (usually in their second year) and then continue studying while the institution embarked on a series of lengthy appeals.

In the 1980s the state established several new universities in the so-called independent homeland areas, such as Bophuthatswana, Transkei, and Venda. These new institutions were intended to accommodate the needs and aspirations of the great majority of black students, of whom only a very small number would be allowed to register at the white institutions. This small number would be admitted via a proposed new regulatory mechanism of quotas, which would replace the old permit system. In essence, this would force the white institutions themselves to assume responsibility for excluding black students. UCT led concerted resistance to the "quota bill," and a key battle against apartheid in higher education was won in that the quota system was never implemented, though it remained, somewhat threateningly, on the statute books until 1994.[4]

During the early 1980s, then, institutions could, to some extent, manipulate the permit system and admit students on merit. However, the Committee of University Principals, comprising the vice-chancellors of the historically white universities, became increasingly alarmed at high and escalating failure rates and very low "throughput" (degree completion) rates at all levels of the system, and in 1985 recommended that universities raise the level of their admissions criteria. Coupled with the already very low levels of performance of black students on the school-leaving examinations of the DET (which was by far the largest and most poorly resourced education department in the segregated system), as well as the growing crisis in black schools, this meant that the great majority of places at white universities continued to be filled by white applicants.[5]

In addition to the problem of the very small numbers of black students meeting the open universities' entry criteria, there were major obstacles to accurately identifying black students who would be likely to succeed. A key obstacle was the unreliability of the school-leaving examinations of the DET as a measure of achieved performance or academic capacity.[6] The consequence of this lack of predictive validity, and the ensuing difficulty of selecting on any principled basis, was that many black students who might have had the potential to succeed were denied access, and the universities were thus the poorer. Conversely, many students were admitted who did not have the ability to succeed, with obvious negative consequences for the institutions and for the students themselves.

The combined effect of these circumstances was expressed in the concept of "educational disadvantage." J. Hofmeyr and R. Spence argue that this concept developed from deficit-based views prevalent in the 1980s, when students were characterized as cognitively deficient in some way.[7] However, while the issue is still sensitive, educational disadvantage is now generally accepted as referring to the outcomes of the long-term under-resourcing, mismanagement, and deliberate oppression of the education system designed for black learners in the years of apartheid.[8] Thus, rather than being due to some lack of capacity within the individual, educational disadvantage is clearly attributable to the environment in which the individual has been forced to undergo her or his educational experiences. As N. S. Ndebele states, failure to specify this leads to a conflation of blackness with disadvantage, falsely implying that black people are innately disadvantaged.[9]

Findings on the impact of educational disadvantage on future academic performance are somewhat difficult to interpret. However, what is generally accepted is that in poor communities, with illiterate or poorly educated adults, the quality of the school has a greater influence on the life chances of a learner than it has in more privileged communities.[10] In such a context, if schools are of poor quality, learners are further disadvantaged. Since it can be considered a general truth that school quality closely reflects a community's access to and ownership of wealth, it is obvious that precisely where school quality could make the greatest positive difference to the lives of learners, it is likely to be poor. In South Africa, where race and resource allocation were inextricably linked, this was starkly obvious.

The consequences of prolonged exposure to poor and chaotic learning conditions have been widely researched. As might be expected, they are not different in kind in South Africa than they are in the United States. They do, however, differ in severity, as can be seen by South Africa's very poor performance on international benchmark tests. Some of the characteristics of educationally disadvantaged students can be seen in a tendency to apply surface learning approaches (such as memorization) to learning tasks and to view the essentially "ill-structured problems" typical of higher education as "puzzles" with a pre-determined outcome that can be reached by using a specific procedure or approach.[11] Additional characteristics are the application of tacit (often incorrect or misleading) rules that tend to override the appropriate rules needed to approach and analyze ill-structured problems, and a tendency to accept text as "given," not to be criticized.

In addition to weak performance in these "contentless processes," students from educationally disadvantaged backgrounds have severely limited content mastery. Among the factors contributing to these poor general conditions are the preponderance of poorly qualified teachers, the high reliance on rote learning and the consequent passivity of learners, the unavailability of appropriate learning materials such as textbooks, and the widespread, ongoing chaos in the school system.[12]

Given these circumstances, the selection challenge was clearly to increase the numbers of black students while minimizing risk in terms of academic performance. The need to increase numbers is clearly illustrated in table A.1, which gives the number of students in 1988, classified by "population group" (the current formal South African measure of equity in terms of race), at all residential universities in South Africa. This shows the very low numbers of black students in the system as a whole, particularly at the historically white universities, and makes it clear that the only real opportunities for black students to gain access to historically white institutions were in the four English-medium, open institutions. The way in which this challenge was taken up at UCT is discussed in the following section.

WIDENING ACCESS AT UCT: FACILITATING
EQUITY IN SELECTION AND ADMISSIONS

In 1986, only 350 students out of a total of 12,500 registered at UCT were black. Several approaches could have been adopted at this stage to address the situation and increase black student numbers. One approach, for example, would have been to increase the size of the student body as a whole, but the limited capacity of the campus prevented this. Another possible response would have been to lower admissions requirements. However, in addition to the high probability that this could have led to the admission of an increased number of white students with mediocre Senior Certificate (SC) results, moving the "bar" for admissions could not deal with the central selection problem: namely, that the SC results of the great majority of DET students who succeeded in obtaining a matriculation exemption fell within a very restricted range of results. This made selection extremely difficult, because there was little to distinguish between applicants using aggregate scores alone.[13]

TABLE A.1
Student Enrollment by Race at South African
Historically White Universities, 1988

Race	English-Medium Universities		Afrikaans-Medium Universities		All Universities	
	Headcount	Percentage of Students	Headcount	Percentage of Students	Headcount	Percentage of Students
African	4,759	10	673	1	90,345	32
Colored	2,384	5	1,497	2	18,166	6
Indian	3,969	8	91	0	19,048	7
White	36,655	77	65,844	97	155,764	55
Total	47,767	100	68,105	100	283,277	100

Source: Adapted from Cooper and Subotzky 2001.

Yet another policy would have been a try-out period of admission. In such a "fail-first" approach, selection would have been delayed.[14] However, delaying selection would not have lessened the impact of rejection —and might actually have made it more severe (for example, students would have accumulated fee debt). Fail-first approaches, in various forms, are in fact still put forward from time to time as an appropriate method of selection. However, the use of expensive higher education resources in the form of places in programs is an inefficient approach to selection. Teaching students with little chance of success does not make economic or educational sense.

None of these options, then, met the requirement that access be widened without undermining quality. It was thus important for innovative strategies to be developed that could go some way toward balancing the demands of equity and excellence. Consequently, UCT's policies came to be based on the early successes of the Academic Support Programme, which had been established in 1980 and was beginning to achieve results in developing educational interventions for educationally disadvantaged students. These successes indicated that special admissions procedures were necessary to make possible the admission of students who did not meet the standard entrance requirements, and approximately 155 places were initially set aside for this purpose.[15] At this stage, the criteria used in the selection of students for special admission included the position of applicants in their last year of school, school reports on their performance in the last three years of schooling, and subject-by-subject analysis of their examination results. However, it rapidly became obvious that the conditions in the DET made any reliance on school-based results problematic, and the university concluded that alternative selection criteria and procedures that did not depend on the dysfunctional school system needed to be developed.

The objectives of this alternative selection system were twofold. First, accurate assessment of the achieved level of skill and performance of applicants with less than a C aggregate in the Senior Certificate was required. Because 95 percent of DET students obtained results below a C aggregate, this meant that virtually all black students would be assessed in this way. Second, it was necessary to gauge the extent to which applicants could benefit from the kinds of academic support that could be offered at the university. Implicitly, this represented a move toward attempting to test potential rather than manifest achievement. This system of assessment and evaluation came to be known as the Alternative Admissions Research Project (AARP). It proved to be a viable means of enabling UCT to admit not only students whose results indicated that they had achieved the required level of performance, but also students who, despite not meeting regular entry criteria, had the potential to succeed provided they were given appropriate support.[16]

With the demise of apartheid came hopes that conditions in South African schools would rapidly improve and the need for alternative admissions procedures and educational development programs would steadily diminish. Despite considerable efforts, however, it was clear that no quick fix would suffice to undo the educational destruction wrought by apartheid. Indeed the very low proficiency levels revealed by South Africa's participation in the 1999 Third International Mathematics and Science Study (TIMSS) tests attested to the fact that schooling in South Africa remained very troubled. Of the 38 countries that participated in TIMSS 1999, South Africa obtained the lowest scores.[17]

Under these conditions, the validation of the Alternative Admissions testing system became even more important. Figure A.1 shows the number and distribution by race of all students who wrote the AARP tests and subsequently registered at UCT (AARP started offering testing to non-DET students only in 1997).

"Survival analysis" research adapted from actuarial techniques has shown that AARP test scores are a better predictor of the academic performance of DET students than the school-leaving results alone. Figure A.2 depicts the successful "survival" over time of categories of former DET students at UCT. "Non-AARP" refers to those former DET students who did not write AARP tests for admission to UCT. "PTEEP Top 30%" refers to those former DET students who wrote the AARP Placement Test in English for Educational Purposes (PTEEP) and obtained a score in deciles 1 to 3 for the cohort. "PTEEP Bottom 30%" refers to those former DET students who obtained a PTEEP score in deciles 8 to 10 for the cohort. Figure A.2 shows statistically significant differences in progression for former DET students who have written the AARP tests and done

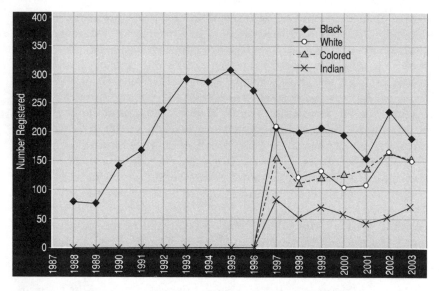

Figure A.1. Total Numbers of Alternative Admissions Research Project (AARP) Test-Writers Who Registered at the University of Cape Town, by Race, 1988–2003

well versus those who have not done well, and also for those who have written the AARP tests and done well versus those who have been admitted on the basis of school-leaving examination results alone. Good performance on an AARP test is clearly better related to successful progression through the curriculum than is poor performance, and good AARP test performance is better related to progression than is conventional school achievement. The AARP tests thus seem to do a better job of identifying talented but educationally disadvantaged students than conventional measures.

As the validity and effectiveness of its tests have become known, AARP has been contracted to undertake selection and placement[18] testing for an increasing number of other South African institutions, including a consortium of leading medical schools. AARP staff have also led a major project funded by the U.S. Agency for International Development[19] that has established placement testing in historically black institutions. Testing venues have been established across South Africa and in several other African countries to allow the recruitment net to be spread wide. The now-extensive AARP database on student assessment and performance provides material for research that can inform national policy on entry-level assessment and access.

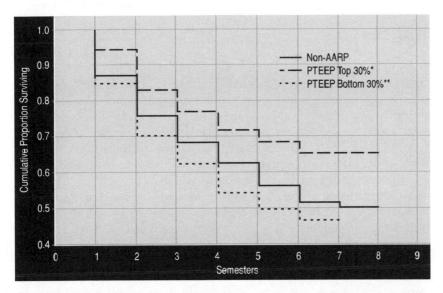

Figure A.2. Survivial of Former Department of Education and Training (DET) Students, by School Achievement or Alternative Admissions Research Project (AARP) Test
    *Refers to those former DET students who wrote the AARP Placement Test in English for Educational Purposes (PTEEP) and obtained a score in deciles 1–3 for the cohort.
    **Refers to those former DET students who obtained a PTEEP score in deciles 8–10 for the cohort.

It is evident that the Alternative Admissions project has made an important contribution to enabling UCT to widen access without compromising its exit standards. Innovative selection would not have been successful, however, without complementary initiatives in curriculum reform, as we discuss in the next section.

WHO SUCCEEDS IN HIGHER EDUCATION? THE TENSION BETWEEN EQUITY AND EXCELLENCE IN THE CURRICULUM

An essential condition for promoting equity is ensuring that talented students, irrespective of their backgrounds, have a fair chance of succeeding in their studies, because access without success is largely a hollow concept. In the current South African context, providing conditions in which students from different backgrounds can succeed may be a key means of promoting excellence as well as equity, through developing the talents of all communities.

As outlined earlier, apartheid legislation had excluded black students (and staff) from the white universities, and thus from the established centers of excellence, throughout the 1960s and much of the 1970s. During the 1970s, then, when opportunities arose to exploit the anomalies of the "separate but equal" ideology, the challenge for the "open" universities like UCT was seen as being principally to provide access, in the sense of places in the university and the material support needed to give disadvantaged students equal opportunity to compete academically with their peers. The poor learning conditions in black schools were also acknowledged, and provided the justification for the establishment of the Academic Support Programme (ASP) at UCT in 1980, with the mission of gaining an understanding of the obstacles faced by black students, organizing help with study skills and additional tutorial support, offering language classes for those black students (the great majority) for whom English was a second language, and co-ordinating material support systems. A similar unit was established at the University of the Witwatersrand at about the same time, and the other two open universities, Natal and Rhodes, soon followed suit, albeit with somewhat different emphases.

The ASP was influenced by affirmative action and minority access programs at a range of leading universities in the United States.[20] The early initiatives of the ASP were modeled partly on such programs and were funded primarily by U.S. charitable foundations and multinational corporations. They took the form mainly of what came to be known as "concurrent" or "add-on" programs: supplementary tutorial support systems that were designed to help disadvantaged students within the regular first-year courses in key subjects. The central aim was to enable talented but disadvantaged students to meet the demands of excellence as embodied in the traditional ethos, approaches, and structures of provision of the university.

The university placed great store in its quality and in the international comparability of its standards, and was sensitive to any developments that might erode these, or might be seen to do so. The admission of "nontraditional" students, particularly via the affirmative action special admissions policy implemented in 1987, and the introduction of intensive tutorial programs, which were vulnerable to being negatively construed as "coaching" or "spoon-feeding," were seen by a range of faculty and staff as a threat to excellence. Even among staff who were strongly supportive of broadening access, there was unease about the implications of affirmative action. The customary tension between excellence and equity that these developments aroused was deepened and complicated by the political and racial conflict that came to a head in South Africa during the 1980s, and the ASP became a lightning rod across the political spectrum.

A key feature of the policies of the early 1980s was that the university's traditional approaches and curriculum structures were taken as a given. Maintaining the status quo was generally equated with maintaining standards. Policies of the time determined that there should be clear limits on how long students would be given support, and that support tutorials and coursework outside the established curriculum—classified formally as "preparatory and remedial instruction"—could not be counted as credits toward a qualification and had to be externally funded. The ideal around which the ASP was originally designed envisaged exceptionally talented students who, with material and some initial academic support, would be able in a short time to overcome the disadvantaging effects of their educational and social backgrounds and "come up to speed" with the traditional student body. Although there certainly were, and have continued to be, students like this, the ideal model was to prove inadequate.

By the mid-1980s, criticism of the original ASP approach had emerged from various quarters, and notably from ASP practitioners themselves. Although the use of supplementary tutorials had grown in sophistication, it had become apparent that this system was effective only for those students who were marginally underprepared (such as black students from the small number of independent non-racial schools). In the case of the majority of the students from the black sectors of the public high school system, particularly those under the DET, the progress they achieved was not enough to overcome the severely disadvantaging effects of their educational backgrounds, which included inappropriate approaches to learning (such as overreliance on rote learning) as well as flawed conceptual knowledge.[21] The key problem was that the concurrent system was bound by the parameters of traditional university courses—particularly the assumptions about students' prior learning on which traditional university curricula were based—which were substantially out of alignment with the black students' educational experience. Particularly in the natural and economic sciences, it was evident that first-year supplementary tutoring, even when the students' standard course workload was reduced, was not sufficient to provide equal opportunities for students from such disparate backgrounds.

The fact that the problem was affecting the majority of the black student intake, even though this was still very small and was drawn from the top-performing echelons of the black school system, indicated the extent of the racial disparities in primary and secondary provision. More radical responses were needed to address inequalities, not only to enable the current black student intake to realize its potential but also to facilitate growth in successful black student participation, the key equity goal.[22] It was equally important, however, that appropriate quality and standards not be sacrificed in the process: it would be a sad irony if, just as higher education was becoming more accessible to black communities, the currency were to be devalued.

At the same time as these educational issues were coming to the fore, the political critique of the higher education system was intensified by anti-apartheid organizations and individuals. Criticism of the open universities focused on the continuing lack of representivity in their student and staff structures (despite their public commitment to non-racism), their institutional culture (which was experienced by black people as exclusionary), and the relevance of their curricula and research to the majority of the South African population. Such criticism included challenges to the traditional concept of excellence that the open universities were seen to espouse, with direct and indirect allegations that it too was unfairly exclusionary.[23]

This starkly highlighted the central point that in South Africa, inequality in access to higher education is not a minority problem. This, in turn, raised the key tension between making the students fit the university and making the university fit the students. H. W. Vilakazi and B. Tema captured the essence of the critique of the status quo in this way: "To gain insight from the study of the experiences of black students in white universities, we have to turn the matter around. . . . The correct starting point should be the realisation that the problem is, first and foremost, not the black student, but the whiteness of the university itself."[24] Leaders of the open universities recognized the pressures and some of the broad implications. For example, as early as 1980 the University of the Witwatersrand's Academic Plan had acknowledged that "we have historically served predominantly the white middle-class community,"[25] and the 1985 UCT vice-chancellor's mission statement encouraged the university to "plan forward . . . so that the University of Cape Town of the future will not merely be a projection of its past but will be in tune with and reflect the changing environment in which it functions."[26] In practice, however, the pressures on the institution were widely seen as a contest between equity and excellence, involving deeply held views on the identity of the university.

The challenge for those who accepted the need for change was how to extend participation without compromising, or being seen to compromise, traditional standards. It had become apparent by the mid-1980s that no significant progress toward greater equity could be made without changes in the structures of provision—that is, without finding alternative routes to reaching the required standards. ASP staff identified the structure of standard South African undergraduate curricula as a central obstacle to access and success for students from the mass black school system.[27] This carried significant implications and raised sensitive questions concerning policy, practice, and values in the university.

There were (and remain) two broad and interlinked areas of contestation. First, given the university's faith in the quality of its provision, there were major concerns about the effects on excellence of any substantial modification of traditional core structures. Second, there was deep-rooted dispute about whether redressing educational inequalities is the responsibility of higher education. A point of view commonly held among academic staff was that, because the root of the problem lay in inequalities and dysfunction in the school system, it was neither productive nor cost-efficient for redress to be attempted at the level of higher education. This argument was applied particularly to leading universities like UCT, which, it was said, should concentrate unequivocally on maintaining internationally recognized excellence. Equity initiatives were seen as bringing a low return on investment and, by drawing away scarce resources, detracting from excellence.

These issues crystallized in what became known as the "articulation gap"—the gap between students' prior learning and the assumptions underlying the university's traditional undergraduate curricula. The articulation gap was complex, involving approaches to learning and academic skills as well as conceptual development and content knowledge. It was manifested in students' underpreparedness for their courses and consequent resorting to surface learning, which undermined their ability ever to gain mastery of their studies. It principally affected black students, and was a key obstacle to equity. The case was made that, although the articulation gap resulted largely from the deficiencies of the school system, it was also attributable to higher education curriculum structures inherited from the colonial past, and was thus essentially a systemic problem for which the higher education sector had to share responsibility.[28]

Most informed parties accepted that in the medium term the school system would not improve sufficiently to ensure a reasonable supply of traditionally well-prepared black students. While there were debates and some isolated initiatives concerning the possibility of establishing an intermediate or community college–style layer that could serve as a partial corrective to the deficiencies of the school system, lack of resources and political will indicated that this was not a realistic prospect, at least in the medium term.[29] The open universities were thus faced with the choice of making no progress toward equity or implementing more substantial and systemic educational development initiatives. The UCT leadership's anti-apartheid commitment meant that the former was not an acceptable option. It did not mean that the university was willing at that stage to consider any significant change in its mainstream educational structures, but there was high-level support for programs designed to substantively address the articulation gap through curriculum development.

The main curriculum-related initiative developed at UCT in the 1980s was the "foundation program" model that came to be introduced in various forms in all the faculties that had large undergraduate enrollments. These programs had their origins in non-credit introductory courses, of half- or full-year duration, that had been devised by ASP science staff in core subjects where black students experienced particular difficulties, including mathematics, physics, and chemistry. These courses were pragmatic responses to the inadequacy of supplementary support. They were designed by skilled educators who were familiar with the demands and assumptions of the regular first-year courses but based their own courses on a realistic understanding of the strengths and weaknesses of their students. They thus, wittingly or not, directly engaged key structural challenges.

In the mid-1980s, because of the promising outcomes of these initiatives and growing recognition of the need for more systemic responses, the ASP focused its work on developing the early foundation courses into comprehensive foundation programs designed for talented but disadvantaged students who were considered to have the academic potential to complete a degree but were not formally qualified, or sufficiently prepared, for direct entry to the regular undergraduate programs. The pioneering program in science was followed over three or four years by similar developments in engineering, commerce, and medicine, with less comprehensive variants in law, arts, and social sciences. Broadly similar programs were introduced at other open universities and one or two technikons at this time, mainly in science and engineering. In most cases, their central components continued to be innovative foundational or "bridging" courses in core subjects, but these were complemented by integrated approaches to developing what have come to be known as key "literacies," particularly academic literacy related to language. Such elements were essential; not only was English not the mother tongue of most black students, but the greatest deficiencies of black schooling were in mathematics and language development, key building blocks for the majority of UCT's most sought-after programs.

The main foundation programs were strongly contextualized within their "home" faculties in both the design of the curriculum and the academic level at which they were pitched, reflecting the importance of linking them as effectively as possible with the regular curricula, and they were incorporated into the university's administrative structures.[30] What they all had in common was that they represented an embryonic but purposeful effort to address the structural problems and inequalities of the education system that were most clearly manifested in the articulation gap. They were thus intended to meet the two interlinked challenges of access and success. They enabled talented but underprepared students to be responsibly admitted to the university, in contrast with the "revolving door" approach of admitting such students to rigid traditional programs from which they were soon excluded through failure, and they were designed to give the students the academic foundations and confidence they needed to realize their potential.

Although the foundation programs and the "special admissions" project had a key role in enabling a four-fold increase in African student enrollment in the latter stage of the apartheid period, numbers were not then the main concern. The central aim was rather to demonstrate —to skeptical faculty, to the university community, to sponsors, and to the students themselves—that the theory was valid, that academic potential was distinguishable from "achieved performance."[31] Given foundational provision that articulated appropriately with their educational backgrounds, talented students from disadvantaged backgrounds could succeed in the full range of degree programs at a selective university like UCT.

The aim was realized in that the small but growing number of graduates who had come through the foundation programs would not have qualified for admission based on the regular criteria, but had met the traditional exit standards. The students' achievements certainly did not convince the academic community as a whole of the validity of the equity agenda—there were, and continue to be, strong criticisms of affirmative action—but such achievements were effective in opening up new perspectives on the issues, especially among the university's leaders. The most effective contributions to changing attitudes arguably came from the performance of particular individuals or classes, as when a rural Science Foundation student, whose school grades were too poor for regular admission, became the first African student to gain an Honors degree in mathematics, or when the Engineering Foundation mathematics class outperformed the regular first-year class for two consecutive years.

However, there was a considerable price to be paid, particularly by the students. As there was no fast track to overcoming their prior disadvantage, the students had to contend with extended academic programs, high levels of stress, and the risk of stigma. Many failed or dropped out. The ironies inherent in this situation, where high achievers from the majority school system were the disadvantaged minority in the university, took their toll. It became clear to the ASP that the performance of many talented black students would be severely constrained by various forms of alienation until such time as the institutional culture and practices came much closer to reflecting the diversity of the population as a whole.[32] In the absence of substantive political change, a key means of progressing toward "normalization" was ensuring that there was a growing number of black students at the university who would be able to hold their own academically and who might in themselves be the most effective agents of positive change.[33]

AFTER APARTHEID:
THE CHALLENGES OF TRANSFORMATION

In the early 1990s, the end of apartheid introduced major change in the significance of equity and the redress of historical inequalities. Those involved in educational development, having previously experienced only opposition from government, were invigorated by the prospect of equity-related work's gaining recognition from the state and hence greater support from the institutions. The public discourse, inside and outside the institutions, rapidly appropriated concepts and terms related to "transformation" that had formerly been frowned on in many universities. It was clear that the opportunity for influencing developments and relating to the state in a new way should not be missed, so a number of educational development specialists needed, for the first time, to divide their time between the institutional and the national levels.

In the latter half of the 1980s, the term *academic development* (AD) had come to be used in most South African higher education institutions in preference to *academic support* because it better indicated the purpose and compass of the field and because *support* had negative connotations. AD became broadly accepted as comprising four inter-related areas of focus: student, staff, curriculum, and institutional development. There was a common aim of improving the effectiveness of the educational process in higher education, to the benefit of all students but with special reference to promoting equity and redress.

The changing political dispensation added new dimensions to AD work. The analysis of what had to be done to achieve acceptable levels of equity in higher education, and how equity could be balanced with other imperatives such as excellence, now had to be undertaken at the national rather than only the institutional level, and carried added significance for two inter-related sets of reasons. First, South Africa had to come to terms with its position as an independent developing country responsible for its own future. Solutions had to be comprehensive, long-term, and sustainable, in comparison with the severely constrained compromises that often had to suffice under apartheid. Second, although equity had been a dominant demand of the anti-apartheid movements, the same movements, coming into government, now had to consider equity in relation to other, potentially competing, requirements of national development.

In AD analysis, a point of departure was the recognition that social and economic inequalities of the kind that had been the source of the major educational problems of the apartheid period would persist. This was of course due to the embeddedness of the apartheid legacy, but it also had to be acknowledged that South Africa was a "less industrialized country" and would have to contend for the foreseeable future with characteristic features of a developing country, including very limited availability of good-quality educational provision and an overarching need to develop latent talent in all communities.

The structural faults in the education system that had been identified in the 1980s, particularly the discontinuity between the secondary and tertiary sectors, remained a key obstacle to inclusiveness and increasing participation in higher education. Ample evidence of the articulation gap was identified, including severe shortages of qualified candidates for key programs, high first-year failure rates, low throughput and graduation rates resulting from inadequate foundations for learning, and a proliferation of (often ad hoc) foundation and bridging programs introduced in response to the mismatch between traditional program demands and the students' prior learning.[34] The problems and inefficiencies were most marked in subject areas where there was the most need for improved output—that is, in science, in engineering and technology, and in high-level management and economics, which were and continue to be identified by government as key requirements for national development. The waste of resources and talent resulting from the poor performance of the system carried a high cost, estimated by the Ministry of Education at well in excess of 10 percent of the state higher education budget.[35]

The new dispensation enabled the arguments about sectoral responsibilities that had begun tentatively in the 1980s to be reviewed and strengthened, on pragmatic and principled grounds. In the first instance it was increasingly evident that, despite the political transition, the school sector would not be in a position to produce the required numbers of traditionally well-prepared students for years or decades to come. The school sector was justifiably pre-occupied with addressing the gross inequalities of the old segregated system and with expansion aimed at achieving universal primary education, and could not reasonably be expected to deliver substantial improvement in output quality at the same time. It was consequently argued that, because it was evident that improving equity in higher education would be a major policy driver, it was in the higher education sector's own interests to take action to address the structural problems that were undermining its performance.

Aside from the pragmatic considerations, it was argued that it was unrealistic to expect a mass school system in a developing country to articulate effectively with a higher education sector that had been designed for completely different conditions. The origins of the higher education framework in South Africa's colonial and apartheid past reinforced the argument that it was important for the sector to be prepared to review its own mainstream structures and assumptions in relation to the country's changing needs. Educational inequalities were neither a minority issue nor a short-term phenomenon, and "normalizing" the system called for productive alignment with the realities of the students that the sector should be expected to accommodate. However, it was critical that greater responsiveness of the institutions to the students must not mean erosion of essential standards. On the contrary, a more representative system had to be expected to improve student responsibility and performance. In summary, it was argued that "it is incumbent on the HE [higher education] sector to take its full share of responsibility for deracialising and normalising the access pathways from lower educational levels" as a key element of its contribution to transformation.[36]

At UCT, in the early 1990s the ASP evolved into the Academic Development Programme (ADP) to take up the broader post-apartheid challenges. As had been the case since the mid-1980s, the ADP saw the educational process, and the curriculum in particular, as the key factor in fostering access and success for talented students from disadvantaged backgrounds. Ensuring productive continuity between secondary and higher education—that is, ensuring that entry-level demands were strongly intellectually challenging but not out of reach—remained a prerequisite, both for enabling disadvantaged students to be admitted to higher education in a responsible manner and for ensuring that they could establish the academic foundations for mastering their disciplines. The continuing inequalities in primary and secondary provision meant that the students who needed and deserved to be given access would be highly diverse in terms of their preparation for higher education, and this in turn called for curricular flexibility, particularly the provision of differential entry levels to match different but legitimate learning needs.

The decade of experience with foundation programs had also shown, however, that the curriculum had to be seen as a whole, that foundational intervention had to be reinforced by sound educational practice at higher levels. For this reason, the concept of the "extended curriculum," in which essential foundational provision was integrated into the mainstream curriculum and influenced its structure, was developed and successfully implemented in various settings, notably in the Academic Support Programme for Engineering in Cape Town (ASPECT) at UCT.

Although in the 1980s there had been no prospect that the calls for equity-related curriculum reform would be heeded, in the mid-1990s the importance attached to equity in the post-apartheid dispensation encouraged AD staff to take the argument to the National Commission on Higher Education (NCHE) through submissions, commissioned papers, and participation in task groups. The case was presented that key equity goals relating to access and success depended, in the medium term, on comprehensive review and redesign of the higher education curriculum framework in relation to required participation rates and representivity targets, and, in the interim, on state recognition of the need for and funding of the provision of extended curricula in selected subject areas.[37] The NCHE accepted the main line of the argument and included some appropriate recommendations in its final report. Some two years later, after various setbacks and revivals, the Ministry of Education's 1997 white paper on higher education, the first major higher education policy statement of the new era, supported the AD position in broad terms.[38] The white paper was historic for AD because it represented the first-ever state recognition of equity-oriented developmental work and, just as important, included a commitment to funding equity-oriented provision.[39]

A further challenge for educational development at the national level under the new dispensation has been the challenge of balancing equity with other imperatives such as excellence. In the early 1990s, when the political transition was in process, there was an exponential increase in the numbers of black youth seeking, and often demanding, access to higher education. The demand for "equality" was at times aggressive, as a result of pent-up need and new expectations, and a number of institutions had effectively no option but to grow exceptionally rapidly. With little or no additional resourcing available from the state, and with the students largely from disadvantaged socioeconomic and educational backgrounds, quality and standards at many institutions were severely at risk. It was in this context that a major contribution to the debate on competing imperatives was made by Harold Wolpe, Saleem Badat, and various colleagues. In various contributions Wolpe and Badat juxtaposed "equality" and "development" (rather than equity and excellence), and analyzed the relationship between them in an effort to foster understanding of the need to balance individual and collective interests and to recognize the importance of quality for the emerging democracy.[40] While "excellence" and "development" in this sense—where it refers to social development and international competitiveness—are closely linked, it is "development" that has turned out in recent years to be arguably a more appropriate concept than "excellence" to juxtapose with "equity."

Finally, a key question that has been debated is whether all higher education institutions should share in the responsibility for achieving equity, or whether a system of institutional differentiation should be introduced that would make equity the responsibility of some and excellence that of a select few. The American system is commonly used as an example of institutional differentiation. In 2000 a task team of the statutory Council on Higher Education made formal recommendations for the establishment of a three-tiered system that would effectively remove research funding from the bottom tier and restrict both research and postgraduate studies in the middle one.[41] The proposal was strongly opposed by a number of groups and not accepted by the Ministry of Education. However, the idea of differentiation remains attractive to various parties as a solution to the tension between equity and excellence.

There is already considerable informal differentiation in South African higher education resulting from the varied origins, missions, and resources of the institutions. While mission differentiation is enriching, statutory differentiation by tier runs the major risk of entrenching social and racial stratification, with the great majority of school-leavers and adult learners from disadvantaged socioeconomic backgrounds (most of whom are black) having access only to under-resourced bottom-tier institutions and having to go via circuitous routes if they are to progress to high-quality qualifications. Given the shortage of well-prepared black students in particular, the key equity goal of fostering representivity across the system requires provision for the inclusion of talented but disadvantaged students in all key programs at all institutions. In the interests of development and equity, it is particularly important for disadvantaged students with high potential to have direct access to extended curricula in selective, high-status programs rather than being faced with the succession of selection hurdles involved in progressing through intermediate institutions. Racial stratification can be reduced if institutions, particularly the leading ones, develop the capacity to accommodate diversity through flexibility in the curriculum framework.[42]

NEW CHALLENGES

In the 1990s the emphasis in relation to equity at UCT shifted toward substantial enrollment increases and economies of scale in foundation and extended curriculum programs. Such planned growth was a step toward "normalization." In addition, as the foundation and extended curriculum programs grew more sophisticated and were more effectively integrated with mainstream curricula, it became possible to open up elements of them to mainstream students (mainly but not exclusively black students) who were struggling with the traditional courses, and some structured "catchnet" curriculum pathways were introduced.[43]

Aided by these developments and some small but rapid growth in black access to quality historically white schools, the overall numbers of black students at UCT increased substantially. Although African enrollment had remained low in absolute terms for much of the 1980s (reaching 900, or 7 percent of total enrollment, in 1988), it rose five-fold in the next 10 years, reaching 5,000, or 28 percent of total enrollment, in 1999, as shown in figure A.3. By the end of the decade, total black enrollment

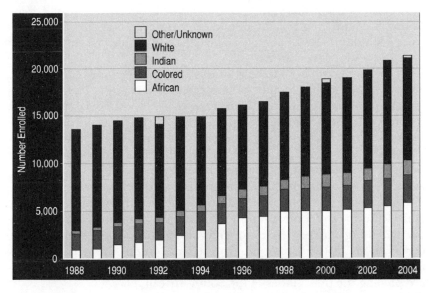

Figure A.3. University of Cape Town Enrollment, by Race, 1988–2004

(including "colored" and "Indian" as well as African students) had lev-
eled off at almost 50 percent.[44]

However, as has been the case across the higher education sector, the
growth in black participation has been concentrated in certain subject
areas, and the promising aggregate figures mask the continuation of racial
(and in some cases gender) imbalances in key programs, notably in high-
status first degrees (such as actuarial science, medicine, and the finance
streams of business science) and in postgraduate studies. Because UCT is
a leader in programs like this, it is felt that it has a particular obligation
to extend their benefits to suitably talented black students who are not
fully qualified or prepared. It has thus become important to provide
extended curricula for the exceptionally selective programs as well.

In this situation, the key challenge for curriculum design and innovation at UCT (and the few similar universities in South Africa) is dealing
effectively with diversity in mainstream provision, rather than relying as
heavily as now on foundation programs. It is evident that to reach reasonable levels of representivity in the student body, UCT has to cater to
a greater range of student preparedness than does almost any comparable university elsewhere. Achieving this without compromising quality
and standards remains a demanding challenge. What is strongly in UCT's
favor, however, and what makes the equity project feasible, is the high

level of latent talent that can be found in the historically oppressed communities. Identifying this talent and offering provision that allows the students to flourish has already yielded significant successes, but there have also been many failures.

These challenges have to be addressed within the context of a higher education system in the midst of unprecedented change. The country's 36 public universities and technikons are to be reduced to 24 institutions through incorporations and mergers. A new sort of institution—a comprehensive university—is to be created. A new funding formula, which will seek to steer publicly funded student places toward national development needs, is being introduced. A new, statutory, quality assurance agency has been launched and is beginning a program of quality audits. A national agency for processing higher education applications is under consideration, and a new, and much changed, curriculum for secondary schooling has been announced, along with a new approach to certification. At the same time, private institutions are proliferating, and entrepreneurial providers from Europe, Australia, and North America are probing the possibilities of the South African market.

New national higher education policy is making strong arguments for a more "responsive and engaged" higher education sector, and, it could be argued, for new ways of understanding the relationship between equity and excellence. The *National Plan for Higher Education in South Africa* and the education white paper, "A Programme for Higher Education Transformation," put forward the following arguments about the role of higher education in contributing to social justice and to economic and social life more generally:

> Higher education, and public higher education especially, has immense
> potential to contribute to the consolidation of democracy and social jus-
> tice, and the growth and development of the economy. . . . These contri-
> butions are complementary. The enhancement of democracy lays the
> basis for greater participation in economic and social life more generally.
> Higher levels of employment and work contribute to political and social
> stability and the capacity of citizens to exercise and enforce democratic
> rights and participate effectively in decision-making. The overall well-being
> of nations is vitally dependent on the contribution of higher education to
> the social, cultural, political and economic development of its citizens.[45]

Institutions such as UCT therefore have an important role to play in addressing issues of equity in a broader sense through supporting new forms of excellence in their policies and practices. They offer individuals the opportunity of moving across the borders of social exclusion. They incubate applied research and technology transfer spin-offs through basic research activities. They act as nodes that link organizations dedicated to the public good (whether government agencies or charitable foundations) with communities. They facilitate the transfer of resources from the "first world" economy to the "third world" (whether the "third world" is in rural Africa or the inner city of a North American metropolis). Inasmuch as this happens, the relationship—or possible relationships—between the twin goals of equity and excellence will be better understood. It might then be possible, through this understanding, to see that the relationship between equity and excellence is part of a larger struggle around the identity and role of (public) higher education institutions.[46]

It is evident that many people in higher education continue to consider that equity and excellence are in competition, particularly for resources, and the dilemmas faced by national and institutional leaders in managing these forces have not yet been resolved. However, in this appendix we have expressed the view that, particularly in the South African context, it is becoming increasingly counter-productive to consider and treat equity and excellence (and the demands of "development") as separate imperatives. In fact, it may well be that the new overarching imperative is to balance equity and excellence.

It is equally clear, however, that there are substantial challenges ahead. In the area of promoting "equity of access" and "equity of outcomes" in the institutions themselves, forthcoming challenges include:

- The probability of a growing tension between equity and efficiency in higher education resulting from changes in the state's approach to funding public services. This probability is evident in the new higher education funding framework in South Africa, and may create testing challenges for equity and/or quality of provision.
- The growing impact of private higher education, which may include drawing away resources from the public higher education sector without contributing substantively to meeting developmental needs.
- The fact that race and social class are no longer virtually coterminous as they were in the apartheid period, which is already creating new tensions, alliances, and challenges in higher education, will require serious reflection on the equity agenda and possibly new equity-related approaches.

We believe that progress will be made not by denying the tensions between equity and excellence that appear as a reality for many in higher education but rather by (1) establishing clear, prioritized, and convincing goals at the national and institutional levels and (2) developing, publicizing, and implementing strong theory- and evidence-based policies and strategies that demonstrate how, or to what extent, the tensions can be reconciled in practice. We believe further that development work done in South Africa and elsewhere, of the kind discussed in this appendix, has identified principles and approaches that can provide a basis for progress, albeit that there are still many serious shortcomings in developmental practices on the ground. It is hoped that international cooperation in this area of work will be able to grow productively as some commonalities emerge between developed and developing countries in relation to widening participation. This should be a goal shared by policy makers and educators in all democratic societies.

Preferences Based on
Socioeconomic Status

Methodological Notes

We simulated the results of admissions policies that give applicants from low–socioeconomic status (SES) backgrounds the same admissions preference that legacy applicants currently receive under four possible regimes: (1) giving the preference to students in the bottom income quartile and maintaining minority preferences; (2) giving the preference to students in the bottom income quartile and eliminating minority preferences; (3) giving the preference to students whose parents did not attend college and maintaining minority preferences; and (4) giving the preference to students whose parents did not attend college and eliminating minority preferences. The two first-generation simulations were done in exactly the same way as the two bottom-quartile simulations, except for the substitution of parental education for income. Accordingly, only the methodologies for the two bottom-quartile simulations will be explained.

MAINTAINING RACE-SENSITIVE PREFERENCES

We began the simulation of bottom-quartile preferences while maintaining minority preferences by applying the current admission rate for legacy students in each combined SAT range of 50 points (with the bottom range coded at "800 and below") at each institution to the non-minority bottom-quartile applicants in that SAT range at that institution. If no admit rate was available for a particular SAT range, the rate was estimated by averaging the admit rates of the two closest available SAT ranges at that institution, with some control for outliers. The resulting non-minority bottom-quartile "admitted students" were assigned the middle SAT score of their 50-point range (those in the "800 and below" range were assigned a score of 700, which reflected the median score in this range at most institutions).

To predict the number and SAT scores of enrolled non-minority bottom-quartile students, the matriculation rate (the yield) of current non-minority bottom-quartile admitted students in each 50-point SAT range at each institution was applied to the predicted non-minority bottom-quartile students in that SAT range at that institution. If no matriculation rate was available for a given SAT range, the rate was estimated by averaging the matriculation rates of the two closest available SAT ranges at that institution, with some control for outliers. The resulting non-minority bottom-quartile "enrolled students" were assigned an SAT score in the same way as the (predicted) admitted students were.

The current admission rates, SAT distribution, and enrollment rates of minority applicants were maintained, as were the admission rates and enrollment rates of non-minority non-bottom-quartile recruited athletes and legacies. The number and SAT distribution of admitted slots were also held constant for each institution. The students admitted with preferences were subtracted from this total, and the remaining spots were assigned to non-minority non-bottom-quartile applicants who did not receive preferences.

Occasionally more "preferred" students were admitted in an SAT range than there were spaces available. When this occurred, the "overflow" was offset by cycling through the other SAT ranges from bottom to top, removing one non-minority non-bottom-quartile admitted student (at random) from each range on each pass until the total number in the overflow was achieved. With this technique we hope to defer in some measure to the judgment of the admissions officer who decided on the allocation of spots by SAT range, using measures of talent and character that we cannot observe.

SAT scores were assigned to the predicted non-minority non-bottom-quartile admitted students again using the middle value of the SAT range. To predict the number and distribution of enrolled students, the current matriculation rates of non-minority non-bottom-quartile students were applied to the predicted admitted students (recruit and legacy matriculation rates were used for recruits and legacies). Because fewer non-minority non-bottom-quartile students were admitted than currently, no correction for missing matriculation rates was necessary. SAT scores were assigned to the predicted enrolled students based on their SAT range.

REMOVING RACE-SENSITIVE PREFERENCES

A similar methodology was used for estimating the effects of an admissions policy in which bottom-quartile students are given the same admission preference as current legacy students while removing race-sensitive preferences, except that bottom-quartile minority applicants were considered together with bottom-quartile non-minority applicants and non-bottom-quartile minority applicants were considered together with non-bottom-quartile non-minority applicants. Current legacy admissions rates in each SAT range were applied to both non-minority and minority bottom-quartile current applicants. The admitted students were assigned an SAT score, and current matriculation rates for non-minority bottom-quartile admitted students and minority bottom-quartile admitted students in each SAT range were applied to the predicted admitted students in that SAT range to determine the numbers and distribution of enrolled students.

The predicted number of bottom-quartile admitted students in each SAT range at each institution was subtracted from the number of current total admitted student spaces in each SAT range at each institution, as was the number of current non-bottom-quartile legacy and recruited athlete admitted students (both non-minority and minority). The remaining admitted student places in each SAT range were given to current non-minority and minority applicants, with the spaces distributed according to the ratio of non-minority to minority applicants in that SAT range. Overflows were offset by cycling through the SAT ranges from bottom to top, removing one non-bottom-quartile admitted student from each range on each pass until the total number in the overflow was achieved (non-minority and minority admitted students were removed according to the ratio of non-minority to minority non-bottom-quartile applicants).

The results were rounded and SAT scores were assigned. The current matriculation rates of non-minority and minority non-bottom-quartile admitted students were applied to the predicted non-bottom-quartile admitted students to determine the number and distribution of enrolled students (recruit and legacy matriculation rates for non-minority and minority students were used for recruit and legacy admitted students in their respective groups). SAT scores were assigned to the predicted enrolled students based on their SAT range.

CALCULATION OF DESCRIPTIVE STATISTICS

Probabilities of admission for bottom-quartile applicants, minority applicants, and non-minority non-bottom-quartile applicants were calculated by dividing the number of the appropriate combination of predicted and current admitted students by the number of current applicants of each type. It is likely that the applicant pools would change under this admissions policy—most notably, the number of bottom-quartile applicants would probably rise to take advantage of the new admissions preference. This is an important consideration, which could potentially be addressed by using a weighted sample of the national pool of SAT-takers as a "predicted" applicant pool. Nevertheless, this simulation probably provides a reasonable estimate of what the actual admissions process would look like, and likely provides an accurate description of what would happen in the first year or few years of a new admissions scheme, before the pool of potential college applicants was able to react to it.

Percentages of admitted and enrolled students were determined using the predicted populations. Using the current matriculation rates to predict enrollment has problems similar to those of using the current applicant pools; under a new policy, there is a non-trivial chance that the matriculation rates of the affected groups would change. This is another important consideration, but one for which it is difficult to account. Again, the enrollment predictions are likely to be reasonable estimates, especially for the early period of a new policy.

Finally, average SAT scores were calculated using actual SAT scores where available for the simulated admitted and enrolled students (a good example is minority SAT scores in the simulation that maintains minority preferences) and using the estimated "middle-of-the-range" distribution where the actual scores were not available. This technique misses some of the nuances of the actual SAT distribution, but given the large number of students and the relatively small SAT ranges, it probably hits pretty close to the target.

OTHER METHODS

The methodology we employed was by no means the only one that could possibly be used. In addition to using different admission rates within SAT intervals (those of minority students, or an index of the admission rates of all groups enjoying an admissions advantage) and estimating different application patterns or matriculation behavior, there are other ways to simulate the admission of the base group of "non-favored" applicants. On the suggestion of Thomas Kane, we simulated the income-sensitive preferences retaining race-sensitive preferences without constraining the size of the pool of admitted students. We then scaled back the number of students admitted (both those who received preferences and those who did not) first by the quotient of the number predicted and the number actually admitted in each SAT range, and then by the overall quotient. Both of these techniques yielded results that were remarkably close to those generated using the methodology described earlier. One could also use regression analysis to produce the admissions probabilities, but we would expect the results obtained to mirror those obtained by using the more mechanical method, only with somewhat greater precision.

Appendix Tables

APPENDIX TABLE 5.1

Number of Non-Foreign Applicants and Enrolled Students,
by Institution, 1995 Entering Cohort

Institution	Non-Foreign Applicants	Non-Foreign Enrolled Students
Private Institutions		
Ivy League universities		
Columbia University	10,066	1,158
Harvard University	15,429	1,511
Princeton University	14,312	1,207
University of Pennsylvania	14,331	2,356
Yale University	12,620	1,364
Liberal arts colleges		
Barnard College	2,973	521
Bowdoin College	3,712	436
Macalester College	2,507	437
Middlebury College	3,222	581
Oberlin College	3,985	725
Pomona College	3,583	392
Smith College	3,334	631
Swarthmore College	2,967	354
Wellesley College	3,371	551
Williams College	4,518	513
All private institutions	**100,930**	**12,737**
Public Universities		
Pennsylvania State University	23,992	4,284
University of California–Los Angeles	25,457	3,695
University of Illinois–Urbana/Champaign	16,936	5,998
University of Virginia	13,249	2,810
All public universities	**79,634**	**16,787**
All institutions	**180,564**	**29,524**

Source: Expanded College and Beyond database.

APPENDIX TABLE 5.2
Percentage of Students from Families in the Bottom Income Quartile,
Percentage Who Were First-Generation College Students, and Overlap Group,
All 19 Institutions, Public versus Private, 1995 Entering Cohort

	Public	*Private*
Applicants		
Bottom income quartile	12.0	11.6
First-generation college student	9.3	5.8
Bottom quartile and first-generation college student	4.0	2.9
Enrolled Students		
Bottom income quartile	11.8	10.6
First-generation college student	8.8	5.5
Bottom quartile and first-generation college student	4.0	2.8

Source: Expanded College and Beyond database.
Note: Percentages based on non-foreign students who provided income and parental education data on the Student Descriptive Questionnaire.

APPENDIX TABLE 5.3a
Percentage of Minority Applicants and Enrolled Students from Low-SES
Backgrounds, All 19 Institutions, 1995 Entering Cohort

	Percentage Bottom Income Quartile	*Percentage First-Generation College*
Applicants		
Minority	25.7	16.4
Non-minority	9.5	4.8
Enrolled Students		
Minority	26.2	16.6
Non-minority	8.8	4.6

APPENDIX TABLE 5.3b
Percentage of Applicants and Enrolled Students from Low-SES Backgrounds
Who Are Minorities, All 19 Institutions, 1995 Entering Cohort

	Percentage Minority
Applicants	
Bottom income quartile	27.7
First-generation college student	32.4
Enrolled Students	
Bottom income quartile	30.4
First-generation college student	35.2

Source: Expanded College and Beyond database.

APPENDIX TABLE 5.4

Average SAT Scores of Enrolled Students and Average Enrollment,
by Family Income and Parental Education, Public versus Private Institutions,
1995 Entering Cohort

	Public Universities	Private Institutions
Family income		
Bottom quartile	1168.8	1228.7
2nd quartile	1214.0	1271.1
3rd quartile	1241.5	1288.3
Top quartile	1259.0	1309.2
Difference between top and bottom	90.3	80.5
Parental education		
First-generation college students	1160.8	1189.5
At least one parent attended college	1239.8	1294.5
Difference between first generation		
and others	79.0	105.0
Average enrollment per class	4,197	849

Source: Expanded College and Beyond database.
Note: Both research universities and small liberal arts colleges are included among the
"Private Institutions," and the average enrollment does not reflect the actual enrollment of
either type. The average enrollment for the five Ivy League universities was 1,519 students
per class, while the average for the 10 liberal arts colleges was 514 students per class.

APPENDIX TABLE 5.5

Distribution of Enrolled Students, by 1989 National Income Quartiles,
11 Overlap Institutions, 1976, 1989, and 1995 Entering Cohorts

	Bottom Quartile	2nd Quartile	3rd Quartile	Top Quartile
1976 entering cohort	10.0%	26.0%	25.1%	38.9%
1989 entering cohort	8.7%	22.6%	22.8%	45.9%
1995 entering cohort	10.8%	22.0%	17.4%	50.0%
Difference 1976–1995	+0.8	−4.0	−7.7	+11.1
Difference 1989–1995	+2.1	−0.6	−5.4	+4.1

Source: College and Beyond database.
Note: Percentages based on non-foreign students who provided income and parental education data on the Student Descriptive Questionnaire. 1976 and 1995 quartile thresholds
are adjusted for Consumers Price Index inflation. Percentages may not add up to 100 percent due to rounding.

APPENDIX TABLE 7.1

Simulation of the Effects of Income-Sensitive Admissions Preferences Based on Legacy Preferences, 18 Institutions, 1995 Entering Cohort

	Current Admissions Policies			Eliminating Race-Sensitive Preferences			Income-Sensitive Preferences, Retaining Race-Sensitive Preferences			Income-Sensitive Preferences, Eliminating Race-Sensitive Preferences		
	Public	Private	All	Public	Private	All	Public	Private	All	Public	Private	All
Admissions Probabilities												
All bottom income quartile	41.7	30.2	**32.1**	38.9	25.8	**27.9**	46.3	46.6	**46.6**	39.7	44.0	**43.3**
All minority	56.8	46.6	**48.3**	27.6	21.9	**22.8**	57.3	47.1	**48.8**	29.0	26.1	**26.6**
Non-minority, non-bottom quartile	43.2	38.6	**39.4**	48.1	41.7	**42.8**	43.1	37.2	**38.2**	48.4	38.9	**40.5**
Percentage of Admitted Students												
All bottom income quartile	11.8	8.7	**9.2**	11.6	7.2	**8.0**	12.2	14.2	**13.8**	10.1	13.7	**13.1**
All minority	17.5	15.0	**15.5**	8.5	6.2	**6.5**	17.6	15.1	**15.5**	9.0	7.8	**8.0**
Non-minority, non-bottom quartile	75.0	79.4	**78.6**	83.1	87.7	**87.0**	74.5	73.9	**74.0**	83.2	80.9	**81.3**
Percentage of Enrolled Students												
All bottom income quartile	12.7	10.2	**10.6**	12.7	8.5	**9.2**	12.6	17.5	**16.7**	10.2	16.8	**15.7**
All minority	17.4	12.5	**13.4**	7.8	4.6	**5.1**	17.0	12.4	**13.2**	8.0	6.9	**7.1**
Non-minority, non-bottom quartile	74.2	80.5	**79.4**	82.6	87.9	**87.0**	74.6	73.3	**73.5**	83.8	79.1	**79.9**

Source: Expanded College and Beyond database.
Note: The University of Illinois is excluded due to missing legacy data. Numbers may not sum correctly or may differ slightly when they should be the same due to rounding.

Simulation of the Effects of Parental Education–Sensitive Admissions Preferences Based on Legacy Preferences, 18 Institutions, 1995 Entering Cohort

	Current Admissions Scheme			Parental Education-Sensitive Preferences, Retaining Race-Sensitive Preferences			Parental Education-Sensitive Preferences, Eliminating Race-Sensitive Preferences		
	Public	Private	All	Public	Private	All	Public	Private	All
Admissions Probabilities									
All first-generation college	37.7	32.1	33.0	44.7	43.7	43.9	38.2	38.4	38.4
All minority	56.8	46.6	48.3	57.3	47.1	48.8	28.0	25.0	25.5
Non-minority, non–first generation	43.5	38.0	38.9	43.2	37.4	38.4	48.3	40.1	41.5
Percentage of Admitted Students									
All first-generation college	8.7	4.7	5.3	9.6	6.8	7.3	7.7	6.2	6.4
All minority	17.5	15.0	15.5	17.6	15.1	15.5	8.8	7.4	7.7
Non-minority, non–first generation	77.3	82.3	81.5	76.3	80.1	79.5	85.2	87.8	87.4
Percentage of Enrolled Students									
All first-generation college	9.6	5.2	5.9	9.4	8.8	8.9	8.0	7.7	7.7
All minority	17.4	12.5	13.4	14.7	13.1	13.4	8.0	6.0	6.3
Non-minority, non–first generation	76.6	84.3	83.0	78.7	80.2	80.0	85.5	87.8	87.4

Source: Expanded College and Beyond database.
Note: The University of Illinois is excluded due to missing legacy data. Numbers may not sum correctly or may differ slightly when they should be the same due to rounding.

Notes

Chapter 1   Framework and Road Map

1. Jeffrey Selingo, "U.S. Public's Confidence in Colleges Remains High," *Chronicle of Higher Education,* May 7, 2004, online edition. Public Agenda and the National Center for Public Policy and Higher Education have also conducted surveys on higher education. An overview of these reports, showing data from 1993–2003, is available in John Immerwahr, *Public Attitudes on Higher Education: A Trend Analysis, 1993 to 2003,* National Center Report no. 04-2, prepared by Public Agenda for The National Center for Public Policy and Higher Education, February 2004. Immerwahr reports that "the vast majority of Americans continue to believe that getting a college education is more important than it was in the past, that the country can never have too many college graduates, and that we should not allow the price of a higher education to exclude qualified and motivated students from getting a college education." At the same time, he reports that "there are signs that the public is becoming more troubled about access to higher education." Quotes on pp. 2 and 3.

2. Selingo.

3. Du Bois made this comment in a speech given at Fisk University in 1933. See W. E. B. Du Bois, *The Education of Black People: Ten Critiques, 1906–1960,* ed. Herbert Aptheker (New York: Monthly Review Press, 2001), p. 112.

4. Thomas Jefferson to Charles Yancey, January 6, 1816, cited in Richard Hofstadter, *Anti-Intellectualism in American Life* (New York: Knopf, 1970; reprint of 1963 ed.), p. 300, and in Jennings L. Wagoner Jr., "Jefferson, Justice, and Enlightened Society," in *Spheres of Justice in Education,* ed. Deborah A. Verstegen and James G. Ward (New York: HarperCollins, 1991), p. 24. Jefferson was not, of course, the only well-known public figure to hold this view. John Dewey, the long-lived pragmatist philosopher and educational reformer, was one of the most ardent supporters of the notion of education as an engine of democracy. See, for example, John Dewey, *Democracy and Education* (New York: Free Press, 1916, 1944).

5. Some years ago, one of us (William Bowen) studied this question at Princeton and found that fully 70 percent of all valedictorians in the classes between 1953 and 1983 had received some form of need-based financial aid. See William G. Bowen, "Maintaining Opportunity: Undergraduate Financial Aid at Princeton," Report of the President, Princeton University, April 1983, p. 4. Of course eligibility for need-based financial aid is not limited to students from poor families; as we will see, the fraction of all students from the lowest income quartile is much smaller than the fraction receiving need-based aid.

6. Thomas Jefferson to John Adams, October 28, 1813, in Thomas Jefferson, *Writings,* selected by Merrill D. Peterson (New York: Library of America, 1984), p. 1305.

7. Thomas Jefferson, letter to William Charles Jarvis, September 28, 1820, in Thomas Jefferson, *The Writings of Thomas Jefferson,* ed. Paul L. Ford (New York: G. P. Putnam's Sons, 1892–99), vol. 10, p. 161.

8. Jefferson observed pointedly that the "the mass of mankind has not been born with saddles on their backs, nor a favored few booted and spurred, ready to ride them." Thomas Jefferson to Roger C. Weightman, June 24, 1826, in Jefferson (1984), p. 1517.

9. And there is considerable questioning of whether in fact higher education is meeting this challenge. President Lawrence H. Summers of Harvard, in a speech at the 2004 Annual Meeting of the American Council on Education, was eloquent in addressing what he called "the manifest inadequacy of higher education's current contribution to equality of opportunity in America." (Lawrence H. Summers, "Higher Education and the American Dream," speech delivered at the 86th Annual Meeting, American Council on Education, Miami, Fla., February 29, 2004, available at http://www.president.harvard.edu/speeches/2004/ace.html, accessed August 9, 2004.) In his words: "The most serious domestic problem in the United States today is the widening gap between the children of the rich and the children of the poor, and education is the most powerful weapon we have to address that problem."

10. A list of the 19 participating colleges and universities and a description of the data used in this study can be found in chapter 5. The original College and Beyond (C&B) database, built by the Mellon Foundation between 1994 and 1997, includes records of more than 80,000 undergraduates who made up the 1951, 1976, and 1989 entering cohorts of 28 academically selective colleges and universities. The database was expanded in 2001 to include records of students in the 1995 cohort obtained from 33 colleges and universities. For the current study, we have expanded the C&B database once again, this time to include both applicants and matriculated students in the 1995 cohort; however, the list of 19 academically selective colleges and universities included in this part of the expanded database differs somewhat from the earlier lists of participating colleges and universities. A full description of the original C&B database can be found in appendix A of William G. Bowen and Derek C. Bok, *The Shape of the River: Long-Term Consequences of Considering Race in College and University Admissions* (Princeton, N.J.: Princeton University Press, 1998). The 2001 expansion of the C&B database is described in William G. Bowen and Sarah A. Levin, *Reclaiming the Game: College Sports and Educational Values* (Princeton, N.J.: Princeton University Press, 2003).

11. Mamphela Ramphele, "Embracing the Future," inaugural address, University of Cape Town, October 11, 1996, available at http://web.uct.ac.za/depts/dpa/publications/mr-instl.htm.

12. The reader who wishes to read the lectures themselves can find them at the Web site of The Andrew W. Mellon Foundation at http://www.mellon.org.

Chapter 2   An Equity and Excellence Time Line

1. See David F. Allmendinger Jr., *Paupers and Scholars: The Transformation of Student Life in Nineteenth-Century New England* (New York: St. Martin's Press, 1975), pp. 11–12. In his superb history of Columbia University, Robert McCaughey notes that, unlike its neighbors and competitors at the College of New Jersey (Princeton), the College of Philadelphia (University of Pennsylvania), Harvard, and Yale, each of whose relatively modest endowments necessitated high enrollments (supported by scholarships and

loans), King's College (Columbia) offered no aid and used its large endowment to limit enrollment. See Robert A. McCaughey, *Stand, Columbia: A History of Columbia University in the City of New York, 1754–2004* (New York: Columbia University Press, 2003), p. 37. See also *The American College in the Nineteenth Century,* ed. Roger L. Geiger (Nashville, Tenn.: Vanderbilt University Press, 2000), p. 1.

2. Stephan Thernstrom, "Poor but Hopefull Scholars," in *Glimpses of the Harvard Past,* ed. Bernard Bailyn, Donald Fleming, Oscar Handlin, and Stephan Thernstrom (Cambridge, Mass.: Harvard University Press, 1986), pp. 116–17.

3. Samuel Eliot Morison, *Three Centuries of Harvard 1636–1936* (Cambridge, Mass.: Belknap Press of Harvard University Press, 1965), p. 199.

4. Jefferson, "Notes on the State of Virginia," 1781–1782, cited in Roy J. Honeywell, *The Educational Work of Thomas Jefferson* (New York: Russell & Russell, 1964; reprint of the Harvard University Press monograph dated 1931), p. 11; and Jefferson, "Bill for the More General Diffusion of Knowledge," 1779, in Honeywell, pp. 199–205, quote on p. 199. See also two works by Jennings L. Wagoner Jr.: "'That Knowledge Most Useful to Us': Thomas Jefferson's Concept of Utility in the Education of Republican Citizens," in *Thomas Jefferson and the Education of a Citizen,* ed. James Gilreath (Washington, D.C.: Library of Congress, 1999), and *Jefferson and Education* (Charlottesville, Va.: Thomas Jefferson Foundation, distributed by the University of North Carolina Press, 2004).

5. In his analysis of public education's evolution in New York City, Carl Kaestle estimates that for the years between 1750 and 1776, approximately 200 New Yorkers (representing approximately 6 percent of all college-age men) attended college; see Carl F. Kaestle, *The Evolution of an Urban School System: New York City, 1750–1850* (Cambridge, Mass.: Harvard University Press, 1973), p. 15, note 40.

6. Lawrence W. Levine, *Unpredictable Past: Explorations in American Cultural History* (New York: Oxford University Press, 1993).

7. Thomas D. Snyder, *120 Years of American Education: A Statistical Portrait* (Washington, D.C.: National Center for Education Statistics, 1993), pp. 76–77.

8. Albert Castel, "The Founding Fathers and the Vision of a National University," *History of Education Quarterly* 4, no. 4 (1964): 280–302. Writing under a pseudonym in the October 29, 1788, *Federal Gazette,* Rush envisioned a collegiate curriculum in which "the youth of America will be employed in acquiring those branches of knowledge which increase the conveniences of life, lessen human misery, improve our country, promote population, exalt the human understanding, and establish domestic, social and political happiness." Rush, quoted in *American Higher Education: A Documentary History,* ed. Richard Hofstadter and Wilson Smith (Chicago: University of Chicago Press, 1961), vol. 1, p. 15.

9. See "A Letter from Thomas Jefferson to the Late Peter Carr," September 7, 1814, in *Early History of the University of Virginia as Contained in the Letters of Thomas Jefferson and Joseph C. Cabell,* ed. Nathaniel Francis Cabell (Richmond, Va.: J. W. Randolph, 1856), p. 385; Jefferson, "A Bill for the More General Diffusion of Knowledge," in Jefferson, *The Writings of Thomas Jefferson,* ed. Paul L. Ford (New York: G. P. Putnam's Sons, 1892–99), vol. 2, pp. 220–29; and Jennings L. Wagoner Jr., *Thomas Jefferson and the Education of a New Nation* (Bloomington, Ind.: Phi Delta Kappa Educational Foundation, 1976).

10. For a discussion of 19th-century social mobility, see Stuart M. Blumin, *The Emergence of the Middle Class: Social Experience in the American City, 1760–1900* (Cambridge, England: Cambridge University Press, 1989); and Sean Wilentz, *Chants Demo-*

cratic: New York City and the Rise of the American Working Class, 1788–1850 (New York: Oxford University Press, 1984).

11. Unlike the ministry, as Colin Burke notes, law and medicine "had more fragile links with liberal education . . . and did not have institutionalized subsidization systems." See Colin B. Burke, *American Collegiate Populations: A Test of the Traditional View* (New York: New York University Press, 1982), p. 101.

12. See Burke, pp. 55–89, and Allmendinger, pp. 8–22.

13. Allmendinger, pp. 28–49. The example of Bowdoin College captures the experiences of many New England institutions. Bowdoin's first scholarships, which were funded by the State of Massachusetts beginning in 1814 (and later renewed by Maine upon becoming an independent state), stipulated that one-fourth of the state's $3,000 annual annuity should be designated for payment of the tuition of "worthy and indigent students." In addition to receiving state aid, Bowdoin created a Benevolent Society (1815–26) that provided loans and other support, such as small amounts of money, furniture, and textbooks. See Louis C. Hatch, *The History of Bowdoin College* (Portland, Me.: Southworth Press, 1927), pp. 229–34. A number of other denominational eastern colleges, including Amherst, Dartmouth, Yale, Colby, Columbia, the University of Pennsylvania, and Williams, continued to benefit from state support, some up to the Civil War. See Burke, pp. 40–52, 106–36.

14. Frederick Rudolph, *The American College and University: A History* (Athens, Ga.: University of Georgia Press, 1990; reprint of Alfred A. Knopf 1962 ed.), pp. 146–50, 202–4; and McCaughey, pp. 81–84. For social class segregation, see Harold S. Wechsler, "An Academic Gresham's Law: Group Repulsion as a Theme in American Higher Education," in *The History of Higher Education*, ed. Lester F. Goodchild and Harold S. Wechsler (Needham, Mass.: Simon & Schuster, 1997), pp. 418–19.

15. Allmendinger, pp. 64–78. James Findlay describes the origins and role of the Society for the Promotion of Collegiate and Theological Education in the West (SPCTEW), a national benevolent society of Presbyterian and Congregational support associations established in 1843 to coordinate the efficient distribution of funds from the East to the colleges of the Mississippi Valley. See Findlay, "The SPCTEW and Western Colleges: Religion and Higher Education in Mid-Nineteenth Century America," *History of Education Quarterly* 17 (Spring 1977): 31–62.

16. Thernstrom, p. 120.

17. See two works by Ronald Story: "Harvard Students, the Boston Elite, and the New England Preparatory System, 1800–1876," *History of Education Quarterly* 15, no. 3 (Autumn 1975): 281–85, quote on p. 284, and *The Forging of an Aristocracy: Harvard and the Boston Upper Class, 1800–1870* (Middletown, Conn.: Wesleyan University Press, 1980).

18. According to Thernstrom, in the 1860s one-third of Harvard undergraduates were public school graduates; two-thirds had attended Andover, Exeter, or other preparatory schools or had been tutored at home. Thernstrom, p. 122; quote on p. 124.

19. See Ruth L. Woodward and Wesley Frank Craven, eds., *Princetonians, 1784–1790: A Biographical Dictionary* (Princeton, N.J.: Princeton University Press, 1991), pp. xxxv–xlv. The quote is from J. Jefferson Looney and Ruth L. Woodward, eds., *Princetonians, 1791–1794: A Biographical Dictionary* (Princeton, N.J.: Princeton University Press, 1991), p. xxxvii.

20. See McCaughey, p. 81. By the 1850s, observes Colin Burke, the University of Virginia and the University of South Carolina, with their links to the plantation cul-

ture, "were perceived to be hostile to members of the new and lower-status denominations." See Burke, pp. 40, 124.

21. See James Findlay, "Agency, Denominations, and the Western Colleges, 1830–1860: Some Connections between Evangelicalism and American Higher Education," in Geiger, ed., pp. 115–26; and Paul H. Mattingly, "The Political Culture of America's Antebellum Colleges," *History of Higher Education Annual* 17 (1997): 73–94.

22. See David B. Potts, "American Colleges in the Nineteenth Century: From Localism to Denominationalism," *History of Education Quarterly* 11 (Winter 1971): 363–80; Jurgen Herbst, "From Religion to Politics: Debates and Confrontations over American College Governance in Mid-Eighteenth Century America," in Goodchild and Wechsler, pp. 53–71; Richard Hofstadter and Walter P. Metzger, *The Development of Academic Freedom in the United States* (New York: Columbia University Press, 1955), pp. 116–19, 152–53; and Rudolph (1990), pp. 68–70. For an interesting analysis of the impact of religion on four Southern state universities, see David W. Bratt, "Southern Souls and State Schools: Religion and Public Higher Education in the Southeast, 1776–1900," PhD dissertation, Yale University, 1999.

23. An important exception to this trend, the increasing demand for doctrinal purity among students, faculty, and administrators in late 19th-century Baptist colleges, is discussed in Potts (1971), pp. 369–71.

24. Hatch, p. 19.

25. Daniel Boorstin captures the early 19th century's "booster" spirit in his description of "upstart" cities whose founders and promoters recklessly built opera houses, railroad terminals, hotels, and even prisons in hopes of attracting residents, businesses, and financial stability. Academies and colleges were created for similar purposes as well-to-do town leaders invested time and money in efforts to secure their personal and familial standing. See Boorstin, *The Americans: The National Experience* (New York: Vintage Books, 1965), pp. 113–68, esp. pp. 152–61; and Richard Hofstadter, *Academic Freedom in the Age of the College* (New York: Columbia University Press, 1961). For an important corrective to Boorstin and Hofstadter's characterization of antebellum Midwestern colleges as being inordinately sectarian and ideologically conservative, see James McLachlan, "The American Colleges in the Nineteenth Century: Towards a Reappraisal," *Teachers College Record* 80, no. 2 (December 1978): 287–306; Robert L. Church and Michael W. Sedlak, "The Antebellum College and Academy," in Goodchild and Wechsler, pp. 131–48, esp. pp. 131, 141–45; and Burke, pp. 38–52.

26. See Peter Dobkin Hall, "Noah Porter Writ Large? Reflections on the Modernization of American Education and Its Critics, 1866–1916," in Geiger, ed., pp. 196–220, esp. 196–97. Hall's monograph *The Organization of American Culture, 1700–1900: Private Institutions, Elites and the Origins of American Nationality* (New York: New York University Press, 1982) places the Yale Report in a broader cultural analysis. For a sympathetic but conflicted view of the Yale Report, see Frederick Rudolph, *Curriculum: A History of the Undergraduate Course of Study since 1636* (San Francisco: Jossey-Bass, 1977), pp. 68–89, and Rudolph's earlier work (1990), pp. 130–35. For a different and more recent interpretation, see Mattingly, pp. 85–89, and David B. Potts, "Curriculum and Enrollment: Assessing the Popularity of Antebellum Colleges," in Geiger, ed., pp. 39–45.

27. For the Yale Report, see Goodchild and Wechsler, pp. 191–99; quote on p. 197. The report originally appeared in "Original Papers in Relation to a Course of Liberal Education," *American Journal of Science and Arts* 15 (January 1829): 312.

28. See Rudolph (1990), p. 207; Mario E. Cosenza, *The Establishment of the College of the City of New York as the Free Academy in 1847, Townsend Harris, Founder* (New York:

Associated Alumni of the College of the City of New York, 1952), pp. 146–47; and Willis Rudy, *The College of the City of New York: A History, 1847–1947* (New York: City College Press, 1949), pp. 19–20.

29. Carl Kaestle found that artisans and factory workers sent their children to the academy almost in proportion to their numbers in the population at large (1855 Census). However, clerical workers' children were slightly overrepresented, the children of "proprietors" were present at twice their proportion of the general population, and the children of professionals and the merchant class were present at three times their proportion of the general population. See Kaestle, pp. 106–7.

30. Henry Adams, *The Education of Henry Adams,* edited and with an introduction and notes by Ira B. Nadel (New York: Oxford University Press, 1999; originally published in 1918), p. 256.

31. Roger Geiger discusses the emergence of "multipurpose" colleges, institutions that combined classical curricula with more practical subjects, including instruction in modern languages, engineering, teacher education, and business, in "The Era of Multipurpose Colleges in American Higher Education, 1850–1890," in Geiger, ed., pp. 127–68.

32. See Robert S. Fletcher, *A History of Oberlin College from Its Foundation through the Civil War,* 2 vols. (Oberlin, Ohio: Oberlin College Press, 1943); W. E. Bigglestone, "Oberlin College and the Negro Student, 1865–1940," *Journal of Negro History* 56, no. 3 (July 1971): 198–219; Ellen N. Lawson and Marlene Merrill, "The Antebellum 'Talented Thousandth': Black College Students at Oberlin before the Civil War," *Journal of Negro Education* 52, no. 2 (Spring 1983): 142–55; and James Oliver Horton, "Black Education at Oberlin College: A Controversial Commitment," *Journal of Negro Education* 54, no. 4 (Autumn 1985): 477–99. Berea College, which from its founding in 1855 drew its students from emancipated slaves and "loyal" (Union) white mountaineers, is another institution whose mid-19th-century policies and practice deserve recognition. See Henry N. Drewry and Humphrey Doermann, *Stand and Prosper: Private Black Colleges and Their Students* (Princeton, N.J.: Princeton University Press, 2001), p. 21; and "The Roller-Coaster Ride of Black Students at Berea College," *Journal of Blacks in Higher Education* 13 (Autumn 1996): 62–64.

33. See Barbara Welter, "The Cult of True Womanhood: 1820–1860," *American Quarterly* 18, no. 2 (Summer 1966): 151–74; Jill Conway, "Perspectives on the History of Women's Education in the United States," *History of Education Quarterly* 14, no. 1 (Spring 1974): 1–12; Patricia A. Graham, "Expansion and Exclusion: A History of Women in American Higher Education," *Signs* 3 (Summer 1978): 759–73; Helen Lefkowitz Horowitz, *Alma Mater: Design and Experience in Women's Colleges from Their Nineteenth-Century Beginnings to the 1930s* (New York: Alfred A. Knopf, 1986); Barbara M. Solomon, *In the Company of Educated Women: A History of Women and Higher Education in America* (New Haven, Conn.: Yale University Press, 1985); Patricia A. Palmieri, "From Republican Motherhood to Race Suicide: Arguments on the Higher Education of Women in the United States, 1820–1920," in Goodchild and Wechsler, pp. 173–82; and Roger L. Geiger, "The 'Superior Instruction of Women' 1836–1890," in Geiger, ed., pp. 183–95.

34. Scholars estimate that in 1870 less than 1 percent of women of college age attended an institution of higher education. See Graham, p. 760; Christopher J. Lucas, *American Higher Education: A History* (New York: St. Martin's Press, 1994), p. 156; and Mabel Newcomer, *A Century of Higher Education for American Women* (New York: Harper and Row, 1959), pp. 46–49 ff.

35. Drewry and Doermann, pp. 32–34.

36. Geiger, "Introduction," in Geiger, ed., pp. 1–36, esp. p. 24.

37. Henry Steele Commager, *The American Mind* (New Haven, Conn.: Yale University Press, 1950), p. 10.

38. Undergraduate calculations based on Integrated Postsecondary Education Data System Enrollment Survey numbers reported in the National Science Foundation's WebCASPAR system (http://webcaspar.nsf.gov) and the *Digest of Education Statistics, 2002*, table 215; doctoral degree data are from Thomas B. Hoffer et al., *Doctorate Recipients from United States Universities: Summary Report 2002* (Chicago: NORC, 2003), appendix table A-7. See also Louis Ferleger and William Lazonick, "Higher Education for an Innovative Economy: Land-Grant Colleges and the Managerial Revolution in America," *Business and Economic History* 23, no. 1 (Fall 1994): 116–28, esp. p. 116.

39. Eldon L. Johnson, "Misconceptions about the Early Land-Grant Colleges," in Goodchild and Wechsler, p. 222.

40. See Roger L. Geiger, "The Rise and Fall of Useful Knowledge: Higher Education for Science, Agriculture, and the Mechanic Arts, 1850–1875," in Geiger, ed., pp. 153–68, esp. pp. 153–54, and Roger L. Williams, *The Origins of Federal Support for Higher Education: George W. Atherton and the Land-Grant College Movement* (University Park, Pa.: Pennsylvania State University Press, 1991).

41. See Eldon Johnson, pp. 222–33, and Scott Key, "Economics or Education: The Establishment of American Land-Grant Universities," *Journal of Higher Education* 67, no. 2 (March–April 1996): 196–220.

42. See Claudia Goldin and Lawrence F. Katz, "The Shaping of Higher Education: The Formative Years in the United States, 1890–1940," *Journal of Economic Perspectives* 13, no. 1 (Winter 1999): 50–51.

43. See Rudolph (1990), pp. 281–82; and Claudia Goldin and Lawrence F. Katz, "The 'Virtues' of the Past: Education in the First Hundred Years of the New Republic," NBER Working Paper no. 9958, September, 2003, pp. 39–47. Roger Geiger estimates that the number of students attending public high school increased by over 167 percent between 1890 and 1900 (representing approximately 11 percent of the 14- to 17-year-old population in 1900), and though only about 30 percent of public high school graduates prepared for college, they quickly emerged as the primary source of potential college students. Since more women than men were graduating from high school, one begins to see the proportion of women and men enrolled in college approaching equality. See Roger L. Geiger, "The Crisis of the Old Order: The Colleges in the 1890s," in Geiger, ed., pp. 264–76, esp. pp. 265–67, and Rudolph (1990), pp. 323–24.

44. Eldon Johnson, pp. 224–25.

45. Rudolph (1990), p. 260.

46. Robert Jenkins contends that the "A&M" colleges' greatest contributions rested in teacher training, where their programs filled the void created by Southern legislatures' purposeful disregard and neglect of black secondary education. See Robert L. Jenkins, "The Black Land-Grant Colleges in Their Formative Years, 1890–1920," *Agricultural History* 65, no. 2 (1991): 63–72; Frederick S. Humphries, "Land-Grant Institutions: Their Struggle for Survival and Equality," in *A Century of Service: Land-Grant-Colleges and Universities, 1890–1990*, ed. Ralph D. Christy and Lionel Williamson (New Brunswick, N.J.: Transaction Publishers, 1992), pp. 3–12; Alan Pifer, *The Higher Education of Blacks in the United States* (New York: Carnegie Corporation, 1973); and Drewry and Doermann, pp. 62–66.

47. James Bryce, *The American Commonwealth* (New York: Macmillan, 1923), vol. 2, p. 716. The land-grant colleges represent an important element of recent revisionist scholarship in the history of higher education. See Roger L. Williams, "The Origins of Federal Support for Higher Education," in Goodchild and Wechsler, pp. 267–72.

48. See Laurence R. Veysey, *The Emergence of the American University* (Chicago: University of Chicago Press, 1965), pp. 12–13, 57–179.

49. Woodrow Wilson, "Princeton in the Nation's Service" (speech given at the Princeton Sesquicentennial Celebration, 1896), as quoted in Ernest Boyer and Fred M. Hechinger, *Higher Learning in the Nation's Service* (Washington, D.C.: Carnegie Foundation for the Advancement of Teaching, 1981), p. 52. Wilson's speech was published in *Forum* 22 (December 1896): 450–66, and is reprinted in Hofstadter and Smith, vol. 2, pp. 684–95.

50. See Derek Bok, *Beyond the Ivory Tower: Social Responsibilities of the Modern University* (Cambridge, Mass.: Harvard University Press, 1982), p. 65.

51. The quote is from Theodore Roosevelt's introduction to Charles McCarthy, *The Wisconsin Idea* (New York: Macmillan, 1912), p. vii. McCarthy was director of the State of Wisconsin's Legislative Reference Library, and later served as one of the commissioners of the U.S. Commission on Industrial Relations (1914–15).

52. See Paula Fass, *Outside In: Minorities and the Transformation of American Education* (New York: Oxford University Press, 1989), p. 7.

53. For enrollment statistics, see U.S. Department of Education, National Center for Education Statistics, *Digest of Education Statistics* (Washington, D.C.: U.S. Government Printing Office, 1973), p. 84, table 100. For the settlement movement, see Allen F. Davis, *Spearheads for Reform: The Social Settlements and the Progressive Movement, 1890–1914* (New Brunswick, N.J.: Rutgers University Press, 1984), 2d ed., and Mina Carson, *Settlement Folk: Social Thought and the American Settlement Movement, 1885–1930* (Chicago: University of Chicago Press, 1990).

54. Harold S. Wechsler, *The Qualified Student: A History of Selective College Admission in America* (New York: Wiley, 1977), pp. xi, 216.

55. See Robert H. Wiebe, *The Search for Order, 1877–1920* (New York: Hill and Wang, 1967); Louis Galambos, "The Emerging Organizational Synthesis in Modern American History," *Business History Review* 44, no. 3 (Autumn 1970): 279–90; Burton J. Bledstein, *The Culture of Professionalism: The Middle Class and the Development of Higher Education in America* (New York: W. W. Norton, 1976); and David O. Levine, *The American College and the Culture of Aspiration, 1915–1940* (Ithaca, N.Y.: Cornell University Press, 1986).

56. In 1920, in the first census in which more Americans resided in urban than rural areas, 61.6 percent of 14- to 17-year-olds living in the nation's largest cities were *enrolled* in high school. See David B. Tyack, *The One Best System: A History of American Urban Education* (Cambridge, Mass.: Harvard University Press, 1974), pp. 182–83. In his history of college admission, Harold Wechsler notes that the percentage of high school graduates doubled between 1910 and the early 1920s and doubled again a decade later, ultimately representing more than half of the 17-year-old age group on the eve of World War II. See Wechsler (1977), p. 238. See also U.S. Census Bureau, *Historical Statistics of the United States, Colonial Times to 1970* (Washington, D.C.: U.S. Government Printing Office, 1975).

57. Richard Angelo, "The Students at the University of Pennsylvania and the Temple College of Philadelphia, 1873–1906: Some Notes on Schooling, Class and Social Mobility in the Late Nineteenth Century," *History of Education Quarterly* 19, no. 2 (Summer 1979): 179–205; quote on p. 194.

58. See Wechsler (1977), pp. 40–49, 121–25.

59. Harold S. Wechsler, "The Rationale for Restriction: Ethnicity and College Admission in America, 1910–1980," *American Quarterly* 36, no. 5 (Winter 1984): 643–67, esp. p. 644.

60. Immigration restriction and discriminatory college admissions are only two examples of the topics that created the sharp social and cultural divisions that bitterly divided Americans in the 1920s. A representative group of topics would also include struggles over the enforcement of Prohibition; the rebirth of the Ku Klux Klan in rural and urban America and its role in states as different as Oklahoma, Oregon, and Massachusetts; the debate over the teaching of evolution in the public schools; the trial and, ultimately, the execution of Nicola Sacco and Bartolomeo Vanzetti, the two Italian immigrants and self-proclaimed anarchists who came to epitomize the nation's hopes and fears; and the deep divisions in national politics, particularly inside the Democratic Party in 1924 and again in 1928 when Al Smith became the first Catholic to run for the presidency. See John Higham, *Strangers in the Land: Patterns of American Nativism, 1860–1925*, 2d ed. (New Brunswick, N.J.: Rutgers University Press, 1988; originally published in 1955); David Burner, *The Politics of Provincialism: The Democratic Party in Transition, 1918–1932* (New York: Alfred A. Knopf, 1968); and David J. Goldberg, *Discontented Americans: The United States in the 1920s* (Baltimore: Johns Hopkins University Press, 1999).

61. Wechsler (1977), p. 66.

62. O. Edgar Reynolds, *The Social and Economic Status of College Students* (New York: Teachers College, Columbia University, 1927), pp. 13–25.

63. Reynolds, p. 34.

64. Reynolds, p. 33. In 1907, Congress created a commission to study the immigration question. After three years of research, endless hearings, and 42 volumes of "evidence," the Dillingham Commission "endorsed the view that the new immigrants threatened the American social and economic fabric." See Oscar Handlin, *Race and Nationality in American Life* (Garden City, N.Y.: Doubleday, 1957); and Morton Keller, *Regulating a New Society: Public Policy and Social Change in America, 1900–1933* (Cambridge, Mass.: Harvard University Press, 1994), p. 225.

65. David Halberstam, *The Teammates* (New York: Hyperion, 2003), p. 5.

66. See Maldwyn Jones, *American Immigration* (Chicago: University of Chicago Press, 1992); Roger Daniels, *Guarding the Golden Door: American Immigration Policy and Immigrants since 1882* (New York: Hill and Wang, 2004); and Alan M. Kraut, *The Huddled Masses: The Immigrant in American Society, 1880–1921* (Arlington Heights, Ill.: Harlan Davidson, 1982).

67. Jerome Karabel, "Status-Group Struggle, Organizational Interests, and the Limits of Institutional Autonomy: The Transformation of Harvard, Yale and Princeton, 1918–1940," *Theory and Society* 13, no. 1 (January 1984): 1–40; Harold S. Wechsler, "An Academic Gresham's Law: Group Repulsion in American Higher Education," *Teachers College Record* 82 (1981): 567–88 (this essay was later included in Goodchild and Wechsler, pp. 416–31). See further Martha Graham Synnott, *The Half-Opened Door: Discrimination and Admissions at Harvard, Yale and Princeton, 1900–1970* (Westport, Conn.: Greenwood Press, 1979).

68. See Synnott, pp. 96, 107, 143, 155, 181–82, as cited in Karabel, p. 10; and McCaughey, p. 257.

69. For the University of Chicago, see Wechsler (1977), pp. 215–36. The University of Pennsylvania's policies and practices are discussed in E. Digby Baltzell, Ellen

Glicksman, and Jacquelyn Litt, "The Jewish Communities of Philadelphia and Boston: A Tale of Two Cities," in *Jewish Life in Philadelphia 1830–1940*, ed. Murray Friedman (Philadelphia: Institute for the Study of Human Issues Press, 1983), pp. 308–10. Robert McCaughey provides a nuanced view of academic nativism and anti-Semitism at Columbia in *Stand, Columbia*, pp. 256–76. Sherry Gorelick examines the experiences of early 20th-century Jewish students from New York who found a more hospitable academic home at the City College of New York in *City College and the Jewish Poor: Education in New York, 1880–1924* (New Brunswick, N.J.: Rutgers University Press, 1981).

70. Wechsler (1984), pp. 646–50; Karabel, p. 15; and Wechsler (1977), pp. 131–85.

71. See Lynn D. Gordon, "Annie Nathan Meyer and Barnard College: Mission and Identity in Women's Higher Education, 1889–1950," *History of Education Quarterly* 26, no. 4 (Winter 1986): 503–22.

72. See Nicholas Lemann, *The Big Test: The Secret History of the American Meritocracy* (New York: Farrar, Straus and Giroux, 1999), for an illuminating account of how educational leaders like Harvard President James Conant hoped to use the Scholastic Aptitude Test (SAT) to identify a true American meritocracy as part of an effort to create a new social vision for postwar society.

73. Keith W. Olson, "The G.I. Bill and Higher Education: Success and Surprise," *American Quarterly* 25, no. 5 (December 1973): 596–610; quote on pp. 597–98.

74. See David M. Kennedy, *Freedom from Fear: The American People in Depression and War, 1929–1945* (New York: Oxford University Press, 1999), pp. 784–86.

75. See Olson (1973), pp. 596–97 and 602, and Olson's monograph *The G.I. Bill, the Veterans, and the Colleges* (Lexington, Ky.: University Press of Kentucky Press, 1974).

76. Olson (1973), p. 605, cites Norman Frederiksen and William B. Schrader, *Adjustment to College* (Princeton, N.J.: Educational Testing Service, 1951).

77. John R. Thelin, *A History of American Higher Education* (Baltimore: Johns Hopkins University Press, 2004), pp. 264–68.

78. Hilary Herbold, "Never a Level Playing Field: Blacks and the G.I. Bill," *Journal of Blacks in Higher Education* 6 (Winter 1994–1995): 104–8; quote on p. 106.

79. Olson (1973), p. 607.

80. See David Onkst, "First a Negro . . . Incidentally a Veteran: Black World War Two Veterans and the G.I. Bill of Rights in the Deep South, 1944–1948," *Journal of Social History* 31, no. 3 (Spring 1998): 517–43.

81. Herbold, p. 106.

82. Sarah Turner and John Bound, "Closing the Gap or Widening the Divide: The Effects of the G.I. Bill and World War II on the Educational Outcomes of Black Americans," *Journal of Economic History* 63, no. 1 (March 2003): 145–77; quote on p. 152. As Turner and Bound observe, Keith Olson's research demonstrates that "an estimated 20,000 black veterans were turned away from the Negro colleges, and a survey of 21 of the southern black colleges indicated that 55 percent of all veteran applicants were turned away for lack of space [particularly family living space], compared to about 28 percent for all colleges and universities" (p. 153). Olson also notes that none of the HBCUs had "an accredited engineering department or a graduate program at the doctoral level, and seven states had no graduate program at all." See Olson (1974), p. 74; and Lizabeth Cohen, *A Consumers' Republic: The Politics of Mass Consumption in Postwar America* (New York: Alfred A. Knopf, 2003).

83. Turner and Bound, p. 172.

84. For interesting insights into the origins and motivations behind the creation of the Truman Commission on Higher Education, see Janet C. Kerr, "From Truman to Johnson: *Ad Hoc* Policy Formulation in Higher Education," in Goodchild and Wechsler, pp. 628–52, esp. 629–32.

85. See Hofstadter and Smith, vol. 2, p. 975.

86. President's Commission on Higher Education, *Higher Education for American Democracy* (Washington, D.C.: U.S. Government Printing Office, 1947), vol. 1, p. 27.

87. President's Commission on Higher Education, vol. 5, pp. 1–2.

88. President's Commission on Higher Education, vol. 1, pp. 40–41 and 25.

89. President's Commission on Higher Education, vol. 1, p. 27, and vol. 2, p. 5.

90. President's Commission on Higher Education, vol. 1, p. 31.

91. President's Commission on Higher Education, vol. 1, p. 32, and vol. 2, p. 18.

92. President's Commission on Higher Education, vol. 1, pp. 67–68.

93. President's Commission on Higher Education, vol. 5, pp. 26–28.

94. President's Commission on Higher Education, vol. 2, pp. 25–26. Four commission members dissented from the majority's statement on racial discrimination that called for an end to segregation by reaffirming their support for "separate but equal" educational facilities. See vol. 2, p. 29.

95. President's Commission on Higher Education, vol. 1, p. 34, and vol. 2, p. 36.

96. President's Commission on Higher Education, vol. 2, p. 36, and vol. 1, p. 35.

97. President's Commission on Higher Education, vol. 2, pp. 38–39. For an illuminating account of how medical schools used standardized testing in the admission process, see Charlotte G. Borst, "Choosing the Student Body: Masculinity, Culture, and the Crisis of Medical School Admissions, 1920–1950," *History of Education Quarterly* 42, no. 2 (Summer 2002): 181–214.

98. President's Commission on Higher Education, vol. 2, p. 40; Snyder, p. 76, table 24.

99. Fass, p. 165, cites *Education and Manpower*, ed. Henry David (New York: Columbia University Press, 1960), p. 267, table 8.

100. See Lynn T. White, *Educating Our Daughters: A Challenge to the Colleges* (New York: Harper, 1950), and Fass, p. 165.

101. Mirra Komarovsky, *Women in the Modern World: Their Education and Their Dilemmas* (Boston: Little, Brown, 1953), pp. 258–73; quotes on pp. viii, 268, 265.

102. Fass, pp. 179–80; and Komarovsky, pp. 4–5.

Chapter 3   In Pursuit of Excellence

1. National Commission on Excellence in Education, *A Nation at Risk: The Imperative for Educational Reform*, Washington, D.C.: U.S. Department of Education, April 1983, p. 13, also available at http://www.ed.gov/pubs/NatatRisk/index.html.

2. We want to say a special word of thanks to our colleagues Neil Rudenstine and Harriet Zuckerman, who have been especially helpful with the analysis presented in this chapter.

3. For an analysis of the founding of various types of institutions (for example, liberal arts colleges, research universities, and community colleges), see William G. Bowen et al., *The Charitable Nonprofits* (San Francisco: Jossey-Bass, 1994), pp. 65–73. This study, which focuses on the founding dates of colleges and universities, plots patterns that show the tendency for institutions of a certain type to be created in spurts

or waves, each "spurt" responding to new needs or new opportunities. Three stages of creation and growth are common to many types of organizations: first, a new institutional model is formed, responding to a particular need; second, there is relatively rapid replication of the model; third, there is a slowdown in the rate of entry as competition increases and the organizational niche is filled. Thus most of the leading liberal arts colleges of today were established in the 19th century, before the Civil War; the spurt in the establishment of research universities occurred in the latter part of the 19th century, after the Civil War; and community colleges were established in large numbers in the 1960s.

4. U.S. Census Bureau, "Table 1: Educational Attainment of the Population 15 Years and Over, by Age, Sex, Race, and Hispanic Origin: 2003," from *Current Population Report*, P20-550, "Educational Attainment: 2003, Detailed Tables" (Washington, D.C.: U.S. Census Bureau, Internet release date June 29, 2004), available at http://www.census.gov/population/www/socdemo/education/cps2003.html. Note the important difference between degrees conferred (the focus here) and college enrollment, which we discuss in chapter 4.

5. Thomas B. Hoffer et al., *Doctorate Recipients from United States Universities: Summary Report 2002* (Chicago: National Opinion Research Center, 2003), table 11. Data on the number of degree-granting institutions are from U.S. Department of Education, National Center for Education Statistics, *Digest of Education Statistics, 2002* (hereafter cited as *Digest of Education Statistics, 2002*), NCES 2003-060 (Washington, D.C.: U.S. Department of Education, National Center for Education Statistics, 2003), table 243. There are also a large number of proprietary institutions, some of which offer degrees.

6. *Digest of Education Statistics, 2002*, table 246.

7. U.S. Census Bureau, Population Division, Education and Social Stratification Branch, *Educational Attainment*, Historical Table A-2, "Percent of People 25 Years and Over Who Have Completed High School or College, by Race, Hispanic Origin and Sex: Selected Years 1940 to 2002," available at http://www.census.gov/population/www/socdemo/educ-attn.html.

8. Educational attainment has also increased for black Americans—more rapidly in relative terms than for white Americans—but only very modestly for Hispanics; however, the absolute attainment rates of both of these minority groups remain well below the rate for whites (roughly half as high). In 2000 there were 36.8 BAs per 100 white 24-year-olds, 19.8 BAs per 100 black 24-year-olds, and 15.8 BAs per 100 Hispanic 24-year-olds. (National Science Board, *Science and Engineering Indicators 2004* [hereafter cited as *S&E Indicators*] [Arlington, Va.: National Science Foundation, 2004], p. 2-20, table 2-8, available at http://www.nsf.gov/sbe/srs/seind04/start.htm.) Demographic changes that increase the share of the population from these groups should be expected, therefore, to exert downward pressure on the overall level of educational attainment in the United States. The Hispanic college-age population is projected to increase by 52 percent between 2000 and 2015, while the comparable white cohort will expand slowly until 2010 and then decline; in 2015, the Hispanic population is expected to be 19.8 percent of the total college-age population (*S&E Indicators*, p. 2-11 and figure 2.3, citing appendix table 2.4); and U.S. Census Bureau, table entitled "Projections of the Total Resident Population by 5-Year Age Groups, Race, and Hispanic Origin with Special Age Categories: Middle Series, 2011 to 2015," from *National Population Projections*, NP-T4 (Washington, D.C.: U.S. Census Bureau, Internet

release date January 13, 2000), available at http://www.census.gov/population/ projections/nation/summary/np-t4-d.txt.

9. Our calculations are based on data in *Digest of Education Statistics, 2002*, table 252.

10. See *Digest of Education Statistics, 2002*, tables 259 and 280. In 2004, according to the Association of American Medical Colleges, women represented 50.4 percent of all applicants, continuing a recent two-year trend. See Katherine S. Mangan, "Applications Rise at Medical Schools, as Female and Minority Students Make Gains," *Chronicle of Higher Education,* October 21, 2004, online edition, available at http://chronicle .com/daily/2004/10/2004102101n.htm.

11. In "Longitudinal Trends in the Applicant Pool for U.S. Medical Schools, 1974–1999," Frances R. Hall and colleagues report that from 1974 to 1999, women applicants to medical schools increased both in number (from 8,712 to 17,433) and as a percentage of the total (from 20 to 45 percent). Men's representation in the applicant pool dropped from 33,912 to 21,096 (from 80 percent to 55 percent). They also mention the findings of a study by Carola Eisenberg, who "showed that, without the increased number of women applicants, medical schools would have experienced difficulty maintaining quality in their entering classes." Frances R. Hall et al., "Longitudinal Trends in the Applicant Pool for U.S. Medical Schools, 1974–1999," *Academic Medicine* 76, no. 8 (August 2001): 829–34.

12. Another reader of an early draft of this chapter observed that the substitution of women for men (as holders of degrees of various kinds) can be regarded as an equal trade-off only if women make the same uses, or equivalent uses, of their degrees. Compensation of women still lags behind compensation of men in many fields, but gaps can be expected to continue to close. And of course market contributions are not the only kinds of contributions that matter.

13. *S&E Indicators,* pp. 5-6, 5-28. See also Richard B. Freeman, Emily Jin, and Chia-Yu Shen, "Where Do New US-Trained Science-Engineering PhDs Come From?" NBER Working Paper no. 10554, June 2004, for an extensive discussion of the changing demographics of science and engineering PhDs.

14. There are some differences within the humanities that deserve more careful exploration than we have been able to give them. It is our impression that history, for example, has come closer to maintaining its share of doctorates than has English literature.

15. Calculations from data in Hoffer et al., *Doctorate Recipients from United States Universities: Summary Report 2002* (Chicago: National Opinion Research Center, 2003), table 5.

16. Another excellent source of information on graduate students is the annual reports compiled by the Council of Graduate Schools. Carefully compiled surveys provide detailed data on enrollment by institution type, field of study, region of the country, and citizenship. (See, for example, Peter D. Syverson, *Graduate Enrollment and Degrees: 1986–2001* [Washington, D.C.: Council of Graduate Schools, Office of Research and Information Services, 2003].)

17. Hoffer et al., p. 18. For background on the history of participation by foreign graduate students in U.S. PhD programs, see William G. Bowen and Neil Rudenstine, *In Pursuit of the Ph.D.* (Princeton, N.J.: Princeton University Press, 1992), esp. chapter 1. In 1958, only 772 non-residents received PhDs from American universities (p. 28).

18. Hoffer et al., table 11. See George J. Borjas, "Do Foreign Students Crowd Out Native Students from Graduate Programs?" NBER Working Paper no. 10349, March

2004, for estimates of the crowding-out effect. See also John Bound and Sarah Turner, "Cohort Crowding: How Resources Affect Collegiate Attainment," Population Studies Center Research Report no. 04-557, April 2004, available at http://www.psc .isr.umich.edu/pubs/papers/rr04-557.pdf.

19. Freeman, Jin, and Shen assert that an exogenously driven decline in the number of qualified U.S. candidates is not the main explanation of the pattern observed here. Instead, they provide evidence that the number of U.S. candidates and the number of foreign-born candidates reflect responses to differing labor market prospects for scientists and engineers in the United States and abroad.

20. Hoffer et al.; quotes and number are from pp. 18–19 and data by field are from table 11.

21. *Survey of Earned Doctorates, 2002,* table 2.

22. *S&E Indicators,* p. 1-4.

23. *S&E Indicators,* p. 2-35. See also appendix table 2-33.

24. *S&E Indicators;* National Science Board, *An Emerging and Critical Problem of the Science and Engineering Labor Force: A Companion to Science and Engineering Indicators 2004* (Arlington, Va.: National Science Foundation, 2004).

25. *S&E Indicators,* p. O-10, figure O-18.

26. *S&E Indicators,* p. O-11.

27. *S&E Indicators,* p. 2-36, figure 2-34.

28. *S&E Indicators,* p. 2-35. The report also notes that today there is a high level of participation by women in many of these countries—as is increasingly the case in the United States.

29. Leo Goedegebuure, Frans Kaiser, Peter Maassen, et al., eds., *Higher Education Policy: An International Comparative Perspective* (Oxford: Pergamon, 1994); Stefan Collini, "HiEdBiz," *London Review of Books,* November 6, 2003, online edition. See also Martin Trow, "The Exceptionalism of American Higher Education," in *University and Society: Essays on the Social Role of Research and Higher Education,* ed. Martin Trow and Thorsten Nybom (London: Jessica Kingsley Publishers, 1991), pp. 156–72.

30. *S&E Indicators,* p. 2-12 and table 2-2. See also pp. 2-20, 2-21.

31. *S&E Indicators,* p. 1-28. Data are from the Third International Mathematics and Science Study—Repeat. *S&E Indicators* reports that "Some evidence suggests that college graduates who enter the teaching profession tend to have lesser academic skills." *S&E Indicators,* p. 1-25, and studies cited there.

32. *S&E Indicators,* pp. 1-13, 1-4.

33. *S&E Indicators,* p. 1-14.

34. *S&E Indicators,* p. 1-4. NAEP stands for National Assessment of Educational Progress. Of course these results surely reflect not just what happens in the schools but influences from home life and neighborhood, which intersect with in-school experiences. We discuss these interacting influences in detail in chapter 4 and then again in chapter 9.

35. *S&E Indicators,* p. 2-13.

36. ACT, *Crisis at the Core: Preparing All Students for College and Work* (Iowa City, Iowa: ACT, 2004), available at http://www.act.org. For a commentary on this report, see Karen W. Arenson, "Study of College Readiness Finds No Progress in Decade," *New York Times,* October 14, 2004, p. A26.

37. *S&E Indicators,* p. O-13.

38. *S&E Indicators,* p. 2-28. We are told that Walter Rosenblith, former provost of MIT, once observed that the lingua franca in the halls of MIT had become Chinese.

39. *S&E Indicators*, appendix table 2-27; Hoffer et al., table 11.

40. Hoffer et al., p. 33 and table 28. See also *S&E Indicators*, figure 2-30.

41. *S&E Indicators*, figure O-24 and p. O-13.

42. Elias A. Zerhouni, "Global Workforce Bolsters U.S. Science," *Science*, May 28, 2004, p. 1211.

43. There are also some quantitative studies of the social and educational origins of members of entities such as the Chinese Academy of Sciences. (See Cong Cao, *China's Scientific Elite* [London: Routledge, 2004].) Of the 970 members elected to the Chinese Academy of Sciences since 1955, 467 (48 percent) were trained outside China. Of these, 251 earned degrees at U.S. universities. The country where training occurred next most frequently was Britain, with 14 percent. It is clear that Chinese students educated in the United States were students not only of U.S. scientists but also of foreign-born scientists who emigrated (Cao, pp. 90–91). More research in this area would be welcome.

44. *S&E Indicators*, pp. 2-25 and 2-26, figure 2-19.

45. *S&E Indicators*, pp. 2-36, 2-37. See also appendix table 2-36 for a country-by-country listing. If we exclude the social and behavioral sciences, the non-U.S. percentage rises to 81 percent. See also figure 2-38 (which shows that in 2001 both Europe and Asia conferred more doctoral degrees in natural sciences and engineering fields than did the United States).

46. *S&E Indicators*, figure 2-37 and text on pp. 2-36 and 2-37, and appendix tables 2-38 and 2-39. In the summer of 2004, the leadership of nine Chinese universities traveled to Yale University for an intensive program on the organization and administration of a modern research university. Madame Chen Zhili, the member of China's State Council who oversees education and technology, has said that her goal is for China to have at least two of the ten best research universities in the world. For a comprehensive discussion of the exceptional progress made by South Korea in building its university and research base, see Alan Brender, "Asia's New High Tech Tiger: South Korea's Ambitious, and Expensive, Effort to Bolster University Research Is Paying Off," *Chronicle of Higher Education*, July 23, 2004, p. A34.

47. In many respects, the growth in graduate programs outside the United States over the past decade or so is reminiscent of what happened in this country between 1950 and 1970. In the past three decades, it may be true that the "top 10" U.S. universities are still stronger than their competitors, but the differences between them and the next 10 to 20 or 30 universities have almost certainly narrowed. This same process may now be occurring globally.

48. Changes in where international students are sending their TOEFL (Test of English as a Foreign Language) scores indicate that domestic institutions as well as universities in Canada and the United Kingdom are increasingly drawing interest from potential applicants. (The TOEFL is an English proficiency exam most international institutions require applicants to take.) Between the 2002 and 2003 academic years, the interest of South Korean students shifted dramatically from American toward Korean institutions, and Japanese students have similarly shifted from U.S. schools to domestic universities. (David G. Payne, "The Flow of Graduate Students and Postdoctoral Scholars to and from the United States," presentation to the National Academies Committee on Policy Implications of Graduate Students and Postdoctoral Scholars in the U.S., Washington, D.C., July 19, 2004.) Although most of the institutions listed at the TOEFL Web site as being approved to receive the test scores are in the United States, some are located in non-English-speaking countries such as France, Japan, Korea, and Thailand. These schools include those operated by

U.S. institutions (e.g., Temple University, Tokyo) and those, like Kyoto University, that operate exchange programs taught in English for international students. Other schools, such as Korea University, offer some classes in English, both for Korean students and for international students. The list of schools accepting TOEFL scores is available at ftp://ftp.ets.org/pub/toefl/0304incod.pdf.

49. *S&E Indicators,* pp. 2-38–2-39.

50. *S&E Indicators,* p. O-14 and table O-1.

51. For example, the University of Illinois at Urbana-Champaign experienced a 30 percent drop in foreign applicants to its graduate programs; the steepest applicant declines were among students from China (nearly 50 percent), India (roughly 30 percent), and South Korea and Taiwan (25 percent each). Pennsylvania State University saw similarly stark declines among students from the same countries, and programs beyond science and engineering were also affected. Foreign applicants to the communications program dropped 54 percent, the liberal arts programs experienced a 32 percent drop, and business administration saw a 15 percent drop. Yale University's 19 percent drop in foreign graduate school applications was largely driven by a 30 percent reduction in Chinese applications; applications from the other three key Asian source countries did not follow a similar pattern. Data on graduate applications supplied to the authors by the universities. See Jeffrey Mervis, "Many Origins, One Destination," *Science,* May 28, 2004, p. 1277.

52. Jennifer Jacobson, "Foreign-Student Enrollment Stagnates," *Chronicle of Higher Education,* November 7, 2003, online edition. See Yudhijit Bhattacharjee, "Foreign Graduate Student Applications Drop," *Science,* March 5, 2004, p. 1453. The article summarizes findings obtained through a survey conducted by five higher education organizations.

53. Jeffrey Mervis, "Is the U.S. Brain Gain Faltering?" *Science,* May 28, 2004, pp. 1278–82.

54. Personal communications with authors, August 6, 2004 (Yale), and August 11, 2004 (Stanford).

55. John Bound, Sarah Turner, and Patrick Walsh are at work on a study that is intended to analyze systematically the market forces that play such a large role in determining the international flows of doctoral students. The model they are using focuses on comparing the "opportunity costs" for a foreign student of pursuing doctoral studies in his or her home country versus the costs of studying in the United States or in some other country. The availability of opportunities at home is clearly a big part of the story. This mode of analysis also helps us to understand why residents of some foreign countries who pursue doctoral studies in the United States are concentrated in the top-tier American universities at the same time that residents of other countries are dispersed more broadly throughout the educational system. (See John Bound, Sarah Turner, and Patrick Walsh, "Internationalization of U.S. Doctorate Education," working draft, November 10, 2004.) Reports published in the fall of 2004 continue to show declines in foreign student enrollment in the United States. Assessments of the recent trends vary, with some reporting that "we've turned the tide" and others convinced that further declines are inevitable. (See Burton Bollag, "Enrollment of Foreign Students Drops in U.S.," *Chronicle of Higher Education,* November 19, 2004, online edition.) Bollag's article is accompanied by detailed information on the latest reports, which were published by the Council on Graduate Schools and the Institute of International Education.

56. The vice-chancellor of a leading African university, who had come to the United States to receive an honorary degree from the American university that he had attended, reported how uncomfortable the current entry process made him feel—and how it made him wonder for the first time if he was welcome. Chinese students have been subjected to lengthy visa delays (generally as a result of Visas Mantis checks related to concerns about inappropriate transmission of sensitive technologies), as have students from European countries. The chairman of Stanford's graduate admissions committee in chemistry is quoted as describing the situation this way: "It's nuts— wastes everybody's time, money, and energy. We used to cherry-pick the most talented people. We want them to stay because they're the best minds in the world. . . . We're shooting ourselves in the foot, or more likely in the head. We're hassling them to death and we're losing talent." (See Dawn Levy, "Foreign Students Share Tales of Visa Woes in a Post-9/11 World," *Stanford Report,* May 25, 2004, online edition.) According to a story in the *Chronicle of Higher Education* (Jacobson), one Saudi architecture student at the University of Colorado was told (mistakenly) by a university staff member that he did not need to notify the Bureau of Citizenship and Naturalization Service that he had returned from vacation; when he discovered the error and went to the nearest immigration office, he was grilled severely and even threatened with jail. He now looks forward to returning home as soon as possible and then pursuing his PhD program in Britain. (See Jacobson.) The acting director of scholarship at the Saudi Ministry of Higher Education is quoted as saying: "We are looking almost everywhere in an effort to provide an alternative to the U.S. for our students wanting to study abroad, especially Canada, Australia, and New Zealand." As Jacobson reports: "Australian officials say that the number of students from countries bordering the Persian Gulf and studying in Australia has increased from slightly more than 100 in 1998 to more than 1,000 in 2003." According to the director of international affairs at the American Physical Society: "The best students may be beginning to decide they don't want the hassle of trying to come to the U.S." Recently, there is some indication that U.S. officials are working to streamline processes and to improve the situation. (See Kelly Field, "U.S. Government Considers Extending Security Clearances for Foreign Students and Scholars," *Chronicle of Higher Education,* August 30, 2004, online edition.)

57. *Report of the Commissioners for the University of Virginia,* August 4, 1818, in Thomas Jefferson, *Writings* (New York: Library of America, 1984), p. 460, as cited in Richard B. Bernstein, *Thomas Jefferson* (New York: Oxford University Press, 2003), p. 174. The "spill-over" benefits of new knowledge are enormous. Jefferson put it best: "He who receives an idea from me, receives instruction himself without lessening mine; as he who lights his taper at mine, receives light without darkening me." Thomas Jefferson to Isaac McPherson, August 13, 1813, in Jefferson (1984), p. 1291.

58. Claudia Goldin and Lawrence F. Katz, "The Shaping of Higher Education: The Formative Years in the United States, 1890–1940," *Journal of Economic Perspectives* 13, no. 1 (Winter 1999): 37–62.

59. Vannevar Bush, "Science: The Endless Frontier," A Report to the President by Vannevar Bush, Director of the Office of Scientific Research and Development (Washington, D.C.: U.S. Government Printing Office, 1945).

60. Sutton Trust, "Nobel Prizes: The Changing Pattern of the Awards," September 2003, esp. tables 3 and 5; quotation on p. 2 of the text.

61. William J. Broad, "U.S. Is Losing Its Dominance in the Sciences," *New York Times,* May 3, 2004, p. A1.

62. Harriet Zuckerman, e-mail message to the authors, June 23, 2004. Another source of data that complements the data on Nobel Prizes describes winners of the Fields Medal in Mathematics, which has been awarded since 1936 to 44 individuals not over the age of 40 in recognition of "both existing work and the promise of future achievement." Of the 43 recipients for whom a primary institutional affiliation at the time of the award was clear, 21, or nearly 50 percent, worked at U.S. institutions. (See http://www.mathunion.org/medals.)

63. *S&E Indicators,* table 5-18. For a good discussion of data and terminology, see the box on p. 5-38. The universe of publications examined is a slowly expanding set of "the world's most influential scientific and technical journals" (over 5,000 journals in 2000) tracked by the Institute for Scientific Information *Science Citation Index* and the *Social Sciences Citation Index.* The existence of "some" English-language bias is acknowledged. The term "author" means "institutional author," and "articles are attributed to countries and sectors by the author's institutional affiliation at the time of publication. . . . Likewise, 'coauthorship' refers to institutional coauthorship."

64. *S&E Indicators,* p. 5-41.

65. *S&E Indicators,* p. 5-38. See also the box on p. 5-41 for a description of the planned study of this phenomenon.

66. See *S&E Indicators,* pp. 5-44 and 5-45, table 5-23, for data for individual countries in 1988, 1994, and 2001. In the specific case of Israel, the U.S. share of co-authored articles was 67 percent in 1988, 60 percent in 1994, and 52 percent in 2001—still a very high level of U.S. collaboration, but obviously a declining one.

67. *S&E Indicators,* pp. 5-48, 5-49.

68. Concern for the future of the humanities is not, of course, limited to the United States. In noting the "gross imbalance" in funding given to the humanities and social sciences as distinct from the sciences in the United Kingdom, Colin Lucas, the recently retired vice-chancellor of Oxford University, has observed that "an exclusively economic benefit-driven, science-oriented emphasis is extraordinarily diminishing of a university's true scope and function." We share Sir Colin's view that "a society that pauperizes the Humanities is in great danger of impoverishing its defences and guarantees for the continued stability of a richly diverse mix." See Colin Lucas, "Oration by the Retiring Vice-Chancellor," *Oxford University Gazette* 4707, supplement 2, October 6, 2004, p. 116.

69. Robert M. Solow, "The Value of *Humanities Indicators,*" in *Making the Humanities Count: The Importance of Data* (Cambridge, Mass.: American Academy of Arts and Sciences, 2002), pp. 1–3. The National Endowment for the Humanities has never had the staffing or budget to take on this task, and efforts by private organizations such as the American Academy of Arts and Sciences have not yet led to a template or to a sustainable plan for collecting data on a regular basis.

70. Patricia Meyer Spacks and Leslie Berlowitz, foreword to *Making the Humanities Count: The Importance of Data* (Cambridge, Mass.: American Academy of Arts and Sciences, 2002), p. v.

71. Organisation for Economic Co-operation and Development (OECD), *Education at a Glance 2004* (Paris: Organisation for Economic Co-operation and Development), table A4.1. Korea ranked first in the percentage of undergraduate degrees conferred in the arts and the humanities (21.4 percent), and Mexico ranked last (2.9 percent).

72. Peter Givler, "University Press Publishing in the United States," in *Scholarly Publishing: Books, Journals, Publishers, and Libraries in the Twentieth Century,* ed. Richard E. Abel and Lyman W. Newlin (New York: Wiley, 2002), p. 117.

73. *Ulrich's International Periodicals Directory,* accessed through Dialog, June 23, 2004. Humanities fields included in the search are art, archaeology, architecture, humanities, philosophy, religions and theology, literature, history, and music.

74. *Arts and Humanities Citation Index,* accessed through Dialog, June 25, 2004.

75. For more information about JSTOR, access their Web site at http://www .jstor.org. See also Roger C. Schonfeld, *JSTOR: A History* (Princeton, N.J.: Princeton University Press, 2003).

76. Nancy Lane Carey, Natalie M. Justh, and Jeffrey W. Williams, *Academic Libraries: 2000,* NCES 2004-317 (Washington, D.C.: U.S. Department of Education, National Center for Education Statistics, 2003), and Margaret W. Cahalan and Natalie M. Justh, *The Status of Academic Libraries in the United States: Results from the 1994 Academic Library Survey with Historical Comparisons,* NCES 98-311 (Washington, D.C.: U.S. Department of Education, Office of Educational Research and Improvement, 1998).

77. OCLC and RLIN holdings information is available at their respective Web sites: http://www.oclc.org and http://www.rlg.org. Figures on abstracting and indexing services derived from a search in *Ulrich's Periodicals Directory,* accessed through Dialog, June 23, 2004.

78. See, for example, Katherine B. Mathae and Catherine L. Birzer, eds., *Reinvigorating the Humanities: Enhancing Research and Education on Campus and Beyond* (Washington, D.C.: Association of American Universities, 2004).

79. Susan H. Anderson, "An Overview of College Rankings," internal memorandum, The Andrew W. Mellon Foundation, May 2003.

80. At the undergraduate level, Ernest T. Pascarella has studied the impact of educational institutions and practices for many years, and his 2001 article in *Change* is a good critique of the "resources and reputations" approach and the "student/alumni outcomes" approach. (See Pascarella, "Identifying Excellence in Undergraduate Education: Are We Even Close?" *Change* 33, no. 3 [May–June 2001]: 19–23.) Alexander Astin and his colleagues at UCLA have also worked hard, over many years, to study the college years. (See Astin, *The Four Critical Years* [San Francisco: Jossey-Bass, 1977].) Another approach to ranking colleges and universities has been proposed in a recent NBER working paper (Christopher Avery, Mark Glickman, Caroline Hoxby, and Andrew Metrick, "A Revealed Preference Ranking of U.S. Colleges and Universities," NBER Working Paper no. 10803, September 2004). The basic idea is to count "wins" (decisions to attend a particular school) and "losses" (decisions to go elsewhere) in head-to-head competitions for students offered admission to more than one school.

81. Daniel Kahneman, a Nobel Prize–winning Princeton economist and psychologist and an expert in measuring what had previously been thought to be immeasurable, suggested one possible methodology for incorporating the "softer" outcomes of higher education into a measure of quality. The first step would be to survey a reference community, such as academic deans, on what they consider the desired outcomes of a college education, as well as evidence of having achieved, to a greater or lesser extent, these outcomes. Using the results of this survey, one would construct an index of college outcomes, the factors of which would be the "evidence" suggested by the survey respondents, scaled based on their relative ranking and weighted according to their popularity in the survey. The index could be applied to existing databases that contain the appropriate variables or to surveys created to fit the index perfectly. For the more subjective elements of the index, multiple surveys could be used (for example, surveys of respondents at different ages, or in different contexts) to triangulate to an unbiased value. One could then group results to determine the relative quality

index rating of different institutions, different types of institutions, or different types of individuals within institutions. Kahneman, conversation with the authors, February 22, 2003.

82. See Bethany Broida, "'Gold Standard' for Rating Doctoral Programs Is Stalled," *Chronicle of Higher Education,* April 9, 2004, online edition. See also an earlier article by Jeffrey Brainard, "Survey of Doctoral Programs Needs Major Changes, Panel Suggests," *Chronicle of Higher Education,* January 10, 2003, online edition. For an interesting attempt to compare different approaches to ranking research universities (broadly, "reputational" versus "quantitative" approaches), see Nancy Diamond and Hugh Davis Graham, "How Should We Rate Research Universities?" available at http://www .vanderbilt.edu/AnS/history/graham/change.htm. The tables at the end of this article suggest that there is much more agreement between the two approaches than is sometimes assumed.

83. Bowen and Rudenstine (1992), p. 58. All of their chapter 4 is concerned with the evolution of programs classified by scale and quality between 1958 and 1988. Freeman, Jin, and Shen, in their recent NBER working paper, provide a more detailed analysis of trends in the distribution of degrees in science and engineering across doctorate-granting programs of different sizes and rankings; their data are also much more current than the data available to Bowen and Rudenstine. One of their major conclusions is: "On the university PhD producing side, the proportion of science and engineering PhDs from traditional leading doctorate institutions declined. These universities tended to maintain the size of their PhD programs in the face of rising graduate enrollments, so that growth of PhDs occurred largely from less prestigious and smaller PhD programs" (p. 19). They also find that the huge increase in the number of PhDs earned by foreign-born students occurred with little decline in the quality of the universities where they earned their PhDs (p. 10). It is not true that the large influx of foreign-born recipients has been concentrated in the less prestigious programs.

84. Bowen and Rudenstine (1992), pp. 59, 67, 74–79. As one of the readers of this manuscript pointed out, it is problematic when weak university departments keep themselves going by attracting marginal foreign graduate students who then use their American PhDs to obtain civil service jobs in poor countries.

85. Freeman, Jin, and Shen, pp. 7–8.

86. Shanghai Jiao Tong University, Institute of Higher Education, *Academic Ranking of World Universities–2004;* rankings and answers to "frequently asked questions" are available at http://ed.sjtu.edu.cn/ranking.htm. The Web site also contains contact information.

87. Robert Stevens, *University to Uni: The Politics of Higher Education in England since 1944* (London: Politico's, 2004), p. xiii.

88. Jennifer Cheeseman Day and Eric C. Newburger, "The Big Payoff: Educational Attainment and Synthetic Estimates of Work-Life Earnings," U.S. Census Bureau, Current Population Reports no. P23-210, July 2002, esp. figure 3 and text on pp. 3–4. Breakdowns are also provided by gender and by race. All estimates are for full-time, year-round workers. None of these figures is discounted for ability bias.

89. J. Bradford DeLong, Claudia Goldin, and Lawrence F. Katz, "Sustaining U.S. Economic Growth," in *Agenda for the Nation,* ed. Henry J. Aaron, James M. Lindsay, and Pietro S. Nivola (Washington, D.C.: Brookings Institution Press, 2003), p. 20. The authors observe: "During the twentieth century, human capital accumulated through formal schooling became a key to economic growth. In determining a nation's success in the increasingly knowledge-driven economy of the twenty-first century, human cap-

ital is likely to remain crucial" (p. 19). The technological revolution in data processing and data communications is widely credited with accelerating productivity growth
in recent years. (See the authors' note 5 for references.)

90. Thomas S. Dee, "Are There Civic Returns to Education?" *Journal of Public
Economics* 88 (2004): 1697–1720. Dee employs geographic proximity to two-year colleges as an instrumental variable in order to counter selection biases.

91. For an alternative formulation of the factors responsible for "the excellence of
US higher education relative to that in other countries," see Charles M. Vest, "Moving
On" (Report of the President for the Academic Years 2002–2004, Massachusetts Institute of Technology, available at http://web.mit.edu/president/communications/
CMVReport2002-04.pdf), p. 2. There is considerable overlap between the list produced by President Vest, drawing on his experience as president of MIT, and the list
that follows. We also agree with President Vest when he writes: "All those who believe
that it is important for the United States to have the best system of higher education
in the world must therefore be constantly vigilant" (p. 3).

92. Sutton Trust, p. 2. This report also cites data on endowments (from an earlier
Sutton report), showing that there is a clear correlation between endowment per student and the prestige ranking of American universities.

93. OECD, table B1.1. These totals include outlays on research and development
(which are also shown separately). This publication contains a wealth of other data on
spending on education at all levels.

94. Bound and Turner.

95. The ideas presented so cryptically here owe much to time that one of us
(Bowen) spent at the London School of Economics in 1962, working with members
of the staff of the Robbins Commission. For a report on Bowen's thinking at the time,
see William G. Bowen, "University Finance in Britain and the United States: Implications of Financing Arrangements for Educational Issues," in *Economic Aspects of Education: Three Essays* (Princeton, N.J.: Industrial Relations Section, Department of Economics, Princeton University, 1964), pp. 41–83; esp. pp. 52–83.

96. When Bowen first visited China in 1974, more or less right after the Cultural
Revolution, and spoke with the leaders of many of that country's leading universities,
he kept asking them: "What is it that really wakes you up at night? What is your greatest worry?" Surprisingly often the answer would be: "How to get the faculty to think
right." William G. Bowen, "University Education in the People's Republic of China:
A Visitor's Impressions," in *Ever the Teacher: William G. Bowen's Writings as President of
Princeton* (Princeton, N.J.: Princeton University Press, 1987), pp. 54–72. That is hardly
what one would hear in the United States, but we would be well advised not to take
our freedoms for granted. For long parts of our history, there were attempts to impose
orthodoxies of one kind or another, and of course McCarthyism is not to be forgotten.
The Vietnam period led, on some campuses, to pressures to "conform" (and oppose
the war) from the opposite end of the political spectrum.

97. See Douglass C. North, "Economic Performance through Time," Nobel Lecture, Stockholm, December 9, 1993, p. 3. North defines *institutions* as "the humanly
devised constraints that structure human interaction. They are made up of formal
constraints (rules, laws, constitutions), informal constraints (norms of behavior, conventions, and self-imposed codes of conduct), and their enforcement characteristics."
(p. 2). North's famous "piracy" example can be found in his "Sources of Productivity
Change in Ocean Shipping, 1600–1850," *Journal of Political Economy* 76, no. 5 (1968):
953–70. In North's formulation it is organizations such as colleges and universities

that are the principal players that act on (and through) the institutional matrix to produce tangible results. North argues persuasively that the combination of these "institutions" (the "rules") and "organizations" ("players") has a great deal to do with economic performance through time.

In higher education, "institutions/rules"—such as the commitment to freedom of
expression, the independence of colleges and universities, and standards of performance and credentialing—are enormously important. South Africa and China are
polar cases in point. The ability of the so-called open universities of South Africa to
maintain their integrity and to continue to function during apartheid was due in no
small part to their status as formidable "institutions," seen inside and outside of South
Africa as members of a worldwide community of colleges and universities committed
to values such as freedom of expression. (See Stuart Saunders's account of the successful resistance of South African universities to government pressures, aided by U.S.
universities, in his *Vice-Chancellor on a Tightrope: A Personal Account of Climactic Years in
South Africa* [Cape Town: David Philip Publishers, 2000], pp. 104–97.) Chinese universities, in contrast, were unable to maintain their standards (and standing) in the face
of the political pressures associated with the Cultural Revolution. As a consequence,
when political circumstances changed, China was forced to send its students to universities outside China for high-quality education. This situation has changed (and is
now changing) markedly.

98. To be sure, there are more "private" institutions of one kind or another spring-
ing up abroad than was the case for many years, but it is important to recognize that
these are generally stand-alone business or management institutes, and do not operate in the expensive fields of science and engineering (which require major investments in laboratories, research infrastructure, and so on).

99. Another factor—often overlooked or underemphasized—is the deep-seated
commitment to freedom of inquiry in the United States. This is particularly important
in fields such as the social sciences and humanities. Criticism of the established order
may not be welcome in authoritarian countries, or in those with powerful religious or
ideological drives. Such countries will have to consider carefully what compromises,
if any, they are prepared to make to create the climate for vigorous debate and
exchange of ideas that is so productive of new knowledge.

100. For a good account of Jefferson's plan for public education, see Jennings L.
Wagoner Jr., "Jefferson, Justice, and the Enlightened Society," in *Spheres of Justice in
Education,* ed. Deborah A. Verstegen and James Gordon Ward (New York: Harper-
Collins, 1991), pp. 11–33. Jefferson's plan is also summarized in Claudia Goldin and
Lawrence F. Katz, "The 'Virtues' of the Past: Education in the First Hundred Years of
the New Republic," NBER Working Paper no. 9958, September 2003, p. 10.

101. See Richard A. Easterlin, "Why Isn't the Whole World Developed?" *Journal of
Economic History* 41, no. 1 (1981): 1–19, esp. figure 1 and appendix table 1, for comparative international enrollment rates for 1830–1975.

102. Goldin and Katz (2003), quote on p. 46. Many scholars have written about
the growth of public education in the United States, most notably Lawrence Cremin
(*American Education,* 3 vols. [New York: Harper and Row, 1970, 1980, and 1988]).
Cremin brings together the threads of this vast literature in an extraordinary way.

103. Goldin and Katz (1999), pp. 50–51. See also Goldin and Katz (2003), p. 44,
and Claudia Goldin, "America's Graduation from High School: The Evolution and
Spread of Secondary Schooling in the Twentieth Century," *Journal of Economic History*
58, no. 2 (June 1998): 345–74.

104. DeLong, Goldin, and Katz, pp. 21–22.

105. DeLong, Goldin, and Katz, p. 21.

106. So-called credit constraints also play a role in preventing students from enrolling in or completing college, and there is a great deal of evidence suggesting that a lack of information about logistics or the benefits of higher education also plays a role. The importance of access to information is demonstrated by the work of Christopher Avery and Thomas Kane in Boston. Students from poor families often lack knowledge about applying to college, applying for student aid, and so on. See Christopher Avery and Thomas J. Kane, "Student Perceptions of College Opportunities: The Boston COACH Program," in *College Choices: The Economics of Where to Go, When to Go, and How to Pay for It,* ed. Caroline M. Hoxby (Chicago: University of Chicago Press, 2004), pp. 355–94. See also Christopher Avery and Caroline M. Hoxby, "Do and Should Financial Aid Packages Affect Students' College Choices?" pp. 239–301 in the same volume.

107. See appendix A for a discussion of this problem in the South African context. It is conceivable that there could be some kind of natural "limit" on how many young people can be prepared adequately for college, but we do not believe that the United States or South Africa is close to any such "limit" (if in fact one knew how to define such a thing). The unequal distribution of individuals from different backgrounds in the "college-eligible" population is one reason we are confident that further expansion is possible. Another reason is the success of other countries (noted earlier in this chapter) in expanding their pools of candidates beyond the level now being achieved in the United States.

108. Goldin and Katz (2003), p. 1. Historians of urban public education have noted the impact of urbanization, immigration, and industrialization in accelerating the consolidation of schools for purposes of achieving economy, efficiency, and social order. See Carl Kaestle, *The Evolution of an Urban School System, New York City, 1750–1850* (Cambridge, Mass.: Harvard University Press, 1973); Stanley K. Schultz, *The Culture Factory: Boston Public Schools, 1789–1860* (New York: Oxford University Press, 1973); and David B. Tyack, *The One Best System: A History of American Urban Education* (Cambridge Mass.: Harvard University Press, 1974).

109. Goldin and Katz (2003), abstract.

Chapter 4 Equity on a National Level: Socioeconomic Status and Race

1. We should note that, although the historically black colleges and universities, such as Morehouse and Spelman, still serve mostly minority students, these institutions are open to anyone who applies.

2. There is persistent debate among policy makers and scholars about the cause of socioeconomically based gaps in enrollment. One side asserts that the major source of the divide is the lack of sufficient preparation (defined in various ways, but generally emphasizing academic preparation) of disadvantaged young people, and that if these individuals could receive better schooling or, as is occasionally argued, if they could be encouraged to take specific steps in moving through the "college pipeline," enrollment gaps would disappear. The other side argues that it is primarily financial problems—specifically, the inability to pay steep college costs—that is keeping disadvantaged students from enrolling. Some have even argued that preparation shortfalls are a *result* of a young student's knowing that he or she will be unable to afford to go to college. See David Glenn, "New Book Accuses Education Dept. of Research

Errors That Skewed Policy Making," *Chronicle of Higher Education,* July 9, 2004, online edition, for a description of a current iteration of this debate. The book referenced in the article (Edward P. St. John, ed., *Public Policy and College Access: Investigating the Federal and State Roles in Equalizing Postsecondary Opportunity, Readings on Equal Education,* vol. 19 [New York: AMS Press, 2004]) contains a series of essays that criticize recent government statistical reports which, the authors allege, present biased results that support the "lack of preparation" argument. As should be apparent from the text, our position is squarely in what comedian Al Franken sometimes refers to as the "mushball middle" of this complicated debate. The research we document suggests that "preparation" (defined by us in a broad way to include non-cognitive as well as cognitive capacities) is the most significant contributor to the socioeconomic gap in enrollment, but that some students truly are "credit constrained." In addition, there is solid evidence that a lack of information and a lack of understanding about the process of applying for college and for financial aid result in sub-optimal college-going decisions.

We do not accept the assumption implicit in many of the arguments on both sides of this debate that simply maximizing enrollment should be the ultimate goal of policy. As we argue later in this chapter, educational attainment is what really matters, and improving attainment depends in part on enrolling students who have sufficiently good preparation to give them a real chance to graduate. Matching of students with institutions matters, too: it is a waste of talent when high-achieving students who are poor are enrolled in resource-starved institutions or in part-time programs owing to financial constraints.

3. Figure 4.1 is based on Tom Mortenson, "Chance for Bachelor's Degree by Age 24 and Family Income, 1970 to 2002," from *Postsecondary Education Opportunity,* available at http://www.postsecondary.org/wn/wn_04.asp, accessed June 25, 2004. The data used by Mortenson are from U.S. Census Bureau school enrollment data obtained through the *Current Population Survey.* A similar figure can be found in College Board, *Trends in College Pricing* (Washington, D.C.: College Board, 2003), p. 17, figure 11. The *Current Population Survey* is not an ideal source for data of this type, since the risk of sampling error is non-trivial. However, this is the best source that we have found for year-by-year enrollment data over such a long period. The enrollment rate of high school graduates understates (slightly) the enrollment gap between wealthy and poor because low-income students are less likely to graduate from high school. Our analysis of data from the National Educational Longitudinal Study of 1988 eighth graders shows that about 80 percent of students from the bottom income quartile in the cohort graduated from high school, compared to about 97 percent of those in the top income quartile. See table 4.1.

4. College Board, *Trends in College Pricing* (2003), p. 4.

5. See also College Board, *Trends in College Pricing* (2003), p. 17, figure 11.

6. David T. Ellwood and Thomas J. Kane, "Who Is Getting a College Education? Family Background and the Growing Gaps in Enrollment," in *Securing the Future: Investing in Children from Birth to College,* ed. Sheldon Danziger and Jane Waldfogel (New York: Russell Sage Foundation, 2000), pp. 283–324; quote on p. 283.

7. See figure 4.1 or College Board, *Trends in College Pricing* (2003), p. 17, figure 11. Student aid trends are relevant in explaining these patterns. For data on student aid, see College Board, *Trends in Student Aid* (Washington, D.C.: College Board, 2004). According to the latter, "Over the past decade, total aid has increased by 122 percent in constant dollars. Grant aid has increased by 84 percent in real terms, while education loan volume has grown by 137 percent" (p. 4).

8. Figure 4.2 is based on College Board, *Trends in College Pricing* (2003), p. 18, figure 12.

9. See Figure 4.2 or College Board, *Trends in College Pricing* (2003), p. 18, figure 12. Interestingly, since the mid-1980s, the African American enrollment rate seems to track the business cycle closely, with drops in enrollment corresponding to recessions. This could be evidence of a strong African American response to public institution tuition, which tends to rise (with falling public subsidies) during recessions.

10. See Figure 4.2 or College Board, *Trends in College Pricing* (2003), p. 18, figure 12.

11. U.S. Census Bureau, "Table FINC-03: Presence of Related Children under 18 Years Old—All Families by Total Money Income in 2003, Type of Family, Work Experience in 2003, Race and Hispanic Origin of Reference Person," from *Annual Demographic Survey, March Supplement* (Washington, D.C.: U.S. Census Bureau, March 2004), available at http://ferret.bls.census.gov/macro/032004/faminc/new03_004.htm.

12. U.S. Census Bureau, "Table 4: Poverty Status of Families, by Type of Family, Presence of Related Children, Race, and Hispanic Origin: 1959 to 2003," from *Current Population Survey*, Annual Social and Economic Supplements (Washington, D.C.: U.S. Census Bureau, Poverty and Health Statistics Branch/HHES Division, 2004), available at http://www.census.gov/hhes/poverty/histpov/hstpov4.html. The poverty threshhold in 2003 was $18,660 for a family of four with two children under 18. See U.S. Census Bureau, *Current Population Survey*, 2004 Annual Social and Economic Supplement, available at http://www.census.gov/hhes/poverty/threshld/thresh03.html.

13. Thomas J. Kane, *The Price of Admission: Rethinking How Americans Pay for College* (Washington, D.C.: Brookings Institution Press, 1999), p. 97.

14. Pedro Carneiro and James J. Heckman, "Human Capital Policy," in James J. Heckman and Alan B. Krueger, *Inequality in America: What Role for Human Capital Policies?* edited and with an introduction by Benjamin M. Friedman (Cambridge, Mass.: MIT Press, 2003), p. 100. We depart somewhat from Heckman and Carneiro in that we believe that the development of college preparedness is a cumulative process that can be exacerbated or ameliorated by experiences at each stage of life. In our view, Heckman and Carneiro tend to overemphasize the importance of early life experiences. See chapter 9 for a fuller discussion of the concept of "accumulating disadvantages" and for an analysis of interventions that can possibly improve the college preparedness of disadvantaged young people.

15. Our calculations using National Educational Longitudinal Study data on 1988 eighth graders.

16. Kevin Carey, "The Funding Gap: Low-Income and Minority Students Still Receive Fewer Dollars in Many States" (Washington, D.C.: The Education Trust, Fall 2004), p. 5, table 2, available at http://www2.edtrust.org/NR/rdonlyres/30B3C1B3-3DA6-4809-AFB9-2DAACF11CF88/0/funding2004.pdf.

17. National Center for Education Statistics, "Public School District Finance Peer Search," Education Finance Statistics Center, available at http://nces.ed.gov/edfin, accessed November 4, 2004.

18. National Center for Education Statistics, "Table 12-2a: Percentage of 4th-Grade Students in the School Eligible for Free or Reduced-Priced Lunch, by Selected School and Teacher Characteristics of Public Schools: 2000," from the National Assessment of Educational Progress (NAEP), 2000 Mathematics Assessment, previously unpublished tabulation, October 2001, available at http://www.nces.ed.gov/programs/coe/2003/section2/tables/t12_2a.asp, accessed June 24, 2004.

19. Beth Aronstamm Young and Thomas M. Smith, "The Social Context of Education," from Findings from *The Condition of Education 1997*, NCES 97-981 (Washington, D.C.: U.S. Department of Education, Office of Educational Research and Improvement, July 1997), pp. 16–18.

20. Aronstamm Young and Smith, p. 25.

21. Jonathan Kozol, *Savage Inequalities: Children in America's Schools* (New York: Crown Publishers, 1991), p. 100. Nationally, 63 percent of schools with more than 70 percent of students receiving free or reduced-price lunches have at least one structural feature that has been deemed "inadequate." Only 45 percent of schools with fewer than 20 percent of students in the free or reduced-price lunch program have an inadequate feature. National Center for Education Statistics, "Table 102: Percent of Public Schools with Building Deficiencies and Renovation Plans, by Level, Enrollment Size, Metropolitan Status, and Free Lunch Eligibility: 1999," from *Fast Response Survey System, Condition of America's Public School Facilities* (Washington, D.C.: National Center for Education Statistics, 1999), available at http://nces.ed.gov/programs/digest/do2/tables/dt102.asp, accessed June 24, 2004.

22. U.S. Department of Education, National Center for Education Statistics, *The Condition of Education 2004*, NCES 2004-077 (Washington, D.C.: U.S. Government Printing Office, 2004), p. 114, table 5-1. Overall, 21 percent of fourth graders attended schools in which more than 75 percent of the students were eligible for free or reduced-price lunches; 47 percent of black students, 51 percent of Hispanic students, and 5 percent of white students attended such schools.

23. Gary Orfield and Chungmei Lee, "*Brown* at 50: King's Dream or *Plessy's* Nightmare?" (Cambridge, Mass.: The Civil Rights Project at Harvard University, February 2004), p. 17, table 6.

24. Orfield and Lee, p. 20, table 8.

25. Erica Frankenberg and Chungmei Lee, "Race in American Public Schools: Rapidly Resegregating School Districts," The Civil Rights Project, Harvard University, August 2002. Frankenberg and Lee find that school districts, particularly those in the South, desegregated rapidly from the early 1970s to the mid-1980s. But from 1986 to 2000, nearly all of the 239 school districts they studied became more racially segregated. In the Topeka school district, black students went to schools with an average of 59 percent white students in 1991, but the average fell to 51 percent in 2001. (Orfield and Lee, p. 12.)

26. National Center for Children in Poverty, "Populations and Income Statistics, Cross-State," from *Let's Invest in Families Today Table Wizard* (New York: National Center for Children in Poverty, Mailman School of Public Health, Columbia University), available at http://nccp.org/wizard/wizard.cgi, accessed May 21, 2004.

27. Federal Interagency Forum on Child and Family Statistics, "America's Children: Key National Indicators of Well-Being, 2002" (Washington, D.C.: U.S. Government Printing Office, 2002), p. 20.

28. U.S. Census Bureau, "POV43: Region, Division and Type of Residence—Poverty Status for People in Families with Related Children under 18 by Family Structure: 2003, Below 200% of Poverty—All Races," from *Current Population Survey, 2004 Annual Social and Economic Supplement* (Washington, D.C.: U.S. Census Bureau, 2004), available at http://ferret.bls.census.gov/macro/032004/pov/new43_200_01.htm, accessed November 4, 2004.

29. Paul A. Jargowsky, "Take the Money and Run: Economic Segregation in U.S. Metropolitan Areas," *American Sociological Review* 61, no. 6 (December 1996): 984–98, esp. p. 990, table 3.

30. Maya Federman et al., "What Does It Mean to Be Poor in America?" *Monthly Labor Review* 119, no. 5 (May 1996): 3–17, esp. p. 9, table 5. The statistics are for 1992.

31. Federman et al., pp. 9–10, table 6. The statistics are for 1993.

32. See College Board, *College-Bound Seniors: National Report* for the years 1987–2003. Note that neither of these figures takes the changing population base of characteristics into account: there is no adjustment for inflation in the income-based figure and no adjustment for changes in the share of the population with different education credentials in the parental education–based figure. Both of these features will tend to bias all trends downward, as larger shares of the population move into higher categories. The highest income category also shifts from "$70,000 or more" to "$100,000 or more" in 1996, with an attendant discontinuous increase in scores. Still, the data indicate clearly that a substantial gap has existed between the SAT scores of advantaged and disadvantaged students in each year studied and that the gap is almost certainly widening.

33. Authors' calculations, using data in the National Educational Longitudinal Study of the 1988 eighth grade cohort (1992 high school seniors). Assuming that socioeconomic status does not change much during the course of a student's high school career, the earlier standardized test scores of low-income students may also be biased downward by environmental effects. Thus, low-income students in the top decile are likely to have greater natural ability than their wealthier peers with similar scores. This means that the gaps in SAT-taking presented here are, in fact, understated.

34. College Board, *College-Bound Seniors* (2003), p. 6, table 4-1, available at http://www.collegeboard.com/prod_downloads/about/news_info/cbsenior/yr2003 /pdf/2003_TOTALGRP_PRD.pdf, accessed June 25, 2004. Hispanic test-takers are separated into "Mexican or Mexican American," "Puerto Rican," and "Latin American, South American, Central American, or Other Hispanic, or Latino," so a "Hispanic" average is not available.

35. Wendy S. Grigg et al., *The Nation's Report Card: Reading 2002*, NCES 2003-521 (Washington, D.C.: U.S. Department of Education, Institute of Education Sciences, National Center for Education Statistics, June 2003), pp. 55–56, table 3.2, available at http://nces.ed.gov/nationsreportcard/pdf/main2002/2003521a.pdf, accessed June 24, 2004.

36. Meredith Phillips et al., "Family Background, Parenting Practices, and the Black-White Test Score Gap," in *The Black-White Test Score Gap*, ed. Christopher Jencks and Meredith Phillips (Washington, D.C.: Brookings Institution Press, 1998), pp. 103–45, esp. pp. 137–38. Phillips and her colleagues use IQ test scores of younger students as their dependent variable. However, Larry Hedges and Amy Nowell, in the same volume, find that family income and parental education also account for about one-third of the test score gap of 17-year-olds in the National Educational Longitudinal Survey of 1992. (Larry V. Hedges and Amy Nowell, "Black-White Test Score Convergence since 1965," in Jencks and Phillips, pp. 161–66.)

37. Phillips et al., pp. 137–38.

38. Roland G. Fryer and Steven D. Levitt, "Understanding the Black-White Test Score Gap in the First Two Years of School," *Review of Economics and Statistics* 86, no. 2 (May 2004): 447–64. The dataset used by Fryer and Levitt is that from the Early Child Longitudinal Study. This study provides data superior to earlier data in that it presents fewer sampling problems and has better co-variants—which presumably explains why this analysis accounts for a much larger part of the test-score gap than earlier studies. The researchers also suspect that there has been some real improvement in early-age black test scores over the past few years.

39. Fryer and Levitt; and James Comer, *Leave No Child Behind: Preparing Today's Youth for Tomorrow's World* (New Haven, Conn.: Yale University Press, 2004).

40. Claude M. Steele and Joshua Aronson, "Stereotype Threat and the Test Performance of Academically Successful African Americans," in Jencks and Phillips, p. 401.

41. Steele and Aronson, p. 403.

42. Steele and Aronson, p. 422. The students involved in these experiments were undergraduates at Stanford—presumably the kind of "school-identified" students that the authors believe will most likely suffer from stereotype threat in academic performance.

43. Steele and Aronson, p. 423.

44. Douglas S. Massey, Camille Z. Charles, Garvey F. Lundy, and Mary J. Fischer, *The Source of the River: The Social Origins of Freshmen at America's Selective Colleges and Universities* (Princeton, N.J.: Princeton University Press, 2003), p. 206.

45. Glenn C. Loury, quoted in J. L. A. Garcia, John McWhorter, and Glenn Loury, "Race & Inequality: An Exchange," *First Things* 123 (May 2002): 22–40, quote on p. 35. In this article Loury explains his purposes in writing his path-breaking book *The Anatomy of Racial Inequality* (Cambridge, Mass.: Harvard University Press, 2002), and defends himself from attacks by some of his critics.

46. See Kane (1999), esp. pp. 96–102. See also Ellwood and Kane for other tabulations and regressions.

47. Heckman presents evidence that disputes Kane's findings concerning the importance of family income. In a 2003 study with Pedro Carneiro that we cited earlier, he found that controlling for ability (as measured by the Armed Forces Qualification Test) and more detailed family background characteristics, such as family structure and place of residence, in addition to parental education, "greatly weaken[s] the relationship between family income and school enrollment." (Carneiro and Heckman, p. 117.) Constructing the analysis in this way is likely to capture much more of the impact of family and community on the development of college preparedness. On the other hand, the data that Heckman and Carneiro use are from the 1970s, and so may not reflect the current situation.

48. Kane (1999), p. 97, table 4.2.

49. An alternative (or perhaps additional) hypothesis, suggested by Michael McPherson, is that there is less discrimination in fields where the average level of education is higher, so minorities who are able to do so are more likely to enroll in college than similarly situated non-minorities. Michael McPherson, personal correspondence with the authors, July 16, 2004.

50. See, for example, Dominic J. Brewer, Eric Eide, and Ronald G. Ehrenberg, "Does It Pay to Attend an Elite Private College? Evidence on the Effects of Undergraduate College Quality on Graduate School Attendance," *Economics of Education Review* 17, no. 4 (October 1998): 371–76; Robert A. Fitzgerald, "College Quality and the Earnings of Recent College Graduates," Research Report no. NCES 2000-043, National Center for Education Statistics, U.S. Department of Education, August 2000, available at http://nces.ed.gov/pubs2000/2000043.pdf; and Caroline M. Hoxby, "The Return to Attending a More Selective College: 1960 to the Present," Harvard University, 1998, available at http://post.economics.harvard.edu/faculty/hoxby/papers/whole.pdf. Stacy Berg Dale and Alan Krueger counter that only disadvantaged students benefit from attending a more selective institution. See Dale and Krueger, "Estimating the Payoff to Attending a More Selective College: An Application of Selection on Observables and Unobservables," *Quarterly Journal of Economics* 117, no. 4 (November 2002): 1491–527.

51. Michael S. McPherson and Morton Owen Schapiro, *Keeping College Affordable: Government and Educational Opportunity* (Washington, D.C.: Brookings Institution Press, 1991), pp. 91–94.

52. Richard R. Spies, "The Effect of Rising Costs on College Choice: The Fourth and Final in a Series of Studies on This Subject," Princeton University, December 2001, p. 22.

53. Caroline M. Hoxby, "Testimony Prepared for U.S. Senate, Committee on Governmental Affairs, Hearing on 'The Rising Cost of College Tuition and the Effectiveness of Government Financial Aid,'" February 9, 2000, in Senate Committee on Governmental Affairs, *Rising Cost of College Tuition and the Effectiveness of Government Financial Aid: Hearings* 106th Cong., 2d sess., 2000 (S. Hrg. 106-515, February 9), pp. 120–28; quote on p. 125. Hoxby's prepared statement is available at: http://govt-aff.senate .gov/020900_hoxby.pdf.

54. Hoxby (2000a), p. 7. Both Hoxby's and Kane's research takes us only to 1992. Unfortunately, sufficiently detailed national-level data do not exist to bring us up to date on this question. Given the overall narrowing in the college enrollment gap shown in the College Board report, it is reasonable to assume that the long-term positive trends that Hoxby found likely continued to some extent in the past decade.

55. College Board, *Trends in College Pricing* (2002), p. 8, table 5. This study contains a wealth of data, by type of school and by region. Tuition clearly rose faster than median family income in both the 1980s and the 1990s (though not in the 1970s).

56. Between 1990 and 2001, the mean income of those in the bottom income quintile increased from $9,833 to $14,021 (in 2001 dollars), a 43 percent increase. During the same time, the mean income of those in the top income quintile changed from $94,404 to $159,644, a 69 percent increase, and the mean income of those in the top 5 percent of the income distribution increased from $148,124 to $280,312, an 89 percent increase. U.S. Census Bureau, "Table F-3: Mean Income Received by Each Fifth and Top 5 Percent of Families (All Races): 1966 to 2001," from *Current Population Survey,* Annual Demographic Supplements (Washington, D.C.: U.S. Census Bureau), available at http://www.census.gov/hhes/income/histinc/f03.html, accessed June 24, 2004.

57. Catharine Hill, Gordon Winston, and Stephanie Boyd, "Affordability: Family Incomes and Net Prices at Highly Selective Private Colleges and Universities," Williams Project on the Economics of Higher Education Discussion Paper no. 66, October 2003. See esp. p. 8, table 2. This study is based on financial aid records of individual students at 28 highly selective private colleges and universities (the COFHE [Consortium on Financing Higher Education] schools). For 2001–02, the authors had 41,401 usable financial aid records in a population of 108,721 matriculated U.S. undergraduates. "Self-help" (loans and jobs) is a component of the "net price" in this study. To the extent that loans can be thought of as having some "grant" characteristics (subsidized interest rates, etc.), the true "net price" is even lower than the Winston study suggests.

58. Hill, Winston, and Boyd (2003), p. 8, table 2.

59. Hill, Winston, and Boyd (2003), p. 23, table 4.

60. Hoxby (2000a), p. 3.

61. Hoxby observes: "Much of the upset over rising college tuition is caused by the fact that commentators focus almost exclusively on the tuition charged for the 10 percent of college places in the United States that are most expensive" (Hoxby [2000a], pp. 4–5). Loan funds obtained by students (and their parents in some cases) are not

included in Hoxby's definition of "institutional aid." To the extent that some of these loans are subsidized and guaranteed, they are more desirable sources of funds than cash or the sale of assets; in this sense, the actual "current" out-of-pocket costs incurred by many students and their parents are less than what is shown in Hoxby's table.

62. See Brewer, Eide, and Ehrenberg; Fitzgerald and Burns; and Hoxby (1998b).

63. See Hoxby's extended discussion of the ways in which more information, better communication, and more mobility have increased competitive forces in higher education and have led to greater stratification of educational institutions within what is increasingly an integrated, "national" market. See Caroline M. Hoxby, "The Effects of Geographic Integration and Increasing Competition in the Market for College Education," May 2000 revision of NBER Working Paper no. 6323.

64. Thomas Kane, personal correspondence with the authors, April 2004.

65. See College Board, *Trends in College Pricing* (2004), p. 8, table 4a. Thomas Kane also provided useful commentary on this point in personal correspondence with the authors, July 15, 2004. *Trends in College Pricing* (2004), released in October 2004, reports that between 2003–04 and 2004–05, tuition and fees at four-year public colleges rose by 10 percent, a smaller increase than the 13 percent of the prior year, but a larger increase than in any of the 10 years before that, when increases ranged from 4 to 9 percent. Tuition at two-year public institutions increased by 9 percent for the second year in a row, again following several years of much smaller increases. The 2004–05 tuition increase at four-year colleges was 6 percent.

66. Kane (1999), p. 105.

67. Kane (1999), p. 106. Kane argues persuasively that the tuition at public two-year colleges is the relevant variable, because this is the level at which most of those on the margin of enrolling or not enrolling will be making their decision. Kane notes that his estimates are in line with the literature.

68. Kane (1999), p. 119. Information about the Pell Grant program, the U.S. federal government's largest need-based student aid program, can be found at http://studentaid.ed.gov/students/publications/student_guide/2004_2005/english/types.htm.

69. See Christopher Avery and Thomas J. Kane, "Student Perceptions of College Opportunity: The Boston COACH Program," in *College Choices: The Economics of Where to Go, When to Go, and How to Pay for It*, ed. Caroline M. Hoxby (Chicago: University of Chicago Press, 2004), pp. 355–94; and Christopher Avery and Caroline M. Hoxby, "Do and Should Financial Aid Packages Affect ?" in the same volume, pp. 239–301.

70. Carneiro and Heckman, p. 119.

71. McPherson and Shapiro (1991), p. 101.

72. Kane (1999), pp. 141–42.

73. Avery and Kane.

74. Avery and Hoxby. Avery also published a book with Andrew Fairbanks and Richard Zeckhauser on early decision programs. They find that early applicants are more likely to gain admission than other similar applicants, and that low-income students are substantially less likely to apply for early decision than other students. See Christopher Avery, Andrew Fairbanks, and Richard Zeckhauser, *The Early Admissions Game: Joining the Elite* (Cambridge, Mass.: Harvard University Press, 2003), pp. 60–62, esp. figures 2.4 and 2.5.

75. Figures based on calculations made by the authors using the National Educational Longitudinal Study (NELS) database. Clifford Adelman found a huge, 56-

percentage-point, difference in bachelor's degree attainment between those in the lowest socioeconomic quintile and those in the highest socioeconomic quintile. The attainment rates were 15.7 percent for those in the lowest quintile and 71.6 percent for those in the highest quintile. See Adelman, *Principal Indicators of Student Academic Histories in Postsecondary Education, 1972–2000* (Washington, D.C.: U.S. Department of Education, Institute of Education Sciences, 2004), p. 34, table 3.1. However, the "base" for Adelman's analysis was all 1992 12th graders, rather than those who enrolled in a four-year institution.

76. Calculations based on 2000 U.S. Census data prepared by Sarah Turner for the authors, delivered in personal correspondence, August 15, 2004.

77. Sarah E. Turner, "Going to College and Finishing College: Explaining Different Educational Outcomes," in Hoxby, ed. (2004), pp. 13–61. Adelman, in his analysis of transcripts of 1972, 1982, and 1992 high school graduates (using data from the National Longitudinal Study of the High School Class of 1972, the High School and Beyond database, and the NELS database), argues that bachelor's degree attainment rates for "nonincidental" students in these three cohorts have remained constant. Adelman arrives at this result only by excluding, *ex ante*, students who earned few credits in postsecondary programs. He finds that, for students who had earned more than 10 undergraduate credits, 48 percent of those from the class of 1972 had obtained bachelor's degrees, compared to 45.3 percent of those from the class of 1982 and 48.7 percent of those from the class of 1992. Attainment rates were even closer for students in the three cohorts who had earned more than 10 credits and for those who had earned any credits from a four-year college at any time. For these students, attainment rates were as follows: 1972, 66.1 percent; 1982, 65.6 percent; 1992, 66.5 percent. (Adelman, p. 18 and p. 20, table 2.1.) A key question, of course, is whether students who "crash and burn" in their first semester have dropped out because of underpreparation, inadequate institutional support, or credit constraints.

78. Turner (2004), p. 13 and figure 1.5.

79. Turner (2004), pp. 13–14.

80. See Kane (1999), p. 144. Winston made this comment to the authors in personal correspondence, July 16, 2004.

81. Turner (2004), pp. 41–42.

Chapter 5 The "Elite" Schools: Engines of Opportunity or Bastions of Privilege?

1. See appendix table 5.1 for data showing the numbers of applicants and the numbers of matriculants at each school. In all cases, we look only at students from the United States. There is of course some overlap in applicants, and there are 103,200 separate individuals in these applicant pools. All descriptive statistics are institution-weighted averages, and the standard errors in all regression analyses are appropriately adjusted for the non-independence of multiple applications submitted by the same individual. The key to our ability to do this kind of fine-grained analysis is linking the Student Descriptive Questionnaire (SDQ) filled out by all students who take the SAT to individual institutional records, including applicant files. The College Board was able to help us link the institutional records provided by individual schools (indicating who applied, who was accepted, who enrolled, and how the matriculants performed in school) to the wealth of data about family backgrounds, test scores, and the like contained in the SDQ. There is much important research that can be done with

this expanded College and Beyond (C&B) dataset that is beyond the scope of this study.

An important statistical note: not every applicant took the SAT, nor did every SAT-taker fill in all of the appropriate questions on the SDQ. Overall, just over 90 percent of applicant records have SDQ data, but just 68.3 percent have data on family income and parental education, our two most important variables. Fortunately, there are two methods we can use to ease concerns about "response bias." First, since we have data from the institutions as well as the SDQ, we can compare the institution-provided characteristics of those students for whom we do not have socioeconomic data to the institution-provided characteristics of those for whom we do have socioeconomic data. On every measure (including race, missing institutional variables, and average SAT scores), those without socioeconomic data are virtually identical to those with socio-economic data. Second, there are cross-institutional differences in the SDQ response rate (ranging from 47 percent to 80 percent) that allow us to compare results on our measures of interest between institutions with high response rates and institutions with low response rates. On every measure, the basic result is the same for the high-response-rate institutions and the low-response-rate institutions. Similarly, different combinations of institutions (such as public and private institutions or women's colleges we have analyzed separately) yield remarkably similar results. To sum up, despite the number of records missing data, there is no reason to believe that there is a systematic bias in the results.

2. Economists Michael McPherson and Morton Schapiro have begun to plan a study of the impact of socioeconomic status on admissions, enrollment, and academic performance at a group of somewhat less selective and less well-endowed institutions. We look forward to their results, and thank them for broadening this research project to include institutions that we were unable to reach.

3. A glance at the curricula vitae of major-party presidential candidates and congressional leaders, especially in the past 20 to 25 years, confirms this. For more quantitative analysis of the income benefits of attending a selective institution, see Dominic J. Brewer, Eric Eide, and Ronald G. Ehrenberg, "Does It Pay to Attend an Elite Private College? Evidence on the Effects of Undergraduate College Quality on Graduate School Attendance," *Economics of Education Review* 17, no. 4 (October 1998): 371–76; Robert A. Fitzgerald and Shelley Burns, *College Quality and the Earnings of Recent College Graduates,* NCES 2000-043 (Washington, D.C.: National Center for Education Statistics, U.S. Department of Education, August 2000), available at http://nces.ed.gov/pubs2000/2000043.pdf; and Caroline M. Hoxby, "The Return to Attending a More Selective College: 1960 to the Present," Harvard University, 1998, available online at http://post.economics.harvard.edu/faculty/hoxby/papers/whole.pdf.

4. Richard R. Spies, "The Effect of Rising Costs on College Choice: The Fourth and Final in a Series of Studies on This Subject," Princeton University, December 2001, p. 22.

5. Spies, p. 17.

6. Spies, p. 17. Spies worked with a sample of 1998 high school graduates who were roughly in the top 15 to 20 percent of all test-takers. Figure 5 on p. 21 of his study shows separate application rates for each income category (by $10,000 intervals), and we see that application rates appear to dip slightly as we move from low family incomes to incomes in the $70,000 to $100,000 range, before rising sharply in the highest income categories. (Some of the category-by-category differences fail to pass tests of statistical significance, but the overall pattern is clear.) Parental education

(measured here by the number of years of schooling of the parent with the highest education level) is also found to have had a positive impact on application probabilities. There was "an 8.5 percentage point difference between the student one of whose parents is a college graduate and the one whose parent did not go to college at all" (p. 24). Knowledge of financial aid opportunities also affects (positively) the odds of students' applying to one of the more selective schools.

7. William R. Fitzsimmons, personal correspondence with the authors, March 17, 2004.

8. Alan Krueger, Jesse Rothstein, and Sarah Turner, "Race, Income and College in 25 Years: The Legacy of Separate and Unequal Schooling," unpublished draft, October 1, 2004. In their paper, the main topic of which will be discussed in more detail in chapter 6, Krueger, Rothstein, and Turner used summary values from the expanded C&B database along with data from the College Board's Test Takers Sample to show the frequency of application of blacks versus the frequency of application of whites to the schools in the expanded C&B database. They found that at the Ivy League universities and the more selective liberal arts colleges, black students are far more likely to apply than white students at each SAT level. At the public universities and the less selective liberal arts colleges, they are slightly more likely to apply at most SAT levels.

9. The national income distribution of families with 16-year-old children is calculated from the Integrated Public Use Microdata Series (IPUMS) sample of 1 percent of the 2000 Census. (Steven Ruggles et al., *Integrated Public Use Microdata Series: Version 3.0* [machine-readable database] [Minneapolis: Minnesota Population Center (producer and distributor), 2004], available at http://www.ipums.org.) The dollar values of the quartile boundaries have been adjusted to 1995 levels using the Consumer Price Index. Due to coding restrictions, the exact real dollar equivalents could not be used. The actual quartile boundaries in 1995 dollars and the estimated boundaries used are as follows:

Income Quartile	Actual Boundaries	Estimated Boundaries
Bottom quartile	<$27,432	<$25,000
2nd quartile	$27,432–$48,661	$25,000–$49,999
3rd quartile	$48,662–$76,926	$50,000–$79,999
Top quartile	>$76,926	>$79,999

10. Our income and parental education data were self-reported by the students taking the SAT or the SAT II. Studies have shown that students are likely to understate their family income above some level. This pattern has been found most recently by Michael McPherson and Jonathan Reischl in working with the National Postsecondary Student Aid Survey 1996 dataset. (Michael McPherson, e-mail correspondence with the authors, March 26, 2004.) In constructing this dataset, some interviews were conducted with an overlapping set of students and their parents. Examination of the scatter plots of the responses indicates that the student and parent estimates of family income were quite close at low income levels, but that there was a consistent underestimation of family income by students as income levels rose. When we compare our student-reported income data with the financial aid records of some of the institutions included in our data (which are based on tax returns), we find that the percentages in the bottom quartile match up quite closely. (C. Anthony Broh, director of research

for the Consortium on Financing Higher Education, personal correspondence with the authors, March 19, 2004.) Further reason for our confidence in the data for the bottom quartile is their consistency with the publicly available data on the distribution of Pell Grants. Donald E. Heller reports that 90 percent of all dependent Pell Grant recipients in 1999–2000 came from families with incomes below $41,000, and 75 percent came from families with incomes below $32,000. (See Donald E. Heller, "Pell Grant Recipients in Selective Colleges and Universities," in *America's Untapped Resource: Low-Income Students in Higher Education,* ed. Richard D. Kahlenberg [New York: Century Foundation Press, 2004], pp. 157–66.) These dollar levels are slightly higher than the dollar cut-off for the bottom quartile, so we would expect there to be slightly more Pell Grant recipients than individuals from the bottom quartile at colleges and universities, and this is exactly the pattern we see. At the 19 institutions in our study, in 1995, 16.7 percent of all undergraduates and 16.1 percent of full-time undergraduates received Pell Grants; this is comparable, given the slightly higher cut-off, with the 10–11 percent figure that we report for the fraction of students from families in the bottom quartile. The situation is murkier at the middle and the top of the income distribution, where we suspect that our self-reported income data understate—perhaps significantly—the concentration of students in the very highest income category. Still, the characteristics of students who report that their families are in the top income quartile and the relationships *across quartiles* in, for example, SAT scores and academic performance should not be distorted in any serious way. We have more confidence in the reporting of parental education, especially in our chosen distinction between having attended college and having no education beyond a high school diploma.

11. Income and parental education distributions are based on the authors' analyses of data on all 16-year-olds included in the IPUMS sample of 1 percent of the 2000 Census. See Ruggles et al.

12. See also appendix table 5.2. Of all students from low-income families enrolled in these schools, only about one-third are also first-generation college-goers; of all first-generation college-goers, only about one-half are also from low-income families. This estimate is consistent with both the data in Anthony P. Carnevale and Stephen J. Rose, "Socioeconomic Status, Race/Ethnicity, and Selective College Admissions," in Kahlenberg, ed., pp. 101–56, and that in Heller, and also with the estimates in William G. Bowen and Derek C. Bok, *The Shape of the River: Long-Term Consequences of Considering Race in College and University Admissions* (Princeton, N.J.: Princeton University Press, 1998), p. 341.

13. The share of the national population of teenagers whose parents had not attended college and whose family income placed them in the bottom income quartile in 1992 is determined by the authors' analyses using data from the National Center for Education Statistics' National Educational Longitudinal Study (NELS) of 1988 eighth graders. We have chosen to present the share of students who are disadvantaged in comparison to the share of the total population that is similarly disadvantaged, but some readers may also be interested in comparing the share who are disadvantaged at *these* highly selective institutions to the share who are disadvantaged at *other* institutions. There are several different sets of data that can be used to make this comparison, but the consensus is that nationally around 20 percent of all college students (those attending two-year and four-year institutions, on a part-time or full-time basis) were from families in the bottom income quartile and 20 percent were first-generation college students during the basic time period under consideration. Analy-

sis of summary data from the College Board's Test Takers Sample provided to us by Princeton economist Jesse Rothstein shows that in 1995, 22 percent of SAT-takers were from families in the bottom income quartile, while 20 percent were potential first-generation college students. Using NELS, we estimate that 25 percent of 1988 eighth graders who ever attended a postsecondary institution had family incomes below $25,000 and that 21.8 percent of these former college students were first-generation college students. Limiting the tabulation to those who ever attended a four-year institution, we find that 19.2 percent were from the bottom income quartile and 15.7 percent were first-generation college students. The U.S. Census Bureau's "Survey of Income and Program Participation" shows that in 1996, 20 percent of dependent enrolled students came from families with incomes below $25,000. (U.S. Census Bureau, 1996 Panel Wave 5, "Enrollment Level by Sex, Race, Hispanic Origin, Age, Marital Status, Relationship to Reference Person, Dependency Status, Labor Force Status, Veteran Status, Annual Family Income, Benefit Receipt, and Financial Aid Receipt for High School Graduates, 1996–1997: All Students," from *Survey of Income and Program Participation* [Washington, D.C.: U.S. Census Bureau, Internet release date October 16, 2002], available at http://www.census.gov/population/ socdemo/school/p70-83/tab01a.pdf.) However, it is important to remember that all of these measures include students with a broad range of abilities, while the institutions in our study enroll students (for the most part) with exceptionally strong academic credentials. Finding an appropriate comparison group is difficult, but one approach is to restrict the group considered to full-time students attending four-year institutions. Using the October 2002 *Current Population Survey* to do so, we find that 11.24 percent of such students are from families with incomes of less than $30,000 (which is approximately the real income equivalent of our bottom income quartile threshold for 1995). (Calculated from U.S. Census Bureau, "Enrollment Status of Dependent Primary Family Members 18 to 24 Years Old, by Family Income, Level of Enrollment, Type of School, Attendance Status, Sex, Race, and Hispanic Origin: October 2002," from *Current Population Survey* [Washington, D.C.: U.S. Census Bureau, Internet release date January 9, 2004], available at http://www.census.gov/population/ socdemo/school/cps2002/tab14-1.pdf.) Looked at in this context, the 19 very selective institutions in our study are doing well in enrolling disadvantaged students (indeed, they are doing better, given their cost and selectivity, than some might have expected them to do). But we believe, as we argue throughout this chapter and throughout this book, that these privileged institutions could do still more to serve their institutional missions and meet societal needs by enrolling larger numbers of well-qualified students from modest backgrounds.

14. See appendix table 5.2. Data reported by David Leonhardt of the *New York Times* suggests that the socioeconomically advantaged character of the student bodies of the four public institutions in our study is typical of the student bodies of selective public institutions across the country. He reports that "at the 42 most selective state universities, including the flagship campuses in California, Colorado, Illinois, Michigan and New York, 40 percent of [2003–04] freshmen come from families making more than $100,000," according to the Higher Education Research Institute, which publishes the *American Freshman* survey. Leonhardt also notes: "More members of [the 2003–04] freshman class at the University of Michigan have parents making at least $200,000 a year than have parents making less than the national median of about $53,000, according to a survey of Michigan students." (Leonhardt, "As Wealthy Fill Top Colleges, Concerns Grow Over Fairness," *New York Times,* April 22, 2004, pp. A1,

A21.) The share of students from families in the top income quartile (income greater than $80,000 in 1995, a somewhat lower bar than the real income equivalent of $100,000 in 2004) at the four public universities in our study was 33.8 percent. However, it must be remembered that this figure likely understates the true share from the top income quartile.

15. Women's colleges enroll a slightly higher percentage of first-generation college students than other private institutions (6.7 percent versus 5.2 percent), but a lower percentage than the public universities (8.8 percent).

16. In the 16 coeducational institutions in our study, women represent over 60 percent of the black applicant pool, compared to just over 50 percent of every other pool. Furthermore, 25 percent of black women come from families in the bottom income quartile versus 21 percent of black men; for every other racial group, men and women applicants are almost equally as likely to come from families in the bottom quartile.

17. Average scores are useful "gross" indicators, but focusing only on averages can lead to serious confusions, as we explain in detail in Bowen and Bok, chapter 2. It is distributions and comparisons on the margins that matter, as we explained in that book by positing an admissions process that focused on the height of applicants and then thinking about how average height would vary by gender even if the marginal applicants (the last ones admitted) were of the same height (p. 16).

18. We define a recruited athelete as a student who, as an applicant, had significant contact with a coach and was strongly recommended for admission. Underrepresented minorities are defined in the conventional way as African American, Hispanic, and Native American students. Legacies are defined as the children or grandchildren of alumni/ae. Note that three institutions (Pomona, Swarthmore, and Wellesley) are missing data on recruited athletes, and one institution (the University of Illinois) is missing legacy data. Early applicants are another special group, but because Penn State, UCLA, and the University of Illinois (three of the four public institutions in our study) are all missing early applicant data, we do not show a graph for this group. Early application is included (and the appropriate institutions are excluded) in the adjusted admissions advantage regression described later in the text.

19. For a full discussion of the admissions advantage concept, and an explanation of how it is calculated through the use of logistic regressions, see Bowen and Bok, pp. 340–43. Citations are to the 2000 paperback edition. See also William G. Bowen and Sarah A. Levin, *Reclaiming the Game: College Sports and Educational Values* (Princeton, N.J.: Princeton University Press, 2003), pp. 69–70 and 345, note 27. In brief, the adjusted admissions advantage is calculated by running a logistic regression (since the outcome variable, admission to an institution, is binary) with the characteristics being observed and other controls as independent variables. The coefficients of a logistic regression are difficult to interpret, so we use them to predict admission probabilities associated with different combinations of characteristics. We use these various probabilities to calculate the adjusted admissions advantage. For example, to predict the adjusted admissions advantage associated with being from a family in the bottom income quartile, we first predict the probability of admission for all applicants as if all applicants were from families in the bottom income quartile; we then predict the probability of admission for all applicants as if all applicants were not from families in the bottom income quartile. Subtracting the second probability from the first leaves

us with the adjusted admissions advantage, which can be interpreted (as we note in the text) as the average advantage—across all combinations of student characteristics for which we control—associated with being from a family in the bottom income quartile.

20. In the analysis reported here, we use binary variables for SAT score ranges of 100 points, which is intended to prevent potential biases resulting from imposing a linear structure on the admission by SAT curve (a possibility if we were to simply include SAT score as a continuous variable). However, when we tried other functional forms—including SAT score as a continuous variable, broadening and narrowing the SAT score ranges, and including both a continuous SAT score variable and an SAT-score-squared variable—the results were barely affected.

21. The primary purpose of announcing a need-blind admissions policy was to reassure applicants from families of moderate means that their financial needs—and the attendant potential obligation of the institution to provide financial aid—would not be held against them in the admissions process. According to institutional Web sites, only UCLA and Oberlin, among the 19 institutions in our study, do not claim to be need-blind. Barnard and Smith claim to be need-blind to a "large extent" and "96–99 percent need-blind," respectively. The other 15 institutions are unequivocally need-blind. When we analyze the admissions dynamics of the four non-need-blind institutions separately, we find that applicants from families with low incomes and low levels of parental education are not disadvantaged there either. In fact, these institutions provide a statistically significant adjusted admissions advantage of four to five points to applicants from low-income and low–parental education backgrounds. Elite institutions are sometimes accused not only of subtly discouraging students with significant levels of high financial need from coming but also of discriminating in favor of applicants at the upper end of the income distribution. Neither charge holds up, at least according to the evidence we have assembled. We discuss further the history and implications of need-blind admissions in chapter 7.

22. Separate probabilities can be calculated for men and women within each of these categories, as Bowen and Levin did in *Reclaiming the Game*, but this further complication seemed unnecessary for our present purposes.

23. The admissions advantage given to recruited athletes (which is very large at all SAT levels above the National Collegiate Athletic Association cut-off) results in less of a fall-off in the share of recruited admittees from low-SES backgrounds than in the share of other admittees who are from low-SES backgrounds. A similar pattern occurs when comparing enrollments (because the yield is so high for recruited athletes); that is, the share of recruited athlete matriculants from low-SES backgrounds is higher than the share of admittees, but it is still lower than the corresponding share of other enrolled students.

24. The percentage of applicants applying early has increased tremendously since 1995. According to Christopher Avery, Andrew Fairbanks, and Richard Zeckhauser, the most selective schools in the country received between 30 and 40 percent of their applications through the early application process in 1999–2000. These authors also found that students who did not apply for financial aid were far more likely to apply early that year. See Avery, Fairbanks, and Zeckhauser, *The Early Admissions Game: Joining the Elite* (Cambridge, Mass.: Harvard University Press, 2003), pp. 61–65, esp. figures 2.4–2.6.

25. Some 27.7 percent of applicants from families in the bottom income quartile

are minorities, and 32.4 percent of first-generation applicants are minorities; the percentages are even higher, although still well below 50 percent, among enrolled students, due to race-sensitive admissions preferences. See appendix tables 5.3a and 5.3b.

26. Using a logistic regression with SES-minority interaction terms, we find that, after controlling for SAT scores, there is almost no difference between the admissions chances of a low-SES non-minority applicant and a high-SES non-minority applicant or between a low-SES minority applicant and a high-SES minority applicant. The within-racial-group admissions advantage is calculated by replacing the first-generation variable, the bottom-income-quartile variable, and the top-income-quartile variable with minority and non-minority interaction variables for each characteristic—for example, first-generation minority and first-generation non-minority—in the regression formula. Non-minority first-generation applicants have an adjusted admissions advantage of 4.6 points over other non-minority applicants, and minority first-generation applicants have an advantage of 2.9 points over other minority applicants. This is not the case for every group of schools, however. In the Ivy League universities, minority first-generation applicants have an adjusted admissions advantage of 9.8 percentage points over other minorities, while non-minority first-generation applicants have an advantage of just 3.7 points over other non-minority applicants. Both of these advantages are significant. Applicants from families in the bottom income quartile do not have a significant advantage over other applicants of the same race whether they are non-minorities or minorities. The bottom-income-quartile coefficient is negative for both minority applicants and non-minority applicants, but the magnitude is larger for non-minority applicants (−2.5 versus −0.6). This explains why a regression analysis (such as in table 5.1) that controls for minority status does not exhibit a negative admissions impact associated with low-income or first-generation status. The interactions between race and SES matter much less for this analysis than one might have thought.

27. The admissions advantage calculations comparing public and private institutions do not include early application as an independent variable. This is due to the fact that three of the four public universities in our study do not have early application data. The University of Illinois has been excluded from the public university regression because it is also missing legacy data.

28. The reason minority applicants to public universities have a similar admissions advantage to but a lower probability of admission than recruited athletes is that the base admissions probability for non-minority applicants is lower than the base admissions probability for non-recruits.

29. We do not have detailed data on financial aid awards, but in another regression we included a variable for the average financial aid award provided by an institution. The inclusion of this variable barely affected the magnitude or standard error of the coefficients for income or parental education. The inclusion of the early application variable seems to be driving the increase in the magnitude of the low-SES coefficients. Indeed, the fact that low-SES admitted students, who were less likely to apply early than more advantaged students, are enrolling at higher rates even in the raw data is quite remarkable.

30. Michael McPherson, personal correspondence with the authors, July 16, 2004.

31. Bowen and Levin, pp. 118–20, esp. figures 5.1a and 5.1b. "High Profile" male sports are football, basketball, and ice hockey; all other male sports are considered "Lower Profile."

32. See Bowen and Levin, pp. 129–32.

33. The result for athletes recruited for High Profile sports does not include data from the three women's colleges (because High Profile sports are, by definition, male sports), nor do they include data from Swarthmore, UCLA, the University of Illinois, or Penn State because of missing variables. Swarthmore is also excluded from the overall recruited athletes statistic for the same reason.

34. See Bowen and Levin, pp. 132–34.

35. For example, male recruited athletes are 25 to 30 percentage points less likely to earn any honors and about 5 to 9 percentage points less likely to earn one of the top honors in the Ivy League universities. Bowen and Levin, p. 142, figure 5.6.

36. We know that SAT scores, for example, are correlated with college grades. Thus, since students from low SES backgrounds have lower average SAT scores, we would expect them to have lower GPAs. Adjusting for this and other factors allows us to determine whether the students are achieving their potential. See Bowen and Bok, pp. 72–78 and appendix B; James L. Shulman and William G. Bowen, *The Game of Life: College Sports and Educational Values* (Princeton, N.J.: Princeton University Press, 2001), pp. 62–77 and 142–50; and Bowen and Levin, chapter 6. See also Nancy W. Burton and Leonard Ramist, *Predicting Success in College: SAT Studies of Classes Graduating Since 1980*, College Board Research Report no. 2001–2 (New York: College Board, 2001).

37. Bowen and Bok, pp. 74–86; and Bowen and Levin, pp. 232–40. There continues to be a lively discussion of whether colleges make too much use of the SAT in admissions, and some schools no longer require the SAT (in our group, Bowdoin and the University of Illinois are the only schools that had adopted this approach at the time of our study). To test the sensitivity of our findings to our reliance on the SAT, we reran regressions substituting other tests and using high school grades. None of these alternative formulations changed the results in any substantive way. (This is also what we found in the work we undertook for Bowen and Levin [see pp. 149–50], when we tried a similar experiment.)

38. Bowen and Levin, pp. 232–39. Underperformance is calculated by running an ordinary least squares regression with rank-in-class as the dependent variable and with binary variables for the socioeconomic characteristics of interest and other control variables as independent variables. The coefficients on the socioeconomic variables (e.g., being from a family in the bottom income quartile) represent the over- or underperformance in rank-in-class percentile points associated with those characteristics, holding the remainder of the independent variables constant. The control variables in our standard underperformance regression were SAT scores, graduation status, field of study, race, athletic recruit status, and institutional dummy variables. We recognize that some of these variables (graduation status and field of study, in particular) could cause endogeneity bias. However, the results reported in the text hold with any combination of these variables; indeed, the basic result is the same when we control for SAT scores alone.

39. For an extended discussion of the factors responsible for underperformance among minority students and recruited athletes—including a discussion of important differences between the two groups—see Bowen and Bok, pp. 72–86 and 262–63; Bowen and Levin, pp. 146–69 and 232–39; and Shulman and Bowen, pp. 62–74, 146–50, 261–62, and 416, note 3.

40. Bowen and Levin, chapter 6, esp. pp. 145–69.

41. Bowen and Levin, p. 163 and appendix table 6.7.

42. Bowen and Levin, chapter 2, chapter 6, and pp. 141–43.

43. Claude M. Steele and Joshua Aronson, "Stereotype Threat and the Test Performance of Academically Successful African Americans," in *The Black-White Test Score Gap*, ed. Christopher Jencks and Meredith Phillips (Washington, D.C.: Brookings Institution Press, 1998), p. 401.

44. Steele and Aronson, p. 403; Douglas S. Massey et al., *The Source of the River: The Social Origins of Freshmen at America's Selective Colleges and Universities* (Princeton, N.J.: Princeton University Press, 2003), p. 206.

45. In fact, Steele's pioneering laboratory studies of stereotype threat were conducted with students at Stanford—an institution very similar to those in our study. Steele and Aronson, p. 422.

46. Or, more accurately, the characteristic of being from a socioeconomically disadvantaged background is not, itself, associated with the factors that we believe lead to underperformance.

47. In earlier days, when campus dress codes required more formal attire, a shabby or poor-quality jacket and tie or dress might have caused a student from a low-SES background to be noticed, or at least self-conscious lest he or she stand out in an unfavorable way.

48. The "striver" label is most commonly applied to students who score higher on the SAT than they would be expected to based on their SES and other characteristics. In the late 1990s, the Educational Testing Service sponsored research conducted by Carnevale on the possibility of developing a "strivers index" that could be used by colleges to identify these overperformers. However, after a minor political storm following a media leak of this research, the project was dropped. See Amy Dockser Marcus, "New Weights Can Alter SAT Scores as Family Factors Determine 'Strivers,'" *Wall Street Journal*, August 31, 1999, online edition; and Ben Gose, "More Points for 'Strivers': The New Affirmative Action?" *Chronicle of Higher Education*, September 17, 1999, online edition.

49. The president of one of the institutions in our study encouraged research on this question during a roundtable discussion on socioeconomically disadvantaged students and elite colleges held at the Century Foundation in New York on June 3, 2004, and attended by two of us (Bowen and Kurzweil). Knowing the characteristics related to overperformance would be particularly helpful should an institution decide to provide a boost to students from low-SES backgrounds in the admissions process, a possibility we discuss in detail in chapter 7.

50. Running the regression with just SAT scores and institutional dummy variables yields an adjusted R-squared value of 0.1297. No other variable alone produces as high an R-squared value, and even after including all of our other control variables, the R-squared value rises to only around 0.19.

51. It is possible that this overperformance characteristic has both a cultural aspect and a cognitive aspect; when we control for both English as a second language and whether a student sought advanced placement credit for studying a foreign language, they are both positive and statistically significant.

52. It is statistically significant at the 90 percent level, but not at the 95 percent level.

53. Our analysis of data from NELS shows that, of the cohort members who enrolled in a four-year college or university, about 44 percent of those from families in the bottom income quartile and 42 percent of first-generation college students even-

tually obtained a bachelor's degree, compared to 78 percent of those from the top income quartile.

54. Graduation rates reflect graduation within five years of enrollment.

55. See Peterson's, *Peterson's Four-Year Colleges 2004* (Princeton, N.J.: Peterson's, 2003).

56. Higher Education Research Institute, Cooperative Institutional Research Program, *The American Freshman: National Norms for 1995* (Los Angeles: Higher Education Research Institute, 1995).

57. We do not have good data on transfers from our institutions, but based on our analysis of the NELS cohort of 1988 eighth graders, we can say that, at the national level, students from families in the bottom income quartile are slightly *less* likely (17 percent versus 21 percent) to transfer from a public four-year institution than those from families in the top income quartile.

58. See appendix table 5.4, bottom panel. The "private institutions" include both 5 research universities and 10 liberal arts colleges. The average enrollment for the 5 Ivy League universities was 1,500, as compared with just over 500 at the liberal arts colleges. Consistent with the line of argument developed in the text, the gap in graduation rates at the Ivies between students from low-income families and those from high-income families was greater than at the selective liberal arts colleges (4 percentage points versus 0 percentage points); but of course 4 points is much different from the 12-point gap at the far larger public universities.

59. Stanley Ikenberry, personal correspondence with the authors, June 17, 2004.

60. Interestingly, the effects of large scale on completion rates can also be seen at the PhD level. See William G. Bowen and Neil L. Rudenstine, *In Pursuit of the Ph.D.* (Princeton, N.J.: Princeton University Press, 1992), pp. 123-41.

61. The 11 institutions are Barnard, Columbia, Oberlin, Penn State, Princeton, Smith, Swarthmore, the University of Pennsylvania, Wellesley, Williams, and Yale. See Bowen and Bok, appendix B, for a description of the original College and Beyond survey and its variables.

62. The survey form asks respondents to include "income from jobs, net income from business, farm or rent, pensions or social security payments." See Bowen and Bok, appendix B. Thus, we use the terms *income* and *earnings* interchangeably in this discussion, because it is impossible to distinguish between them.

63. The parental income quartiles described above are actually the 1976 real income equivalents (deflated using the Consumer Price Index) of the 1989 income quartile thresholds. The 1976 boundaries were: bottom quartile, less than $9,000; second quartile, $9,000–$17,999; third quartile, $18,000–$27,999; and top quartile, $28,000 and over. Only full-time workers were included in the analysis. The individual earnings of women (who were more likely at that time than men not to work) may not accurately reflect the financial returns to their college education, which could be thought to include the income of a spouse met at or through college. To correct for this we also checked household earnings of all former students, whether working or not. The pattern is similar, with those from the bottom quartile earning about $15,000 less, and those from the top quartile earning about $15,000 more, than those in the middle quartiles.

64. Melvin Oliver and Thomas Shapiro found that wealth (the measure of held assets) exacerbates income inequality tremendously. For example, they show that in 1988, households with incomes below $11,611 had an average net worth of just

$5,700, and those with incomes between $11,611 and $25,000 had a net worth of $21,500. In contrast, households in the top income category they included (incomes over $49,999) had an average net worth of $118,700, about 20 times that of those in the bottom category. (Oliver and Shapiro, *Black Wealth/White Wealth* [New York: Routledge, 1995], p. 74, figure 4.1.) There is also a substantial racial wealth gap (which is responsible, in part, for the large income-based wealth gap). Oliver and Shapiro note that the ratio of black median income to white median income was 0.62 ($15,630 to $25,384) in 1988, but the ratio of black median net worth to white median net worth was a stunning 0.08 ($3,700 to $43,800) (p. 86, table 4.4).

65. The average income of working college graduates was found using the IPUMS sample of 1 percent of the 1990 Census. The income value for individuals with at least a bachelor's degree who were between the ages of 37 and 39 was adjusted for inflation using the Consumer Price Index value of 22.9 percent. A similar technique was used for comparison purposes in Bowen and Bok, p. 124 and appendix B.

66. The survey, which was conducted by the National Opinion Research Council, is described in Bowen and Bok, appendix A.

67. An earnings variable is not included in this regression.

68. National voting statistics are from U.S. Census Bureau, "Table A-1: Reported Voting and Registration by Race, Hispanic Origin, Sex and Age Groups: November 1964 to 2000," from *Current Population Report* (Washington, D.C.: U.S. Census Bureau, November 2000 and earlier reports), available at http://www.census.gov/population/socdemo/voting/tabA-1.pdf, accessed June 24, 2004.

69. Our logistic regression for voting has very little predictive power, with a log pseudo-likelihood of –626.5 and a pseudo-R-squared of just 0.0328.

70. Bowen and Bok, p. 157.

71. Bowen and Bok, p. 160.

72. See appendix table 5.5. McPherson and Schapiro demonstrate that over a similar period, this downward shift in the share of students from middle-income families does not imply a downward shift in the share of these students who are attending top institutions. Indeed, the fraction of students attending highly selective institutions has increased at all income levels—but the share of students from low-income and high-income families who attend these institutions has grown more than the share of students from middle-income families. Michael S. McPherson and Morton O. Schapiro, "The End of the Student Aid Era? Higher Education Finance in the United States," in *A Faithful Mirror: Reflections on the College Board and Education in America,* ed. Michael C. Johanek (New York: College Board, 2001), pp. 335–76.

73. Higher Education Research Institute, Cooperative Institutional Research Program, *The American Freshman: National Norms for 1981* (also *1989, 1995,* and *2002*) (Los Angeles: Higher Education Research Institute, 1981, 1989, 1995, and 2002).

74. A list of the 145 most selective schools can be found in Heller, pp. 160–66.

75. Tabulations made using data provided to the authors by the U.S. Department of Education's Federal Student Aid Office. The Barron's group of 145 institutions is the group used by Carnevale and Rose. The percentage of students who receive Pell Grants is not a reliable statistic for determining the share of students who are disadvantaged. (See Jeffrey Tebbs and Sarah Turner, "College Education for Low Income Students: A Caution on the Use of Data on Pell Grant Recipients," University of Virginia, mimeo, 2004.) But it is nevertheless comforting that the basic trends found by looking at Pell Grant data are similar to those revealed by our data.

76. Ruggles et al.

77. The gap found in the 1976 cohort is not statistically significant after controlling for race, gender, athletic status, and SAT scores. However, the 1989 gap remains after the inclusion of these controls.

78. Caroline M. Hoxby, "The Effects of Geographic Integration and Increasing Competition in the Market for College Education," revision of NBER Working Paper no. 6323, Harvard University, May 2000.

79. See appendix table 5.5. We believe that figures of this kind, using self-reported data, underestimate the proportion of students who come from families in the top quartile because of the tendency for students from wealthy families to understate family income.

Chapter 6   Race in American Higher Education: The Future of Affirmative Action

1. See chapter 2 and Henry Drewry and Humphrey Doermann, *Stand and Prosper: Private Black Colleges and Their Students* (Princeton, N.J.: Princeton University Press, 2001).

2. In his recent biography, Richard B. Bernstein writes: "He [Jefferson] stressed the central difference between masters and slaves—that of race, or what he called "'the real distinctions which nature has made' between whites and blacks. Jefferson claimed that Africans were inferior to Europeans, listing such differences as skin color, facial features, body type, and habits. But his list was not neutral or scientific, though he wrote as if it were. Rather, he skewed his results to tip the balance, every time, for whites and against blacks, cloaking his bias with the appearance of scientific impartiality." Bernstein then quotes from Jefferson's *Notes on the State of Virginia*, Query XIV: Laws: "I advance it therefore as a suspicion only, that the blacks, whether originally a distinct race, or made distinct by time and circumstances, are inferior to the whites in the endowments both of body and mind. It is not against experience to suppose that different species of the same genus, or varieties of the same species, may possess different qualifications. Will not a lover of natural history, then, one who views the gradations in all the races of animals with the eye of philosophy, excuse an effort to keep those in the department of man as distinct as nature has formed them? This unfortunate difference of colour, and perhaps of faculty, is a powerful obstacle to the emancipation of these people." Bernstein, *Thomas Jefferson* (New York: Oxford University Press, 2003), pp. 61–62; Bernstein quoting Thomas Jefferson, *Writings* (New York: Library of America, 1984), pp. 256–75, esp. pp. 264–70 (quotes on pp. 264, 270).

3. President's Commission on Higher Education, *Higher Education for American Democracy* (Washington, D.C.: U.S. Government Printing Office), vol. 2, pp. 25–26.

4. Sarah Turner and John Bound, "Closing the Gap or Widening the Divide: The Effects of the G.I. Bill and World War II on the Educational Outcomes of Black Americans," *Journal of Economic History* 63, no. 1 (March 2003): 145–77.

5. William G. Bowen and Derek Bok, *The Shape of the River: Long-Term Consequences of Considering Race in College and University Admissions* (Princeton, N.J.: Princeton University Press, 1998), p. 4. The 19 institutions come from the full database of 28 institutions, which include Barnard College, Bryn Mawr College, Columbia University, Denison University, Duke University, Emory University, Hamilton College, Kenyon College, Miami University (Ohio), Northwestern University, Oberlin College, Pennsylvania State University, Princeton University, Rice University, Smith College, Stanford University, Swarthmore College, Tufts University, Tulane University, the University of

Michigan at Ann Arbor, the University of North Carolina at Chapel Hill, the University of Pennsylvania, Vanderbilt University, Washington University in St. Louis, Wellesley College, Wesleyan University, Williams College, and Yale University.

6. John Payton, "Night of Brown v. Board of Education: 50 Years Later: Remarks of John Payton," speech delivered at the Thurgood Marshall Center Trust, January 31, 2004, esp. pp. 3, 8–9. See also John Payton, "Brown v. Board of Education: The True Legacy of Charles Hamilton Houston: Remarks of John Payton," speech delivered at the Washington Bar Association Law Day Dinner, May 1, 2004. See also Sara Hebel's review article ("Segregation's Legacy Still Troubles Campuses," *Chronicle of Higher Education,* May 14, 2004) for an informative history of previous litigation, much of it aimed at demonstrating that separate law schools were inferior. Earl Lewis has also written an excellent account of the long path to *Brown* and then to the Michigan decisions; see his "Why History Remains a Factor in the Search for Racial Equality," in *Defending Diversity: Affirmative Action at the University of Michigan,* by Patricia Gurin et al. (Ann Arbor: University of Michigan Press, 2004), pp. 17–59.

7. Payton (2004b), pp. 4–7. See also Herbert Wechsler, "Toward Neutral Principles of Constitutional Law," *Harvard Law Review* 73, no. 1 (November 1959): 1–35.

8. Payton (2004b), p. 6.

9. Two people died during the riots that erupted when, in 1962, James Meredith became the first black student to enroll in the University of Mississippi. See William Doyle, *An American Insurrection: The Battle of Oxford, Mississippi, 1962* (New York: Doubleday, 2001). Charlayne Hunter-Gault, one of the first two black undergraduates to enroll in the University of Georgia, spoke at the University 25 years later, of both the past and the present: "For centuries, we shared a world of courtesy and difference established on utter tragedy. As Blacks, we gave to the white world, and that world gave to us. But the gifts were ambiguous weighted as they were with the force of unequal tradition. You were not ours, but we were yours. Then, slowly, painfully, came the furious dawn of recognition. We saw, half hidden in the blazing noonday sun, the true outline of our burden. . . . No one here today would pretend that the Old South is dead and buried, that the events of the past twenty-five years, even my presence here today, have transformed our peculiar world into one that is beyond recognition." Hunter-Gault, quoted in Lewis, pp. 40–41.

10. The realities of the post-*Brown* period contrast dramatically with the optimism that was expressed immediately after the decision about how fast progress would be made. Thurgood Marshall was quoted in the *New York Times* as saying that it might take "up to five years" for segregation in education to be ended for the entire country. The story went on to say: "He [Marshall] predicted that, by the time the 100th anniversary of the Emancipation Proclamation was observed in 1963, segregation in all its forms would have been eliminated from the nation." ("N.A.A.C.P. Sets Advanced Goals," *New York Times,* May 18, 1954, p. 16.)

11. Marvin Krislov, vice-president and general counsel of the University of Michigan, recently reminded us: "Not only does residential and educational segregation continue, but recent studies suggest that, even though overtly biased attitudes have declined, clear racial discrimination persists. One study sponsored by the National Bureau of Economic Research found that applicants with traditionally 'white-sounding' names were fifty percent more likely to get called for an initial interview than applicants with 'African American sounding names.'" (Krislov, "Affirmative Action in Higher Education: The Value, the Method, and the Future," *University of Cincinnati Law Review* 72, no. 3 [Spring 2004]: 899–907; quote on p. 906.) The NBER study to which Krislov

referred was done by Marianne Bertrand and Sendhil Mullainathan and bears the apt title "Are Emily and Greg More Employable than Lakisha and Jamal? A Field Experiment on Labor Market Discrimination" (NBER Working Paper no. 98732, July 2003).

12. Ronald Dworkin, "Affirming Affirmative Action," *New York Review of Books* 45, no. 16 (October 22, 1998), pp. 91-102; quote on pp. 99–100.

13. Glenn C. Loury, *The Anatomy of Racial Inequality* (Cambridge, Mass.: Harvard University Press, 2002). Loury's quote appears in the foreword to the paperback (2000) edition of Bowen and Bok, p. xxvii.

14. We have resisted using the term *affirmative action* to talk about "race-conscious" or "race-sensitive" admissions because of the much broader meaning often associated with *affirmative action,* which is still often thought about in an employment context. In fact, the issues involved in thinking about "affirmative action" in employment are different in many respects from the issues associated with admissions. Also, some people react negatively to the broad concept of affirmative action as applied to all kinds of situations (employment, awarding of contracts, etc.), although they may in fact favor taking account of race in admissions. For these reasons, it seemed best to avoid the broad brush of the term *affirmative action* when speaking about admissions and to talk instead about race-sensitive, or race-conscious admissions. See Bowen and Bok, notes on pp. liii and liv. By now, however, the term *affirmative action* has become so widely used in discussing race-sensitive admissions policies of various kinds that it seems foolish to insist on different terminology.

15. Geoffrey Kabaservice, *The Guardians: Kingman Brewster, His Circle, and the Rise of the Liberal Establishment* (New York: Henry Holt, 2004), pp. 259, 261, 263–71. For an informative review of this book, see Alan Brinkley, "The End of an Elite," *New Republic,* June 7, 2004, online edition. Brinkley ends by observing: "Although the United States still remains very far from being a true meritocracy, neither is it any longer a society ruled by an inherited aristocracy of leadership. Evidence of that is visible in Brewster's own cohort—Ivy League presidents—among whom there is no one today whose social profile looks even remotely like his. Women, Jews, African-Americans, public school graduates, and others from backgrounds far different from those of Brewster and his establishment circle now occupy virtually all the major university presidencies, and a similar transformation has occurred in many other areas of society. But Kingman Brewster, who could easily have become—like some of his contemporaries— a victim of this change, was in fact an agent of it. Cautiously, sometimes boldly, occasionally rashly, he advanced the very goals that most threatened his own social world."

16. Calculations from the College and Beyond (C&B) database. Hispanics accounted for less than 0.1 percent in the '51 cohort and about 1.6 percent of the '76 cohort. Native Americans were even less common. In 1951, there were no Native American students in the C&B institutions, and by 1976, the share who were Native American was just 0.09 percent. By the 1970s, most selective institutions had expanded their aggressive recruitment policies to include Hispanics and Native Americans, but there were still very small numbers in the U.S. population. Subsequent population shifts resulting from increased immigration from Latin American countries greatly increased the pool of potential applicants, and accordingly, their presence at selective colleges and universities. See Bowen and Bok, pp. 9–10.

17. Ansley Coale, the son of a Presbyterian minister, is one example of the former. A scholarship student both at Princeton and at Mercersburg Academy, which he attended for a year prior to entering Princeton in order to brush up on his Vergil and Cicero, Coale supplemented his undergraduate scholarship by waiting tables at the

student dining halls and by tutoring. Far from being isolated at Princeton, when he arrived there, Coale was able to count "eighteen companions from Mercersburg." (See Coale's *Ansley J. Coale: An Autobiography* [Philadelphia: American Philosophical Society, 2000], pp. 3, 6–7.) For a chilling portrait of the experiences of black students at Princeton after World War II, see the student-made video *Looking Back: Reflections of Black Princeton Alumni* (video [VHS] produced by Media Genesis Productions. Published by the Trustees of Princeton University, 1997).

18. See Marvin W. Peterson, Robert T. Blackburn, Zelda F. Gramson, et al., *Black Students on White Campuses: The Impacts of Increased Black Enrollments* (Ann Arbor: Survey Research Center Institute for Social Research, University of Michigan, 1978), for a detailed analysis of the period between 1968 and 1975.

19. *Regents of the University of California v. Bakke*, 438 U.S. 265 (1978).

20. For an excellent analysis of the Court's view of race in education, and especially of the legality of race-sensitive admissions, see Joel K. Goldstein, "Beyond *Bakke:* *Grutter-Gratz* and the Promise of *Brown*," *Saint Louis University Law Journal* 48, no. 3 (Spring 2004): 899–954. Goldstein carefully traces the evolution of thinking from *Brown* to the present day and offers a detailed assessment of the arguments presented in each of the major cases.

21. U.S. Census Bureau, Population Division, Educational Attainment Historical Table A-2, "Percent of People 25 Years Old and Over Who Have Completed High School or College, by Race, Hispanic Origin and Sex: Selected Years 1940 to 2003" (Washington, D.C.: U.S. Census Bureau), available at http://www.census.gov/population/socdemo/education/tabA-2.pdf.

22. Robert M. O'Neil, "Preferential Admissions: Equalizing Access to Legal Education," *University of Toledo Law Review* (Spring–Summer 1970): 281–320, esp. p. 300; Herbert W. Nickens, Timothy P. Ready, and Robert G. Petersdorf, "Project 3000 by 2000: Racial and Ethnic Diversity in U.S. Medical Schools," *New England Journal of Medicine* 331, no. 7 (1994): 472–76; data cited on p. 472.

23. The American Bar Association reports that the enrollment of African Americans in U.S. law schools stood at 3,744 in 1971–72 and at 9,412 in 2001–02. The number of Hispanic law students grew from 1,156 to 7,434 during the same period. (American Bar Association, "Minority Enrollment 1971–2002," available at http://www.abanet.org/legaled/statistics/ministats.html; U.S. Census Bureau, *Statistical Abstract of the United States: 2003* [Washington, D.C.: Government Printing Office, 2004].) The number of black students enrolled in U.S. medical schools grew from 3,587 in 1978 to 4,779 in 2002; the number of Hispanic medical students grew from 2,052 to 4,220 during the same period. (Association of American Medical Colleges [AAMC], *Minority Students in Medical Education: Facts and Figures XII* [Washington, D.C.: AAMC, 2002].)

24. The percentage of doctorates outside the field of education earned by U.S. citizens who were black grew from 2.6 percent in 1982 to 4.7 percent in 2002. During the same period, the share of doctorates earned by Hispanics grew from 2 percent to 4.5 percent. Thomas B. Hoffer et al., *Doctorate Recipients from United States Universities: Summary Report 2002* (Chicago: National Opinion Research Center, 2003), table 8.

25. See appendix A of Bowen and Bok for a full discussion of the original C&B database, including the list of schools included in it, survey methodology, and weighting conventions used at the large public universities. Subsequently we created an expanded C&B database, for 1995 applicants as well as matriculants, to study socioeconomic status of enrollees. It is this expanded C&B database that was used to make the calculations reported in chapter 5.

26. This summary draws in part from the paper that Bowen wrote with Neil Rudenstine in an effort to summarize principal propositions that we believed deserved consideration as the U.S. Supreme Court was considering the University of Michigan cases. See William G. Bowen and Neil L. Rudenstine, "Race-Sensitive Admissions: Back to Basics," *Chronicle of Higher Education,* February 7, 2003, online edition, also available at The Andrew W. Mellon Foundation Web site, http://www.mellon.org.

27. Patricia Gurin, with Eric L. Dey, Gerald Gurin, and Sylvia Hurtado, "The Educational Value of Diversity," in Gurin et al., p. 175. This nearly 90-page essay is an impressive recounting of Gurin's own extensive research and also a compilation of the findings of many other scholars. Professor Gurin makes extensive use of amicus briefs filed by social science organizations and others. In addition, she examines in detail the criticisms of her work, and of related work, offered on behalf of the plaintiffs.

28. Bowen and Bok, chapters 4, 5, and 6.

29. For valuable insight into Jefferson's ideas about and passion for education, see Jennings L. Wagoner, Jr., *Jefferson and Education* (Charlottesville, Va.: Thomas Jefferson Foundation, distributed by University of North Carolina Press, Chapel Hill, 2004).

30. Bowen and Bok, pp. xxxi–xxxii, 60–61, 110–11, 138–40, 198–201.

31. At the 2004 American Sociological Association meetings, Marta Tienda and Sigal Alon presented results of their study that found that black and Hispanic students who attended selective colleges were more likely to stay in school than were black and Hispanic students who attended nonselective institutions. David Glenn, "Minority Students Fare Better at Selective Colleges, Sociologists Find," *Chronicle of Higher Education,* August 16, 2004, online edition.

32. Bowen and Bok, pp. 281–82. See the accompanying text for a definition of *race-neutral* and an explanation of the methodology used to estimate the characteristics of "retrospectively rejected" minority students.

33. One major misconception is that all, or almost all, minority candidates who are "over threshold" are admitted. On the contrary, newly available data show that well over half of all high-scoring minority students in the 1999 applicant pools at the selective schools in the C&B database were turned down; for example, among male minority applicants with combined SAT scores in the 1200–1299 range, the odds of admission were only about 35 percent. Calculations based on data collected for William G. Bowen and Sarah A. Levin, *Reclaiming the Game: College Sports and Educational Values* (Princeton, N.J.: Princeton University Press, 2003).

34. Bowen and Bok, p. 26; Bowen and Levin, p. 233, table 9.3, and p. 136, table 5.1.

35. This result implies that "underperformance" by black students (defined as academic outcomes that fall short of what would have been predicted on the basis of entering credentials such as test scores and high school rank-in-class) has decreased somewhat over time. This is correct, but underperformance remains a serious problem that must be addressed. Data in this paragraph are from Bowen and Levin, p. 237, table 9.5.

36. The 10 institutions for which we have 1999 admissions records are Amherst, Bates, Carleton, Colby, Princeton, Swarthmore, Trinity, Wellesley, Wesleyan, and Yale.

37. Story recounted in the introduction to the paperback edition of Bowen and Bok, p. xxxiii. Another vignette makes much the same point. When Bowen was preparing to go to Chicago to speak to the trustees of the University of Chicago and Northwestern, a former Princeton undergraduate who had been in one of his Economics 101 sections, Jerry Blakemore, called Bowen's office. Blakemore is an African American who had come from the South Side of Chicago to study at Princeton in the

fall of 1972. He is the son of parents who had no experience of higher education and could not imagine why he was going to Princeton. In the telephone conversation, Blakemore said: "I am now the chairman of the Board of Higher Education in the State of Illinois, and I wonder if we could arrange for you to speak to our Board too." After Bowen agreed to meet with his trustees, Blakemore thanked him and then, after a long pause, added: "President Bowen, your book is about *me*." He spoke with great feeling, and the data in *Shape of the River* tell us that there are large numbers of Jerry Blakemores out there, individuals who have succeeded professionally and are also actively involved in a host of civic, community, and not-for-profit activities. (See introduction to the paperback [2000] edition of Bowen and Bok, pp. xxxii–xxxiii.) Such stories continue. For example, the *Boston Globe* published a story in late May 2004 recounting the highly positive effects of attending Boston College on two students, Juan De Jesus and Drudys Nicolas, who have now headed for Wall Street (De Jesus) and a nursing career (Nicolas). Both are effusive in their praise of the "leg up" that Boston College gave them. (See Adrian Walker, "45 Graduates Seize the Day," *Boston Globe*, May 27, 2004, p. B1.)

38. The United States is by no means the only country struggling with the issues of preferences or quotas in university admissions. A recent article in the *Chronicle of Higher Education* (Beth McMurtrie, "The Quota Quandary," February 13, 2004, p. A38) describes in detail the active debates going on today in Brazil, India, and Malaysia—which represent three radically different situations. There is apparently much more willingness to use quotas in these countries (though that situation is now changing in Malaysia) than there is in the United States.

39. In a talk given on Martin Luther King Day (February 14) 2003, President Vest recalled: "When I began my career as a Teaching Fellow and then as a young assistant professor at the University of Michigan in the 1960s it was extraordinary if I had more than one African American student in my classes every couple of years. . . . In that context, when I look around today at an MIT student body whose undergraduates are . . . 6 percent African-American, 11 percent Hispanic American, 2 percent Native American—a student body that is remarkably diverse in so many other dimensions as well—it seems to me that a miracle has happened. But that is just the point. It is not a miracle. It is not a natural occurrence. It is the result of determined, conscientious effort, over more than three decades, often against seemingly insurmountable odds." The metaphor of the thread and the scissors is from this same talk. (Charles M. Vest, "MIT's 29th Annual Celebration of the Life and Legacy of Dr. Martin Luther King, Jr.: Remarks by President Charles M. Vest," speech delivered at Massachusetts Institute of Technology, February 14, 2003, available at http://web.mit.edu/newsoffice/2003/mlk-cmv.html, accessed November 9, 2004.)

40. Linda Greenhouse, "The Supreme Court: Affirmative Action: Justices Back Affirmative Action by 5 to 4, but Wider Vote Bans a Racial Point System," *New York Times*, June 24, 2003, p. A1.

41. *Grutter v. Bollinger et al.*, 539 U.S. 306 (2003) at 328.

42. *Grutter*, 539 U.S. at 343. Also: "When race-based action is necessary to further a compelling governmental interest, such action does not violate the constitutional guarantee of equal protection so long as the narrow-tailoring requirement is also satisfied" (*Grutter*, 539 U.S. at 327).

43. *Gratz v. Bollinger et al.*, 539 U.S. 244 (2003).

44. *Gratz*, 539 U.S., esp. at 268–75.

45. Other schools that used point systems have been busily replacing them. See, for example, the discussion of admissions policies at the University of Massachusetts

at Amherst (Jenna Russell, "UMass Finds Its Minority Level Even," *Boston Globe,* April 20, 2004, p. A1).

46. See Scott Jaschik, "Affirmative Reactions: A Year after the Supreme Court Upheld Affirmative Action at the University of Michigan, Why Has Minority Enrollment Gone Down?" *Boston Globe,* June 13, 2004, p. H1. It is also possible, as one of our colleagues has suggested, that expectations of rejection could have had an effect. See also Marvin Krislov's description of the changes in undergraduate admissions made by the University of Michigan (Krislov, p. 901).

47. Gurin, p. 99.

48. See Goldstein, pp. 949 ff. As Derek Bok writes in a paper published shortly before the Supreme Court heard arguments in the Michigan cases: "[There is] an established tradition of trying to serve the needs of important professions and occupations in the society. Serving such needs has been a fundamental aim of American higher education ever since the Puritan fathers founded Harvard College in 1636 to prepare young men to teach in their schools and preach in their churches. Similar aims inspired the lawmakers who authorized the creation of land-grant universities in the 19th century in an effort to meet the needs of an industrializing nation. They continue to represent the principal reason why states appropriate vast sums of public money each year to maintain and improve the medical schools, law schools, business schools, and other university programs that prepare students for the ever more stringent requirements of hospitals, law firms, corporations, and other demanding places of employment." (Derek Bok, "The Uncertain Future of Race-Sensitive Admissions," January 20, 2003, available at http://www.nacua.org/documents/Uncertain_Future_of_Race_Sensitive_Admissions_Revised.pdf, p. 3.) Bok then points out that today, in defining its needs, "every major profession in the United States has made known a desire for more diversity within its ranks" (p. 4). He goes on to document this claim by referencing statements adopted by professional associations and citing numerous amicus briefs. One particularly eloquent statement was prepared in 1998 by the American Bar Association (ABA) Committee on Diversity of Legal Education: "The need to diversify the legal profession is not a vague liberal ideal; it is an essential component of the administration of justice. The legal profession must not be the preserve of any one segment of our society. Instead, we must confront the reality that if we are to remain a government under law in a multicultural society, the concept of justice must be one that is shared by all our citizens. Unless law schools—the gateway to the profession—are able to maintain diversity by providing broad access to legal education, these goals will be unattainable." (*ABA Report of the Committee on Diversity in Legal Education* [1998], pp. 7–8, cited by Bok on p. 6 of his paper.)

49. For a fascinating history of the debate over what the 14th Amendment really means, going back to *Brown v. Board of Education,* and of the interplay between these two ways of thinking about the 14th Amendment, see Reva B. Siegel, "Equality Talk: Antisubordination and Anticlassification Values in Constitutional Struggles over *Brown,*" *Harvard Law Review* 117, no. 5 (May 2004): 1470–543. For a convincing repudiation of the idea that the Equal Protection Clause should operate symmetrically for whites and blacks, see Goldstein, pp. 906, 927–28. Goldstein emphasizes the difference between "programs of exclusion and those of inclusion," and he quotes Justice Stevens's formulation, which notes the difference between "a No Trespassing sign and a welcome mat."

50. But we must also recognize that at least one other opinion, Justice Clarence Thomas's dissent, fails to address at all the overwhelming empirical evidence in Bowen and Bok and in other publications cited by Gurin, among others, demonstrating how

well most minority students have fared under race-sensitive programs—and how well *they* think they have fared. Indeed, one of the most compelling statistical findings in Bowen and Bok is the one cited earlier in this chapter, showing that, *in given SAT ranges,* minority students do better in life and are more satisfied, the more selective the schools they attended as undergraduates. Nonetheless, Justice Thomas writes: "The Law School tantalizes unprepared students with the promise of a University of Michigan degree and all of the opportunities that it offers. These overmatched students take the bait, only to find that they cannot succeed in the cauldron of competition." Dissenting opinion of Justice Thomas, *Grutter,* 539 U.S. at 372. It is nothing less than astonishing that a bald statement of this kind can be made by a Supreme Court Justice without any supporting evidence. As various commentators have observed, Justice Thomas appears to be acting on a personal agenda, or reflecting personal views (insecurities?) that hardly constitute "evidence." Maureen Dowd describes Justice Thomas's dissent as "a clinical study of a man who has been driven barking mad by the beneficial treatment he received. It's poignant, really. It makes him crazy that people think he is where he is because of his race, but he is where he is because of his race." (Dowd, "Could Thomas Be Right?" *New York Times,* June 25, 2003, p. A25.) Linda Greenhouse writes: "Justice Thomas, whose impassioned 31-page dissenting opinion in the law school case was almost precisely the length of Justice O'Connor's majority opinion, took as his text not the briefs but his own life story." Greenhouse then refers to "a remarkable series of paragraphs, most without footnotes, statistics or outside references, about the pain and stigma suffered by recipients of affirmative action." (Greenhouse, "The Supreme Court: The Justices; Context and the Court," *New York Times,* June 25, 2003, p. A1.) This strange piece of judicial history is a telling reminder of how important it is to move beyond "the anecdote range" and focus not on individual cases, which may represent, as in this instance, outliers, but rather on the weight of evidence. We are fond of quoting Damon Runyon as having observed: "It may be that the race is not always to the swift, nor the battle to the strong—but that is the way to bet." (Runyon, quoted in Christopher Avery, Andrew Fairbanks, and Richard Zeckhauser, *The Early Admissions Game: Joining the Elite* [Cambridge, Mass.: Harvard University Press, 2003], pp. 161–62.)

51. For an extended analysis of the role played by amicus briefs in the Michigan cases, and of the criteria relevant to deciding when such briefs can be especially helpful, see Jonathan Alger and Marvin Krislov, "You've Got to Have Friends: Lessons Learned from the Role of Amici in the University of Michigan Cases," *Journal of College and University Law* 30, no. 3 (2004): 503–29.

52. Payton (2004a), p. 12. At least 85 companies, including 65 Fortune 500 corporations, filed amicus briefs in support of the University of Michigan. See University of Michigan, "Chronology of Key Rulings in the University of Michigan Affirmative Action Lawsuits and Other Higher Education Affirmative Action Suits," from University of Michigan Admissions Lawsuits Web site (Ann Arbor: University of Michigan, last revised October 23, 2003), available at http://www.umich.edu/~urel/admissions/faqs/chronology.html.

53. *Grutter,* 539 U.S. at 331.

54. *Grutter,* 539 U.S. at 331. In a nice twist, the Court then cites the U.S. government's brief as affirming that "ensuring that public institutions are open and available to all segments of American society, including people of all races and ethnicities, represents a paramount government objective."

55. *Grutter,* 539 U.S. at 332.

56. *Grutter,* 539 U.S. at 339. There is a serious problem of semantics here. What the Court calls "race neutral" we would prefer to call "race blind" (in the sense that the race of the candidate is not taken explicitly into account). Race-blind policies can have major effects on the racial composition of a student body, and so are not race neutral in this regard. For an excellent discussion of this distinction, and of its importance, see Glenn Loury's foreword to the paperback edition of Bowen and Bok, pp. xxii–xxiv.

57. *Grutter,* 539 U.S. at 339.

58. *Grutter,* 539 U.S. at 340.

59. See Glenn Loury et al., "Brief of Social Scientists Glenn C. Loury, Nathan Glazer, John F. Kain, Thomas J. Kane, Douglas Massey, Marta Tienda, and Brian Bucks as *Amici Curiae* in support of Respondents," submitted to the U.S. Supreme Court in *Barbara Grutter v. Lee Bollinger, et al.,* and *Jennifer Gratz and Patrick Hamacher v. Lee Bollinger, et al.,* February 2003. The brief argues that percent plans are not race neutral, that they are "less effective and less efficient" than current affirmative action plans, that they are too focused on one criterion of success at the expense of numerous others, that they depend on a segregated minority high school population, that they necessitate expensive financial aid and recruitment programs, and that they are too new for their effects to be fully known. In sum, the authors of the brief argue that these percentage plans are less "narrowly tailored" than current race-sensitive preferences (p. 3).

60. See Jonathan D. Glater, "Diversity Plan Shaped in Texas Is Under Attack," *New York Times,* June 13, 2004, section 1, p. 1.

61. Roland Fryer Jr., Glenn C. Loury, and Tolga Yuret, "Color-Blind Affirmative Action," NBER Working Paper no. 10103, November 2003. Fryer, Loury, and Yuret use data from the '89 C&B entering cohort to analyze the efficiency cost of using a race-blind admissions policy to achieve racial diversity. Replacing conventional race-sensitive college admissions policies with race-blind alternatives will increase the weight admissions committees seeking racial diversity will place on factors that are correlated with race but not necessarily the best predictors of academic achievement. Fryer, Loury, and Yuret assess the efficiency implications of both race-blind and race-sensitive policies, measuring efficiency in terms of the average class rank of those admitted to a constructed cohort half the size of each school's original entering class. Replicating the race composition of the actual entering classes of seven C&B schools using a retroactively race-blind admissions policy led to short-run efficiency losses four to five times greater than those incurred by a race-sensitive policy. In changing the relative importance of many academic and socioeconomic factors in the admissions process, race-blind policies lead to long-run efficiency losses, because students face muddled incentives for acquiring the traits and characteristics valued by admissions committees that may not lead to greater success in college—undermining efficiency on the supply side as well.

62. *Grutter,* 539 U.S. at 328.

63. Dissenting opinion of Justice Scalia, *Grutter,* 539 U.S. at 348.

64. See Peter Schmidt, "Advocacy Groups Pressure Colleges to Disclose Affirmative-Action Policies," *Chronicle of Higher Education,* April 2, 2004, p. A26. An ominous development occurred earlier (in February 2004) when an assistant to one of the members of the U.S. Commission on Civil Rights distributed a survey to 40 selective colleges asking about their affirmative action policies. The survey was not authorized by the commission and was denounced by the leader of the commission's panel, Mary

Berry, who encouraged the colleges not to respond to it. Peter Schmidt, "Head of Civil-Rights Panel Denounces Affirmative Action Survey Sent Out on Panel's Letterhead," *Chronicle of Higher Education*, February 13, 2004, online edition.

65. William Kidder, Susan Kiyomi Serrano, and Angelon Ancheta, "In California, a Misguided Battle over Race," *Chronicle of Higher Education*, May 21, 2004, p. B16. Moores claimed that the university system was "discriminating blatantly against Asians," a tactic labeled "racial mascotting" by the legal scholar Sumi Cho.

66. Alyson Klein, "Affirmative-Action Opponents Suffer Setbacks in Colorado and Michigan," *Chronicle of Higher Education*, April 9, 2004, online edition.

67. The Supreme Court received a record number of 107 amicus curiae briefs before the case was decided in June 2003. Among the more than 70 briefs in support of the University of Michigan were those submitted by 65 Fortune 500 companies, retired military leaders, MTV, labor unions, states and cities, as well as universities and professional and academic associations such as the American Bar Association and the American Sociological Association. See Tony Mauro, "Court Affirms Continued Need for Preferences," *New York Law Journal*, June 24, 2003, p. A1; Leslie T. Thornton, "With Friends Like These . . . ," *Legal Times*, March 31, 2003, p. 70; University of Michigan, "*Grutter* and *Gratz:* Amicus Briefs," from University of Michigan Admissions Lawsuits Web site, available at http://www.umich.edu/~urel/admissions/legal/amicus.html.

68. For press accounts of the MIT situation, see Michael A. Fletcher, "MIT to End Programs' Racial Exclusiveness," *Washington Post*, February 12, 2003, p. A03; Peter Schmidt and Jeffrey R. Young, "MIT and Princeton Open 2 Summer Programs to Students of All Races," *Chronicle of Higher Education*, February 21, 2003, online edition; and MIT News Office, "MIT to Open Pre-College Summer Enrichment Programs to All Races," February 11, 2003, available at http://web.mit.edu/newsoffice/2003/programs.html. Fletcher quotes Robert P. Redwine, MIT's dean of undergraduate education, as saying: "Our best advice was that for racially exclusive programs, our chances of winning were essentially zero." There is likely no university in the United States more committed to addressing racial disparities than MIT, and President Vest and others at MIT were determined to preserve the essentials of their highly successful program. After interminable discussions, huge investments of time, and what can only be construed as threats to shut down the program, MIT continued its program in all essential respects, but only after modifying it to make disadvantaged students from other groups eligible as well. Critics of decisions by many colleges and universities (not only MIT) to eliminate race exclusivity should study this history and recognize that continuing to insist on race exclusivity not only entails the risk of litigation, but also risks the termination of programs through the use of injunctions.

69. For a recent account of the history of this program, and of its accomplishments, see The Andrew W. Mellon Foundation, *Report of The Andrew W. Mellon Foundation 2003* (New York: The Andrew W. Mellon Foundation, 2003), pp. 34–46. Since its inception, MMUF has had over 2,000 participating students, and the attrition rate continues to be extremely low. In addition to the more than 100 MMUF participants who have already obtained their PhDs, approximately 500 are currently in graduate school (with many more completing their undergraduate studies or taking time off before going on to graduate school), and the number earning PhDs each year continues to accelerate. Today, MMUF "alums" teach in a variety of fields at a wide range of colleges and universities. The two fields with the largest numbers of MMUF faculty are English/literature and history. But there are also significant numbers in fields

such as anthropology, physics/chemistry, mathematics, music, and art history. The 40 colleges and universities that have recruited former MMUF students to their faculties constitute a veritable "Who's Who" of American higher education; the roster includes Bryn Mawr, Clark-Atlanta, Harvard, Queens (CUNY), and the Universities of Chicago, Michigan, and New Mexico, to name just a few that illustrate the range of the institutions served.

These results have been brought about in large degree because of the quality and the commitment of the mentors who have worked with individual students. One early MMUF student from Oberlin credited his mentor with "bringing my mind to life." Equally important have been the distinguishing features of the program itself: delegation of responsibility for personalized selection of candidates to individual campuses, where campus coordinators are chosen and put in charge; targeted recruitment of promising students in their sophomore year; careful identification of mentors who pay close attention to their MMUF students; provision of opportunities for academic involvement (teaching or research) during both the academic year and the summer, with modest financial subventions provided by the Foundation; annual conferences that lead to intellectual stimulation, practice in writing and presenting papers, and the strengthening of support networks; the promise of the Foundation that it will repay, in a staged manner, undergraduate debt of up to $10,000 incurred by MMUF students as they progress through their PhD programs; and, more recently, targeted support for research by MMUF students during graduate study and after they obtain initial faculty appointments. But much experience has taught us that the campus coordinators have been most important of all.

70. It was the colleges and universities participating in MMUF that were primarily at risk of being found to have violated Title VI of the Civil Rights Act of 1964, not the Foundation itself (since the Foundation receives no federal funds). But of course the Foundation did not want to create problems for its participating colleges and universities through the structure of the MMUF program, and without the active participation of the individual colleges and universities, MMUF could not continue to operate as effectively as it has in the past.

71. For a much fuller account of how the Foundation approached the reconceptualization of MMUF, please see the Foundation's 2003 report, cited earlier.

72. For a short biography of Dr. Mays, see Orville Vernon Burton, "Mays, Benjamin Elijah," from *American National Biography Online*, available at http://www.anb.org/articles/homc.html, last updated February 2000. Dr. Mays seems an excellent model for MMUF, in part because it is said that "at an early age [he] developed an 'insatiable desire' for education." Overcoming obstacles of every kind, he earned an undergraduate degree from Bates College and, at age 40, a PhD from the University of Chicago. He was a great teacher, and one student inspired by Mays was Martin Luther King Jr. At King's funeral, Dr. Mays gave the eulogy. Dr. Mays was president of Morehouse College for 27 years.

73. Programs like MMUF clearly convey additional "benefits" to their participants, and in this sense are "cousins" to an admissions process at an academically selective institution. By now, many other "preparation" and "enrichment" programs have also been redesigned to end their racial exclusivity. See, for example, the account of the opening up of the Harvard Business School's summer program (Peter Schmidt, "Harvard Business School Opens Summer Program to White and Asian Students in Response to Complaint," *Chronicle of Higher Education*, February 18, 2004, online edition).

74. The Law and Society Association (LSA)/National Science Foundation Minority Pre-Dissertation and Mentoring Program was canceled "due to concerns that have been raised about the constitutionality of the race-exclusive eligibility requirements." (Memo from Howard Erlanger, president of LSA, March 25, 2004; see also the LSA Web site, http://lawandsociety.org/fellowship/announce.htm.) The effects of modifications in programs that were once race-exclusive obviously depend on how the programs are modified and on the continuing commitment of resources to them. We agree with those who believe that careful modifications of programs, with careful attention to their original objectives, can succeed. For a lengthy discussion of this subject, see Jodi S. Cohen, "Minority Programs Eroding on Campus," *Chicago Tribune,* September 29, 2004, p. C1.

75. See Alyson Klein, "Foes of Affirmative Action Take Aim at Scholarship Offered by Pepperdine U.," *Chronicle of Higher Education,* January 23, 2004, online edition. Paris Dennard, an African American student at Pepperdine, is a staunch defender of the Pepperdine scholarships and critical of those who oppose them, saying, "There are people who are on the right, and there are people on the extreme right." (Stuart Silverstein, "Pepperdine Defends Its Minority Scholarships," *Los Angeles Times,* January 22, 2004, p. B1.) According to press reports, a number of other colleges and universities have modified scholarship programs to open them to non-minority students. (See Daniel Golden, "Colleges Cut Back Minority Programs after Court Rulings," *Wall Street Journal,* December 30, 2003, online edition.) Very recently, Washington University in St. Louis announced that "on guidance from the U.S. Education Department, it would begin letting members of any race apply for scholarships previously reserved for black students." (Peter Schmidt, "Federal Pressure Prompts Washington U. in St. Louis to Open Minority-Scholarship Program to all Races," *Chronicle of Higher Education,* April 5, 2004, online edition.)

76. Washington University has been a leader in increasing opportunities of every kind for minority students, and yet it decided, in the spring of 2004—following a visit by lawyers from the Office for Civil Rights to discuss complaints filed by the Center for Equal Opportunity and the American Civil Rights Institute—to make the university's John B. Ervin Scholarships available to students of any race. However, preference will be given to applicants "who are interested in a career in education or are active in community service and have shown an interest in helping the less fortunate." See Peter Schmidt (2004d), p. A23. This decision is, we believe, likely to prove a harbinger of similar decisions by other colleges and universities.

77. *Grutter,* 539 U.S. at 343.

78. We can underline the extent of the uncertainty about the correct interpretation by noting that two of the justices who joined the majority opinion argue in a concurring opinion that the "25 years" comment is not binding; two other justices who dissented from the majority opinion state that the 25-year limit is "a holding." (Ginsburg concur, *Grutter,* 539 U.S. at 344; Thomas, concur and dissent, *Grutter,* 539 U.S. at 351 and 377.) We are left with seven justices endorsing the specific language of the sentence that referred to 25 years, two who see it as a hopeful, non-binding dictum; two who see it as a firm, legal limit; and three who endorse the ambiguous statement without commentary. Goldstein does not believe that the 25-year limit is binding, and he writes: "Justice Thomas' repeated characterization of the Court's 'holding' that race preferences in higher education 'will be illegal in 25 years,' reflected either wishful thinking, sloppy reading, or deliberate deception" (p. 931).

79. Derek Bok, "Closing the Nagging Gap in Minority Achievement," *Chronicle of Higher Education*, October 24, 2003, online edition. Bok sees the 25-year limit as serving "to push educators into doing what they should have been attending to all along"; in this sense, he thinks that "the *Grutter* case may prove to be an even greater boon than any of us could have dared to hope." See also Glenn C. Loury, "Affirmed . . . For Now the Supreme Court's Decision Made Affirmative Action Resoundingly Legal. Now Comes the Hard Part—Making It Unnecessary," *Boston Globe*, June 29, 2003, p. D1. Loury writes: "Affirmative action isn't going away soon, but it will not last forever."

80. We are indebted to Alan Krueger, Jesse Rothstein, and Sarah Turner for permission to reproduce this figure from their paper "Race, Income and College in 25 Years: The Legacy of Separate and Unequal Schooling" (unpublished draft, October 1, 2004, figure 4).

81. This group includes three public universities (Pennsylvania State University, UCLA, and the University of Virginia) and 14 private colleges and universities (Barnard, Bowdoin, Columbia, Harvard, Middlebury, Oberlin, Pomona, Princeton, Smith, Swarthmore, Wellesley, Williams, the University of Pennsylvania, and Yale). These schools are part of the expanded College & Beyond database described in chapter 5. In the main, for reasons explained originally in *The Shape of the River* (appendix A), we aggregate data by assigning the results for each school an equal weight. However, the results are so similar across schools that the weighting system is of no great consequence.

82. Krueger, Rothstein, and Turner, p. 18. This paper contains an extensive discussion of the work on intergenerational transmissions of income that is the basis for this assumption. It should be noted that in fact there has been little convergence of family incomes over the past three or four decades. The ratio of the median income for black families with one child to the median income for similar white families was 0.63 in 1967 and 0.62 in 2001 (p. 6). Over the same period, however, there was considerable convergence of earnings for black and white workers. The other variable that has inhibited convergence of family incomes is changes in family structure. As Krueger, Rothstein, and Turner explain, the likelihood of living in a two-parent family has decreased much more sharply for black families over these decades than it has for white families; hence, black families have been much less likely to be able to count on two paychecks than white families. We agree with the authors that continued relative deterioration of black family structures is unlikely, and that for this reason it is plausible to believe that over the next 25 years there will be some real convergence of family incomes. However, we also agree with the authors that their estimate of 50 percent convergence may be "on the optimistic side."

83. Krueger, Rothstein, and Turner limit all of their projections to black and white population groups, excluding Hispanics and Asians. They adopt this approach to avoid having to deal with the manifold complications associated with immigration. For the very rough purposes of this discussion, we treat data for blacks as a proxy for data for Hispanics and data for whites as a proxy for data for Asians. This is clearly a gross oversimplification, but it is the only way to generate the ball-park estimates of the need for racial preferences in 25 years that are our objective.

84. The entire set of simulations by Krueger, Rothstein, and Turner is summarized in table 1 of their paper; we have aggregated their data, which are presented for separate sets of schools defined by selectivity, by using the same weighting system employed throughout our analysis (with data from each school given an equal weight).

85. Recall, however, that median family incomes have not converged much if at all over this period; thus we are less concerned than Krueger, Rothstein, and Turner about the possible "double counting" of income convergence.

86. Larry V. Hedges and Amy Nowell, "Black-White Test Score Convergence since 1965," in *The Black-White Test Score Gap*, ed. Christopher Jencks and Meredith Phillips (Washington, D.C.: Brookings Institution Press, 1998), p. 154. See figure 1 of the paper by Krueger, Rothstein, and Turner for a useful plot of test score changes since 1970. The lack of convergence in recent years is evident.

87. The reasons for the convergence that did occur prior to the late 1980s are also relevant. Social scientists who have studied this question conclude that changes in family characteristics (median family income, parental education, and so on) had only a limited impact. Changes in school resources and peer effects probably also played some role, but David Grissmer and his colleagues point to the civil rights movement and large-scale anti-poverty programs as the main causes of the reduced gap. They hypothesize that the symbolic value of these progressive reforms, perhaps even more than their direct effects, was responsible for the narrowing of the test score gap—that "a nationwide shift in beliefs, attitudes, and motivations among black parents and students, as well as their teachers, . . . significantly changed the educational experience of black children." (David Grissmer, Ann Flanagan, and Stephanie Williamson, "Why Did the Black-White Score Gap Narrow in the 1970s and 1980s?" in Jencks and Phillips, pp. 198–222.) Active government support for initiatives of this kind has unquestionably diminished in recent decades. Other scholars agree that changes in family characteristics alone were less significant than is sometimes thought. Michael Cook and William Evans find that the narrowing of the parental education gap accounted for no more than 25 percent of the narrowing in National Assessment of Educational Progress scores from 1972 to 1990. (Michael D. Cook and William N. Evans, "Families or Schools? Explaining the Convergence in White and Black Academic Performance," *Journal of Labor Economics* 18, no. 4 [October 2000]: 749.) Alan Krueger and Diane Whitmore find that black students benefit more than white students from the provision of additional school resources and that much of the decline in the black-white gap can be accounted for by the decline in the pupil-teacher ratio. (See Alan B. Krueger and Diane M. Whitmore, "Would Smaller Classes Help Close the Black-White Achievement Gap?" Princeton University, Industrial Relations Section, Working Paper no. 451, March 2001, available at http://www.irs.princeton.edu/pubs/pdfs/451.pdf.) However, the average pupil-teacher ratio for blacks and whites is now virtually the same.

88. Hedges and Nowell, p. 159.

89. As sociologist Christopher Jencks commented in reaction to the opinion in *Grutter:* "I hope we won't need preferences in five years. But if there's something we should all be doing in the next 25 years to produce this result, she [Justice O'Connor] didn't mention it, and we haven't found it yet." (Jencks, quoted in Patrick Healy, "Justice's 'Deadline' Confounds Colleges," *Boston Globe,* June 29, 2003, p. A1.) In their concurring opinion, Justices Ruth Bader Ginsburg and Stephen Breyer wrote: "From today's vantage point, one may hope, but not firmly forecast, that over the next generation's span, progress toward nondiscrimination and genuinely equal opportunity will make it safe to sunset affirmative action" (*Grutter,* 539 U.S. at 346).

90. See Ginsburg's concurrence for an extended discussion of the pre-college schooling problem (along with many references) that without question contributes to

the preparation gap. Ginsburg concludes that "it remains the current reality that many minority students encounter markedly inadequate and unequal educational opportunities" (*Grutter*, 539 U.S. at 346).

91. Erica Frankenberg and Chungmei Lee, "Race in American Public Schools: Rapidly Resegregating School Districts" (Cambridge, Mass.: Civil Rights Project, Harvard University, August), available at http://www.civilrightsproject.harvard.edu/research/deseg/Race_in_American_Public_Schools1.pdf.

92. Payton (2004a), p. 13.

93. See Bok (2003b) for a discussion of this subject, as well as other aspects of this problem.

94. See Freeman A. Hrabowski, "Supporting the Talented Tenth: The Role of Research Universities in Promoting High Achievement among Minorities in Science and Engineering," David Dodds Henry Lecture, University of Illinois at Urbana-Champaign, November 5, 2003. See also Freeman A. Hrabowski, Kenneth I. Maton, Monica L. Greene, and Geoffrey L. Greif, *Overcoming the Odds: Raising Academically Successful African American Young Women* (New York: Oxford University Press, 2002); and Freeman A. Hrabowski, Kenneth I. Maton, and Geoffrey L. Greif, *Beating the Odds: Raising Academically Successful African American Males* (New York: Oxford University Press, 1998).

95. We also suggest that American colleges and universities look more closely than they have to date at policies that have worked elsewhere. South Africa is an excellent example of a country facing far more difficult problems of lack of preparation and an immediate legacy of a racially bifurcated population than anyone in the United States can imagine. The University of Cape Town has devoted an enormous amount of effort to developing a test that aims to identify academic potential in students who do not perform well on traditional measures of college preparation—in this case, the South African high school matriculation exam. The new test attempts to measure not academic achievement or the current ability of the test-taker, but rather his or her potential to achieve with proper support. This objective is achieved through "scaffolding"—building questions on material provided in the test itself, rather than knowledge acquired elsewhere. See the separate essay in this volume that discusses experiences in South Africa (appendix A).

96. The lessons to be learned to date from such research are summarized in chapter 9, where we discuss alternative approaches to improving early education and pre-collegiate preparation.

97. Loury (2000), esp. pp. xxviii–xxix. Loury writes: "No understanding of the social order in which we operate is possible that does not make use of racial categories because these socially constructed categories are embedded in the consciousness of the individuals with whom we must reckon. Because *they* use race to articulate their own self-understandings, *we* must be mindful of race as we conduct our public affairs. This is a cognitive, not a normative, point. One can hold that race is irrelevant to an individual's moral worth, that individuals and not groups are the bearers of rights, and nevertheless affirm that, to deal effectively with these autonomous individuals, account must be taken of the categories of thought in which they understand themselves" (p. xxviii).

98. A phrase attributed to the historian David Kennedy by Jonathan Rieder in his review of three books about Martin Luther King Jr. (Rieder, "Righteousness Like a Mighty Stream," *New York Times Book Review*, February 8, 2004, p. 6.)

99. Rieder, p. 6.

Chapter 7   Broadening the Quest for Equity at the Institutional Level:
Socioeconomic Status, Admissions Preferences, and Financial Aid

1. This is the title of the excellent study of college admissions and financial aid
policies of 16 liberal arts colleges between 1955 and 1994 by Elizabeth A. Duffy and
Idana Goldberg, *Crafting a Class: College Admissions and Financial Aid, 1955–1994*
(Princeton, N.J.: Princeton University Press, 1998).

2. See William G. Bowen, "Maintaining Opportunity: Undergraduate Financial
Aid at Princeton," *Report of the President,* Princeton University, April 1983.

3. South Africa's National Plan for Higher Education states: "Higher Education
. . . has immense potential to contribute to the consolidation of democracy and social
justice, and the growth and development of the economy. . . . The overall well-being
of nations is vitally dependent on the contribution of higher education to the social,
cultural, political and economic development of its citizens." Council on Higher Education (South Africa), *Towards a New Higher Education Landscape: Meeting the Equity,
Quality and Social Development Imperatives of South Africa in the 21st Century* (Pretoria:
Council on Higher Education, 2000), pp. 25–26. For an extended discussion of the
South African experience, see appendix A.

4. Woodrow Wilson made the case for diversity this way: "One of the things that
makes us unserviceable citizens is that there are certain classes of men with whom we
have never been able to associate and whom we have, therefore, never been able to
understand. I believe that the process of a university should be a process of unchosen
contacts with modern thought and life." Wilson, quoted in Bowen (1983), p. 7.

5. President Lawrence H. Summers of Harvard described this concern eloquently in his speech to the American Council on Education in February 2004.
Lawrence H. Summers, "Higher Education and the American Dream," speech delivered at the 86th Annual Meeting, American Council on Education, Miami, Fla., February 29, 2004, available at http://www.president.harvard.edu/speeches/2004/
ace.html, accessed August 9, 2004.

6. Nationally, over 80 percent of the institutions included in a recent broad-
based survey of admissions policies and practices indicated that "aid had no influence
on the admissions decision," and 69 percent reported that "admissions and financial
aid decisions were completely unrelated." (See Hunter Breland et al., *Trends in College
Admission 2000: A Report of a National Survey of Undergraduate Admission Policies, Practices,
and Procedures* [Alexandria, Va.: National Association for College Admission Counseling, March 2002]), quotes on pp. 115 and 118. "Demonstrated need" can of course
be met through various combinations of grant aid, loans, and work opportunities. The
schools in our study differ in some degree in their reliance on loans, in part as a consequence of differences in resources and in part because of differences in philosophies. (See the discussion, and the references, near the end of the chapter concerning decisions by Harvard and the University of Virginia to replace loans with grants for
families in the bottom part of the income distribution; see also the broader discussion
of "packaging" that is part of the discussion of merit aid.)

7. In May of 1991, the Antitrust Division of the Department of Justice sued the
eight Ivy League schools and the Massachusetts Institute of Technology (MIT) under
Section I of the Sherman Act for price-fixing. All of the Ivies ended up signing a con-
sent decree in which they agreed to halt the activities of the Overlap Group. MIT
refused to sign and was involved in a lengthy legal dispute that concluded when that
school also settled with the government after an initial guilty verdict was found to have

been based on an erroneous reading of the law, and sent back for retrial. Subsequently, Congress passed an exemption ("section 568" of an unrelated bill) that allowed a set of private institutions that were committed to need-blind admissions to meet to discuss financial aid policies and the formula for awarding financial aid—but not the awards made to specific students. (See Dennis W. Carlton, Gustavo E. Bamberger and Roy J. Epstein, "Antitrust and Higher Education: Was There a Conspiracy to Restrict Financial Aid?" *RAND Journal of Economics* 26, no. 1 [Spring 1995]: 131–47; and Eric Hoover, "28 Private Colleges Agree to Use Common Approaches to Student Aid," *Chronicle of Higher Education,* July 20, 2001, online edition.) We will not debate the pros and cons of this complex set of events, except to note that we believe there are good reasons for certain kinds of collaborations among non-profit institutions seeking to serve societal goals. (Full disclosure: Bowen was a witness for MIT in the appeals phase of the judicial process.) Caroline Hoxby puts forward a strong argument in favor of cooperation on financial aid in "Benevolent Colluders? The Effects of Antitrust Action on College Financial Aid and Tuition," NBER Working Paper no. 7754, June 2000.

8. Geoffrey Kabaservice, *The Guardians: Kingman Brewster, His Circle, and the Rise of the Liberal Establishment* (New York: Henry Holt, 2004), p. 261. Claudia Goldin (as described in personal correspondence with the authors, July 14, 2004), studied a sample of Bronx Science graduates from the classes of 1951, 1963, 1985, and 1992. From her class (1963), only 14 percent of the female graduates and 24 percent of the male graduates went to "elite" colleges and universities. By contrast, 65 percent of the females and 51 percent of the males went to "All CUNY & SUNY" schools. In 1992 (the most recent class that Goldin studied), 34 percent of the females and 45 percent of the males went to "elite" schools; the percentages going to "All CUNY & SUNY" schools had fallen to 26 percent for the females and 12 percent for the males. Goldin warns that these figures are based on reunion samples, and that she does not believe the figures are biased in any major way. She also observed that in her class "the 'elites' would not have included many going to Yale, Princeton, and Harvard, although there were some."

9. Yale was particularly aggressive in taking on the financial aid issue. When the Yale Corporation approved President Brewster's proposal for need-blind admissions in 1966, it did so on the understanding that "there would be no quota on the number of scholarship students to be accepted, nor any limit on the amount of money available for gifts and loans." (Kabaservice, p. 264.) Kabaservice then observes that this policy's "financial implications were seriously underestimated." Brewster is said to have credited the need-blind admissions policy for having a very large effect on Yale's ability to attract students from less affluent backgrounds (p. 264).

10. Princeton was generally unable (because of resource constraints) to meet the full needs of admitted students in the 1950s and early 1960s. According to the Princeton President's Report for 1983: "Over almost all the years since 1970, the University has been able to meet—from one source or another—the demonstrated needs of all [American] undergraduates." At this point there is a footnote that reads: "In 1971, there were insufficient scholarship funds to meet the full needs of all admitted freshmen, and fifty-one students were put on a financial aid waiting list. The Undergraduate Association [UGA] . . . held a fund-raising drive in support of the principle of meeting full need. By September, the UGA scholarships and the normal process of attrition had enabled the University to meet the needs of all eligible students." The text of the report continues: "While we remain strongly committed to attempting to

sustain this policy, it is by no means certain that ways can in fact be found to do so" (p. 14).

11. See Duffy and Goldberg, esp. chapter 6, for a highly textured discussion of the evolution of financial aid policies at liberal arts colleges in Massachusetts and Ohio over a period of 40 years. This book also provides a very clear picture of the considerations that went into shaping admissions policies.

12. Juliette Wallack, "Brown U. Implements Need-Blind Policy Beginning with Class of '07," *Brown Daily Herald*, February 25, 2002, online edition.

13. Personal conversation with President Lawrence Bacow. See also Marjorie Howard, "A Great University: It's Time to Take 'Prudent Risks,' President Says," *Tufts Journal*, April 2003, online edition.

14. To answer one question that we have been asked several times: black applicants from poor families do not appear to enjoy a larger admissions advantage than black applicants from rich families. However, minority applicants who are first-generation college students enjoy an admissions advantage that is a statistically significant 2.9 points higher than that of other minority applicants. But the racial preference clearly dominates the parental education preference.

15. Refer back to table 5.1. First-generation applicants enjoy a very small admissions advantage (about 4 points on a base admissions probability of about 40 percent), but this advantage is not anything like the advantage enjoyed by other "special groups" such as legacies, recruited athletes, and underrepresented minorities.

16. As we observed before (in chapter 5), this may well not be true at schools operating under greater financial pressure. Subsequent research, especially that being carried out by Michael McPherson and his colleagues, may help answer this question. It is also true that within the highly selective schools (including the 19 in our study), special attention is often given to "development cases" (applicants from families that have been exceedingly generous to the school or are expected to be exceedingly generous). But apparently the number of such cases is so small, relative to the size of the total pool of applicants, that this kind of "quiet" preference does not have a measurable effect on the statistical results. The policy issues raised by development cases are discussed later.

17. Later we also report and discuss the admissions advantage enjoyed by a fourth special group—early applicants. The data for the early applicants come from a slightly different set of schools (a subset of our 19), which is why they need to be treated separately.

18. As mentioned in chapter 5, the adjusted legacy admissions advantage differs substantially between the public and private institutions. At the public universities, the legacy advantage is just 5.5 percentage points, while at the private institutions it is 21 percentage points.

19. See Glenn C. Loury, *The Anatomy of Racial Inequality* (Cambridge, Mass.: Harvard University Press, 2003), for a thoughtful and evocative assessment of the deep springs that continue to feed racial stereotypes and stigmas, and thus affect minorities at every level of society. When the eminent social psychologist Kenneth Clark was asked by an interviewer interested in nomenclature, "What is the best thing for blacks to call themselves?" Clark replied: "White." Clark, quoted in William G. Bowen and Derek C. Bok, *The Shape of the River: Long-Term Consequences of Considering Race in College and University Admissions* (Princeton, N.J.: Princeton University Press, 1998; paperback edition, 2000), p. li of the paperback edition.

20. Quoted in Daniel Golden, "Admissions Preferences Given to Alumni Children Draws Fire," *Wall Street Journal,* January 15, 2003, online edition.

21. The University of Illinois did not provide legacy data. We must re-emphasize that we suspect that the percentage of students who report that they are from the top income quartile is quite a bit *lower* than the actual share of students from the top income quartile. But there is no reason to believe that legacies would understate their income more or less than non-legacies, so the comparison of reported shares should be valid.

22. Cameron Howell and Sarah A. Turner, "Legacies in Black and White: The Racial Composition of the Legacy Pool," NBER Working Paper no. 9448, January 2003.

23. In mentioning the Breyer exchange, Daniel Golden also notes that five of the nine justices or their children themselves "qualified for . . . 'legacy preference.'" (Golden, "For Five Supreme Court Justices, Affirmative Action Isn't Academic," *Wall Street Journal,* May 14, 2003, online edition.) James Traub has argued that a single, "combined" choice has to be made: "So which is it to be—no to legacies and affirmative action, or yes to both?" (See Traub, "The Way We Live Now: 2-29-04: The Pull of Family," *New York Times Magazine,* February 29, 2004, p. 22.) We do not see the choices this way. The two kinds of preferences raise quite different issues.

24. Edwards is quoted in Jacques Steinberg, "Of Sheepskins and Greenbacks," *New York Times,* February 13, 2003, p. A24, and the Shaw quote is from Golden (2003a). Michael Lind is also quoted by Steinberg as saying: "Legacies are a relic of white supremacy and Northeastern establishment dominance." Senator Edward M. Kennedy has filed a bill that would require colleges and universities to report on the race and economic status of first-year students who are relatives of alumni or were admitted under early decision programs. Daniel Golden, "Bill Would Make Colleges Report Legacies and Early Admissions," *Wall Street Journal,* October 29, 2003, online edition.

25. Eliminating legacy preferences can make it easier for those who favor race-sensitive admissions to accept a race-blind approach to admissions. This is what happened at Texas A&M when the university coupled its decision not to embark on race-sensitive admissions for undergraduates (following the University of Michigan decisions) with a decision to stop awarding bonus points to applicants whose relatives had attended A&M. From the perspective of minority students, this action brought an end to an illegitimate form of affirmative action for those who needed it least. See Scott Jaschik, "Affirmative Reactions: A Year after the Supreme Court Upheld Affirmative Action at the University of Michigan, Why Has Minority Enrollment Gone Down?" *Boston Globe,* June 13, 2004, p. H1.

26. Golden (2003a).

27. To avoid confusion, it is necessary to distinguish ratios of admit rates from absolute measures of admissions advantage. In the case of the 13 schools for which we have all the data needed to run the regressions used to estimate admissions advantage, the base (non-legacy) admit rate is 44 percent; adding the legacy admissions advantage of 20 percentile points results in an adjusted admit rate for legacies of 64 percent. The ratio of these admit rates is 3 to 2. The comparable ratio in the Ivies is more like 2 to 1. But even so, these ratios are lower than the ones publicized by the schools and the media.

28. Golden (2003a).

29. The adjusted admissions advantage for legacies in different SAT categories was found by running a logistic regression that included the standard admissions advantage controls. SAT variables were collapsed into the three SAT categories described in the text, and the legacy variable was divided into three interaction variables for legacies in each of the three SAT categories. This functional form allows us to predict the probability of admission for every student as if that student were a legacy in a particular SAT range and compare it to the predicted probability of admission for every student as if that student were a non-legacy in that SAT range. The difference between these two values, for each SAT range, is the adjusted legacy admissions advantage for that SAT range.

30. Kabaservice, p. 262. The rest of this paragraph draws on the same source, pp. 262–67.

31. The Brewster and Clark reforms of the Yale admissions process in the 1960s apparently led to a fine-grained approach to legacy preferences that is rather similar to what our data reveal the situation is today. Kabaservice quotes one of Clark's faculty admissions committee members as noting: "Yale sons have a much harder time of it than I thought. They won, it seemed to me, very little special consideration. If they were good enough, they didn't need it; if they were poor enough, we didn't think it wise to give it to them. The in-between range in which special consideration could be decisive turned out to be a very narrow range indeed." (Memo by Charles E. Lindblom, March 30, 1966, Brewster Presidential Records, quoted in Kabaservice, pp. 269–70.) One difference is that competition for admission is so much keener today that even legacy candidates with extremely impressive credentials may need at least a modest boost if they are to get in; this is Fitzsimmons's "tie-breaker" point.

32. See, for example, Debra Thomas and Terry Shephard, "Legacy Admissions Are Defensible, Because the Process Can't Be 'Fair,'" *Chronicle of Higher Education,* March 14, 2003, p. B15. Both Thomas and Shephard work at Rice University.

33. Quoted in Steinberg, p. A24. We did not find that any systematic preference was given to applicants from families in the top income quartile, but of course this does not mean that no preference was given to some small number of applicants from extremely rich families.

34. Daniel Golden, "Many Colleges Bend Rules to Admit Rich Applicants," *Wall Street Journal,* February 20, 2003, online edition.

35. Golden (2003b).

36. These issues exist in many countries, and an article on China (Paul Mooney, "Extortion Scandal in China Shakes Public Confidence in Fairness of University Admissions," *Chronicle of Higher Education,* August 20, 2004, online edition) reports a public outcry and hail of criticism in the media "when it was alleged that officials at one institution had attempted to extort thousands of dollars from the family of a newly admitted student." To be sure, this is an extreme version of efforts to tie admission to financial support for a university!

37. For an extended discussion of the different rationales for giving admissions advantages to underrepresented minorities and recruited athletes, see William G. Bowen and Sarah A. Levin, *Reclaiming the Game: College Sports and Educational Values* (Princeton, N.J.: Princeton University Press, 2003), pp. 232–40.

38. See James L. Shulman and William G. Bowen, *The Game of Life: College Sports and Educational Values* (Princeton, N.J.: Princeton University Press, 2001), pp. 220–26, and the references cited therein, including "Winning and Giving," the work on which was done principally by Sarah Turner. See Sarah E. Turner, Lauren A. Meserve, and

William G. Bowen, "Winning and Giving: Football Results and Alumni Giving at Selective Private Colleges and Universities," *Social Science Quarterly* 82, no. 4 (December 2001): 812–26.

39. See Shulman and Bowen and, more recently published, Bowen and Levin. See also Thomas J. Espenshade, Chang Y. Chung, and Joan L. Walling, "Admission Preferences for Minority Students, Athletes, and Legacies at Elite Universities," *Social Science Quarterly* 85, no. 5 (December 2004), 1422–46.

40. Bowen and Levin, p. 105 and table 4.1.

41. See, for example, Alvin A. Rosenfeld and Nicole Wise, *The Over-Scheduled Child: Avoiding the Hyper-Parenting Trap* (New York: St. Martin's Press, 2001).

42. Christopher Avery, Andrew Fairbanks, and Richard Zeckhauser, *The Early Admissions Game: Joining the Elite* (Cambridge, Mass.: Harvard University Press, 2003), esp. chapter 5. It is worth emphasizing that similarities in average SAT scores between students admitted through early decision programs and students admitted in the "regular" round (a statistic commonly presented in discussions about early application) tell us very little about the degree of advantage associated with applying early. The right question is this: what is the probability of an applicant with given characteristics being admitted if the applicant applies early, and what is the probability if the applicant applies in the regular round? The answer depends on how many other applicants with similar characteristics are in the two pools. For example, an applicant with combined SAT scores of 1300 might have a 1-in-3 chance of being admitted through early decision but a 1-in-10 chance of being admitted in the regular round.

43. Due to a small number of observations, we combine early decision and early action programs. Avery, Fairbanks, and Zeckhauser found that early decision provides more of an admissions preference than early action; thus our statistic likely understates the true advantage provided to those who apply through a binding early decision program.

44. See Avery, Fairbanks, and Zeckhauser (2003), pp. 60–61, figures 2.4, 2.5.

45. See Bowen and Levin, pp. 79–82.

46. For a discussion of black students and early decision programs, see "Black Students Are Beginning to Seize the Early Admission Advantage," *Journal of Blacks in Higher Education* 43 (Spring 2004): 81–85. More black applicants than before are applying early. However, because of the financial aid considerations noted in the text, the authors conclude that black students would be better off if early decision programs were ended and all students competed in one admissions cycle.

47. Karen W. Arenson, "Yale President Wants to End Early Decisions for Admissions," *New York Times*, December 13, 2001, p. D1.

48. "Brief of Harvard University, Brown University, The University of Chicago, Dartmouth College, Duke University, The University of Pennsylvania, Princeton University, and Yale University as Amici Curiae Supporting Respondents," submitted to the U.S. Supreme Court in *Grutter v. Bollinger, et al.*, and *Gratz v. Bollinger, et al.*," p. 20.

49. We are reminded of John Payton's comment about the lack of law review articles praising the *Brown* decision when it was rendered. At that time, in the mid-1950s, there were very few champions (certainly very few black champions) of desegregation teaching on law school faculties.

50. President Summers emphasized this point strongly in his 2004 commencement address at Harvard. He spoke about increasing inequality in America and the threat it poses to achieving "the American Dream." Then he added: "Yet education

may in fact be adding to the problem. For the linkage between education and economic success has become much stronger. . . . In the 1930s and '40s almost half of American CEOs and founders of leading businesses had no college degree. Now almost all top business leaders have college degrees, and 70 percent have an MBA, J.D., or other advanced degree. This is not just a question of credential inflation. Rather it is the result of a cognitive revolution in the workplace itself, as success in every sphere from finance to baseball depends more and more on powers of analysis. Indeed, the return for completing college has more than doubled over the last generation. . . . The return for attending selective colleges is even greater." Lawrence H. Summers, "Reaffirming the Commitment to Opportunity," Harvard University Commencement Address, June 10, 2004.

51. One of the earliest and most complete statements of the case for class-based affirmative action was provided eight years ago by Richard Kahlenberg in *The Remedy: Class, Race, and Affirmative Action* (New York: Basic Books, 1996). A more recent formulation of the case for "economic affirmative action" is Anthony P. Carnevale and Stephen J. Rose, "Socioeconomic Status, Race/Ethnicity, and Selective College Admissions," in *America's Untapped Resource: Low-Income Students in Higher Education,* ed. Richard D. Kahlenberg (New York: Century Foundation Press, 2004), pp. 101–56. See also Richard D. Kahlenberg, "Toward Affirmative Action for Economic Diversity," *Chronicle of Higher Education,* March 19, 2004, p. B11. This latter piece summarizes the study by Carnevale and Rose and adds some further commentary.

52. There are of course a limitless number of other kinds and sizes of thumbs that one could imagine. One other obvious approach would be to give applicants from lower-SES backgrounds the same admissions advantage now given to minority students, but this has the disadvantage of suggesting to some people that we are pitting students from low-income families against minority students in a "them against us" contest. Another alternative we considered was to assign students from low-income families the same admissions advantage given to recruited athletes, but the admissions advantage enjoyed by these athletes at some of the schools in our study, even at very low SAT levels, is so great that the resulting calculations for applicants from low-income families would be meaningless (refer to the lower SAT ranges of figure 5.7). Finally, we also considered the suggestion that we just boost the SAT scores of applicants from low-income families by some arbitrary number. The overriding objection to this approach is that it smacks of the kind of "point-score" advantage rejected by the Supreme Court in *Gratz v. Bollinger.* An important caveat about using legacy preferences to estimate the effects of giving some advantage to low SES applicants is that the preferences provided to legacies by public institutions are far smaller than the preferences provided by private institutions. This situation is complicated further by different in-state and out-of-state admissions policies. We do not think these differences affect our simulations, but in practice, public institutions are unlikely to use legacy preferences as even a rough guideline for any low SES preferences they might want to adopt.

53. We provide a detailed explanation of the methodology used to make these simulations in appendix B, which also discusses other possible ways of running simulations. Different methods of simulating the admission of applicants, and different assumptions about application and enrollment rates, will of course affect the results; what we offer is one way of carrying out such an analysis. We start out by focusing on students from low-income families solely to simplify the exposition. We have made comparable calculations for first-generation college-goers, with very similar results. We do

not mean to pass lightly over the question of whether it would be better to use income or parental education (or some combination) as a measure of SES for the purpose of making admissions decisions. Thomas Kane (in e-mail correspondence with the authors, March 20, 2004) has emphasized the desirability of using "verifiable" measures, since this is both a fair approach and one that discourages manipulation and "gaming." In this spirit, Kane suggests that more active consideration of SES at the time admissions decisions are being made (rather than only at the time financial aid is being awarded) might both justify and require asking applicants and their families to provide income tax returns (even year-old returns) when they apply.

54. We would hope that admitting more high-achieving students from struggling public high schools would, in turn, encourage more students from such schools to apply to selective colleges and universities. There is evidence of effects in the opposite direction related to changes in the preferences given to minority students. When minority preferences were eliminated at the University of California, and when the "point boost" for minority students at the University of Michigan was ended, applications from minority students declined. See University of California, "Undergraduate Access to the University of California After the Elimination of Race-Conscious Policies," University of California, Office of the President, March 2003; and Jaschik, p. H1.

55. The result of admitting more applicants from low-SES backgrounds from middle to high SAT ranges is actually a slight increase in average SAT scores. A final, minor source of the slight boost in SAT scores is the fact that, in simulating the admission of applicants from non-low-income families, lower-scoring applicants who were admitted under current policies were made slightly more likely than higher-scoring applicants to give up their place to someone from a preferred group.

56. It is of course the case that, in admitting the current group of students from low-SES categories, admissions officers are not choosing randomly. They are "picking and choosing" the candidates whom they believe are the most suitable ones for their schools on the basis not only of the observable characteristics known to them but also on the basis of letters of recommendation, trajectories in achievement, and so on. For this reason, it is entirely possible that any additional admits, even if they had the same test scores and other formal qualifications as those admitted before, would be marginally less desirable candidates. The simulations/projections made by Carnevale and Rose seem much more subject to this qualification, however, than do the simulations shown here. For one thing, Carnevale and Rose selected additional students from low-SES categories on the basis of an absolute standard (SAT scores over 1000, a high school grade point average of at least 3.0 in core courses, and strong recommendations) that may fall well short of the admissions standards applied generally by the selective schools in our study. As they say, their model "assumes a fairly aggressive use of economic affirmative action," which is projected to result in increasing the share of students from the bottom two income quartiles from 10 percent to 38 percent—nearly quadrupling the share from the bottom half of the income distribution (p. 149). We wonder whether it is realistic to assume that such a large additional intake of students with preparation, as measured by test scores, well below the averages for the kinds of institutions in our study, could be accommodated without a considerable impact on academic achievement. For example, the fact that the students currently enrolled in these schools with similar credentials (e.g., below-average SATs) graduate in large numbers does not convince us that all other students with similar credentials, who may not even have applied to such schools, would fare nearly as well. "Unobserv-

ables" of all kinds could produce quite different results. Carnevale and Rose recognize that their simulations are "more a thought experiment than a true representation of what actually takes place in the admissions office at selective colleges . . . and do not reflect the complexity of the real college admissions process" (p. 139).

57. These calculations were made based on the income distribution, net price by income, and list tuition of institutions in the Consortium on Financing Higher Education reported by Catharine Hill, Gordon Winston, and Stephanie Boyd in "Affordability: Family Incomes and Net Prices at Highly Selective Private Colleges and Universities," Williams Project on the Economics of Higher Education, Discussion Paper no. 66, October 2003, pp. 5 and 8.

58. We thank Caroline Hoxby for bringing this question to our attention in personal correspondence, April 2004.

59. The institutions are Barnard, Oberlin, Princeton, Smith, Swarthmore, the University of Pennsylvania, Wellesley, Williams, and Yale .

60. The regression also includes institutional dummy variables. Of course admissions officers do not know what the future employment choices and income streams of applicants will be. When we re-ran the regression for giving rates, including as variables only those characteristics that would be evident at the time of application (SAT scores, gender, and race), we found that students from the top income quartile do have a statistically significant higher giving rate in this more limited functional form. However, there is no statistically significant difference among the giving rates of those in the bottom three quartiles.

61. See Karen W. Arenson, "Harvard Says Poor Parents Won't Have to Pay," *New York Times*, February 29, 2004, section 1, p. 14; and Amy Argetsinger, "U-Va. Acts to Ease Students' Debt Load: Scholarships to Replace Loans," *Washington Post*, February 7, 2004, p. A01.

62. In commenting on an early draft of this chapter, Michael McPherson pointed out that if we had examined similar applications and admissions data for less selective and less wealthy institutions, we might well have found that a number of these colleges and universities give an admissions advantage to applicants from high-income families. McPherson's point is simply that many such schools have to search for "full-pay" students to meet their budget goals. Thought about in this way, the "neutral" admissions-advantage results related to family income that we obtain for the selective, expensive (and generally wealthy) schools in our study are probably "as good as it gets." It would be much more difficult for schools below the top tier that we have studied to favor applicants from low-income families.

63. See appendix table 5.3. Of all minority applicants, 26 percent are from families in the bottom income quartile, and 17 percent are first-generation applicants. Of all applicants with family incomes in the bottom quartile, 28 percent are members of minorities; of all first-generation applicants, 32 percent are members of minorities.

64. These percentages differ from those used in the simulations reported in chapter 6 because here we are examining the overall number of underrepresented minorities (black, Hispanic, and Native American students) as a percentage of all students; in chapter 6 we focused on black students as a percentage of all black and white students.

65. See appendix table 7.1.

66. This difference is likely an artifact of our decision to use legacy admission preferences as the reference point for low-income preferences. Legacy preferences are

smaller at public universities, so the minority students from low-income families who are applying to these institutions do not get as much of a boost in our simulation as those applying to private institutions.

67. Kane, correspondence with the authors, March 2004. See also Kane's earlier work on this subject: Thomas J. Kane, "Racial and Ethnic Preferences in College Admissions," in *The Black-White Test Score Gap,* ed. Christopher Jencks and Meredith Phillips (Washington, D.C.: Brookings Institution Press, 1998), pp. 431–56. Carnevale and Rose (2004) agree that "Race and ethnicity matter in the distribution of opportunity, independent of other characteristics" (p. 132). In their discussion of policy, they are clear that they favor maintaining racial affirmative action (p. 153). It is distressing to see that, after all the research that has been done, some commentators continue to believe (hope?) that the problem of racial diversity will be taken care of "automatically" if we only do more to enroll students from lower-income families. (See, for example, the column by James Traub, p. 21.)

68. See appendix table 7.2.

69. See Jaschik, p. H1.

70. See Sara Rimer and Karen W. Arenson, "Top Colleges Take More Blacks, but Which Ones?" *New York Times,* June 24, 2004, p. A1.

71. Douglas S. Massey et al., *The Source of the River: The Social Origins of Freshmen at America's Selective Colleges and Universities* (Princeton, N.J.: Princeton University Press, 2003), pp. 39–40. Massey reports that "nationwide only 3% of African Americans are foreign born."

72. See Rimer and Arenson.

73. Quoted by Joel Goldstein in his article on the Supreme Court's handling of the major cases involving race and admissions, "Beyond *Bakke: Grutter-Gratz* and the Promise of *Brown,*" *Saint Louis University Law Journal* 48, no. 3 (Spring): 899–954; quote on p. 912.

74. Bowen and Bok, p. 283.

75. Because the definition of "merit" is so hazy and so subjective, some prefer to avoid the term altogether and to speak only of "non-need" aid, but we use both terms, more or less interchangeably.

76. Michael McPherson, personal correspondence with the authors, July 30, 2004.

77. The quoted passage is from a memorandum sent to Bowen by Michael McPherson on July 30, 2004, accompanying preliminary results from ongoing research by McPherson and Morton Schapiro. See also Michael S. McPherson and Morton Owen Schapiro, "The Blurring Line between Merit and Need in Financial Aid," *Change* 34, no. 2 (March–April 2002): 39–46.

78. See Duffy and Goldberg, esp. chapters 6 and 7. (The quotation in the text is from p. 205.) The book by Duffy and Goldberg contains references to much of the rest of the literature on this subject, including the important work done by Sandra Baum. See also Michael S. McPherson and Morton Owen Schapiro, *The Student Aid Game* (Princeton, N.J.: Princeton University Press, 1998), esp. chapters 9 and 10. Chapter 10 cites a most interesting summary of student aid history contained in a paper by Philip G. Wick, the long-time director of financial aid at Williams College.

79. Breland et al., p. 118.

80. Breland et al., p. 122, table 6.13. The pattern for four-year public institutions is similar, and all the percentages are higher; for example, 57 percent of the public institutions made no-need awards to athletes.

81. Breland et al., p. 119, table 6.11. (In looking at table 6.11, note that the far right-hand columns are mislabeled: they show data for all two-year and all four-year institutions surveyed, not just all four-year institutions.)

82. Laura Horn and Katharin Peter, *What Colleges Contribute: Institutional Aid to Full-Time Undergraduates Attending 4-Year Colleges and Universities*, NCES 2003-157 (Washington, D.C.: U.S. Department of Education, National Center for Education Statistics, April 2003), pp. xii–xiii.

83. All of these data are for private institutions in the year 2000. Also, unlike data in the other sources cited earlier, these data do not treat athletic scholarships as "no-need" or "merit" aid. The institutional coverage of the National Postsecondary Student Aid Study (NPSAS), on which McPherson and Schapiro draw, is broad. Details about the study's methodology, including the varied sources tapped (such as institutional records and phone interviews), are available from the NPSAS section of the NCES Web site, http://nces.ed.gov/surveys/npsas/index.asp. The three SAT bands used by McPherson and Schapiro are less than 900, 900–1100, and 1100 and over. The income categories (under $30,000, $30,000 to $60,000, $60,000 to $100,000, and over $100,000) are all adjusted for inflation. All values are expressed in 1999–2000 academic year dollars.

84. Memorandum sent by Michael McPherson to Bowen, July 30, 2004.

85. All of the data in this paragraph are from preliminary tables sent to Bowen by McPherson, July 30, 2004, and the quotation is from the accompanying memorandum. When McPherson and Schapiro complete their research, it will be possible for the first time to understand trends in merit-aid defined *empirically* (in relation to academic achievement, the selectivity and cost of the school attended, and family income) rather than on the basis of the label attached to a particular award. In e-mail correspondence after the transmittal of the data, McPherson pointed out that including government grants in the analysis would change somewhat the patterns reported here (which deal only with "institutional aid") in that government grants are more heavily concentrated on students from poor families; however, as McPherson puts it, "Government grants too have migrated to some degree up the income stream."

86. McPherson and Schapiro (1998), p. 91.

87. See Gordon C. Winston and David J. Zimmerman, "Where Is Aggressive Price Competition Taking Higher Education?" *Change* 32, no. 4 (July–August 2000): 10–18; and, by Winston, "Subsidies, Hierarchy and Peers: The Awkward Economics of Higher Education," *Journal of Economic Perspectives* 13, no. 1 (Winter 1999): 13–36.

88. Duffy and Goldberg, pp. 207–8.

89. Duffy and Goldberg, pp. 226–27.

90. See David Zimmerman, David Rosenblum, and Preston Hillman, "Institutional Ethos, Peers and Individual Outcomes," Williams Project on the Economics of Higher Education (WPEHE) Discussion Paper no. 68, June 2004, as well as other Williams Project discussion papers by Zimmerman, Gordon Winston, and others, at the WPEHE Web site, http://www.williams.edu/wpehe; Eric A. Hanushek et al., "Does Peer Ability Affect Student Achievement?" *Journal of Applied Econometrics* 18, no. 5 (September–October 2003): 527–44; and Bruce Sacerdote, "Peer Effects with Random Assignment: Results for Dartmouth Roommates," *Quarterly Journal of Economics* 116, no. 2 (May 2001): 681–704. See also McPherson and Schapiro (1998), pp. 109–15, for a full discussion of these issues. McPherson and Schapiro come to essentially the same conclusion as Duffy and Goldberg concerning the appropriateness of the use of merit aid in some contexts but not in others.

91. See Duffy and Goldberg, p. 226. A highly preliminary examination of more recent statistics generated by McPherson and Schapiro using the NPSAS suggests that, among the private institutions studied, there was a substantial increase in need-based aid between 1992 and 1996 but some retrenchment thereafter. On the other hand, non-need-based awards (merit aid) increased unambiguously between 1992 and 1996 and between 1996 and 2000. This is a less encouraging picture than the one presented by Duffy and Goldberg.

92. Michael McPherson also pointed out (in personal e-mail correspondence with the authors) that interpretations of anti-trust laws may make this situation worse. Schools have been frightened away from pursuing collective approaches to financial aid policies that could be in the broader interests of society at large. We return to this subject in chapter 10.

Chapter 8   Government Support of Higher Education

1. Caroline Hoxby puts these goals in more succinct and technical terms: "Higher education initiatives should be analyzed with the goal of determining whether they induce people to invest in the amount of education that is optimal for them." Hoxby, "Tax Incentives for Higher Education," in *Tax Policy and the Economy,* ed. James M. Poterba (Cambridge, Mass.: MIT Press, 1998), pp. 49–81; quote on p. 50.

2. State Higher Education Executive Officers (SHEEO), *State Higher Education Finance FY 2003* (Denver: SHEEO, 2004), p. 17, available at http://www.sheeo.org/finance/shef.pdf. In fiscal year 2000, approximately one-third (34 percent) of all current fund revenues for four-year public institutions came from state governments, and the percentage obtained from state governments rises to 36 percent when we consider all public degree-granting institutions. In contrast, the federal government provided just under 11 percent of current fund revenues to all public degree-granting institutions and 12 percent to the four-year institutions. (The federal figures do not include Pell Grants, which are shown as part of tuition and fees, and which, in totality, contribute around 18 percent of current revenues.) These figures are from State Higher Education Executive Officers, table 3.

3. Susan Dynarski, "The New Merit Aid," in *College Choices: The Economics of Where to Go, When to Go, and How to Pay for It,* ed. Caroline M. Hoxby (Chicago: University of Chicago Press, 2004), pp. 63–100.

4. Dynarski (2004a), p. 64.

5. The federal Hope program provides tax credits of up to $1,500 per student to families with a dependent in his or her first two years of college, and the Lifetime Learning Credit allows for a credit of 20 percent on the first $10,000 of tuition for families with students beyond their first two years. Both are phased out for joint tax-filers with $80,000 to $100,000 of income and for single filers with $40,000 to $50,000 of income. See Thomas J. Kane, *The Price of Admission: Rethinking How Americans Pay for College* (Washington, D.C.: Brookings Institution Press, 1999), p. 42; see also Alan B. Krueger and Cecilia E. Rouse, "Education and Labor Policy in the 1990s," in *American Economic Policy in the 1990s,* ed. Jeffrey A. Frankel and Peter R. Orszag (Cambridge, Mass.: MIT Press, 2002), pp. 690–92. The fact that both the Georgia program and the federal program bear the "Hope" name can be confusing. We generally refer to the Georgia program as "HOPE" and the federal program as "Hope."

6. Kane (1999), p. 43. In fact, "approximately one million low-income first and second-year dependent students and one million independent students in college [in

2001] are not eligible to receive the HOPE Scholarship." (Thomas R. Wolanin, "Rhetoric and Reality: Effects and Consequences of the HOPE Scholarship," Institute for Higher Education Policy Working Paper, April 2001, available at http://www.ihep .com/Pubs/PDF/Hope.pdf.) In his 2004 presidential campaign platform, John Kerry proposed providing a $4,000 tax credit each year for tuition payments, which would be refundable so that families with little or no tax liability would benefit alongside families with sizable tax bills. See Kerry-Edwards Campaign, "College Opportunity for All," available from the Kerry-Edwards Campaign Web site at http://www.johnkerry.com/issues/ education/college.html; see also Jeffrey Selingo, "Senator Kerry Proposes Student Loan Auctions," *Chronicle of Higher Education,* April 23, 2004, online edition.

7. Susan M. Dynarski, "Who Benefits from the Education Savings Incentives? Income, Educational Expectations, and the Value of the 529 and Coverdell," NBER Working Paper no. 10470, May 2004. One stunning finding is that, due to the higher marginal tax rates on higher-income families and the structure of the penalties for not using the funds on schooling, "those in the top two tax brackets gain more from *nonqualified* use of a 529 or Coverdell than those in the bottom bracket gain from *qualified* use." Dynarski (2004b), p. 1.

8. See Dynarski (2004a), pp. 68–70.

9. Bridget Terry Long, "The Impact of Federal Tax Credits for Higher Education Expenses," in Hoxby, ed. (2004), pp. 101–68. To some degree the ineffectiveness of the Hope and Lifetime Learning credits was anticipated by Clinton administration officials; however, "the focus on tax incentives rather than other approaches to expanding access to higher education reflected political realities regarding the attractiveness of tax incentives relative to spending increases." They were also a response to the across-the-board tax cuts proposed by Senator Bob Dole during his presidential candidacy. See Frankel and Orszag (2002), pp. 1009–11.

10. Dynarski (2004a), pp. 68–70, 74–82. Another study has found that the Georgia HOPE Scholarship program increases the number of Pell Grant recipients (almost all of whom are from very low-income families) attending Georgia colleges and universities. See Larry D. Singell Jr., Glen R. Waddell, and Bradley R. Curs, "Hope for the Pell? The Impact of Merit-Aid on Needy Students," paper presented at the NBER Higher Education Meeting, April 30, 2004, version dated March 2004. It is unclear, however, whether the additional students holding Pell Grants are students who otherwise would not have gone to college or whether they are students who just would not have applied for Pell Grants (perhaps because they would not have known how to apply) in the absence of requirements associated with getting a HOPE Scholarship. Completing the Free Application for Federal Student Aid (FAFSA) was a requirement for HOPE scholars with family incomes below $50,000 during the years studied. Whether or not the HOPE program induced them to enroll, these students may not have received any money from the HOPE program itself (because there is a dollar-for-dollar reduction in the HOPE award when need-based financial aid is received).

11. Dynarski (2004a), p. 94. For a limited review of further literature on the HOPE scholarship and other merit aid programs, see Avery and Kane, table 8.1.

12. Dynarski (2004a), p. 91.

13. See Christopher Cornwell and David Mustard, "Merit-Based College Scholarships and Car Sales," research paper, University of Georgia, 2002, cited by Dynarski (2004a), p. 90.

14. See Melissa Binder and Philip Ganderton with Kristin Hutchens, "Incentive Effects of New Mexico's Merit-Based State Scholarship Program: Who Responds and

How?" in *Who Should We Help? The Negative Social Consequences of Merit Scholarships,* ed. Donald E. Heller and Patricia Marin (Cambridge, Mass.: Harvard University, 2002), pp. 43–56. This study is cited by Dynarski (2004a), pp. 90–91, who notes that it is the "only conclusive empirical research regarding the question of effect of merit programs on academic effort in college."

15. See Singell, Waddell, and Curs.

16. Jeffrey Selingo, "Georgia Lawmakers Alter Scholarships," *Chronicle of Higher Education,* April 23, 2004, online edition.

17. See Theda Skocpol, "Targeting within Universalism: Politically Viable Policies to Combat Poverty in the United States," in *The Urban Underclass,* ed. Christopher Jencks and Paul Peterson (Washington, D.C.: Brookings Institution Press, 1991), pp. 411–36; and William Julius Wilson, *The Truly Disadvantaged: The Inner City, the Underclass, and Public Policy* (Chicago: University of Chicago Press, 1987).

18. Michael McPherson has pointed out (in personal correspondence with the authors) that some students of this subject have argued that the whole package of federal support for college enrollment represents proper "targeting within universality." The argument is that when one groups together the Pell Grants, the loans, and the tax breaks, the result is a system that is close enough to universal, and that on balance does the most possible for the disadvantaged. This is a different perspective from that gained by looking at one program at a time, and we are doubtful that this "holistic" perspective is a good way to look at the issue, because in fact these programs are quite separate, with the oversight of tax and expenditure programs so completely separate in Congress. McPherson believes that when the tax breaks were being seriously debated in the late 1990s, it would have made great sense to have a Pell program that extended further into the middle class, giving more voters and politicians a stake of the kind that Skocpol and Wilson advocate. Had that happened, we might have had a better chance of putting more money into Pell Grants rather than into tax breaks. By now the tax breaks have become entrenched, and it is unlikely that the government will switch away from them in favor of expanding expenditure programs. As one of our colleagues puts it, now that these tax breaks have found a constituency, we appear to be condemned to the realm of the second-best. The incremental tax-based reforms proposed by both President George W. Bush and Senator John Kerry during their campaigns are evidence of the entrenchment.

19. The distribution of Pell Grant recipients among institution types differs from the distribution of non-recipients, with the strongest disparity appearing in the choice of for-profit institutions: 21 percent of Pell Grant recipients and only 6 percent of non-recipients who entered college in 1995–96 enrolled in less-than-four-year proprietary schools. The percentage of Pell Grant recipients is also much higher (57 percent) at less-than-four-year for-profit institutions than it is at public and private non-profit institutions, where it is about 25 percent. (Christina Chang Wei and Laura Horn, *Persistence and Attainment of Beginning Students with Pell Grants,* NCES 2002-169 [Washington, D.C.: National Center for Education Statistics, 2002], pp. 10–12.) Furthermore, 14 percent of Pell Grant funding goes to for-profit institutions, which is close to triple the percentage of undergraduates enrolled in for-profit institutions (about 5 percent). (Jacqueline E. King, *2003 Status Report on the Pell Grant Program* [Washington, D.C.: American Council on Education, October 2003].) Not much is known about the consequences of investments in proprietary schools for labor market or other outcomes.

20. See Stephen Burd, "For-Profit Colleges Spend Big and Win Big on Capitol Hill," *Chronicle of Higher Education,* July 30, 2004, online edition. Burd explains that

for-profit colleges donated more than $350,000 to the leadership of the House Committee on Education and the Workforce during the process of reauthorizing the Higher Education Act, which governs most federal financial aid. Many commentators feel that, as a result, certain measures in the reauthorization bill unduly favor these proprietary institutions.

21. See Kane (1999), p. 118; see also Thomas J. Kane, "A Quasi-Experimental Estimate of the Impact of Financial Aid on College-Going," NBER Working Paper no. 9703, May 2003, table 1, for a review of the literature on the effectiveness of the Pell Grant program and other government subsidization of higher education.

22. National Center for Public Policy and Higher Education. *Losing Ground: A National Status Report on the Affordability of American Higher Education* (San Jose, Calif.: The Center, 2002), p. 6, table 3.

23. Kane (1999), pp. 95–99; Kane (2003), table 1. Comparing the average Pell Grant to average tuition is virtually meaningless. What is of interest is the share of actual college costs that the Pell Grant covers for each recipient, averaged across all recipients. Using this approach, we see that Pell Grants cover only 39 to 49 percent of the costs of the average student from a low-income family, depending on the type of institution attended. Susan P. Choy and Ali M. Berker, *How Families of Low- and Middle-Income Undergraduates Pay for College: Full-Time Dependent Students in 1999–2000* (Washington, D.C.: National Center for Education Statistics, U.S. Department of Education, June 2003), table 11.

24. Kane (2003), pp. 35–36.

25. See Gary Orfield, "Money, Equity, and College Access," *Harvard Educational Review* 72 (Fall 1992): 337–72, cited by Kane (1999), p. 95.

26. Kane (1999), p. 95. Kane notes that one way in which financial aid forms are more complicated is that they require information on both income from assets and on the value of assets themselves. The findings of Singell, Waddell, and Curs on increased Pell Grant program participation resulting from the HOPE Scholarship can be taken as evidence of the burden of applying for aid: when they are required to do so, many more students who are eligible apply.

27. Kane (1999), p. 141.

28. Advisory Committee on Student Financial Assistance, *Access Denied: Restoring the Nation's Commitment to Equal Educational Opportunity* (Washington, D.C.: Advisory Committee on Student Financial Assistance, February 2001), pp. 14, 19. As "proof" of the ease of application, the committee states that, as a result of the FAFSA, 95 percent of aid recipients receive the full amount of aid they can receive (p. 14). But this finding does not tell us whether the FAFSA has encouraged students to apply for aid and enroll in college, which is the outcome of primary interest.

29. Christopher Avery and Thomas J. Kane, "Students' Perceptions of College Opportunity: The Boston COACH Program," in Hoxby, ed. (2004), pp. 355–94.

30. See Singell, Waddell, and Curs.

31. Thomas Kane, personal correspondence with the authors, June 30, 2004. For example, if assets were dropped from the formula, the benefit reduction rate applied to family income could be raised to offset the additional costs. In this correspondence Kane also contrasts the inexpensive policies he advocates with expensive and long-term interventions like the Upward Bound program, which has been shown to have some success in increasing college enrollment, but at a cost of about $20,000 to $25,000 per student.

32. National Center for Public Policy and Higher Education, p. 7.

33. One can also make the case for loans on the principle of market efficiency. The benefits of education largely accrue to the individual in terms of greater lifetime earnings; thus optimal education decisions are better made when individuals take the full cost and benefit of education into account. Government resources spent on loans ease short-term credit constraints with very little market interference, while grants change the cost-benefit calculus of college-going more drastically and may thus lead to sub-optimal decision making.

34. Kane (1999), pp. 146–51. In practice, this kind of income-contingent loan scheme would work best through the tax system. Either indebted former students whose loan payments exceed a certain portion of their income could be given a tax credit to cover the remainder of their loan or the "forgiven" portion could be capitalized into the loan amount. (Kane, personal correspondence with the authors, July 23, 2004.) See Robin Wilson, "Amid Debate over New Income-Contingent Loans, Many Students Say They Just Want the Money," *Chronicle of Higher Education*, December 9, 1987, p. A19; Jamie P. Merisotis, "Income Contingent Loans: A Hot 'New' Idea and Its Cold Realities," *Change* 19, no. 2 (March–April 1987): 10–11; and William B. Simpson, "Income-Contingent Student Loans: Context, Potential and Limits," *Higher Education* 15, no. 6 (1987): 699–721.

35. See Department for Education and Skills (DfES), *Widening Participation in Higher Education* (London: DfES, April 2003), p. 3; and DfES, "Future of Universities Secured Today as Higher Education Act Is Approved by Parliament–Clarke," Press Notice no. 2004/0127, DfES, July 1, 2004, available at http://www.dfes.gov.uk/hegateway/uploads/SF%20Web-words-final%20v.pdf, accessed July 20, 2004

36. A similar argument is often made in favor of a burdensome process for obtaining welfare benefits, such as food stamps. See Albert L. Nichols and Richard J. Zeckhauser, "Targeting Transfers through Restrictions on Recipients," *American Economic Review* 72, no. 2 (May 1982): 372–77.

37. Of course students with wealthy parents have, in effect, full grants to attend college, but one rarely hears commentators declare that this "low barrier" represents a moral hazard.

38. Greg Winter, "A Windfall for a Student Loan Program," *New York Times*, August 27, 2004, p. C1.

39. U.S. Congress, Congressional Budget Office (CBO), "Using Auctions to Reduce the Cost of the Federal Family Education Loan Program," analysis prepared by the CBO at the request of Senator Edward M. Kennedy, July 1998, available at http://www.cbo.gov/ftpdocs/6xx/doc644/ffelauct.pdf.

40. In October 2004, President Bush signed into law a bill to temporarily close this loophole while Congress works to close the loophole permanently as part of the reauthorization of the Higher Education Act. See Susana Duff Barnett, "Legislation: Bush Signs Law Closing Student Loan Loophole," *Bond Buyer*, November 2, 2004, p. 5; Greg Winter, "Congress Passes Bill to Tighten Lending Rules," *New York Times*, October 12, 2004, p. A19.

41. U.S. Department of Education. National Center for Education Statistics, *Digest of Education Statistics, 2002*, NCES 2003-060, table 330, "Current-Fund Revenue of Public Degree-Granting Institutions, by Source: 1980–81 to 1999–2000."

42. Thomas J. Kane and Peter R. Orszag, "Funding Restrictions at Public Universities: Effects and Policy Implications," Brookings Institution Working Paper, mimeo, September 2003.

43. Thomas J. Kane, Peter R. Orszag, and David Gunter, "State Fiscal Constraints and Higher Education Spending," Urban-Brookings Tax Policy Center Discussion Paper no. 11, May 2003, p. 1.

44. See Kane and Orszag, p. 4, and the references cited therein.

45. See Kane and Orszag, pp. 3–14.

46. The Carnegie Commission on Higher Education observed: "[The] United States has the great advantage of a decentralized system of administrative responsibility for higher education through the 50 states and through hundreds of private institutions." See the Commission's *Priorities for Action: The Final Report of the Carnegie Commission on Higher Education* (New York: Carnegie Foundation for the Advancement of Teaching, 1973), p. 59.

47. See Sarah E. Turner, "Going to College and Finishing College: Explaining Different Educational Outcomes," in Hoxby, ed. (2004), pp. 13–61.

48. See Charles T. Clotfelter, *Buying the Best: Cost Escalation in Elite Higher Education* (Princeton, N.J.: Princeton University Press, 1996), for an insightful analysis of the forces driving costs ever higher.

49. In 1968, Bowen completed a study for the Carnegie Commission on Higher Education (*The Economics of the Major Private Universities*) that led Clark Kerr to formulate what he called "Bowen's Law." Examination of data for three research universities going back to the early 1900s revealed that the cost per student consistently rose faster than an economy-wide cost index. The basic reasons were the same as those William Baumol and Bowen advanced to explain why the costs of chamber orchestras also kept rising faster than inflation. (See William J. Baumol and William G. Bowen, *Performing Arts, The Economic Dilemma: A Study of Problems Common to Theater, Opera, Music, and Dance* [New York: Twentieth Century Fund, 1966].) The underlying phenomenon —driven by differences in productivity gains between service industries and the economy at large—came to be called "Baumol's Disease." In recent years, advances in information technology and in data management may have led to a fundamental change in productivity prospects for the service industries—possibly including even parts of higher education. (See Hal Varian, "Information Technology May Have Been What Cured Low Service-Sector Productivity," *New York Times,* February 12, 2004, p. C2.) New digital projects such as JSTOR offer the prospect of substantial savings in scholarly communications and library operations. (See also William G. Bowen, "At a Slight Angle to the Universe: The University in a Digitized, Commercialized Age," Romanes Lecture, University of Oxford, October 17, 2000; reprinted by Princeton University Press, 2001.)

50. See, for example, Sara Hebel, "Virginia Governor Announces Budget Cuts for Public Colleges," *Chronicle of Higher Education,* October 17, 2002, online edition; and Hebel, "California Governor's Revised Budget Keeps Tuition Increases and Many University Cuts," *Chronicle of Higher Education,* May 17, 2004, online edition.

51. "A Revolt of the Flagships," *New York Times,* February 16, 2004, p. A20.

52. Alyson Klein, "States Move to Limit Increases in Tuition," *Chronicle of Higher Education,* March 5, 2004, online edition. See also Kristina Goetz, "Miami U. Raises Tuition 8.5%," *Cincinnati Enquirer,* February 28, 2004, online edition; Alan B. Krueger, "Market Forces Press State Colleges to Raise Tuition and Give Financial Aid; Politics Presses to Keep Tuition Low," *New York Times,* May 1, 2003, p. C2; Jeffrey Selingo, "New Illinois Law Will Freeze Public-College Tuition for Each Incoming Class," *Chronicle of Higher Education,* July 24, 2003, online edition.

53. For an elaboration of this line of argument in the New York State context, see Sarah E. Turner, "Will We Pay Too Much for SUNY's Low Tuition?" *Newsday* (New York), February 12, 2001, p. A20. In recent years both major political parties have proposed that the *federal* government should enforce a tuition cap. (See Stephen Burd, "Republican Introduces Bill to Penalize Colleges for Tuition Increases," *Chronicle of Higher Education*, October 24, 2003, online edition; Burd, "Plan to Punish Big Increases in Tuition Is Dropped," *Chronicle of Higher Education*, March 12, 2004, online edition; and Jeffrey Selingo, "Kerry Offers Proposal to Hold Down Tuition," *Chronicle of Higher Education*, July 9, 2004, online edition.) The caps typically limit tuition growth at public and/or private institutions to some multiple of inflation, with the threat of decreased funding or no new funding for non-compliance. As in the case of state-enforced tuition caps, these federal constraints on tuition growth would prevent institutions from raising the money they need to provide the kind of education for which their students enroll.

54. Greg Winter, "As State Colleges Cut Classes, Students Struggle to Finish," *New York Times*, August 24, 2003, section 1, p. 1.

55. Of course there is nothing to prevent a graduate of a state institution from moving to a different state after graduation. Besides, in terms of effectiveness in educating a workforce that will remain in the state, some programs are more attractive candidates for state support than others. See John Bound et al., "Trade in University Training: Cross-State Variation in the Production and Stock of College-Educated Labor," *Journal of Econometrics* 121, nos. 1–2 (2004): 143–73.

56. "A Revolt of the Flagships," p. A20. See also Erin Strout, "U. of Virginia Unexpectedly Opens $3-Billion Campaign to Become a Private Public University," *Chronicle of Higher Education*, June 15, 2004, online edition.

57. David W. Breneman, "Are the States and Public Higher Education Striking a New Bargain?" AGB Public Policy Paper no. 04-02, June 2004.

58. Over half (54 percent) of Miami University families are said to earn $100,000 or more. See David W. Breneman, "Why a Public College Wants to Send In-State Tuition Soaring," *Chronicle of Higher Education*, April 25, 2003, p. B20.

59. See W. Lee Hansen and Burton Weisbrod, "The Distribution of Costs and Direct Benefits of Public Higher Education," *Journal of Human Resources* 4 (Spring 1969): 176–91.

60. See Miami University of Ohio, "New Tuition and Scholarship Plan," available at http://www.miami.muohio.edu/tuitionplan/ohiofamilies.cfm, accessed August 2, 2004, and "Innovative Tuition & Scholarship Program," available at http://www.miami.muohio.edu/tuitionplan/specifics.cfm, accessed October 26, 2004.

61. So, too, is David Breneman, who has written the most insightful analysis of the Miami proposal. See Breneman (2003).

62. See Kate Zernike, "At Auburn, a Challenge to a Trustee's Reign," *New York Times*, July 26, 2002, p. A12; Thomas Bartlett and Megan Rooney, "Runaway Board? Unilateral Actions at Virginia Tech Raise Questions about the Proper Role of Trustees," *Chronicle of Higher Education*, March 28, 2003, online edition; and Burton Bollag, "Grambling Regains Its Accreditation; Auburn Put on Probation for Trustee Meddling," *Chronicle of Higher Education*, December 19, 2003, online edition.

63. See Michael Arnone, "Keeping Searches Secret," *Chronicle of Higher Education*, July 9, 2004, online edition.

64. Of the students who began their studies at non-doctorate-granting public

institutions in 1995–96, 19 percent were able to graduate from those institutions within four years, and 40 percent graduated within six years. Students in the same cohort who enrolled in public doctorate-granting institutions showed higher completion rates: 27 percent graduated from the college where they began within four years, and 55 percent graduated within six years. Lutz Berkner, Shirley He, and Emily Forrest Cataldi, *Descriptive Summary of 1995–96 Beginning Postsecondary Students: Six Years Later,* NCES 2003–151 (Washington, D.C.: U.S. Department of Education, National Center for Education Statistics, 2002), p. viii.

65. The benefits to the state in pursuing this policy are clear—the students at the public institutions are the most likely to stay in the state and become a part of its labor force. Jeffrey A. Groen, "The Effect of College Location on Migration of College-Educated Labor," *Journal of Econometrics* 121 (2004): 125–42.

66. Martin Wolf, "Set Universities Free to Compete," *Financial Times,* November 28, 2003, p. 19.

67. In 2004, the modest government-capped fee was £1,125 ($2,025 in 2004 dollars). Even with the introduction of top-up fees, the actual cost of a university education—estimated at the best institutions to be more than £10,000 per annum ($18,000 in 2004 dollars)—will still significantly exceed what universities are permitted to charge.

68. See John F. Halsey and W. Bruce Leslie, "Britain's White Paper Turns Higher Education Away from the EU," *International Higher Education* 32 (Summer 2003): 10–12, available at http://www.bc.edu/bc_org/avp/soe/cihe/newsletter/news/text006.htm, accessed July 20, 2004; and Ken Mayhew, Cécile Deer, and Mehak Dua, "The Move to Mass Higher Education in the UK: Many Questions and Some Answers," *Oxford Review of Education* 30, no. 1 (March 2004): 65–82, esp. p. 67.

69. In 1960, one in twenty "school-leavers" (5 percent of the college-age cohort) went to university; that rose to one in seven in the early 1970s, one in five in 1990, and one in three by 2002. (See "Higher Education White Paper: From Student Grants to Tuition Fees," *Guardian,* January 23, 2003, p. 11; and Martin Wolf, "Let the Top Universities Off the Funding Leash," *Financial Times,* March 6, 2000, p. 23.) While higher education enrollment has soared—from fewer than a half-million students in the mid-1960s to more than two million in 2004—a debate about the consistency of these numbers has arisen. For most of the past 40 years, the government has used one measure—the Age Participation Index (API)—to measure the proportion of young people electing higher education. Though the API had three distinct divisions or bands, the most commonly used band measured full-time and "sandwich" students (those engaged in cooperative, work-related internships) who were under 21 and resided in the United Kingdom. Once the Labour government embraced "life-long learning" as part of its pledge to reach 50 percent participation in higher and "further" education, the API's utility as a policy vehicle became problematic. The API was replaced by the short-lived Initial Entry Rate, which expanded the age cohort to 17 to 30, defined higher education as a course of one year or more, included part-time students, and covered all universities in the United Kingdom. But it, too, was compromised by inaccuracies and lack of clarity. In 2003, the DfES introduced a more refined Higher Education Initial Participation Rate, which measures participation rather than entry. (See David Jobbins, "Who Really Counts?" *Times Higher Education Supplement,* June 11, 2004, p. 1.)

For the purposes of historical consistency, we use the API: 1960 (5.4 percent), 1970 (8.4 percent), 1980 (12.4 percent), 1990 (19.3 percent), 2000 (33.0 percent).

See David Robertson and Josh Hillman, "Widening Participation in Higher Education for Students from Lower Socio-Economic Groups and Students with Disabilities," Report 6 of the National Committee of Inquiry into Higher Education, *Higher Education in the Learning Society* (Dearing Report) (London: Her Majesty's Stationery Office, June 1997).

70. "The Ruin of Britain's Universities," *Economist,* November 16, 2002, p. 29. In 2000, according to the *Financial Times,* "the proportion of gross domestic product spent on UK universities was the second lowest among all advanced countries, after Italy at 1 percent, compared with 2.7 percent of gross domestic product (GDP) in the United States and 2.6 percent in Canada. Only Japan's public sector spent a lower share of GDP than the UK." (See Wolf [2003d].) It is estimated that the unfunded expansion in student enrollment over the past 20 years has created a "funding gap" of approximately £10 billion ($18 billion). (See "Who Pays to Study?" *Economist,* January 24, 2004, p. 23.)

71. For a discussion of the origins of Britain's official social class categorization scheme, see David Rose, "Official Social Classification in the UK," *Social Research Update* (July 1995), available at http://www.soc.surrey.ac.uk/sru/SRU9.html, accessed July 8, 2004.

72. William Beveridge, *Social Insurance and Allied Services,* report presented to Parliament by command of His Majesty, Cmnd. 6404, November 1942, summary available at http://www.weasel.cwc.net/beveridge.htm, accessed July 12, 2004; and Stefan Collini, "HiEdBiz," *London Review of Books,* November 6, 2003, online edition.

73. Robert Stevens, *University to Uni: The Politics of Higher Education in England since 1944* (London: Politico's, 2004), p. 13.

74. Stevens, p. 14.

75. George Walden, *We Should Know Better: Solving the Education Crisis* (London: Fourth Estate, 1996), pp. 3, 13.

76. Walden, pp. 22, 170; and "Few Are Chosen; British Education," *Economist,* July 3, 2004, p. 15.

77. Collini.

78. Walden, p. 169.

79. Martin Wolf, "The Omens Look Good for UK Universities," *Financial Times,* January 20, 2003, p. 21.

80. Martin Trow, "Trust, Markets and Accountability in Higher Education: A Comparative Perspective," *Higher Education Policy* 9, no. 4 (1996): 309–24; quote on p. 310.

81. "Equality or Efficiency?" *Economist,* January 25, 2003, p. 32.

82. Universities UK, "Universities UK's Response to 'The Future of Higher Education': DfES White Paper" (Universities UK, April 2003), p. 47, available at http://www.UniversitiesUK.ac.uk/consultations/responses, accessed July 19, 2004.

83. Martin Wolf, "A Morally Bankrupt Education Policy," *Financial Times,* May 26, 2003, p. 17.

84. Trow (1996), pp. 312–13.

85. Martin Trow, "The Dearing Report: A Transatlantic View," *Higher Education Quarterly* 52, no. 1 (January 1998): 93–117; and Stevens, pp. 88–92.

86. Wolf (2003c), p. 17.

87. "Affirmative Action, Negative Reaction," *Economist,* March 8, 2003, p. 16.

88. The new variable fee will replace the £1,125 ($2,045 in 2004 dollars) means-tested fixed tuition fee, but the first £1,100 in "graduate contributions" will still be means tested. This way, low-income students will pay back a maximum of £1,900

($3,420 in 2004 dollars) in fees at current prices. See "Universities 'Critical' to UK's Success," *Guardian,* January 23, 2003. This means-tested repayment is similar to the concept of income-contingent loans discussed earlier in the chapter. The major difference between the British plan and the policy we advocate is that the British plan more explicitly subsidizes the tuition repayment of lower-income graduates with the tuition repayment of higher-income graduates. In addition, the British policy is universal, counteracting the adverse selection one might see in a similarly progressive plan that was voluntary. The Higher Education Funding Council for England (HEFCE) is the government's principal funding body for universities. HEFCE's allocation agreements are based on the number of students enrolled and the subjects taught. Universities bid for additional funded places, and funding is conditional upon meeting those recruitment objectives. Nearly all research funding is related to quality and volume. See "Higher Education in the United Kingdom," HEFCE, available at http://www.hefce.ac.uk/pubs/hefce/2004/HEinUK/HEinUK.pdf, accessed July 20, 2004; and "Core Funding/Operations, Framework for Accountability," HEFCE, available at http://www.hefce.ac.uk/pubs/hefce/2004/04_28, accessed July 20, 2004.

89. The National Union of Students (NUS) cited a 1995 report by the American Association of State Colleges and Universities. See Independent Committee of Inquiry into Student Finance, "Student Finance: Fairness for the Future" (the "Cubie" report), Independent Committee of Inquiry, Edinburgh, December 1999, available at http://www.esib.org/links/cubie_full_report.pdf, accessed August 4, 2004; and National Union of Students, "Briefing: Higher Education—The Big Picture." Funding the Future Campaign, March 2004, available at http://www2.nusonline.co.uk/resource/resources/pdf/4750.pdf, accessed November 5, 2004.

90. See the NUS Web site, stopfeesnow.com, "Latest Campaign" blog entry, http://www.nusonline.co.uk/subsites/stopfeesnow/, accessed July 28, 2004. Australia introduced a Higher Education Contribution Scheme (HECS) in 1989. Under the original plan, students were expected to make a contribution toward the cost of their tertiary education, and were given the choice of paying up front or taking out a loan from the commonwealth. Effective in 2005, the Australian government will no longer set student contributions through HECS; instead, institutions will set their own contribution levels for each band of study (band 1: arts, humanities, social science and education; band 2: math, computer science, health science, agriculture, science and engineering, and business and economics; and band 3: law, medicine, dentistry, and veterinary medicine). HECS was designed to minimize the adverse effect of fees and loans on the participation of relatively disadvantaged students. Research to date suggests that students from low-SES backgrounds are participating in higher education at or above pre-fee rates, and that participation has expanded for members of all socioeconomic groups. (See Bruce Chapman and Chris Ryan, "Income-Contingent Financing of Student Charges for Higher Education: Assessing the Australian Innovation," Australian National University, Centre for Economic Policy Research Discussion Paper no. 449, May 2002, available at http://cepr.anu.edu.au/pdf/DP449.pdf, accessed September 2, 2004.) On a less positive note, recent longitudinal data suggest that students with large loans are purchasing homes at a later stage in life than in the pre-loan era. (See Council of Australian Postgraduate Associations [CAPA], "The Social and Economic Impact of Student Debt," CAPA research paper, March 2003.)

91. See Department for Education and Skills (2004).

92. NUS Web site, "Latest Campaign blog entry."

93. "Charles Clarke's Statement to the Commons," *Guardian,* January 22, 2003, online edition.

94. Peter Scott, "Conclusion: Triumph and Retreat," in *The State of UK Higher Education: Managing Diversity and Change,* ed. David Warner and David Palfreyman (Buckingham, England: Society for Research into Higher Education and Open University Press, 2001), pp. 187–204, esp. p. 193.

95. In chapter 4 we report strikingly similar findings in our analysis of the effects of growing up poor on academic preparedness. For the British experience, see Department for Education and Skills (DfES), *Widening Participation in Higher Education* (London: DfES, April 2003), available at http://www.dfes.gov.uk/hegateway/uploads/White%20Pape.pdf, accessed November 14, 2004, pp. 7–8. The General Certificate of Secondary Education (GCSE) is based on an examination, which is normally taken at the age of 16, and is required of all students upon completion of secondary school. After completing the GCSE, some students leave school, while others enter technical colleges, and still others continue their post-16 education for an additional two years of A-level study in preparation for taking a university degree.

96. Department for Education and Skills (2003), p. 8. See our discussion in chapter 9 of the effects of the Head Start program on improving college preparedness. In an unpublished study by the DfES of the effect of educational and socioeconomic disadvantage on pre-entry achievement in the United Kingdom, the data show that "lower-income pupils are over-represented in schools that add the least value to pupils' performance." The data also demonstrate that students from both lower-income and higher-income families perform better in schools with a low percentage of students on free meal plans. Scholars have found similar patterns in the United States. See Admissions to Higher Education Steering Group, "Consultation on Key Issues Relating to Fair Admissions to Higher Education," September 2003, p. 18, available at http://www.admissions-review.org.uk/downloads/Headmissions_consultation.doc, accessed July 22, 2004.

97. In an effort to raise standards, the government urged the country's secondary schools to become independent specialists in at least one subject, and the DfES promised a major expansion of (up to 200) state-funded "city academies" by 2010. A small number of these high-quality schools, which are designed to offer the children of inner-city families the choice and advantage of independent schools, have been introduced in London and are likely to appear in other deprived urban areas if Labour is kept in office. For their part, the Tories have responded with their "Right to Choose" initiative, which would give every school grant-maintained status, enabling them to control their own budgets and select pupils by ability. Critics of this plan argue that it will lead to "cream-skimming," or selection of the best students, with adverse results for students who are less able academically and/or whose families are less involved in their education. See these pieces by BBC News: "More Freedom in School Reforms," *BBC News,* July 8, 2004, available at http://news.bbc.co.uk/1/hi/education/3875073/stm, accessed July 19, 2004; "200 City Academies Promised," BBC News, June 28, 2004, available at http://news.bbc.co.uk/1/education/3848195/stm, accessed July 19, 2004; and "Parent Choice Tops Tory Package," BBC News, June 29, 2004, available at http://news.bbc.co.uk/1/uk_politics/3847885.stm, accessed July 19, 2004.

98. Admissions to Higher Education Steering Group, p. 42.

99. Students usually concentrate in three or four A-level subject areas in the two years of study known as "sixth form." A-level results determine eligibility for and admission to university. See Department for Education and Skills (2003), p. 10.

100. Admissions to Higher Education Steering Group. These findings are very similar to the results from our analysis of 19 selective American institutions discussed in chapter 5.

101. The Sutton Trust, which was created in 1997, supports educational opportunities for academically able students from non-privileged backgrounds. The universities chosen for the study by the DfES included Birmingham, Bristol, Cambridge, Durham, Edinburgh, Imperial College, the London School of Economics, Nottingham, Oxford, St. Andrews, University College London, Warwick, and York. In August 2004 the Sutton Trust published a report that demonstrated the continuing disparities in aspirations and attainment between students in Britain's state and independent schools. While 45 percent of independent school students who obtain the equivalent of an A and two Bs go to one of the nation's 13 leading universities, only 26 percent of state school students achieving the same grades do so. For a provocative analysis of this imbalance and its likely consequences, see Sutton Trust, "The Missing 3000: State School Students Under-Represented at Leading Universities," Sutton Trust, August 2004, and an op-ed piece by the trust's founder and chairman, Sir Peter Lampl, "Imbalance of Talent," *Times Higher Education Supplement,* August 20, 2004, p. 16.

102. Research comparing applications and admissions data for 2000–2001 by the DfES demonstrated that 16 percent of those admitted by the 19 Russell Group universities were from the three social classes representing the most disadvantaged groups. This compares unfavorably with the benchmark of 19 percent established by HEFCE. (See Department for Education and Skills [2003], p. 11; and Tony Halpin, "Universities 'Must Show They Are Open to All,'" *Times* [London], April 9, 2003, p. 15.) The older and more established "Russell Group" universities are Birmingham; Bristol; Cambridge; Cardiff; Edinburgh; Glasgow; Imperial College, London; Kings College, London; Leeds; Liverpool; the London School of Economics and Political Science; Manchester; Newcastle; Nottingham; Oxford; Sheffield; Southampton; University College London; and Warwick.

103. See Department for Education and Skills (2003), p. 13. The Admissions to Higher Education Steering Group, which Education Secretary Charles Clarke created in the spring of 2003 to review admission policies and criteria, reported that while 7 percent of the school population (all ages) attend independent schools, students from independent schools account for 18 percent of the young, full-time university population. The steering group concluded that some of the nation's leading universities were recruiting fewer students from state schools and colleges than might be expected given HEFCE indicators. See Admissions to Higher Education Steering Group, p. 44. In an effort to close the gap in preparedness and opportunity that separate students in the United Kingdom's state and independent schools, the Sutton Trust has proposed a public-private partnership known as "Open Access" that would open 100 of the top independent day schools on a competitive basis regardless of a family's ability to pay. The Sutton Trust says that "fees for successful applicants would be charged on a sliding scale, with the richest paying the same as before, shading off to the poorest, who would pay nothing." In essence, the cost for opening up the United Kingdom's private schools would be shared among the school, paying parents, and the government. See the Sutton Trust paper "Open Access: A Practical Way Forward, New Developments," Sutton Trust, June 2004, p. 20.

104. See "Universities UK's Response to 'The Future of Higher Education.'" Well before issuance of this government white paper in January 2003, HEFCE had set "benchmark" targets for the proportion of state-school applicants universities should

take, and ranked the institutions accordingly. One of HEFCE's incentives—the "Postcode Premium"—paid any university a 5 percent bonus for every student taken from a "low-participation (poor) postcode area." HEFCE also joined with private foundations like the Sutton Trust to promote university access at state schools. For its part, DfES initiated the "Aimhigher" Program to encourage inner-city students to believe "that going to university is a good idea." See "Bending the Rules," *Economist,* August 24, 2002, p. 28, and the Aimhigher Web site, http://www.dfes.gov.uk/aimhigherprogramme/.

105. See Martin Wolf, "How to Save the British Universities," *Times* (London), April 9, 2003, p. 15; and Halpin (2003b).

106. Department for Education and Skills (2003), p. 13. The Sutton Trust is also investing its resources in such initiatives as "specialist schools" and in independent and state school partnerships.

107. See Tim Miles, "Oxbridge Must Lose Brideshead Reputation," *Evening Standard,* April 8, 2003, p. 15. The reference is to the Evelyn Waugh novel *Brideshead Revisited* and to the 1981 Granada television series that evoked Waugh's sentimental and nostalgic longing for Edwardian England.

108. Tony Halpin, "Oxbridge Alarm at Quotas," *Times* (London), January 23, 2003, p. 4.

109. In May 2004, the Sutton Trust issued a report analyzing results from the Organisation for Economic Co-operation and Development's 2001 Programme for International Student Assessment. The data demonstrated marked improvement in the comparative performance of U.K. secondary school children, but the findings also raised continuing concern about the qualitative differences in the experiences provided students in the independent and the government-maintained schools: "Across all countries (with the exception of Japan), independent-school pupils did better than those in maintained [government-supported] schools, and those in England did best of all with the gap from the maintained sector the widest." See Alan Smithers, "England's Education: What Can Be Learned by Comparing Countries?" Centre for Education and Employment Research, University of Liverpool, commissioned by the Sutton Trust, May 2004, pp. 25–26, 34.

110. See "Entry to Leading Universities," the Sutton Trust, May 2000, p. 1, available at http://www.suttontrust.com/reports/entrytoleadingunis.pdf, accessed July 27, 2004; Anthony Smith, "The Laura Spence Affair and the Contemporary Political Mind," in *Education! Education! Education! Managerial Ethics and the Law of Unintended Consequences,* ed. Stephen Prickett and Patricia Erskine-Hill (Thorverton, England: Imprint Academic, 2002), p. 32; see also pp. 29–37.

111. Smith, p. 34.

112. See Department for Education and Skills (2004).

113. "Who Pays to Study?" *Economist,* January 24, 2004, p. 23, and Research Tools Backgrounders, "Britain's Universities," *Economist,* September 22, 2004, available at http://www.economist.com/research/backgrounders/displaybackgrounder.cfm?bg= 1452940, accessed November 14, 2004. In 1999, when one of us (Tobin) was on sabbatical in England studying the role of liberal education in the British university system, his Oxford acquaintances frequently steered the conversation to subjects of interest to their institutions, such as charitable giving, particularly planned gifts, alumni development and career counseling, corporation and foundation relations, prospect research, and stewardship.

114. See Cristina Odone, "College Ties That Bind," *Observer,* December 8, 2002, available at http://education.guardian.co.uk/universitiesincrisis/story/0,12028,

856687,00.html, accessed July 22, 2004. Many observers of the United Kingdom and the United States have noted that no British university's endowment, other than those of Oxford and Cambridge, would rank in the top 150 in the United States, and that Oxbridge's endowment would not rank in the top dozen. See Halsey and Leslie, pp. 10–12.

115. Wolf (2003c), p. 17.

116. "Degrees of Access: Universities Cannot Make Up for Poorly Performing Schools," *Financial Times,* January 23, 2003, p. 18.

Chapter 9   Improving College Preparedness

1. Special thanks are owed to Mellon Foundation Research Associate Nirupama Rao, who provided invaluable reviews of the relevant literature and assisted with the drafting of this chapter.

2. Richard J. Herrnstein and Charles Murray, *The Bell Curve: Intelligence and Class Structure in American Life* (New York: Free Press, 1994).

3. See, for example, James J. Heckman, "Lessons from *The Bell Curve,*" *Journal of Political Economy* 103, no. 5 (October 1995): 1091–120; Sanders Korenman and Christopher Winship, "A Reanalysis of *The Bell Curve,*" NBER Working Paper no. 5230, August 1995; Janet Currie and Duncan Thomas, "The Intergenerational Transmission of 'Intelligence': Down the Slippery Slopes of *The Bell Curve,*" *Industrial Relations* 38, no. 3 (July 1999): 297–330; Nicholas Lemann, "*The Bell Curve* Flattened: Subsequent Research Has Seriously Undercut the Claims of the Controversial Best Seller," *MSN Slate Magazine,* January 18, 1997, online edition, available at http://slate.msn.com/id/2416/.

4. For example, see Pedro Carneiro and James Heckman, "Human Capital Policy," in *Inequality in America: What Role for Human Capital Policies?* by James Heckman and Alan Krueger (Cambridge, Mass.: MIT Press, 2003); see also James Traub, "What No School Can Do," *New York Times Magazine,* January 16, 2000, p. 52.

5. Our notion of "accumulating advantages and disadvantages" is similar to ideas proposed by Swedish social scientist and Nobel laureate Gunnar Myrdal in *An American Dilemma: The Negro Problem and Modern Democracy* (New York: Harper, 1944). Robert Merton and our colleague Harriet Zuckerman have been influential in developing this way of thinking. See Robert K. Merton, "The Matthew Effect in Science," *Science,* January 5, 1968, pp. 56–63. (This is the first clear-cut formulation of accumulation of advantage and disadvantage as a general pattern.) See also Robert K. Merton, "The Matthew Effect in Science II: Cumulative Advantage and the Symbolism of Intellectual Property," *Isis* 79, no. 4 (December 1988): 606–23; Harriet Zuckerman, *Scientific Elite: Nobel Laureates in the United States* (New York: Free Press, 1977), esp. chapter 8, "The Nobel Prize and the Accumulation of Advantage" (in which Zuckerman discusses the additive and multiplicative cumulation of advantage and disadvantage); and Zuckerman, "Accumulation of Advantage and Disadvantage: The Theory and Its Intellectual Biography," in *Robert K. Merton and Contemporary Sociology,* ed. Carlo Mongardini and Simonetta Tabboni (New Brunswick, N.J.: Transaction Publishers, 1998), pp. 139–61.

6. We owe a particular debt of gratitude to two of these scholars, Caroline Hoxby and Lawrence Katz of Harvard, for helping us understand a range of issues and for ensuring that our description of them is both more accurate and more nuanced than it would have been without their help.

7. William J. Wilson, *The Truly Disadvantaged: The Inner City, the Underclass, and Public Policy* (Chicago: University of Chicago Press, 1987).

8. U.S. Department of Agriculture, Economic Research Service, "Rural Poverty at a Glance," Rural Development Research Report no. 100, July 2004. "Persistent poverty" is defined as a sustained poverty rate of 20 percent or more over the past 30 years.

9. Tom Loveless, *The 2003 Brown Center Report on American Education: How Well Are American Students Learning?* (Washington, D.C.: Brookings Institution Press, October 2003), pp. 1–12.

10. For initial evaluation of Moving to Opportunity, see Lawrence F. Katz, Jeffrey R. Kling, and Jeffrey B. Liebman, "Moving to Opportunity in Boston: Early Results of a Randomized Mobility Experiment," NBER Working Paper no. 7973, October 2000; final version published in *Quarterly Journal of Economics* (May 2001): 607–54; and Jens Ludwig, Helen F. Ladd, and Greg J. Duncan, "Urban Poverty and Educational Outcomes," in *Brookings-Wharton Papers on Urban Affairs: 2001*, ed. William G. Gale and Janet Rothenberg Pack (Washington, D.C.: Brookings Institution Press, 2001), pp. 147–201.

11. Jeffrey R. Kling, Jens Ludwig, and Lawrence F. Katz, "Neighborhood Effects on Crime for Female and Male Youth: Evidence from a Randomized Housing Voucher Experiment," *Quarterly Journal of Economics* 130, no. 1 (February 2005).

12. Lisa Sanbonmatsu et al., "Neighborhoods and Academic Achievement: Results from the Moving to Opportunity Experiment," Princeton Industrial Relations Section Working Paper no. 492, August 2004.

13. Eric A. Hanushek, John F. Kain, Jacob M. Markman, and Steven G. Rivkin, "Does Peer Ability Affect Student Achievement?" *Journal of Applied Econometrics* 18, no. 5 (September–October 2003): 527–44. See also Caroline M. Hoxby, "Peer Effects in the Classroom: Learning from Gender and Race Variation," NBER Working Paper no. 7867, August 2000. Two studies of college roommates found similar peer effects: Bruce M. Sacerdote, "Peer Effects with Random Assignment: Results for Dartmouth Roommates," *Quarterly Journal of Economics* 116, no. 2 (May 2000): 681–704; and Gordon C. Winston and David J. Zimmerman, "Peer Effects in Higher Education," in *College Choices: The Economics of Where to Go, When to Go, and How to Pay for It,* ed. Caroline Hoxby (Chicago: University of Chicago Press, 2004), pp. 394–421.

14. Jonathan Guryan, "Desegregation and Black Dropout Rates," NBER Working Paper no. 8345, June 2001.

15. Joshua D. Angrist and Kevin Lang, "How Important Are Classroom Peer Effects? Evidence from Boston's Metco Program," NBER Working Paper no. 9263, October 2002.

16. Julie Berry Cullen, Brian A. Jacob, and Steven Levitt, "The Effect of School Choice on Student Outcomes: Evidence from Randomized Lotteries," NBER Working Paper no. 10113, November 2003.

17. Janet Currie and Mark Stabile, "Socioeconomic Status and Health: Why Is the Relationship Stronger for Older Children?" NBER Working Paper no. 9098, August 2002. See also Anne Case, Darren Lubotsky, and Christina Paxson, "Economic Status and Health in Childhood: The Origins of the Gradient," *American Economic Review* 92, no. 5 (December 2002): 1308–34; and Anne Case, Angela Fertig, and Christina Paxson, "From Cradle to Grave? The Lasting Impact of Childhood Health and Circumstance," NBER Working Paper no. 9788, June 2003.

18. Ellen A. Meara, "Why Is Health Related to Socioeconomic Status?" NBER Working Paper no. 8231, April 2001. See also Roland G. Fryer Jr. and Steven D. Levitt,

"Understanding the Black-White Test Score Gap in the First Two Years of School," *Review of Economics and Statistics* 86, no. 2 (May 2004): 447–64, p. 455, table 5, for evidence of the link between birth weight and test scores.

19. Currie and Stabile.

20. Leighton Ku and Sashi Nimalendran, "Improving Children's Health: A Chartbook about the Roles of Medicaid and SCHIP," Center for Budget and Policy Priorities, January 15, 2004.

21. Kaiser Family Foundation State Health Facts Online, "SCHIP Expenditures, FFY 2002," available at: http://www.statehealthfacts.org; and Marilyn Ellwood, Angela Merrill, and Wendy Conroy, *SCHIP's Steady Enrollment Growth Continues: Final Report,* MPR no. 8644–500 (Cambridge, Mass.: Mathematica Policy Research, May 2003).

22. U.S. Department of Education, National Center for Education Statistics, *The Condition of Education, 1995,* NCES 95-273 (Washington, D.C.: U.S. Government Printing Office, 1995), p. 28. "High-income" is defined as the upper quintile of the income distribution, while "low-income" is the bottom quintile of the distribution. Data exactly like those reported for 1993 in *The Condition of Education, 1995* are not available for more recent years. However, data from the National Center for Education Statistics, *The Condition of Education, 2002* (NCES 2002-025 [Washington, D.C.: U.S. Government Printing Office, 2002]) indicate that between 1993 and 2001 there was no significant change in the rates at which children below and above the poverty line and between ages three and five attended center-based early childhood care and education programs.

23. Ron Haskins and Isabel Sawhill, "The Future of Head Start," Brookings Institution Policy Brief no. 27: Welfare Reform & Beyond, July 2003, p. 1, available at http://apps49.brookings.edu/dybdocroot/es/wrb/publications/pb/pb27.pdf.

24. Janet Currie and Duncan Thomas, "Does Head Start Make a Difference?" *American Economic Review* 85, no. 3 (June 1995): 341–64. The researchers conditioned on a variety of demographic characteristics, including income.

25. Currie and Thomas (1995).

26. Currie and Thomas (1995).

27. Currie and Thomas (1995).

28. Janet Currie and Duncan Thomas, "School Quality and the Longer-Term Effects of Head Start," *Journal of Human Resources* 35, no. 4 (Autumn 2000): 755–74.

29. Barbara Wolfe and Scott Scrivner, "Providing Universal Preschool for Four-Year-Olds," in *One Percent for the Kids,* ed. Isabel Sawhill (Washington, D.C.: Brookings Institution Press, 2003), pp. 113–135. Oklahoma incrementally expanded its existing early childhood education programs into a universal pre-K system that is administrated at the school district level. It now ranks first in the country in terms of the fraction of four-year-olds in preschool programs. Whether this system—which relies on superintendents to voluntarily offer preschool programs—is more effective is an open question also worthy of further investigation. For further information regarding Oklahoma's universal preschool initiative, see David L. Kirp, "You're Doing Fine, Oklahoma!" *American Prospect,* November 1, 2004, online edition.

30. Doris Entwisle, Karl Alexander, and Linda Olson, *Children, Schools and Inequality* (Boulder, Colo.: Westview, 1997). Referenced in Alan Krueger, "Inequality, Too Much of a Good Thing?" essay dated August 4, 2002, later published in Heckman and Krueger.

31. Brian A. Jacob and Lars Lefgren, "Remedial Education and Student Achievement: A Regression-Discontinuity Analysis," NBER Working Paper no. 8918, May

2002. At the same time that the remedial summer school policy was instituted, the Chicago Public Schools also imposed stricter grade retention policies, confounding attempts to isolate the effect of each individual policy. Researchers attempted to account for this simultaneity, and their estimates based on these methods are reported here.

32. Harris Cooper et al., "Making the Most of Summer School: A Meta-Analytic and Narrative Review," *Monographs of the Society for Research in Child Development* 65, no. 1 (serial no. 260, 1997): 1–118, referenced in Krueger (2002), pp. 30–32.

33. Tiebout developed his theory in Charles M. Tiebout, "A Pure Theory of Local Public Expenditures," *Journal of Political Economy* 64, no. 5 (October 1956): 416–24. A good example of the formal application of the theory to schooling is Thomas Nechyba, "Public School Finance in a General Equilibrium Tiebout World: Equalization Programs, Peer Effects and Private School Vouchers," NBER Working Paper no. 5642, June 1996. The prime example of an empirical treatment of Tiebout's theory applied to education is Caroline M. Hoxby, "Does Competition among Public Schools Benefit Students and Taxpayers?" *American Economic Review* 90, no. 5 (December 2000): 1209–38.

34. Hoxby (2000e). The robustness of Hoxby's results have been challenged by other economic researchers. In a commentary piece Jesse Rothstein concludes, based on his re-estimation and extension of Hoxby's findings, that "Hoxby's estimated effect of interdistrict competition on school output is not robust [to different sample constructions and estimation tactics], and that a fair read of the National Educational Longitudinal Survey evidence does not support claims of a large or significant effect." For further detail, please see Rothstein, "Does Competition among Public Schools Benefit Students and Taxpayers? Comment," Princeton University, mimeo, February 2004, available at http://www.princeton.edu/~jrothst/rothstein_hoxbycomment.pdf.

35. Hoxby (2000e).

36. Caroline M. Hoxby, "All School Finance Equalizations Are Not Created Equal," *Quarterly Journal of Economics* 116, no. 4 (November 2001): 1189–231. Hoxby cites California as the prime example of this kind of leveling down. Texas's so-called Robin Hood school finance equalization scheme provides another extreme example of the negative consequences and imbedded inefficiencies of such poorly conceived plans. Under the Texas system, districts set their own property tax rates (subject to a rate ceiling) but they may keep only the revenue generated on the first $280,000 of property value per pupil (students with disabilities are given additional weight in the calculation), while the state confiscates any additional revenue—an effective 100 percent marginal tax rate. State funds are then allocated to property-poor districts through a matching scheme that encourages them to set property tax rates at the state maximum (which, in and of itself, distorts the educational investment decisions they make), transferring funds from districts with strong preferences for education to districts with weaker educational preferences. The scheme is dynamically unstable, because the capitalization of tax burdens and spending restrictions into property values shrinks the tax base and leads the state to face chronic revenue shortfalls. Because capitalization causes land value to more quickly reflect tax burdens, the property tax base shrinks much faster than the bases of other taxes, such as income or sales taxes. These shortfalls beget property tax rate increases until the rate cap is reached, at which point educational spending can no longer be increased through taxation. The weighting scheme, however, allows the district to increase funding by classifying more students as "special needs"—a perverse incentive if ever there was one. While some "special

needs" conditions do not require subjective judgment, such as blindness, 95 percent of the difference between weighted and actual pupils can be attributed to classifications that require judgment, such as learning disabilities, limited English proficiency, speech impairment, or emotional disturbance. See Caroline M. Hoxby and Ilyana Kuziemko, "Robin Hood and His Not-So-Merry Plan: Capitalization and the Self-Destruction of Texas' School Finance Equalization Plan, Harvard University Department of Economics, February 2004, updated July 2004, available at http://post.economics.harvard.edu/faculty/hoxby/papers/txpaper.pdf, pp. 9–12, 17. In short, because the Robin Hood scheme cannibalizes its tax base to fund distorted investments, it uses evaporating resources to support less productive districts. It can even have counterproductive effects in the case of students misclassified as disabled.

37. Other studies that treated school finance equalization as an event and used a regression discontinuity approach found more positive achievement effects than Hoxby's method of calculating and using the exact tax-price changes of each district. Please see David Card and A. Abigail Payne, "School Finance Reform, the Distribution of School Spending, and the Distribution of SAT Scores," NBER Working Paper no. 6766, October 1998; Sheila E. Murray, William N. Evans, and Robert M. Schwab, "Education Finance Reform and the Distribution of Education Resources," *American Economic Review* 88, no. 4 (September 1998): 789–812; Thomas A. Downes and David N. Figlio, "School Finance Reform, Tax Limits and Student Performance: Do Reforms Level Up or Dumb Down?" unpublished working paper, Department of Economics, University of Oregon, February 1997, later released as Institute for Research on Poverty Discussion Paper no. 1142–97, September 1997.

38. Douglas S. Reed, "Court-Ordered School Finance Equalization: Judicial Activism and Democratic Opposition," in *Developments in School Finance 1996*, ed. William J. Fowler Jr. (Washington, D.C.: U.S. Department of Education, National Center for Educational Statistics), pp. 93–120.

39. There is a clear trade-off between providing additional funds for all students with disabilities who are more difficult to educate and eliminating incentives (or opportunities) for districts to artificially inflate the number of students who fall into "special needs" categories by misclassifying marginal students. Relying on more immutable characteristics, such as blindness, that are less susceptible to improper diagnosis minimizes the incentives for misclassification, but also means that districts may not be fully compensated for educating students with more subjective conditions such as attention deficit disorder. See, for example, Julie Berry Cullen, "The Impact of Fiscal Incentives on Student Disability Rates," NBER Working Paper no. 7173, June 1999. Redistribution can also be based on student characteristics that are harmlessly mutable at the district level, for example, the percentage of students qualifying for reduced-price lunches; districts could receive more state funds if they recruited more students from low-income families, but this does not work against the state's educational objectives.

40. Hoxby (2001), p. 1229.

41. Alan B. Krueger, "Reassessing the View That American Schools Are Broken," Princeton University Industrial Relations Section Working Paper no. 395, January 1998, p. 4.

42. Among the National Education Goals agreed to by President George H. W. Bush and the governors in 1990 was the goal that, by 2000, 90 percent of 18- to 24-year-olds would have attained a high school education. The percentage stagnated at around 85 percent throughout the 1990s. See the National Education Goals Panel Web site, http://www.negp.gov/, accessed September 4, 2004. See also our figure 3.7 for a chart of educational attainment by birth cohort.

43. Spending increased from $3,782 per pupil to $7,591 per pupil (in 2001 dollars) between 1970 and 2000. Eric A. Hanushek, "The Failure of Input-Based Schooling Policies," NBER Working Paper no. 9040, July 2002, table 1.

44. Hanushek.

45. Krueger (2002).

46. Alan B. Krueger and Diane M. Whitmore, "Would Smaller Classes Help Close the Black-White Achievement Gap?" Princeton University, Industrial Relations Section, Working Paper no. 451, March 2001, available at http://www.irs.princeton.edu/pubs/pdfs/451.pdf.

47. Alan B. Krueger and Diane M. Whitmore, "The Effect of Attending a Small Class in the Early Grades on College-Test Taking and Middle School Test Results: Evidence from Project STAR," NBER Working Paper no. 7656, April 2000.

48. Caroline M. Hoxby, "The Effects of Class Size on Student Achievement: New Evidence from Population Variation," *Quarterly Journal of Economics* 115, no. 4 (November 2000): 1239–85.

49. David Sims, "How Flexible Is Education Production? Combination Class and Class Size Reduction in California," MIT Department of Economics, mimeo, January 2004.

50. We should add that we think it is unwise to place too much emphasis on improving macro-level productivity measures as a policy goal. High macro-level productivity is consistent with both perfectly equitable and perfectly inequitable distributions of resources and enhancement of college preparedness. At the same time, low marginal productivity for spending on advantaged, well-prepared students, coupled with high productivity for spending on disadvantaged, poorly prepared students, suggests the desirability of allocating more resources for the disadvantaged—which would be a win for both equity and efficiency.

51. See Luis A. Crouch and Thabo Mabogoane, "Aspects of Internal Efficiency Indicators in South African Schools: Analysis of Historical and Current Data," *EduSource Data News* 19 (1997): 4–28; and Johan Muller and Jennifer Roberts, "The Sound and Fury of International School Reform: A Critical Review," report prepared for the Joint Education Trust, 2000.

52. U.S. Department of Education. National Center for Education Statistics. *Public School Districts in the United States: A Statistical Profile, 1987–88 to 1993–94* (Washington, D.C.: National Center for Education Statistics, 1998).

53. It is probably no coincidence that the rise of teachers' unions in the 1960s (following a wave of legalization of collective bargaining) was virtually contemporaneous with the decline in macro-level productivity. See Caroline M. Hoxby, "How Teachers' Unions Affect Education Production," *Quarterly Journal of Economics* 111, no. 3 (August 1996): 671–718.

54. James Walsh and Ron Nixon, "School Contracts: Pricing Out Young Teachers," *Star Tribune* (Minneapolis), May 23, 2004, p. A1; Fermin Leal, "Santa Ana Teachers OK 4% Pay Cut; Concessions Allow Smaller Classes and Prevent Layoffs as the District Faces a Budget Shortfall," *Orange County Register*, March 14, 2004, online edition; Megan Tench, "With No Pact, Boston Teachers Weigh Staging 1-Day Strike; Pay, Class, Size, Overtime Are among the Issues," *Boston Globe*, February 27, 2004, p. B3. Unions are not the only institution shifting the flow of money; school districts may also have to adjust their spending to comply with state mandates, such as the one to limit class sizes that is currently in effect in Florida. Jeffrey S. Solochek, "Class Size Limit Straining System," *St. Petersburg Times*, April 22, 2004, p. 1.

55. Hoxby (1996).

56. As Susan Moore Johnson and Susan M. Kardos point out, "industrial bargaining" agreements that work best in a manufacturing setting have been replaced in a number of districts by "reform bargaining" agreements that recognize that a school is not a factory and that teachers are not interchangeable. See Johnson and Kardos, "Reform Bargaining and Its Promise for School Improvement," in *Conflicting Missions? Teachers Unions and Educational Reform,* ed. Tom Loveless (Washington, D.C.: Brookings Institution Press, 2000), pp. 7–46. An analogous labor-management relationship is found in symphony orchestras, where presumably shared artistic goals can be compromised by adversarial (or simply absent) relationships between players and management. Over the past five years, the Mellon Foundation's Program for Symphony Orchestras has supported efforts by a number of orchestras to bring musicians, music directors, and management together to clarify and to better articulate their artistic identities and goals and to help them create an internal culture wherein these goals can most effectively be achieved. One lesson that has already been learned from this program is that well-established lines of communication throughout an organization, along with the possibility for shared decision making, enhance the organization's ability to respond effectively to financial and other crises.

57. U.S. Department of Education, National Center for Education Statistics, *Digest of Education Statistics, 2002,* NCES 2003-060 (Washington, D.C.: U.S. Department of Education, National Center for Education Statistics, 2003), table 3, "Enrollment in Educational Institutions, by Level and Control of Institution: 1869–70 to Fall 2012."

58. See Caroline M. Hoxby, "The Effects of School Choice on Curriculum and Atmosphere," in *Earning and Learning: How Schools Matter,* ed. Susan Mayer and Paul Peterson (Washington, D.C.: Brookings Institution Press, 1999), pp. 281–316. See also Caroline M. Hoxby, "School Choice and School Productivity: Could School Choice Be a Rising Tide That Lifts All Boats?" in *The Economics of School Choice,* ed. Hoxby (Chicago: University of Chicago Press, 2003), pp. 287–341.

59. Caroline M. Hoxby, "School Choice and School Competition: Evidence from the United States," *Swedish Economic Policy Review* 10, no. 2 (2003): 9–65.

60. Hoxby (2003a), p. 15.

61. See Eric A. Hanushek and Steven G. Rivkin, "Does Public School Competition Affect Teacher Quality?" and Paul E. Peterson, William G. Howell, Patrick J. Wolf, and David E. Campbell, "School Vouchers: Results from Randomized Experiments," in Hoxby, ed. (2003b), pp. 23–47 and 107–44. See also Caroline M. Hoxby and Jonah E. Rockoff, "Impact of Charter Schools on Student Achievement," May 2004, available at http://post.economics.harvard.edu/faculty/hoxby/papers/hoxbyrockoffcharters .pdf. Other researchers dispute these findings or present findings of non-effects using other data. See Alan B. Krueger and Pei Zhu, "Another Look at the New York City School Voucher Experiment," NBER Working Paper no. 9418, December 2002.

62. Hoxby (2003a).

63. Cecilia Rouse, "Private School Vouchers and Student Achievement: An Evaluation of the Milwaukee Parental Choice Program," *Quarterly Journal of Economics* 113, no. 2 (May 1998): 553–602. Rouse acknowledges several caveats to her conclusions, including the possible effects of attrition bias and data imperfections.

64. Hoxby (2003b).

65. For example, Mathematica Policy Research has contracted to conduct a comprehensive study of the effect of charter schools on student achievement. Other evaluative efforts are detailed in a Department of Education press release, "More than

"$8 Million in Grants Awarded to Expand Charter Schools, Study Charter School Achievement," October 9, 2003, available at http://www.ed.gov/news/pressreleases/2003/10/10092003a.html.

66. George M. Holmes, Jeff DeSimone, and Nicholas G. Rupp, "Does School Choice Increase School Quality?" NBER Working Paper no. 9683, May 2003.

67. Hoxby (2004).

68. Dennis Epple and Richard Romano, "Competition between Private and Public Schools, Vouchers, and Peer-Group Effects," *American Economic Review* 88, no. 1 (March 1998): 33–62. See also Epple and Romano, "Educational Vouchers and Cream Skimming," NBER Working Paper no. 9354, November 2002.

69. As Rouse points out, future studies must take into account the high mobility among students and collect outcome data for a relevant control group to minimize sample attrition and allow accurate comparisons to be drawn. Rouse, p. 593.

70. See Diana Jean Schemo, "Charter Schools Trail in Results, U.S. Data Reveals," *New York Times,* August 17, 2004, p. A6; and Schemo, "Education Secretary Defends Charter Schools," *New York Times,* August 18, 2004, p. A3.

71. See the full-page advertisement titled "Charter School Evaluation Reported by the *New York Times* Fails to Meet Professional Standards," *New York Times,* August 25, 2004, p. A17.

72. Gene V. Glass, as quoted by Samuel G. Freedman, "Report Offers No Clear Victory for Charter School Opponents," *New York Times,* August 25, 2004, p. B8. The ad in the *New York Times* questioning the conclusions of the American Federation of Teachers (AFT) report was "sponsored" by The Center for Education Reform, an organization well known for its strong support of the charter school movement. Of course the AFT has its own constituency and its own interests to serve.

73. Alan Krueger has made this suggestion in discussing terrorism data. Missteps in the analysis and measurement of terrorist incidents prompted debates regarding the legitimacy of current evaluation methods and agency independence. Krueger's description of the controversy and his recommendations for rectifying the situation are detailed in Alan B. Krueger and David D. Laitin, "'Misunderestimating' Terrorism," *Foreign Affairs* 83, no. 5 (September–October, 2004): 8–13.

74. In other words, the accountability movement can be thought of as a reaction to Katz and Goldin's "virtue" of leniency toward academic and disciplinary mistakes.

75. See Eric A. Hanushek and Margaret E. Raymond, "Does School Accountability Lead to Improved Student Performance?" NBER Working Paper no. 10591, June 2004; Brian A. Jacob, "Accountability, Incentives, and Behavior: The Impact of High-Stakes Testing in the Chicago Public Schools," NBER Working Paper no. 8968, June 2002; and Meredith Phillips, "What Makes Schools Effective? A Comparison of the Relationships of Communitarian Climate and Academic Climate to Mathematics Achievement and Attendance during Middle School," *American Educational Research Journal* 34, no. 4 (Winter 1997): 633–62.

76. See David N. Figlio and Lawrence S. Getzler, "Accountability, Ability, and Disability: Gaming the System," NBER Working Paper no. 9307, October 2002; and Jacob. Figlio and Getzler found that Florida schools classified students as needing special education at much higher rates following the introduction of the "Sunshine State Standards." This increase was especially pronounced at impoverished schools. Jacob found that low-achieving students at poor schools in Chicago were more likely to be classified as special education students following the introduction of high-stakes testing.

77. Jacob.

78. James Comer, *Leave No Child Behind: Preparing Today's Youth for Tomorrow's World* (New Haven, Conn.: Yale University Press, 2004), p. 7.

79. Comer, pp. 86–92.

80. See Comer, chapters 6 and 7.

81. Comer, p. 85.

82. See Geoffrey D. Borman et al., "Comprehensive School Reform and Student Achievement: A Meta-Analysis," Center for Research on the Education of Students Placed at Risk, Technical Report no. 59, November 2002, pp. 1–4 and table 3, available at http://www.csos.jhu.edu/crespar/techReports/Report59.pdf, accessed July 21, 2004.

83. Meredith Phillips provides a detailed review and commentary on the literature as of 1997 in Phillips (1997), pp. 635–39. She reports that three studies found positive but statistically unreliable effects from communitarian characteristics, and one study found statistically unreliable negative effects.

84. One feature that casts doubt on Phillips's analysis is that she controls for seventh-grade test scores and attendance rates when her dependant variables are eighth-grade test scores and attendance rates, yet there is no indication that any change in policy occurred between seventh and eighth grade that would impact the various communitarian characteristics she uses as independent variables. In other words, there may have been no change in test scores or attendance because there was no change in policy, not because the policy does not work. See Phillips (1997).

85. Borman et al., tables 3 and 5. The other two programs in the "Strongest Evidence of Effectiveness" category are Direct Instruction and Success for All.

86. Joseph Tierney and Jean Grossman, *Making a Difference: An Impact Study of Big Brothers/Big Sisters* (Philadelphia: Public/Private Ventures, 1995), as referenced in Carneiro and Heckman.

87. Amy Johnson, *An Evaluation of the Long-Term Impacts of the Sponsor-a-Scholar Program on Student Performance* (Princeton, N.J.: Mathematica Policy Research, 1996), as referenced in Carneiro and Heckman.

88. For the Prep for Prep story, see Gary Simons, *Be the Dream: Prep for Prep Graduates Share Their Stories* (Chapel Hill, N.C.: Algonquin Books of Chapel Hill, 2003).

89. See Christopher Avery and Thomas J. Kane, "Students' Perceptions of College Opportunity: The Boston COACH Program," in Hoxby, ed. (2004), pp. 355–94.

90. See Karen W. Arenson, "Study of College Readiness Finds No Progress in Decade," *New York Times*, October 14, 2004, p. A26.

Chapter 10 Concluding Thoughts

1. Lawrence A. Cremin, ed., *The Republic and the School: Horace Mann and the Education of Free Men* (New York: Teachers College, Columbia University Press, 1957), p. 8.

2. Judith Sealander, "Making Public Education Mandatory: The Consequences of a Foundation-Supported Idea in City Schools," paper presented at the conference "Philanthropy and the City: An Historical Overview," Rockefeller Archive Center, September 25–26, 2000, p. 4, available at http://archive.rockefeller.edu/publications/conferences/sealander.pdf, accessed August 6, 2004.

3. Sealander, p. 4. See also U.S. Department of Education, National Center for Education Statistics, *Digest of Education Statistics, 1992* (Washington, D.C.: U.S. Department of Education, National Center for Education Statistics, 1992), pp. 108–10.

4. Sealander, p. 5, and Michael Katz, *A History of Compulsory Education Laws* (Bloomington, Ind.: Phi Delta Kappa Educational Foundation, 1976).

5. Sealander, pp. 5–6, cites Federal Security Agency, Office of Education, *Vitalizing Secondary Education,* Report of the First Commission on Life Adjustment Education for Youth (Washington, D.C.: Federal Security Agency, Office of Education, 1951), pp. 4–6. See also U.S. Department of Education (1992), pp. 108–10.

6. Claudia Goldin and Lawrence F. Katz, "The 'Virtues' of the Past: Education in the First Hundred Years of the New Republic," NBER Working Paper no. 9958, September 2003, and other references cited in chapter 3.

7. In dividing up the "blame" for excluding various groups from the opportunities that higher education confers, we should pay some heed to the self-interests and stated missions of colleges and universities. For example, historical decisions to exclude, which clearly run counter to modern equity and excellence objectives, were, in their myopic way, consistent with the way schools saw their mission of "educating society's future leaders" in periods when leadership opportunities were themselves largely confined to white men of the right religion. By the end of World War II, as society evolved and as leadership opportunities broadened, there was a growing realization, or at least a gradual recognition, that knocking down discriminatory barriers to access was consistent with strengthening standards of excellence as well as promoting opportunity.

8. "Who Pays to Study?" *Economist,* January 24, 2004, p. 23.

9. This point was made by Derek Bok, who is writing a book on undergraduate education, in personal correspondence with the authors, September 6, 2004.

10. College Board, *Trends in College Pricing* (Washington, D.C.: College Board, 2003), p. 4. See also chapter 4.

11. In South Africa there has been a tension between "making the students fit the university and making the university fit the students" (see appendix A, section headed "Who Succeeds in Higher Education? The Tension between Equity and Excellence in the Curriculum"). Initially, faculty assumed that there was no reason to change the way they taught; but experience convinced many that in their context they simply had to take account of the backgrounds of the African students whom they now, following apartheid, must educate successfully. Needless to say, the "college preparedness" of the African students is very different from the preparedness of the white students. Also, the society (and the world) that new graduates of South African universities will enter is very different from what it used to be. For all of these reasons, it has been argued more recently that "it is incumbent on the HE [higher education] sector to take its full share of responsibility for deracialising and normalising the access pathways from lower educational levels" as a key element of its contribution to transformation (see appendix A, section headed "After Apartheid: The Challenges of Transformation").

12. J. Bradford DeLong, Claudia Goldin, and Lawrence F. Katz, "Sustaining U.S. Economic Growth," in *Agenda for the Nation,* ed. Henry J. Aaron, James M. Lindsay, and Pietro S. Nivola (Washington, D.C.: Brookings Institution Press), pp. 17–60, esp. pp. 19–20.

13. Jennifer Cheeseman Day and Eric C. Newburger, "The Big Payoff: Educational Attainment and Synthetic Estimates of Work-Life Earnings," Current Population Report no. P23-210, U.S. Census Bureau, July 2002, available at http://www .census.gov/prod/2002pubs/p23-210.pdf, esp. figure 3 and text on pp. 3–4.

14. Lawrence H. Summers, "Higher Education and the American Dream," speech delivered at the 86th Annual Meeting, American Council on Education, Miami, Fla.,

February 29, 2004, available at http://www.president.harvard.edu/speeches/2004/ace.html, accessed August 9, 2004. President Summers reiterated this same theme at the June 2004 Harvard commencement.

15. Another subject that we believe deserves careful rethinking is competition versus collaboration in different contexts within higher education. There is a real need, in our judgment, for a clear-headed analytical study of the optimal forms and degrees of competition—and collaboration. Certainly competition among institutions for faculty and resources has been a great driver of higher standards, which is one reason why many of us are concerned about the declining position of a number of leading public universities, seen in relation to their private university peers. Growing international competition can also have positive effects in stimulating fresh thinking about graduate programs and in providing new centers of good work with which to collaborate as well as to compete.

At the same time, the debate engendered by the "Overlap Group" approach (see chapter 7) to providing student aid at the undergraduate level demonstrated that standard anti-trust laws, designed to prevent for-profit entities from harming consumers, have limited relevance in a predominantly not-for-profit sector in which institutions are seeking to maximize values other than profit. Indeed there is a strong case to be made for benign collusion at the undergraduate level, where, unlike at the graduate level, there is a history of taking family resources into consideration in making financial aid awards. We believe that such forms of cooperation will discourage price wars and permit educational institutions to husband their scarce resources for worthy purposes, such as increasing the enrollment of students from low-income backgrounds. Unfortunately, the Overlap Group antitrust case has had a chilling effect on the willingness of colleges and universities to re-examine what might and might not be permissible in this realm—even though the case was returned to the d istrict court on appeal.

Some other forms of competition for students at the undergraduate level can also have untoward effects on both excellence and equity objectives. We have in mind, for example, the tendency to cater to the "consumer" mentality of some students and their families by creating more and more expensive social and recreational facilities on campus. The same problem extends—powerfully—into the athletic realm. If one school in a conference gets a "turf" field for field hockey (or a super weight room for athletes in general), the pressure is on others to provide the same amenities—whether or not such outlays are the best way to advance the fundamental educational goals of the institution. Of course there are myriad judgments involved in making such decisions, and we certainly do not propose that any particular set of values be imposed on everyone—an impossible task in any case. But we do wonder if this is another area in which benign collusion might be helpful.

In the realm of libraries, research facilities, software development, and scholarly communication, the case for pursuing collaborative approaches to common problems seems overwhelming. Such collaborations can improve the quality of what is done and also free up resources for other uses. For example, the provision of new digital resources that can benefit a wide array of institutions, here and abroad, has only positive consequences. The history of JSTOR, a Mellon Foundation–sponsored initiative that has led to the creation of a massive, highly searchable database of scholarly literature, is an excellent case in point. JSTOR, which is an independent not-for-profit entity, pursues a policy of "value-based pricing," whereby it charges lower prices to smaller, poorer institutions than to larger, wealthier ones. Its goal is to make its database widely available while at the same time collecting enough resources from a broad-based community of users to ensure sustainability and the capacity to migrate to new electronic platforms as time goes on. The ability of JSTOR to serve equity as well as excellence objectives is illustrated by the heavy use made of the database both among Appalachian colleges in this country and in the libraries of South Africa. Students at these institutions now have access to literature that otherwise would have been either entirely inaccessible or very difficult to obtain (through, for example, interlibrary loans).

These comments about competition at the higher education level also have some resonance at pre-college levels. Here, however, we are less concerned about too much competition than we are about too little. Fostering experiments of all kinds seems eminently sensible, and one would certainly hope that the successes of at least some charter schools would have a salutary effect on entire school systems through the healthy kinds of competition. Care has to be taken, needless to say, to be sure that competition does not serve to further disadvantage poor families and minority groups, but this observation suggests only the need for careful attention to the details of proposed programs and careful monitoring of outcomes.

16. Ramphele.

Appendix A   Equity and Excellence in Higher Education: The Case of the University of Cape Town

Ian Scott is associate professor and director of the Academic Development Programme; Nan Yeld is associate professor and dean of higher education development; Janice McMillan is senior lecturer in the Centre for Higher Education Development; and Martin Hall is deputy vice-chancellor and professor in the Graduate School of Humanities at the University of Cape Town.

1. Stuart J. Saunders, *Vice-Chancellor on a Tightrope: A Personal Account of Climactic Years in South Africa* (Cape Town: David Philip Publishers, 2000).

2. On its election in 1994, South Africa's first democratic government inherited a fragmented, bureaucratically chaotic situation in respect to higher education administration and control. See National Education Coordinating Committee (NECC), *The National Education Policy Investigation: Framework Report and Final Report Summaries* (Cape Town: Oxford University Press/NECC, 1993), p. 206. The legislative framework of "own affairs" and "general affairs" determined how post-secondary institutions were governed. In essence, this meant that educational matters relating directly to the white, colored, and Indian population groups were deemed to be "an own affair within the group's own cultural and value framework," and were administered by a minister who was a member of the Council of Ministers of the relevant group authority: the House of Assembly for whites, the House of Representatives for coloreds, and the House of Delegates for Indians. In contrast, the educational affairs of Africans (in respect to "own affairs") were administered by a cabinet minister (the Minister of Cooperation, Development and Education) in the central government. To make the position even more complicated, educational matters deemed to affect more than one of the three minority population groups and Africans outside the black "homelands" or so-called national states (e.g., Gazankulu, KaNgwane, Lebowa, QwaQwa, KwaNdebele, and KwaZulu) were termed "general affairs" and were administered by the Minister of National Education. Apart from the "homeland" authorities, there were thus five ministers responsible for education, four for "own affairs" and one for

"general affairs." It is perhaps no wonder, then, that "the apartheid model led to a situation of divided and unequal control as far as educational institutions were concerned." See I. Bunting, *A Legacy of Inequality: Higher Education in South Africa* (Rondebosch, South Africa: University of Cape Town Press, 1994), p. 9.

3. P. Christie, *The Right to Learn: The Struggle for Education in South Africa* (Johannesburg: The SACHED Trust, 1986).

4. Saunders.

5. By way of illustration, in 1983 some 95 percent of the Department of Education and Training (DET) students who obtained a matriculation exemption (the statutory minimum requirement for eligibility for degree study) attained aggregate grades of D or E—that is, they obtained aggregate scores of less than 60 percent. In South Africa, the aggregate results of school-leaving examinations are classified and used as the main criterion for entry to higher education, and a C aggregate has generally allowed access to most programs. Thus the profile of results for DET students was below the aggregate level required by the white institutions. At this time, moreover, of the students writing the Senior Certificate examination at the end of grade 12, only between 8 percent and 13 percent obtained an exemption. The fact that only about a tenth of the tiny group of survivors of the dysfunctional DET school system (1.4 percent of those who started school) would be eligible for regular admission to a white university shows just how elite this group was. Compounding this, the very poor state of mathematics and science education in DET schools meant that even if students attained a high enough aggregate to be considered, they would be unlikely to achieve the kinds of results in these key subjects that they needed to be considered eligible for admission to many high-status academic programs. See N. Badsha, A. Williams, and N. Yeld, "Alternative Admissions Research Project: A Work in Progress Report," paper presented at the Academic Support Programme Annual Conference, Grahamstown, 1987; and M. Bot, "Standard Examination Results, 1981–1991," *EduSource* 1 (1992): 6.

6. The widespread suspicion that DET Senior Certificate results did not effectively predict future academic performance was supported by a growing body of evidence. (See N. Badsha, G. T. W. Blake, and J. G. Brock-Utne, "Evaluation of the African Matriculation as a Predictor of Performance in the University of Natal Medical School," *South African Journal of Science* 82 [1986]: 220–21; I. Shochet, "Manifest and Potential Performance in Advantaged and Disadvantaged Students," unpublished PhD dissertation, University of the Witwatersrand, Johannesburg, 1986; and C. S. Potter and A. N. Jamotte, "African Matric Results: Dubious Indicators of Academic Merit," *Indicator South Africa*, 3, no. 1 [1985]: 10–13.) This view was trenchantly expressed in 1987 by the principal of the University of the Witwatersrand, who stated that "for students produced by the system offered by the Department of Education and Training, matriculation can only be regarded as a random statistic." (*Star* [Johannesburg], May 25, 1987.) In addition to the structural and legislative factors impacting the access of black learners to historically white universities, the chaotic and repressive conditions in DET schools ensured that black learners were inadequately prepared for university study. The universities were therefore faced with the unsatisfactory situation of having to select students on a basis known to be unreliable. To make matters worse, the DET examinations produced a restricted range of scores in a restricted set of subjects, making selection largely arbitrary because there was little to distinguish one applicant from another.

7. See J. Hofmeyr and R. Spence, "Bridges to the Future," *Optima* 37, no. 1 (1989): 37–48.

8. The underresourcing is best captured in pupil-teacher ratios and per capita expenditure (Christie). In 1971 the pupil-teacher ratios were 58 to 1 in DET schools and 20 to 1 in white schools. In 1983 the ratios were 43 to 1 in DET schools and 18 to 1 in white schools. In 1971 the per capita expenditure was R17 ($378 in 2004 dollars) for DET students and R282 ($6,275) for white students, and in 1983 it was R146 ($433) and R1,211 ($3,592), respectively.

9. N. S. Ndebele, "Maintaining Domination through Language," *Academic Development* 1, no. 1 (1995): 3–5.

10. Luis A. Crouch and Thabo Mabogoane, "Aspects of Internal Efficiency Indicators in South African Schools: Analysis of Historical and Current Data," *EduSource Data News* 19 (1997): 4–28.

11. F. Marton and R. Säljö, "On Qualitative Differences in Learning—I: Outcome and Process," *British Journal of Educational Psychology* 46 (1976): 4–11.

12. See two works by R. Kapp, "'With English You Can Go Everywhere': An Analysis of the Role and Status of English at a Former DET School," *South African Journal of Education* 25 (2000): 227–59, and "'Reading on the Line' in a South African English Second Language Literature Class," unpublished manuscript, University of Cape Town, 2000. See also P. Vinjevold, "Language Issues in South African Classrooms," in *Getting Learning Right: Report of the President's Education Initiative Research Project*, ed. N. Taylor and P. Vinjevold (Johannesburg: Joint Education Trust, 1999), 205–26; and C. A. MacDonald, *Crossing the Threshold into Standard Three* (Pretoria: Human Sciences Research Council, 1990).

13. N. Cloete and S. Pillay, "Can Wits Have a More Representative Student Body within the Existing Structures: Optimistic or Pessimistic?" unpublished manuscript, University of the Witwatersrand, Johannesburg, 1987.

14. The Teach-Test-Teach (TTT) project at the University of Natal was in its early years a version of this approach. See two works by H. Griesel: "Access to University: A Review of Selection Procedures," unpublished manuscript, University of Natal, Durban, South Africa, 1991; and *Access and the Higher Education Sector: A South African Case Study on Innovative Policy and Programmes* (Pretoria: Association for the Development of Education in Africa [ADEA] and South African Department of Education, 1999); and H. Zaaiman, *Selecting Students for Mathematics and Science: The Challenge Facing Higher Education in South Africa* (Pretoria: Human Sciences Research Council, 1998). A large group of students was tested, put through a fortnight of instruction, then retested. Selection was planned to take place after this two-week tryout period. See Griesel (1991).

15. University of Cape Town, Academic Planning Office, "Proposal for a Research Project to Devise Alternative Selection Procedures for Entry to UCT," University of Cape Town, Academic Planning Office, 1986.

16. See T. Barsby, W. Haeck, and N. Yeld, eds., *Accountability in Testing: The Contribution of Tests to Increased Access to Post Secondary Education*, South African Association for Academic Development, Workshop Publication Series no. 2 (Cape Town: University of Cape Town, 1994). The prevalence and severity of educational disadvantage in South Africa, and the adverse impact this has on the ability of candidates to demonstrate their underlying abilities, made the development of an alternative system of testing an extremely complex undertaking. Initially it was believed that a large part of

the problem of the restricted range of scores obtained by black Senior Certificate candidates would be overcome by a more rigorous assessment system—in other words, that the flawed DET examination was the primary problem. But it rapidly became clear that a new approach to probing underlying ability was needed, rather than simply improved conventional testing procedures. As Yeld and Haeck pointed out, traditional testing approaches tend to elicit "fairly uniformly dismal performances . . . [which] blur the distinction between better and weaker candidates." The Alternative Admissions Research Project (AARP) therefore adopted a "scaffolding" approach, whereby tasks are created within the tests. This "scaffolding," it was reasoned, "enables candidates to engage with the . . . tasks in ways which are different from those which would have been employed had the scaffolding exercises not been worked through." (See N. Yeld and W. Haeck, "Educational Histories and Academic Potential: Can Tests Deliver?" *Assessment and Evaluation in Higher Education* 22 [1997]: 5–16, esp. p. 9.) The approach, while recognizing the limitations of in-test opportunities to really shift performance, attempts to take students from a performance level based on their prior opportunities to one more closely approximating their underlying ability. It was decided to use the skill areas of language and numeracy in early test development, as these were of general value in the curriculum and represented core areas of academic ability. In a comprehensive validation study of this approach, it was concluded that "the use of scaffolding within a test, for talented educationally disadvantaged students, can significantly enhance test performance." (See N. Yeld, "Equity, Assessment and Language of Learning: Key Issues for Higher Education Selection and Access in South Africa," unpublished PhD dissertation, University of Cape Town, 2001, p. 307.) The study also concluded that the AARP tests were effective in predicting academic success, and, more specifically, that "students who score in the top quintile of their candidate pool are more likely to graduate than are students who are admitted on the basis of their Senior Certificate results alone" (Yeld, p. 308).

17. The basic statistics from the 2001 cohort writing the Senior Certificate examination confirmed these disquieting results. Only about 15 percent (67,700) of South Africa's school-leaving examination candidates achieved the minimum requirement for entry into higher education. This represented less than 8 percent of the age cohort, far short of South Africa's target higher education participation rate of 20 percent. (See Ministry of Education [MoE], South Africa, *National Plan for Higher Education in South Africa* [Pretoria: MoE, 2001].) Only about half of those who achieved the minimum entry requirement for higher education were black students—about 33,000 in total. Fully 51 percent of the age cohort did not write the examination. It was not reported whether those who did not write the examination were at school in lower grades, or not in school at all. See I. V. S. Mullis, *TIMSS 1999 International Mathematics Report* (Chestnut Hill, Mass.: International Study Center, Boston College, 2000); and N. Taylor and P. Vinjevold, "Teaching and Learning in South African Schools," in Taylor and Vinjevold, pp. 131–62.

18. "Placement" here refers to placing new students in first-year courses with an entry level that matches their prior learning, thus enabling the students to gain a firm foundation for their studies as well as allowing for responsible widening of access.

19. Part of the Tertiary Education Linkages Project.

20. Saunders, pp. 76, 85.

21. See, for example, P. Hunter, "The Transformation of Learning: The Evolution of an Academic Support Programme," *South African Journal of Higher Education* 3, no. 2 (1989): 68–75.

22. I. Scott, "Tinkering or Transforming? The Contribution of Academic Support Programmes to 'Opening the Doors of Learning and of Culture,'" *Aspects* 7 (1986): 10–26, University of Natal, Pietermaritzburg.

23. See Vusi Khanyile, untitled keynote address presented at 1986 Academic Support Programmes Conference, *Aspects* 7 (1986): 1–9, University of Natal, Pietermaritzburg; M. Mboya, "Open Non-Racial Universities: A Myth or Reality?" *Monday Paper*, 5 (1986): 28, University of Cape Town; and "Tomorrow Begins at Wits Today? The Role of the University in a Changing Society," *Perception of Wits*, University of the Witwatersrand, Johannesburg, 1986.

24. H. W. Vilakazi and B. Tema, "White Universities and the Black Revolution," paper presented at the 1985 Academic Support Programmes Conference, University of the Witwatersrand, Johannesburg, 1985.

25. F. R. N. Nabarro, "An Outline of the Academic Plan," University of the Witwatersrand, Johannesburg, 1980.

26. *Vice-Chancellor's Report for 1985*, University of Cape Town, p. 2.

27. See Scott (1986), pp. 21–22.

28. I. Scott, "The Interface between Higher Education and Secondary/Further Education as a Key Determinant of Access to and Success in Higher Education," paper commissioned by Task Group 5 of the National Commission on Higher Education, 1995, available at http://star.hsrc.ac.za/nche/final/tg5/systems/papers.html. It was argued that the articulation gap was partly attributable to the higher education sector's historical lack of alignment with South African educational realities. Mainstream university programs had never articulated successfully with the black school sector. The main reason for this was that the core of the higher education qualification framework had been adopted early in the 20th century (based on the Scottish system) for institutions that were serving a small, predominantly white middle-class community. South Africa's higher education qualification structure was (and remains) based on a three-year first degree followed by an "Honors" year benchmarked on the British honors degree. Critical curriculum parameters and assumptions were based on a largely homogeneous and well-prepared student intake, and were not valid for the majority of the black students who would need to be admitted in increasing numbers if any significant equity progress was to be made.

29. G. Fisher and I. Scott, "Approaches to the Development of Intermediate Post-Secondary Education in South Africa," *South African Journal of Higher Education* 7, no. 1 (1993, Research Supplement): 43–58.

30. See, for example, A. Sass, "Academic Support in Engineering at the University of Cape Town," *South African Journal of Higher Education* 2, no. 1 (1988): 25–29.

31. Shochet.

32. See, for example, F. Badenhorst, D. Foster, and S. Lea, "Factors Affecting Academic Performance in First-Year Psychology at the University of Cape Town," *South African Journal of Higher Education* 4, no. 1 (1990): 39–45.

33. Scott (1986), p. 22.

34. South African Association for Academic Development (SAAAD), "Facilitating Academic Development as a Key Element of Transformation in Higher Education," submission to the National Commission on Higher Education by the South African Association for Academic Development, 1995.

35. Ministry of Education (2001), p. 2.1.3.

36. Scott (1995), p. 11.

37. SAAAD; Scott (1995); National Commission on Higher Education (NCHE), *Report of (Task Group 5) Technical Committee 2 on Student Access, Support and Development*

(Pretoria: NCHE, 1995), available at http://star.hsrc.ac.za/nche/final/tg5/systems/chao2/html.

38. National Commission on Higher Education (NCHE), *A Framework for Transformation* (Pretoria: Human Sciences Research Council, 1996); and Ministry of Education (MoE), *Education White Paper 3: A Programme for the Transformation of Higher Education, General Notice 1196* (Pretoria: MoE, 1997).

39. In 2004—seven years after producing the white paper and a decade and a half after the University of Cape Town, through its vice-chancellor, first argued for state funding of academic development in the then-statutory higher education advisory body—the Department of Education made available the first major tranche of funding for foundation programs, as provided for in the new funding framework: a total of some R270 million, or more than $44.6 million, for the 2004–06 triennium.

40. See H. Wolpe, S. Badat, and Z. Barends, *The Post-Secondary Education System: Beyond the Equality vs. Development Impasse and Towards Policy Formulation for Equality and Development* (Cape Town: Education Policy Unit, University of the Western Cape, 1993).

41. Council on Higher Education, South Africa, *Towards a New Higher Education Landscape: Meeting the Equity, Quality and Social Development Imperatives of South Africa in the 21st Century* (Pretoria: Council on Higher Education, 2000).

42. See Fisher and Scott (1993), and Ian Scott, "Balancing Excellence, Equity and Enterprise in a Less-Industrialised Country: The Case of South Africa," in *The Enterprising University: Reform, Excellence and Equity*, ed. G. Williams (Buckingham, England: Society for Research into Higher Education and Open University Press, 2003), pp. 40–53.

43. For example, the direct intake into the Science Foundation Programme grew from under 30 students in the 1980s to around 120 in the late 1990s, representing up to 30 percent of the total science intake. The growing numbers of "mainstream" students transferring into the program have effectively doubled the size of some of the component courses, reflecting the need for this form of provision.

44. The contributors of Academic Development Programme (ADP) to the successful participation of black students cannot be accurately quantified in summary form because of major variance in the extent to which students in different categories and programs make use of ADP provision. By way of example, however, cohort studies of the five most recent intakes to have completed their program (the 1995–99 intakes) show that in science and engineering—areas where black representation has historically been very low—around 60 percent of the African graduates came through the full ADP program. This shows that talented but disadvantaged students who do not meet regular entry criteria can reach the exit standards of academically demanding programs if they have appropriate provision. This is seen as significant in that future growth in African enrollment will come mainly from this category of students, at least in the medium term.

45. Ministry of Education (2001) and (1997). The quotation is from Council on Higher Education (2000), pp. 25–26.

46. Martin Hall, "Boundary Institutions: Universities and Social Change," discussion paper, University of Cape Town, 2003.

References

Aaron, Henry J., James M. Lindsay, and Pietro S. Nivola, eds. 2003. *Agenda for the Nation*. Washington, D.C.: Brookings Institution Press.

Abel, Richard E., and Lyman W. Newlin, eds. 2002. *Scholarly Publishing: Books, Journals, Publishers, and Libraries in the Twentieth Century*. New York: Wiley.

ACT. 2004. *Crisis at the Core: Preparing All Students for College and Work*. Iowa City, Iowa: ACT, 2004. Available at http://www.act.org.

Adams, Henry. 1999. *The Education of Henry Adams*. Edited and with an introduction and notes by Ira B. Nadel. New York: Oxford University Press. Originally published in 1918.

Adelman, Clifford. 2004. *Principal Indicators of Student Academic Histories in Postsecondary Education, 1972–2000*. Washington, D.C.: U.S. Department of Education, Institute of Education Series, January. Available at http://www.ed.gov/rschstat/research/pubs/prinindicat/prinindicat.pdf.

Admissions to Higher Education Steering Group. 2003. "Consultation on Key Issues Relating to Fair Admissions to Higher Education." September. Available at http://www.admissions-review.org.uk/downloads/HE_docu.pdf. Accessed August 24, 2004.

Advisory Committee on Student Financial Assistance. 2001. *Access Denied: Restoring the Nation's Commitment to Equal Educational Opportunity*. Washington, D.C.: Advisory Committee on Student Financial Assistance, February.

"Affirmative Action, Negative Reaction." 2003. *Economist*, March 8, p. 16.

Alger, Jonathan, and Marvin Krislov. 2004. "You've Got to Have Friends: Lessons Learned from the Role of Amici in the University of Michigan Cases." *Journal of College and University Law* 30, no. 3: 503–29.

Allmendinger, David F., Jr. 1975. *Paupers and Scholars: The Transformation of Student Life in Nineteenth-Century New England*. New York: St. Martin's Press.

Anderson, Susan. 2003. "An Overview of College Rankings." Report from The Andrew W. Mellon Foundation, May 22.

Angelo, Richard. 1979. "The Students at the University of Pennsylvania and the Temple College of Philadelphia, 1873–1906: Some Notes on Schooling, Class and Social Mobility in the Late Nineteenth Century." *History of Education Quarterly* 19, no. 2 (Summer): 179–205.

Angrist, Joshua D., and Kevin Lang. 2002. "How Important Are Classroom Peer Effects? Evidence from Boston's Metco Program." NBER Working Paper no. 9263, October.

Angrist, Joshua D., and Victor Lavy. 1999. "Using Maimonides' Rule to Estimate the Effect of Class Size on Student Achievement." *Quarterly Journal of Economics* 114, no. 2 (May): 533–75.

Arenson, Karen W. 2001. "Yale President Wants to End Early Decisions for Admissions." *New York Times,* December 13, p. D1.

———. 2004a. "Harvard Says Poor Parents Won't Have to Pay." *New York Times,* February 29, section 1, p. 14.

———. 2004b. "Study of College Readiness Finds No Progress in Decade." *New York Times,* October 14, p. A26.

Argetsinger, Amy. 2004. "U-Va. Acts to Ease Students' Debt Load: Scholarships to Replace Loans." *Washington Post,* p. A01.

Arnone, Michael. 2004. "Keeping Searches Secret." *Chronicle of Higher Education,* July 9, p. A25.

Association of American Medical Colleges (AAMC). 2002. *Minority Students in Medical Education: Facts and Figures XII.* Washington, D.C.: AAMC.

Astin, Alexander W. 1977. *Four Critical Years.* San Francisco: Jossey-Bass.

Avery, Christopher, and Caroline M. Hoxby. 2004. "Do and Should Financial Aid Packages Affect Students' College Choices?" In *College Choices: The Economics of Where to Go, When to Go, and How to Pay for It,* ed. Caroline M. Hoxby, 239–301. Chicago: University of Chicago Press.

Avery, Christopher, and Thomas J. Kane. 2004. "Student Perceptions of College Opportunities: The Boston COACH Program." In *College Choices: The Economics of Where to Go, When to Go, and How to Pay for It,* ed. Caroline M. Hoxby, 355–94. Chicago: University of Chicago Press.

Avery, Christopher, Andrew Fairbanks, and Richard Zeckhauser. 2003. *The Early Admissions Game: Joining the Elite.* Cambridge, Mass.: Harvard University Press.

Avery, Christopher, Mark Glickman, Caroline M. Hoxby, and Andrew Metrick. 2004. "A Revealed Preference Ranking of U.S. Colleges and Universities." NBER Working Paper no. 10803, September.

Badenhorst, F., D. Foster, and S. Lea. 1990. "Factors Affecting Academic Performance in First-Year Psychology at the University of Cape Town." *South African Journal of Higher Education* 4, no. 1: 39–45.

Badsha, N., G. T. W. Blake, and J. G. Brock-Utne. 1986. "Evaluation of the African Matriculation as a Predictor of Performance in the University of Natal Medical School." *South African Journal of Science* 82: 220–21.

Badsha, N., A. Williams, and N. Yeld. 1987. "Alternative Admissions Research Project: A Work in Progress Report." Paper presented at the Academic Support Programme Annual Conference, Grahamstown.

Bailyn, Bernard, Donald Fleming, Oscar Handlin, and Stephan Thernstrom, eds. 1986. *Glimpses of the Harvard Past.* Cambridge, Mass.: Harvard University Press.

Baltzell, E. Digby, Allen Glicksman, and Jacquelyn Litt. 1983. "The Jewish Communities of Philadelphia and Boston: A Tale of Two Cities." In *Jewish Life in Philadelphia 1830–1940,* ed. Murray Friedman, 290–313. Philadelphia: Institute for the Study of Human Issues.

Barnett, Susan Duff. 2004. "Legislation: Bush Signs Law Closing Student Loan Loophole." *Bond Buyer,* November 2, p. 5.

Barsby, T., W. Haeck, and N. Yeld, eds. 1994. *Accountability in Testing: The Contribution of Tests to Increased Access to Post Secondary Education.* South African Association for Academic Development, Workshop Publication Series no. 2. Cape Town: University of Cape Town.

Bartlett, Thomas, and Megan Rooney. 2003. "Runaway Board? Unilateral Actions at Virginia Tech Raise Questions about the Proper Role of Trustees." *Chronicle of Higher Education,* March 28, p. A25.

Baumol, William J., and William G. Bowen. 1966. *Performing Arts, the Economic Dilemma: A Study of Problems Common to Theater, Opera, Music, and Dance.* New York: Twentieth Century Fund.

BBC News. 2004a. "200 City Academies Promised." *BBC News,* June 28. Available at http://news.bbc.co.uk/1/hi/education/3848195.stm. Accessed July 19.

———. 2004b. "Parent Choice Tops Tory Package." *BBC News,* June 29. Available at http://news.bbc.co.uk/1/hi/uk_politics/3847885.stm. Accessed July 19.

———. 2004c. "More Freedom in School Reforms." *BBC News,* July 8. Available at http://news.bbc.co.uk/1/hi/education/3875073.stm. Accessed July 19.

"Bending the Rules." 2002. *Economist,* August 24, p. 28

Berkner, Lutz, Shirley He, and Emily Forrest Cataldi. 2002. *Descriptive Summary of 1995–96 Beginning Postsecondary Students: Six Years Later.* NCES 2003-151. Washington, D.C.: U.S. Department of Education, National Center for Education Statistics, December.

Bernstein, Richard B. 2003. *Thomas Jefferson.* New York: Oxford University Press.

Bertrand, Marianne, and Sendhil Mullainathan. 2003. "Are Emily and Greg More Employable than Lakisha and Jamal? A Field Experiment on Labor Market Discrimination." NBER Working Paper no. 9873, July.

Beveridge, William. 1942. *Social Insurance and Allied Services.* Report presented to Parliament by command of His Majesty. Cmnd. 6404, November. Summary available at http://www.weasel.cwc.net/beveridge.htm, accessed July 12, 2004.

Bhattacharjee, Yudhijit. 2004. "Foreign Graduate Student Applications Drop." *Science,* March 5, p. 1453.

Bigglestone, W. E. 1971. "Oberlin College and the Negro Student, 1865–1940." *Journal of Negro History* 56, no. 3: 198–219.

Binder, Melissa, and Philip T. Ganderton, with Kristin Hutchens. 2002. "Incentive Effects of New Mexico's Merit-Based State Scholarship Program: Who Responds and How?" In *Who Should We Help? The Negative Social Consequences of Merit Aid Scholarships,* ed. Donald E. Heller and Patricia Marin, 43–56. Cambridge, Mass.: Civil Rights Project, Harvard University Press.

"Black Students Are Beginning to Seize the Early Admission Advantage." 2004. *Journal of Blacks in Higher Education* 43 (Spring). 81–85.

Bledstein, Burton J. 1976. *The Culture of Professionalism: The Middle Class and the Development of Higher Education in America.* New York: W. W. Norton.

Blumin, Stuart M. 1989. *The Emergence of the Middle Class: Social Experience in the American City, 1760–1900.* Cambridge, England: Cambridge University Press.

Bok, Derek C. 1982. *Beyond the Ivory Tower: Social Responsibilities of the Modern University.* Cambridge, Mass.: Harvard University Press.

———. 2003a. "The Uncertain Future of Race-Sensitive Admissions." Unpublished report, January 20. Available at http://www.nacua.org/documents/Unceratin_Future_of_Race_Sensitive_Admissions_Revised.pdf.

———. 2003b. "Closing the Nagging Gap in Minority Achievement." *Chronicle of Higher Education,* October 24, p. B20.

Bollag, Burton. 2003. "Grambling Regains Its Accreditation; Auburn Put on Probation for Trustee Meddling." *Chronicle of Higher Education,* December 19, p. A29.

———. 2004. "Enrollment of Foreign Students Drops in U.S." *Chronicle of Higher Education,* November 19, online edition.

Boorstin, Daniel J. 1965. *The Americans: The National Experience.* New York: Vintage Books.

Borjas, George J. 2004. "Do Foreign Students Crowd Out Native Students from Graduate Programs?" NBER Working Paper no. 10349, March.

Borman, Geoffrey D., Gina M. Hewes, Laura T. Overman, and Shelly Brown. 2002. "Comprehensive School Reform and Student Achievement: A Meta-Analysis." Center for Research on the Education of Students Placed at Risk, Technical Report no. 59, November. Available at http://www.csos.jhu.edu/crespar/techReports/Report59.pdf, accessed July 21, 2004.

Borst, Charlotte G. 2002. "Choosing the Student Body: Masculinity, Culture, and the Crisis of Medical School Admissions, 1920–1950." *History of Education Quarterly* 42, no. 2 (Summer): 181–214.

Bot, Monica. 1992. "Standard Examination Results, 1981–1991." *EduSource Data News* 1: 6.

Bound, John, and Sarah E. Turner. 2004. "Cohort Crowding: How Resources Affect Collegiate Attainment." PSC Research Report no. 04-557, April. Available at http://www.psc.isr.umich.edu/pubs/papers/rr04-557.pdf.

Bound, John, Jeffrey Groen, Gábor Kézdi, and Sarah E. Turner. 2004. "Trade in University Training: Cross-State Variation in the Production and Stock of College-Educated Labor." *Journal of Econometrics* 121, nos. 1–2 (July–August): 143–73.

Bound, John, Sarah Turner, and Patrick Walsh. 2004. "Internationalization of U.S. Doctorate Education." Working draft. November 10.

Bowen, William G. 1964. "University Finance in Britain and the United States: Implications of Financing Arrangements for Educational Issues." In *Economic Aspects of Education: Three Essays,* 41–83. Princeton, N.J.: Industrial Relations Section, Department of Economics, Princeton University.

———. 1968. *The Economics of the Major Private Universities.* Berkeley, Calif.: Carnegie Commission on Higher Education.

———. 1983. "Maintaining Opportunity: Undergraduate Financial Aid at Princeton." Report of the President, Princeton University, April.

———. 1987a. *Ever the Teacher: William G. Bowen's Writings as President of Princeton.* Princeton, N.J.: Princeton University Press.

———. 1987b. "University Education in the People's Republic of China: A Visitor's Impressions." In *Ever the Teacher: William G. Bowen's Writings as President of Princeton,* 54–72. Princeton, N.J.: Princeton University Press.

———. 2000. "At a Slight Angle to the Universe: The University in a Digitized, Commercialized Age." Romanes Lecture, University of Oxford, October 17. Reprinted by Princeton University Press, 2001.

Bowen, William G., and Derek C. Bok. 1998. *The Shape of the River: Long-Term Consequences of Considering Race in College and University Admissions.* Princeton, N.J.: Princeton University Press. (Paperback edition, 2000.)

Bowen, William G., and Sarah A. Levin. 2003. *Reclaiming the Game: College Sports and Educational Values.* Princeton, N.J.: Princeton University Press.

Bowen, William G., and Neil L. Rudenstine. 1992. *In Pursuit of the Ph.D.* Princeton, N.J.: Princeton University Press.

———. 2003. "Race-Sensitive Admissions: Back to Basics." *Chronicle of Higher Education,* February 7, pp. B7–B9.

Bowen, William G., Thomas I. Nygren, Sarah E. Turner, and Elizabeth A. Duffy. 1994. *The Charitable Nonprofits: An Analysis of Institutional Dynamics and Characteristics.* San Francisco: Jossey-Bass.

Boyer, Ernest L., and Fred M. Hechinger. 1981. *Higher Learning in the Nation's Service.* Washington, D.C.: Carnegie Foundation for the Advancement of Teaching.

Brainard, Jeffrey. 2003. "Survey of Doctoral Programs Needs Major Changes, Panel Suggests." *Chronicle of Higher Education,* January 10, p. A10.

Bratt, David W. 1999. "Southern Souls and State Schools: Religion and Public Higher Education in the Southeast, 1776–1900." PhD dissertation, Yale University.

Breland, Hunter, James Maxey, Renee Gernand, Tammie Cumming, and Catherine Trapani. 2002. *Trends in College Admission 2000: A Report of a National Survey of Undergraduate Admission Policies, Practices, and Procedures.* Alexandria, Va.: National Association for College Admission Counseling, March.

Brender, Alan. 2004. "Asia's New High Tech Tiger: South Korea's Ambitious, and Expensive, Effort to Bolster University Research Is Paying Off." *Chronicle of Higher Education,* July 23, p. A34.

Breneman, David W. 2003. "Why a Public College Wants to Send In-State Tuition Soaring." *Chronicle of Higher Education,* April 25, p. B20.

———. 2004. "Are the States and Public Higher Education Striking a New Bargain?" AGB Public Policy Paper no. 04-02, June.

Brewer, Dominic J., Eric Eide, and Ronald G. Ehrenberg. 1998. "Does It Pay to Attend an Elite Private College? Evidence on the Effects of Undergraduate College Quality on Graduate School Attendance." *Economics of Education Review* 17, no. 4 (October): 371–76.

Brinkley, Alan. 2004. "The End of an Elite." *New Republic,* June 7, online edition.

Broad, William J. 2004. "U.S. Is Losing Its Dominance in the Sciences." *New York Times,* May 3, p. A1.

Broida, Bethany. 2004. "'Gold Standard' for Rating Doctoral Programs Is Stalled." *Chronicle of Higher Education,* April 9, p. A10.

Bryce, James. 1923. *The American Commonwealth.* 2 vols. New York: Macmillan.

Bunting, Ian. 1994. *A Legacy of Inequality: Higher Education in South Africa.* Rondebosch, South Africa: University of Cape Town Press.

Burd, Stephen. 2003. "Republican Introduces Bill to Penalize Colleges for Tuition Increases." *Chronicle of Higher Education,* October 24, online edition.

———. 2004a. "Plan to Punish Big Increases in Tuition Is Dropped." *Chronicle of Higher Education,* March 12, online edition.

———. 2004b. "For-Profit Colleges Spend Big and Win Big on Capitol Hill." *Chronicle of Higher Education,* July 30, online edition.

Burke, Colin B. 1982. *American Collegiate Populations: A Test of the Traditional View.* New York: New York University Press.

Burner, David. 1968. *The Politics of Provincialism: The Democratic Party in Transition, 1918–1932.* New York: Knopf.

Burton, Nancy W., and Leonard Ramist. 2001. *Predicting Success in College: SAT Studies of Classes Graduating since 1980.* College Board Research Report no. 2001-2. New York: College Board.

Burton, Orville Vernon. 2000. "Mays, Benjamin Elijah." *American National Biography Online.* Available at http://www.anb.org/articles/home.html. Last updated February.

Bush, Vannevar. 1945. *Science: The Endless Frontier.* Washington, D.C.: U.S. Government Printing Office, July. Available at http://www.nsf.gov/od/lpa/nsf50/vbush1945.htm.

Cabell, Nathaniel Francis, ed. 1856. *Early History of the University of Virginia as Contained in the Letters of Thomas Jefferson and Joseph C. Cabell.* Richmond, Va.: J. W. Randolph.

Cahalan, Margaret W., and Natalie M. Justh. 1998. *The Status of Academic Libraries in the United States: Results from the 1994 Academic Library Survey with Historical Comparisons.* NCES 98-311. Washington, D.C.: U.S. Department of Education, Office of Educational Research and Improvement, September.

Cao, Cong. 2004. *China's Scientific Elite.* London: Routledge.

Card, David, and A. Abigail Payne. 1998. "School Finance Reform, the Distribution of School Spending, and the Distribution of SAT Scores." NBER Working Paper no. 6766, October.

Carey, Kevin. 2004. "The Funding Gap: Low-Income and Minority Students Still Receive Fewer Dollars in Many States." Washington, D.C.: The Education Trust, Fall. Available at http://www2.edtrust.org/NR/rdonlyres/30B3C1B3-3DA6-4809-AFB9-2DAACF11CF88/0/funding2004.pdf.

Carey, Nancy Lane, Natalie M. Justh, and Jeffrey W. Williams. 2003. *Academic Libraries: 2000.* NCES 2004-317. Washington, D.C.: U.S. Department of Education, National Center for Education Statistics.

Carlton, Dennis W., Gustavo E. Bamberger, and Roy J. Epstein. 1995. "Antitrust and Higher Education: Was There a Conspiracy to Restrict Financial Aid?" *RAND Journal of Economics* 26, no. 1 (Spring): 131–47.

Carnegie Commission on Higher Education. 1973. *Priorities for Action: The Final Report of the Carnegie Commission on Higher Education.* New York: Carnegie Foundation for the Advancement of Teaching.

Carneiro, Pedro, and James J. Heckman. 2003. "Human Capital Policy." In James Heckman and Alan Krueger, *Inequality in America: What Role for Human Capital Policies?* ed. Benjamin M. Friedman, 77–239. Cambridge, Mass.: MIT Press.

Carnevale, Anthony P., and Stephen J. Rose. 2004. "Socioeconomic Status, Race/Ethnicity, and Selective College Admissions." In *America's Untapped Resource: Low-Income Students in Higher Education,* ed. Richard D. Kahlenberg, 101–56. New York: Century Foundation Press.

Carson, Mina Julia. 1990. *Settlement Folk: Social Thought and the American Settlement Movement, 1885–1930.* Chicago: University of Chicago Press.

Case, Anne, Angela Fertig, and Christina Paxson. 2003. "From Cradle to Grave? The Lasting Impact of Childhood Health and Circumstance." NBER Working Paper no. 9788, June.

Case, Anne, Darren Lubotsky, and Christina Paxson. 2002. "Economic Status and Health in Childhood: The Origins of the Gradient." *American Economic Review* 92, no. 5 (December): 1303–34.

Castel, Albert. 1964. "The Founding Fathers and the Vision of a National University." *History of Education Quarterly* 4, no. 4: 280–302.

Chapman, Bruce, and Chris Ryan. 2002. "Income-Contingent Financing of Student Charges for Higher Education: Assessing the Australian Innovation." Australian National University, Centre For Economic Policy Research Discussion Paper no. 449, May.

"Charles Clarke's Statement to the Commons." 2003. *Guardian,* January 22, online edition.

Choy, Susan P., and Ali M. Berker. 2003. *How Families of Low- and Middle-Income Undergraduates Pay for College: Full-Time Dependent Students in 1999–2000.* Washington, D.C.: U.S. Department of Education, National Center for Education Statistics.

Christie, Pam. 1986. *The Right to Learn: The Struggle for Education in South Africa.* Johannesburg: The SACHED Trust.

Christy, Ralph D., and Lionel Williamson, eds. 1992. *A Century of Service: Land-Grant Colleges and Universities, 1890–1990.* New Brunswick, N.J.: Transaction Publishers.

Church, Robert L., and Michael W. Sedlak. 1997. "The Antebellum College and Academy." In *The History of Higher Education,* ed. Lester F. Goodchild and Harold S. Wechsler, 131–48. Needham Heights, Mass.: Simon & Schuster.

Cloete, N., and S. Pillay. 1987. "Can Wits Have a More Representative Student Body within the Existing Structures: Optimistic or Pessimistic?" Unpublished manuscript, University of the Witwatersrand, Johannesburg.

Clotfelter, Charles T. 1996. *Buying the Best: Cost Escalation in Elite Higher Education.* Princeton, N.J.: Princeton University Press.

Coale, Ansley J. 2000. *Ansley J. Coale: An Autobiography.* Philadelphia: American Philosophical Society.

Cohen, Jodi S. 2004. "Minority Programs Eroding on Campus." *Chicago Tribune,* September 29, p. C1.

Cohen, Lizabeth. 2003. *A Consumers' Republic: The Politics of Mass Consumption in Postwar America.* New York: Knopf.

College Board. 1983–2003. *College-Bound Seniors: National Report.* New York: Admissions Testing Program, College Board.

———. 2002–04. *Trends in College Pricing.* Washington, D.C.: College Board.

———. 2004. *Trends in Student Aid.* Washington, D.C.: College Board.

Collini, Stefan. 2003. "HiEdBiz." *London Review of Books,* November 6, online edition.

Comer, James P. 2004. *Leave No Child Behind: Preparing Today's Youth for Tomorrow's World.* New Haven, Conn.: Yale University Press.

Commager, Henry Steele. 1950. *The American Mind: An Interpretation of American Thought and Character since the 1880's.* New Haven, Conn.: Yale University Press.

Conway, Jill K. 1974. "Perspectives on the History of Women's Education in the United States." *History of Education Quarterly* 14, no. 1 (Spring): 1–12.

Cook, Michael D., and William N. Evans. 2000. "Families or Schools? Explaining the Convergence in White and Black Academic Performance." *Journal of Labor Economics* 18, no. 4 (October): 729–54.

Cooper, D., and G. Subotzky. 2001. *The Skewed Revolution: Trends in South African Higher Education.* Bellville, South Africa: Educational Policy Unit, University of the Western Cape.

Cooper, Harris, Kelly Charlton, Jeff Valentine, and Laura Muhlenbruck. 1997. "Making the Most of Summer School: A Meta-Analytic and Narrative Review." *Monographs of the Society for Research in Child Development* 65, no. 1 (serial no. 260): 1–118.

Cornwell, Christopher, and David B. Mustard. 2002. "Merit-Based College Scholarships and Car Sales." Preliminary draft, Department of Economics, University of Georgia, July 16. Available at http://www.terry.uga.edu/hope/hope.cars.pdf.

Cosenza, Mario Emilio. 1925. *The Establishment of the College of the City of New York as the Free Academy in 1847, Townsend Harris, Founder.* New York: Associate Alumni of the College of the City of New York.

Council of Australian Postgraduate Associations (CAPA). 2003. "The Social and Economic Impact of Student Debt." CAPA research paper, March.

Council on Higher Education (South Africa). 2000. *Towards a New Higher Education Landscape: Meeting the Equity, Quality and Social Development Imperatives of South Africa in the 21st Century.* Pretoria: Council on Higher Education.

Cremin, Lawrence A. 1970, 1980, and 1988. *American Education,* 3 vols. New York: Harper and Row.

Cremin, Lawrence A., ed. 1957. *The Republic and the School: Horace Mann on the Education of Free Men.* New York: Teachers College, Columbia University.

Crouch, Luis A., and Thabo Mabogoane. 1997. "Aspects of Internal Efficiency Indicators in South African Schools: Analysis of Historical and Current Data." *EduSource Data News* 19: 4–28.

Cullen, Julie Berry. 1999. "The Impact of Fiscal Incentives on Student Disability Rates." NBER Working Paper no. 7173, June.

Cullen, Julie Berry, Brian A. Jacob, and Steven Levitt. 2003. "The Effect of School Choice on Student Outcomes: Evidence from Randomized Lotteries." NBER Working Paper no. 10113, November.

Currie, Janet, and Mark Stabile. 2002. "Socioeconomic Status and Health: Why Is the Relationship Stronger for Older Children?" NBER Working Paper no. 9098, August.

Currie, Janet, and Duncan Thomas. 1995. "Does Head Start Make a Difference?" *American Economic Review* 85, no. 3 (June): 341–64.

———. 1999. "The Intergenerational Transmission of 'Intelligence' Down the Slippery Slopes of *The Bell Curve.*" *Industrial Relations* 38, no. 3 (July): 297–330.

———. 2000. "School Quality and the Longer-Term Effects of Head Start." *Journal of Human Resources* 35, no. 4 (Autumn): 755–74.

Dale, Stacy Berg, and Alan B. Krueger. 2002. "Estimating the Payoff to Attending a More Selective College: An Application of Selection on Observables and Unobservables." *Quarterly Journal of Economics* 117, no. 4 (November): 1491–527.

Daniels, Roger. 2004. *Guarding the Golden Door: American Immigration Policy and Immigrants since 1882.* New York: Hill and Wang.

David, Henry, ed. 1960. *Education and Manpower.* New York: Columbia University Press.

Davis, Allen Freeman. 1984. *Spearheads for Reform: The Social Settlements and the Progressive Movement, 1890–1914*, 2d ed. New Brunswick, N.J.: Rutgers University Press.

Day, Jennifer Cheeseman, and Eric C. Newburger. 2002. "The Big Payoff: Educational Attainment and Synthetic Estimates of Work-Life Earnings." Current Population Report no. P23-210. U.S. Census Bureau, July. Available at http://www.census.gov/prod/2002pubs/p23-210.pdf.

Dee, Thomas S. 2004. "Are There Civic Returns to Education?" *Journal of Public Economics* 88 (August): 1697–720.

"Degrees of Access: Universities Cannot Make Up for Poorly Performing Schools." 2003. *Financial Times,* January 23, p. 18.

DeLong, J. Bradford, Claudia Goldin, and Lawrence F. Katz. 2003. "Sustaining U.S. Economic Growth." In *Agenda for the Nation,* ed. Henry J. Aaron, James M. Lindsay, and Pietro S. Nivola, 17–60. Washington, D.C.: Brookings Institution Press.

Department for Education and Skills (DfES). 2003. *Widening Participation in Higher Education.* London: DfES, April. Available at http://www.dfes.gov.uk/hegateway/uploads/White%20Pape.pdf. Accessed November 14, 2004.

———. 2004. "Future of Universities Secured Today as Higher Education Act Is Approved by Parliament–Clarke." Press Notice no. 2004/0127, DfES, July 1. Available at http://www.dfes.gov.uk/pns/DisplayPN.cgi?pn_id=2004_0127.

Dewey, John. 1997. *Democracy and Education: An Introduction to the Philosophy of Education.* New York: Free Press.

Diamond, Nancy, and Hugh Davis Graham. 2004. "How Should We Rate Research Universities?" Available at http://www.vanderbilt.edu/AnS/history/graham/change.htm. Accessed August 24.

Dowd, Maureen. 2003. "Could Thomas Be Right?" *New York Times,* June 25, p. A25.

Downes, Thomas A., and David N. Figlio. 1997. "School Finance Reform, Tax Limits, and Student Performance: Do Reforms Level Up or Dumb Down?" Unpublished working paper, Department of Economics, University of Oregon, February. Later released as Institute for Research on Poverty Discussion Paper no. 1142–97, September 1997.

Doyle, William. 2001. *An American Insurrection: The Battle of Oxford, Mississippi, 1962.* New York: Doubleday.

Drewry, Henry, and Humphrey Doermann. 2001. *Stand and Prosper: Private Black Colleges and Their Students.* Princeton, N.J.: Princeton University Press.

Du Bois, W. E. B. 2001. *The Education of Black People: Ten Critiques, 1906–1960,* ed. Herbert Aptheker. New York: Monthly Review Press

Duffy, Elizabeth A., and Idana Goldberg. 1998. *Crafting a Class: College Admissions and Financial Aid, 1955–1994.* Princeton, N.J.: Princeton University Press.

Dworkin, Ronald. 1998. "Affirming Affirmative Action." *New York Review of Books* 45, no. 16 (October 22): 91–102.

Dynarski, Susan M. 2004a. "The New Merit Aid." In *College Choices: The Economics of Where to Go, When to Go, and How to Pay for It,* ed. Caroline M. Hoxby, 63–100. Chicago: University of Chicago Press.

———. 2004b. "Who Benefits from the Education Saving Incentives? Income, Educational Expectations, and the Value of the 529 and Coverdell." NBER Working Paper no. 10470, May.

Easterlin, Richard A. 1981. "Why Isn't the Whole World Developed?" *Journal of Economic History* 41, no. 1 (March): 1–19.

Ellwood, David T., and Thomas J. Kane. 2000. "Who Is Getting a College Education? Family Background and the Growing Gaps in Enrollment." In *Securing the Future: Investing in Children from Birth to College,* ed. Sheldon Danziger and Jane Waldfogel, 283–324. New York: Russell Sage Foundation.

Ellwood, Marilyn, Angela Merrill, and Wendy Conroy. 2003. *SCHIP's Steady Enrollment Growth Continues: Final Report.* MPR no. 8644–500. Cambridge, Mass.: Mathematica Policy Research, May.

Entwisle, Doris R., Karl L. Alexander, and Linda Steffel Olson. 1997. *Children, Schools, and Inequality.* Boulder, Colo.: Westview Press.

Epple, Dennis, and Richard E. Romano. 1998. "Competition between Private and Public Schools, Vouchers, and Peer-Group Effects." *American Economic Review* 88, no. 1 (March): 33–62.

———. 2002. "Educational Vouchers and Cream Skimming." NBER Working Paper no. 9354, November.

"Equality or Efficiency?" 2003. *Economist,* January 25, p. 32.

Espenshade, Thomas J., Chang Y. Chung, and Joan L. Walling. 2004. "Admission Preferences for Minority Students, Athletes, and Legacies at Elite Universities." *Social Science Quarterly* 85, no. 5 (December): 1422–46.

Fass, Paula S. 1989. *Outside In: Minorities and the Transformation of American Education.* New York: Oxford University Press.

Federal Interagency Forum on Child and Family Statistics. 2002. "America's Children: Key National Indicators of Well-Being, 2002." Washington, D.C.: Federal Interagency Forum on Child and Family Statistics, U.S. Government Printing Office. Available at http://childstats.gov/ac2002/pdf/ac2002.pdf.

Federal Security Agency, Office of Education. 1951. *Vitalizing Secondary Education.* Report of the First Commission on Life Adjustment Education for Youth. Washington, D.C.: Federal Security Agency, Office of Education.

Federman, Maya, Thesia I. Garner, Kathleen Short, W. Bornan Cutter, IV, John Kiely, David Levine, Duane McGough, and Marilyn McMillen. 1996. "What Does It Mean to Be Poor in America?" *Monthly Labor Review* 119, no. 5 (May): 3–17.

Ferleger, Louis, and William Lazonick. 1994. "Higher Education for an Innovative Economy: Land-Grant Colleges and the Managerial Revolution in America." *Business and Economic History* 23, no. 1 (Fall): 116–28.

"Few Are Chosen; British Education." 2004. *Economist,* July 3, p. 15.

Field, Kelly. 2004. "U.S. Government Considers Extending Security Clearances for Foreign Students and Scholars." *Chronicle of Higher Education,* August 30, online edition.

Figlio, David N., and Lawrence S. Getzler. 2002. "Accountability, Ability, and Disability: Gaming the System." NBER Working Paper no. 9307, October.

Findlay, James. 1977. "The SPCTEW and Western Colleges: Religion and Higher Education in Mid-Nineteenth Century America." *History of Education Quarterly* 17, no. 1 (Spring): 31–62.

———. 2000. "Agency, Denominations, and the Western Colleges, 1830–1860: Some Connections between Evangelicalism and American Higher Education."

In *The American College in the Nineteenth Century,* ed. Roger L. Geiger, 115–26. Nashville, Tenn.: Vanderbilt University Press.

Fisher, G., and I. Scott. 1993. "Approaches to the Development of Intermediate Post-Secondary Education in South Africa." *South African Journal of Higher Education* 7, no. 1 (Research Supplement): 43–58.

Fitzgerald, Robert A. 2000. *College Quality and the Earnings of Recent College Graduates.* NCES 2000-043. Washington, D.C.: U.S. Department of Education, National Center for Education Statistics, August. Available at http://nces .ed.gov/pubs2000/2000043.pdf.

Fletcher, Michael A. 2003. "MIT to End Programs' Racial Exclusiveness: Nonminority Students to Be Accepted." *Washington Post,* February 12, p. A03.

Fletcher, Robert Samuel. 1943. *A History of Oberlin College from Its Foundation through the Civil War.* 2 vols. Oberlin, Ohio: Oberlin College Press.

Frankel, Jeffrey A., and Peter R. Orszag, eds. 2002. *American Economic Policy in the 1990s.* Cambridge, Mass.: MIT Press.

Frankenberg, Erica, and Chungmei Lee. 2002. "Race in American Public Schools: Rapidly Resegregating School Districts." Cambridge, Mass.: Civil Rights Project, Harvard University, August. Available at http://www.civilrightsproject .harvard.edu/research/ deseg/Race_in_American_Public_Schools1.pdf.

Frederiksen, Norman, and William Benton Schrader. 1951. *Adjustment to College: A Study of 10,000 Veteran and Nonveteran Students in Sixteen American Colleges.* Princeton, N.J.: Educational Testing Service.

Freedman, Samuel G. 2004. "Report Offers No Clear Victory for Charter School Opponents." *New York Times,* August 25, p. B8.

Freeman, Richard B., Emily Jin, and Chia-Yu Shen. 2004. "Where Do New US-Trained Science-Engineering PhDs Come From?" NBER Working Paper no. 10554, June.

Fryer, Roland G., Jr., and Steven D. Levitt. 2004. "Understanding the Black-White Test Score Gap in the First Two Years of School." *Review of Economics and Statistics* 86, no. 2 (May): 447–64.

Fryer, Roland G., Jr., Glenn C. Loury, and Tolga Yuret. 2003. "Color-Blind Affirmative Action." NBER Working Paper no. 10103, November.

Galambos, Louis. 1970. "The Emerging Organizational Synthesis in Modern American History." *Business History Review* 44, no. 3 (Autumn): 279–90.

Garcia, J. L. A., John McWhorter, and Glenn Loury. 2002. "Race & Inequality: An Exchange." *First Things* 123 (May): 22–40.

Geiger, Roger L. 2000a. "The Crisis of the Old Order: The Colleges in the 1890s." In *The American College in the Nineteenth Century,* ed. Roger L. Geiger, 264–76. Nashville, Tenn.: Vanderbilt University Press.

———. 2000b. "The Era of Multipurpose Colleges in American Higher Education, 1850–1980." In *The American College in the Nineteenth Century,* ed. Roger L. Geiger, 127–68. Nashville, Tenn.: Vanderbilt University Press.

———. 2000c. "Introduction: New Themes in the History of Nineteenth-Century Colleges." In *The American College in the Nineteenth Century,* ed. Roger L. Geiger, 1–36. Nashville, Tenn.: Vanderbilt University Press.

———. 2000d. "The Rise and Fall of Useful Knowledge: Higher Education for Science, Agriculture, and the Mechanic Arts, 1850–1875." In *The American Col-*

lege in the Nineteenth Century, ed. Roger L. Geiger, 153–68. Nashville, Tenn.: Vanderbilt University Press.

———. 2000e. "The 'Superior Instruction of Women' 1836–1890." In *The American College in the Nineteenth Century,* ed. Roger L. Geiger, 183–95. Nashville, Tenn.: Vanderbilt University Press.

Geiger, Roger L., ed. 2000. *The American College in the Nineteenth Century.* Nashville, Tenn.: Vanderbilt University Press.

Gilreath, James, ed. 1999. *Thomas Jefferson and the Education of a Citizen.* Washington, D.C.: Library of Congress.

Givler, Peter. 2002. "University Press Publishing in the United States." In *Scholarly Publishing: Books, Journals, Publishers and Libraries in the Twentieth Century,* ed. Richard E. Abel and Lyman W. Newlin, 107–20. New York: Wiley.

Glater, Jonathan D. 2004. "Diversity Plan Shaped in Texas Is Under Attack." *New York Times,* June 13, section 1, p. 1.

Glenn, David. 2004a. "Minority Students Fare Better at Selective Colleges, Sociologists Find." *Chronicle of Higher Education,* August 16, online edition.

———. 2004b. "New Book Accuses Education Dept. of Research Errors That Skewed Policy Making." *Chronicle of Higher Education,* July 9, online edition.

Goedegebuure, Leo, Frans Kaiser, Peter Maassen, Lynn Meek, Frans van Vught, and Egbert de Weert, eds. 1994. *Higher Education Policy: An International Comparative Perspective.* Oxford: Pergamon.

Goetz, Kristina. 2004. "Miami U. Raises Tuition 8.5%." *Cincinnati Enquirer,* February 28, p. 1A.

Goldberg, David J. 1999. *Discontented America: The United States in the 1920s.* Baltimore: Johns Hopkins University Press.

Golden, Daniel. 2003a. "Admissions Preferences Given to Alumni Children Draws Fire." *Wall Street Journal,* January 15, online edition.

———. 2003b. "Many Colleges Bend Rules to Admit Rich Applicants." *Wall Street Journal,* February 20, online edition.

———. 2003c. "For Five Supreme Court Justices, Affirmative Action Isn't Academic." *Wall Street Journal,* May 14, online edition.

———. 2003d. "Bill Would Make College Report Legacies and Early Admissions." *Wall Street Journal,* October 23, online edition.

———. 2003e. "Colleges Cut Back Minority Programs after Court Rulings." *Wall Street Journal,* December 30, online edition.

Goldin, Claudia. 1998. "America's Graduation from High School: The Evolution and Spread of Secondary Schooling in the Twentieth Century." *Journal of Economic History* 58, no. 2 (June): 345–74.

Goldin, Claudia, and Lawrence F. Katz. 1999. "The Shaping of Higher Education: The Formative Years in the United States, 1890 to 1940." *Journal of Economic Perspectives* 13, no. 1 (Winter): 37–62.

———. 2003. "The 'Virtues' of the Past: Education in the First Hundred Years of the New Republic." NBER Working Paper no. 9958, September.

Goldstein, Joel K. 2004. "Beyond *Bakke: Grutter-Gratz* and the Promise of *Brown.*" *Saint Louis University Law Journal* 48, no. 3 (Spring): 899–954.

Goodchild, Lester F., and Harold S. Wechsler, eds. 1997. *The History of Higher Education.* Needham Heights, Mass.: Simon & Schuster.

Gordon, Lynn D. 1986. "Annie Nathan Meyer and Barnard College: Mission and Identity in Women's Higher Education, 1889–1950." *History of Education Quarterly* 26, no. 4 (Winter): 503–22.

Gorelick, Sherry. 1981. *City College and the Jewish Poor: Education in New York, 1880–1924*. New Brunswick, N.J.: Rutgers University Press.

Gose, Ben. 1999. "More Points for 'Strivers': The New Affirmative Action?" *Chronicle of Higher Education,* September 17, online edition.

Graham, Patricia Albjerg. 1978. "Expansion and Exclusion: A History of Women in American Higher Education." *Signs* 3, no. 4: 759–73.

Greenhouse, Linda. 2003a. "The Supreme Court: Affirmative Action: Justices Back Affirmative Action by 5 to 4, but Wider Vote Bans a Racial Point System." *New York Times,* June 24, p. 1.

———. 2003b. "The Supreme Court: The Justices: Context and the Court." *New York Times,* June 25, p. A1.

Griesel, H. 1991. "Access to University: A Review of Selection Procedures." Unpublished manuscript, University of Natal, Durban, South Africa.

———. 1999. *Access and the Higher Education Sector: A South African Case Study on Innovative Policy and Programmes*. Pretoria: Association for the Development of Education in Africa and South African Department of Education.

Grigg, Wendy S., Mary C. Daane, Ying Jin, and Jay R. Campbell. 2003. *The Nation's Report Card: Reading 2002*. NCES 2003-521. Washington, D.C.: U.S. Department of Education, Institute of Education Sciences, National Center for Education Statistics, June. Available at http://nces.ed.gov/nationsreportcard/pdf/main2002/2003521a.pdf, accessed June 24, 2004.

Grissmer, David, Ann Flanagan, and Stephanie Williamson. 1998. "Why Did the Black-White Score Gap Narrow in the 1970s and 1980s?" In *The Black-White Test Score Gap,* ed. Christopher Jencks and Meredith Phillips, 198–222. Washington, D.C.: Brookings Institution Press.

Groen, Jeffrey A. 2004. "The Effect of College Location on Migration of College-Educated Labor." *Journal of Econometrics* 121: 125–41.

Gurin, Patricia, with Gerald Gurin, Eric L. Dey, and Sylvia Hurtado. 2004. "The Educational Value of Diversity." In *Defending Diversity: Affirmative Action at the University of Michigan,* by Patricia Gurin, Jeffrey S. Lehman, and Earl Lewis, with Gerald Gurin, Eric L. Dey, and Sylvia Hurtado, 97–188. Ann Arbor: University of Michigan Press.

Gurin, Patricia, Jeffrey S. Lehman, and Earl Lewis, with Gerald Gurin, Eric L. Dey and Sylvia Hurtado. 2004. *Defending Diversity: Affirmative Action at the University of Michigan*. Ann Arbor: University of Michigan Press.

Guryan, Jonathan. 2001. "Desegregation and Black Dropout Rates." NBER Working Paper no. 8345, June.

Halberstam, David. 2003. *The Teammates*. New York: Hyperion.

Hall, Frances R., Collins Mikesell, Pamela Cranston, Ellen Julian, and Carol Elam. 2001. "Longitudinal Trends in the Applicant Pool for U.S. Medical Schools, 1974–1999." *Academic Medicine* 76, no. 8 (August): 829–34.

Hall, Martin. 2003. "Boundary Institutions: Universities and Social Change." Discussion paper, University of Cape Town.

Hall, Peter Dobkin. 1982. *The Organization of American Culture, 1700–1900: Private*

Institutions, Elites, and the Origins of American Nationality. New York: New York University Press.

———. 2000. "Noah Porter Writ Large? Reflections on the Modernization of American Education and Its Critics, 1866–1916." In *The American College in the Nineteenth Century,* ed. Roger L. Geiger, 196–220. Nashville, Tenn.: Vanderbilt University Press.

Halpin, Tony. 2003a. "Oxbridge Alarm at Quotas." *Times* (London), January 23, p. 4.

———. 2003b. "Universities 'Must Show They Are Open to All.'" *Times* (London), April 9, p. 15.

Halsey, John F., and W. Bruce Leslie. 2003. "Britain's White Paper Turns Higher Education Away from the EU." *International Higher Education* 32 (Summer): 10–12.

Handlin, Oscar. 1957. *Race and Nationality in American Life.* Garden City, N.Y.: Doubleday.

Hansen, W. Lee, and Burton Weisbrod. 1969. "The Distribution of Costs and Direct Benefits of Public Higher Education." *Journal of Human Resources* 4 (Spring): 176–91.

Hanushek, Eric A. 2002. "The Failure of Input-Based Schooling Policies." NBER Working Paper no. 9040, July.

Hanushek, Eric A., and Margaret E. Raymond. 2004. "Does School Accountability Lead to Improved Student Performance?" NBER Working Paper no. 10591, June.

Hanushek, Eric A., and Steven G. Rivkin. 2003. "Does Public School Competition Affect Teacher Quality?" In *The Economics of School Choice,* ed. Caroline M. Hoxby, 23–47. Chicago: University of Chicago Press.

Hanushek, Eric A., John F. Kain, Jacob M. Markman, and Steven G. Rivkin. 2003. "Does Peer Ability Affect Student Achievement?" *Journal of Applied Econometrics* 18, no. 5 (September–October): 527–44.

Haskins, Ron, and Isabel Sawhill. 2003. "The Future of Head Start." Brookings Institute Policy Brief no. 27: Welfare Reform and Beyond Brief, July.

Hatch, Louis Clinton. 1927. *The History of Bowdoin College.* Portland, Me.: Southworth Press.

Healy, Patrick. 2003. "Justice's 'Deadline' Confounds Colleges." *Boston Globe,* June 29, p. A1.

Hebel, Sara. 2002. "Virginia Governor Announces Budget Cuts for Public Colleges." *Chronicle of Higher Education,* October 17, online edition.

———. 2004a. "Segregation's Legacy Still Troubles Campuses." *Chronicle of Higher Education,* May 14, p. A24.

———. 2004b. "California Governor's Revised Budget Keeps Tuition Increases and Many University Cuts." *Chronicle of Higher Education,* May 17, online edition.

Heckman, James J. 1995. "Lessons from the Bell Curve." *Journal of Political Economy* 103, no. 5 (October): 1091–120.

Heckman, James J., and Alan B. Krueger. 2003. *Inequality in America: What Role for Human Capital Policies?* Ed. Benjamin M. Friedman. Cambridge, Mass.: MIT Press.

Hedges, Larry V., and Amy Nowell. 1998. "Black-White Test Score Convergence since 1965." In *The Black-White Test Score Gap,* ed. Christopher Jencks and Meredith Phillips, 149–81. Washington, D.C.: Brookings Institution Press.

Heller, Donald E. 2004. "Pell Grant Recipients in Selective Colleges and Universities." In *America's Untapped Resources: Low Income Students in Higher Education,* ed. Richard D. Kahlenberg, 157–66. New York: Century Foundation Press.

Heller, Donald E., and Patricia Marin, eds. 2002. *Who Should We Help? The Negative Social Consequences of Merit Aid Scholarships.* Cambridge, Mass.: Civil Rights Project, Harvard University Press.

Herbold, Hilary. 1994. "Never a Level Playing Field: Blacks and the G.I. Bill." *Journal of Blacks in Higher Education* 6 (Winter): 104–8.

Herbst, Jurgen. 1997. "From Religion to Politics: Debates and Confrontations over American College Governance in Mid-Eighteenth Century America." In *The History of Higher Education,* ed. Lester F. Goodchild and Harold S. Wechsler, 53–71. Needham Heights, Mass.: Simon & Schuster.

Herrnstein, Richard J., and Charles A. Murray. 1994. *The Bell Curve: Intelligence and Class Structure in American Life.* New York: Free Press.

Higham, John. 1988. *Strangers in the Land: Patterns of American Nativism, 1860–1925,* 2d ed. New Brunswick, N.J.: Rutgers University Press. Originally published in 1955.

Higher Education Research Institute. 1981. *The American Freshman: National Norms for 1981.* Los Angeles: Higher Education Research Institute.

———. 1989. *The American Freshman: National Norms for 1989.* Los Angeles: Higher Education Research Institute.

———. 1995. *The American Freshman: National Norms for 1995.* Los Angeles: Higher Education Research Institute.

———. 2002. *The American Freshman: National Norms for 2002.* Los Angeles: Higher Education Research Institute.

"Higher Education White Paper: From Student Grants to Tuition Fees." 2003. *Guardian,* January 23, p. 11

Hill, Catharine, Gordon Winston, and Stephanie Boyd. 2003. "Affordability: Family Incomes and Net Prices at Highly Selective Private Colleges and Universities." Williams Project on the Economics of Higher Education Discussion Paper no. 66, October.

Hoffer, Thomas B., Scott Sederstrom, Lance Selfa, Vince Welch, Mary Hess, Shana Brown, Sergio Reyes, Kristy Webber, and Isabel Guzman-Barron. 2003. *Doctorate Recipients from United States Universities: Summary Report 2002.* Chicago: National Opinion Research Center.

Hofmeyr, J., and R. Spence. 1989. "Bridges to the Future." *Optima* 37, no. 1: 37–48.

Hofstadter, Richard. 1961. *Academic Freedom in the Age of the College.* New York: Columbia University Press.

———. 1970. *Anti-Intellectualism in American Life.* New York: Knopf. Reprint of 1963 ed.

Hofstadter, Richard, and Walter P. Metzger. 1955. *The Development of Academic Freedom in the United States.* New York: Columbia University Press.

Hofstadter, Richard, and Wilson Smith, eds. 1961. *American Higher Education: A Documentary History.* 2 vols. Chicago: University of Chicago Press.

Holmes, George M., Jeff DeSimone, and Nicholas G. Rupp. 2003. "Does School Choice Increase School Quality?" NBER Working Paper no. 9683, May.

Honeywell, Roy J. 1964. *The Educational Work of Thomas Jefferson.* New York: Russell & Russell. Reissue of a Harvard University Press monograph from 1931.

Hoover, Eric. 2001. "28 Private Colleges Agree to Use Common Approaches to Student Aid." *Chronicle of Higher Education,* July 20, p. A33.

Horn, Laura, and Katharin Peter. 2003. *What Colleges Contribute: Institutional Aid to Full-Time Undergraduates Attending 4-Year Colleges and Universities.* NCES 2003-157. Washington, D.C.: U.S. Department of Education, National Center for Education Statistics, April.

Horowitz, Helen Lefkowitz. 1986. *Alma Mater: Design and Experience in the Women's Colleges from Their Nineteenth-Century Beginnings to the 1930s.* Boston: Beacon Press.

Horton, James Oliver. 1985. "Black Education at Oberlin College: A Controversial Commitment." *Journal of Negro Education* 54, no. 4: 477–99.

Howard, Marjorie. 2003. "A Great University: It's Time to Take 'Prudent Risks,' President Says." *Tufts Journal,* April, online edition.

Howell, Cameron, and Sarah E. Turner. 2003. "Legacies in Black and White: The Racial Composition of the Legacy Pool." NBER Working Paper no. 9448, January.

Hoxby, Caroline M. 1996. "How Teachers' Unions Affect Education Production." *Quarterly Journal of Economics* 111, no. 3 (August): 671–718.

———. 1998a. "Tax Incentives for Higher Education." In *Tax Policy and the Economy,* ed. James M. Poterba, 49–81. Cambridge, Mass.: MIT Press.

———. 1998b. "The Return to Attending a More Selective College: 1960 to the Present." Harvard University. Available at http://post.economics.harvard.edu/faculty/hoxby/ papers/whole.pdf.

———. 1999. "The Effects of School Choice on Curriculum and Atmosphere." In *Earning and Learning: How Schools Matter,* ed. Susan Mayer and Paul Peterson, 281–316. Washington, D.C.: Brookings Institution Press.

———. 2000a. "Testimony Prepared for U.S. Senate, Committee on Governmental Affairs, Hearing on 'The Rising Cost of College Tuition and the Effectiveness of Government Financial Aid.'" In Senate Committee on Governmental Affairs, *Rising Cost of College Tuition and the Effectiveness of Government Financial Aid: Hearings.* 106th Cong., 2d sess., 2000 (S. Hrg. 106-515, February 9), pp. 120–28.

———. 2000b. "The Effects of Geographic Integration and Increasing Competition in the Market for College Education." Revision of NBER Working Paper no. 6323. Harvard University, May.

———. 2000c. "Benevolent Colluders? The Effects of Antitrust Action on College Financial Aid and Tuition." NBER Working Paper no. 7754, June.

———. 2000d. "Peer Effects in the Classroom: Learning from Gender and Race Variation." NBER Working Paper no. 7867, August.

———. 2000e. "Does Competition among Public Schools Benefit Students and Taxpayers?" *American Economic Review* 90, no. 5 (December): 1209–38.

———. 2001. "All School Finance Equalizations Are Not Created Equal." *Quarterly Journal of Economics* 116, no. 4 (November): 1189–231.

———. 2003a. "School Choice and School Competition: Evidence from the United States." *Swedish Economic Policy Review* 10, no. 2: 9–65.

———. 2003b. "School Choice and School Productivity: Could School Choice Be a Rising Tide that Lifts All Boats?" In *The Economics of School Choice,* ed. Hoxby, 287–341. Chicago: University of Chicago Press.

———. 2004. "A Straightforward Comparison of Charter Schools and Regular Public Schools in the United States." Department of Economics, Harvard University, September. Available at http://post.economics.harvard.edu/faculty/hoxby/papers/hoxbyallcharters.pdf.

Hoxby, Caroline M., ed. 2003. *The Economics of School Choice.* Chicago: University of Chicago Press.

———. 2004. *College Choices: The Economics of Where to Go, When to Go, and How to Pay for It.* Chicago: University of Chicago Press.

Hoxby, Caroline M., and Ilyana Kuziemko. 2004. "Robin Hood and His Not-So-Merry Plan: Capitalization and the Self-Destruction of Texas' School Finance Equalization Plan." Department of Economics, Harvard University, February (updated July). Available at http://post.economics.harvard.edu/faculty/hoxby/papers/txpaper.pdf.

Hoxby, Caroline M., and Jonah E. Rockoff. 2004. "Impact of Charter Schools on Student Achievement." May. Available at http://post.economics.harvard.edu/faculty/hoxby/papers/hoxbyrockoffcharters.pdf.

Hrabowski, Freeman A. 2003. "Supporting the Talented Tenth: The Role of Research Universities in Promoting Higher Achievement among Minor in Science and Engineering." David Dodds Henry Lecture, University of Illinois at Urbana-Champaign, November 5.

Hrabowski, Freeman A., Kenneth I. Maton, and Geoffrey L. Greif. 1998. *Beating the Odds: Raising Academically Successful African American Males.* New York: Oxford University Press.

Hrabowski, Freeman A., Kenneth I. Maton, Monica L. Greene, and Geoffrey L. Greif. 2002. *Overcoming the Odds: Raising Academically Successful African American Young Women.* New York: Oxford University Press.

Humphries, Frederick S. 1992. "Land-Grant Institutions: Their Struggle for Survival and Equality." In *A Century of Service: Land-Grant Colleges and Universities, 1890–1990,* ed. Ralph D. Christy and Lionel Williamson, 3–12. New Brunswick, N.J.: Transaction Publishers.

Hunter, P. 1989. "The Transformation of Learning: The Evolution of an Academic Support Programme." *South African Journal of Higher Education* 3, no. 2: 68–75.

Immerwahr, John. 2004. *Public Attitudes on Higher Education: A Trend Analysis, 1993 to 2003.* National Center Report no. 04-2. Prepared by Public Agenda for the National Center for Public Policy and Higher Education, February.

Independent Committee of Inquiry into Student Finance. 1999. "Student Finance: Fairness for the Future." Independent Committee of Inquiry, Edinburgh, December. Available at http://www.esib.org/links/cubie_full_report.pdf. Accessed August 4, 2004.

Jacob, Brian A. 2002. "Accountability, Incentives, and Behavior: The Impact of High-Stakes Testing in the Chicago Public Schools." NBER Working Paper no. 8968, June.

Jacob, Brian A., and Lars Lefgren. 2002. "Remedial Education and Student Achievement: A Regression-Discontinuity Analysis." NBER Working Paper no. 8918, May.

Jacobson, Jennifer. 2003. "Foreign-Student Enrollment Stagnates." *Chronicle of Higher Education,* November 7, online edition.

Jargowsky, Paul A. 1996. "Take the Money and Run: Economic Segregation in U.S. Metropolitan Areas." *American Sociological Review* 61, no. 6 (December): 984–98.

Jaschik, Scott. 2004. "Affirmative Reactions: A Year after the Supreme Court Upheld Affirmative Action at the University of Michigan, Why Has Minority Enrollment Gone Down?" *Boston Globe,* June 13, p. H1.

Jefferson, Thomas. 1892–99. *The Writings of Thomas Jefferson.* 10 vols. Ed. Paul L. Ford. New York.

———. 1984. *Writings.* Selected by Merrill D. Peterson. New York: Library of America .

Jencks, Christopher, and Meredith Phillips, eds. 1998. *The Black-White Test Score Gap.* Washington, D.C.: Brookings Institution Press.

Jenkins, Robert L. 1991. "The Black Land-Grant Colleges in Their Formative Years, 1890–1920." *Agricultural History* 65, no. 2: 63–72.

Jobbins, David. 2004. "Who Really Counts?" *Times Higher Education Supplement,* June 11, p. 1.

Johanek, Michael C., ed. 2001. *A Faithful Mirror: Reflections on the College Board and Education in America.* New York: College Board.

Johnson, Amy W. 1996. *An Evaluation of the Long-Term Impacts of the Sponsor-a-Scholar Program on Student Performance.* Princeton, N.J.: Mathematica Policy Research.

Johnson, Eldon L. 1997. "Misconceptions about the Early Land Grant Colleges." In *The History of Higher Education,* ed. Lester F. Goodchild and Harold S. Wechsler, 222–33. Needham Heights, Mass.: Simon & Schuster.

Johnson, Susan Moore, and Susan M. Kardos. 2000. "Reform Bargaining and Its Promise for School Improvement." In *Conflicting Missions? Teachers Unions and Educational Reform,* ed. Tom Loveless, 7–46. Washington, D.C.: Brookings Institution Press.

Jones, Calvin C. 2002. "A Report to the American Academy: Evaluation of Existing Datasets for Policy Research on Humanities Fields." In *Making the Humanities Count: The Importance of Data,* by Robert M. Solow, Francis Oakley, Phyllis Franklin, John D'Arms, and Calvin C. Jones, 25–99. Cambridge, Mass.: American Academy of Arts & Sciences.

Jones, Maldwyn Allen. 1992. *American Immigration.* Chicago: University of Chicago Press.

Kabaservice, Geoffrey M. 2004. *The Guardians: Kingman Brewster, His Circle, and the Rise of the Liberal Establishment.* New York: Henry Holt.

Kaestle, Carl F. 1973. *The Evolution of an Urban School System: New York City, 1750–1850.* Cambridge, Mass.: Harvard University Press.

Kahlenberg, Richard D. 1996. *The Remedy: Class, Race, and Affirmative Action.* New York: Basic Books.

———. 2004. "Toward Affirmative Action for Economic Diversity." *Chronicle of Higher Education,* March 19, p. B11.

Kahlenberg, Richard D., ed. 2004. *America's Untapped Resource: Low-Income Students in Higher Education.* New York: Century Foundation Press.

Kane, Thomas J. 1998. "Racial and Ethnic Preferences in College Admissions." In *The Black-White Test Score Gap*, ed. Christopher Jencks and Meredith Phillips, 431–56. Washington, D.C.: Brookings Institution Press.

———. 1999. *The Price of Admission: Rethinking How Americans Pay for College*. Washington, D.C.: Brookings Institution Press.

———. 2003. "A Quasi-Experimental Estimate of the Impact of Financial Aid on College-Going." NBER Working Paper no. 9703, November.

Kane, Thomas J., and Peter R. Orszag. 2003. "Funding Restrictions at Public Universities: Effects and Policy Implications." Brookings Institution Working Paper. Mimeo. September.

Kane, Thomas J., Peter R. Orszag, and David L. Gunter. 2003. "State Fiscal Constraints and Higher Education: The Role of Medicaid and the Business Cycle." Discussion Paper no. 11, May.

Kapp, R. 2000a. "'Reading on the Line' in a South African English Second Language Literature Class." Unpublished manuscript, University of Cape Town.

———. 2000b. "'With English You Can Go Everywhere': An Analysis of the Role and Status of English at a Former DET School." *South African Journal of Education* 25: 227–59.

Karabel, Jerome. 1984. "Status-Group Struggle, Organizational Interests, and the Limits of Institutional Autonomy: The Transformation of Harvard, Yale, and Princeton, 1918–1940." *Theory and Society* 13, no. 1 (January): 1–40.

Katz, Lawrence F., Jeffrey R. Kling, and Jeffrey B. Liebman. 2000. "Moving to Opportunity in Boston: Early Results of a Randomized Mobility Experiment." NBER Working Paper no. 7973, October. Final version published in *Quarterly Journal of Economics* (May 2001): 607–54.

Katz, Michael S. 1976. *A History of Compulsory Education Laws*. Bloomington, Ind.: Phi Delta Kappa Educational Foundation.

Keller, Morton. 1994. *Regulating a New Society: Public Policy and Social Change in America, 1900–1933*. Cambridge, Mass.: Harvard University Press.

Kennedy, David M. 1999. *Freedom from Fear: The American People in Depression and War, 1929–1945*. New York: Oxford University Press.

Kerr, Janet C. 1997. "From Truman to Johnson: Ad Hoc Policy Formulation in Higher Education." In *The History of Higher Education*, ed. Lester F. Goodchild and Harold S. Wechsler, 628–52. Needham Heights, Mass.: Simon & Schuster.

Key, Scott. 1996. "Economics or Education: The Establishment of American Land-Grant Universities." *Journal of Higher Education* 67, no. 2 (March–April): 196–220.

Khanyile, Vusi. 1986. Untitled keynote address presented at the 1986 Academic Support Programmes Conference. *Aspects* 7: 1–9. University of Natal, Pietermaritzburg.

Kidder, William, Susan Kiyomi Serrano, and Angelo N. Ancheita. 2004. "In California, a Misguided Battle over Race." *Chronicle of Higher Education*, May 21, p. B16.

King, Jacqueline E. 2003. *2003 Status Report on the Pell Grant Program*. Washington, D.C.: American Council on Education, October.

Kirp, David L. 2004. "You're Doing Fine, Oklahoma!" *American Prospect*, November 1, online edition.

Klein, Alyson. 2004a. "Foes of Affirmative Action Take Aim at Scholarship Offered by Pepperdine U." *Chronicle of Higher Education,* January 23, online edition.

————. 2004b. "States Move to Limit Increases in Tuition." *Chronicle of Higher Education,* March 5, p. A1.

————. 2004c. "Affirmative-Action Opponents Suffer Setbacks in Colorado and Michigan." *Chronicle of Higher Education,* April 9, online edition.

Kling, Jeffrey R., Jens Ludwig, and Lawrence F. Katz. 2005. "Neighborhood Effects on Crime for Female and Male Youth: Evidence from a Randomized Housing Voucher Experiment." *Quarterly Journal of Economics* 130, no. 1 (February).

Komarovsky, Mirra. 1953. *Women in the Modern World: Their Education and Their Dilemmas.* Boston: Little Brown.

Korenman, Sanders, and Christopher Winship. 1995. "A Reanalysis of *The Bell Curve.*" NBER Working Paper no. 5230, August.

Kozol, Jonathan. 1991. *Savage Inequalities: Children in America's Schools.* New York: Crown Publishers.

Kraut, Alan M. 1982. *The Huddled Masses: The Immigrant in American Society, 1880–1921.* Arlington Heights, Ill.: Harlan Davidson.

Krislov, Martin. 2004. "Affirmative Action in Higher Education: The Value, the Method, and the Future." *University of Cincinnati Law Review* 72, no. 3 (Spring): 899–907.

Krueger, Alan B. 1998. "Reassessing the View That American Schools Are Broken." Princeton University, Industrial Relations Section, Working Paper no. 395, January.

————. 2002. "Inequality, Too Much of a Good Thing." Essay, August 4. Published in James Heckman and Alan Krueger, *Inequality in America: What Role for Human Capital Policies?* ed. Benjamin M. Friedman, 1–75. Cambridge, Mass.: MIT Press, 2003.

————. 2003. "Market Forces Press State Colleges to Raise Tuition and Give Financial Aid; Politics Presses to Keep Tuition Low." *New York Times,* May 1, p. C2.

Krueger, Alan B., and David D. Laitin. 2004. "'Misunderestimating' Terrorism." *Foreign Affairs* 83, no. 5 (September–October): 8–13.

Krueger, Alan B., and Cecilia E. Rouse. 2002. "Education and Labor Policy in the 1990s." In *American Economic Policy in the 1990s,* ed. Jeffrey A. Frankel and Peter R. Orszag, 690–92. Cambridge, Mass.: MIT Press.

Krueger, Alan B., and Diane M. Whitmore. 2000. "The Effect of Attending a Small Class in the Early Grades on College-Test Taking and Middle School Test Results: Evidence from Project STAR." NBER Working Paper no. 7656, April.

————. 2001. "Would Smaller Classes Help Close the Black-White Achievement Gap?" Princeton University, Industrial Relations Section, Working Paper no. 451, March. Available at http://www.irs.princeton.edu/pubs/pdfs/451.pdf.

Krueger, Alan B., and Pei Zhu. 2002. "Another Look at the New York City School Voucher Experiment." NBER Working Paper no. 9418, December.

Krueger, Alan B., Jesse Rothstein, and Sarah E. Turner. 2004. "Race, Income and College in 25 Years: The Legacy of Separate and Unequal Schooling." Unpublished draft, October 1.

Ku, Leighton, and Sashi Nimalendran. 2004. "Improving Children's Health: A Chartbook about the Roles of Medicaid and SCHIP." Center for Budget and Policy Priorities, January 15.

Lampl, Peter. 2004. "Imbalance of Talent." *Times Higher Education Supplement,* August 20, p. 16.

Lawson, Ellen N., and Marlene Merrill. 1983. "The Antebellum 'Talented Thousandth': Black College Students at Oberlin before the Civil War." *Journal of Negro Education* 52, no. 2 (Spring): 142–55.

Leal, Fermin. 2004. "Santa Ana Teachers OK 4% Cut; Concessions Allow Smaller Classes and Prevent Layoffs as the District Faces a Budget Shortfall." *Orange County Register,* March 14, online edition.

Lemann, Nicholas. 1997. "*The Bell Curve* Flattened: Subsequent Research Has Seriously Undercut the Claims of the Controversial Best Seller." *MSN Slate Magazine,* January 18, online edition. Available at http://slate.msn.com/id/2416/.

———. 1999. *The Big Test: The Secret History of the American Meritocracy.* New York: Farrar Straus and Giroux.

Leonhardt, David. 2004. "As Wealthy Fill Top Colleges, Concerns Grow over Fairness." *New York Times,* April 22, pp. A1, A21.

Levine, David O. 1986. *The American College and the Culture of Aspiration, 1915–1940.* Ithaca, N.Y.: Cornell University Press.

Levine, Lawrence W. 1993. *The Unpredictable Past: Explorations in American Cultural History.* New York: Oxford University Press.

Levy, Dawn. 2004. "Foreign Students Share Tales of Visa Woes in a Post-9/11 World." *Stanford Report,* May 25, online edition.

Lewis, Earl. 2004. "Why History Remains a Factor in the Search for Racial Equality." In *Defending Diversity: Affirmative Action at the University of Michigan,* by Patricia Gurin, Jeffrey S. Lehman, and Earl Lewis, with Gerald Gurin, Eric L. Dey, and Sylvia Hurtado, 17–59. Ann Arbor: University of Michigan Press.

Long, Bridget Terry. 2004. "The Impact of Federal Tax Credits for Higher Education Expenses." In *College Choices: The Economics of Where to Go, When to Go, and How to Pay for It,* ed. Caroline M. Hoxby, 101–68. Chicago: University of Chicago Press.

Looking Back: Reflections of Black Princeton Alumni. 1997. Video (VHS) produced by Media Genesis Productions, Brooklyn, N.Y. Published by the Trustees of Princeton University.

Looney, J. Jefferson, and Ruth L. Woodward, eds. 1991. *Princetonians, 1791–1794: A Biographical Dictionary.* Princeton, N.J.: Princeton University Press.

Loury, Glenn C. 2000. Foreword to *The Shape of the River: Long-Term Consequences of Considering Race in College and University Admissions,* by William G. Bowen and Derek Bok. Paperback edition. Princeton, N.J.: Princeton University Press.

———. 2002. *The Anatomy of Racial Inequality.* Cambridge, Mass.: Harvard University Press.

———. 2003. "Affirmed . . . For Now the Supreme Court's Decision Made Affirmative Action Resoundingly Legal. Now Comes the Hard Part—Making It Unnecessary." *Boston Globe,* June 29, p. D1.

Loury, Glenn C., Nathan Glazer, John F. Kain, Thomas J. Kane, Douglas Massey, Marta Tienda, and Brian Bucks. 2003. "Brief of Social Scientists Glenn C. Loury, Nathan Glazer, John F. Kain, Thomas J. Kane, Douglas Massey, Marta Tienda, and Brian Bucks as *Amici Curiae* in Support of Respondents." Submitted to the U.S. Supreme Court in *Gratz v. Bollinger, et al.* and *Grutter v. Bollinger, et al.,* February.

Loveless, Tom. 2003. *The 2003 Brown Center Report on American Education: How Well Are American Students Learning?* Washington, D.C.: Brookings Institution Press, October.

Loveless, Tom, ed. 2000. *Conflicting Missions? Teachers Unions and Educational Reform.* Washington, D.C.: Brookings Institution Press.

Lucas, Christopher J. 1994. *American Higher Education: A History.* New York: St. Martin's Press.

Lucas, Colin. 2004. "Retiring Vice-Chancellor's Oration." *Oxford University Gazette* 4707, supplement 2, October 6.

Ludwig, Jens, Helen F. Ladd, and Greg J. Duncan. 2001. "Urban Poverty and Educational Outcomes." In *Brookings-Wharton Papers on Urban Affairs: 2001,* ed. William G. Gale and Janet Rothenberg Pack, 147–201. Washington, D.C.: Brookings Institution Press.

Macdonald, C. A. 1990. *Crossing the Threshold into Standard Three.* Pretoria: Human Sciences Research Council.

Mangan, Katherine S. 2004. "Applications Rise at Medical Schools, as Female and Minority Students Make Gains." *Chronicle of Higher Education,* October 21, online edition.

Marcus, Amy Dockser. 1999. "New Weights Can Alter SAT Scores as Family Factors Determine 'Strivers.'" *Wall Street Journal,* August 31, online edition.

Marton, F., and R. Säljö. 1976. "On Qualitative Differences in Learning—I: Outcome and Process." *British Journal of Educational Psychology* 46: 4–11.

Massachusetts Institute of Technology, News Office. 2003. "MIT to Open Pre-College Summer Enrichment Programs to All Races." Available at http://web.mit.edu/newsoffice/2003/programs.html.

Massey, Douglas S., Camille Z. Charles, Garvey F. Lundy, and Mary J. Fischer. 2003. *The Source of the River: The Social Origins of Freshmen at America's Selective Colleges and Universities.* Princeton, N.J.: Princeton University Press.

Mathae, Katherine B., and Catherine L. Birzer, eds. 2004. *Reinvigorating the Humanities: Enhancing Research and Education on Campus and Beyond.* Washington, D.C.: Association of American Universities.

Mattingly, Paul H. 1997. "The Political Culture of America's Antebellum Colleges." *History of Higher Education Annual* 17: 73–96.

Mauro, Tony. 2003. "Court Affirms Continued Need for Preferences." *New York Law Journal,* June 24, p. 1.

Mayer, Susan, and Paul Peterson. 1999. *Earning and Learning: How Schools Matter.* Washington, D.C.: Brookings Institution Press.

Mayhew, Ken, Cécile Deer, and Mehak Dua. 2004. "The Move to Mass Higher Education in the UK: Many Questions and Some Answers." *Oxford Review of Education* 30, no. 1 (May): 65–82.

Mboya, M. 1986. "Open Non-Racial Universities: A Myth or Reality?" *Monday Paper* 5: 28, University of Cape Town.

McCarthy, Charles. 1912. *The Wisconsin Idea.* New York: Macmillan.

McCaughey, Robert A. 2003. *Stand, Columbia: A History of Columbia University in the City of New York, 1754–2004.* New York: Columbia University Press.

McLachlan, James. 1978. "The American Colleges in the Nineteenth Century: Towards a Reappraisal." *Teachers College Record* 80, no. 2 (December): 287–306.

McMurtrie, Beth. 2004. "The Quota Quandary." *Chronicle of Higher Education,* February 13, p. A38.

McPherson, Michael S., and Morton Owen Schapiro. 1991. *Keeping College Affordable: Government and Educational Opportunity.* Washington, D.C.: Brookings Institution Press.

———. 1998. *The Student Aid Game: Meeting Need and Rewarding Talent in American Higher Education.* Princeton, N.J.: Princeton University Press.

———. 2001. "The End of the Student Aid Era? Higher Education Finance in the United States." In *A Faithful Mirror: Reflections on the College Board and Education in America,* ed. Michael C. Johanek, 335–76. New York: College Board.

———. 2002. "The Blurring Line between Merit and Need in Financial Aid." *Change* 34, no. 2 (March–April): 38–46.

Meara, Ellen. 2001. "Why Is Health Related to Socioeconomic Status?" NBER Working Paper no. 8231, April.

Mellon Foundation, The Andrew W. 2004a. Web site. Available at http://www.mellon.org. Accessed August 20.

———. 2004b. *Report of The Andrew W. Mellon Foundation 2003.* New York: The Andrew W. Mellon Foundation.

Merisotis, Jamie P. 1987. "Income Contingent Loans: A Hot 'New' Idea and Its Cold Realities." *Change* 19, no. 2 (March–April): 10–11.

Merton, Robert K. 1968. "The Matthew Effect in Science." *Science,* January 5, pp. 56–63.

———. 1988. "The Matthew Effect in Science, II: Cumulative Advantage and the Symbolism of Intellectual Property." *Isis* 79, no. 4 (December): 606–23.

Mervis, Jeffrey. 2004a. "Many Origins, One Destination." *Science,* May 28, p. 1277.

———. 2004b. "Is the U.S. Brain Gain Faltering?" *Science,* May 28, pp. 1278–82.

Miami University at Ohio. 2004a. "Innovative Tuition & Scholarship Program." Available at http://www.miami.muohio.edu/tuitionplan/specifics.cfm. Accessed October 26.

———. 2004b. "New Tuition and Scholarship Plan." Available at http://www.miami.muohio.edu/tuitionplan/ohiofamilies.cfm. Accessed August 2.

Miles, Tim. 2003. "Oxbridge Must Lose Brideshead Reputation." *Evening Standard,* April 8, p. 15.

Ministry of Education (MoE), South Africa. 1997. Education White Paper 3: A Programme for the Transformation of Higher Education, General Notice 1196. Pretoria: MoE.

———. 2001. *National Plan for Higher Education in South Africa.* Pretoria: MoE.

Mongardini, Carlo, and Simonetta Tabboni, eds. 1998. *Robert K. Merton & Contemporary Sociology.* New Brunswick, N.J.: Transaction Publishers.

Mooney, Paul. 2004. "Extortion Scandal in China Shakes Public Confidence in Fairness of University Admissions." *Chronicle of Higher Education,* August 20, online edition.

Morison, Samuel Eliot. 1965. *Three Centuries of Harvard 1636–1936.* Cambridge, Mass.: Belknap Press of Harvard University Press.

Muller, Johan, and Jennifer Roberts. 2000. "The Sound and Fury of International School Reform: A Critical Review." Report prepared for the Joint Education Trust, February.

Mullis, Ina V. S., Michael O. Martin, Eugenio J. Gonzalez, Kelvin D. Gregory, Robert A. Garden, Kathleen M. O'Connor, Steven J. Chrostowski, and Teresa A. Smith. 2000. *TIMSS 1999 International Mathematics Report.* Chestnut Hill, Mass.: International Study Center, Boston College.

Murray, Sheila E., William N. Evans, and Robert M. Schwab. 1997. "Education Finance Reform and the Distribution of Education Resources." *American Economic Review* 88, no. 4 (September 1998): 789–812.

Myrdal, Gunnar. 1944. *An American Dilemma: The Negro Problem and Modern Democracy.* New York: Harper.

"N.A.A.C.P. Sets Advanced Goals." 1954. *New York Times,* May 18, p. 16.

Nabarro, F. R. N. 1980. "An Outline of the Academic Plan." University of the Witwatersrand, Johannesburg.

National Center for Education Statistics. 2004. "Public School District Finance Peer Search." Washington, D.C.: U.S. Department of Education, National Center for Education Statistics, 2000–01. Available at http://nces.ed.gov/edfin. Accessed November 4.

National Center for Public Policy and Higher Education. 2002. *Losing Ground: A National Status Report on the Affordability of American Higher Education.* San Jose, Calif.: The Center.

National Commission on Excellence in Education. 1983. *A Nation at Risk: The Imperative for Educational Reform.* Washington, D.C.: National Commission on Excellence in Education, April. Also available at http://www.ed.gov/pubs/NatatRisk/index.html. Accessed June 24, 2004.

National Commission on Higher Education (NCHE). 1995. *Report of (Task Force Group 5) Technical Committee 2 on Student Access, Support and Development.* Pretoria: NCHE. Available at http://star.hsrc.ac.za/nche/final/tg5/systems/chao2/html.

———. 1996. *A Framework for Transformation.* Pretoria: Human Sciences Research Council.

National Education Coordinating Committee (NECC). 1993. *The National Education Policy Investigation: Framework Report and Final Report Summaries.* Cape Town: Oxford University Press/NECC.

National Education Goals Panel. 2004. Web site. Available at http://www.negp.gov/. Accessed September 4.

National Science Board. 2004a. *An Emerging and Critical Problem of the Science and Engineering Labor Force: A Companion to Science and Engineering Indicators 2004.* Arlington, Va.: National Science Foundation.

———. 2004b. *Science and Engineering Indicators 2004.* 2 vols. (Vol. 1: NSB 04-1; vol. 2: NSB 04-1A.) Arlington, Va.: National Science Foundation. Available at http://www.nsf.gov/sbe/srs/seind04/start.htm.

National Union of Students. 2004a. "Briefing: Higher Education—The Big Picture." Funding the Future Campaign, March. Available at http://www2.nusonline.co.uk/resource/resources/pdf/4750.pdf. Accessed November 5.

———. 2004b. "Latest Campaign." Available at http://www.nusonline.co.uk/subsites/stopfeesnow/. Accessed July 28.

Ndebele, N. S. 1995. "Maintaining Domination through Language." *Academic Development* 1, no. 1: 3–5.

Nechyba, Thomas J. 1996. "Public School Finance in a General Equilibrium Tiebout World: Equalization Programs, Peer Effects and Private School Vouchers." NBER Working Paper no. 5642, June.

Newcomer, Mabel. 1959. *A Century of Higher Education for American Women*. New York: Harper.

Nichols, Albert L., and Richard J. Zeckhauser. 1982. "Targeting Transfers through Restrictions on Recipients." *American Economic Review* 72, no. 2 (May): 372–77.

Nickens, Herbert W., Timothy P. Ready, and Robert G. Petersdorf. 1994. "Project 3000 by 2000: Racial and Ethnic Diversity in U.S. Medical Schools." *New England Journal of Medicine* 331, no. 7: 472–76.

North, Douglass C. 1968. "Sources of Productivity Change in Ocean Shipping, 1600–1850." *Journal of Political Economy* 76, no. 5 (September–October): 953–70.

———. 1993. "Economic Performance through Time." Nobel Lecture, Stockholm, December 9.

Oakley, Francis. 2002. "Data Deprivation and *Humanities Indicators*." In *Making the Humanities Count: The Importance of Data*, by Robert M. Solow, Francis Oakley, Phyllis Franklin, John D'Arms, and Calvin C. Jones, 5–16. Cambridge, Mass.: American Academy of Arts & Sciences.

Odone, Cristina. 2002. "College Ties That Bind." *Observer,* December 8, p. 27. Available at http://education.guardian.co.uk/universitiesincrisis/story/0,12028,856687,00.html. Accessed July 22, 2004.

Oliver, Melvin L., and Thomas M. Shapiro. 1995. *Black Wealth/White Wealth: A New Perspective on Racial Inequality.* New York: Routledge.

Olson, Keith W. 1973. "The G.I. Bill and Higher Education: Success and Surprise." *American Quarterly* 25, no. 5 (December): 596–610.

———. 1974. *The G.I. Bill, the Veterans, and the Colleges.* Lexington, Ky.: University Press of Kentucky.

O'Neil, Robert M. 1970. "Preferential Admissions: Equalizing Access to Legal Education." *University of Toledo Law Review* (Spring–Summer): 281–320.

Onkst, David H. 1998. "'First a Negro . . . Incidentally a Veteran': Black World War Two Veterans and the G.I. Bill of Rights in the Deep South, 1944–1948." *Journal of Social History* 31, no. 3 (Spring): 517–43.

Orfield, Gary. 1992. "Money, Equity, and College Access." *Harvard Educational Review* 72 (Fall): 337–72.

Orfield, Gary, and Chungmei Lee. 2004. "*Brown* at 50: King's Dream or *Plessy's* Nightmare." Cambridge, Mass.: Civil Rights Project, Harvard University, January. Available at http://www.civilrightsproject.harvard.edu/research/resego4/brown50.pdf.

"Original Papers in Relation to a Course of Liberal Education." 1829. *American Journal of Science* 15 (January): 297–351.

Organisation for Economic Co-operation and Development. 2003. *Education at a Glance 2003*. Paris: Organisation for Economic Co-Operation and Development. Available at http://www.oecd.org/edu/eag2003.

———. 2004. *Education at a Glance 2004*. Paris: Organisation for Economic Co-Operation and Development. Available at http://www.oecd.org/edu/eag2004.

Palmieri, Patricia A. 1997. "From Republican Motherhood to Race Suicide: Arguments on the Higher Education of Women in the United States, 1820–1920." In *The History of Higher Education,* ed. Lester F. Goodchild and Harold S. Wechsler, 173–82. Needham Heights, Mass.: Simon & Schuster.

Pascarella, Ernest T. 2001. "Identifying Excellence in Undergraduate Education: Are We Even Close?" *Change* 33, no. 3 (May–June): 19–23.

Payne, David G. 2004. "The Flow of Graduate Students and Postdoctoral Scholars to and from the United States." Presentation to the National Academies Committee on Policy Implications of Graduate Students and Postdoctoral Scholars in the U.S. Washington, D.C., July 19.

Payton, John. 2004a. "Night of *Brown v. Board of Education:* 50 Years Later: Remarks of John Payton." Speech delivered at the Thurgood Marshall Center Trust, January 31.

——. 2004b. "*Brown v. Board of Education:* The True Legacy of Charles Hamilton Houston: Remarks of John Payton." Speech delivered at the Washington Bar Association Law Day Dinner, May 1.

Peterson, Marvin W., Robert T. Blackburn, Zelda F. Gramson, Carlos H. Arce, Roselle W. Davenport, and James R. Mingle. 1978. *Black Students on White Campuses: The Impacts of Increased Black Enrollments.* Ann Arbor: Survey Research Center Institute for Social Research, University of Michigan.

Peterson, Paul E., William G. Howell, Patrick J. Wolf, and David R. Campbell. 2003. "School Vouchers: Results from Randomized Experiments." In *The Economics of School Choice,* ed. Caroline M. Hoxby, 107–44. Chicago: University of Chicago Press.

Peterson's. 2003. *Peterson's Four-Year Colleges 2004.* Princeton, N.J.: Peterson's.

Phillips, Meredith. 1997. "What Makes Schools Effective? A Comparison of the Relationships of Communitarian Climate and Academic Climate to Mathematics Achievement and Attendance during Middle School." *American Educational Research Journal* 34, no. 4 (Winter): 633–62.

Phillips, Meredith, Jeanne Brooks-Gunn, Greg J. Duncan, Pamela Klebanov, and Jonathan Crane. 1998. "Family Background, Parenting Practices, and the Black-White Test Score Gap." In *The Black-White Test Score Gap,* ed. Christopher Jencks and Meredith Phillips, 103–45. Washington, D.C.: Brookings Institution Press.

Pifer, Alan J. 1973. *The Higher Education of Blacks in the United States.* New York: Carnegie Corporation of New York.

Poterba, James M., ed. 1998. *Tax Policy and the Economy.* Cambridge, Mass.: MIT Press.

Potter, C. S., and A. N. Jamotte. 1985. "African Matric Results: Dubious Indicators of Academic Merit." *Indicator South Africa* 3, no. 1: 10–13.

Potts, David B. 1971. "American Colleges in the Nineteenth Century: From Localism to Denominationalism." *History of Education Quarterly* 11, no. 4 (Winter): 363–80.

——. 2000. "Curriculum and Enrollment: Assessing the Popularity of Antebellum Colleges." In *The American College in the Nineteenth Century,* ed. Roger L. Geiger, 39–45. Nashville, Tenn.: Vanderbilt University Press.

President's Commission on Higher Education. 1947. *Higher Education for American Democracy.* 6 vols. Washington, D.C.: U.S. Government Printing Office.

Ramphele, Mamphela. 1996. "Embracing the Future." Inaugural address, University of Cape Town, October 11. Available at http://web.uct.ac.za/depts/dpa/publications/mr-instl.htm.

Reed, Douglas S. 1997. "Court-Ordered School Finance Authorization: Judicial Activism and Democratic Opposition." In *Developments in School Finance 1996*, ed. William J. Fowler Jr., 93–120. Washington, D.C.: U.S. Department of Education, National Center for Education Statistics.

Research Tools Backgrounders. 2004. "Britain's Universities." *Economist*, September 22. Available at http://www.economist.com/research/backgrounders/displaybackgrounder.cfm?bg=1452940. Accessed November 14.

"A Revolt of the Flagships." 2004. *New York Times*, February 16, p. A20.

Reynolds, O. Edgar. 1927. *The Social and Economic Status of College Students*. New York: Teachers College, Columbia University.

Rieder, Jonathan. 2004. "Righteousness Like a Mighty Stream." *New York Times Book Review*, February 8, p. 6.

Rimer, Sara, and Karen W. Arenson. 2004. "Top Colleges Take More Blacks, but Which Ones?" *New York Times*, June 24, p. A1.

Robertson, David, and Josh Hillman. 1997. "Widening Participation in Higher Education for Students from Lower Socio-Economic Groups and Students with Disabilities." Report 6 of the National Committee of Inquiry into Higher Education, *Higher Education in the Learning Society* (Dearing Report). London: Her Majesty's Stationery Office, June.

"The Roller-Coaster Ride of Black Students at Berea College." 1996. *Journal of Blacks in Higher Education* 13 (Autumn): 62–64.

Rosenfeld, Alvin A., and Nicole Wise. 2001. *The Over-Scheduled Child: Avoiding the Hyper-Parenting Trap*. New York: St. Martin's Press.

Rothstein, Jesse. 2004. "Does Competition Among Public Schools Benefit Students and Taxpayers? Comment." Industrial Relations Section, Princeton University. Mimeo. February. Available at http://www.princeton.edu/~jrothst/rothstein_hoxbycomment.pdf.

Rouse, Cecilia E. 1998. "Private School Vouchers and Student Achievement: An Evaluation of the Milwaukee Parental Choice Program." *Quarterly Journal of Economics* 113, no. 2 (May): 553–602.

Rudolph, Frederick. 1977. *Curriculum: A History of the American Undergraduate Course of Study since 1636*. San Francisco: Jossey-Bass Publishers.

———. 1990. *The American College and University: A History*. Athens, Ga.: University of Georgia Press. Reprint of 1962 ed.

Rudy, Willis. 1949. *The College of the City of New York. A History, 1847–1947*. New York: City College Press.

Ruggles, Steven, Matthew Sobek, Trent Alexander, Catherine A. Fitch, Ronald Goeken, Patricia Kelly Hall, Miriam King, and Chad Ronnander. 2004. *Integrated Public Use Microdata Series: Version 3.0* [machine-readable database]. Minneapolis: Minnesota Population Center [producer and distributor]. Available at http://www.ipums.org.

"The Ruin of Britain's Universities." 2002. *Economist*, November 16, p. 29.

Russell, Jenna. 2004. "UMass Finds Its Minority Level Even." *Boston Globe*, April 20, p. A1.

SAAD (South African Association for Academic Development). 1995. "Facilitating Academic Development as a Key Element of Transformation in Higher
Education." Submission to the National Commission on Higher Education by
the South Africa Association for Academic Development.

Sacerdote, Bruce. 2000. "Peer Effects with Random Assignment: Results for Dartmouth Roommates." *Quarterly Journal of Economics* 116, no. 2 (May): 681–704.

St. John, Edward P., ed. 2004. *Public Policy and College Access: Investigating the Federal and State Roles in Equalizing Postsecondary Opportunity.* Vol. 19 of *Readings on
Equal Education.* New York: AMS Press.

Sanbonmatsu, Lisa, Jeanne Brooks-Gunn, Greg J. Duncan, and Jeffrey R. Kling.
2004. "Neighborhoods and Academic Achievement: Results from the Moving
to Opportunity Experiment." Princeton Industrial Relations Section Working
Paper no. 492, August.

Sass, A. 1988. "Academic Support in Engineering at the University of Cape
Town." *South African Journal of Higher Education* 2, no. 1: 25–29.

Saunders, Stuart. 2000. *Vice-Chancellor on a Tightrope: A Personal Account of Climactic Years in South Africa.* Cape Town: David Philip Publishers.

Sawhill, Isabel, ed. 2003. *One Percent for the Kids.* Washington, D.C.: Brookings
Institution Press.

Schemo, Diana Jean. 2004a. "Charter Schools Trail in Results, U.S. Data Reveals."
New York Times, August 17, p. A6.

———. 2004b. "Education Secretary Defends Charter Schools." *New York Times,*
August 18, p. A3.

Schmidt, Peter. 2004a. "Head of Civil-Rights Panel Denounces Affirmative-Action
Survey Sent Out on Panel's Letterhead." *Chronicle of Higher Education,* February
13, online edition.

———. 2004b. "Harvard Business School Opens Summer Program to White and
Asian Students in Response to Complaint." *Chronicle of Higher Education,* February 18, online edition.

———. 2004c. "Advocacy Groups Pressure Colleges to Disclose Affirmative-
Action Policies." *Chronicle of Higher Education,* April 4, p. A26.

———. 2004d. "Federal Pressure Prompts Washington U. in St. Louis to Open
Minority-Scholarship Program to All Races." *Chronicle of Higher Education,* April 5,
online edition.

Schmidt, Peter, and Jeffrey R. Young. 2003. "MIT and Princeton Open 2 Summer
Programs to Students of All Races." *Chronicle of Higher Education,* February 21,
p. A31.

Schonfeld, Roger C. 2003. *JSTOR: A History.* Princeton, N.J.: Princeton University
Press.

Schultz, Stanley K. 1973. *The Culture Factory: Boston Public Schools, 1789–1860.*
New York: Oxford University Press.

Scott, Ian. 1986. "Tinkering or Transforming? The Contribution of Academic
Support Programmes to 'Opening the Doors of Learning and of Culture.'"
Aspects 7: 10–26. University of Natal, Pietermaritzburg.

———. 2003. "Balancing Excellence, Equity and Enterprise in a Less-
Industrialised Country: The Case of South Africa." In *The Enterprising University:
Reform, Excellence and Equity,* ed. G. Williams, 40–53. Buckingham, England:
Society for Research into Higher Education and Open University Press.

Scott, Peter. 2001. "Conclusion: Triumph and Retreat." In *The State of UK Higher Education: Managing Change and Diversity,* ed. David Warner and David Palfreyman, 187–204. Buckingham, England: Society for Research into Higher Education and Open University Press.

Sealander, Judith. 2000. "Making Public Education Mandatory: The Consequences of a Foundation-Supported Idea in City Schools." Paper presented at the conference "Philanthropy and the City: An Historical Overview," Rockefeller Archive Center, September 25–26. Available at http://archive.rockefeller .edu/publications/conferences/sealander.pdf. Accessed August 6, 2004.

Selingo, Jeffrey. 2003. "New Illinois Law Will Freeze Public-College Tuition for Each Incoming Class." *Chronicle of Higher Education,* July 24, online edition.

———. 2004a. "Georgia Lawmakers Alter Scholarships." *Chronicle of Higher Education,* April 23, p. A28.

———. 2004b. "Senator Kerry Proposes Student-Loan Auctions." *Chronicle of Higher Education,* April 23, online edition.

———. 2004c. "U.S. Public's Confidence in Colleges Remains High." *Chronicle of Higher Education,* May 7, p. A1.

———. 2004d. "Kerry Offers Proposal to Hold Down Tuition." *Chronicle of Higher Education,* July 9, online edition.

Shanghai Jiao Tong University, Institute of Higher Education. 2004. *Academic Ranking of World Universities–2004.* Available at http://ed.sjtu.edu.cn/ranking .htm. Accessed August 20.

Shochet, I. 1986. "Manifest and Potential Performance in Advantaged and Disadvantaged Students." Unpublished PhD dissertation, University of the Witwatersrand, Johannesburg.

Shulman, James L., and William G. Bowen. 2001. *The Game of Life: College Sports and Educational Values.* Princeton, N.J.: Princeton University Press.

Siegel, Reva B. 2004. "Equality Talk: Antisubordination and Anticlassification Values in Constitutional Struggles over *Brown.*" *Harvard Law Review* 117, no. 5 (May): 1470–543.

Silverstein, Stuart. 2004. "Pepperdine Defends Its Minority Scholarships." *Los Angeles Times,* January 22, p. B1.

Simons, Gary. 2003. *Be the Dream: Prep for Prep Graduates Share Their Stories.* Chapel Hill, N.C.: Algonquin Books of Chapel Hill.

Simpson, William B. 1987. "Income-Contingent Student Loans: Context, Potential and Limits." *Higher Education* 15, no. 6: 699–721.

Sims, David. 2004. "How Flexible Is Education Production? Combination Class and Class Size Reduction in California." MIT, Department of Economics. Mimeo. January.

Singell, Larry D., Jr., Glen R. Waddell, and Bradley R. Curs. 2004. "Hope for the Pell? The Impact of Merit-Aid on Needy Students." Paper presented at the NBER Higher Education Meeting, April 30. Version dated March.

Skocpol, Theda. 1991. "Targeting within Universalism: Politically Viable Policies to Combat Poverty in the United States." In *The Urban Underclass,* ed. Christopher Jencks and Paul E. Peterson, 411–36. Washington, D.C.: Brookings Institution Press.

Smith, Anthony. 2002. "The Laura Spence Affair." In *Education! Education! Education! Managerial Ethics and the Law of Unintended Consequences,* ed. Stephen

Prickett and Patricia Erskine-Hill, 29–37. Thorverton, England: Imprint Academic.

Smithers, Alan. 2004. "England's Education: What Can Be Learned by Comparing Countries?" Centre for Education and Employment Research, University of Liverpool, commissioned by the Sutton Trust, May.

Snyder, Thomas D., ed. 1993. *120 Years of American Education: A Statistical Portrait.* Washington, D.C.: National Center for Education Statistics.

Solochek, Jeffrey S. 2004. "Class Size Limit Straining System." *St. Petersburg Times* (Florida), April 22, p. 1.

Solomon, Barbara M. 1985. *In the Company of Educated Women: A History of Women and Higher Education in America.* New Haven, Conn.: Yale University Press.

Solow, Robert M. 2002. "The Value of *Humanities Indicators.*" In *Making the Humanities Count: The Importance of Data,* by Robert M. Solow, Francis Oakley, Phyllis Franklin, John D'Arms, and Calvin C. Jones, 1–3. Cambridge, Mass.: American Academy of Arts & Sciences.

Solow, Robert M., Francis Oakley, Phyllis Franklin, John D'Arms, and Calvin C. Jones. 2002. *Making the Humanities Count: The Importance of Data.* Cambridge, Mass.: American Academy of Arts & Sciences.

Spacks, Patricia Meyer, and Leslie C. Berlowitz. 2002. Foreword to *Making the Humanities Count: The Importance of Data,* by Robert M. Solow, Francis Oakley, Phyllis Franklin, John D'Arms, and Calvin C. Jones, v–viii. Cambridge, Mass.: American Academy of Arts & Sciences.

Spies, Richard R. 2001. "The Effect of Rising Costs on College Choice." Research Report Series no. 117. Princeton, N.J.: Princeton University, December.

Star (Johannesburg). 1987. May 25.

State Higher Education Executive Officers (SHEEO). 2004. *State Higher Education Finance FY 2003.* Denver: SHEEO. Available at http://www.sheeo.org/finance/shef.pdf.

Steele, Claude M., and Joshua Aronson. 1998. "Stereotype Threat and the Test Performance of Academically Successful African Americans." In *The Black-White Test Score Gap,* ed. Christopher Jencks and Meredith Phillips, 401–28. Washington, D.C.: Brookings Institution Press.

Steinberg, Jacques. 2003. "Of Sheepskins and Greenbacks." *New York Times,* February 13, p. A24.

Stevens, Robert. 2004. *University to Uni: The Politics of Higher Education in England since 1944.* London: Politico's.

Story, Ronald. 1975. "Harvard Students, the Boston Elite, and the New England Preparatory System, 1800–1870." *History of Education Quarterly* 15, no. 3: 281–98.

———. 1980. *The Forging of an Aristocracy: Harvard and the Boston Upper Class, 1800–1870.* Middletown, Conn.: Wesleyan University Press.

Strout, Erin. 2004. "U. of Virginia Unexpectedly Opens $3-Billion Campaign to Become a Private Public University." *Chronicle of Higher Education,* June 15, online edition.

Summers, Lawrence H. 2004a. "Higher Education and the American Dream." Speech delivered at the 86th Annual Meeting, American Council on Education, Miami, Fla., February 29. Available at http://www.president.harvard.edu/speeches/2004/ace.html. Accessed August 9.

———. 2004b. "Reaffirming the Commitment to Opportunity." Harvard University Commencement Address, June 10. Available at http://www.president.harvard.edu/speeches/2004/commencement.html. Accessed August 9.

Sutton Trust. 2000. "Entry to Leading Universities." Sutton Trust, May. Available at http://www.suttontrust.com/reports/entrytoleadingunis.pdf. Accessed July 27, 2004.

———. 2003. "Nobel Prizes: The Changing Pattern of Awards." Sutton Trust, September. Available at http://www.suttontrust.com/reports/nobel.doc.

———. 2004a. "Open Access: A Practical Way Forward, New Developments." Sutton Trust, June.

———. 2004b. "The Missing 3000: State School Students Under-Represented at Leading Universities." Sutton Trust, August.

Synnott, Marcia Graham. 1979. *The Half-Opened Door: Discrimination and Admissions at Harvard, Yale, and Princeton, 1900–1970*. Westport, Conn.: Greenwood Press.

Syverson, Peter D. 2003. *Graduate Enrollment and Degrees: 1986–2001*. Washington, D.C.: Council of Graduate Schools Office of Research and Information Services.

Taylor, Nick, and Penny Vinjevold. 1999a. *Getting Learning Right: Report of the President's Education Initiative Research Project*, ed. Nick Taylor and Penny Vinjevold, 205–26. Johannesburg: Joint Education Trust.

———. 1999b. "Teaching and Learning in South African Schools." In *Getting Learning Right: Report of the President's Education Initiative Research Project*, ed. Nick Taylor and Penny Vinjevold, 131–62. Johannesburg: Joint Education Trust.

Tebbs, Jeffrey, and Sarah E. Turner. 2004. "College Education for Low Income Students: A Caution on the Use of Data on Pell Grant Recipients." University of Virginia. Mimeo.

Tench, Megan. 2004. "With No Pact, Boston Teachers Weigh Staging 1-Day Strike; Pay, Class Size, Overtime Are among the Issues." *Boston Globe*, February 27, p. B3.

Thelin, John R. 2004. *A History of American Higher Education*. Baltimore: Johns Hopkins University Press.

Thernstrom, Stephan. 1986. "Poor but Hopefull [*sic*] Scholars." In *Glimpses of the Harvard Past*, ed. Bernard Bailyn, Donald Fleming, Oscar Handlin, and Stephan Thernstrom, 115–28. Cambridge, Mass.: Harvard University Press.

Thomas, Debra, and Terry Shepard. 2009. "Legacy Admissions Are Defensible, Because the Process Can't Be 'Fair.'" *Chronicle of Higher Education*, March 14, p. B15.

Thornton, Leslie T. 2003. "With Friends Like These. . . ." *Legal Times*, March 31, p. 70.

Tiebout, Charles M. 1956. "A Pure Theory of Local Expenditures." *Journal of Political Economy* 64, no. 5 (October): 416–24.

Tierney, Joseph, and Jean Grossman, with Nancy L. Resch. 1995. *Making a Difference: An Impact Study of Big Brothers/Big Sisters*. Philadelphia: Public/Private Ventures.

"Tomorrow Begins at Wits Today? The Role of the University in a Changing Society." 1986. *Perception of Wits*. University of Witwatersrand, Johannesburg.

Traub, James. 2000. "What No School Can Do." *New York Times Magazine,* January 16, p. 52.

———. 2004. "The Way We Live Now: 2-29-04: The Pull of Family." *New York Times Magazine,* February 29, p. 21.

Trow, Martin. 1991. "The Exceptionalism of American Higher Education." In *University and Society: Essays on the Social Role of Research and Higher Education,* ed. Martin Trow and Thorsten Nybom, 156–72. London: Jessica Kingsley Publishers.

———. 1996. "Trust, Markets and Accountability in Higher Education: A Comparative Perspective." *Higher Education Policy* 9, no. 4: 309–24.

———. 1998. "The Dearing Report: A Transatlantic View." *Higher Education Quarterly* 52, no. 1 (January): 93–117.

Trow, Martin, and Thorsten Nybom, eds. 1991. *University and Society: Essays on the Social Role of Research and Higher Education.* London: Jessica Kingsley Publishers.

Turner, Sarah E. 2001. "Will We Pay Too Much for SUNY's Low Tuition?" *Newsday* (New York), February 12, p. A20.

———. 2004. "Going to College and Finishing College: Explaining Different Educational Outcomes." In *College Decisions: How Students Actually Make Them and How They Could,* ed. Caroline M. Hoxby, 13–61. Chicago: University of Chicago Press.

Turner, Sarah E., and John Bound. 2003. "Closing the Gap or Widening the Divide: The Effects of the G.I. Bill and World War II on the Educational Outcomes of Black Americans." *Journal of Economic History* 63, no. 1 (March): 145–77.

Turner, Sarah E., Lauren A. Meserve, and William G. Bowen. 2001. "Winning and Giving: Football Results and Alumni Giving at Selective Private Colleges and Universities." *Social Science Quarterly* 82, no. 4 (December): 812–26.

Tyack, David B. 1974. *The One Best System: A History of American Urban Education.* Cambridge, Mass.: Harvard University Press.

Universities UK. 2003. "Universities UK's Response to 'The Future of Higher Education': DfES White Paper." Universities UK, April. Available at http://image.guardian.co.uk/sys-files/education/documents/2003/04/10/uuk.pdf. Accessed July 19, 2004.

University of California. 2003. "Undergraduate Access to the University of California after the Elimination of Race-Conscious Policies." University of California, Office of the President, March.

University of Cape Town, Academic Planning Office. 1986. "Proposal for a Research Project to Devise Alternative Selection Procedures for Entry to UCT." University of Cape Town, Academic Planning Office.

U.S. Census Bureau. 1975. *Historical Statistics of the United States, Colonial Times to 1970.* Washington, D.C.: U.S. Census Bureau, U.S. Government Printing Office.

———. 2004. *Statistical Abstract of the United States: 2003.* Washington, D.C.: Government Printing Office.

U.S. Census Bureau, Demographics Survey Division. 2004. "Survey of Income and Program Participation (SIPP)." Washington, D.C.: U.S. Census Bureau, last updated February 5. Available at http://www.sipp.census.gov/sipp/.

U.S. Census Bureau, Population Division, Education and Social Stratification Branch. 2004. *Educational Attainment: Current Population Survey.* Washington, D.C.: U.S. Census Bureau, last updated June 29. Available at http://www.census .gov/population/www/socdemo/educ-attn.html.

U.S. Congress, Congressional Budget Office (CBO). 1998. "Using Auctions to Reduce the Cost of the Federal Family Education Loan Program." Analysis prepared by the CBO at the request of Senator Edward M. Kennedy, July. Available at http://www.cbo.gov/ftpdocs/6xx/doc644/ffelauct.pdf.

U.S. Department of Agriculture, Economic Research Service. 2004. "Rural Poverty at a Glance." Rural Development Research Report no. 100, July.

U.S. Department of Education. National Center for Education Statistics. 1973. *Digest of Education Statistics, 1973.* Washington, D.C.: U.S. Department of Health, Education and Welfare, National Center for Education Statistics.

———. 1992. *Digest of Education Statistics, 1992.* NCES 92-097. Washington, D.C.: U.S. Department of Education, National Center for Education Statistics.

———. 1995. *The Condition of Education 1995.* NCES 95-273. Washington, D.C.: U.S. Government Printing Office.

———. 1998. *Public School Districts in the United States: A Statistical Profile, 1987–88 to 1993–94.* NCES 98-203. Washington, D.C.: National Center for Education Statistics.

———. 2002. *The Condition of Education 2002.* NCES 2002-025. Washington, D.C.: U.S. Government Printing Office.

———. 2003. *Digest of Education Statistics, 2002.* NCES 2003-060. Washington, D.C.: U.S. Department of Education, National Center for Education Statistics.

———. 2004. *The Condition of Education 2004.* NCES 2004-077. Washington, D.C.: U.S. Government Printing Office.

"Universities 'Critical' to UK's Success." 2003. *Guardian,* January 23.

Varian, Hal R. 2004. "Information Technology May Have Been What Cured Low Service-Sector Productivity." *New York Times,* February 12, p. C2.

Verstegen, Deborah A., and James G. Ward, eds. 1991. *Spheres of Justice in Education.* New York: HarperBusiness.

Vest, Charles M. 2003. "MIT's 29th Annual Celebration of the Life and Legacy of Dr. Martin Luther King, Jr.: Remarks by President Charles M. Vest." Speech delivered at Massachusetts Institute of Technology, February 14. Available at http://web.mit.edu/newsoffice/2003/mlk-cmv.htm. Accessed November 9, 2004.

———. 2004. "Moving On." Report of the President for the Academic Years 2002–2004. Massachusetts Institute of Technology. Available at http://web .mit.edu/president/communications/CMVReport2002-04.pdf.

Veysey, Laurence R. 1965. *The Emergence of the American University.* Chicago: University of Chicago Press.

Vice-Chancellor's Report. 1985. University of Cape Town.

Vilakazi, H. W., and B. Tema. 1985. "White Universities and the Black Revolution." Paper presented at the 1985 Academic Support Programmes Conference, University of the Witwatersrand.

Vinjevold, Penny. 1999. "Language Issues in South African Classrooms." In *Getting Learning Right: Report of the President's Education Initiative Research Project,* ed. Nick Taylor and Penny Vinjevold, 205–26. Johannesburg: Joint Education Trust.

Wagoner, Jennings L. Jr. 1976. *Thomas Jefferson and the Education of a New Nation.* Bloomington, Ind.: Phi Delta Kappa Educational Foundation.

———. 1991. "Jefferson, Justice, and the Enlightened Society." In *Spheres of Justice in Education,* ed. Deborah A. Verstegen and James G. Ward, 11–33. New York: HarperBusiness.

———. 1999. "'That Knowledge Most Useful to Us': Thomas Jefferson's Concept of Utility in the Education of Republican Citizens." In *Thomas Jefferson and the Education of a Citizen,* ed. James Gilreath, 115–31. Washington, D.C.: Library of Congress.

———. 2004. *Jefferson and Education.* Charlottesville, Va.: Thomas Jefferson Foundation. Distributed by University of North Carolina Press, Chapel Hill.

Walden, George. 1996. *We Should Know Better: Solving the Education Crisis.* London: Fourth Estate.

Walker, Adrian. 2004. "45 Graduates Seize the Day." *Boston Globe,* May 27, p. B1.

Wallack, Juliette. 2002. "Brown U. Implements Need-Blind Policy Beginning with Class of '07." *Brown Daily Herald,* February 25, online edition.

Walsh, James, and Ron Nixon. 2004. "School Contracts: Pricing Out Young Teachers." *Star Tribune* (Minneapolis), May 23, p. 1A.

Wechsler, Harold S. 1977. *The Qualified Student: A History of Selective College Admission in America.* New York: Wiley.

———. 1981. "An Academic Gresham's Law: Group Repulsion as a Theme in American Higher Education." *Teachers College Record* 82 (Summer): 567–88. Reprinted in *History of Higher Education,* ed. Lester F. Goodchild and Harold S. Wechsler, 416–31. Needham Heights, Mass.: Simon & Schuster.

———. 1984. "The Rationale for Restriction: Ethnicity and College Admission in America, 1910–1980." *American Quarterly* 36, no. 5: 643–67.

Wechsler, Herbert. 1959. "Toward Neutral Principles of Constitutional Law." *Harvard Law Review* 73, no. 1 (November): 1–35.

Wei, Christina Chang, and Laura Horn. 2002. *Persistence and Attainment of Beginning Students with Pell Grants.* NCES 2002-169. Washington, D.C.: National Center for Education Statistics.

Welter, Barbara. 1966. "The Cult of True Womanhood: 1820–1860." *American Quarterly* 18, no. 2, part 1 (Summer): 151–74.

White, Lynn Townsend. 1950. *Educating Our Daughters: A Challenge to the Colleges.* New York: Harper.

"Who Pays to Study?" 2004. *Economist,* January 24, p. 23.

Wiebe, Robert H. 1967. *The Search for Order, 1877–1920.* New York: Hill and Wang.

Wilentz, Sean. 1984. *Chants Democratic: New York City and the Rise of the American Working Class, 1788–1850.* New York: Oxford University Press.

Williams, G., ed. 2003. *The Enterprising University: Reform, Excellence and Equity.* Buckingham, England: Society for Research into Higher Education and Open University Press.

Williams, Roger L. 1991. *The Origins of Federal Support for Higher Education: George W. Atherton and the Land-Grant College Movement.* University Park, Pa.: Pennsylvania State University Press.

———. 1997. "The Origins of Federal Support for Higher Education." In *The History of Higher Education,* ed. Lester F. Goodchild and Harold S. Wechsler, 267–72. Needham Heights, Mass.: Simon & Schuster.

Wilson, Robin. 1987. "Amid Debate over New Income-Contingent Loans, Many Students Say They Just Want the Money." *Chronicle of Higher Education,* December 9, p. A19.

Wilson, William J. 1987. *The Truly Disadvantaged: The Inner City, the Underclass, and Public Policy.* Chicago: University of Chicago Press.

Winston, Gordon C. 1999. "Subsidies, Hierarchy and Peers: The Awkward Economics of Higher Education." *Journal of Economic Perspectives* 13, no. 1 (Winter): 13–36.

Winston, Gordon C., and David J. Zimmerman. 2000. "Where Is Aggressive Price Competition Taking Higher Education?" *Change* 32, no. 4 (July–August): 10–18.

———. 2004. "Peer Effects in Higher Education." In *College Choices: The Economics of Where to Go, When to Go, and How to Pay for It,* ed. Caroline M. Hoxby, 395–423. Chicago: University of Chicago Press.

Winter, Greg. 2003. "As State Colleges Cut Classes, Students Struggle to Finish." *New York Times,* August 24, section 1, p. 1.

———. 2004a. "A Windfall for a Student Loan Program." *New York Times,* August 27, p. c1.

———. 2004b. "Congress Passes Bill to Tighten Lending Rules." *New York Times,* October 12, p. A19.

Wolanin, Thomas R. 2001. "Rhetoric and Reality: Effects and Consequences of the HOPE Scholarship." New Millennium Project Working Paper. Washington, D.C.: Institute for Higher Education Policy, April. Available at http://www.ihep.com/Pubs/PDF/Hope.pdf.

Wolf, Martin. 2000. "Let the Top Universities Off the Funding Leash." *Financial Times,* March 6, p. 23.

———. 2003a. "The Omens Look Good for UK Universities." *Financial Times,* January 20, p. 21.

———. 2003b. "How to Save the British Universities." *Times* (London), April 9, p. 15.

———. 2003c. "A Morally Bankrupt Education Policy." *Financial Times,* May 26, p. 17.

———. 2003d. "Set Universities Free to Compete." *Financial Times,* November 28, p. 19.

Wolfe, Barbara, and Scott Scrivner. 2003. "Providing Universal Preschool for Four-Year-Olds." In *One Percent for the Kids,* ed. Isabel Sawhill, 119 95. Washington, D.C.: Brookings Institution Press.

Wolpe, H., S. Badat, and Z. Barends. 1993. *The Post-Secondary Education System: Beyond the Equality vs. Development Impasse and Towards Policy Formulation for Equality and Development.* Cape Town: Education Policy Unit, University of the Western Cape.

Woodward, Ruth L., and Wesley Frank Craven, eds. 1991. *Princetonians, 1784–1790: A Biographical Dictionary.* Princeton, N.J.: Princeton University Press.

Yeld, Nan. 2001. "Equity Assessment and Language of Learning: Key Issues for Higher Education Selection and Access in South Africa." Unpublished PhD dissertation, University of Cape Town.

Yeld, Nan, and Wim Haeck. 1997. "Educational Histories and Academic Potential: Can Tests Deliver?" *Assessment and Evaluation in Higher Education* 22: 5–16.

Young, Beth Aronstamm, and Thomas M. Smith. 1997. "The Social Context of Education." Findings from *The Condition of Education 1997*. Washington, D.C.: U.S. Department of Education, Office of Educational Research and Improvement.

Zaaiman, H. 1998. *Selecting Students for Mathematics and Science: The Challenge Facing Higher Education in South Africa*. Pretoria: Human Sciences Research Council.

Zerhouni, Elias A. 2004. "Global Workforce Bolsters U.S. Science." *Science*, May 28, p. 1211.

Zernike, Kate. 2002. "At Auburn, a Challenge to a Trustee's Reign." *New York Times*, July 26, p. A12.

Zimmerman, David J., David Rosenblum, and Preston Hillman. 2004. "Institutional Ethos, Peers and Individual Outcomes." Williams Project on the Economics of Higher Education Discussion Paper no. 68, June.

Zuckerman, Harriet. 1977. *Scientific Elite: Nobel Laureates in the United States*. New York: Free Press.

———. 1998. "Accumulation of Advantage and Disadvantage: The Theory and Its Intellectual Biography." In *Robert K. Merton & Contemporary Sociology*, ed. Carlo Mongardini and Simonetta Tabboni, 139–61. New Brunswick, N.J.: Transaction Publishers.

LEGAL CASES CITED

Brown v. Board of Education, 347 U.S. 483 (1954).
Gratz v. Bollinger et al., 539 U.S. 244 (2003).
Grutter v. Bollinger et al., 539 U.S. 306 (2003).
Regents of the University of California v. Bakke, 438 U.S. 265 (1978).

Index

Page numbers for entries occurring in figures are suffixed by an *f;* those for entries in notes, by an *n,* with the number of the note(s) following; and those for entries in tables, by a *t.*

Thomas Jefferson Foundation
Distinguished Lecture Series

Across the Continent: Jefferson, Lewis and Clark, and the Making of America
Douglas Seefeldt, Jeffrey L. Hantman, and Peter S. Onuf, editors

Equity and Excellence in American Higher Education
William G. Bowen, Martin A. Kurzweil, and Eugene M. Tobin